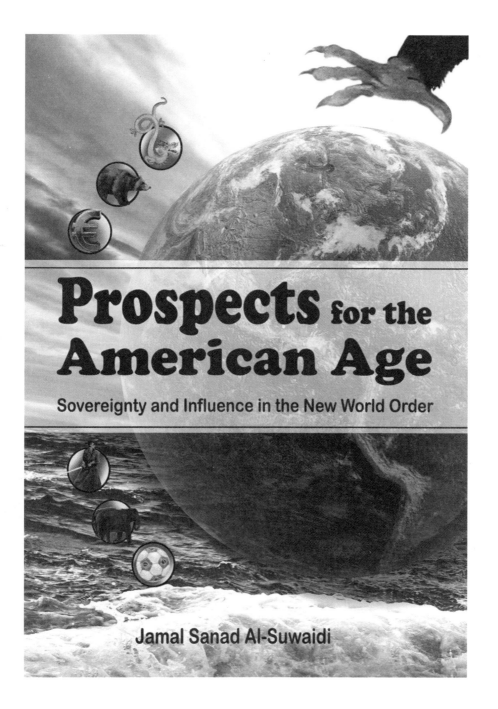

Prospects for the American Age

Sovereignty and Influence in the New World Order

Jamal Sanad Al-Suwaidi

ISBN 978–9948–14–858–6 Paperback Edition
ISBN 978–9948–14–859–3 Hardback Edition
ISBN 978–9948–14–860–9 Electronic Edition

All correspondence may be directed to:
Office of the Director General
PO Box: 4567, Abu Dhabi
United Arab Emirates
E-mail: jamalalsuwaidi@ecssr.ae

With my very best wishes

26 February 2014

PROSPECTS FOR THE AMERICAN AGE

SOVEREIGNTY AND INFLUENCE IN THE NEW WORLD ORDER

JAMAL SANAD AL-SUWAIDI

Acknowledgments

I wish to express my gratitude and appreciation to my family, who have provided invaluable support and encouragement for my research endeavors, and who have been an endless source of support to me all throughout my scholarly life. I also extend my thanks to the editors, proof-readers, information specialists and reviewers who assisted me by providing the scholarly material required to produce this book, and who have crafted its language to achieve the desired form. In particular I would like to extend my thanks and gratitude to all my fellow academics and researchers, both within the United Arab Emirates and abroad, who provided me with their insights and opinions regarding this book, from which I benefited considerably. I firmly believe that such intellectual engagement and scholarly interaction can significantly contribute to the development of accurate perspectives and clear-cut visions to achieve the ends that we all seek; namely a good life for our peoples, a glorious future for our Arab nation, and a better tomorrow for coming generations.

Dedicated to

Mohammed Bin Zayed Al Nahyan

CONTENTS

PREFACE

The universe is in a state of continuous flux, and the world undergoes periods of change at a pace that varies according to current events and developments. Hence there are states, powers, institutions, agencies, mentalities and theories that evolve quickly, undergo gradual change, or perhaps choose to remain static. This does not alter the reality of the change taking place around us, which is the main inspiration for presenting this vision of the current and future features of the new world order.

In this book I have sought to present an informed view that is comprehensive, objective and analytical—one that is based on statistics, data and information, rather than casual personal impressions, biases or opinions. Nevertheless, I recognize that readers are free to agree or disagree with the views adopted herein. Indeed, this is a natural process for any research effort that seeks to shed light on the structure, course and composition of power, sovereignty and influence in the world in the coming decades with a view to contributing to an understanding of global and regional developments and the ongoing need for clear strategic views of the future.

Some may consider research on the 'new world order' to be necessarily out of date, being a subject discussed by untold numbers of intellectuals, experts, researchers and scholars in the existing literature. Yet the concept can be readily applied to the world we live in today, as well as that of the future; we are discussing a theme that continues to flow through the lives of nations, peoples and even individuals. This order is not just an idea confined to the pages of books; rather, it involves strategies, plans and programs that are implemented in reality, affecting – directly or indirectly – the lives of billions of people worldwide.

Undoubtedly, this study's view of the subject differs from earlier readings of the topic offered by others, barring some general commonalities in terms of conclusions regarding the United States of America and its role in the global order. Controversy over the phenomenon of globalization continues to rage among theorists, researchers and businessmen with regard to its nature, effects and dimensions, as well as the means by which to maximize its returns. On the other hand, there are those who look inward in an attempt to avoid the impacts associated with globalization, to by-pass it or hide from it, not realizing that its strength and speed are such that no natural or artificial barrier may stem its momentum.

In my book *From Tribe to Facebook: The Transformational Role of Social Networks*, I discussed the various effects of social networking as one of the manifestations of globalization in the realm of media. In this book, I shall chart some of the political, economic and cultural impacts of the phenomenon, and how it has come to represent a vital and historic turning point in terms of the evolving structure of the new world order. So significant is globalization in this context that some researchers consider it to be the main driver of the new world order—the opposite side of the same coin. Others consider it to be a symbol of the hegemony and supremacy of the foremost superpower in that order. In either case, globalization remains a basic and integral element affecting the prospects of the American age, the profile of which is still being defined today.

In this book I do not attempt to draw plans for the future—the pace of change and the enormous developments witnessed by the world can transcend any planning, exposing estimations to rapid fluctuation and instability. The future is outlined by the present and the past. In this scholarly effort I seek to shed light on the givens of the present while drawing on the lessons of the past; yet I avoid delving into the past too deeply, recognizing its ability to hinder one's efforts to plan for the future in light of its inevitable focus on former burdens – and perhaps failures – that, once evoked, can easily result in an unhealthy pessimism, or over-caution, *vis-à-vis* the future.

Rather than seeking to produce a roadmap for the future, I aim to clarify the facts and shed light on statistical and analytical indicators. Readers are free to accept or disregard these indicators, but it is difficult to ignore or deny their significance and impact in any rational discussion of the new world order, either in its present or future incarnations. They are relevant to discussing the causes of conflict and are both numerous and diverse in their variety, be they cultural, economic, military, scientific or educational, or issues wherein all or some of those dimensions overlap. These elements can be useful in clarifying whether potential global conflicts between nations and states will emerge, and whether they will revolve around culture, religion, economic interests or political influence and the associated interactions of globalization.

What is certain is that we cannot live in isolation from events occurring in the world around us—such an approach is virtually suicidal for individuals and states alike, and it is unimaginable that anyone would voluntarily choose this in the present age. The world is experiencing a rapid convergence, aligning within a single model that is difficult to resist—at least for those who have been swept along by all the manifestations of globalization. Many talk of the declining role of the state and its institutions in a world where the lines have become blurred between traditional concepts such as the boundaries between sovereignty, citizenship, and national, supra-national or sub-national influence. This has occurred to such an extent that the research debate is no longer confined to the limits of state sovereignty; rather, it now encompasses the very existence of sovereignty in light of the economic manifestations of globalization, the growing influence of multinational companies and international organizations, and the many other variables which all point to the erosion of the concept of state sovereignty. There are numerous victims born of such developments; foremost among them are advocates of isolation—those who seek to resist change under the pretext of avoiding 'Westernization' and external dependency as a result of globalization at a time when involvement in the world economy and its mechanisms is vital to development and growth.

The new world order is an increasingly globalized one. Yet disagreement remains over how to describe the phenomenon of globalization, and whether it is a mutual endeavor or the repressive imposition of an American–Western model. Is globalization essentially a form of cultural subservience, with all the negative connotations that implies?

Is the age of America over, or does it enjoy further prospects? Will future developments force China to accept the American cultural model and its values, or will the West give in to China's culture and ancient civilization? Perhaps these, and other questions, have been the focus of scholarly discussion in recent years. They are also questions that will remain in the future, and may not produce clear-cut conclusions. Nonetheless, in this book I have attempted to develop objective answers in an attempt to satisfy a clear void in the catalogue of strategic, forward-looking Arab research, particularly in relation to the structure of power and influence in the new world order and the related impacts on the world's countries and regions. This is born of a desire to establish a methodological approach that will contribute to a deeper understanding of the interactions and changes occurring within the new world order, in the hope that this will help Arab states and societies avoid paying the enormous costs of misreading global strategic realities.

Identifying the various dimensions, trends and potential strategic consequences of change, and exploring the prospects for the new world order in a scholarly and methodological way, may offer the opportunity to preserve our interests. Undertaking an analysis of the realities, indicators and manifestations of the present age inevitably forces us to consider the future. In this regard, however, I do not aim to present a vision that is beyond discussion or debate, neither do I claim to possess the absolute truth; the future is open to all, yet the understanding thereof is reserved for those who believe in the methodology of a scholarly approach.

Jamal Sanad Al-Suwaidi
January 2014

INTRODUCTION: A THESIS ON THE POWER STRUCTURE OF THE NEW WORLD ORDER

Introduction

A Thesis on the Power Structure of the New World Order

When an expert attempts to understand a particular phenomenon related to the political and social sciences, he resorts to research in order to understand how that phenomenon may manifest itself now and in the future. This research sometimes unearths contradicting, and more often conflicting views, and perhaps much repetition and redundant material. These are all matters that require academic analysis in order to bring clarity to the matter in question.

The scholar always depends on logic in order to gather evidence and reach conclusions on a theoretical approach that can be used as a model for measurement. Therefore, why not subject the new world order to such thinking, in light of the research available today, in an attempt to predict its development? To achieve this, our academic 'laboratory' will conduct its work within the pages of this book, where facts and theory meet, dialogue is promoted between East and West, North and South, and the past, present and future are considered. For these reasons, the approach taken herein will not be traditional; the study of the new world order is characterized by an overlap between strategy, politics, economy, military affairs, technology, culture, science, ideology and geography, and by the development of concepts and networks of relationships—from the level of state citizens up to global citizens.[1]

History has witnessed prominent turning points that have resulted in three major developments: the emergence of world powers, the birth of a new global order, and changes among those powers and in their ranking within the order. The new world order was not born out of the present moment; rather, it is the product of an accumulation of historical events which have seen some powers disappear, the regression of others, and some rise up to preserve their status, role and strength.

Today, the world faces an increasingly complex, overlapping and expanding raft of challenges, risks and threats that are shaping the future. Some of these are domestic in origin, but are characterized by their spread across borders, nationalities and sects—such as the ethnic and sectarian conflicts witnessed in Iraq, Myanmar, Sudan and a number of African countries including Rwanda, Burundi and Uganda, as well as in Kosovo from 1998 to 1999. This has led to a debate about citizenship and human rights, and the spread of cross-border crime affecting global security – directly or indirectly – to varying degrees, be they conventional crimes such as human trafficking, drugs or arms smuggling and money-laundering, or non-conventional crimes that have emerged in cyberspace such as the various types of cyber-crime, cyber sabotage and online espionage, in addition to crimes of a compound nature which employ both conventional and cyber tools such as global terrorism.

Other threats and challenges occur vertically within the hierarchy of states or groups of states at differing levels of development due to competition for strategic interests, the existence of border disputes, or hegemonic pursuits by major international powers regardless of the interests of others. For example, when the United States of America invaded Iraq on March 20, 2003, it did so to strengthen its interests in the Middle East and without taking into consideration the effect on the Iraqi state or its neighbors, or the international community's response to the violation of a state's national sovereignty and disregard for world organizations – primarily the United Nations (UN) – which were established to guarantee the interests of all and achieve international stability and security.

Objective of the Book

International interactions stretching over more than six decades since the end of World War II – with the surrender of Japan on September 2, 1945[2] – encompass the Cold War between the United States of America and the Soviet Union, and have led to the transformation of an 'international system,' where interactions took place between states' official institutions, to a 'new world order' where national and international interests overlap and where economics, communications, media, education, culture and values are globalized.

In this new world order, the internal and external borders of countries disappear, allowing societies, civilizations, individuals and sub-state organizations to interact regardless of national sovereignty, heralding the emergence of a global civil society.[3] The role of the state has overlapped in one way or another with the global community, and the state is no longer solely responsible for building international relations. Thus, there is a need for a revision of certain concepts such as the status and position of the state, national sovereignty and security, in order to conform with the shrinking role of the state in monopolizing foreign relations with other nations in tackling common challenges and global threats, namely food, water and energy security, cyber-security, poverty, refugees, illegal migration, overpopulation, climate change, desertification, organized crime, terrorism, and the spread of weapons of mass destruction (WMD) and their means of delivery.[4]

Herein lies the importance of studying the past, present and future of the new world order, to understand its structure and the factors affecting its formation and development; one may examine how it affects international relations, as well as its role in countering global phenomena that threaten human existence such as climate change, global warming, depletion of energy, water and food resources, and the widening of both social and economic imbalances, especially between rich and poor countries.

By shedding light on the structure of the new world order, I seek to build a new concept of its power structure, sovereignty and influence over the coming two decades. I believe that the foundations of overall power held by the United States of America – the dominant player of the new world order – still qualify it to continue holding the reins and manage its affairs in spite of various hegemonic and unipolar behavior within the balance of power and conflict between major powers like China, the European Union (EU), Russia and Japan, as well as emerging economies like India and Brazil on the one hand, and the interests of the United States of America as the hegemonic pole, on the other.

The Problem,
the Questions and the Assumptions

The term 'new world order' raises many questions, including over the very existence of such a system in the first place; and if it does exist, what are the factors behind its emergence and who is responsible for it? Who leads it, and does its leadership necessitate the imposition of rights and duties by countries at the global level, or is the new world order itself the product of a dominant power? Who are its actors and is the order fixed or fluid? What are its defining characteristics and what is the difference between the new world order and the 'international system'? Finally, what is the future of the new world order and what are its effects on society?

We should also wonder to what extent the existence of the new world order will affect global security and stability, and what the implications of this system might be on vital and strategic interests. Moreover, we should examine the future of the state itself as an effective entity in light of this new world order and any possible notion of a 'global citizen' in a 'global civil society.' It is also important to question whether there is a single world order, or in fact several; namely an economic world order, another political, a third financial, a fourth informational, a fifth military, and so on. If so, which of these dominates the others? Or is the new world order the product of the integration and interaction of all these orders? Moreover, how do countries and their populations view this order?

Certainly, when examining such vital themes, assumptions multiply; some are constant and basic, many are variant and dependent. The main assumption here is based on the substance of this new world order. It aims to measure the extent of change in the structure and patterns of power that in turn affect contemporary international relations and global values. It also aims to measure the extent of the transformations and patterns of interaction established as part of the prevailing value system of the new order, and through which it seeks to achieve global stability and the objectives and interests of the major poles of the order. Another assumption relates to the formation, determinants, foundations and pillars of the order, its current structure, and the ranking of powers within it. According to these assumptions, there are several criteria that determine the structure of the new world order, international relations and the balance of power, including the geographical barriers separating countries, peoples, societies and individuals. Yet a third assumption relates to the political, economic, social, military, educational and cultural effects of the new world order, namely new systems and mechanisms that affect the interaction between states and individuals in all fields. These are the questions, assumptions and problems that this book will attempt to answer, in addition to other questions regarding the future of the new world order.

The New World Order:
Principles and Foundations

In contemporary history, divergent views have emerged over the exact nature of the new world order. Former Soviet Premier Mikhail Sergeyevich Gorbachev defined the new world order in terms of the following principles: a balance of international relations rather than a balance of powers;[5] tackling global issues affecting the future of civilization and culture; and a speeding up of the normalization of international relations in the fields of economics, media, culture, education and the environment based on widespread internationalization—that is, a global financial system, international culture, a globalized vision of education, and global cooperation on the limitation of environmental pollution—ultimately, the replacement of globalization with internationalization.[6]

In Gorbachev's vision, the international system overlaps with the new world order, where the best guarantee of security is disarmament, and especially nuclear disarmament.[7] Moreover, he demands the provision of mutual security for all through the recognition of peoples' interests and equality in international relations, which is essential to any new world order. In addition, he stresses the need for a country's security to be associated with the security of all members of the international community, along with non-intervention in the domestic affairs of other states.[8]

Although the collective treaties of the Peace of Westphalia concluded in 1648 granted countries the right of national sovereignty within the international community – which is of particular importance to smaller states – former US President George Herbert Bush [Sr.] sees the essence of the new world order lying in the holistic vision of a world without borders, envisioning an order in which there is freedom from terror, a valiant pursuit of justice, and more security in the quest for peace.[9] It is an order in which the nations of the world can prosper and live in harmony, work on the peaceful settlement of disputes, and focus on international solidarity in the face of aggression; where the principles of justice and free co-existence prevail, and in which the weak should be protected from the strong. That is, a world where the UN would be freed from the Cold War stalemate, where freedom and respect for human rights would spread, and where peoples would be treated justly.[10]

The new world order was also understood in line with the changes that accompanied the post-Cold War period—the imbalance of powers, the expansion of world markets, the disintegration of states and the rise of nationalism, technological advances, and the spread of globalization. Hence, Joseph Samuel Nye's comment that, "the world order is the product of a stable distribution of power among the major states," with "… relations among peoples as well as states" and the spread of "broad values like democracy and human rights," the application of international law and the empowerment of its institutions, such as the UN.[11]

Nye asserts that a new world order is built around the interests and relations of peoples and societies, which form the foundations upon which governments build their foreign relations. This formation necessitates the spread of democracy and human rights, stability and freedom from prejudice through a balance in the distribution of power and a commitment to international justice via the UN.[12] In addition, Nye believes the new world order's international legitimacy is represented by the UN and not by any other interests.[13]

Meanwhile, Lawrence David Freedman suggests that the concept of the new world order presumes that "international institutions and, in particular, the United Nations, will be taking a more active and important role in global management."[14] He adds that "the phrase 'new world order' is merely descriptive, requiring no more than acceptance that the current situation is unique and clearly different in critical respects from the one that obtained just a few years ago."[15]

Freedman argues that the essence of the new world order lies in the effectiveness of the UN as the sole global administrative representative in accordance with international values that no particular power should dominate; i.e., the superpowers would disappear from the top of the pyramid in the new world order to be replaced by the UN—an order completely different from the current international system, according to Freedman.[16] This proposition is based on the fact that the UN represents all peoples of the world and that it is possible to formulate *ideal* international values. However, such an outcome appears highly improbable, at least for the time being, owing to the realities of politics and international relations.

Samuel Phillips Huntington believes that the new world order is a natural product of the clash of civilizations[17]—that the development of global politics after the Cold War is based on a world of civilizations whose culture, language, religion and identity shape models of disintegration, engagement and conflict. Thus, a world order is now emerging based on civilization—societies with common cultural links cooperating and mobilizing themselves around the leading power within their civilization. Thus, the preservation of the new world order and the avoidance of conflict between civilizations depend on the acceptance and cooperation by global leaders to preserve the advantages of civilizational pluralism in world politics.[18]

Huntington's vision of the world order refutes the rise of a universal civilization based on the concept of globalization—if the world revolved in a bi-polar orbit during the Cold War, it later faced a state of flux that led to the emergence of new alliances and blocs representative of the cultural entities to which they belong,[19] including the emergence of religion or language-based alliances, such as the Organization of the Islamic Conference or the Arab League, and other regional unions based on common values and a unified religion or language. Religion, language, values, tradition, populations and resources formed the basis of these major entities.

According to Huntington, the new world order is based on civilizations, i.e. coexistence within a system of different civilizations, each with one or more leading state. Therefore, relations within this new world order will be built according to levels of loyalty and hostility between countries and societies that belong to differing cultures. Ultimately, this means that the new world order reproduces that found at the dawn of history, where the point of conflict formed the border separating different civilizations—whether sectarian, civil or ethnic. A world order based on civilizations is the safe haven against the eruption of a new world war.[20]

Yoshihiro Francis Fukuyama doubts the ability of the UN to form the foundation of a new world order[21] and argues that if we want to set up a league of nations that would not suffer from the fatal flaws of earlier international organizations, it would have to look much more like the North Atlantic Treaty Organization (NATO) than the UN; that is, a league of truly free states brought together by their common commitment to liberal principles and free economy. Such a league should be more capable of forceful action to protect its collective security from threats arising from the non-democratic world. The foundation for the establishment of this new world order is based on the clear linkage between industrial democracies and judicial instruments that regulate their mutual economic relations.[22]

Moreover, Fukuyama believes that the United States of America and other liberal democracies will have to come to terms with the fact that, with the collapse of communism, the world in which they live is less familiar, and the rules of the past cannot be applied to the present. Current major issues will be economic in nature – promoting competitiveness and innovation, managing internal and external deficits, etc. – or will involve dealing cooperatively with grave environmental problems. It is a new world order in which rational and pragmatic dealings have replaced the struggle for domination.[23]

Meanwhile, former US National Security Advisor, Zbigniew Kazimierz Brzezinski, sees a new world order based on American supremacy with a number of special features, namely: a collective security system, regional economic cooperation, US domination over international decision-making, and a rudimentary global constitutional and judicial structure.[24]

Thomas Loren Friedman, on the other hand, considers globalization to be the new world order. He argues that the world has become 'flat' in light of a universal technological revolution, and that there are ten factors which have contributed to the emergence of this flat world:[25]

1. The fall of the Berlin Wall on November 9, 1989 and its political consequences.

2. The emergence and development of the internet in the early 1970s.

3. The development of information technology (IT) systems that allowed individuals to work together in virtual time, regardless of their geographical location.[26]

4. The emergence of free and open participation of creative and commercial ideas over the internet.

5. Assigning work and services to organizations and individuals that carry them out effectively.

6. Establishing factories in other countries to lower production costs, as witnessed by major Western aluminum and microelectronic industry companies, which have opened up factories in countries such as China, India, Malaysia and Vietnam due to their low labor costs.

7. Supply chaining, which has allowed retailers to benefit from individual products rapidly and at a lower cost.

8. The attempt by companies to work outside the framework of their area of operations with a view to expanding their services by forging alliances with other suppliers.

9. The availability of information, especially through the services provided by search engines such as Google, Yahoo, etc.

10. The new inventions in the field of digital technology and software.

According to Friedman, the existence of the flat world will have inevitable consequences, including greater contact between different cultures,[27] including relations between the Islamic and Western worlds. From his point of view, if we imagine the global community as city neighborhoods: "Western Europe would be an assisted-living facility, with an aging population lavishly attended to by Turkish nurses ... the United States of America would be a gated community, with a metal detector at the front gate and a lot of people sitting in their front yards complaining about how lazy everyone else was, even though out back there was a small opening in the fence for Mexican labor and other energetic immigrants ... Latin America would be the fun part of town, the club district, where the work day doesn't begin until ten p.m. and everyone sleeps until midmorning ... the landlords in this neighborhood almost never reinvest their profits here, but keep them in a bank across town ... The Arab street would be a dark alley where outsiders fear to tread, except for a few side streets called Dubai, Jordan, Bahrain, Qatar, and Morocco. The only new businesses are gas stations, whose owners, like the elites in the Latin neighborhood, rarely reinvest their funds in the neighborhood ... Africa, sadly, is that part of town where the businesses are boarded up, life expectancy is declining ... India, China, and East Asia would be ... a big teeming market, made up of small shops and one-room factories, interspersed with Stanley Kaplan SAT prep schools and engineering colleges. Nobody ever sleeps in this neighborhood, everyone lives in extended families, and everyone is working and saving to get to 'the right side of the tracks.'" [28]

Friedman argues that the path of globalization since 2000 has exceeded all expectations, that it is still accelerating and that its impact is difficult to assess. The manifestations of globalization are rapidly felt and they encompass the whole world, which has effectively been reduced to a 'global village.' Diversified forms of communication between organizations and individuals have become fast and accessible, regardless of geography. Billions of humans live in this global village in a new world order characterized by a single horizon where governments and civil organizations can cooperate and trade beyond geographical borders, which have effectively vanished due to the incursion of globalization and its economic effects at the local and international levels.[29]

At a time when the world's size has diminished due to successive waves of globalization, it has witnessed a new age characterized by an exchange of information, services and labor forces taking place with greater ease than the exchange of traditional goods. In spite of any country's ability to benefit from the 'flatness' of the world – as long as it conforms to the rules of this system – it is the industrial countries that lead in terms of possessing the technological innovation and skills base required to play an effective role in managing this new world order.[30]

While former US President George Herbert Bush [Sr.] had spoken about the emergence of a new world order on September 11, 1990,[31] indicating that it was a system in which freedom and peace for all peoples would prevail,[32] during the presidency of his son, George Walker Bush [Jr.], 'constructive' or 'creative' chaos[33] emerged as one of the main features of the new world order.[34] This approach allowed the contradictions taking place within socio-economic structures in any domestically unstable authoritarian country to manifest freely without constraints from the existing political system, thus leading to the emergence of new dynamics that express the true socio-economic reality hidden by the authoritarian state. Thus, a new political system is re-made in light of deliberately created chaos[35] in a process of destruction and re-construction. Perhaps this explains some of what is happening in many countries in the world in terms of chaos and the pursuit of change.

The world is witnessing today changes in global values as a result of the emergence of a new world order characterized by the dominance of the service economy in the field of development, technology in the field of science, the internet in the field of communications, and chaos and hesitation in the field of crisis settlement, as witnessed by the US position towards the crises in Libya, Egypt and Tunisia, where hesitation and caution – and sometimes even clumsiness – have dominated US reactions towards the conditions witnessed by those countries in recent years.

The UN believes that progress towards a global vision of development, peace and human rights depends on certain fundamental values essential to international relations in the 21st century, namely:[36]

- Democratic and participatory governance based on the will of the people that guarantees freedom for men and women and the right to live their lives in dignity, free from hunger or the fear of violence, oppression or injustice—in essence, a liberal system.

- Equality, so that no individual and no nation may be denied the opportunity to benefit from development, and equal rights and opportunities for men and women must be assured.

- Global solidarity in the face of common challenges in a way that fairly distributes the costs and burdens, in accordance with basic principles of equity and social justice.

- Promoting a culture of peace and dialogue among all civilizations, and respect for diversity of belief, culture and language.

- Preservation of the environment through the effective management of all living species and natural resources in accordance with the tenets of sustainable development.

- Sharing of responsibility among nations of the world for the management of global economic and social development as well as threats to international peace and security.

- Allowing people freedom to live life in accordance with their own choices and providing them with the opportunities to make those choices.

- Enabling members of religious or ethnic minorities or migrants to make a political contribution at local and national levels to enhance decisions affecting their lives.

- To create an influential and effective role for civil society organizations with regard to their influence over global transparency, their ability to set rules on aid, debt, human rights, health and climate change. Hence, civil society networks can take advantage of new media and new communications technologies to establish links between activists at the local level, as well as at a level that transcends the limits of state sovereignty, and allow individuals and groups to share ideas and concerns and to generate collective perspectives on a global and comprehensive scale.

Enshrining these values leads to a new world order that not only depends on relations between governments, but is a world that extends horizontally to encompass all elements, including a cross-border role for the individual, society and civil society organizations that transcends the approaches, positions and role of one's country, to formulate a global public opinion that supports the new world order, enhances its cause and helps to alleviate its concerns. This will have negative consequences for authoritarian regimes, which will no longer be able to hide activities that deny human and civil rights. Global civil society will play its role in delegitimizing such regimes, depending on the positions of local civil society organizations. Thus, it will become meaningless to talk about what is internal or external in terms of the nation state, since national and international interests will become intertwined, allowing powers that dominate the new world order to intervene without the need for international legitimacy.[37]

Therefore, the emergence of a new world order clash of generations is possible, as distinct from the clash of civilizations—namely a conflict between the older generation (over 40 years old) and the younger generation (those aged below 40) – Chapter V of this book sheds light on the views of different generations towards international issues. Undoubtedly, the aforementioned clash of generations essentially emanates from the different convictions of each generation with regard to the political circumstances in which each was raised, the understanding of the new world order by each generation, and the extent to which it is influenced by that generation's values and principles. Media availability and access to information have enabled the younger generation to transcend the limits of place and time and encouraged the exchange of opinions with counterparts around the world—a state of affairs reflected by the sedentary state of the elderly compared to the incessant motion that characterizes the young.

This conflict will lead to influential cultural and political interactions inside the new world order that will encourage greater partnership, cooperation, integration, democracy, demands for human rights and gender equality, and recognition of identity differences leading to the creation of integrated and culturally diversified societies. It could be that authoritarian regimes and dictatorships will completely disappear, and a high expectation placed on states and governments to explain their policies, decisions and approaches to two different generations, each with its own culture and convictions.

The New World Order: Determinants and Foundations

The determinants of the general framework within which interactions take place between the components of the new world order represent limitations or opportunities resulting from the overlap of a multitude of factors and circumstances. Force – and skill in its use – was one of the foundations of the world order during the Cold War, manifested in mutual deterrence. In the post-Cold War era, crisis management became one of the determinants of the new world order, and persistent international attempts were made by certain major powers to impose hegemony, in the belief that this would achieve a balance of power,[38] particularly following the transition to a unipolar world order.

In this new world order, states in the traditional sovereign sense lose their capacity to maneuver, and thus become prisoners to the global and regional interests of the single dominant superpower. The role of international organizations, such as the UN, the International Monetary Fund (IMF) and the World Bank, is reduced to simply realizing the interests of the dominant pole. Thus, the interests of other states, peoples and constituent units of the new world order depend on the acceptance or rejection of the hegemonic superpower – i.e. the United States of America – and whichever party violates its vision must suffer the consequences. While the new unipolar world order claims to distinguish between governments, individuals and peoples in its actions within the international system, there is a price to be paid when a government rejects the approaches of that dominant pole by refusing to give in to its will, or even by remaining neutral—it is a system based on the principle: 'you are either with us or against us.'[39]

Among the main determinants of the new world order is the nature of relations between the superpower and the major powers. The superpower possesses dominant capabilities and effective military, economic, technological, educational and cultural influences; the great powers sit relatively lower in the power rankings, but their role is globally effective. Other determinants are the extent of competition, convergence, consensus, agreement or conflict between the interests of the superpower and major powers, and the means of realizing, imposing or protecting those interests. Thus, the product of the interaction is an implicit recognition of the existence of the order and those controlling it.

Since the beginning of human history, global systems have always produced a major power or groups of powers to assume control, either as a result of military or economic conflicts, cultural, scientific or educational hegemony, or because some actors or parties possess global power and influence in the military, economic, cultural, educational, energy and transport fields that is difficult to challenge. Such influences can be employed by such powers within a universal strategy in order to realize their interests – for example, in settling international crises – and thereby obtain implicit global recognition of their position at the head of the world order—a position difficult for others to challenge.

For a deeper understanding of the nature, formation determinants and mechanisms of the new world order, a brief review of related vocabulary and terminology is useful. The term 'new world order' is made up of several components. It is an order[40] according to which the functioning of several units or countries is organized in line with specific laws, rules, values and frameworks; these have been formulated according to the prevailing ranking of powers and in such a way as to reflect the priorities and interests of the superpower that dominates the new world order. The same is true for the major powers.[41] The adjective 'global' reflects all that pertains to the world and its dimensions—sea, land (above and below) and cyberspace; i.e., a power that bears the responsibility to take a 'global decision' or undertake responsibility for 'world affairs.'

The word 'order,' rather than 'system,' has been used, since it expresses a form of organization of international relations under a particular pattern of values and behavior governing the interactions between the system's components.[42] Boutros Boutros-Ghali, the former UN Secretary-General, stated that, "nations that have the lead in the world have sufficient capability, resources and creativity to shape a new world order. Yet the question does not relate to capability, but rather to perseverance, commitment and will."[43]

Former US President George Herbert Bush [Sr.] used the term 'new world order' when he declared the foundation of a new world order in his speech before the US House of Representatives on January 16, 1991,[44] stating that: "We have before us the opportunity to forge for ourselves and for future generations a new world order – a world where the rule of law, not the law of the jungle, governs the conduct of nations. When we are successful – and we will be – we have a real chance at this new world order, an order in which a credible United Nations can use its peacekeeping role to fulfill the promise and vision of the UN's founders."[45] Based on this interpretation there are many determinants affecting the formation of this new world order. These represent limitations or opportunities resulting from geostrategic factors, circumstances and elements, namely:

1. The existence of powers with global interests that develop strategies to achieve those interests according to their vision of the world. Such powers therefore work to re-shape the world in accordance with their will, and possess the capacity to apply both hard and soft power to achieve this.

2. A competitive environment that leads to the division of the world between powers such as the five permanent members of the UN Security Council (that have the 'right of veto') plus Germany (P5+1); powers that have a regional role such as India and Japan; emerging powers and economies such as Brazil, Indonesia, Turkey, South Africa, the United Arab Emirates and Saudi Arabia; failed states such as Somalia and Afghanistan; and a developed world, a developing world, and a non-developing world.

3. International institutions that express the will of the international community, such as the UN and its affiliated organizations, particularly the Security Council, the IMF, the World Bank and the World Trade Organization (WTO).

4. The need for stability and security in the face of colonial greed and behavior.

The new world order has its fundamentals and foundations based on the following core elements:[46]

1. Global consensus over international pacts, treaties and international law.

2. Strategic balance in military forces as opposed to balance of interests.

3. Interactions and activities that drive towards the emergence of global organizations, alliances and structures, and therefore international behavior that alters according to international circumstances.

4. The shift to globalization at the cultural, media, commercial and economic level.

5. A world trade system—for example, with the WTO at its head.

6. A global financial system made up of an integrated network of national central banks, regional financial alliances, an international monetary fund, a world bank, and a globally circulated reference currency – namely the US dollar – as the unit against which other currencies are measured.

The Structure of the New World Order

The fall of the Berlin Wall on November 9, 1989 – 28 years after it was constructed – is perhaps the starting point for the emergence of the new world order. East and West Germany were re-united into one state on October 3, 1990, after the youth of East Germany decided to rid themselves of dictatorship, embrace freedom in the Western sense, and re-unite a country. There followed the collapse of the Soviet Union and its disintegration on December 25, 1991,[47] ending the era of the bi-polar international system. These events were accompanied in 1991 by the end of the Japanese economic miracle and the succession of China – after the massacre in Tiananmen Square on June 4, 1989 – as an export-driven, high-growth economy. The Maastricht Treaty was drafted and signed on February 7, 1992 to structure the EU, and the US-led international coalition forced Iraq to withdraw from Kuwait and allow its liberation on February 26, 1991.[48]

Three phenomena can be examined which have determined the shape of the new world order since the end of the Cold War, namely: the emergence of various additional components of US power of the United States of America; the rise of China as a hub for low-wage, global economic growth; and the emergence of the EU as an integrated major economic power, particularly after the launch of the single currency, the euro (€), on January 1, 1999. The structure of the new world order is hierarchical, with the United States of America occupying the top spot due to its comprehensive power represented by a military force that exceeds any other in the history of the world, a unique culture and education, the largest economy in the world, incomparable technological leadership, unprecedented global supremacy in the energy and transport sectors, and significant contribution to global innovation. This has been most apparent since the ideological conflict between communism, socialism and liberal capitalism ended, and the political, economic and military power of the former US adversary – the Soviet Union – disintegrated.[49] The sole remaining superpower imposed its control militarily, economically, technologically and politically, and the market economy and capitalism controlled global economic conditions.[50]

After the end of the first decade of the 21st century, the United States of America is still the sole superpower of the new world order. Although other major powers such as China, Russia and the EU have attempted to rival the United States of America' preeminent position, it is difficult – as the following chapters will explain – to displace this single pole and assume its global role, or even develop any sort of partnership with it to lead the new world order. The reason for this is that the United States of America continues to retain its supremacy in terms of power, sovereignty and influence in the new world order. The current hierarchy of power is likely to endure for at least the next 50 years, unless the United States of America decides not to retain its leadership role, or if it opts to employ an approach that is less confrontational with potential competitors seeking to establish a multipolar world order, namely China.

Therefore, the central proposition of this book is that the United States of America is the dominant pole in the new world order, and that the world is still living in an American age, which in the author's opinion will likely endure for a long time to come (at least five decades). There are indications to support this proposition, in particular the fact that the power structure in the unipolar world order tilts clearly in favor of the United States of America and its power and influence in the military, economic, cultural, educational, energy and transport fields. For example, the US defense budget exceeds the total combined defense budgets of the six next largest defense spenders.

Table 1
Military Spending of the United States of America and Other Major Powers, 2012[51]

Superpower/major powers	Defense expenditure in US dollars (billions)
United States of America	645.7
European Union	280.1
China	102.4
Russia	59.9
Japan	59.4
India	38.5
Brazil	35.3
Total (excluding the United States of America)	575.6

In addition, US gross domestic product in 2012 ($15.685 trillion) is more than eight times the GDP of India, nearly seven times that of Britain, five times that of Germany, three times that of Japan, and more than twice that of China.[52] Moreover, in terms of innovation, creativity and commercial competitiveness the United States of America ranks first. In 2003 alone, the United States of America launched 24 spacecraft, compared to just six launched by China, four by France, and two by India.[53] The United States of America also contributes around a quarter of the UN's budget.[54]

Some analysts, including the American economist A. Gary Shilling,[55] argue that the United States of America has several long-term advantages over its competitors, primarily the strong dollar, which constitutes a significant long-term comparative advantage for the United States of America, as the dollar reflects US economic and political power. It is the leading reserve currency and is expected to retain this position for years to come. Another advantage, according to Shilling is the demographic composition, considering that the United States of America has been one of the countries most open to, and benefitting from, new immigrants, who are usually young with high birth rates. Most immigrants have jobs and pay taxes that naturally help to provide benefits to pensioners of the baby boomer generation.[56] Another advantage is labor availability which, according to estimates by the US Bureau of Labor Statistics, means working-age population in the United States of America will increase by around 2.2 million annually, equaling 1.4 million new job-seekers. This figure almost equates to labor demand.[57]

Another comparative US advantage, according to Shilling, is an innovative spirit, and in spite of projections of economic recession, the country is still far ahead of any state ranked in terms of innovation. This advantage starts with an educational system that promotes scholarly research and affords opportunities to challenge accepted ideas, which distinguishes it from any corresponding system in other developed countries.

There is also the flexibility of the US labor market. The role of labor unions in the United States of America has declined and almost vanished, particularly in the private sector. As a result, wages have become downwardly flexible and studies have shown that many of those unemployed for six months or more are willing to accept work for lower pay than they used to earn. In the other competing countries and China in particular, there is less flexibility, according to Shilling.[58]

Moreover, another advantage enjoyed by the United States of America is the fact that its currency, the dollar, is the leading global reserve currency. US Treasury Bonds are considered the safest reserve asset for financial investors, both countries and financial institutions.[59] This advantage, which the United States of America has drawn from the strength of its economy and its relative size, in addition to its developed markets and financial institutions, allows the US government to finance its budget deficit, and allows its central bank – the Federal Reserve – to determine its own monetary policy, given the significant global demand on investment in US government debt securities (i.e. US government bills and bonds). This huge demand reduces US government borrowing to a minimum. It also allows it to influence movements in the global markets through its monetary policy. However, it is noted that the advantage of low-cost borrowing sometimes leads to increased US government spending, which also increases the government's financial deficit, the deficit in the trade balance, and sometimes also in the current account in the balance of payments. This is known as the double or 'twin' deficits, a phenomenon that will be explained in detail in Chapter IV. In order to combat this phenomenon, and strengthen the position of the economy, US interest rates would have to rise. Increasing savings would reduce spending, including on imports, which would lead to a reduction in the US trade balance deficit (approximately $741 billion in 2012, representing 4.7% of GDP), and the current account deficit (nearly $440 billion in the same year, representing approximately 3% of GDP).[60]

There are several features, often intrinsic to shaping the new world order, that the United States of America is unique in commanding, primarily:[61]

1. The United States of America will remain a dominant power in several domains; it is globally superior in terms of education, culture, technology, economy, military power and transportation—although it will learn to recognize the difference between superiority and absolute authority.

2. The EU (28 countries) is still trying to regain a balance between its competing countries.

3. Russia will rise again through the recovery of its economy and the rebuilding of its military capabilities.

4. China will focus on managing its global economic position and preserving its economic prosperity. It will remain more of a universal actor than a superpower, since it lacks soft power due to the absence of global familiarity with the Chinese language, as well as an unsophisticated Chinese state media that is largely ignored elsewhere in the world.[62]

5. A large number of countries, such as South American states (especially Brazil), India, South Africa and certain Southeast Asian countries, will compete with China to become low-cost, high-growth global hubs.

6. A decline in the role of the UN and its affiliates as a 'referee,' in order to better serve the interests of the United States of America.[63]

Yet from both a procedural and a thematic standpoint, the structure of the new world order includes a number of elements, the most important of which are:

1. The presence of a single dominant power and rival major powers that may or may not be hostile (the dominant power being that which possesses universal capabilities, while lesser but major powers compete with the dominant power).

2. Global financial, economic and trade institutions and structures, such as the WTO, the IMF, and the World Bank Group—which comprises the International Bank for Reconstruction and Development, the International Centre for Settlement of Investment Disputes, the International Development Association, the International Finance Corporation, and the Multilateral Investment Guarantee Agency.

3. The UN and its organizations, such as the General Assembly, the Security Council, the International Court of Justice, and specialist agencies such as the United Nations Food and Agriculture Organization (FAO); the International Civil Aviation Organization; the International Fund for Agricultural Development; the International Labor Organization (ILO);

the World Health Organization (WHO); the International Maritime Organization; the United Nations Educational, Scientific and Cultural Organization (UNESCO); the United Nations Industrial Development Organization (UNIDO); the Universal Postal Union; the International Atomic Energy Agency (IAEA); the Organization for the Prohibition of Chemical Weapons; the World Intellectual Property Organization (WIPO); the World Tourism Organization; the World Meteorological Organization; the United Nations Fund for Democracy; and the United Nations Fund for International Partnerships.[64]

4. Military alliances, such as the North Atlantic Treaty Organization (NATO), the Organization for Security and Cooperation in Europe (OSCE), and the Common Defense Agreement of the Cooperation Council of the Arab States of the Gulf (GCC).[65]

5. The International Criminal Court (ICC), which is an independent body established in 2002 and is not affiliated to the United Nations.

6. Regional and international economic groupings, such as the group of eight industrialized nations (G8), the group of twenty (G20), the North American Free Trade Agreement (NAFTA), the Association of Southeast Asian Nations (ASEAN), and the Asia–Pacific Economic Cooperation (APEC).[66]

7. Non-governmental organizations (NGOs) concerned with human rights, women and children, the fight against corruption, the environment, labor, health, and press freedom. Such NGOs include: Médecins Sans Frontières (MSF), the Development Group Organization, Norwegian People's Aid (NPA), CARE International, Save the Children Fund, Amnesty International, the International Committee of the Red Cross, Greenpeace, the World Organization against Torture, Reporters without Borders, the International Solidarity Movement, Transparency International, and Human Rights Watch.

8. Global, transnational and cross-border companies such as: Sony Corporation, Daimler Chrysler, General Motors, ExxonMobil, and General Electric.[67]

9. Media and social networking that influence global public opinion, such as satellite TV channels, the Internet, Facebook, Twitter and YouTube.

The structure of the new world order is more often determined by the pattern of power distribution between the major powers that are positioned at the top. It is a pattern that in turn determines the distribution of polarity in the new world order. As the major countries acquire global superiority through comprehensive military, technological, economic, educational and cultural strength, they become increasingly able to impose their hegemony on the new world order. The

United States of America stands undisputedly at the top of the system, and can impose its will and pursue its interests, thanks to its military, technological and economic advantages that separate it from the other major powers, as well as the possession of cumulative experience in the management of global affairs and international crises. Moreover, the United States of America has a universal strategy for the future direction of world affairs. It is known that the Central Intelligence Agency (CIA), and certain US think tanks that have influence in strategic decision-making, issue strategic and in-depth studies or forecasts that may look 30–50 years into the future, and it is upon these that US strategists develop a universal strategy to guarantee the continuity of US dominance over the new world order.

Any superpower, such as the United States of America – and before it the United Kingdom, France and Spain, and before them all the Ottoman Empire – divides the world into spheres of direct and indirect influence, areas of strategic interests, regions of conciliation, and areas of competition and conflict. Each one of these areas has its unique features and position within the structure of the new world order.

Some major powers have direct areas of influence, the implication being that they have the right of action in those areas, while areas of indirect influence are where major powers seek control. For instance, the United States of America considers Central America as part of its sphere of direct influence—which explains its history of military intervention and intelligence gathering in the region, from Argentina in 1890 to Honduras in 2009.[68] It considers the Middle East to be an area of indirect influence, therefore the United States of America has sought to retain a military presence in the region and be a key player in managing crises. As for the Soviet Union before its disintegration in the early 1990s, it saw Eastern Europe as under its direct influence and invaded Czechoslovakia on August 20, 1968 when the latter announced the adoption of more liberal policies.[69] Likewise, the invasion of Afghanistan in 1979 falls within the framework of indirect influence of the Soviet Union. As for China, it regards Southeast Asia, particularly countries with a majority population of Chinese origin, as private areas of influence and considers the US role in such areas as a strategic challenge. The same is true for some parts of Africa that are witnessing competition between China and the United States of America.[70]

The policy of political, diplomatic and intellectual détente between the United States of America and the Soviet Union emerged during the late 1960s and early 1970s according to the vision of former Secretary of State Henry Alfred Kissinger.[71] The US administration sought to establish relations with the Soviet Union on the basis of negotiation instead of confrontation, and to work on building a peace based on political, economic, cultural and technical cooperation. They agreed to hold consultations and negotiations to resolve any differences on any bilateral or global matters of concern through direct contact or through agreed diplomatic channels;[72] hence, the idea of establishing a hotline in 1963 between Washington and Moscow following the Cuban missile crisis, in order to avoid any escalation or subsequent repercussions. Indeed, the idea of this hotline was also proposed between Moscow and Paris in 1966, and between Moscow and London in 1967, in order to prevent a nuclear strike due to miscalculation or error. The hotline continued to gain importance over the ten years from 1963 until 1973.[73]

Power Ranking in the New World Order

Global criteria certainly exist upon which the power structure of the new world order is based. They are the main measurements that determine the status of a nation within the order, or through which the structure of the new world order is formulated. Accordingly, a pyramidical structure indicating the ranking of powers in the new world order is proposed.

A country's ranking is based on its all of these criteria, since a country's ranking can be high in one aspect and behind in another. When ranking by individual criteria, however, the power rankings in the new world order are as listed below.

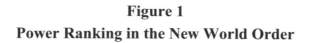

Figure 1
Power Ranking in the New World Order

1. Education and Culture

In terms of education indicators, the United States of America has 83 universities listed among the top 400 worldwide, in addition to an unmatched number of publications produced annually.

2011 statistics indicate that the number of titles issued for the first time in the United States of America was 347,178, while the number of books published in the Arab world (22 countries) was around 15,000 in 2011, and in Greece (included for the sake of comparison due to its history, civilization and present economic situation) produced 8,333 titles.[74] These statistics reveal a huge gap in terms of knowledge, culture and publishing between the superpower dominating the new world order and selected states in comparison.

Table 2

Superpower and Major Powers' Spending

on Education and Research[75]

World power	Spending on education as a percentage of GDP (%) 2011	Spending on research and development as a percentage of GDP (%)[76]	Number of universities among the world's top 400 universities in 2012	Number of patents in 2011	Number of patents recorded per million persons in 2011
United States of America	5.40	2.77	83	224,505	707.6
Russia	4.10	1.12	5	29,999	212.1
China	4	1.7	9	172,113	100.7
European Union	6.2	2	156	62,112	93.8
India	3.3	0.8	5	5,168	5.1
Brazil	5.6	1.2	3	3,439	16.7
Japan	3.8	3.26	16	238,323	1,760

In terms of spending on education and research, the previous table highlights US dominance in most aspects, specifically those directly associated with education and research. Its only competitor is Japan, which overtakes the United States of America in terms of the number of patents, innovations and spending on research and development (R&D). The EU also appears as a competitor to the United States of America in terms of the best universities worldwide. More than 224,505 patents were recorded in the United States of America, which also produced 707.6 innovations per million individuals.[77] The previous table lists the most important education and research indicators of states by world order rank.

2. Economy

The main economic indicators for world powers, particularly in terms of GDP for 2012, indicate that the United States of America ($15.685 trillion) comes second after the EU ($16.641 trillion).[78] The United States of America has the highest per capita GDP, and ranks first in terms of the world human development index (HDI). The US economy is also the world's largest in terms of money supply (M3).[79] Table 3 indicates the main economic indicators for major powers in the new world order.

Table 3

Superpower and Major Powers' Main

Economic Indicators, 2012[80]

World power	GDP (trillion US dollars)	Per capita GDP (US dollars)	Human Development Index value, 2012
United States of America	15.685	49,922	0.937
Russia	2.015	14,247	0.788
China	8.227	6,076	0.699
European Union	16.641	32,518	0.845
India	1.842	1,492	0.554
Brazil	2.253	12,079	0.730
Japan	5.960	46,736	0.912

3. Technology

The United States of America is home to most of the biggest global companies in the field of software and networking technology (Microsoft, Apple, Google, etc.), ranks first in the world in terms of the number of personal computers per 100 individuals, and comes second after Japan in terms of internet users per 100 individuals. Table 4 lists the main technology indicators for the major powers.

Table 4
Superpower and Major Powers' Main
Technological Indicators[81]

World power	Number of personal computers per 100 individuals, 2002–2009	Number of internet users per 100 individuals, 2010
United States of America	80.6	74.2
Russia	13.3	43.4
China	5.7	34.4
European Union	22.3	43.4
India	3.2	7.5
Brazil	16.1	40.7
Japan	40.7	77.6

Figure 2
Main Technological Indicators
for the United States of America and Major Powers

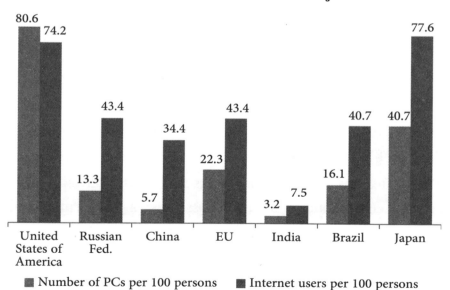

4. Military

All indicators for measuring military capabilities highlight the decisive supremacy of the United States of America over all other actors in the world order, in addition to its possession of the most advanced military technology. Table 5 lists the main military indicators for the ranked powers.

Table 5
Major Military Indicators
in the New World Order[82]

World power	Defense expenditure as a percentage of GDP (%)	Total manpower in armed forces	'Global firepower' ranking	Total number of aircraft carriers	Total number of combat aircraft	Total number of main navy vessels	Possession of space military capabilities	Possession of nuclear military capabilities
United States of America	4.12	1,520,100	1	11	2,851	173	+	+
Russia	3.06	845,000	2	1	1,372	96	+	+
China	1.24	2,285,000	3	1	1,455	118	–	+
European Union	1.52	2,206,000	–	5	2,618	670	–	+
India	1.98	1,325,000	4	1	618	43	+	+
Brazil	1.45	318,500	10	1	234	24	–	–
Japan	0.99	247,450	17	2	552	50	–	–

5. Energy

The United States of America ranks first worldwide in terms of energy consumption. It also possesses a high production capability in energy compared to other competing powers. Table 6 lists the main energy indicators for the major powers in the new world order.

Table 6

Major Energy Indicators

According to Power Rankings

in the New World Order, 2012[83]

World power	Oil production (mbpd)	Oil consumption (mbpd)	Gas production (bcf/y)	Gas consumption (bcf/y)
United States of America	10.136	18.949	22,902	24,385
Russia	10.239	3.115	22,213	17,975
China	4.347	9.852	3,629	4,624
European Union	1.692	13.48	5,474	15,817
India	0.996	3.411	1,682	2,261
Brazil	2.685	2.722	515	885
Japan	0.136	4.481	176	4,361

6. Transport

The United States of America possesses strategic air and maritime transport capabilities that give it global reach. It has the highest number of large-scale and paved-runway airports,[84] as found in Atlanta, Chicago, New York, Houston, San Francisco and Los Angeles; and the longest railways and highways in the world. Table 7 lists the main transport indicators for the ranked powers in the new world order.

Table 7
Major Transport Indicators According to Power Rankings in the New World Order, 2012[85]

World power	Number of airports (paved & unpaved runways)	Number of airports (paved runways)	Number of transport aircraft	Railways (km)	Expressways (km)
United States of America	13,513	5,194	1,795	224,792	75,238
Russia	3,035	462	765	223,270	85,000
China	1,218	601	337	87,157	29,000
European Union	507	452	186	86,000	84,946
India	346	251	238	63,974	200
Brazil	4,093	713	142	28,538	not available
Japan	175	144	86	27,182	7,383

Figure 3
Major Transport Indicators According to Power Rankings in the New World Order

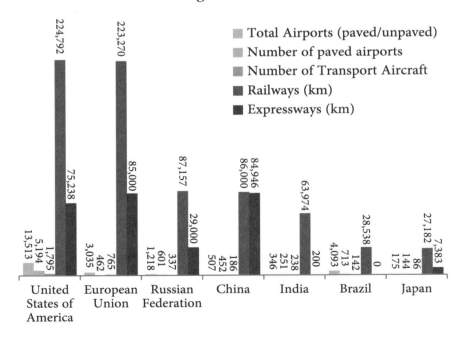

62

US political sociologist George Friedman, in his book *The Next 100 Years: A Forecast for the 21st Century*,[86] describes how the United States of America, as a power that stands alone at the head of the new world order, has five strategic geopolitical goals that drive its grand strategy. The realization of these goals has become increasingly more difficult, just as the goals have become more ambitious over time. Below are the most important aspects mentioned by Friedman regarding the realization of US goals:

1. The Complete Domination of North America by the US Army

Had not the borders of the United States of America extended from the eastern to the western coast of North America (it takes 5 hours and 47 minutes to traverse by air)[87] it would have been extremely unlikely that the United States of America would have survived as a nation state. Its geographical location between two large oceans – namely the Atlantic and the Pacific – has contributed to the preservation of its political cohesion and to its protection, unlike the former Soviet Union and empires both ancient and modern. In the 19th century, two important events took place that shaped the future of the United States of America: 1) the defeat of the British in the Battle of New Orleans (1814/15), which gave the United States of America complete control over the network of rivers in North America; and 2) the defeat of the Mexican army, whereby Mexico lost large areas of its northern lands to the United States of America, including the current State of Texas. Foremost among the clashes with Mexico was the Mexican–American War in which the United States of America invaded Mexico in 1847,[88] confirming the US army as the dominant military power in North America and securing the American continent for the United States of America, creating a vast and wealthy country that could not be strategically challenged regionally.[89]

2. The Elimination of any Threat to the United States of America by any Power in the Western Hemisphere

In reality, Latin America does not constitute any threat whatsoever to the United States of America for geographical reasons. Latin America has difficult terrain, which renders it impassable by large armies, such as an inter-continental force. The only eventuality in Latin America that would concern the United States of America is the establishment of bases by a foreign power.[90]

3. Complete Naval Control of the Maritime Approaches to the United States of America to Deter any Potential Invasion

In the war of 1812, the British Navy sailed past Chesapeake to Baltimore, landing a force to destroy public buildings in Washington, DC on their way,[91] including the White House and the Capitol, which was under construction in March 1814.[92] In the 19th century, the United States of America was very concerned that the British would shut off its access to the oceans, thereby strangling it completely. It therefore secured its Pacific approaches by acquiring Alaska within the framework of a financial deal with Russia on March 30, 1867,[93] and then annexed Hawaii in 1898.[94] During World War II, American military growth put an end to British naval dominance off its East Coast, and thus the United States of America became effectively invulnerable to foreign invasion.[95]

4. Complete Domination of the World's Oceans to Further Secure the United States of America, Protect its Interests and Guarantee Control over International Trade

The United States of America emerged from World War II with the largest network of naval bases in the world. Globally, this is the single most important geopolitical fact; the United States of America controls the world's oceans, and maintaining that geopolitical control is of immense importance.[96]

5. The Prevention of any other Nation from Challenging US Naval Power

"Having achieved domination of all the world's oceans, the US wanted to preserve this domination. Part of this strategy is preventing another power the resources to invest in and build a navy that can challenge this domination. The US works to create shifting allegiances to tie down any potential regional hegemon. Having systematically achieved its strategic goals, the US has the ultimate aim of preventing any major power in Eurasia. The goal of its interventions is never to achieve something – despite political rhetoric – but rather to prevent something. The US wants to prevent stability in areas where another power might emerge. Its goal is not to stabilize, but to destabilize."[97] American intervention was based on preventing sudden or unexpected events; the United States of America wants to achieve stability in areas where other competing powers might emerge.

The New World Order and International Relations

The new world order has a key role in structuring international relations and in determining the balance of power. It is notable that the new world order works toward achieving stability and guaranteeing security in areas where its vital strategic interests lie. Meanwhile, it ignores conflicts in areas not affecting its interests. In other words, the structuring of international relations is directly proportional to the strategic importance of the interests of major powers influencing the new world order. The more the international system has strategic interests in an area, the bigger the role of the powers of that system in achieving or imposing stability.

The new world order has an interest in the balance of power but not at the expense of the balance of interests.[98] This results in either real peace between balanced powers where conflicts of interest still exist and may require crisis management; or to a perfect and comprehensive peace, where mutual deterrence is present in the power balance, which leads to the disappearance of conflict within the international community.[99] In our current unipolar world the degree of maneuver available between opposing or competing forces has reduced. The quality and structure of international relations depend on how close to the dominant power one stands; moreover, international politics also lack balance in any approach to crises and international relations restructuring.

Although other powers retain influence in the global order – such as China, Russia and the EU – they have not as yet been able to assume a role that in any way compares to that of the United States of America. Thus, they sometimes appear to hinder or negotiate their support for actions by the dominant power for the sake of strategic interest or gain. Because of this and their domestic problems that limit their aspirations and influence in the new world order, they stand on the sidelines of the global arena against the United States of America.[100]

The end of the ideological conflict between East and West does not mean the disappearance of the role of ideology (political doctrine) as a driving factor of relations within the new world order.[101] Conflicts have shifted from the very top of the global system to bottom, that is, they have moved to sub-regions which directly affect the structure of international relations. Perhaps what is taking place in the world today stems from nationalism and religion, and is a natural product of the structure of the new world order under a unipolar system, which operates according to the interests of the dominant power. Thus, it works in favor of one party at the expense of another, or stands as a neutral observer as long as the interests of this strategic power remain unaffected. Because of this, parties that feel a sense of grievance concerning international injustice pursue their own interests by the use of violence based on sectarian, nationalistic, ethnic and tribal affiliations in order to achieve their aims.

In addition, there is the role of the new world order in promoting the struggle over energy resources and even the search for alternative energy sources.[102] Oil has been at the center of many global events due to its role at the heart of the global economy, and therefore it comprises one of the factors influencing international relations and the distribution of power. For these reasons, the major powers have sought to impose their own pricing and supply controls on oil to ensure economic superiority on the one hand, and economic control over competing powers on the other.

Moisés R. Naím argues in his book *The End of Power...*[103] that "the nature of power in the new world order is decaying and shifting from West to East and North to South, from presidential palaces to public squares, from large stable armies to loose bands of insurgents, from formidable corporate behemoths to nimble agile start-ups, and from brawn to brains."[104]

68

Table 8
Average Daily Oil Production
and Consumption, 2012[105]

Country	Average daily production (thousand barrels)	Country	Average daily consumption (thousand barrels)
Saudi Arabia	11,530	United States of America	18,555
Russia	10,643	China	10,221
United States of America	8,905	Japan	4,714
China	4,155	India	3,652
Canada	3,741	Russia	3,174
Iran	3,680	Saudi Arabia	2,935
United Arab Emirates	3,380	Brazil	2,805
Kuwait	3,127	South Korea	2,458
Iraq	3,115	Canada	2,412
Mexico	2,911	Germany	2,358
Venezuela	2,725	Mexico	2,074
Nigeria	2,417	Iran	1,971
Brazil	2,149	France	1,687
Qatar	1,966	Indonesia	1,565
Norway	1,916	United Kingdom	1,468
Rest of the world	19,792	Rest of the world	27,725
World total	**86,152**	**World total**	**89,774**

Figure 4
Average Daily Oil Production, 2012 (kbpd)

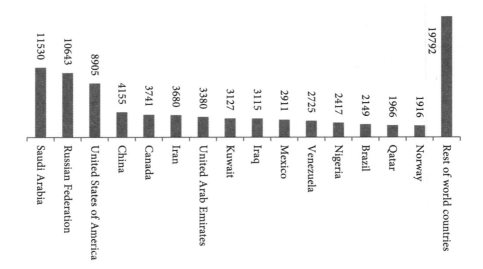

Figure 5
Average Daily Oil Consumption, 2012 (kbpd)

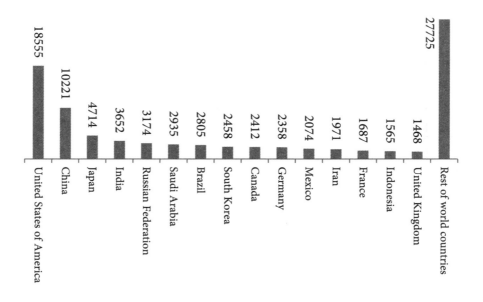

However, the shift in power from the West to the East, and from the North to the South, along with other changes, as Naím argues, do not negate the dominance of the United States of America over the mechanisms of this shift. Neither do they diminish its control and hegemony or its leading role in the world order.

According to Naím, "Power is shifting, becoming harder to use and easier to lose. As a result, all leaders have less power than their predecessors, and the potential for upheaval is unprecedented."[106] Demonstrations against state institutions in small countries might lead to the overthrow of tyrannical regimes, eliminate monopolistic and corrupt practices and create new opportunities for state-building. However, they may also result in chaos and paralysis. Internal events and changes in some Arab countries over the last few years indicate that the waves of change resulting from the shift in power patterns from the governing regimes to the streets, sometimes lead to forms of chaos and unrest that are very hard to control. They may last for years and even jeopardize the cohesion, stability and regional status of countries. Based on the same logic, and as a result of the shift in power patterns, according to Naím, the latest round of UN talks on climate change have not resulted in any convergence in opinion between countries on how to address the phenomenon of global warming.[107]

In addition, power is declining on the battlefields around the world and even among corporate boards. A study conducted in 2001 by political scientist Prof. Ivan M. Arreguin-Toft[108] of Boston University on 197 asymmetrical (non-traditional) wars[109] discovered that, "between 1800 and 1849 the weaker side (in terms of soldiers and weapons) achieved its strategic goals in only 12% of cases. But in the wars that erupted between 1950 and 1998, the weaker side prevailed more often: 55% of the time."[110] Therefore, military power has been seen to alter radically, and the same can be applied to companies. In 1980 the American company Raytheon was rated among the top 20 companies in terms of size and industry. After two decades, the company's ranking had fallen by 25% and the average length of stay of the company's CEO dropped from around ten years in the 1990s to five and a half years in recent years.[111]

This drop in the impact of traditional power has clearly emerged in the new world order, where al-Qaeda has been able to threaten the impervious image of the United States of America; the Taliban was able to inflict heavy losses on US and coalition forces and deprived them of total victory; and Somali pirates with outdated boats and AK-47 rifles have managed to limit the operational effectiveness of modern multinational naval vessels – including naval ships belonging to the largest military power in history, the United States of America – that have been mobilized to counter maritime piracy in that area. Furthermore, EU leaders failed to contain the economic crisis that emanated from the relatively small Greek economy. When the world is unable to agree on how to reduce carbon emissions, it becomes clear that something is happening to power in the new world order beyond any Sino-American competition based on a zero-sum equation. This decline in power and influence may be the result of three concurrent revolutions: ease of access and availability of information and goods, mobility of ideas and people, and profound changes in attitudes and ideas among the general populace.[112]

The 'More' Revolution

The 21st century is characterized by an abundance of everything, from people to literacy, products in markets, and political parties. The global middle class is expanding and by 2050 the world population will be four times what it was 100 years earlier.[113] According to the World Bank, the proportion of the population living in extreme poverty is expected to decrease by 16.3% in 2015[114]—the first fall since statistics on poverty have been available. Since 2006, 28 low-income countries have been reclassified as middle income[115] and the resulting new middle class is both well-informed and eager for progress beyond what governments are able to deliver. The intolerance shown by this middle class towards corruption has transformed into an effective force behind a number of political changes occurring in the developing world during the first decade of the 21st century.[116]

The 'Mobility' Revolution

There is revolutionary human mobility in the new world order – represented by the unprecedented movement of people – and one that is very difficult to control. The UN estimates that there are 214 million migrants around the world who live in places other than their country of origin—an increase of 37% in the past two decades.[117] Ethnic, religious, and professional migrations, along with political migrations as a result of various types of conflicts and developmental pressures, change the distribution of power within a population, allowing migrants to assume power regardless of race, color, creed or sect.

The 'Mentality' Revolution

In the new world order, individuals are able to access more sources of information and knowledge than ever before, culminating in what is termed the 'knowledge economy.' Knowledge has become the main driver of economic growth, whether in production or services, and is a result of scientific research, technology and innovation.[118] This phenomenon has in turn resulted in an enormous global cognitive and mental transformation. The *World Values Survey 2010* has revealed growing global consensus on the importance of individual freedoms and gender equality, and a widespread intolerance of dictatorial regimes.[119] Dissatisfaction with political systems, social norms, and government institutions is also growing universally, an example of which is the increased empowerment of women in many countries. However, divorce rates have increased to reach 20% in Saudi Arabia, 26% in the United Arab Emirates (UAE), and 37% in Kuwait in 2010.[120] Certainly these indicators work against the empowerment of women in those countries, or at least reduce the effectiveness of those efforts.

The combination of these three revolutions has contributed to the weakening of barriers that formerly shielded the powerful from their competitors. The 'abundance revolution' helps those competitors to sweep away such barriers; the mobility revolution helps them to circumvent those barriers; while the cognitive revolution helps them to undermine such barriers.

While I think that the above proposition regarding the limits of power in the new world order includes immovable realities, it is also necessary to note that this overlooks the drastic change in the nature of power and the fact that the decline in the components of traditional power does not mean a corresponding absolute decline in state power, especially considering the fact that the United States of America has realized these changes early, as supported by numerous US studies and research within this context.[121] The changes in the concept of power concern the limits of its use, the re-invention of power, combining US hard and soft power, and the emergence of what is described as 'smart power.'[122]

Humanitarian Intervention in the New World Order

The principle of humanitarian intervention has emerged as an important element in the new world order after the end of the Cold War and subsequent domination by the United States of America. The fall of communism resulted in the outbreak of internal conflicts and ethnic violence in many countries. The obligation has fallen on states and international organizations to protect these minorities and populations exposed to human rights violations, as witnessed in Kosovo and Libya. The United States of America, in collaboration with certain other major powers, has the ability to intervene anywhere in the world – namely areas witnessing natural, industrial, political, military or economic disasters that threaten the lives of the population or that are facing a state of insecurity that is hard to control under the pretext of humanitarian assistance and peace-keeping, as occurred in northern Iraq in 1991, Somalia in 1992, and Kosovo in 1999.[123]

The principle of intervention for humanitarian purposes has collided with the concepts of sovereignty, independence, non-interference in the internal affairs of states, and a number of recognized international conventions. It is these concepts that certain leaders exploit when taking hardened positions against political opposition movements, or ethnic, religious or sectarian minorities. Therefore, advocates of the principle of humanitarian intervention overlay a layer of ethical compliance to justify invasive operations, and legitimize their decisions by pressuring the UN Security Council and other international organizations to adopt damning resolutions, thus allowing for intervention on the pretext of improving humanitarian conditions. Yet the selective implementation of these humanitarian principles reveals the existence of implicit interests to be achieved through their application, thereby allowing intervention by the UN and other international organizations.[124]

However, the principle of humanitarian intervention in all circumstances collides with historical and cultural contexts. Foreign troops without the cover of international legitimacy, and undertaking operations using the pretext of creating a secure environment for humanitarian assistance, do not take into account the historical, cultural, social and ethnic nature of the conflict occurring inside the state whose sovereignty has been penetrated. This usually leads to failure on the one hand, and increases the challenges facing the exit strategy on the other. There are numerous examples of this, such as Somalia, Bosnia, Kosovo, Iraq and Afghanistan. The possession by some regimes of weapons of mass destruction (WMD) and their use against civilians is considered one of the justifications for legitimate humanitarian intervention in accordance with international law. The possession of WMDs and their use by certain regimes against civilians are considered one justification for humanitarian intervention in accordance with international approval; this is exactly the issue that has raised such tremendous controversy in the Syrian crisis.

These facts raise many questions about humanitarian intervention, namely, what are the humanitarian situations in which major powers choose to use military might? When is UN legitimacy required for intervention? To what extent are the major powers willing to bear the risks of intervention? What procedures and time period are required for military success? And what is the impact on the population whose national sovereignty is being transgressed?

Table 9

Major World Hedge Fund Institutions

by Size of Assets Managed, October 2011[125]

Hedge Fund	Managed Assets (billion dollars)
Bridgewater Associates (United States of America)	77.6
The Man Group (United Kingdom)	64.5
JP Morgan Asset Management (United States of America)	46.6
Brevan Howard Asset Management LLP (United Kingdom)	32.6
Och-Ziff Capital Management Group (United States of America)	28.5

While the number of sovereign states has more than quadrupled since the 1940s – from 41 to 194 countries[126] – the new world order has sometimes required certain states to relinquish aspects of sovereignty for the sake of global security and stability. This erosion of national sovereignty witnessed through the influence of certain international bodies such as the IMF, high-risk investment funds, sovereign wealth funds, and even organized crime, entails compliance with the conditions laid down by such bodies, which implies a transgression of state sovereignty.

Moreover, the ruling authority in any country is no longer absolute; it now operates under internal restrictions and external determinants that can topple it, if ignored. In 1977, there were 89 countries subject to authoritarian rule,[127] but by 2011 that number had fallen to 22. Today, more than half of the world's population lives under a form of democratic rule.[128] In addition, democratic elections were conducted in 117 out of 193 countries in 2011, compared to 69 out of 167 countries in 1989.[129]

The decline of the governing power in any country is due not only to democracy and empowerment made available via the internet; communication technology and social networks are also important tools. But for them to have an effect, these tools need users, and these in turn need guidance and motivation. The use of social networking was a key factor in empowering demonstrators during the 'Arab Awakening.' However, the circumstances that prompted those protesters to take to the street were domestic and personal, such as unemployment, poor living conditions, the deterioration of the economic situation, and the expectations of the fast-growing and better-educated middle class not being met. However, the very technology that enabled citizens to monitor the state and its actions also helped Iran, for example, identify those who took part in the 'Green Revolution' in 2009, and imprison them.[130]

As the leading power of the new world order has sought to structure international relations according to its interests, the issues of political reform, achieving democracy and preserving human rights have been raised. These are issues that affect the image of the new world order on the one hand, and allow doubts to be raised about the legitimacy of certain regimes on the other. Therefore, for example, we have seen the United States of America use force against Haiti to impose democracy (September 1994–March 1995)[131] in an attempt to confer international legitimacy on its role in the new world order by acting under the umbrella of the UN and its affiliates. This has meant molding the work of such international bodies and organizations to achieve US strategic interests and prevent any objection by major powers to its approach to global issues.[132]

Effects of the New World Order

Today's global system has various different effects on society, some of which stem from the structure of the new world order itself, and some of which result from the behavior of the actors within it. These effects are as follows:

1. *Political effects:* terms such as transparency, governance, good governance,[133] democracy, political reform, human rights, and the rights of women and minorities have become

widespread. Thus, many countries have been strategically exposed to the requirements of the new world order.

2. *Economic effects:* the global economic crisis that began in 2007 has had a global effect; its repercussions are still felt today, including in the form of currency wars within the global financial system.

3. *Social effects:* we are living in a global village and therefore societal isolation is difficult. Interactions between individuals and communities allow both sides to influence and be influenced, and help build international public opinion that has an effect on the role of the new world order.

4. *Military effects:* the use of armed force has become a key feature in the new world order and is relied upon to impose the interests of major powers. The UN Security Council has been adapted to legitimize military intervention. UN Security Council Resolution 794 of 1992 gave legitimacy to US military intervention in Somalia under the name 'Operation Restore Hope,' as well as UN Security Council Resolution 940 of 1994, which authorized the military intervention in Haiti, resulting in the US intervention in May 1994.[134] Resolution 1368 in September 2001 granted the United States of America legitimacy to invade Afghanistan, and Resolution 1441, issued on November 8, 2002, which the United States of America used as a justification to invade Iraq in March 2003. The global imbalance of power led states to form alliances and coalitions.

5. *Media effects:* the impact of audiovisual, print and online media on how the world is able to connect regardless of borders, time and place or hierarchy has become prominent. The revolution in telecommunications is also a direct effect on the new world order. After the collapse of artificial barriers between communities and the availability of capabilities to transcend sovereign boundaries, the world has become a global village within the system of the new world order.

The Divisions of this Book

This volume has been divided into seven main chapters in addition to the Preface, Introduction and Conclusion.

In this Introduction the focus is on the central proposition of the book, namely the primacy of the United States of America in the new world order in the presence of major powers such as China, EU, Russia, Japan and emerging countries of international weight such as India and Brazil, ranked in accordance with the proposed criteria determining the world order, namely: education, culture, economy, technology, military capability, energy and transport. These criteria are considered the main benchmarks against which a country's position can be gauged within the hierarchy of the new world order.

Chapter I, entitled "The New World Order: Features and Concepts," has been divided into two themes: the first deals with the concepts of the new world order by means of an essential introduction to determine the nature of its structure, the differences between the new world order and the international system, the concept of the 'universal actor' and the superpower, where the former is a participant with an opinion, while the latter is dominant and has a global strategy that it strives to achieve using tools with global effects.

The second theme deals with the most prominent features of the new world order, including global civil society, globalization, the civilizational and ideological conflicts of the new world order and their repercussions for the international community, the controversial relationship between globalization and state sovereignty, and interactions between globalization, realism and liberalism. It discusses the theory of the 'end of history,' the conflict between Islam and the West, the proliferation of ethnic, factional and sectarian conflicts, and the growth of extremist trends and ideologies – particularly the emergence of the US far right – where the new world order faces challenges and risks as a result of new and existing conflicts of varying degrees of severity, effect and implications. This theme also deals with scenarios resulting from the impact of ideologies in international relations, including: the continuation of the 'business-as-usual' scenario, the 'retreating role of ideology' scenario, and a third scenario in which progressive and humanitarian ideologies are able to regain the political initiative.

As part of this theme, I also discuss the role of the United States of America as a unipolar actor at the top of the new world order and a leading country in the field of research and development, higher education and entrepreneurial activities. It allies itself with the largest two entities that possess a per capita gross national income (GNI) close to that of the United States of America, namely the EU and Japan. Therefore it is difficult to say that we live in 'the post-US world'; rather we explore the prospects for the American era. However, the United States of America has to face its own internal problems, such as debt and political problems, and maintain the development of quality secondary education.

Chapter II, entitled "Factors Influencing the Structure of the New World Order," examines the issues affecting the makeup of the new world order and the extent of their effects on the conduct of international relations. This leads to an analysis of the relations between countries and their various dimensions in the new world order, the strategic opportunities and constraints with regard to the management of foreign policy, and how common global challenges might be addressed. The chapter also discusses relations between civilizations, and deals with levels of power in international relations – including how they affect the structure of the new world order – economic factors, strategic military superiority, as well as societal effects of scientific and technological progress and related impacts on the structure of the new world order. Whoever enjoys scientific progress and technological development controls knowledge, and whoever controls knowledge controls the world and the future. The new world order also faces new challenges, namely: partnerships, the geostrategic situation, national sovereignty, security, terrorism, and globalization.

Chapter III, entitled "The New World Order: Decisive Junctures," contains a historical analysis of significant milestones in the history of the new world order, with a view to identifying those events that affected – and perhaps continue to affect – the formation of the new world order, in order to better understand the foundations of this order and the impact of history on its future. The Cold War period cast a shadow over the world order and ultimately led to an imbalance of power. Nuclear weapons became the dominant factor in military relations between countries and crises became widespread. The Gulf War of 1991 came to form a new milestone in the evolution of the new world order, whereby the United States of America assembled an international military alliance of 34 countries to restore regional security in the Middle East. New universal values emerged from this effort, based on peace, stability, human rights, humanitarian intervention and global responsibility to protect vulnerable states. Later, the spread of globalization was to have a clear impact on the world order in terms of the development of relations and the spread of a single cultural model in a manner that reflects the erosion of national sovereignty, the spread of global communications, and growing cross-border issues.

Chapter IV, entitled "The New World Order: Economy, Trade and Energy," studies in detail the role of money, trade and the economy in the structure of the new world order. Economics plays a key role in shaping the structure of the order and is the locomotive that drives unipolar power. The global financial system, associated currency conflicts, and the role of international financial institutions directly affect the nature of the management of the new world order. The same is true of trade, its various dimensions, global lines of passage and what it reflects in terms of consensus or competition within the international system. The economic system is itself a complementary global system that exists in parallel to the political world order. Each of them influences the other; it depends on global economic growth and various forms of energy – be they conventional hydrocarbons or unconventional resources – rates of production and consumption, the extent of self-sufficiency, strategic exposure, the gap between energy production and consumption up to 2030, government budgets, the size of public debt, the balance of trade, and strategic transport capacities and their diversity. The power of a state is affected by its possession of transport capabilities of a global nature in order to be able to control global freedom of trade and expand into markets.

Chapter V, entitled "Public Opinion and the New World Order: A Survey of the UAE Population" offers a detailed study of public opinion polls of different age groups within the multinational population (nationals and expatriates) of the UAE. The study examines the prevailing perception of values and ethics in the new world order to identify people's viewpoint regarding the nature and working mechanisms of the order and to what extent that viewpoint is in harmony with the reality of that order. The importance of individuals and their influence in the new world order has emerged in light of interest in rights, maintaining freedoms and upholding their independence in a world in which the barriers of space and time have been reduced via the realms of cyberspace.

Chapter VI, "Prospective Structural Changes and their Consequences for the New World Order," studies the projected strategic effects on countries around the world as a result of the structural changes expected in the new world order, examining the positions and roles of nations and the potential, capabilities and sources of wealth that they might contribute to this system, resulting in the identification of clear variations in their strategic vulnerability to change. The chapter also argues that the new world order is merely a set of social, economic, political and geographical realities governing relations within the global community; yet these do not occur in a universal vacuum—rather they affect (and are affected by) the main actors in the system, taking into account the dominant role of the single superpower that controls the current hierarchical structure of the present global system.

One of the most important structural changes expected in the new world order is its division into two parts: the first part will consist of those allied or affiliated to the dominant power – or at least those that are neutral – while the second will be equivalent and opposing; attempting to match up to the accelerating progress of the single pole. Yet the relations of interdependence between the various units of both parts may play a decisive role in determining the nature of relations and patterns of interaction within a world order that has several distinctive features, including dependence on market economy, democracy and political liberalism, enabling individuals to exercise their freedoms and rights and participate in the decisions affecting them, as well as the promotion of political pluralism, popular sovereignty, a return to economic blocs, and the emergence of a political role for sovereign wealth funds.

The economic dimension will become more influential than the political factor in shaping relations and policies within the system. US military power will maintain its superiority in the new world order, and will stick to a preemptive military strategy in facing major threats. Nuclear arms may become more widespread, which will increase global instability. As the United States of America upholds its ideology, it is likely that this influence will increase within the system and it will reflect on cultural, media, educational and political fields.

The roles of religion, nationalism and sectarianism are expected to grow as a result of the increasing overlap between communities, rather than as a consequence of the failure of certain states to fulfill their social and economic functions. The spread of new technology will accelerate and the risks to global stability will increase as a result of a further deterioration in human living conditions, especially in the poorest countries, as migration to urban areas, combined with a population explosion, leads to an increase in the numbers of disadvantaged and the existence of hundreds of millions of young unemployed.

The most important mechanisms of strategic influence in the new world order are: hard power, soft power, smart power, international institutions and bodies, media, the internet, the establishment of new blocs and alliances, bilateral and multilateral conventions, parallel diplomacy and proxy war, conference and seminar diplomacy, and direct and indirect military intervention. Therefore, the chapter charts the possible strategic effects of the future of the new world order for the UN, the EU, South America, the Russian Federation, China, Japan, India, Eurasia, and Africa.

Chapter VII, "The New World Order: Future Outlook," explores the potential future of the global system and reviews its determinants and characteristics, employing a mid-term forecast based on the current situation and taking into account the various factors affecting the system's evolution. It reveals the most important features of the future order to be a system that tends toward unipolarity; increasing reliance on technology and non-conventional systems of production and communication, as well as genetic engineering, cloning and nanotechnology; growing pressure on the capitalist system to reform in light of the recent global financial crisis; a decline in conventional military conflicts; increased reliance on technology and soft power; and employing a military force to act as a deterrent in order to facilitate negotiation and the resolution of conflicts and crises.

Finally, the Conclusion sheds further light on many of the observations that can be drawn from the preceding chapters of the book, namely that the world is heading towards increasingly fierce rivalry between economies. Integration into the global economy is no longer an option that can be disregarded; rather, adapting to globalization in all its manifestations has become an increasingly urgent necessity. It is also suggested that the globalization of international issues and affairs has not occurred as a direct result of the interests of a certain bloc or category of countries; rather, there is a key parallel motive, which is the need to face emerging global challenges via effective international cooperation. Further emphasis is given to the current research debate on the nature of the new world order, the reality of US hegemony over this order, and the recognition – implicitly or explicitly – by the major powers of the US role within this framework. The Conclusion also indicates that the world order is currently passing through a pivotal stage that could be very significant to its development over the coming years and decades.

There is no doubt that the Syrian crisis is a significant milestone that has tested the limits of US power in the face of Sino-Russian resistance and refusal to sanction the use of military force against the regime of president Bashar al-Assad. The Conclusion confirms that it is premature to say that this ongoing struggle of wills between the world's sole superpower and its allies on the one hand, and additional major powers on the other, will be a harbinger of a multipolar world order, or spell the emergence of a formula for the sharing of power and influence between the United States of America and certain other major powers, especially considering the fact that the military solutions that have contributed to the decline in US influence following its involvement in Afghanistan and Iraq have themselves been the focus of debate in connection with the Syrian crisis. Thus, any approach other than a military response to crises would also be of interest to the United States of America and its allies, which now adopt smart power to achieve their strategic interests. Hard power is no longer the sole way forward; US supremacy in the economic, military, technological, scientific, cultural and educational areas, as well as in energy and transport, and the ability of the United States of America to renew and adapt, all cast doubt on the chances of a power-sharing arrangement to lead the new world order, at least in the foreseeable future.

THE NEW WORLD ORDER:
FEATURES AND CONCEPTS

Chapter I

The New World Order:
Features and Concepts

When the topic of the new world order is put forward for study, controversy and debate soon ensue regarding its nature – indeed, sometimes its very existence – and how it differs from the international system in terms of its concepts and general framework, and whether there are facts that testify to the validity of such characterizations. Therefore, there is a need to identify the key concepts and their dimensions, and arrange these in various theoretical frameworks which might engender both agreement and disagreement in the world of research. Yet this commendable debate does not alter the fact that it is the outcome of an academic pursuit, which at its heart does not rely on an absolute definition of concepts as rigid terms. In parallel to the above, they pose questions regarding the most salient features and manifestations of this order. It seems appropriate in this chapter to deal with this issue based on two themes: the first relates to concepts, in an attempt to discover and comprehend the realities of the new world order in its various guises. The second focuses on the most prominent features of this order, addressing, *inter alia*, global civil society, globalization, civilizational and ideological conflicts, the controversial relationship between globalization and state sovereignty, interactions between globalization, realism and liberalism, the debate on the notion of a clash between civilizations, the controversy of the relationship between Islam and the West, ethnic, factional and sectarian conflicts, and the growth of extremist trends and ideologies in the new world order, using the US far right as an example.

Theme #1: Concepts

Most political and social science literature agrees on the existence of the so-called 'new world order,' but differs in terms of the timing and causes of its advent.

There are three main approaches to explain the development of this order, namely:[1]

The first approach argues that the emergence of 'nation-states' from the treaties of Westphalia in 1648 marks the real beginning of an international system. It may not be clearly defined in terms of having dominant powers that manage its affairs, yet the nature of the system's interactions indicates its presence. Advocates of this approach refer to the armed conflicts that took place in the wake of these treaties, such as the wars of Bismarck in the mid-19th century and World War I (1914–1918), which resulted in the emergence of the League of Nations.[2]

Those who oppose this view believe that the treaties of Westphalia were the first diplomatic agreement in modern history, coming after religious wars that lasted for three decades,[3] and established a new system in central Europe in accordance with the principles of equality between states, respect for national sovereignty and non-intervention in the internal affairs of other states. The House of Bourbon emerged as a superpower in control of Europe[4] at the time and France's status in Europe rose, becoming a strong competitor to Germany, and resulting in the emergence of regional major powers rather than a global system.[5] France was able to extend its borders, achieve unity, instigate discord in the constituent states of the German Empire by agitating conflict between rulers of the states and the German emperor, as well as the dispute between the Protestant north and the Catholic south. This protected France from the threat of a united Germany on the one hand, and ensured France's superiority as a dominant regional power in Europe on the other.[6]

The rapid US withdrawal after 1919 from its external obligations, and the parallel isolationist Soviet orientation under the Bolsheviks after 1917, left behind a global system that was disconnected from economic reality.[7] The other powers in the global system at the time, such as Britain and France, had to face German and Japanese challenges and therefore to expand as soon as possible if they wanted to be free from the influence of the two continental giants – the United States of America and Russia – which possessed huge industrial power.[8]

The new world order came about as a natural consequence of the evolution of the international system that developed after World War I with the creation of the League of Nations, which emerged after the Paris Peace Conference of January 18–21, 1919.[9] By February 23, 1935, the number of countries that had joined the League of Nations reached 58.[10] The most important objectives of the League of Nations were to prevent the outbreak of war by ensuring common security between states, arms control, and the settlement of international disputes through negotiations and international arbitration. Later, the United Nations was born on June 26, 1945 with the signing of an agreement in San Francisco in the presence of representatives of some 50 countries.[11] The pursuit of a global civil society led to the birth of a new world order that now transcends geography and history and works to establish a single global model that takes into consideration different societal, political, economic, military, educational, cultural and media frameworks.[12]

The second approach advocates that the new world order has emerged in the wake of the Cold War following the break-up of the Soviet Union into several countries of marginal global influence; the end of the ideological struggle between communism and capitalism; and the eventual rise of the United States of America to the top of the new world order in 1990[13] after the Soviet Union transitioned from being a superpower to merely another global player. Yoshihiro Francis Fukuyama even went as far as to suggest that the

1990s heralded not just the end of the Cold War, but the 'end of history' as we knew it. The ideological struggle that had governed the world since the advent of Marxism in the second half of the 19th century[14] – followed by the Bolshevik Revolution in February 1917, the establishment of Socialist International (SI) and the emergence of the Eastern bloc after the end of World War II – reached its limit and subsequent demise with the rise of the liberal capitalist system and the market economy.[15] However, opponents of this opinion argue that this system did not emerge as a result of the end of the Cold War, the fall of the Soviet Union and the decline of its role as a world superpower due to deteriorating economic conditions; rather it was the result of US involvement in the Gulf War, which highlighted its dominance and role in mobilizing the international community against the Iraqi invasion of Kuwait on August 2, 1990.[16]

The third approach, therefore confirmed the emergence of the new world order after former US President George Herbert Bush [Sr.] mobilized international efforts to achieve US interests in the Middle East and liberate Kuwait from Iraqi occupation on February 26, 1991. He announced in three consecutive speeches the emergence of a new world order, which would realize the universal strategic objectives of the United States of America in making the twenty-first century an American age.[17] Stressing the role of the United States of America and its leadership in a speech on April 13, 1992, at Montgomery Air Force base in Alabama,[18] the US president spoke about a new world order in the making, the end of four decades of the Cold War and the fact that the conflict with the Communist bloc, including the Warsaw Pact, had now passed into the pages of history. He highlighted the suffering in countries such as Iraq and the responsibilities of the United States of America – after its major success in ending the Cold War, the triumph of liberal values and the market economy, and the liberation of Kuwait – to promote commitment to the principles of international legitimacy, respect for international law, adherence to the principle of collective security, solidarity in the face of aggression, and arms reduction and control, while emphasizing the guarantees of freedom, democracy, development and human rights.[19]

However, critics of this approach believe that the new world order had already emerged economically before it was even announced by the former US President. They argue that the General Agreement on Tariffs and Trade (GATT) and the World Trade Organization (WTO)[20] are elements of this global economic system that materialized over the course of more than five decades. The tendency towards globalization of trade subsequently grew under the complete control of the United States of America, the IMF and the World Bank.[21]

There is another line of thought that denies a new world order has emerged at all. It considers the world today as simply going through a transitional stage – a harbinger of the emergence of the new world order – basing its claims on such current realities as international monetary liquidity, anarchy, and a lack of clarity in US universal strategy. This claim views the new world order as still passing through an evolutionary stage in which its development is marked by differentiating itself from the heritage of the bipolar system. Where efforts are made to formulate its structure and hierarchy, its inherent rules and foundations differ from the previous world order, particularly in terms of the current promotion of values and principles linked to the achievement of peace, an end to global conflict, and the imposition of international law and human rights.[22]

One final opinion asserts that the origins of the new world order could date back to the 1960s, as a result of academic development, the emergence of global movements, the proliferation of regional and international blocs, and growing competition between the major powers for sources of overall strength. Thus, the global events witnessed at the end of the 1980s and early 1990s, such as the fall of the Berlin Wall and the break-up of the Soviet Union, merely shaped the environment for the existence of this new world order, with all peoples and nations contributing to its existence through their struggle for cultural, political, economic and social causes.[23]

Despite differences in opinion, all confirm the existence of a new world order by its presence in international diplomacy, world crisis management, the globalization of the economy, the dissemination of political, social, cultural and educational values and media (both traditional and digital), the global spread of democracy and civil society, and successive technological revolutions in communications and information.

What is the New World Order?

Any system consists of an interactive set of elements, including governing general principles that interact with each other in accordance with specific objectives and common interests.[24]

A system may also contain sub-systems, each with different functions within a larger framework. If we apply this 'systems theory' to the new world order, we discover that it is an interactive group within the global environment, affected by common interests, that works to address crises affecting humanity, establish decision-making processes, and enact the strategies of different parties in a system in which sub-state level powers have a significant impact over its direction.[25]

Therefore, the new world order is primarily the result of major transformations arising as a result of new global challenges. It has unique characteristics formed by the rules, structures and levels of relations that bind its actors, and a clear consensus between the United States of America as a major force and a limited number of less influential countries and groupings (such as the EU, China, Russia, Japan, India and Brazil) – most of which are politically advanced and technologically developed – over a set of rules organizing the relations of these countries with each other and the rest of the world.[26]

The Concept of the New World Order: Multiple Perspectives

International interactions over the last 50 years indicate a transition from an international system to a truly global order. However, scholars differ in their approach to developing an integrated and comprehensive definition of this order. In the wake of the announcement by George Herbert Bush [Sr.] of the emergence of a new world order, former Secretary of State Henry Alfred Kissinger commented that this new world order was evident in the transformations taking place in the world, but that it was still in the process of formation and had not yet fully materialized.[27] It is difficult to talk about a system that is not yet complete.

Kissinger also believed that the new world order would reward or punish its participants according to economic criteria. However, such criteria do not stimulate loyalty or support in individuals,[28] as they indicate the development of an order under state control, rather than one under the control of the individual and civil society.

Joseph M. Frankel defines the new world order as a set of independent political events that interact with each other on a regular basis.[29] That is, the order determines its own system according to the results of the interactions of events. Although this may have historical precedent, any system has a leadership that manages its operations and whose change needs to take place over long periods of time.[30]

Others have defined the new world order as a set of rules for international dealings, both in times of conflict and cooperation, that are laid down by the major powers in the international community and imposed on their contemporaries.[31] Here, the new world order is looked upon as an international system, despite the obvious difference between them, recognizing implicitly the impact of international conventions on relations between the main and subsidiary actors in the system. This international system deals with states, whereas the new world order includes not only states, but also populations, civil society organizations and individuals.[32]

Many researchers and intellectuals confirm the existence of a new unipolar world order[33] with the United States of America undisputedly at its top. Its position is supported by Western allies on the one hand, and its ability to use its military power to resolve conflict and maintain global stability on the other.[34] This view is based on the fact that the disappearance of the Soviet Union has provided a unique opportunity for the United States of America to assume global power, control and status. It has become capable of employing the elements of power in its possession to fulfill its responsibilities in the organization and management of world affairs without any substantive competition or challenge from any other international power, and has thus assumed an undisputed position at the top of the new world order.

According to a more comprehensive concept, we may define the new world order as the product of all interactions between nations, peoples, individuals, and community organizations without discrimination, based on universal values and common interests that are concentrated in the pursuit of international justice and equality among nations and the spread of democracy. These interactions are a natural result of a growing awareness due to global progress in the realms of satellite media, telecommunications and information and cross-border social networking that represent, in turn, a seemingly infinite development in cyber-technology under the direction of global powers with a universal strategy.

What is the Difference between the International System and the New World Order?

There are many criteria by which the fundamental differences between the international system and the new world order may be measured. Most important among these are: major actors, international decision-making, the nature of international relations, the role of civil society, the economy, national sovereignty, the relationship between the internal and external security of states, the prevalence of global values, and the legal regime.

In the international system, the state and its official representatives appear at the forefront, dealing with international organizations – primarily the UN and its institutions, agencies and bodies – in accordance with international conventions. On the other hand, the prominent actor in the new world order is civil society, both local and global, the individual, popular will, domestic and international public opinion, and local organizations. All these now have influential roles and interact more widely within the new world order than ever before.

Recent movements in international law demonstrate its close ties to international relations, and therefore with the new world order. While international law has traditionally been focused on the sovereignty of states, and was not intended to end wars but to reduce their likelihood by balancing power, it managed, at the end of the 20th century, to achieve the goal of establishing a relative balance of justice in numerous cases of crisis, and currently seeks to achieve the target of mutual cooperation and coordination between states, as well as guarantee a certain degree of integration of power.[35] An example of such cooperation can been seen in the international alliances formed to support humanitarian intervention – for example in Kosovo and Libya – or to uphold international justice, as in the case of the ejection of Iraqi occupying forces from Kuwait.

The ongoing technological revolution has led to both positive and negative consequences for international law. The development of new, ever more powerful WMDs was initially pursued to emphasize the role of coercion in global politics at the expense of legal principles. Countries now seek a better balance between law and politics, with a view to forming a more coherent and therefore more secure global system. Most probably the international legal system will become, within the foreseeable future, more effective in strengthening relations between countries, as well as in safeguarding their interdependence.[36]

Decision-making within the international system is based on debate, and attempts to impose international justice according to the vision of the five major powers that are influential in the management of the international system. It is a *relative* justice that is sometimes applied by the UN and its international institutions (particularly the Security Council, the decisions of which are controlled by the five major countries with permanent membership and the 'right of veto'). However, in the new world order decisions are often made according to the vision of the sole superpower that dominates and the international system. This means that the dominant superpower is the party that, in consultation or coordination with the major powers and within the limits of its interests and objectives, undertakes to manage the affairs of the new world order through its diplomatic, military, economic, media, educational, cultural and technological capabilities so that it may impose its own interests, with or without international legitimacy, as dictated by regional and international circumstances.[37]

Therefore, the nature of international relations in the international system differs from that in the new world order. In the former, we find that diplomatic tools have priority in determining the nature and evolution of this relationship, while in the latter, the role of informal relations, the media, social networking, non-governmental organizations, civil society institutions, and transnational corporations are prominent in the formulation of a country's status within the global system. The interests of the superpower dominating the new world order will be directly or indirectly present in all international interactions.[38]

The influence of the role of civil society in the new world order is certainly much stronger when compared with the international system. In the presence of national, regional and global organizations interested in human rights and working to protect rights and maintain human dignity and freedom of worship, without distinction in terms of color, sex or race, concern is for the individual and therefore the community, expressed by non-governmental organizations under a new world order that acknowledges the role of this civil society. Under the international system, dealings are carried out through states, their governments and official representatives. Economic globalization has formed the economy witnessed today, which was previously classified according to the prevailing antithetical ideologies of communism and capitalism, leading to the ideologies of liberal capitalism and mixed economy (socialist–capitalist, as in the Swedish and Austrian models)[39] and the market economy, democracy and economic openness in the new world order.[40]

The national sovereignty of states in the new world order has diminished—many factors have made it difficult for states to control cross-border activities owing to cyber/media accessibility and proliferation, including the advent of the 24-hour news cycle. No country is able to hide what is going on within its borders or prevent its communities from being affected by events elsewhere. The strategic behavior of countries has become exposed to the world, and therefore no country in the new world order can live or act in isolation;

regional and global blocs will become a central feature of the new world order.

As a result, the lines separating the internal and external security of countries have blurred; challenges, risks and threats have proliferated. Internal instability and insecurity in one country can have implications for the security of neighboring states—and at times for regional security, such as Iraq after the overthrow of the regime of Saddam Hussein Al-Tikriti.

It is possible that events could deteriorate so far as to threaten global security and stability, particularly in cases such as: refugee crises, as witnessed in Somalia and Syria; and the destruction of objects of cultural heritage—as in Afghanistan when the Taliban destroyed the Buddhas of Bamiyan, drawing the attention of global cultural organizations, and indeed harming Islam itself by presenting it as hostile to other cultures and civilizations. Besides, chaos and internal instability lead to the outbreak of conflicts based on religion and minority rights, leading to loss of human life which the world cannot ignore due to live reportage of the suffering via the media and social networks, as seen in Libya, Syria, Tunisia and Egypt. All these eventualities fall under the responsibility of the new world order and, by extension, the state leading it. Under the previous international system, these responsibilities were confined to the nation in whose geographical boundaries such crises occurred. Thus, they were subject to that country's ability to hide any nefarious responses from the world, including the confiscation of freedoms and rights. At the same time, traditional approaches to security have fallen by the wayside and belong to a time when foreign policies focused on containment and wars of national liberation.[41]

The proliferation of universal values was limited under the international system to conventions made applicable to a state, which defined rights over land, people and government within a single code. These values were applicable at the national level, concerning sovereignty, non-intervention in the internal affairs of states, and the settlement of crises and disputes by diplomatic means, etc. However, in the new order, an integrated system of universal values emerged, which included: the spread of democracy; peaceful transfer of power; respect for personal freedoms; protection of human rights; transparency; anti-corruption; good governance; rule of law and global citizenship; development; concern over climate change, environmental pollution and public health; engagement via social media; attention to global trends; and adhering to a balance of interests rather than a balance of power.

Within the legal arena, the international system was based on the International Court of Justice (ICJ). Founded on June 26, 1945 and comprising the official judicial arm of the UN, the ICJ decides on legal disputes that arise between states, and provides advisory opinions on legal matters that may be referred to it by the UN and its agencies, performing its functions in accordance with the provisions of international law.[42] It was preceded by the Permanent Court of International Justice in 1920 under the auspices of the League of Nations.

In the new world order the quest to preserve the legal rights of the individual and society has resulted in the creation of the International Criminal Court (ICC), established on April 11, 2002, which is an independent body not affiliated to the UN.[43] It is the first international judicial body to maintain a universal mandate without a time limit. Its jurisdiction encompasses prosecuting individuals accused of crimes of genocide, crimes against humanity, war crimes and crimes of aggression. It is considered the court of legal last resort in cases where national courts fail in their functions, and seeks to put an end to the culture of impunity for crimes committed by the state. A number of leaders of the Bolshevik Revolution and the Nazi regime who committed genocide escaped justice before the advent of the ICC.[44] The United States of America has refused to sign up to the ICC for fear that members of its armed forces who took part in military operations in Afghanistan and Iraq could be tried by the Court. The international debate surrounding the role of the ICC perhaps explains the decision of the African Union to reject the request that the Kenyan president Uhuru Muigui Kenyatta appear before the Court. The African Union held an emergency summit on October 11, 2013 to discuss Africa's relations with the ICC, which was accused of targeting Africans in an unfair manner while largely overlooking the crimes taking place in other parts of the world. Africans claim that the Court adopts double standards, and indicate that as yet it has only condemned one individual who is in charge of an African militia, and all those accused by the ICC so far have been Africans.[45]

Based on the above, the fundamental differences between the international system and the new world order become clear, although there are similarities between them that will endure as long as international law and the UN Charter continue to constitute the two main foundations governing relations between nations. The state has not disappeared completely under the new world order, although its role and status have declined. Examples of these similarities include: selectivity (the policy of double standards); the weakness of international justice, which explains the rejection by Saudi Arabia to accept the rotating seat on the UN Security Council in October 2013; the proliferation of crises; international competition; proliferation of armed conflict; and the survival of countries under authoritarian and dictatorial rule.[46]

Foundations of the New World Order

There are several criteria that determine the hierarchy of power in the new world order, currently topped by the United States of America. These include progress in the fields of: education, culture, economy, technology, military capacity, energy and logistics capability. According to these criteria, we find that the new world order is pyramidal in shape, as shown in Figure 1 in the Introduction.

The United States of America did not wait, passively, for the new world order to emerge; it actively sought to create this order according to a universal strategic vision aimed at maintaining US superiority in the face of other major powers, working to prevent the emergence of a rival superpower, and arranging matters of global importance to serve its interests. Therefore, the United States of America has adopted a variety of means for the formulation of the new world order to ensure that its objectives are achieved, namely:

1. Political Foundations

The United States of America has employed a number of political approaches in creating a new world order in keeping with its interests, including:

A. Benefitting from the weakness of the UN and its agencies *vis-à-vis* the United States of America, which supplies 22–25% of the organization's budget.[47] UN weakness allows the United States of America to achieve its interests and hegemony over the world order via the cover of international legitimacy in military activities carried out and sanctions imposed. In fact, international bodies and institutions, especially the UN Security Council, have merely become a tool for the implementation of US foreign policy.[48]

B. Exercising pressure on the permanent members of the UN Security Council to support US strategy, while also manipulating evidence. Examples of this include the role played by President George Herbert Bush [Sr.] in persuading former French President François Maurice Mitterrand to support him by providing false satellite imagery indicating Iraqi armaments, or the false evidence provided by former US Secretary of State Colin Luther Powell to the UN Security Council about Iraq's possession of WMDs in order to secure a resolution under Chapter VII allowing the use of military force.[49]

C. Lobbying friendly nations and allies by providing support and assistance in various forms—provided this falls within the scope of US interests.

D. Strengthening relations with international powers, particularly the EU, Japan and India, to ensure their support for US global strategy.

E. Continued close coordination with China and Russia and the adoption of summit diplomacy to reduce the impacts of their influence on US global interests. The Western alliance had previously intervened in countries such as Kosovo, Libya and Iraq despite strong objections by China and Russia. Russian technicians and experts had also been expelled from countries such as

Egypt – with no reaction from Moscow[50] – during the Anwar Mohammed El-Sadat presidency in July 1972; indeed, Russia and China withdrew their experts from vital facilities in Iraq, Iran and Syria for fear that those facilities would be subject to Western military strikes.

F. The promotion of US political values,[51] ensuring greater US political influence in the world.

G. Exercising the US role as 'global policeman,'[52] relying on the doctrine of humanitarian intervention in order to benefit from an advanced US military presence.

H. Reliance on active diplomatic intervention to resolve political crises between countries.

I. Attention to broader international issues that correspond with vital US interests in order to ensure that the United States of America wins over smaller countries by their acceptance of US hegemony.

J. A number of experts believe that the success and global spread of democracy are not due to any desire by political regimes to embrace democratic values and principles – such as women's rights, for example – but rather because the United States of America is itself a liberal democracy and acts as a model to follow; indeed, the global spread of democracy would not have occurred without US support and influence.[53]

2. Military Foundations

As a result of the US desire to maintain its military superiority – the US defense budget for 2013 amounts to $645.7 billion[54] – and underline its ability to impose its interests through hard power, the United States of America relies on several military capabilities, namely:[55]

A. The spread of permanent and mobile US military bases and the possession of a strategic intercontinental ballistic missile capability, and the capability to deploy militarily to any part of the world.

B. Possession of conventional and non-conventional military capabilities that would guarantee it qualitative superiority and the continuous development thereof, representing a global deterrent.

C. Perpetual development of military technology ahead of other nations in order to maintain US military superiority over other nations.

D. Imposition of restrictions on the proliferation of WMDs and their means of delivery.

E. Ongoing training with the armed forces of other nations in political hot spots around the world to ensure its participation with these countries in the event of armed crises.

Table 1.1
Global Distribution of Permanent US Bases,* 2012[56]

Location	Base type	Quantity
United Kingdom	Airbase	5
Germany	Land forces base	8
	Airbase	2
Italy	Land forces base	2
	Airbase	3
	Naval base	2
Turkey	Airbase	1
Portugal	Airbase	1
Spain	Air and naval base	1
The Netherlands	Land forces base	1
Greece	Air and naval base	1
Kuwait	Land forces base	3
	Airbase	1
Qatar	Airbase	1
Bahrain	Airbase	1
	Naval base	1
Oman	Airbase	1
Iraq	Land forces base	5
	Airbase	2
Afghanistan	Land forces base	2
	Airbase	1
Kyrgyzstan	Airbase	1
South Korea	Land forces base	4
	Airbase	2
Japan	Land forces base	2
	Airbase	2
	Navy base	3
	Air and naval base	1
	Marine base	5
Djibouti	Air and naval base	1

Location	Base type	Quantity
Kenya	Airbase	1
Honduras	Airbase	1
Cuba	Navy base	1
Indian Ocean	Air and naval base	1
Australia	Marine base	1
Pakistan	Airbase	2
The Philippines	Airbase	1
Singapore	Airbase	1
Panama	Air and naval base	1
Chile	Air and naval base	1
Kosovo	Airbase	1

* The data do not include certain facilities granted for use by US troops in some countries.

Table 1.2
Global Distribution of Mobile US Bases, 2013[57]

Aircraft carrier	Commissioned	Home port
USS *Nimitz*	1975	Naval Station Everett, Washington
USS *Dwight D. Eisenhower*	1977	Naval Station Norfolk, Virginia
USS *Carl Vinson*	1982	San Diego, California
USS *Theodore Roosevelt*	1986	Naval Station Norfolk, Virginia
USS *Abraham Lincoln*	1989	Naval Station Norfolk, Virginia
USS *George Washington*	1992	Yokosuka, Japan
USS *John C. Stennis*	1995	Bremerton, Washington
USS *Harry S. Truman*	1998	Naval Station Norfolk, Virginia
USS *Ronald Reagan*	2003	San Diego, California
USS *George H.W. Bush*	2009	Naval Station Norfolk, Virginia

A. The difficulty for any country in matching US military spending, allowing the United States of America to retain military superiority on the one hand, and engender fear among the rest of the world on the other.

B. The diversity of US military power, which allows it to undertake any form of modern warfare with equal efficiency. The US military also has the potential to conduct operations remotely, thus reducing its human and material losses, and possesses effective resources to allow engagement in more than one major war at a time (such as the concurrent use of US armed forces in Afghanistan and Iraq), and in a form that establishes massive US military superiority.

C. The availability of substantial ground, air and space reconnaissance potential, and significant intelligence superiority, providing accurate and timely information and allowing decisive intervention when needed.

D. Benefitting from the fall of the Warsaw Pact by maintaining NATO as an arm of US hegemony. This has involved extending the alliance to include other countries in Eastern Europe at the expense of Russia, such as Slovakia, Estonia, Romania, the Czech Republic and Hungary. The alliance expanded within a formula of partnership and cooperation with Middle Eastern states as part of the Istanbul Initiative, including the GCC.[58] NATO's role has been recalibrated to allow its intervention in the affairs of nations outside its usual remit.

E. Building a global anti-missile system – Missile Defense Shield[59] – to establish US military dominance by reducing the political and military influence of other major powers.

3. Economic Foundations

The United States of America considers itself a major actor in the global economy, given its manufacturing, production and export capabilities. It accounts for 25–30% of the global economy,[60] and there are many economic foundations for its continued hegemony over the new world order, namely:[61]

A. Its control over the global monetary system and international institutions such as the IMF and the World Bank. Through its indirect influence in these two institutions, the United States of America imposes its own accession conditions, therefore no other country may join without satisfying its criteria.

B. Direct supervision of the WTO and the politicization of its role at the regional and international levels, such as controlling global trade, accession negotiations of major powers such as China and Russia, and directing negotiations in line with US interests.

C. Promotion of globalization – especially economic – which allows the United States of America to achieve its global strategic economic objectives.

D. Direct and indirect control of energy sources on which competing powers (China, India and the EU) depend as a means to control the world economy, including the economies of these rival powers.[62]

E. Seeking to impose its hegemony on world markets through the development of US industries and the provision of political protection to ward off competitors.

F. Enshrining free-market capitalism, as advocated by the United States of America, as the most effective mechanism for continued economic growth, and therefore standards of living,[63] thus ensuring the link between the global economic system and the US economy.

G. Supporting the spread of multinational and cross-border companies, especially US companies – such as Boeing, American Express, Exxon Mobil and General Electric – which act as a strong incentive to achieve economic globalization under US control.[64]

4. Cultural and Technological Foundations

Many indicators show that the United States of America is by a wide measure ahead of all other countries when it comes to technological development,[65] and it was among the first to participate in the information and knowledge revolution. This is reflected in all forms of US strategic power, especially economic and military affairs. Therefore, the most important cultural and technological starting points to establish its hegemony on the new world order have come as a natural result of this progress. Most important among these foundations are:

A. The global dissemination of US culture, values and way of life, such as the proliferation of US clothing brands and the work done by various US research centers, such as the Carnegie Middle East Center in Qatar, to educate young people about the values of Western democracy, human rights, the protection of freedoms, etc.

B. The rapid transfer of US culture in terms of ideas, policy, books, magazines, music and movies over the internet, and the use of satellite media to influence the culture of communities, ensuring the achievement of cultural hegemony.

C. Proliferation of fast-food chains such as McDonald's and Kentucky Fried Chicken (KFC) to establish US culinary culture and related societal values.

D. Promoting the political values of the US liberal model in the international community, particularly with regard to human rights, Western democracy and respect for freedoms—positioning the United States of America as the 'gatekeeper' of these values, thereby increasing its cultural/political dominance.

E. Encouraging foreign students from various countries around the world to study at US universities through the provision of grants and educational–cultural exchange programs to establish US academic hegemony.[66] For instance, estimates indicate that the total enrollment of Arab students in US universities from academic years 1949/1950 to 2011/2012 amounted to 1,098,653.[67]

Frameworks of the New World Order

There are several frameworks within which the concept of the new world order may be understood; some are linked to form, while many are based on content, of which the most important include:

1. Cognitive Framework

This framework aims to enable a comprehensive understanding of the new world order, and attempts to identify the realities of the existence of the system and the relationship between it and the world. Thus, it consists of three elements: the system, the world, and the interaction between the two.

The system is made up of a matrix representing states and sub-state powers such as individuals, society, and civil society organizations. In addition, the world can be considered to have five basic dimensions: land, water, air, space and cyber. Thus, interaction between the system and the world demands the existence of various actors with different political, economic, military and technical capacities. The cognitive framework of the new world order therefore imposes the need to dismantle the elements of that order and understand the interactive relationships that exist between its components.

2. Methodological Framework

The methodological framework is the approach, plan or set of rules on which the new world order is based; i.e. the methodological structure of this order is a combination of the steps that led to its creation on the one hand, and the time period over which it remains coherent on the other. Therefore, the concept of a new world order according to the methodological framework indicates the existence of a systematic plan by the power or powers that control the order, the imposition of rules that underlie the order, and the steps followed by those powers to guarantee the working nature of the order in accordance with their needs, and with the implicit recognition of other competing interests.

It is notable that the United States of America did not simply wait to take advantage by reacting to a changing world; instead, it sought – according to a systematic plan – to shape the world in accordance with US interests, as and when its power and influence allowed.[68]

3. Systematic Framework

In this framework the 'system' represents the main object of analysis of the new world order, defined as a set of political, economic and military interactions that occur within the international community and under which global policy is formed. In this framework there exist six components, namely: inputs, processing, outputs, feedback, environment and limits.[69]

The environment represents the historical circumstances of the new world order that both directly and indirectly affect the range of inputs – reflecting the beliefs and attitudes of the upper echelons of power, and their support or opposition – as well as the capabilities and resources available. Since the new world order does not exist in a universal vacuum, there are limits to this system resulting from the interaction between its components and the global geostrategic situation. These conditions are affected by prevailing economic, social and cultural values.

Processing refers to the conversion of those inputs (i.e., resources, capabilities and demands) into outputs (i.e. decisions and policies issued by dominant powers) to ensure the preservation of the order to face related challenges, risks and threats.

Feedback, meanwhile, consists of the resultant positive or negative impacts of outputs (decisions, policies and behavior) on inputs.

Figure 1.1 illustrates the functional make-up of the new world order according to the systematic framework.

Figure 1.1
The New World Order According
to the Systematic Framework

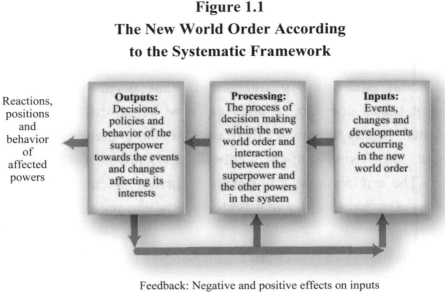

Feedback: Negative and positive effects on inputs
resulting from the process

As an expression of the reality of the systematic framework in interpreting the new world order, Zbigniew Kazimierz Brzezinski concludes that it would be difficult to do without the balancing effect of US power on global stability,[70] although the main challenge to this power will emanate from within the United States of America itself, either because US democracy will reject power; because the US power is misused; or because global threats disappear.[71] Therefore, the current world system imposes adherence by the United States of America to the legitimacy of its use of force on the one hand, and drives it to mobilize the efforts of the other powers in a joint effort to formulate a more secure global system on the other.

4. Formal Framework

Under this framework, we find that the structure of the new world order stems from the nature of its structure, whether it is unipolar, bipolar or multipolar, as well as from: the composition of the global community; vertical and horizontal interactions; the hierarchy within the system as indicated in the Introduction; and the working mechanisms within the new world order based on concepts such as integration, partnership, interdependence, adaptation, growth, deterioration, crisis, collapse, stability and balance.[72]

Three fundamental structural transformations have occurred in terms of the politics and distribution of power that have shaped the global order over the past five centuries. The first was witnessed between the beginning of the 15th and the late 18th centuries, with the rise of Western powers. This led to the spread of science, technology, commerce, capitalism and the agricultural and industrial revolutions.[73] The second structural transformation began in the early 19th century and lasted until the end of the 20th century. The third began with the shift to the new world order under the United States of America following the collapse of the Soviet Union, US domination of the global economy and global politics, the growth of its economic, scientific, cultural and educational and military strength, and the imposition of US values and interests on the world. The latest transformation has come as a result of the rise of other powers achieving unforeseen rates of economic growth –

especially in Asia (e.g. China) – as well as the emergence of sub-state actors such as terrorist organizations and transnational corporations, and the challenges to state sovereignty posed by international organizations.[74]

In this context, Brzezinski argues that attempts by the United States of America to restructure the new world order entail consideration of geo-strategically important questions[75] such as: will the EU remain the main ally of the United States of America, particularly given instances of disagreement with France and Germany on the nature and level of global threats? This issue was recently brought into focus by the news that the United States of America has been spying on certain European allies, exposed in early August 2013 by a whistleblower who sought asylum in Russia.[76] Indeed, further questions relate to when some form of accommodation might be found between the Russia and the EU, and how Russia might help in promoting stability in Eurasia. Elsewhere, how might the United States of America maintain a balance with China? Japan relies on the United States of America and stands ready to develop as a military power; the ongoing hostility on the Korean Peninsula raises questions of stability; and India and Brazil aspire to play a role in the new world order. Might the development of greater stability in Europe, driven by the expansion of the Euro-Atlantic group to include Russia, eventually become associated with security issues in the Far East? Naturally, such questions are related to the situation in the Middle East, particularly in terms of any restructuring of the new world order, and whether the prevailing regional equations endure.

This proposition suggests that the concept of a new world order according to the formal framework is affected, directly and indirectly, by the relations between the power dominating it and the major powers that influence decision-making within it. This implies that the concept of a formal framework is not static in terms of its global political, economic, military, cultural and educational interactions, but rather may differ from one field to another; albeit the superpower may maintain its position and role within each field.

5. Philosophical Framework

Within this framework the new world order is defined as a set of functions operating in accordance with periods of change and stability, i.e., it is the 'life cycle of the new world order,' which is based on a range of important and vital functions that no global system can survive without. This is a working philosophy of the new world order, which demonstrates the extent to which it achieves its objectives, resulting in an increasing or decreasing sense of satisfaction among the international community, and therefore an increase or reduction in support and advocacy for the new world order. In other words, the longevity of the global system under its present philosophy is closely associated with its achievement of the interests of the majority, and in such a way as to retain the acceptance and satisfaction of members of the global community. A number of experts[77] believe that with the fall of communism and the accompanying end to ideological conflict, globalization became for the United States of America an attractive mechanism and philosophical approach through which to interpret the global situation resulting from this conflict[78]—representing, as it does, a new reality of increasing interdependence, largely driven by modern communications technology, in which boundaries between states have become reduced to lines on maps rather than true geographic barriers to personal mobility, free trade, and the movement of financial and intellectual capital.[79] Hence, the philosophical framework of the concept of a new world order stems from the various dimensions of the role played by globalization in the order's structure. Ultimately, globalization is fundamental to the global order of the 21st century.

6. Intellectual Framework

The intellectual framework interprets the new world order as a natural product of creative and innovative activity in response to the political, economic, social, military, security, technological, cultural and educational needs of the components of this system. This leads to the arrangement of the components of the global community in pyramidal form, as indicated in Figure 1 of the Introduction. In other words, it can be said that the new world order comprises the result of all the innovative processes performed to support the establishment and spread of a single cultural model across the world—namely globalization in its numerous manifestations and with its various associated phenomena.

Samuel Phillips Huntington argues in *The Clash of Civilizations and the Remaking of World Order* that in the new world order, cultural identities (ethnic, nationalist, religious and civilizational) are the central powers, and where relations of cultural convergence shape alliances, lead to hostile conflicts and guide the policies of states.[80]

Meanwhile, Yoshihiro Francis Fukuyama argues in *The End of History and the Last Man*,[81] that the new world order is the product of an ideological and intellectual struggle; and that the United States of America has begun to bring about the end of history and the establishment of this new order by spreading liberal thought, democracy and capitalism. Fukuyama concludes that the universal and hegemonic world of the new order – which represents the end of history – appears as a result of two main factors: liberal economics alongside liberal politics.[82]

For his part, Avram Noam Chomsky claims that in the new world order the United States of America, as the sole superpower, acts unilaterally without taking into account the ideas, opinions or interests of others. Since the 1990s, the United States of America had imagined a world subject to its own financial ascendancy; however, when the financial crisis occurred in 2007 it threatened the US global position. This reoccurred when neoconservatives, during the term of former US President George Walker Bush [Jr.], aspired to global military domination without attempting to win the 'battle for hearts and minds,' resulting in further disasters for the United States of America.[83]

Brzezinski views the United States of America as a global cultural magnet. US social influence in the world represents an alluring intellectual and cultural revolution, characterized by its continuity and ability to bring about deep-felt change. It does not depend on political direction or propaganda, but rather relies on convincing others to accept its authority. It works to redefine social traditions, cultural values, human behavior and the individual aspirations of many young people around the world, regardless of their existing standard of living.[84]

All of the above indicates the existence of an intellectual framework for the new world order based on a unilateral US vision that seeks to unify ideas, cultures, and social–political values into an intellectual and ideological template for the expectations and aspirations of the younger generation. Through the National Democratic Institute (NDI), the International Republican Institute (IRI) and other US centers of research[85] large numbers of young people from all over the world are being educated on US values. In mid-2013, more than 120 young people from more than 20 countries[86] were been brought together to be educated on the social, political and cultural ideas and values of American society in order to immerse them in the American cultural model, so that they might spread these values in their own countries, societies and communities.[87]

7. Analytical Framework

This framework is divided into two sub-components: micro-analysis and macro-analysis.[88] At the micro-analytical level, the new world order consists of the interaction between states, peoples and civil society organizations – such as human rights groups and NGOs – individuals, and the dominant power(s) of the order that dictate international agendas, issues, challenges, risks and threats. According to this approach, the new world order is a natural product of this interaction, whereby the rights and responsibilities of governments are equal to the rights and responsibilities of individuals. In this case, we find that the order seeks to recognize each of its components, and deal with them all without discrimination.

At the macro-analytical level, the new world order is a product of a set of international interactions that occurred during a specific time period, which led to major developments that resulted in the preeminence of a single superpower that today controls the order and its interests, whilst also ensuring its stability and security. Therefore, the macro-level analysis identifies a series of global and regional events during the 1990s that led to the emergence of the new world order and the United States of America as its dominant power.

8. Historical Framework

This framework is concerned with the natural evolution of human needs over different ages imposed by the domestic environment of individual countries as well as external global conditions born of the balance or imbalance between world powers.[89] Within the historical framework, the concept of the new world order has passed through several stages, the most important of which are the three major historical periods that were heavily influenced by events in Europe:

A. The first period stretches from the end of the Thirty Years' War in Europe – which had continued from 1618 and ended with the conclusion of the Peace of Westphalia on October 24, 1648 – to the beginning of World War II on September 1, 1939. The world order was then considered a multi-polar system with Europe at its heart, according to the traditional balance of powers.

B. The second period stretches from the end of World War II in 1945 up to 1990. The world order was then defined as a bi-polar system which saw competition between the United States of America and the Soviet Union over political and economic ideologies.

C. The third period stretches from 1991 until the present. Bipolarity collapsed and the system became defined as a unipolar world order in which states and peoples have little political and strategic opportunity to achieve interests that conflict with the dominant superpower. Increasing compliance with the objectives and strategies of the superpower is required, the alternative being US sanctions—the principle of carrot and stick, set against the backdrop of the decline of the influence of international organizations.[90]

It is upon this historical framework that Paul Michael Kennedy bases his *The Rise and Fall of the Great Powers*, which charts the rise of major powers over 500 years until their eventual decline before the advent of the new world order.[91] He argues that wealth, economic and military power are all relative with respect to the new world order, and that because of this relativity there is no fixed international balance. In light of the competitive nature of nations, each century will witness debate about the composition of the world order against the rise and fall of powers in a chaotic world.[92]

Fukuyama, on the other hand, argues that the new world order will remain prey to a variety of religious, national and ideological conflicts, depending on the stage of development of the particular countries concerned. The old rules of power politics will continue to apply, and the nation-state will continue to be the chief locus of political identification in that order.[93]

In sum, all of these conceptual approaches to the defining the world order comprise a broad spectrum of frameworks that offer a unique perspective on the order's structure and nature, and that of today's emergent global civil society.

Theme #2: The Most Prominent Features of the New World Order

This theme deals in detail with the salient features of the new world order that play an important role in its internal interactions, and at the same time set the boundaries separating it from the preceding historical phases of the global system.

Global Civil Society

The phrase 'global civil society' is often used to represent one of the main actors and features of the new world order. Civil society has emerged at the level of global politics and has begun to play an influential role in political development; but what is global civil society? Political literature suggests that it comprises:[94]

1. Local civil society organizations whose activities extend beyond the borders of their countries, such as environmental conservation groups and 'green' organizations.

2. Cross-border non-governmental organizations (NGOs). These are organizations that were established mainly to exercise activities outside their home countries, such as the American Association for the International Commission of Jurists, and the United States of America Commission on International Religious Freedom.

3. Non-governmental international organizations whose membership is open to individuals from any country, such as Amnesty International and Médecins Sans Frontières.

4. Global federations of national organizations, such as international labor unions.

5. Permanent or temporary international fora of civil society organizations, such as the conferences organized by the UN (the Conference on Environment and Development [Earth Summit], the International Conference on Population and Development, the World Economic Forum and the World Social Forum).

6. Permanent and temporary social movements that include groups of individuals, organizations and institutions with common aims or values, such as the anti-globalization movement, the 'Stop the War' coalition, and peace movements.

Global civil society emerged as a result of several developments, notably the globalization of online social networking and exchange born of the communications revolution, which has led to intensive and unprecedented social interaction among tens of millions of people sharing common concerns over global events, topics and challenges.[95] Just as influential has been the role played by local civil society organizations in educating the public regarding freedom of assembly, and the ongoing collective activities of organizations from several countries to spread the values of human rights, civil liberties, equality, democracy and social justice.[96]

An active role has emerged for global civil society in the new world order, although it is still in the process of development. Civil society organizations' most prominent achievements include:[97]

1. Participation in the activities of international bodies; many national and regional civil society organizations are involved with UN organizations in an advisory capacity. They offer their opinions, present their positions and coordinate informally with other countries to reach decisions that are compatible with the mutual demands of these organizations.

2. Acting as a parallel organization to governments, they are able to express the positions of global public opinion by convening conferences that are held alongside international gatherings, which are usually only attended by the official representatives of governments. These alternative conferences held by civil society organizations work to mobilize world public opinion on the issues at hand, and have run simultaneously alongside the Earth Summit in 1992, the World Conference on Human Rights in 1993, the World Social Summit in 1995, the Conference on Women in 1995, and the World Conference Against Racism in 2001.[98]

3. Arranging regional and global protests to pressure governments to take positions in line with their goals. Examples of this include the protests against globalization and the WTO in 1999 in Seattle, and in 2005 in Hong Kong, and the rejection of the US war in Iraq in 2003.

4. Working to raise local issues that affect freedoms, rights, the environment, living conditions, etc. to the global level, and then influencing world public opinion regarding these issues and topics. The threat of the negative image that might be attributed to countries that contradict world opinion drives governments to change domestic policies, as witnessed by the various reactions to human rights and development reports issued by local and international organizations.

5. Reducing the influence of major powers on decision-making in the new world order, particularly with respect to the militarization of world politics.

The frameworks and concepts put forward in this chapter represent an analysis of the various prevailing approaches circulating in international politics and social sciences literature concerning the new world order. Such an analysis is necessarily based on the recognition of the world order as distinct from the 'international system,' as well as the identification of its key actors. There is talk today the 21st century being known as the 'American century,'[99] implying the continued dominance of the world order by the United States of

America. Yet some researchers indicate that such an 'American' era will be limited, or even predict its imminent demise—such as Stephen Martin Walt in his article "The End of the American Era,"[100] which charts the growing challenges to US global hegemony. However, this does not necessarily imply an acknowledgement of declining US power; true understanding requires closers introspection and understanding of what is happening in the world, as emphasized by the reports of the US National Intelligence Council.[101] Nor does this mean that the world order will be of an exclusively American character as a result of its military, cultural, educational, media and economic influence. Nonetheless, objectivity requires recognition of American hegemony over the world order, and it goes without saying that US influence dramatically affects the formulation of the conceptual and value-based frameworks of this system.

The Controversial Relationship between Globalization and State Sovereignty

There is a clear controversial relationship between globalization and state sovereignty. A large part of the growing discussions on the effects of globalization is related to the implications of this phenomenon on the state in its Westphalian sense, its functional role, and consequently on the concept of national sovereignty, which falls into a gradual decline despite any polemic over the ranking of the role of the state in influencing the structure of the new world order.

It is conceived that there is a close correlation between the state and the phenomenon of globalization, whereby the role of the former declines as the latter dominates and expands. Doubtlessly, demonstrations of globalization – particularly in terms of its global economic dimension reflected in multinational and transcontinental corporations and international economic institutions such as the World Trade Organization (WTO), the World Bank, the International Monetary Fund, civil society groups, and other organizations – are considered factors that strongly contribute to the decline of the state's structural and functional role[102] since the Treaties of Westphalia and the emergence of the concept of the state in its historical sense. This concept has traditionally been linked to the concept of state sovereignty, i.e. the possession by the state of a supreme sovereignty whereby it exercises overall, unlimited and exclusive authority over its territories and the citizens living in them.[103] From this perspective specifically, the impact of globalization is evident, whereby it consigned this relatively traditional concept of sovereignty to history. Although the state survived, the established criteria for sovereignty since the Treaties of Westphalia no longer exist. Indeed, it cannot be revived under the globalization of the contemporary world, since it requires absolute control over events and developments taking place within the state. Meanwhile, the cross-border flow of, *inter alia*, information, goods, funds and people – within international exchangeable frameworks or in cyberspace – surpasses traditional borders and removes the vital domain that allows for the exercise of sovereignty by the state, while imposing on it new frameworks that now govern this role, both internally and externally.[104]

Regardless of the prevailing controversy over how the state deals with the effects of globalization – whether by adapting to it, integrating into the global economy and benefitting from ensuing opportunities and developmental returns, or by resisting changes imposed by globalization and regarding it as a pervasive evil to developing countries whose risks and threats far exceed its advantages – it is hard to ignore the effects it has brought about on all countries without exception. From the cultural point of view, we find that globalization tends to undermine and weaken local cultures, formulate a Western universal culture, and create a global identity.

Naturally, this does not negate those indications suggesting the existence of a cultural resistance to the waves of globalization through the promotion of ethnic, religious and nationalist identities in order to immunize against Westernization.[105] From an economic perspective, there is sufficient evidence of the existence of economic activities that conflict with the concept of state sovereignty, particularly in view of the rapid and significant expansion of transcontinental and multinational corporations, outsourcing and servicing activities, commercial exchange networks, and the pegging of local currencies, with all the implications thereof for national economies.[106] Economic power is obviously related to a country's sovereignty and independence, as seen when countries undergo an embargo or face economic pressures to force them to adopt particular policies or suffer punishment for policies they adopt. Economic sanctions become a tool of compulsion and a mechanism to exercise hegemony and tighten control over the new world order on the part of the hegemonic power, whether it exercises it by itself or through the employment of the institutions and tools of this order, such as the United Nations Security Council. At the same time, this tool constitutes an explicit reduction in state sovereignty.[107]

While multinational corporations, transnational lobbies, global media networks and civil society organizations are symbols of globalization, they are themselves the main competitor of the state in its vital domain. Indeed, there are those who argue that multinational corporations no longer depend on the directions of the nation-state, as was the case in the past. They now compete with the state in determining the present and future of the global economy. At best, these companies ally themselves with the state and gradually obtain legitimacy and roles parallel to that of the state, which acknowledged sharing its role with international organizations, multinational networks and cross-border socio-political movements.[108]

The relationship between globalization and state sovereignty became more obvious after the fall of the Iron Curtain, which used to separate societies during the Cold War era. The fall of the Iron Curtain revealed societies that for decades were used to living apart under a specific authority, and all of a sudden met face-to-face.[109] Triggered by globalization, this fall unveiled gaps between the developed and least-developed countries. It was natural for the latter to fear hegemony as the stronger – not necessarily only military – will automatically dominate the weaker; this is the nature of competition in an unrestricted world.[110] Moreover, this also entails compliance to collective charters, rules and commitments resulting from membership in international institutions and organizations, including acquiescence to the dominant will, even if this contradicts their own will and interests. This means giving up part of the absolute right of sovereignty to a majority voice, which contradicts the traditional concept of sovereignty whereby the state has the right to act independently in all situations and under any circumstances.[111]

In summary, globalization is not irrelevant to shaping the problematic conceptual and functional position of the state. Therefore, the state under globalization needs a restructuring of its institutional, functional and structural architecture so that it can deal with the variables of globalization and the consequent effects and interactions in all their manifestations.[112] Discussion is not just about the end of the state or geography; it is also focused on the weaknesses of the state and the decline of its role. It is the concept of territorial land and its relationship to sovereignty that have been subject to change after globalization, resulting in preventing borders from carrying out their absolute function and reducing their political, economic and security roles against the backdrop of the flow of relations that cross those borders and the domination of the financial networks and economic and media traffic.[113]

On the other hand, globalization has become an expanding phenomenon—there is no means to downsize it or stop its spread; indeed no-one should even consider this, especially as there are those who link globalization to the evolution of humanity itself, and thus people who seek to obstruct the path of globalization are seen as trying to obstruct the path of man's development itself.[114] However, in my opinion this does not mean absolute surrender to what globalization imposes in terms of cultural, economic, social and educational patterns. Indeed, its advantages in terms of, *inter alia*, the economy, technology, culture, education or universal communications should be utilized without giving up one's cultural uniqueness or inherent identity.[115]

Mutual Interactions between Globalization, Realism and Liberalism

Against this backdrop, questions are raised regarding the relation between globalization and political trends and theories such as realism and liberalism, in order to explain the relation that links globalization to those intellectual trends and the consequences of this on international relations, the role of the state and the concept of sovereignty. Here it could be observed that globalization stands in contradiction to classical and contemporary realism, which proclaims that states will remain the dominant actors in international politics and that states can, if their interests change, alter institutions.[116] Therefore, globalization theorists and neo-liberalists who advocate international interdependence represent, since the beginning of the 1970s, a challenge to the realist perspective when studying international politics.

The obvious point of disagreement in this proposition centers around the concept of state sovereignty and its centrality for neo-realists when examining international relations and the role of the state as a major actor in international politics. On the other hand, globalization theorists claim that this sovereignty has been eroded, and therefore the role of the state in determining the output of international politics has diminished. Those theorists substantiate their point by referring to the growth and sophistication of the international trade exchanges as evidence of the erosion of sovereignty and the decline of the nation-state.[117] In other words, the controversy between proponents of these intellectual schools is focused on the role of the state, the limits of its relationship, and the extent to which it is affected by the growing role of international institutions. Every group cites evidence to support its assumption. Neo-realists believe that international institutions in the new world order are merely the means that states employ to achieve their interests and objectives. They cite the role of the UN and how the power of the organization is strongly linked to the objectives of the United States of America, which has played a most prominent role in the projection of UN power when it suited US objectives, as happened in conflicts such as the Gulf War in March 1991 and the former Yugoslavia and East Timor. In contrast, the UN was completely ignored by Washington during the war against Iraq in 2003 when the Security Council did not authorize the United States of America to use military force. Indeed, it is observed that the Security Council is marginalized with the widening gap between US power and interests on the one hand and the power and interests of the major powers in the new world order on the other.[118]

Another aspect that constitutes, in its economic aspect, a challenge to the idea of realism is that states think of themselves as independent economic units with their own resources. This idea is no longer valid in the post-Cold War world. Globalization constitutes a major challenge to state sovereignty and legitimacy and has threatened its national identity and political independence.[119]

The conflict between the concepts of realism and globalization is largely due to historical variations. Realism was the dominant theory in international relations during the

Cold War era. It is a concept of international relations taken from a pessimistic perspective, which views it simply as a power struggle, and argues that those relations will never be without conflicts and wars. This clear domination of realism during that era is attributed to the fact that it was the appropriate theoretical framework to explain some of the international phenomena of the time, such as military alliances, and to its relevance to competitive US–Soviet relations.[120] Thus, it considers the state as the main unit for analysis. Military power is the prime characteristic in any realist analysis that positions issues of stability, sovereignty and power as top priorities. Realists reject any change at the level of the bipolar international system that prevailed during the Cold War era.[121]

It would appear that the scenario witnessed at the end of the Cold War, which represented a challenge to realist thinking, contributed to the driving force behind globalization. The shift from a bipolar global system to a unipolar new world order was considered the worst development for realists; what happened was contrary to all their expectations. Kenneth Neal Waltz's theory on the system of power balance was based primarily on the preference of the bipolar system over other systems.

Therefore, this theory suffered a dilemma after the end of the Cold War and the transformation of the global system into a unipolar order led by the United States of America.[122] The debate over globalization and realism will remain, in the view of the author, subject to the prevailing controversy over the extent of change taking place in the concept of sovereignty of the nation-state. This debate is between those who argue that it disappeared or declined, and those who think that the nation-state still has the upper hand in international relations, which implies that realist logic continues to be valid with the shift in balance of power in the economic domain instead of the military domain.[123]

To talk of the continued role of the nation-state, in its former sense, as a main actor in international relations is to overlook the realities of the last two decades. The unit of analysis has shifted gradually from the state to political blocs, groups and globalization powers that have re-demarcated the borders between states using new means and techniques in the media and communications. This renders realist concepts inconsistent with those huge transformations which have brought about followers describing certain third-world countries as states with deficient sovereignty, or even as countries which are about to disappear from the world map under the pressure of lacking the fundamentals for any technical sovereignty over their borders.[124]

It is also believed here that the dependence of realist thinking on the factor of military power in achieving the interests and objectives of countries, or defending those interests and objectives, makes it difficult to rely on realism in understanding the transformations being witnessed in international relations in the last few years, unless the intellectual pattern of power encompasses other manifestations of power that have become more important, mainly that of knowledge, technology and economic power.

Neo-liberalism is based on the assumption that market powers will lead economic growth. It is viewed by its proponents as a universal theory contributing to the powers of globalization. Indeed, there are those who claim that neo-liberalism and globalization are two sides of the same coin. Neo-liberalism argues that the world will be better, and that markets will make it better, without intervention by countries.[125] There are those who argue that neoliberalism is not merely an ideology that has the support of a group of economic intellectuals; it is a global policy that is binding to all governments of the world, regardless of the system under which they operate. They also believe that the source of obligation is the domination by global economic institutions – such as the World Bank and the International Monetary Fund – over the economies of many third-world countries, and that the World Trade Organization (WTO), the basis of a treaty that was signed by most countries worldwide, has become the real guardian and primary defender of the principle of trade liberalization.[126]

Therefore, some researchers argue that the theory of neo-liberalism is the product of the interactions of globalization, and that the United States of America makes every effort to ensure this theory is the prevailing ideology in all contemporary societies without exception.[127]

150

The starting point for the dissemination of this theory is the liquidation of the welfare state in all its variations (socialist and capitalist), the liquidation of the theory of socialist thinking, and the termination of public-sector projects through privatization, economic liberalization and a focus on market freedom. Some researchers believe that liberalism, represented by the Davos Forum in its annual conferences, has led to enormous problems for the peoples of developing nations, with those countries being transformed into mere markets for global capitalist corporations under the auspices of the WTO.[128]

Inter-civilizational and Ideological Conflict and International Relations

Conflict is a major feature of international relations, but the nature and causes of conflict vary from one historical epoch to another. The advent of the new world order reveals the pivotal role played by ideological conflict in international relations, and the development it has undergone during the transition from the old order to the new.

The world order in the 20th century witnessed two major conflicts, namely World War I (1914–1918) and World War II (1939–1945), as well as the Cold War, which lasted from the end of World War II until the fall of the Soviet Union in December 1991. Each of these conflicts heralded a transition from one world order to another. Following World War I, the Austro-Hungarian Empire collapsed, and the United States of

America emerged as a major power on the international stage—albeit one that chose to pursue a policy of isolationism,[129] allowing the balance of power to remain in Europe. However, after World War II obliterated the influence of both the French and the British empires, the world bore witness to the rise of a bipolar world divided by two superpowers – the United States of America and the Soviet Union – that were to dominate Europe and through it the world from 1945 until the dissolution of the Soviet Union on December 25, 1991.[130]

Conflict was the dominant feature in relations between the world powers during this period, and primarily took the form of an ideological struggle between nations and territories governed by totalitarian and democratic regimes. Ideology, therefore, formed the foundations of the animosity that led to the outbreak of both world wars.[131] Nevertheless, ideology was not the only cause of these episodes of violence; the interests of major powers, and their corresponding competition for influence, were also to blame for the escalation of rivalry that led to two world wars.

The second half of the 20th century witnessed radical transformations; the Communist bloc disintegrated, the Warsaw Pact dissolved, Eastern European states headed towards democracy and a market economy, and the United States of America assumed leadership in a new unipolar world order. Together, these events induced a major shift in the nature of the world order, representing a decisive victory for capitalism over communism.[132] Many Western intellectuals in Europe and the United States of America became convinced after the end of the Cold War that the world had settled once and for all on one system, united by universal values born of the ruins of totalitarian ideologies associated with communism and totalitarianism. These values included individual and economic freedom, intellectual and political pluralism, and respect for human rights.[133]

The Gulf War of 1991 was the most important event of its decade in terms of the evolution of the new world order, particularly as it coincided with the dissolution of the Soviet Union. These two events inaugurated a new phase in international relations characterized by complete US dominance,[134] cementing its place as the single superpower in the new order. There is no doubt that the complete US dominance following the Gulf War promoted a single ideology based on capitalism. Nevertheless, this did not spell the end of ideological and cultural conflict; indeed, the world has witnessed a proliferation of such conflicts since the bipolar era, many of them based on extremist ideologies and ideas. Hence, this shift in the world order represents: "a change from within … a certain order … so that events are shaped and concepts are developed according to [the desires and decisions of] the new center"—in this case the United States of America.[135]

The most significant risks facing the new world order include terrorism, organized crime, the proliferation of WMDs, illegal immigration, as well as environmental issues and the spread of deadly infectious diseases (such as AIDS and other diseases).[136]

The new world order was meant to fill the vacuum in influence left behind by the collapse of the Soviet Union. It was born in practice during the First Gulf War, with George Herbert Bush [Sr.] and his administration taking the first steps toward what they viewed as the 'American century.'[137] This new order has since witnessed a multitude of forms of cultural, educational, ideological and civilizational conflict.[138]

The Relationship between Civilizations: Clash or a Dialogue?

With the end of the Cold War came a raft of theories and ideas as to how the new world order might develop. These include Samuel Phillips Huntington's above-mentioned prediction of a 'clash of civilizations,' in which global conflict would escalate from conventional conflict over resources and ideologies to an altogether broader stage—a clash of civilizations.[139]

In the summer of 1993, Huntington, a famous Cold-War era theorist, published an article entitled "The Clash of Civilizations?" in the influential American journal *Foreign Affairs*.[140] His theory was that after the end of the East–West struggle, international relations would move into a new era. The main global fault line during the Cold War was between the Eastern and Western camps, while third-world countries were forced to seek protection by forging alliances and blocs.[141] It was no longer a matter of class-based or ideological

154

antagonisms, but rather a matter of cultural and civilizational divisions. According to Huntington, major future wars will occur as a result of these divisions, and the conflict between civilizations will be fuelled by many factors including rapid population growth and globalization.[142]

Huntington posits that the fundamental differences between communities will be the primary cause of this clash of civilizations, particularly as a result of intensified interaction as the world becomes more interconnected, given the effects of globalization on international relations.[143] Huntington argues that this eventuality will also come as a result of the constant and accelerating economic modernization and social change occurring around the world, which serves to separate individuals from their identities. A further aggravating factor, according to Huntington, was the growth of so-called 'civilization consciousness,' born of the realization that although the West and its capitalist system has achieved the peak of its power, it is confronted by different civilizations that increasingly have the desire to shape the world, thus the inevitable clash of civilizations.[144]

It is worth noting that Huntington's clash of civilizations theory was inspired by the famous Jewish Orientalist Maxime Rodinson, who was the first to liken the relationship between the Islamic and the Christian worlds to the ideological conflict between capitalism and communism.[145]

Talk of a clash between civilizations leads us to another theory which is Yoshihiro Francis Fukuyama's "end of history," fully developed in his 1989 book, *The End of History and the Last Man.*[146] Fukuyama argues that American capitalist democracy is the "end point of mankind's ideological evolution" and the "final form of human government," and thus it represents the end of history.[147]

According to Fukuyama, this implies that the changes the world will witness will merely represent a chance for other peoples to follow the ultimate (Western) model, because there will be no further progress in the development of the underlying global principles and institutions.[148]

Fukuyama draws links between democracy and development, concluding that there can be no development in the absence of democracy, and confirms that "…capitalism is a path toward economic development that is potentially available to all countries," provided that they "play by the rules of economic liberalism."[149]

These two theories are based on the victory of Western civilization as a consequence of the end of the Cold War. For Fukuyama, the end of history represents the triumph of democratic values. The 'history' he refers to is a scene of massive conflict between values, practices and interests, which has reached its inevitable end.[150]

As previously mentioned, the clash of civilizations theory has been met with substantial criticism, most notably the following:

1. The desired relationship between civilizations comprises meaningful dialogue among them and positive interaction between cultures based on mutual respect.[151] It also

156

requires international legitimacy and the application of international law, as these are the common denominators between peoples and governments in the world today. They are the agreed reference; however cultural, civilizational and religious references remain a source of dispute, and even of conflict and intolerance.[152]

2. Huntington also promulgated another blunder by considering human history to have begun with the history of Europe. Indeed, archaeological discoveries have proved that Eastern peoples in general and the people of the Middle East and North Africa in particular, can be credited with laying the foundations of human civilization during the first rise of the east between 3100 and 330 BC.[153]

Another significant criticism that can be leveled at the clash of civilizations theory is the fact that human history is not just dictated by a conflict in the world of ideas. Physical human conflict and its various incarnations lead to evolution in the world of ideas,[154] which in turn leads to historical progress, leaving non-resilient ideas to wither.[155] In the same context, the clash of civilizations proposition is incompatible with both the present age and the future to which we aspire, as we live in a world in which Western civilization represents only one – albeit significant – part.[156]

There is no doubt that Huntington, over the years, came to realize the core differences between the concepts of religion and civilization, and that his concept of civilization would appear to be confused with that of culture, a realization supported by the definition outlined by Sir Edward Burnett

Tylor in his book, *Primitive Civilization*[157]: "[T]hat complex whole which includes knowledge, belief, art, law, morals, custom, and any other capabilities and habits acquired by man as a member of society."[158] This realization led Huntington to review his thesis of an inevitable clash between civilizations, admitting that although he said that Islam would inevitably end in his original book,[159] he had since concluded that he had been wrong. He said that others had made similar mistakes, that some had claimed Islam as a religion and a 'nation' ended when Mustafa Kemal Ataturk abolished the Caliphate in 1924, but that recent events had confirmed that the Islamic civilization was not dead, but was instead renewable.[160] Ultimately, Huntington's theory of a clash of civilizations began to fade away and dwindle in the run-up to his death on December 24, 2008.[161]

As for Fukuyama's theory of "the end of history," it has been heavily criticized for being based exclusively on the American model of Western democracy. His supporters defend his theory by saying that it is misunderstood, as Fukuyama believes that the world will witness more democracies developing in various forms in Turkey, Ghana, Venezuela and other countries in different regions of the world.[162]

Fukuyama is also criticized, as for a long period of his life he was considered a neo-conservative, calling alongside his like-minded hard-liners on President Bush to take action to remove Saddam Hussein Al-Tikriti's regime in the wake of the September 11, 2001 attacks—even though there was nothing to connect the Iraqi regime with the attackers.[163]

The "end of history" theory has faced much criticism because of the rapid political transformations witnessed by Western capitalist nations, the most prominent of which being the emergence of a new political ideology called the "third way," which attempted to reconcile socialist principles and the dynamics of capitalism, such as focusing on individual motivation as the basis for progress.[164] In the same context, the "end of history" theory was met with harsh criticism following the escalation of ethnic and religious conflicts following the Cold War. This led some to question the efficacy of ideology and liberal and democratic ideas as a means of achieving harmony and concordance among the nations and peoples of the world.[165]

Controversy about the relationship between Islam and the West

The first signs of interaction and clash between the Western and nascent Islamic civilizations began early. Since the emergence of the Islamic Dawah, Western Christendom had perceived the Muslim world as a menace threatening its very existence.[166]

The Western view of Islam evolved in parallel with the general mentality of the time. During the feudal era the Church's view of Islam prevailed, characterizing it as a nomadic development of Judaism, or as one of the various eastern Christian heresies.[167] Meanwhile, the Arab attitude, through various ages, portrayed those of the West as 'infidel,' or 'foreigner,' then 'European,' and later as 'Westerner,' and the duality of acceptance and rejection of the other is evident in each historical era.[168]

The West's view of Islam and Muslims was formed over long periods, during which clergymen, politicians and Orientalists all espoused differing perceptions and eventually resulted in the West attributing to itself the characteristics of 'truth,' 'centrality,' and 'reason' while describing the other as 'aberrant,' and 'backward.'[169]

The dispute between Islam and the West lies at the core of the dispute between the Western and Islamic civilizations—Western civilization broke with its dark past by entirely alienating religion. While Islamic civilization was founded on the basis of bypassing the darker phases and building a civilization beyond them, leading to an historical era of glory. Most of the pioneers of the renaissance in the Levant in the modern era relied in one way or another on religion, unlike their Western counterparts. The intellectual restoration associated with Arab civilization considered religion as a main facilitator, given the role it plays in the Arab and Islamic societies. The goal of revival was to rid the mind of its rigid view toward religion, and to rely on reason in discussion life's issues.[170]

The fundamental controversy between Islamic and Western civilizations remained a source of contradiction between the Arabs and Muslims on the one hand, and the West on the other. Tension and confrontation between the two parties escalated

160

when the situation evolved into a political struggle against imperialism. With the struggle for independence, Arabs and Muslims consistently countered the West's colonial discourse with even more hyperbolic nationalist discourse.[171]

Some Western authors use the term 'Islamic fundamentalism' to describe the Islamic awakening,[172] in an attempt to associate it with fanatical Christian fundamentalist movement that has emerged in the West, with all the negative connotations this carries in the American psyche, and that of the Christian West in general.[173] Islam has been perceived, from its inception, as a militant religion, and its followers as engaged in spreading their faith and their law by might.[174] Despite the fact that there are extremist religious Islamic groups, the problem lies in generalization and describing Islam and Islamic civilization as fundamentalist.

In 1991, the well-known French historian Jean-Christophe Rufin authored a book entitled *The Empire and the New Barbarians*. In his book, Rufin considered the civilization of the North and West to be the 'empire,' while the barbarians represented the peoples of the South or developing countries, the populations of which are increasing at a rate that frightens the countries of the north.[175] For Rufin, the most threatening issue is the risk of 'population explosion' taking place in the countries of the South. He bluntly states that: "What we stand for, in fact, is our standard of living."[176] The South that Rufin refers to includes Islamic countries such as the states of the Arab Maghreb, Turkey and Iran.[177]

Another new source of tension between Islam and the West is the presence of large numbers of Muslim minority communities in the Western world. The number of such minorities is increasing; while the population in the West is declining due to falling birth rates.[178]

The post-Cold War era brought increased tension between Islam and the West. After the collapse of the Soviet Union, Islam replaced the communist threat.[179] The September 11, 2001 attacks saw a further widening of the rift between the West and the East; many parties capitalized on those events to tarnish the image of Islam and Muslims.[180]

US journalist Thomas Loren Friedman described the attacks as representing "a third world war."[181] He went on to say that this new world war "does not pit us against another superpower. It pits us – the world's only superpower" against angry people who "... do not share our values, they resent America's influence ... not to mention our support for Israel, and they often blame America for the failure of their societies..."[182] Friedman goes on to argue that "what makes them super-empowered, though, is their genius at using the networked world, the internet and the very high technology they hate, to attack us. They turned our most advanced civilian planes into human-directed, precision-guided cruise missiles" to destroy civilian American targets.[183]

In fact, the solution to the problem of the relationship between Islam and the West does not lie within the political sphere. It is rather a long-term historical process which requires, above all, the Arabs to restore their self-confidence in order to attain a sense of parity.[184] The two sides must also recognize that there is diversity and difference in the values, standards and cultures of different peoples, and thus arises a fundamental right for nations, peoples and cultural entities to be distinctive and different.[185]

There is no doubt that the reality of the complex relationship between Islam and the West raises a number of problems and issues. First, it seems that inter-religious dialogue must be reviewed. It is obvious that such dialogue is confined to elites, and very little of the rapprochement filters down to the public.[186] Even if it occurred to centrist and moderate Islam that rapprochement was possible with the Vatican (as a representative of Christians), the Vatican is not the only point of reference for all Christians—it cannot compel Western governments to abide by anything. Furthermore, the hotbeds of Christian fanaticism do not follow it.[187] An example of such bigotry is the statement attributed to US congressman Thomas Gerard "Tom" Tancredo, who said that if Islamic terrorists used nuclear weapons against US cities, the United States of America should retaliate against Mecca.[188]

Second, historical legacies endure from the period of the Crusades, the colonial era suffered by Muslim countries, and also from the Islamic conquests (Constantinople, Poitiers, Andalusia, etc.)[189] that contribute to the development of hostility and hatred, and their constant reiteration by both sides via their curricula. In modern history, the deconstruction of the old form of colonization (decolonization) coincided with the creation of Israel and the transformation from the old colonization into its latest, indirect form. Israel's control of

Jerusalem represents the achievement of the objectives of the Crusaders, and the culmination of what the term 'Christian–Jewish civilization' represents.[190]

Third, and finally, Islam has today jumped to the forefront of the concerns of Western societies owing to the growing number of Muslims in many Western states. This is referred to as the 'immigration problem' – as mentioned earlier – and is often referenced in connection with 'terrorism' and its concepts.[191] Although Islam, as a religion, has nothing to do with this issue, there is an entrenched impression that the common denominator between countries that fail to respect freedoms or to establish regular economies is the fact that they are 'Islamic.' Perhaps the reason behind this increased focus on Islam is that some Muslim immigrants seek – wherever their numbers multiply – to impose manifestations of their religion leading to such problems as periodically arise regarding the veil in France, for example.[192]

In fact, "many of the judgments made by the West on Islamic civilization are the result of conflicting powers between the colonial West and Islamic countries securing their independence ... The West generalized the history of Islamic civilization and its future from the perspective of current conflict of powers."[193] The West generalized in considering the entire Islamic culture as fundamentalist, comprising "rejection of modernity, obsession with religious practice, acceptance of violence domestically and internationally, and dubbing the society as infidel."[194]

Therefore, people must resort to reason in order to "safeguard their faiths and nations from all attempts at ridiculing faiths. The United Nations should take serious steps against any affront to religious sanctities. Muslims should also try to ignore advocates of the 'clash of civilizations.' They should foil their plans of inciting conflict between cultures and religions."[195]

Ethnic and Sectarian Conflicts

Most of the world's countries include minorities of different ethnic and national origins, cultures, religions and sects. However, the presence of a religious, ethnic or sectarian minority does not necessarily lead to political problems. Indeed, there are minorities described as politically active and others as benign or inactive at the political level, and there are minorities seeking to preserve their own character, and others are more open to a high level of sociopolitical integration with the community they live in.[196]

Ethnic and sectarian conflicts were rare during the Cold War era because the dominant ideologies were an important factor in preserving national unity. Leadership in this period was characterized by a charisma, enabling a balanced formula of coexistence among different ethnicities. Moreover, the confrontation between capitalism and communism and between East and West imposed a degree of internal coherence in both blocs.[197] As the Cold War came to an end, ethnic groups began expressing themselves, and ethnic problems exploded with demands that the authorities recognize their uniqueness and identity, with a view to promoting their distinctiveness and representing their presence in the political arena.[198]

In this context, it is important to refer to the definition of the ethnic group, as the term 'ethnicity' is used to describe a "population group characterized by common biological features that stem from genetic factors."[199] Others define an ethnic group as a "human group whose members have common customs and traditions, language or religion or any other distinctive attributes including origin and physical features, and these individuals are aware of the difference between their group and other groups in any of these features which lends them a sense of belonging, each to his own group."[200] The reasons for ethnic conflict can be generally summarized by as follows:[201]

1. **Political reasons:** these are one of the key reasons of many of the world's conflicts, such as the problem over the status of territory, political exclusion or persecuting minorities.[202] A more dangerous dimension, in this context, is that some people or groups seeking to dominate sects have short-sighted interests. These people will operate in favor of their sects without considering the consequent risks, and they rely on sectarian identity rather than national collective identities. This problem is further exacerbated if the social environment suffers underdevelopment.[203] The absence of a strategic vision of the parties involved in sectarian sedition is a major problem, as it makes such parties respond to the

actions of other parties in a confused manner, and thus contributes to igniting sectarian strife.[204]

2. **Religious reasons**: religion is one of the central elements controlling the most profound needs, values and aspirations of human beings; and its impact will remain present and tangible in both the individual and collective areas of life.[205] Religion provides ideals, identity, values and principles in varying degrees.[206] Religious beliefs have a major impact on patterns of group behavior, and in some cases this impact is even higher than that of language or dynasty. Perhaps what confirms that the religious factor is the reason for aggravating so many conflicts is the tendency witnessed in international relations, especially after September 11, 2001, to associate Islam with terrorism.[207]

3. **Economic reasons:** a number of scholars argue that ethnic conflicts, at their roots, are for access to economic resources.[208] They also think that political language is often used to express economic inequalities. Among the economic issues that may be in dispute is employment discrimination in government institutions.[209] There is no doubt that injustice in the distribution of state resources will result in the emergence of richer areas and poorer areas, and hence the people of poor areas will feel a sense of injustice. If the inhabitants of such areas are minorities, they are likely to develop a sense of marginalization.[210]

4. **Historical reasons**: communities are causally linked to historical legacies, rendering them trapped or dependent on history, as if it were able to change the present status quo, such as the issue of Imamate and Caliphate between Sunni and Shiite Muslims, and the issue of mind and soul (religion or science) between Catholics, Protestants and Orthodox Christians.[211] In the same vein, the feelings of some national, sectarian, religious or confessional minorities that there is a history of injustice against their communities leads to a quest for primacy that results in clashes with members of other minorities.

5. **Cultural reasons:** culture plays a critical role in tensions and conflicts, such as when there is a tangible threat to the interests of an ethnic community by another ethnic group or by government.[212] The absence of intellectual pluralism plays a dangerous role in this regard, as it necessarily means a lack of acceptance of social and cultural pluralism.[213] Societal pluralism on an ethnic, sectarian, religious or other basis can be employed in favor of building strong communities.

It has been pointed out that there are several options, in terms of policy at the state level, that could potentially dissuade and alleviate ethnic conflict. These include the following political, cultural, economic, military and educational solutions:

1. Political Solutions

A wide variety of democratic electoral systems can facilitate ethnic accommodation and harmony in diverse settings, such as the proportional representation system, in which the number of parliamentary seats is proportionate to the number of votes.[214]

In this regard, a critical issue is the need to pursue political consensus between all components of society. This is the only option available, as a cultural consensus cannot be established among people because diversity is the nature of communities; working to establish a political consensus is more important than fabricating an illusion of cultural consensus.[215]

Solving the problem of ethnic, religious and sectarian conflict in the communities that suffer such problems – be it evident or implicit, with the potential to explode at the political level – essentially requires the adoption of political pluralism in particular, and communal pluralism in general, meaning it is inevitable that diversity be recognized, no matter what foundations a society is based on, due to the presence of the multiple affiliations within a single identity.[216]

There is no doubt that democracy represents the most effective solution to the problem of minorities. Democracy is a key mechanism aimed at addressing sectarianism entirely – not partially – and without it all plans to solve such a problem may fail. The democratic system is a formula that protects and recognizes the widest possible diversity, and it allows all components of society to participate in creating the identity of the community and its future.[217]

2. Military Solutions

The military is the symbol of hard power in any society, and if the state fails to control its military, conflict can be severe.[218] As the military has such a central position, it is dangerous for it to be dominated by a particular sect, who might use it to protect itself and its interests in the face of rivals. The Syrian situation represents a prominent Arab model of this. After Hafez Al-Assad assumed power in 1970, he entrenched a tribal and sectarian structure in the ranks of the security and military institutions, where the percentage of Alawite officers is about 80%, while the remaining 20% is distributed among other sects of the country.[219]

3. Cultural Solutions

Cultural policies aimed at avoiding sectarian conflicts include those dealing with cultural practices, such as religion, education and language.[220] What is required here, in brief, is the need to understand the difference between negative sectarianism and positive sectarianism. Negative sectarianism means "transforming sectarianism to a backward sociopolitical system based on treating the individual and the group as parts of a category that acts on their behalf regarding their political positions; as such, sectarianism governs the personal life of the individual. However, positive sectarianism concentrates on establishing a cohesive society based on considerations of citizenship and loyalty to one center only, which is the state."[221]

4. Educational Solutions

There is no doubt that education at all levels is an important tool in eliminating sectarianism and bringing about societal progress in general. All human experiences prove that education is a significant and effective way to accomplish integration and harmony between the various components and spectra of society.[222]

5. Economic Solutions

It is generally agreed that economic development extinguishes sectarian and ethnic strife by changing the priorities and values of the population as a result of an increasing proportion of literate people, hence raising their acceptance of the principles of tolerance and moderation.[223] In the same context, the increase in wealth generated from economic development curbs the struggle for power and political influence. Economic development also leads to the emergence of a large number of non-governmental organizations, which increase political participation and produce and disseminate new ideas.[224]

The Growth of Extremist Trends and Ideologies: The American Right as a Model

The new world order has witnessed the emergence of many radical ideologies and intellectual currents, the most dangerous of which is the extreme right in the United States of America, which dominated the US administration of former President George Walker Bush [Jr.][225] Its principles formed the content of the so-called 'Bush Doctrine' of a global war on terror, encapsulated by the line: "Either you are with us, or you are with the terrorists. ... any nation that continues to harbor or support terrorism will be regarded by the United States of America as a hostile regime."[226] This brought about massive shifts in American foreign policy, primarily focusing on the Middle East, where Washington sought to change the nature of existing regimes, claiming that it seeks to convert them into democratic regimes—Iraq in 2003, for example. However, the real goal was to integrate Israel in the region.[227]

In fact, the birth of the neoconservatives dates back to the 1940s. One of the main reasons that led the neoconservatives to turn against their liberal affiliation was their position toward communism. For them, communism represented a real threat to the very existence of America,[228] a confrontational ideology with which there was no room for conciliation or coexistence, and which therefore must be eliminated—otherwise it would eliminate the United States of America.[229]

The religious right enjoyed a remarkable rise during the 1980 presidential campaign of Ronald Wilson Reagan, under the slogan 'The Born Again Christians.' Supporters of this trend divide the world into two camps: the good camp – which includes Christians – and the evil camp, which includes other religions.[230]

Several key factors contributed to the emergence of the Christian–Zionist movement within the fundamentalist and evangelical churches. These factors include the Israeli occupation of Jerusalem in June 1967, and the assumption of power by US President James Earl "Jimmy" Carter in 1977,[231] along with his support for the Christian Zionists and for Israel. Another factor is Menachem Wolfovich Begin's election as Israeli prime minister in 1977, which legitimized religious extremism, and strengthened Israel's relations with the Christian Zionism movement. Also, the emergence and spread of 'TV evangelism,' led by the stars of religious TV programs, referred to as 'televangelists.' The majority of the material produced by such programs is political in nature, despite their religious titles, and they have reflect Zionist ideological trends.[232] Such programs and networks include The 700 Club on the Christian Broadcasting Network (CBN), co-hosted by Pat Robertson, Gordon Robertson and Terry Meeuwsen, and Fox News, which is one of the most prominent US channels to broadcast such programs.[233]

The inauguration of George Walker Bush [Jr.] as President in January 2001, was a clear testament to the success of the American right – both in its political incarnation as 'neoconservative,' and its religious form as the 'New Christian Right' – in reaching the highest institutions of power and government in the United States of America. Both branches are known for their extremism, and for their ideological views on various issues, including what they see as the global role that should be assumed by the United States of America. The Bush administration included many figures who belonged to the conservative right.[234] The most prominent figures of the 'neocons' included Vice President Richard Bruce "Dick" Cheney, Secretary of Defense Donald Henry Rumsfeld, Assistant Secretary of Defense Paul Dundez Wolfowitz, and Attorney General John David Ashcroft.[235]

Controversy about the Role of Ideology in International Relations

Is it possible to determine whether the ideological and civilizational struggle witnessed in the new world order will improve or worsen in the future?

In answer to this question, it can be said that the collapse of the Soviet Union and the disintegration of the Eastern bloc in Europe put an end to the ideological conflict between East and West, identified by Fukuyama as the 'end of history.'

Fukuyama argues that the end of ideological conflict between East and West was a decisive, definitive victory for liberalism. With the end of this ideological conflict, the Cold War ended.[236]

Talk of the end of ideological conflict and an 'end to history' coincided with that of a clash of civilizations.

Huntington is considered one of the main proponents of this latter notion. He argues that the main source of conflict in the post-Cold War era will be neither ideological nor economic, but cultural.[237]

It is fitting to point out at the end of this chapter that the concept of a clash between civilizations and cultures in the new world order has actually brought about an appreciation of the need for dialogue among civilizations and for peaceful coexistence among different cultures. For example, Dr. Abdulaziz bin Othman Altwaijri emphasizes the need for a civilized dialogue which reflects the evolution and maturity of civilizations and societies. Altwaijri believes that dialogue should be based on mutual respect, fairness, justice and the rejection of bigotry and hatred. He says that that the objective of the dialogue is to achieve welfare, wellbeing, peace, security, prosperity and tranquility for all people.[238]

However, efforts to initiate such a dialogue have been marred by a number of obstacles, such as: an overlap of doctrinal and intellectual issues, at a time when debate should avoid such controversial and immovable aspects. The debate must also uphold what is already agreed and can represent common denominators among all.[239]

Perhaps what makes it difficult is that many such dialogues are left to religious scholars and personalities, whose primary concern is to defend their beliefs and religious doctrine. This does not mean that religious belief should be entirely separated from dialogue; rather, it should be confined to one aspect of the dialogue, allowing for a general focus on cultural issues and matters of mutual interest in all fields.[240]

Conclusion

In its first theme, this chapter reviewed the literature dealing with the emergence of the global system from the Treaties of Westphalia in 1648 up to the present. It also explored the controversy surrounding the nature of that system and the distribution of power within it, including the view that refutes the establishment of a new world order in favor of a period of transition characterized by international fluidity and chaos, and the alternative opinion that the beginnings of the new world order may be found in the 1960s, and its existence becoming clear in the late 1980s and early 1990s with the fall of the Berlin Wall and the disintegration of the Soviet Union.

This theme deals in some detail with the concept of the new world order, both in terms of its constituent units and the nature of the relations and interactions between those units. It concludes that the new world order is the product of all the interactions between countries, peoples, individuals and community organizations. These interactions are influenced by a set of important factors such as global progress in the field of satellite media, information and communications technology, and cross-border social media networks.

This theme explains the different frameworks through which the concept of the new world order may be understood. These include: the cognitive framework required to identify and characterize this order and its global orientation; the methodological framework used to determine the strategy of major powers in imposing the rules on which the new order is based; and the framework of systems within which political, economic and military interaction occurs within the international community. Other frameworks include: the structure of the world order that determines whether it is unipolar, bipolar or multipolar; the philosophical framework that considers the world order as a set of vital functions that must be undertaken to ensure the survival of the international system; the intellectual framework that regards the new world order as a natural product of creative and innovative activities in response to the political, economic, social, military, security, technical and cultural needs of the components of the order; and the analytical framework that regards the order from one of two perspectives: the first based on the interaction between countries, peoples and civil society organizations, and the second on international interactions that have taken place during a limited period, which have led to deep historical transformations.

The first theme also deals with the various criteria influencing the shape of the new world order, including political, military, economic, cultural, educational, technical and energy dimensions, and how the United States of America has successfully employed these tools to shape the world order in accordance with a universal strategic vision that aims to preserve US supremacy in the face of the other major powers, prevent the emergence of competitors, and re-arrange the world in a way that serves its interests. This theme concludes that US hegemony clearly influences the value system of the world order.

The second theme of this chapter dealt with the most prominent contemporary features of the new world order, namely: the growing role of global civil society; the relationship between globalization and state sovereignty, and between globalization, realism and liberalism; civilizational and ideological conflict and related controversy; the growth of extremist trends and ideologies in the new world order, using the US far right as an example of this trend; and finally the controversy over the role of ideology in international relations. It is believed here that shedding light on those features is necessary in understanding much of the interaction taking place in the new world order. It is also affords an opportunity to disentangle the working mechanisms of the global system in its various stages of development, culminating in the unique features of the present world order that play an influential role in directing the policies and relations between its various constituents.

II

FACTORS INFLUENCING THE STRUCTURE OF THE NEW WORLD ORDER

Chapter II

Factors Influencing the Structure of the New World Order

Whereas the new world order is a reflection of the distribution of power between its main actors, there are many other factors that influence – either directly or indirectly – the basic structure of that system. This has been dealt with extensively in the Introduction and Chapter I entitled "The New World Order: Features and Concepts." It is attempted in this chapter to identify the most important of these factors and discuss their influence and manifestations in the global order. In doing so, it seeks to inform the intellectual understanding of the new world order, its dynamics and construction.

The Relationships between Civilizations

Some researchers, including Samuel Phillips Huntington,[1] argue that the post-Cold War world consists of eight civilizations, namely: the Chinese, the Japanese, the Indian, the Islamic, the Western, the Latin American, the Orthodox and the African.[2] Huntington posits that the development of international interests, animosities and alliances will be drawn in the future according to the relationships between these civilizations and the levels of mutual interest and/or hostility between them. He believes that civilizational interactions have played an influential role since the beginning of history in shaping the features of the world—for example, through invasion or subjugation.[3] The result, according to Huntington, is that global politics has become multi-polar as well as multi-civilizational. Many Western researchers agree with Huntington regarding the impact of the civilizational and cultural factors in international conflicts. Yoshihiro Francis Fukuyama argues that there are indeed cultural issues at play in the clash between the West and terrorists.[4] He believes that the September 11, 2001 attacks destroyed the idea held by Americans that, "their institutions and values – democracy, individual rights, the rule of law and prosperity based on economic freedom – represent universal aspirations that will ultimately be shared by people all over the world."[5] Fukuyama believes that culture, which includes, "religious beliefs, social habits and longstanding traditions, is the last area of convergence, and also the weakest. Societies are loathed to give up deeply rooted values, and it would be extremely naïve to think that American popular culture ... will soon engulf the entire world,"[6] and that, "the spread of McDonald's and Hollywood ... has provoked a considerable backlash against the very prospect of globalization."[7] As for the views of Arab researchers, Abdul Wahab Mohammed El-Messiri believes that the spread of the manifestations of globalization and US culture is associated primarily with increasing US military,

184

civilizational and cultural dominance. It is also a manifestation of the transition from an age of privacy to one of publicity, from solidity to liquidity, modernism to postmodernism, and ultimately to secular nationalism.[8]

Thus, it can be said that the spread of US culture (or the process of 'Americanization'), is in fact synonymous with globalization, as an evolution that removes the barriers between peoples, as well as between man and objects, removing any sense of privacy or identity.[9] This perhaps sheds light on the dislike of globalization among Arabs, Muslims and peoples across the world referred to by Fukuyama. To a certain degree, such sentiments were manifested in the Seattle demonstrations against the World Trade Organization (WTO) Conference in November–December 1999 that called for amendments to WTO agreements. The proponents of globalization and unipolarity considered these and subsequent demonstrations to be early evidence of a major crisis facing globalization.[10]

Despite the proliferation of claims of a clash of civilizations, some specialists, having debated the foundations of this mindset, reach the opposite conclusion. Huntington's assumption has been widely criticized for its pessimistic conclusions. Although he identified several non-Western civilizations that might enter into conflict with the West, he cited Islam as the single most serious threat, ignoring the diversity, multiplicity and change found in Islam, the Muslim world,[11] and Islamic fundamentalism—the latter providing an example of how the proponents of globalization characterize Middle Eastern and Islamic culture. In doing so, he employs an easy means of portraying the Middle East as a major, unchangeable obstacle to globalization.[12]

Mohammed Abed al-Jabri criticized Huntington's seminal article, published in the Summer 1993 issue of *Foreign Affairs*,[13] describing the body of the text as among the worst he had read.[14] He justified this by saying that the article was rife with repetition, the ideas 'scrambling,' the evidence overlapping, the analysis troubled, the interpolation raving, and noted that it was loaded with fallacy, all of which suggests that the underlying principle of Huntington's text was nothing more than that 'ends would justify means.'[15] Indeed, Al-Jabri argues that Huntington confused the definitions of culture and civilization, resorted to low academic standards and grave fallacies, failed to use religion as a measure to distinguish between civilizations except in relation to Islam—attributing the defining aspects of other civilizations to geography in the case of Western civilization, the country in the case of Japan and India, or person in the case of Confucian civilization.[16] Huntington ascribes the Latin American and African civilizations to a continent and a race,[17] and in this Al-Jabri's viewpoint seems logical, but one must admit that although Huntington's ideas show racial bias, they also exhibit a

186

tangible realism; hence the difficulty in dealing with such theories.

In parallel to this criticism, the intellectual Harald Müller[18] accuses Huntington of building his theory on a lone and limited thematic basis by adopting a vision of the future that is portrayed as an inescapable inevitability, namely what has been described as the 'Civilizational Cold War' between the West and Islam, pitting Islam as the West's enemy—one that it must be ready to face.[19] Müller described Huntington's theory of a clash of civilizations between the Western and Islamic worlds as imaginary, pointing out that the real contemporary clash has not occurred between two worlds, but between two specific movements, represented by Al-Qaeda leader Osama bin Laden on the one hand, and President George Walker Bush [Jr.] and the neoconservatives on the other.[20]

According to Harald Müller, coexistence between civilizations is indeed possible. There is no better place than the Middle East to prove this, provided that a just peace can be achieved as an imperative to a relationship between the West and the Arabs/Muslims that has evolved from tension to friendship. Unlike Huntington, Müller believes that culture is not a key player in international politics; it cannot be effective in international politics, he argues, and therefore talk about a clash of cultures is nothing more than a politically irrelevant metaphor.[21]

Harald Müller's intellectual approach is supported by a broad range of researchers and intellectuals, including Redwan Naif Al-Sayyed, who believes that civilizations are not separate units among which conflicts arise; rather, he states they are long-lived cultures and structures that do not compete or conflict with each other, but instead interact, overlap and are influenced by one another—neither eliminating the other.[22] Conflicts, on the other hand, break out between states, nations and peoples for political, economic, strategic or military reasons, not for cultural or civilizational reasons. Al-Sayyed supports this by arguing that the great wars of the 20th century took place within a single civilization, between its countries and nations for political, economic and strategic reasons. Indeed, the ideological dimensions given to these wars – communism versus liberalism – only appeared later to cover up the true causes.[23]

The intellectual Edward Wadie Said believed that Huntington failed to substantiate his proposition about the clash of civilizations. According to Said, Huntington only proved himself to be a poor writer and an unskilled thinker expressing his lofty view of civilizations and cultures as, "Sealed-off entities that have been purged of the myriad currents and countercurrents that animate human history, which is ignored in the rush to highlight the ludicrously compressed and constricted warfare that 'the clash of civilisations' argues is the reality."[24] Said was astonished at Huntington's extremely superficial treatment of two large identities, namely Islam and the West. He indicates that issues as complex as identity and culture should not be treated like warring cartoon characters, the more courageous of whom is inevitably the victor. He touches upon an extremely important point in this discussion, namely the heritage of the monotheistic religions, "where each religion is a successor haunted by what came before; for Muslims, Islam fulfills and ends the line of prophecy. There is still no decent history or demystification of the many-sided contest among these three followers."[25] So far, there is no logical history or analysis of the multi-faceted clash between followers of the three Abrahamic religions, since they each constitute not a single coherent unit but a group of similar approaches. Said concludes that the proposition of the clash of civilizations is a farce that does not provide a critical understanding of the impressive interrelation seen in our times.

Regardless of this intellectual controversy over the inevitability of a clash of civilizations (and the validity of Huntington's argument that the conflict between the superpowers has been replaced by such a clash)[26] and Müller's approach, the relationship between civilizations remains one of the pivotal factors influencing the structure of international relations, conflict management and alliance-building in the 21st century. It seems clear that cultural factors are increasingly shaping global political interactions due to the emergence of cultural identity as a source of conflict within and between societies. The disappearance of the ideological struggle of the Cold War has led to the revival of national, ethnic, religious and sectarian identities that have lent new momentum to disputes of a cultural nature in a number of regions of the world, while violence in the name of nationalism and culture has also escalated.[27]

The conflict does not appear to be so much among civilizations, but among major centers of capitalism and economic power. Therefore, whilst the cultural variable is of a dialectic nature – in agreement with Huntington – it is difficult to accept or acknowledge the validity that it is a singular and inevitable variable.[28] There is no doubt that this environment has played a role in the emergence of the proposition of a 'dialogue among civilizations' or 'dialogue of cultures'[29] advocated by a number of researchers in the face of Huntington's argument. Those researchers believe that such an approach comprises a realistic intellectual alternative. Within this framework, some Arab researchers, including Ammar Ali Hassan,[30] believe that attempts to link political conflicts (as seemingly permanent features of human interaction, be it between nations or empires) to civilizations pose a threat to the idea of true dialogue, and are employed by major powers to control and dominate smaller states. In other words, the 'dialogue of civilizations' is merely a tactic in an overall strategy, or a detail of an integrated political concept based on a strong desire to dominate, employed within an environment of political polarization to bring some countries under the influence of the single superpower while believing they are only participating in a formula for international dialogue and discussion.[31]

The potential of a dialogue among civilizations represents a timely question in an age witnessing the impacts of globalization, including the amalgamation and reformulation of cultural structures within communities into a single cultural mold. Globalization has taken over all fields, as Thomas Loren Friedman illustrated when he suggested that the world was becoming 'flat':[32] "... in today's world, having an Indian company led by a Hungarian servicing American banks with Montevidean engineers managed by Indian technologists who have learned to eat Uruguayan veggie [*sic*] is just the new normal"[33] —an idea which has been dealt with extensively in the Introduction to this volume. Globalization continues to provide new opportunities for cultures, but it has also produced huge challenges for these cultures, asking sensitive and decisive questions regarding the position of culture in the contemporary world, the fate of cultural peculiarities, and the future of global cultural diversity.[34]

The intensity of links between cultures will increase rapidly, unleashing social forces that will drive dialogue forward and away from the influence of politics. Transnational movements will be established and will overlap, common human values will grow. In this regard, the ICT revolution continues to play a key role in the convergence of cultures. The world has become a global digital society which has in turn produced a "digital citizenry."[35] Communication has become a global societal current from which no-one can remain isolated; indeed an over-abundance of communication has become a phenomena of the modern age.[36]

In keeping with the view of Mohamed Sa'adi Al-Hassan, the dialogue between cultures is essential in establishing new rules to address disputes and differences without resorting to war, fanaticism and violence, and in building trust between the various actors in the international arena to ensure coexistence and peace between nations.[37] The world seems to be in urgent need of such a dialogue. In Germany, for example, there are about four million Muslims, mostly of Turkish origin[38]—a good example of globalization. There are other examples in France, Britain, the Netherlands, and also in non-European countries such as the six GCC states,[39] at the forefront of which is the United Arab Emirates, where followers of most of the Abrahamic religions from different cultures reside among more than 200 nationalities.[40]

What enhances the need for a genuine dialogue between civilizations is the fact that the points of view of Western theorists such as Yoshihiro Francis Fukuyama in refuting the assumption of the clash of civilizations appear, in their essence, contradictory (even though Fukuyama's talk of nations' cultural identities seems to admit a victory for multilateralism). Fukuyama's vision is far from objective, particularly when he considers, "The struggle between Western liberal democracy and Islamo-fascism is not between two equally viable cultural systems, both of which can master modern science and technology, create wealth and deal with the de-facto diversity of the contemporary world,"[41] but rather, "Western institutions hold all the cards and for that reason will continue to spread across the globe in the long run."[42] He also states that, in the short-term, "courage and a determination to fight for the values that make modern democratic societies possible,"[43] despite the presence of exceptions in the Muslim world that confirm the possibility of communication with the West on the basis of science and the production of wealth and knowledge (e.g., Turkey, Malaysia and Indonesia).

Fukuyama is not even-handed when he reduces the Islamic world to 'fascist organizations' and terrorist groups – moving away from his rational proposition based on the preservation of civilizational identity and the rejection of hegemony – and considers Western civilization the sole platform from which to embrace diversity in the contemporary world. It also seems that Fukuyama is oblivious to the reality of political trends and realities on the ground, particularly when he talks of Iran as a candidate for the leadership of the Islamic world through the development of, "a modern and tolerant form of Islam … as a powerful example to the rest of the Muslim world."[44]

Furthermore, Fukuyama does not understand the nature of the relationship between Islamic denominations and the sensitivities that exist therein. He does not realize that Iran, which adheres to the Shiite denomination,[45] cannot lead an Islamic world whose overwhelming majority belong to the Sunni denomination. Furthermore, he asserts that Al-Qaeda's former leader Osama bin Laden gained 'immense popularity' throughout the Muslim world as a result of the terrorist attacks of September 11, 2001.[46] This argument must be refuted, because acknowledging it will lead to the extremely grave conclusion that all Muslims believe in the ideologies of terrorists and extremist organizations, which is simply not true.

Fukuyama's controversial conclusion confuses 'popularity' (which has a positive connotation in the sense that there are numerous supporters of your reasoning and approach) and 'notoriety,' with both its negative and positive connotations and abstract media sense—in this case that an ideological position reaches a large segment of the public because of a particular act, regardless of the opinion toward it. For instance, it cannot be said that the widespread awareness of the name of the Swedish cartoonist Lars Endel Roger Vilks[47] means that he won any kind of popularity among Muslims throughout the world when he drew cartoons degrading the Prophet Mohammed (peace be upon him).[48] Above all, Fukuyama's proposition regarding Osama Bin Laden's 'popularity' does not apply at all to many states and communities in the Islamic world, since they appear more inclined to reject the model of radical Islam and renounce terrorism and violence. No-one can say, for example, that an open Arab Muslim society, characterized by tolerance and capable of human coexistence, has received the attacks of September 11, 2001 with any degree of satisfaction or happiness.[49]

Herein lies the importance of a dialogue that can lead to greater understanding, peaceful co-existence and mutual respect, because the absence of such a dialogue means that current illusions will become further entrenched and false stereotypes promoted. It will also spell growing mistrust and ignorance between parties. There is therefore no alternative to dialogue, because it is the gateway to understanding and a necessity in avoiding conflict. In the absence of dialogue, the idea of conflict between people or civilizations will start to emerge and spread.[50] Hence the importance of international efforts made to achieve civilizational convergence and address the forces that fuel violence, extremism and conflict across the world.[51]

The Role of Force
in International Relations

Power may be defined as the ability to attain outcomes sought by policy planners.[52] It has several forms and manifestations, but power forms the foundation of all states. Power politics play a prominent role in the structure of the world order, which reflects the power and authority – actual or potential – of countries, forming a matrix built on the full understanding by each state of its own relative position, commitment to the preservation and limits of that position, and awareness and respect for the roles of the other actors within the order.[53]

Some researchers state that hierarchies of power within the structure of the new world order cannot be determined by mathematical calculations; rather, it is a structure achieved through mutual agreement, often at international conferences culminating in the conclusion of peace treaties governing the distribution of power between states – such as those comprising the Peace of Westphalia concluded in 1648[54] – and other seminal moments launching new eras in the global order. These treaties have inducted new states into the list of major powers while excluding others—permanently or temporarily. The idea of a balance of power, emerging in the wake of the Peace of Westphalia, became one of the most important mechanisms under which the system has operated in all historical periods since. However, as one of the most prominent mechanisms of international relations, this concept cannot be understood in its idealistic form. It has been applied in various different incarnations in different eras; as former US Secretary of State Condoleezza Rice states, it has been used in a military, economic and geostrategic sense (i.e. the actual balance of capabilities between opponents and competitors), as well as to denote strategies aimed at preventing the emergence of a dominant power—for example, the alliance between Russia, Austria, Prussia (whose territory is presently shared by Germany and other countries) and Britain in 1813 with the aim of defeating France and restoring the balance of power, employing the concept for self-defense against the arbitrary actions of a regional power.[55] The balance of power concept has also been used by major powers to justify expansionist policies. The concept was also used during the Cold War to signify the need for Western superiority over the communist bloc countries, especially at the military level. Thus, 'balance of power' is not actually indicative of balance, but of an imbalance of power in favor of the party employing the concept—such as in the case of Israel, the dominant regional power in the Middle East.[56]

The emergence of the nation-state in Europe following the Peace of Westphalia led to the demarcation of borders between states, the identification of the sovereignty of each state, and recognition of states' natural proclivity to develop their strength in line with the demands of national sentiments.[57] The balance between states achieved by force has become the means of preserving borders, sovereignty and the interests of other countries. This was legally framed by the Treaty of Utrecht in 1713,[58] signed by France, Spain, the United Kingdom, Austria and Holland. In essence, a balance of power is based on the recognition of states' interests, as the distinctive characteristics in international relations. Indeed, international relations would not only be dictated by differences in the national interests of countries, but also by each country's attempt to reinforce its national power at the expense of others.'[59] Consequently, if a single state is capable of gaining overwhelming superiority, this will drive it to threaten the freedom and independence of other nations. It is this challenge that inspires countries to confront force with force through the development of individual power, or the creation of strong coalitions capable of meeting the challenge emanating from a given strategic foe.[60]

In general, superpowers and major powers in every age, such as the United States of America, the European Union, Russia, China and Japan today, have tailored the form of the global system to serve their interests. In the 16th century, Spain redefined basic concepts of justice and universality so as to justify the conquest of indigenous Americans. In the 18th century, France developed its concept of borders and the balance of power to suit its principally continental strengths. In the 19th century, Britain forged new rules on piracy, neutrality, and colonialism—again, to suit its particular interests as the predominant power of the time.[61] This is perhaps the case with the United States of America today; since the end of the Cold War, it has become the world's single undisputed superpower. Thus, it has sought to achieve a number of goals that serve its strategic interests. These goals could not have been achieved were it not for such an international structure. This also explains the changes to the notion of the use of force and its governance brought about by the administration of President George Herbert Bush [Sr.].

In fact, the US monopoly on leadership of the new world order is not the only reason that such changes have been possible. The broad international sympathy gained by the United States of America in the wake of the attacks of September 11, 2001, and mounting international concerns about the spread of terrorism have also since contributed, allowing the United States of America to achieve a long sought-after goal, namely an expansion in the right to self-defense to include military responses against states that support or harbor terrorist groups.[62]

Some researchers cite the term 'rogue state' as key to the US understanding of this new form of military action. Iraq provided a clear example; the United States of America considered Iraq an outlaw nation that had to be apprehended by the guardians of the new world order.[63] Therefore, the United States of America acted outside the appropriate legal framework in dealing with Iraq; namely the United Nations Charter that through Articles 41, 42 and 51 governs how states should deal with such cases,[64] which states in Article 39: "The Security Council shall determine the existence of any threat to the peace, or act of aggression and shall make recommendations, or decide what measures shall be taken in accordance with Articles 41 and 42, to maintain or restore international peace and security."[65] However, the United States of America referred to Article 51 of the Charter, which provides for the only exception to this rule: "Nothing in the present Charter shall impair the inherent right of individual or collective self-defense if an armed attack occurs against a Member of the United Nations ..."[66]

The Charter states that such acts of self-defense should be 'reported' to the Security Council immediately; but the right to use force in self defense is open to interpretation in terms of its necessity and proportionality,[67] which are determined via frameworks that are naturally tailored in accordance with the balance of international power and the nature of the world order.

Hence, some researchers view the US invasion of Iraq in 2003 as a turning point in determining the nature of the new world order. They consider it the beginning of a new proclivity for upholding the logic of force over that of legitimacy. The United States of America, as the most powerful country in the world, now had the first word and last word in the new world order. The equation had become based on the assumption that US decisions represented law, justice and international legitimacy, and that such decisions would also define lawlessness, injustice and international illegitimacy.[68]

Indeed, the precursors to this new direction could be seen in earlier events. For example, then US representative to the UN, but later US Secretary of State, Madeleine Korbel Albright,[69] when addressing the United Nations Security Council during debates on events in Iraq in 1994, said: "We will behave ... multilaterally when we can and unilaterally when we must"[70]; and President William Jefferson "Bill" Clinton[71] expressed the same sentiment when he said: "Everyone would understand that then the United States of America, and hopefully all of our allies, would have the unilateral right to respond at a time, place and manner of our own choosing,"[72] commenting on an agreement signed between UN Secretary General Kofi Atta Annan and Iraqi President Saddam Hussein Al-Tikriti in February 1998.[73] It was as if Clinton considered Washington to be the only judge deciding the extent of commitment by Saddam Hussein Al-Tikriti's regime to the implementation of the agreement reached with the United Nations.

Economic Factors

Bipolarity was based on three fundamental pillars: namely ideology, the immensely destructive power of nuclear weapons, and economic capabilities. The role of the economy in the relations between East and West was no less than that of military might or ideology. The division of Europe into two conflicting camps was also economic— based on two patterns of global economy, namely market economics and capitalism vs. socialist production.[74] The many failures of the communist economic system shook the convictions of its proponents, and capitalism ultimately prevailed against the backdrop of the collapse of the Communist bloc.[75] Thereafter the influential role of economic factors in international relations increased, partly owing to the relative decline of the roles of ideology and military power.

British Prime Minister David William Cameron[76] makes a direct link between his country's influence on the international scene and the strength of its economy. In a speech on British foreign policy delivered in the City of London on November 15, 2010, Cameron said that while some claimed that Britain's global role was declining "... Britain will remain a great economic power," but needed to 'sort out' its economy if it wanted to "carry weight in the world."[77] He also indicated that one way to achieve this was to strengthen ties with emerging economies.

This clear link between economy, influence and international standing is supported by a report issued in November 2008 by the US National Intelligence Council entitled "Global Trends 2025: A Transformed World."[78] In the report, experts concluded that US influence would decline over the following two decades. One of the reasons behind this expectation was that the dollar would lose its status as the world's main currency. The report also concluded that the world was likely to experience more conflicts over trade, investment, innovation and access to technology.[79]

Many researchers agree that the critical factors in determining the hierarchy of the new world order are economic, scientific, military, demographic, cultural and educational. However, such resources are useless if not effectively and actively invested in the development of national economies.[80] In demonstrating US superiority, some cite mainly economic considerations, pointing out that US gross domestic product (US $15.685 trillion) is roughly equal to the combined GDP of China, Japan and Russia ($16.202 trillion). Indeed, it is also almost equal to the GDP of the 28 countries of the European Union ($16.641 trillion).[81]

The United States of America considers the most serious threat in economic terms to be the European Union and China, both of which – according to the US viewpoint – possess the necessary capabilities to become independent players at the global level.[82] The most serious threat to the United States of America in this respect is the fact that the economies of each are key to their global power, as is also the case for the United States of America. The increasing strength of the euro and the yuan could gradually lead to their replacing the dollar as the global reserve currency, spelling a resultant reduction in the ability of the United States of America to secure financial reserves in hard currency and control global lending operations, debt and world trade. US fears in this regard could perhaps signal the possibility of a trade war between Europe and China on the one hand, and the United States of America on the other.

The EU and China realize that their common weak point is energy, and that all US schemes revolve around the energy sources on which they depend. Therefore, searching for alternatives, they have turned towards Russia—which has no less than ten billion tons of oil reserves and the world's largest reserves of natural gas (more than 40 trillion cubic meters). Russia also has the infrastructure required to supply energy resources to the West.[83] The countries of the former Soviet Union satisfied around 41% of EU countries' natural gas needs in 2011 and around 51% of their oil needs in the same year.[84]

To demonstrate the importance of energy in the strategies of the major powers, researchers suggest that the oil reserves of

Saudi Arabia are equivalent in strategic terms in the international arena to the possession of nuclear weapons.[85] Indeed, its reserves may constitute a weapon of deterrence in the face of those who might threaten the interests of the Kingdom, specifically those associated with its role within the Organization of the Petroleum Exporting Countries (OPEC). The Kingdom has used its resource production efficiency to maintain its position within the Organization over the decades, and forced countries such as Russia and Venezuela to abandon any race to increase production.

Media reports claim that Prince Bandar bin Sultan bin Abdulaziz Al Saud, Secretary-General of the National Security Council and Head of the Saudi Intelligence Agency, met with Russian President Vladimir Vladimirovich Putin in July 2013 in Moscow, where it was reported that Prince Bandar presented an overview of the various aspects of potential cooperation between the two countries. They reached an understanding on a number of regional issues, including on Syria. Other areas of agreement included oil and investment cooperation between the two countries; Prince Bandar offered cooperation in terms of oil pricing and production to help maintain a stable price on global markets, and discussions ensued on Russian gas pipelines to Europe, the establishment of refineries and petrochemical industries, and the provision of huge multi-billion dollar investments in various Russian markets, in exchange for political understanding with regard to a number of issues, including those involving Syria and Iran.[86]

It may be noted that the recent glut of political literature on the decline of US power has been accompanied primarily by indications of a decline in the US economy against the growing economic power of other countries and blocs, such as China, the European Union and Russia. This raises a conceptual research problem, in that the rise of major economic powers may spell an equal decline in that of the superpower. Although this notion is not new to the US scholarly community – particularly considering its appearance in the 1980s during the rise of the Japanese economic power – China's economic rise may indeed represent a factor affecting the future of US influence, coinciding as it does with deep crises in the US economy, and the rise of emerging economies such as the BRICS.[87] Some experts predict that these countries will occupy the top spots in the world economy by 2050.[88] This is a new development of an economic nature that may play a role in the structure of the new world order in the future. These countries seek to attain global leadership through international financial institutions such as the World Bank and the International Monetary Fund (IMF).

The debates taking place in the various fora of these institutions reflect the ambitions of emerging countries to graduate from the back seats of discussions on the nature of the global financial system. In other words, these countries seek to gain economic influence that could subsequently be translated into political and strategic influence in the new world order.

However, evidence confirms that achieving such ambitions will be much more difficult in reality, at least in the coming two decades. Hence, such expectations should be approached with caution; "Instead of dominant powerhouses it is possible that China, India, Brazil and Russia may end up like Japan: huge economic growth [*sic*] that is not accompanied by extended geopolitical power and influence."[89]

Possessing economic power is one thing, utilizing it to enhance a country's status and influence in the world is quite another; the first does not translate directly into the second. That being said, relevant historical examples should be considered according to the specific circumstances in which they occurred. Germany, for example, responded to the dominant influence of Great Britain in the early 20th century, which ultimately led to the outbreak of the First World War.[90] Similar reasons and circumstances prevailed and subsequently led to the outbreak of World War II. Yet such an analysis necessarily leads to other scenarios that may lack corresponding historical evidence but are nonetheless possible, albeit due to changing international developments and circumstances.

A strong economy is not necessarily matched by growing military strength or global political influence. Japan, as mentioned above, is a good example. Furthermore, a strong economy does not necessarily produce a strong army that is capable of confronting great powers. Most of all, the economic rise of a particular country does not necessarily lead to the outbreak of a new world conflict, in view of overlapping interests. Besides, war is no longer necessarily a result of the desire by an emerging power to demonstrate its strength and expand its sphere of influence.

Whatever the perspective of analysis, however, what is certain is that the military power and political influence of a given country are based primarily on economic strength. According to Paul Kennedy, the ability of nations to exercise and maintain global control remain ultimately dependent on their productive capability,[91] as mentioned in the Chapter entitled "The New World Order: Features and Concepts."

There are those who believe that the economy has played the most prominent role in international relations in recent decades. They recall the second oil crisis of 1979,[92] and the announcement by China's leader Deng Xiaoping of the adoption of a new policy based on a market economy.[93] They consider this Chinese orientation to be the most prominent strategic shift to have occurred in recent decades by virtue of the effects it had on the global balance of power, manifested in the rise of China in 2008 to the second largest world economy at a time when the United States of America and the European Union were suffering the consequences of an acute financial crisis.[94] Indeed, there are those who divide modern economic history into two periods: 'before China' and 'after China,' with the year 1978 representing an economic milestone.[95] The strategic value of China's move toward a market economy was enhanced by the emergence of a growing role for emerging economies. This essentially economic variable, in addition to the consequences of US military intervention in Afghanistan and Iraq, has brought the United States of America a step closer to sharing influence on the international stage with major powers such as the European Union, China and Russia, albeit retaining the status of the leading global power.[96]

Ultimately, the economy has become a key driver of international relations and the first and most influential product of those relations. Hence, it is a prominent factor guiding the new world order. The past two decades have witnessed dramatic shifts in the definition and components of economic interests; indeed, it would not be an exaggeration to say that some radical changes have occurred in the understanding of the very nature of the economic interests of countries. The global economy has become increasingly dependent on electronic networks, involving the interconnection of huge numbers of people across a virtual space that, by definition, does not have a presidency or headquarters. In such a space, each user feels that they are at the center of the cyber universe; indeed, small businesses now have the opportunity to overtake huge international bureaucratic corporations, jeopardizing their immense trade influence.[97]

Cyber networks have contributed to the advent of the knowledge economy, featuring increased reliance on information, creativity and innovation as sources of wealth for states, individuals and institutions alike. This evolution comes at the expense of the traditional 'goods and services' economy owing to the adoption of advanced technologies and the increasing demand for knowledge and information, to the extent that information becomes an extremely important strategic 'commodity' in itself, and a key pillar in the competitive environment of the 21st century.[98]

Companies comprising just a handful of individuals have turned into extremely influential actors in the global economy. For many years now, nearly 50% of US exports have originated from companies employing 19 or fewer employees, while companies with 500 or more employees account for only 7% of total exports.[99] This in turn means that the traditional concept of the international corporation has begun to fade, as did its predecessors that were confined to particular economies or markets. Thus, we are dealing with a new equation of economic power, wielded by productive individuals anywhere in the world. Consequently, it has become extremely difficult to determine the structure of the new world order according to considerations of economic superiority, a pursuit subject to continuous change and adaptation.

Calculations of states' interests, as well as the general balance of power, have played a prominent role in determining the structure of the global order throughout history, which has been finalized only after broad-ranging debates among the major powers. At each stage, the global order has reflected the role, principles, foundations, limits and interests of each party in such a way as to ensure genuine partnerships that maintain the pre-agreed structure of the order, be it unipolar, bipolar or multipolar.[100]

Some cases serve as examples of highly influential economic priorities, with the 28 EU member states going further than the creation of a closely interdependent and integrated financial zone by launching a single European currency (the euro).[101] The aim is also to speak with one voice and act as one bloc with respect to political and military issues. Signed on February 7, 1992, the Maastricht Treaty[102] sought not just to introduce the single currency in the EU countries, but also to promote the adoption of a common foreign and security policy.[103] However, free trade and the rise of Asia have pushed some euro-zone members to the margins of the world economy, and undermined stalwarts such as France and Italy.[104]

Despite the role of economic factors in the structure of the new world order, and contrary to those who believe the rise of China as an international power could rival US dominance in the wake of the financial crisis,[105] Joseph Samuel Nye doubts the viability of China's challenge. He believes China has a long road to travel in this regard, given the problems it faces on the development front, the issue of rural degradation, and its various demographic challenges.[106] As mentioned earlier, in

210

terms of technology, standards of living and military power, China falls well behind the United States of America. Its military is weak by comparison; while the United States of America has 11 aircraft carriers, as of the end of 2012 China had one—a single re-fitted Ukrainian-made former Soviet aircraft carrier called "Liaoning."[107] (Although China is working toward producing its own, larger carrier that will be capable of accommodating more aircraft.)[108]

Nonetheless, recent decades have seen a clear change in the primacy of military power in achieving the strategic objectives of states, with an increased focus on economic power, which has come to assume a position of equal standing among the tools of foreign policy. Some countries with strong economies have moved up the global decision-making hierarchy based on this fact alone. Germany and Japan are clear examples of this transformation. Also noticeable is the decline in the international focus on military alliances in favor of regional or international economic alliances, such as the BRICS and ASEAN.

Some specialists and researchers, including Sayed Yaseen,[109] and Martin Jacques[110] (in his book *When China Rules the World: The End of the Western World and the Birth of a New Global Order*)[111] assert that China now has qualities that will allow it to bring about an historic transition, moving to the forefront of the new world order by virtue of its military strength and impressive economic achievements, and bringing with it an integrated strategic theory for an international multipolar world. Indeed, Goldman Sachs has predicted that the Chinese economy will overtake that of the United States of America by 2027.[112]

Talk of the rise of China challenges the prevailing US theory of a unipolar world. Some researchers believe that regardless of whether China or other major states harbor visions of some form of multipolar evolution, change will not occur in the absence of an organized international movement that systematically reconsiders the structure of the world order, its constituent units, and its prevailing ideology, which at present renders the United States of America both a leader and an adversary.[113]

This theory largely supports that which this book adopts regarding the position of the United States of America at the top of the new world order. China remains reluctant to cooperate in the face of global challenges, maintaining a process of calculation quite distinct from that of the United States of America and other major powers, including when considering issues such as sovereignty, global terrorism, humanitarian intervention and the proliferation of WMDs.

There is much evidence, however, that the views of Sayed Yaseen, Martin Jacques and others overlook many aspects of China's situation, strategic thinking and behavior.[114] China faces numerous obstacles and suffers a variety of restrictions that will likely prevent it from assuming a prominent position in the new world order. Global security challenges, such as those relating to energy and environmental security, have begun to have negative impacts on the internal situation in the country, which also faces increasing internal unrest, as well as concerns about the inability to meet the ambitions of its people and their ever-increasing expectations. These are major challenges that could perhaps push China – albeit to a limited extent – towards introversion and a more limited role on the world stage. At best, it could postpone China's strategic ambitions in this regard.[115] Regardless, the influence of the rise of China or the growing role of global economic blocs such as the G8 and G20 in determining the structure of the new world order should not be ignored.

Practically speaking, there are also a number of stable features of the order, including the economic weight of the US financial system, which is reflected in its political dominance of the global order. The funds upon which commerce and industry depend often pass via Manhattan,[116] and are affected by decisions taken in Wall Street,[117] Washington, DC, and by the US Federal Reserve, the repercussions of which instantly resonate around the world. Major US companies such as ExxonMobil, Microsoft and Apple, as well as the regulatory infrastructure supporting them and the funds driving them, constitute an influence that dominates economic policies in Europe, Asia, South America and around the world.

The World Trade Center in New York was the symbol of the network of global trade and finance until 2001.[118] It was chosen by terrorists as a target through which to impact the free market system and the political system associated with it, which – in turn – is closely intertwined with the United States of America. Since the beginning of the 21st century, almost all countries of the world have remained loyal to a world order based on the concept of the market economy, not just because each country has benefitted or hopes to benefit from the system, but also because there has been no other practical alternative that would offer nations the same opportunity to compete, grow and promote their interests.[119]

More importantly, the world remains dependent on the dollar as its global reserve currency. Talk about the role of the Chinese yuan in this regard is still highly controversial—no significant change has occurred in the status of the dollar, which accounted for nearly 60% of global foreign exchange reserves as of 2010.[120] Despite the financial problems experienced by the United States of America in recent years, the dollar is still seen as a safe haven in times of crisis, and it seems unlikely that the yuan could dislodge the US dollar from this position in the next ten years.[121]

Nonetheless, this does not mean that the future will not belong to China, or that it is not progressing in that direction at a measured pace. We should not ignore the fact that China considers time in different terms to the West;[122] it has a long history – 5,000 years of civilization – and an equally long memory. It is also patient, and trusts that history will stand on its side. These attributes have been inherent in the Chinese psyche since time immemorial.[123] Perhaps this explains, albeit partially, the immense popularity of the new slogan coined by current Chinese Premier Xí Jìnpíng: 'The Chinese Dream.' Indeed, local researchers believe the dream refers to the ambition of installing China as a dominant global power.[124]

Military Superiority

There is no doubt, as mentioned earlier, that the extent of states' military development continues to play a prominent role in laying the foundations of the new world order and in determining the relationships between countries, be they world or regional powers. The United States of America would not enjoy its unique contemporary status had it not been for its huge qualitative military, economic, technological, cultural and educational superiority. The United States of America is unmatched militarily, and as experts confirm, its monumental arsenal of missiles and precision-guided munitions is capable of defeating any adversary without sustaining heavy losses.[125]

There are various indications that it would take a very long time to weaken the US military – which includes the most powerful army in history – and thus bring about an actual decline in the influence of a country whose total military spending exceeds that of China, Russia, Britain, Japan, France,

India, Germany, Italy, South Korea and Australia combined,[126] amounting to nearly $633 billion in 2014,[127] and representing about 40% of global defense expenditure.[128] The US defense budget is about three times the size of the EU countries combined, and exceeds by six times the defense budget of China (which ranks third in the world after the United States of America and the European Union in terms of military spending).[129]

Thanks to its enormous defense budget, the United States of America is the only country that is able to achieve sustained progress in the development of military technology, ensuring its ongoing superiority and domination. This is no temporary trend; US military expenditure in 1997 exceeded that of the next five or six biggest defense spenders (China, Russia, France, Japan, the United Kingdom and Germany), whose combined defense budget in 1997 was nearly $267 billion.[130] By 2000, it had risen to $354 billion, above the combined expenditure of the next eight largest defense spenders. While the defense budgets of most states are either stable or in decline, the US military budget is constantly rising, and a number of researchers agree that no other country or group of countries can hope to compete with US military–technological progress for at least a generation.[131]

Nevertheless, it is necessary to point out that military force no longer enjoys the same status as in the age of bipolarity. While the relative importance of military power is decreasing within the power equation of states, the importance of economic, technical, educational and cultural power is growing. This has led to a rearrangement of state power in the new world order. The rise of several economic competitors to the United States of America – including China, Japan, the European Union and Russia – has contributed to a decline in US economic power.

There is no doubt that the proliferation of Western liberal concepts and the rise of economic globalization have contributed to the rise of economic might at the expense of military power; so much so that developed countries have begun restructuring the roles of their armed forces and revising their military doctrines to better suit an era of non-traditional threats, as well as the decline of the traditional role of military power in opening up foreign markets and extending influence and domination—this role now being undertaken by multinational companies, unopposed except in their particular business areas.[132]

Furthermore, the concept of conventional warfare itself has changed, both in terms of the threats (such as terrorism, organized crime, etc.) and major developments in information technology, manifested militarily in the advent of cyber warfare. Such is the level of strategic threat posed by cyber attack and electronic espionage that US President Barack Hussein Obama[133] has declared that any electronic attack on the United States of America will be treated in the same way as a conventional assault, and that the United States of America will respond by any means it deems necessary according to the nature and extent of the provocation.[134]

According to press reports, a confidential legal review concluded that the President enjoys the power to order electronic pre-emptive strikes in the event that the United States of America discovers evidence of a potential attack of this kind.[135] A US official was quoted as saying that the new US policy would also determine how intelligence agencies will monitor computer networks in other countries to identify potential cyber attacks on the United States of America and examine the possibility of launching a preventive war against enemies.[136] Further testament to the magnitude of the threat posed by cyber attacks was evident in warnings by Russian expert Eugene Kaspersky[137] in June 2012 at a cybersecurity conference organized by Tel Aviv University on June 6, 2012,[138] that the continued development and proliferation of cyber weapons would alter the face of the world as we know it, and that infrastructure around the world remains dangerously exposed to such weapons.[139]

Scientific Development and Technological Progress

Although scientific–technological progress and development have always been vital in determining the overall power of states, their influence has grown in recent decades— particularly in light of the information and communications revolution in developed economies. For example, the US economy witnessed phenomenal growth during the 1990s with the momentum generated by advances in information technology, pushing the New York Stock Exchange and NASDAQ indices to record levels. The contribution of the information sector to US GDP grew from 3.4% in 1991 to around 4.3% in 1999,[140] a pattern also seen in several other countries. Aspects of technical progress have enabled the least-developed countries to make significant jumps forward. Advances in technology and communications have also brought about a parallel revolution in other fields such as medicine, engineering, scientific research and genetics.[141]

This progress has produced enormous shifts and radical changes in the patterns of thinking and interaction among humans in the political, social, security, media, economic and educational fields. The knowledge-based economy has become a resource that countries consider a significant source of power and national income.[142]

Another variable influencing the structure of the new world order relates to the level of technological progress achieved not by states but by the cross-border organizations and groups that since the attacks of September 11, 2001 have become key players affecting the conduct of international relations. It is now highly likely that countries are vulnerable to electronic attacks waged by terrorist groups. As mentioned above, some senior US officials, including former Secretary of

Defense Leon Edward Panetta, have even warned of the vulnerability of the United States of America to a "cyber Pearl Harbor."[143]

Some experts consider this a likely scenario, but not all. The main concern surrounding the possibility is the vulnerability of critical infrastructure, such as power and communications grids, air traffic control, banking, and water or electricity networks. A successful attack on these networks – which represent the backbone of an economy – would lead to complete paralysis and chaos. Some refer to this as part of an increasing 'globalization of crime' and virtual conflict over the internet.[144]

The severity of the strategic threat posed by countries with clear scientific–technological superiority, and the potential for such states to capitalize on this advantage to secure greater international status and influence conflict, are encapsulated in the comment of Richard Alan Clarke, Former US National Coordinator for Security, Infrastructure Protection and Counter-terrorism,[145] that the age of cyberwar has already begun.[146] He has cautioned states to take precautions against electronic attacks immediately, as some had already begun 'preparing the battlefield' by hacking into each other's networks and infrastructures and laying in wait; occurring during peacetime, such actions have already blurred the boundaries between war and peace, adding a new dimension to global security and stability.[147]

There is no doubt that cyber attacks pose an unprecedented challenge for the new world order, particularly considering the difficulty in determining the identity of those responsible, and the absence of international legislation to hold the countries or institutions that carry out such attacks to account; there are therefore limited means with which to prosecute perpetrators, unlike in other forms of warfare.[148] This opens the door to unilateral action, and heightens the determination of major powers to emphasize the right to self-defense outside international law, which ultimately provides safeguards that achieve global security and stability through the relatively stable international relations they ensure.

The technological–knowledge revolution has changed every aspect of human life, from methods of production and consumption to the perceptions of ideological and moral values, political and legal systems, means of warfare and military strategy. Just as the birth of capitalism was associated with the beginnings of the technological and knowledge revolutions, its own successes and crises have been associated with the momentum achieved by the deployment of those technologies; its future prospects will be linked to this accelerating technological revolution.

It is difficult to understand the current dynamics of globalization – or even the recent global financial crisis – in isolation from the information revolution which has allowed for the daily, instant movement of thousands of billions of dollars, complicating the task of monitoring the trajectories of financial transfers. Nor is it possible to appreciate the nuances of strategies controlling oil resources and corridors without considering expensive alternative energy technologies in the coming decades, or to imagine future military deployments by major powers in the world without considering the effects of the communications revolution.

The world stands at the threshold of an era of accelerated scientific progress that will dictate future global developments – be they in terms of production, industry, trade, or extending global power (or criteria for the employment thereof) and influence over world public opinion – driving some researchers to claim that the hierarchy of the global order will become increasingly based on states' levels of scientific and technological achievement. This may come at the expense of those nations that fail to understand or act upon the need to engage in the ongoing technological competition, or merely cannot afford to keep up, ultimately falling behind the development curve and becoming marginalized in the world order.[149]

New Challenges and Variables

New challenges and variables – such as the introduction of ever-more advanced information and communications technologies, as well as the various manifestations of globalization – play an influential role in determining the structure of the new world order. Indeed, the concept of the global village is fast becoming a reality as a result of the massive proliferation of means of advanced communication, which will render Western lifestyles and values universal.

This homogenization is also encouraged by the emergence of common global challenges, such as poverty, environmental pollution, global warming and illegal migration, bringing about a trend toward global governance and a corresponding fall in the role of the nation-state that has prevailed since the Westphalian treaties of 1648. Some claim this new inclination toward centralized global authority raises the prospect of global decision-making via multinational organizations spread across the world—such as NATO. Others, however, believe that such a proposition is unlikely, mainly in view of the failure of the United Nations (as the most important global organization in recent times) to act independently of the superpower that drives it, namely the United States of America.[150]

Nevertheless, the concept of global partnership still finds advocates among theorists who focus their discussions on the fact that rapid developments in telecommunications have come to represent the greatest influence on world affairs during the current era. They argue that the future promises a world where divisions and fault lines will not occur between civilizations, as Huntington claimed, or between ethnic, religious, or national groups, but between those who consider themselves part of the world wide web and those who do not; there are some 1.483

billion users of Facebook – the most popular social network – 982 million users of Twitter, and 340 million users of Google+, all living in a single electronic community.[151]

Others argue that the conceptual framework for the model of the global village and a 'universal' community ignores two key facts:[152] first, personal authority of the individual or the institution is still subject to the authority of the state, and citizens can only act in ways permitted by the legislative infrastructure that allows a state to limit – if it so wishes – the actions of individuals; second, the business of transferring power is not a zero-sum game, as an increase in the influence and authority of individuals within the state does not necessarily mean that government will cede any of its traditional control. Therefore, the state will not disappear, but its role and the extent of its involvement in the affairs of justice and legislation may shrink.[153]

Some researchers believe that the 'new reality' created by international non-governmental organizations, transnational corporations and new means of social communication will transform the world order into an informal global system or, more precisely, lead to the development of a global civil society, governed by companies and institutions, in light of the decay of the state and its sovereignty in recent decades. They base this, in part, on the vision put forward in the 1990s by US national security adviser Zbigniew Kazimierz Brzezinski, of a new geopolitical map of the world—the so-called "Grand

Chessboard."[154] Some claim that this vision has already begun to be realized, citing the example of Google (the number-one search engine in the world, which handles a billion search requests each month),[155] which has garnered great political and economic influence in the international arena, and has even become embroiled in disputes with states—as in the case of China, owing to issues relating to internet censorship.[156]

Ultimately, global communication networks, open financial markets and the proliferation of transport and communications infrastructure are all factors that increase the vulnerability of the state in the face of threats posed by external actors. For example, de-regulation in the broadcasting and communications industries has deprived nation states of their ability to monitor and control communications within their own borders. Private telecommunications networks now constitute new communities of interests that are only nominally linked to a given territory or country, and many people today are identified by their virtual addresses more than by their geographical locations.[157]

The decline of the nation-state becomes more pronounced in the realms of trade, where international companies are able to pressure governments to make major concessions that further weaken their traditional sovereign rights. International conventions and treaties, such as the General Agreement on Tariffs and Trade (GATT), have deprived governments of their right to impose local restrictions that hinder global free trade.

Similarly, institutions such as the WTO, the successor to the afore-mentioned GATT, can impose sanctions on countries that violate the conventions of international trade. Furthermore, globalized communications have produced new and non-traditional security threats that emanate not from states but from the internet or commercial interests.

Joseph Samuel Nye alludes to this problem in his proposition that the world is witnessing two shifts in power – a "transition" and a "diffusion,"[158] wherein a "transition of power from one dominant state to another is a familiar historical pattern, but power diffusion is a more novel process."[159] This diffusion of power refers to its distribution – be it soft, hard or 'smart' power – including through the emergence on the international stage of new actors such as terrorist organizations, multinational corporations and non-governmental organizations.

Nye believes the "problem for all states today is that more is happening outside the control of even the most powerful of them … For all the fashionable predictions that China … will surpass the United States of America in the coming decades, the greatest threats may come from … non-state actors. In an information-based world of cyber-insecurity, power diffusion may be a greater threat than power transition."[160] This view has merit; the strategic danger that is most threatening to US security today is not from the rise of China or other powers, but is primarily due to the geographical spread and qualitative variation of power. The threat no longer emanates from a single source and location – as was the case during the Cold War era – but from cyber, biological, military and terrorist threats coming from a variety of sources.

As mentioned above, this adds to the weakening of the importance of states' military capabilities and their control over national security and the fundamentals of sovereignty.[161] Today, events in one country can directly affect the economies of others. An example of this is the Asian financial crisis in 1997–1998[162] in which the psychological factor played a major role in its diffusion and effects as a result of mutual exposure between markets.

Among the changes that have occurred in recent decades and that now also cast a shadow on the structure of the new world order is the proliferation of international terrorism, which has taken on a global character. Its perpetrators are neither national nor regional actors, and do not operate through state institutions, yet they represent influential independent variables in the structure of the new world order.[163] A number of researchers, including Fukuyama, believe that the challenge facing the United States of America and other Western governments since the attacks of September 11, 2001 goes beyond a straightforward conflict with a small group of terrorists. Fukuyama believes that the environment of Islamic fascism in which terrorists thrive poses a sharper ideological challenge, in many ways, than that previously posed by communism.[164]

While the premier of the then Soviet Union, Nikita Khrushchev, once promised to "bury" the United States of America, "he never did act on the threat."[165] However, Osama bin Mohammed bin Laden, the former Saudi leader of Al-Qaeda, managed to achieve something that the mighty USSR had not—"the mass murder of Americans on American soil."[166] Therefore, in the days following the attacks of September 11, 2001, US strategic confusion in determining the source and nature of the next global threat in the post-Cold War world vanished. As with the principle of containment, a new principle took shape to combat a new threat: the global threat of communism and the Soviet Union was replaced by the existential threat of Islamofascism.

However, the most dangerous effect of terrorism for the new world order was economic in nature—i.e., its impact on global financial markets through the reduction of foreign cash flows across national borders, transactions that exceed $1.3 trillion per day.[167] Terrorism has therefore become a threat to the globalization of financial markets and the welfare of states, as well as to their security, politics and culture.

Reference must also be made to another variable determining the state of the new order—the effects of the forces of globalization, which pose challenges to governance worldwide, especially to authoritarian political systems. The need to rely increasingly on global free trade and foreign investment flows will reduce authoritarian control, as it requires a degree of societal freedom. To compete effectively, in some cases states must relinquish elements of their sovereignty. This scenario understandably disturbs authoritarian regimes,[168] which may succeed, temporarily, in containing the pressures of globalization or turning them to their advantage. However, they will ultimately be unsuccessful, as new challenges to these regimes will emerge as a result of their exposure to globalization. For example, some major economic powers, such as China, have had to join the WTO[169] after agreeing to sign the International Covenants on Human Rights in the end of the 1990s.[170] This indicates a willingness to join the global alignment, and an implicit acknowledgement of global governance, not just over economic practice, but also the political behavior of states.[171]

All of the above testifies to the effects of globalization as influential variables in the structure of the new world order. The collapse of the Soviet Union resulted in what can be described as a global shift towards liberal democracy. The regimes that had preserved themselves through alliance with one of the superpowers found themselves exposed and vulnerable to the long-suppressed demands of their own people for democracy. These regimes were afforded no assistance from the powers that had long competed for their allegiance in order to secure strategic advantages in the bipolar era. At the same time, the free movement of capital and technology has led to the creation of new wealth, as well as a worldwide demand for economic and political equality. Together, these variables have contributed to transforming the very role of the state. Existing equations changed with the expansion of the global market; countries no longer had control over the economic interaction taking place within their borders, leading to a reduction in the importance of the role of the state in the management of its economic destiny, and a consequent weakness of government in the face of global economic forces.[172]

Another important variable in the new world order is the growing importance of environmental issues, namely climate change and the intense international debate on how best to mitigate its effects. Some researchers characterize this as an area of economic conflict,[173] it being a natural result of existing conflicts between classes and the fact that domestic and foreign policy is the product of the economic interests of the dominant class. Fearing the outbreak of conflict and unrest in the event of the failure of international cooperation to solve the problem of global warming and its consequences, some call for the promotion of a balance of *interests* over the balance of *power* that presently governs the strategic thinking of major powers.[174]

The Behavior of the Superpower
and Major Powers in the New World Order

When we discuss the factors governing or affecting the structure of the new world order, we must also discuss the behavior of the dominant superpower of the age, as well as the other influential powers of the order, firstly in terms of their status and, secondly, their opponents or competitors. This is an important determinant of the nature of the world order, both in terms of the continuation of the dominance of certain powers, and the participation of other parties, either as a result of a specific US policy, or through a strategic retreat that allows other powers to fill the vacuum. As has been discussed, states are no longer the main actors on the international stage in light of the "privatization of international relations,"[175] that has seen certain responsibilities delegated to private sector and civil society organizations. States no longer enjoy a monopoly on influence. Rather, international institutions such as the IMF and the World Bank guide the financial and monetary decisions of states, inhibiting their ability to keep up with the evolving dynamics of globalization on the one hand, and the maneuvering of non-state actors on the other.[176]

In terms of the hierarchy of the new world order, the dominant superpower still seeks to exert control over that order. Following the fall of the Soviet Union (on December 25, 1991), the US Department of Defense developed a comprehensive strategy aimed at maintaining US superiority by preventing the emergence of global rivals.[177] However, the influence of this controversial plan was eventually to diminish, following questions over its efficacy, and the use of supremacist vocabulary was ultimately abandoned by the United States of America, which instead began to talk of itself as simply a 'leader' or an 'indispensable nation.'[178]

Some researchers point out that the United States of America retains a margin of superiority over all other major powers combined, one that exceeds that of any other power of the past two centuries.[179] It is the first leading power in modern history to achieve decisive superiority in all aspects of power: education, culture, economy, technology, military capability, energy and transport. Hence, some researchers are naturally dubious of any questioning of the foundations of US superiority, although there are those who believe that the United States of America deliberately focuses on the idea of unipolarity in order to discourage conflict born of other countries' ambitions to establish themselves as counterweights to the arrogance of the dominant state.[180]

The ongoing debate concerning the US role in the new world order, which has continued for several decades, revolves in part around the concept and framework of a global balance of power, and from the assumption that a lack of balance is dangerous. One theory is that countries affected by the balance of power must ally themselves to oppose the dominant state, or take other measures that will enhance their ability to resist an aggressor—any state can choose its role in terms of the balance of power by changing its alliances, when the need arises, in order to maintain this balance.[181] However, with the collapse of the USSR, the affected states chose to follow the behavior of the most dominant and influential powers, indicating a recognition of the reality of the situation—that there is no benefit derived from debating the nature of the balance of power and whether the new world order should be unipolar or pluralistic. The truth is that we are dealing with a world order in which the United States of America stands at the top of the pyramid, unchallenged.

Researchers indicate that the famous quote by former US President George Walker Bush [Jr.] – "either you are with us, or against us"[182] – illustrated the US stance as the only international point of reference for determining right from wrong in terms of the behavior of states. In this respect, Bush followed a similar course to that of Ronald Wilson Reagan in terms of a distinct unilateral orientation.[183] Some studies draw a connection between this and the declaration in the US National Security Strategy in the fall of 2002 of its intention to maintain its dominance: "Our forces will be strong enough to dissuade potential adversaries from pursuing a military build-up in hopes of surpassing, or equaling the power of the United States of America."[184] Avram Noam Chomsky quotes G. John Ikenberry, an expert in international relations, as saying that

US doctrine in this regard dismisses international law and its institutions "as of little value," and that "the new imperial grand strategy presents the United States of America [as] a revisionist state seeking to parlay its momentary advantages into a world order in which it runs the show."[185] Chomsky believes that the grand US strategy "asserts the right of the United States of America to undertake 'preventive war' at will," stressing the concept of preventive, rather than pre-emptive, action as "pre-emptive war might fall within the framework of international law."[186] Perhaps the most dangerous aspect of this framework, however, is the US approach of waging preventive cyber wars to protect its interests and defend against external threats.

Within this framework, Chomsky claims that the defenders of this strategy "recognize that it runs roughshod over international law but see no problem in that." They consider "international law ... [as] just 'hot air.'"[187] Representing an approach that supports unilateral US behavior, several Western studies indicate that as long as the United States of America is the leader of the enlightened world, any attempt to restrict its use of force should be resisted. Perhaps this is the basis of what Chomsky meant when he said that "the enlightened leader is also free to change the rules at will"; hence, "contempt for international law and institutions was particularly flagrant" during the terms of both Ronald Wilson Reagan and George Walker Bush [Jr.]. Washington "continued to make it clear that the US reserved the right to act 'unilaterally when needed,' including the unilateral use of military power to defend such vital interests 'as ensuring uninhibited access to key markets, energy supplies, and strategic resources.'"[188]

With regard to who has the right to set standards and rules of behavior within the new world order, researchers such as Chomsky believe that "it is an exaggeration to say that only the most powerful are granted the authority to establish norms of appropriate behavior for themselves" in the new world order; "the authority is sometimes delegated to reliable clients."[189] In this regard, Israel is cited as being permitted to establish its own norms, such as "its regular resort to 'targeted killing,'" an act considered a terrorist atrocity "when carried out by the wrong hands."[190] Indeed, the leader of the new world order, which grants such powers, may in turn benefit from precedents established by the client – in the way that the United States of America benefits from Israeli precedents in terms of assassinations, carrying out similar actions in other countries on the grounds that this is established behavior in the new world as a result of Israel's actions.[191]

Furthermore, standards change according to international circumstances and the political positions of the powers dominating the new world order. For example, Israel's bombing of the Iraqi Osirak nuclear reactor in June 1981 was in violation of international law at the time. With former president Saddam Hussein Al-Tikriti's transformation from a friend of the West to an enemy in August 1990 by invading the State of Kuwait, the reaction to the bombing of Osirak also changed: what was once "a [minor] crime," was now a norm, and was greatly praised for having impeded Saddam Hussein Al-Tikriti's nuclear weapons program.[192]

In any case, the implications of the changes taking place in the information and telecommunications sector, and other manifestations of the knowledge economy, will play a prominent role in the structure of the new world order, perhaps even to an extent comparable to the influence of the dominant powers on this order. The greatest victims of expansion in this field will be the small countries that will lose – without doubt – a degree of their function in the world order to other players, such as international corporations, institutions and organizations.

To emphasize the importance of the behavior of the great powers in determining the structure of the new world order, some state that the system itself is purely a US–Western construct, born of the change in US policy from containment of the Soviet Union to advocate for democracy in the post-Cold War era, as part of an omnipresent aim to maintain US global hegemony. This policy has endured since the end of World War II, sometimes under the cover of the United Nations, sometimes outside its reach (if so warranted by the circumstances and US interests). According to those who advance this view, the United States of America promotes the existence of a new world order so that it might take advantage of the effects of globalization which – advanced by the Western media and modern communication technologies – has effectively transformed the world into a global village.[193]

One need look no further than China to demonstrate the importance of the behavior of international actors. Many researchers emphasize the fact that China is undergoing extensive development that will inevitably produce a major power that affects the path and features of the new world order, and that China's status renders it open to intense scrutiny as a result.[194] On the other hand, China has not yet chosen an appropriate moment to impose its new power. It does not want to take the risk of entering into a costly strategic and political competition with the United States of America. Therefore, it favors appeasement, flexibility and balance.[195]

Despite all the above, the behavior of the great powers is not limited to the physical balance of power on the ground, or the positions they adopt *vis-à-vis* their competitors and adversaries; it is also visible within international institutions. By way of an example some cite the ongoing management of the conflict in Syria, assuming that the United Nations could play a prominent role in the rebuilding of a multipolar new world order through the decisions and positions it adopts in relation to this conflict. Advocates of this view base their opinion on what they see as the failure of the United States of

America and its allies to impose their will on the UN Security Council and adopt resolutions permitting military intervention against President Bashar al-Assad to overthrow his regime, which is supported by Iran, Russia and Hezbollah. On this basis, some researchers believe that the common position of Russia and China in preventing foreign military intervention in Syria via the UN Security Council establishes a new phase of conflict within international organizations—the Security Council being the most influential body in the structure of the new world order.[196] Indeed, the rejection by Saudi Arabia of its non-permanent seat on the Security Council in October 2013 would appear to support this.

Yet relying on interactions in the Security Council relating to the Syrian crisis in determining the current global balance of power is unlikely to produce sound analysis; indeed, there is ample evidence confirming US leadership of the new world order in its ability to impose its will and vision, regardless of the positions of Russia or China in the Security Council. Perhaps its diplomatic success in reaching a formula to dispense with Syria's chemical weapons reflects the status of the United States of America at the top of the new world order.

The United States of America threatened to launch a military strike against the Syrian regime after accusing it of being responsible for a chemical attack on the outskirts of Damascus, described by the United Nations as a 'war crime.' However, it then proceeded to reach an agreement with Russia to avoid military action. International experts were quoted as saying that Syria has about 1,000 tons of mustard, VX (nerve agent) and Sarin gas, which UN inspectors confirm was used in the East Ghouta attack in Rif Dimashq in August 2013.[197]

The behavior of the United States of America in the decades following the era of the George Herbert Bush [Sr.] administration suggests that it has been seeking to change the new world order. In this regard, observers such as Bilal Saeed Al-Hassan[198] believe that the United States of America seeks to abolish the United Nations and replace it with a new international body under its direct control, as a true representation of its power in the post-Cold War era. Washington no longer accepts the idea of a global system that allows − institutionally − five countries to share veto rights in the Security Council; perhaps that is why it still has reservations over granting Germany permanent membership. This would also explain the establishment of the new world order proclaimed by President George Herbert Bush [Sr.] in 1991 − the foundations and principles of which he outlined − and the announcement of his son, George Walker Bush [Jr.], in 2002 that everyone must accept a changed world—a new world order built on new international institutions, a new global charter, and singular US leadership.[199]

It is paradoxical to note that the major powers themselves may well see any disruption of the new world order or decline in US influence as an added burden, forcing them to exert more effort to protect their interests and values. For example, Jan Techau, Director of the European Center of the Carnegie Endowment for International Peace, believes that those concerned with EU foreign policy assumed for years that Europe could rely for its freedom, stability and prosperity on a global liberal democratic system which it could not secure on its own. The expectation was that the system could depend on the United States of America as the main guarantor of its stability, but as it becomes weaker it also becomes less inclined to provide 'free' security services to its European allies. This means that further imbalances in the new world order will force Europe to offer more in exchange for the protection of its interests. Yet Techau believes that the United States of America is not in decline; rather, it will proceed to reinforce its status as the world's sole superpower. He cites several factors in this regard. First, the shale gas revolution in North America will reduce energy costs and lead to a significant boost in US manufacturing;[200] tax revenue will rise, the deficit will shrink and the US economy will achieve strong growth. Second, the United States of America will not give in to the temptations of isolationism; it will maintain a global economic, political and militarily presence; the US economy will achieve huge gains from the globalization of markets, and Washington will remain responsible for ensuring the security and stability of the world, rather than seeking the help of others. Third, considering China's recognition that it has benefited greatly from the peace

240

provided under US power during the past 30 years, Beijing's ambitions to become a competing superpower will remain limited and its focus will remain on its own geographical neighborhood. China's leaders will find that managing international crises is a laborious and expensive process, to the point that it would be difficult to compete with the United States of America in terms of global leadership. Fourth, thanks to trade and investment partnerships across the Atlantic, as well as Trans-Pacific partnerships, the United States of America will remain both the world's referee and a nation to which other countries will gravitate. Furthermore, Techau believes it will be beneficial for Europe if the United States of America retains its status, influence and superiority,[201] because for Europe to achieve global stature and influence, its only choice will be to unify its foreign policy, improve its strategic thinking and acquire better security and military capabilities.

Conclusion

This chapter has dealt with the various factors directly or indirectly influencing the architecture of the new world order in terms of its structure and the patterns of interaction within it. The discussion of these factors was not intended to raise one over another or to rank them in terms of their importance. Rather, the objective was to analyze the dimensions of those factors and the extent of their influence in shaping the structure of the new world order, especially in light of the complexity that has characterized the working mechanisms of that order over the last two decades with the emergence of extremely influential variables, whether in terms of re-defining the concept of power or the importance of new factors and variables at the expense of those that have long played the most prominent role in global decision-making, such as military power. Against the backdrop of what I have put forward in this chapter, I believe that power, with its new patterns and concepts, continues to constitute the cornerstone of the structure of the new world order; policies dictating the use of power, as previously mentioned, are the basis for the interactions between primary and secondary tier nations within this system.

The new world order no longer depends on one or more of the recognized factors that traditionally influence its structure and hierarchy. The order's structure is now shaped in accordance with a mixture of overlapping factors arising from interactions within it. Some of those factors now constitute the basis of interactions in the new world order, such as the economic factors, educational development and technological progress—vital factors which have played a leading role in determining the pyramidical status of that order. This has contributed to enormous qualitative transformations in the patterns of international relations, whether as a direct result of developments in knowledge, technology and associated influential variables such as globalization in its various manifestations, – particularly in the fields of economy, communications, media, education and culture – or because those developments have played a counteractive role affecting the concept of power itself. For instance, hard power no longer enjoys primacy within the strategies of the dominant superpower. It has become a supporting tool in the mixture of approaches that constitute smart power – as applied by the United States of America – or become but one factor of political action, as in fourth generation warfare, which relies on all forms of power, and in which hard power is not at the forefront of strategic thinking.

THE NEW WORLD ORDER: DECISIVE JUNCTURES

Chapter III

The New World Order: Decisive Junctures

History indicates that power has traditionally been, and remains, the central pillar of strategies and the main driver of policies and relations among countries and societies. The stronger party uses its power to impose its interests on others with no regard to their own interests or the damage it could inflict on them. Interactions among nations and societies have thus been based on the principle of "might makes right" since ancient times.[1] My implication here is that the world order has not taken shape or fully developed over a specific period of time, but rather has passed through a gradual historical process, gaining from the lessons of each era and progressing to reach its complex incarnation at the end of the 20th century. The first international treaty was signed in 1258 BC between the Egyptian Pharaoh, Ramesses II and the Hittite King, Muwatallis,[2] after which emerged the city-states in the ancient east, prior to the establishment of the state in its modern form. Historians note that the first treaty between these city-states was between the settlements of Lagash and Umma[3] (in what is now Iraq) in 3100 BC.[4] Within this historical process, it is imperative to highlight the contribution of ancient eastern civilizations, especially the Chinese and Indian, in instilling the rules of international relations. One cannot ignore, for example, the ideas of Confucius,[5] who famously spoke of the existence of a universal common law for the whole world, laying the foundation for a strong state based on justice and equality.

While I will discuss in this chapter the historic milestones of the world order in its various stages, old and new, a key focal point is the emergence of states or independent political communities, each of which maintains its own government and exercises its internal and external sovereignty over a specific geographic territory and population. In this sense, independent political communities considered as states historically included city-states in Ancient Greece,[6] Ancient Rome,[7] or Renaissance Italy,[8] in addition to those of the modern era, which included states whose governments were based on the principle of legitimacy derived from ruling dynasties—prevalent in most parts of Europe until the French Revolution in 1789.[9] In addition, there were city-states whose governments were based on the principle of legitimacy derived from their people, such as the type that still exists in Europe and in multinational communities such as the European colonial empires in the 19th century.[10]

The Ancient Greeks were the first to establish an organized political community, when Greek philosophy paved the way for the creation of a pioneering form of democracy[11] that was manifested, to a greater or lesser degree, in Athens, Sparta and other Ancient Greek cities. Greece also organized its relations with neighboring states on the basis of commitments, and set a law to resolve disputes through arbitration, while the Romans defined sovereignty in terms freedom, independence and authority. Despite all their shortcomings and limitations, the scope of these ideas bore a resemblance to modern thinking, albeit slight. However, no-one could argue that the Greeks and the Romans recognized the nation-state in its modern sense, despite the existence of many manifestations of such. Democracy in Ancient Greece was limited to free citizens and their right to govern, without the acknowledgement of individual rights or freedoms. However, the Greeks are credited with inventing some of the legal ideas and principles which are well-established in today's world, such as democracy, freedom and equality, among others; although theirs fell short of the modern concepts and their comprehensive natures.[12]

The State in the Muslim World

The Abbasid State, officially established on the 12th day of Rabi Al-Awwal 132 AH (750 AD),[13] arguably marked the beginning of statehood in its modern sense in the Muslim world.[14] The Abbasids officially named their new system a "state,"[15] ushering in a new era of history by espousing urban civic values in society more than ever before. This period in Islamic history has been rightly dubbed one of civilizational prosperity, or an era of renaissance in Islam, which reached its zenith in the 10th century (4th century AH).[16] This shows

Islamic civilization to be urban, with cities being the center of commercial and industrial activity,[17] whilst the state came to provide security and stability—both of which are important elements in the development of any civilization. The Islamic military establishment also underwent significant transformation and improvement in the early stage of the Abbasid period whereby a professional army was formed for the first time in the history of the Islamic state. Both Arabs and *Mawali* (non-Arab Muslims) from Khorasan joined the army as individuals rather than tribesmen. They were registered in *Diwan Al-Jund* (the troop records) according to the names of their towns and villages, not their tribes, implying a bond of allegiance to the state, which provided them with training, supplies and equipment.[18] In other words, the state in the Abbasid period changed from an Arab nationalist social institution with an Islamic ideology into a cosmopolitan seat of empire,[19] bearing no characteristics of any specific nationality. It espoused Islam as a religion and culture on the basis of equality among all peoples and ethnicities, and was subject to the sublime will of the ruling Caliph in his capacity as a sovereign guardian of lives, possessions, land and faith.[20]

The functions of the ruler and the nature of his authority evolved during the Abbasid state, as well as the state's functions and roles in the lives of its subject peoples and communities. Arabism and Islam had been inseparable in the Islamic State of Medina, established by the Prophet

Mohammed and during the period of the first four Caliphs (The Rashidun Caliphate/the 'Rightly-guided' Caliphate). The state still remained Arab–Islamic in character through the Umayyad Caliphate that followed, but other peoples and ethnicities converted to Islam and hence Arabism and Islam were no longer of one form. Non-Arab Muslims became equal in number to Arab Muslims, and some of the Arabs themselves were non-Muslims,[21] but the Arabs remained the leaders of the Islamic state. However, in the Abbasid era, and after the revolt in which the Mawali played a prominent role[22] against the Arabs' control, the Caliph became a religious symbol for all Muslims, and Arabism was demoted to a linguistic and cultural element of the Islamic state.[23]

Although the Abbasids stressed that their Caliphate was an extension to the Rashidun Caliphate (the rightly guided Caliphate) and the Umayyad period, they also asserted that their authority was derived from Allah, who ordered people to obey them because they were the heirs of the Prophet. The Abbasid Caliph Abu Jaafar Al-Mansur once said to the people of Hijaz in one of his sermons: "Men, I am the Authority of Allah on His earth and I rule you according to success and guidance from Him. So ask Him to direct me to the path of rectitude and wisdom, and imbue me with compassion and kindness to you."[24] Another anecdote describes the Abbasid Caliph Al-Mutawakkil as "a rope extending between Allah and His creation."[25] Thus, the Caliph in the Abbasid era changed from being an Arab ruler governing his people through the advice of noble and influential Arab Muslims into a ruler deriving his authority directly from Allah, supported by a strong organized army and a large class of administrative functionaries. Unlike the Roman emperors or the Persian Shahanshahs of the Sasanian Empire, the Abbasid Caliph's authority was restricted by the principles of Islamic Sharia, the interpretation of which he entrusted to reliable scholars, while he acted as the guarantor of its implementation.[26]

The Ottoman Empire

In his book *The Ottomans*, Andrew Wheatcroft considers the conquest of Constantinople in 1453 as the beginning of the Ottoman Empire proper. Researchers indisputably agree that its final collapse was in March 1924 when the Turkish parliament voted to abolish the Caliphate system, after Mustafa Kemal Atatürk announced the establishment of the Republic of Turkey.[27]

Other researchers trace the shape of the Ottoman Empire, the formation of its structures, the birth of its ambitions and the status of its Sultan to after the conquest of Constantinople in 1453, when "the Sultan had become the source of authority since then."[28] Moreover, the conquest of Constantinople in 1453 was a defining milestone in the rise of the Ottoman Empire, which previously was on the verge of disintegration following the humiliating defeat and capture of Sultan Bayezid I by Tamerlane on July 28, 1402 near Ankara. However, the

Ottomans managed to restore their strength and to establish their new empire by conquering Constantinople.[29]

Ottoman rule included most of the Islamic regions. It was considered an era of the Islamic Caliphate and its ruler was the caliph of all Muslims.[30] The Ottoman Empire was to become the strongest Islamic state of its time, and was considered one of the world's major powers, if not the greatest.[31] From its heartland in modern-day Turkey, its territories included the entire Arab region, except Morocco, in addition to East Africa and parts of Chad, most of the Caucasus regions, including areas north of the Black Sea, Cyprus and parts of Europe. It covered an area of more than 20 million square kilometers. Out of all the existing Islamic regions of the time, only Southeast Asia, Morocco, Central Asia, Iran and Afghanistan were not part of the Ottoman Empire.[32]

During the reign of Suleiman the Magnificent (1520–1566), the Ottoman State became an international power, thanks to its vast territories extending from Central Europe to the Indian Ocean.[33] The Ottoman state was transformed into a true transcontinental empire or cosmopolitan state, treating religions and ethnicities as one unit and conjoining Orthodox Christians in the Balkans with the Anatolian Muslims into one country.[34]

The *Encyclopedia of Military, Political and Civilizational History of the Ottoman Empire, 629–1341 AH/1231–1922 AD* cites the Austrian historian Baron Joseph von Hammer-

Purgstall, author of the most famous books on Ottoman history, as saying that the Ottoman Empire was vast and of infinite importance, like a giant embracing three continents simultaneously in its mighty arms (as described in a book in 1835, according to the encyclopedia), and ruling over regions larger than those territories of even the Byzantine Empire at the height of its glory.[35] Ottoman armies were the largest in number, as well as the best trained, equipped and organized. In the name of Islam, these armies achieved great victories and many European territories fell before them, with the Ottomans' Islamic, military and political presence becoming a reality in these areas for several centuries.[36]

The same source cites a variety of Orientalists and scholars who have noted that in retrospect the Ottoman Empire may be described as one of the biggest empires in history, the largest and most stable state in Islamic history, and a major global power. British historian and philosopher Arnold Joseph Toynbee considered the Ottoman state the true successor to the Roman Empire.[37]

The rise of the Ottoman Empire as a world power was a prominent feature of international relations during that period, as it almost coincided with the emergence of new political units in Europe in the form of nation-states, which paved the way for a new political thinking on the continent. No doubt this affected the course of international relations, especially considering the newly emergent European political climate of secularism and the disappearance of church authority forever. This secular trend dominated all aspects of life in European societies and completely dominated its politics.[38]

State and Sovereignty in the Middle Ages

During the 15th century the world witnessed the expansion of the Spanish Empire,[39] which comprised the territories directly ruled by Spain in Europe, the Americas, Africa, Asia and Oceania. At the height of its power, the Spanish Empire was one of the largest in history.[40] It existed from the 15th century up to the loss of its last African colonies towards the end of the 20th century. Spain emerged as a unified state following the fall of the kingdoms of Andalusia after the Granada War on January 2, 1492.[41] That year marked an historic milestone towards the establishment of the Spanish Empire, the influence of which grew at the hands of Holy Roman Emperor Charles V.[42] At that time Christopher Columbus started his exploratory trips across the Atlantic Ocean,[43] opening the door for European colonization of the Americas, which became the central focus of the Spanish Crown following the discovery of what is now known as San Salvador in November 1482. Those discoveries, along with other developments, served to change the face of the world and the strategic balance calculus. In this era, however, symptoms of religious conflict in Europe began to brew against the backdrop of tension between church authorities and religious reform movements in the 16th century.[44] There Thirty Years' War that followed[45] (1618–1648), was the most destructive conflict to befall Europe before the two World Wars of the 20th century, and ended with the treaties comprising the Peace of Westphalia in 1648.[46]

Almost concurrent with the Spanish Empire, the Portuguese Empire (also known as the Portuguese Overseas Empire) was established. It was the first global empire in history and one of the longest-surviving of the modern European colonial empires, spanning almost six centuries, from the capture of Ceuta in 1415 to the handover of Macau in 1999, and spread throughout a vast number of territories across the world. Between 1580 and 1640 Portugal formed a union with Spain, known as the Iberian Union, although the two empires continued to administer their territories separately.[47]

Origins of the World Order

The world order is a hypothetical concept, in the sense that it doesn't imply a physical entity, but rather an underlying one. In other words, the new world order is an abstract, only identifiable within changing global structures. Each structure has features that may be characterized by certain phenomena on the global stage, such as: wars, international alliances, cooperation, coordination, threats, negotiation and integration, etc.[48]

The concept of the world order refers to international political interactions and activities which lead to the emergence of different forms and patterns of relationships based on specific regulatory frameworks, institutional structures and international rules of conduct. Such rules may evolve over time as required by changing realities, developments and events.[49]

It seems logical that any historical review of how the world order has arisen should begin by charting the signs indicating its point of origin, including interaction or communication between states whereby one country's decisions have influenced the behavior of another. In such cases, wherein each country's behavior becomes an important element in the other's calculations, one may begin to talk about the contours of a "system" taking shape that involves these states.[50]

In the earlier stages of history, societies began by seeking to achieve their goals and resolve their differences within the framework of a coherent social system based on a certain hierarchy of controlling forces, which then developed into a relatively more flexible and equitable system, albeit one still hierarchical in nature. At the peak of the feudal system in the 15th century, societies were stratified into strict classes, with members of the nobility enjoying an exceptional and privileged status compared to other classes, whilst also maintaining the right to defend their interests. Although the nobility was inclined to infighting, it was united against all protests leveled by the lower classes against it. During that period the world system began to take shape, and the primitive form of interaction between classes developed into what was to become known as international relations,[51] as defined at the conference that resulted in the treaties of Westphalia in 1648.[52] This basic form of world system continued to function for nearly 300 years without undergoing any radical changes.

Events in the 20th century contributed to a growing unease concerning the absence of any mechanisms through which to manage relationships among countries; the old system and the traditional forms of power and influence were incapable of dealing with the world developments then taking place, resulting in the aggravation of every problem or issue that found its way into calculations of the relations between major powers.

Thus, the world system has begun to change, due mainly to two intersecting and mutually reinforcing trends.[53] First, unlike in the past, war is no longer considered or viewed as a useful tool of policy implementation due to the growing role of other influences such as the knowledge economy and information technology; second, a host of new issues have emerged on the world stage that are higher in priority than any strategic rivalry among major powers. Given the disappearance of the traditional importance of geographic barriers and the different perception of interests and their nature, war can no longer be viewed as a viable means to achieve the goals of the major powers. In addition, the emergence of cyber-threats and their associated risks have contributed to the decline of the traditional impact of military operations in terms of operational deterrence. As a result, policy implementation has become linked to tools and mechanisms of modern times, such as the technological, scientific and economic dominance of the United States of America and other major powers.[54]

However, the emergence of worldwide challenges such as global warming, global terrorism, drug trafficking, organized crime, illegal migration, human trafficking etc., have contributed to promoting cooperation and understanding instead of conflict and rivalry in the new world order.

Since the beginnings of its formation, the global system has comprised an ever-expanding politico-historical phenomenon built upon balances of power. It has also become increasingly interconnected, to the extent that any major shift in one part of the system inevitably affects the others. Researchers refer to various historical examples in this respect;[55] as the colonial plunder of third-world countries contributed to the affluence and prosperity of Europe, so it equally contributed to the impoverishment and underdevelopment of those countries. While World War I disrupted the balance of power in Europe, it also inspired the system of collective security represented by the League of Nations—its effects extending to parts of the third world through trusteeship, and the system of protectorates and mandates established by victors to ensure their colonial control over those territories.[56] There are many examples of colonial exploitation and the resultant sensitivities created between former imperial powers and their colonies, which can still be witnessed today in regions previously dominated by France, Britain, Portugal and Spain.

World War II permanently disrupted the European balance of power, and its political, economic and military consequences led to the birth of a new global superpower bipolarity, which drew most parts of the world into its inherent global struggle for influence.[57] The collapse of the Soviet Union and the end of the Cold War produced the greatest change in world power relationships since World War II. The disintegration of the Soviet Union on December 25, 1991 led to its fall from superpower status, which it shared only with the United States of America, and with it the bipolar structure that had shaped the security policies of the major powers for nearly half a century ceased to exist. Commentators were quick to recognize that a new unipolar moment of unprecedented American power had arrived,[58] and today some even argue that the United States of America suffers from "imperial overstretch."[59]

The term 'new world order' refers to the product of the overarching developments and interactions that have taken place in the structure of the world system since the end of the Cold War and the collapse of the Soviet Union, and the transition from the bipolar system to a new world order. The most salient of those developments and trends are as follows:

The Cold War Era

World War II culminated in the victory of the Allied Forces[60] and the defeat of German Nazism, Italian fascism and Japanese militarism. That war ended with their surrender and their subjection to the terms and diktats of the victors. Following their victory, the leaders of the Allied countries – the United States of America, the Soviet Union and Great Britain – assembled on July 17, 1945 in the German city of Potsdam as part of a series of meetings to discuss the new international situation resulting from the war, particularly in Europe.[61] This meeting built upon the result of a summit conference in the Soviet city of Yalta on the north coast of the Black Sea, which was held on February 4–11, 1945,[62] before the Potsdam meeting. During the meetings, deep political and ideological differences unfolded among the United States of America and Great Britain on one hand and the Soviet Union on the other.[63] However, due to considerations relating to the international balance of power, the influence, calculations and territories held by each party, and the role each had played in the war, the participants had no option but to sign the Yalta agreement on February 11, 1945,[64] demarcating geographical and political boundaries in Europe and beyond.

The end of World War II also brought an end to this artificially created alliance, formed in response to Nazi aggression against the United States of America, the West and the Soviet Union.[65] After the defeat of Nazism, contradictions in both interests and ideologies between the previously allied countries began to emerge, differences that would eventually give rise to the Cold War between the capitalist bloc – led by the United States of America – and the Communist bloc, led by the Soviet Union. The philosophy of the Cold War was based on the mobilization of each bloc's forces and capabilities against the other.[66] Europe was its main battlefield, as the Soviet Union began to impose its ideological, political and economic influence on eastern European countries, and communism expanded after the triumph of the revolution in China and its consequent alliance with the Soviet Union. The confrontation between these two blocs also extended into Asia in the form of war between the two Koreas in 1950–1953. Each bloc had formed its own military alliance; on April 4, 1947 the North Atlantic Treaty Organization (NATO)[67] was formed with the signing of the Washington Treaty, and included 12 countries at first. In response, the Warsaw Pact was created on May 14, 1955.[68] The accession of West Germany at the time to NATO on May 9, 1955 provided an incentive to speed up the formation of the Warsaw Pact.

The Cold War also spread to the Middle East. The launch of the Eisenhower Doctrine in January 1957[69] was an expression of this rivalry between the two superpowers, according to which a country could request American economic assistance or aid from US military forces if it was threatened by another state; the aim of the Doctrine was to protect the Middle East from Soviet designs.[70] The atmosphere of the Cold War had a significant effect on Europe, particularly Germany during what was known as the Berlin Crisis in 1960 and the construction of the Berlin Wall by the German Democratic Republic to separate East and West Berlin on August 13, 1961, a structure that came to symbolize the division of Europe. However, the Cold War reached its peak in the Caribbean, with the Cuban missile crisis of 1962.[71] The crisis reflected the calculus of interests between the two superpowers,[72] and was ultimately to alter their behavior by forcing them to confront the need to establish the means of avoiding such crises in the future, lest they should lead to nuclear Armageddon. The most important development in the wake of the crisis, as noted in the Introduction, was the establishment of a direct hotline of communication on June 20, 1963[73] between Washington, DC and Moscow in order to avoid any inadvertent misinterpretations that could lead to terminal consequences.[74]

In addition to the acquiescence of the Soviet Union to the United States of America' superior nuclear capability, a number of other factors contributed to the resolution of the crisis, the most important of which was the two superpowers' relative perceptions of threat, whereby the United States of America felt a greater level of threat from neighboring Cuba than from the Soviet Union. The United States of America could rely on its conventional forces, the naval blockade, and even a potential American invasion, all of which strengthened the credibility of US deterrence, placing the psychological burden on the Soviet Union.[75]

The struggle between capitalism and communism was not only military, but also economic, ideological, cultural and educational. Capitalism, democracy and a set of military alliances across the world with NATO at its head stood for decades against communism, led by the Warsaw Pact. Eventually, the economic weakness of the communist model in the Soviet Union led to the victory of capitalism, the spread of democracy, the collapse of the Warsaw Pact in March 1991 and the ultimate dissolution of the Soviet Union itself.[76] Nearly three decades after the Cuban missile crisis, the collapse of the Soviet Union brought the Cold War era to an end. The world had become 'purely' capitalist and no longer governed by the ideological conflict that had prevailed during the preceding era. Russia adopted capitalism under former President Boris Yeltsin after the dissolution of the Soviet Union,[77] and China too was to become capitalist – or has adopted a mixed system closer to the capitalist system – after integrating itself into the global capitalist economy.[78]

The United States of America worked hard to achieve global supremacy after the collapse of the Soviet Union by establishing a unipolar world, making use of the subsequent power vacuum and the weakness of other capitalist countries. The end of the Cold War had not only resulted in the collapse of the Communist bloc, but also led to a revision of the intellectual and values system of communism. Capitalist countries, led by the United States of America, sought to consolidate their victory and superiority by setting out new approaches to governing international interactions politically and economically. In the context of these new global developments, the United States of America used its military superiority to achieve its political and economic interests[79] and ensure the continuity of its dominance over the new world system by making liberal ideology, democratic values and the free-market capitalist economy an ideal model for countries around the world to embrace. To that end, the United States of America used both the UN as a political and military tool,[80] and donor international financial institutions, such as the IMF and the World Bank, as economic tools.[81]

The end of the Cold War thus marked a huge transformation in international relations with the demise of bipolarity and its consequent outcomes at the level of strategic thinking. Some Western thinkers, including Fukuyama, believe that this era did not only mean the end to the Cold War, but also to history itself,[82] as discussed in the chapter entitled 'Factors Influencing the Structure of the New World Order,' and that the ideological struggle that had dominated the world since the spread of Marxist thought in the 19th century, the outbreak of the Bolshevik Revolution in October 1917,[83] and the establishment of communism and the eastern bloc after the end of World War II, had ended with the decisive victory of the liberal capitalist system after the official dissolution of the Soviet Union.[84]

The effects of globalization on all walks of life in the post-Cold War era have seen attempts to impose American dominance and culture on the world, and an economic regime that advances the interests of American monopolistic corporations; although domination has sometimes taken the form of direct military intervention and the forward deployment of military bases.[85] Following the fall of the Berlin Wall in November 1989, and with it the Soviet threat, the administration of President George Herbert Bush [Sr.][86] submitted its annual budget request to Congress asking for the allocation of a huge budget to the Department of Defense, entailing an increase in spending in 1990 to around $480 billion.[87] The administration justified that request by saying that in this new phase of history the use of US armed forces was unlikely to be related to the Soviet Union, but instead to the third world, which would require new capabilities and methods of action.[88] The fall of the Berlin Wall was a symbolic end to an era of international relations in which events occurred under the Cold War and the danger of nuclear annihilation shrouding the competing poles at that time; it also marked the beginning of a new era fraught with events and transformations,[89] with increasing calls for the creation of a new world order.

Such sentiments were indicated in early 1990s by the non-governmental South Commission chaired by former Tanzanian President Julius Kambarage Nyerere.[90] The Commission consisted of economists, planners, clerics and other third-world elites who called for a new world order that was more responsive to the demands of the South for justice, equality and democracy within the international community. The calls soon faded, yet they revealed that the world continued to operate according to the system constructed after World War II and outlined by former British Prime Minister, Sir Winston Leonard Churchill,[91] who said: "The government of the world must be entrusted to satisfied nations, who wished nothing more for themselves than they had. If the world government were left in the hands of hungry nations, there would always be danger. But none of us had any reason to seek for anything more. The peace would be kept by peoples who lived in their own way and were not ambitious. Our power placed us above the rest. We were like rich men dwelling at peace within their habitations."[92]

History has shown that the term 'new world order' has been habitually employed in the West by states after emerging victorious from a major conflict. The term was used during the administration of the 28th American President, Thomas Woodrow Wilson[93] (March 4, 1913 to March 4, 1921) to describe the concept of collective security which the United States of America advocated as an alternative to the European balance of power after World War II, and when the then British Prime Minister, Sir Winston Leonard Churchill, stressed the need for a new, post-war economic world order.[94] However, a short while after the South Commission's call for a new order based on the principles of justice, equality and democracy, President George Herbert Bush [Sr.] used this term as a rhetorical cover for war in the Gulf, when he declared that the United States of America would lead a new world order in which all diverse nations of the world would be brought together in common cause to achieve the aspirations of the peoples of the world—peace, security, freedom and the rule of law.[95] The American Secretary of State at the time, James Addison Baker III,[96] was describing this new world order when he said we live in "an era full of promise," and "one of those rare transforming moments in history."[97] Thomas Loren Friedman suggests that the principal notion guiding Bush [Sr.] during the Gulf War was that "unless the international boundaries between sovereign nation-states are respected, the alternative is chaos."[98]

The end of the Cold War has not given birth to new institutions based on a new world order. Traditional institutions have continued to exist, although there have been attempts to reform them in order to cope with realities of a post-Cold War world.[99] For example, attempts are still being made to reform the United Nations and make it more democratic by expanding the Security Council in order to reflect the new international balance of powers, adding new influential states such as Germany and Japan and other emerging countries like India, South Africa or Brazil. Of course, the United States of America would strongly voice its reservations in any discussions on this topic, especially given that the accession of any emerging major powers or countries to permanent membership of the UN Security Council would affect international decision-making and thus the structure of the new world order. Debate and discussion are ongoing on the reform mechanisms of international institutions, including the selection and candidacy criteria for membership. This discussion essentially reflects a desire to create a power structure different from that agreed after World War II. Some institutions, such as NATO after the end of the Cold War era, have faced problems of legitimacy— NATO being a symbol of a bygone era.

The collapse of the Soviet Union caused profound disruption in the international balance of power, and the United States of America capitalized on this, deploying its military capabilities for missions outside its borders in a manner that would not have been possible in the face of potential conflict with the Soviets.[100] The war in Afghanistan, launched on October 7, 2001, and the invasion of Iraq on March 20, 2003, are two examples of the free military movement and political maneuvering that the United States of America has enjoyed since the collapse of the Soviet Union. The same trend also applies to NATO, which has often become a tool for implementing the US agenda, directly or indirectly. In addition, one of the significant outcomes of the end of the Cold War was the rise of the economy's role in international relations as a natural result of the decaying influence of ideology following the decline of Marxism–Leninism and the collapse of most international security strategies that were based on might and power. This led major powers to rethink their priorities and transform from economies supporting security to those supporting politics and interests.[101]

Some researchers argue that the new world order in the post-Cold War era has several distinctive characteristics, including:[102]

1. US dominance in the absence of the Soviet Union as an influential balancing power in international politics, marking the end of 'bipolarity' and the beginning of 'unipolarity' represented by the United States of America and its declared strategy to spread democracy, human rights and the principles of the free-market economy.[103] Many experts consider the new world order to be a continuation of global US hegemonic policy since the end of World War II under the cover of the UN.

   George Herbert Bush [Sr.] expressed the prevailing American policy and world view when he said: "This is a new and different world. Not since 1945 have we seen the real possibility of using the United Nations as it was designed, as a center for international collective security."[104] Some commentators have suggested that this indicated US intent to achieve global control and dominance through this international institution.[105]

The main features of this US project to establish a new world order comprise: (1) imposing an immediate transition to a global market economy; (2) promoting Western-style democracy and political liberalism as desired by the West, while being selective when imposing these arrangements— this has increased in recent years through American pressure on Middle Eastern countries, in particular, to move towards adopting political pluralism or democratic governance; (3) restructuring of the institutional and regulatory framework of international relations to concentrate power among a limited number of countries.[106]

Indeed, there are several indications that confirm the desire of the United States of America to control the new world order and remain the only 'pole' in international relations. Such indications include: harnessing the UN to achieve US interests under the guise of legitimacy based on upholding human rights; using other international organizations to pressure international powers competing with Washington; and seeking to make the UN and the Security Council tools for the implementation of US foreign policy.[107] The United States of America also attempts to play the role of global policeman and spread the American model by imposing US values and influence across the world, particularly in regions of strategic importance.[108] It is also modernizing its military power, and continues to undertake an ambitious project launched in the last century to create a new force described as the 'twenty-first century army,' the vanguard of which is to take shape in the period 2010–2016. This force will make use of the rapid and massive technological development and radical changes resulting from the technological revolution. One example of advancement in military technology derived from such developments is the recent US success in producing a remotely-operated F-16 fighter jet.[109]

2. The spread of state power in the new world order, with the consequence that the single superpower is less able to tighten its control and secure its influence and dominance over the order. This has given rise to the role of exclusive groups and fora, such as the G-7, which have started to have a major bearing on the fate of the world economy and much of international politics, to the extent that the new world order sometimes seems to be controlled by this small group of economic powers rather than the single superpower or the UN. The G-7 has sometimes monopolized international decision-making, and international relations have moved towards a form of minority rule.[110]

3. The global promotion of Western lifestyle and democratic values as the ideal political model, coupled with the shift to a market economy and liberal economic policies. International financial institutions have supported this trend by pressuring countries to develop in this way. A similar shift in countries' interests has occurred, from safeguarding sovereign rights and national security to interests that serve the goals of interdependence and economic prosperity, which can only be achieved through international cooperation and resolving global problems through international systems.[111]

4. Limiting the role of the nation-state; the globalization of information and communications technology and satellite broadcasting, for example, has raised broad national concerns and fears in third-world countries regarding what is described as 'cultural invasion,' a weakening of national identities, and of other inherent features of the nation-state.

Academic discussions on the negative effects of the world becoming a global village have proliferated; ironically, it was the major economic powers which started this trend. With the spread of globalization and the decline of the role of military power, the concept of a professional army has become more widespread. France suspended military conscription in 1996[112] – which was a product of the

French Revolution – because the state no longer needed a large military force to open up foreign markets, given the ability of multinational corporations to enter any country facing only competition from international rivals. Some states have also discarded a symbol of their sovereignty by joining a single common regional currency.[113] International interdependence has even contributed to changing the very concept of the state, as new transnational interactions have emerged in which none of the parties involved represents a state or an intergovernmental organization. All this has weakened the legal sovereignty of the state and made control over the economy in the globalized era a matter that surpasses geopolitical boundaries.

The decline of the state's role is one of the most prominent features of the post-Cold War era, where pressing new developments have undermined the state's monopoly of politics at the international level, and its capacity as the main actor on the world stage. New players have appeared, some of which are supra-national actors such as regional groups that seize a vital part of the state's sovereign functions, such as the European Union.[114]

The world has entered a period characterized by the privatization of international relations,[115] and the process is no longer limited to ceding aspects of the state's functions and roles to external actors, but also to local actors in the form of NGOs, civil society organizations, branches of multinational corporations and the like.[116] Moreover, some advocates of globalization (globalists) believe that state boundaries are eroding because of the increasing presence of non-state actors on the international stage, and the resulting pressure of the interaction between globalization and new media and communication technologies.[117] The researcher James Nathan Rosenau argues that the changing dynamics of the post-Cold War era have weakened the state's abilities and efficiency, making its borders more permeable and less important.[118] Hence, academic debate has grown on redefining the concept of national sovereignty, which has been based for centuries on the two principles of monopoly and exclusion; that is, the domestic monopoly on power by the state, and the state's enjoyment of absolute right of representation abroad.[119]

The decline of the state's role at home and abroad and its engagement in wars against people whom it is supposed to protect – as happened in the former Yugoslavia, Libya, and is happening still in Syria and elsewhere – have sparked controversy about the concept of state sovereignty and the related issue of regulating the right of humanitarian intervention to ensure that it is not misused to interfere in other countries' sovereign affairs.

Some European researchers argue that the issue of military intervention for humanitarian reasons has become one of the most persistent and controversial in international relations, particularly in light of the Libyan and Syrian crises. In this respect, the researcher Jean–Baptiste Jeangène Vilmer, says in his book, *War in the Name of Humanity: Kill or Let Die*,[120] that throughout history, military intervention has been justified on humanitarian grounds, from ancient China through to Babylon, by the Hittites, the Ancient Greeks and the Romans.[121] He points out that countries always intervene to serve their own interests, even if they justify their intervention on humanitarian grounds. Humankind does not launch war—states do. History shows that it is impossible to separate between humanitarian motives and self-interested goals of intervening states, and there have always been political, economic and geostrategic motives behind good intentions. Vilmer believes that the solution lies in reforming international institutions, particularly the UN Security Council, in order to lend more support, credibility and legitimacy to humanitarian intervention.[122]

5. Fragmentation of multi-ethnic states: following the disintegration of the huge entity that was the Soviet Union, fragile states – especially those suffering from nation-state crises – have succumbed to a tendency to fragment and disintegrate. This leads to a retreat under subnational umbrellas and greater sectarianism, ethnicity, tribalism and localism/regionalism,[123] as witnessed in Iraq. It is possible

to identify various reasons behind this trend, including: cases of collapse and chaos witnessed by several countries after the dissolution of the Soviet Union and resultant attempts to assert national identity; and the fact that the nation-state in its modern sense has essentially come into existence following the decline and collapse of empires, as mentioned in previous chapters. Another reason is the erosion of political and legal constraints associated with the bipolar system, allowing the formation of national political, religious and sectarian movements that seek to achieve their objectives of self-determination and freedom as a direct result of the disappearance of an important rule in international relations—that of the inviolability of existing boundaries between nation-states. This rule was associated with the interests of the two competing 'poles' of the bipolar era, and has been vital for many countries in securing control over their religiously or ethnically diverse societies. With the demise of this rule, the sanctity of the nation-state vanished, and an international setting based on the implosion and disintegration of multi-ethnic countries has emerged.[124]

6. The spread of human rights is a direct reaction to attempts to promote the values of the victor in the ideological struggle. A common American argument is that democracies do not go to war against each other.[125] The World Conference on Human Rights held in Vienna on June 14–

25, 1993[126] proclaimed for the first time in the history of international relations that democracy is the basis for a legitimate government system, since it is the best foundation for ensuring human rights. Thus, the issue of human rights has become universal in nature, and no longer based on the principles stated in national constitutions and international declarations, but on the protection of international law through various international treaties and conventions.[127] This focus on human rights was embodied by the creation of the office of the High Commissioner for Human Rights at the United Nations in 1994,[128] in addition to the roles played by international NGOs in the field of human rights monitoring. This trend has gained greater depth with the United States of America considering human rights a main guiding element of its foreign policy, as well as its provision of economic assistance to other countries, and facilitation of borrowing from international donor institutions.[129]

The new world order has given rise to various new issues of importance that were previously not of sufficient interest – or of any interest – to the bipolar international system. It should be noted here that the collapse of the Soviet Union contributed to international attention regarding issues such as environmental concerns, human rights, democracy and terrorism.[130] However, this does not mean that national, regional and international security issues or political issues in general have been marginalized.[131] The liberation of Kuwait from Iraqi occupation proved that these issues would remain at the top of the international agenda when exacerbated. The war also proved that, in a reversal of the prevailing calculus, economic security issues have become a driver of strategic security issues; yet the war also clearly showed that nationalistic sentiments have not receded.[132]

In the context of the growing focus on the primacy of democracy in the new world order, several US and European initiatives have been created to support the process of democratic development in the Middle East. Among these initiatives is the US Greater Middle East Initiative announced by former George Walker Bush [Jr.] on February 6, 2004 at the National Endowment for Democracy.[133] In the same month Washington provided the draft proposal of the initiative to the G-8[134] for their feedback in preparation for discussion at the 30th G-8 summit held in the United States of America on June 2004 on Sea Island, and to be presented at the NATO Istanbul Summit in June 2004.[135]

The basis for the Initiative was the inevitability of reform in the Middle East in view of a belief that the region had become a breeding ground for terrorism, organized crime, illegal immigration, and other problems that have become a security threat to the United States of America itself and a source of concern to the 'civilized' world.[136] The Initiative justified the need for reform on the grounds of the 'severe backwardness' suffered by Middle Eastern countries, as highlighted by the two UN-funded Arab Human Development Reports of 2002 and 2003, which exposed the lack of freedom, knowledge, empowerment of women, etc., in the region.[137]

This interest of the West in general, and the United States of America in particular, in the political reform and democratization of the Middle East has provoked heated debate over whether the United States of America has any real intention to support the process of democratic reform in the region; as democracy has never been a priority in US foreign policy, since it has formed alliances with many nondemocratic regimes in the Middle East and elsewhere.[138]

Following the dissolution of the Soviet Union, international politics have been affected by three major facts.[139] The first is the great imbalance of power in the world. Not since the Roman Empire has a single country had almost total global control;[140] second is the existence of nuclear weapons – most of which form part of the US arsenal – and their spread to other countries.[141] The increasing impact of terrorism has not changed this fact in international politics—that nuclear weapons govern military relations between nuclear states.

Although the terrorist attacks of September 11, 2001 were not a conventional means of attack, the Bush (Jr.) administration used terrorism as a political cover to abandon the Anti-Ballistic Missile Treaty.[142] Third, the spread of crises across the world and the involvement of the United States of America, directly or indirectly, in the majority of them. Terrorists have not changed the nature of ongoing crises, but by tracking down terrorists and threatening the countries hosting them, new crises have been added to a long existing list. However, some scholars believe that terrorism as an international challenge does not really represent a serious threat to the security of nations, and there is no implication that the global balance of power will change. Such scholars believe that the commitment of the coalition in the war against terrorism, albeit broad in number, is only skin deep.[143]

If the end of the Cold War has led to the collapse of bipolarity, as mentioned before, it also confirmed at the same time the unipolarity of the new world order and its inter-relations. This event has not only led to major transformations in Europe, but also contributed to the marginalization of the third world and its plight as a helpless bystander in the face of Western powers' aspirations to globalize the system politically, economically, culturally and educationally, in line with the values and traditions of their own brand of liberalism.[144]

The end of the Cold War led to an imbalance in the new world order. Indeed, some believe that balance no longer exists at the regional level, as the absence of the joint factors of military power and ideology in international politics has driven most countries to adopt more realistic approaches to their relations with each other, and a distance from previous political and ideological discourses that constrained their national interests in the past; in other words, countries have chosen to give priority to a balance of interests in their relations with others, at the expense of a balance of power.[145]

However, I believe that the hypothesis of realism in international relations should be treated with caution, owing to evidence – at least at the Arab regional level – that proves the continued prevalence of an ideological–political discourse at the expense of national interests in many countries. Perhaps the most obvious examples have been Iraq during the rule of its former President Saddam Hussein Al-Tikriti, and Libya under the rule of former President Muammar Mohammed Al-Gaddafi.

Although most researchers differ in their opinions when analyzing the dimensions of post-Cold War international politics, they increasingly agree on the prevailing view of unipolarity (regardless of any possible shift from unipolarity or even if it has already shifted) that it tends to create conflict, as other countries seek to counterbalance the arrogant power of the dominant country.[146] The assumption that unipolarity leads to instability is the subject of a wider debate about the nature of international politics in the post-Cold War era since 1991 until now.[147]

As previously mentioned, along with the ongoing controversy over world leadership in the post-bipolar era it is also necessary to touch upon some related phenomena, such as the weak or failed states, which have become the most serious problem in the new world order. These states commit gross human rights violations, attack their neighbors, lead to huge waves of migration out of their territories, and are frequently the source of humanitarian disasters. It has also become clear that some weak or failed states host terrorists who threaten the United States of America and other advanced countries.[148] There are many examples in this regard, such as Iraq under Saddam Hussein Al-Tikriti, Syria, and various African countries, such as Rwanda and Burundi, among others.

In this context, it may be noted that the vast majority of global crises that occurred during the period between the fall of the Berlin Wall and the attacks of September 11, 2001 were actually related to failed or weak states. Reference can be made to a long list of such states, including Somalia, Cambodia, Bosnia, Kosovo, Rwanda, Liberia, Sierra Leone, the Congo, East Timor and Afghanistan. Most of these countries have experienced international interventions, and in some of them power was practically seized and native rulers were removed from power in order to avoid further human rights violations, as was the case with the regime of Saddam Hussein Al-Tikriti.[149]

Fukuyama argues that the logic of US foreign policy since the September 11, 2001 attacks has put it in a position of responsibility for the governance of failed states.[150] He sees that despite repeated American denial of imperialism, the United States of America explicitly expressed such motives in the speech delivered by George Walker Bush [Jr.] at West Point Military Academy on June 1, 2002 when he said: "We must uncover terror cells in 60 or more countries, using every tool of finance, intelligence and law enforcement."[151] In that speech, Bush in fact spoke about a wider security vision than that of previous US administrations: "All nations that decide for aggression and terror will pay a price ... We will not leave the safety of America and the peace of the planet at the mercy of a few mad terrorists and tyrants."[152]

These trends were also visible in the National Security Strategy of the United States of America in 2002, which adopted the principle of pre-emptive war, essentially granting the United States of America the right to rule over hostile peoples in countries considered to pose a terrorist threat, of which Iraq and Afghanistan are two examples.

Globalization and the New World Order

The Cold War was an important historic milestone in the development of the new world order, but it is difficult to imagine any discussion of the order's defining characteristics without examining the more recent implications of a phenomenon that has had an enormous impact—globalization. By its very nature, globalization creates rivalry and forces countries to constantly change their policies and principles in order to remain competitive and creative in a global market where information and technology have made the knowledge economy a common currency in the new world order.[153]

The term 'globalization' came into use in the second half of the 20th century and became widespread in the 1980s. Therefore, globalization – in terms of its makeup and manifestations – has coincided with the advent of the post-Cold War era and the collapse of the Soviet Union. This may explain why some researchers have not accorded it the requisite priority when considering the vital historic junctures in the development of the new world order.

Globalization is considered one of the main features of the new world order and plays a growing role in its continued existence. In its simplest sense, the globalization implies the growth and homogenization of an intellectual, cultural, political, economic or social pattern of a certain group or nation to encompass the entire world. In its practical sense, globalization implies a trend towards the deepening of capitalism after having spread globally, and an increasing international dependency on capitalist theory.[154] This means that internationalization is no longer limited to distribution and exchange, but has gone further to cover production and redistribution, thus causing a global shift towards capitalism under the dominance, leadership and control of major world powers and a new global system characterized by unequal exchange.[155]

Another definition of globalization describes it as, "the current stage of development of the world capitalist system in which the core states seek to remove all barriers, obstacles and constraints that prevent the movement of goods and capital beyond their national borders, which is a basic necessity for the continuation of capital accumulation."[156] This necessity led to a capitalism-induced crisis at the local level, where unemployment rocketed, domestic demand for products plummeted, profit rates in the commodity sector declined, budget deficits grew, and rates of investment and growth worsened.[157]

It could be said that globalization in essence means the domination of the Western and American cultural model over the rest of the world through the adoption of its liberal economic system, backed by the dominance of Western culture. Another dimension of globalization is the use of modern science and technology in the field of communications.[158] Although the general idea behind the spread of globalization is clear, it is doubtful whether globalization and dependency can be directly linked. What many Arab intellectuals and elites imply when they twin globalization with concepts such as control and hegemony is the subordination of developing countries to Western influence in general and US influence in particular. I believe that the real threat posed by globalization stems from the danger it poses to the principle of state sovereignty, which has for nearly two decades faced a totally unprecedented threat that is different to any seen in previous centuries. State sovereignty faces a true threat from economic globalization, market liberalization, the explosive growth of international trade, successive waves of technological revolution in the fields of communications and transport – with their associated effects on the movement of capital and investments – and the consequent growth of financial markets that pay no regard to countries' economic and trade interests.[159]

There can be no doubt that sovereignty in its historical Westphalian sense is no longer consistent with the movements of investment, trade and the global economy. Therefore, the question is not related to the problem of globalization and dependency, but to the continuity of the system established by the Westphalian treaties and based on the principle of state sovereignty; i.e., the redefinition of sovereignty according to new international developments that are specific to a particular historical period, designed to set an absolute distinction between matters domestic (internal affairs) and external (foreign affairs or relations between leaders and peoples).

However, this distinction has become blurred as a result of the ongoing proliferation of communication technologies. Therefore, questions have been raised as to whether the nation-state is a remnant of history, or a relic of a bygone historical era.[160] Developing the mechanics of the principle of sovereignty will contribute to resolving the problems of globalization and dependency, and may provide opportunities for developing countries to benefit from globalization without infringing on their economic sovereignty, as well as their right to utilize their wealth and natural resources for their own development.[161]

Some scholars argue that the prevailing capitalist character of globalization represents nothing but a repeat of the past, that the call for market liberalization is in fact the objective basis on which the international system was established and maintained up to the Bolshevik Revolution of October 1917, and that market liberalization is seen yet again as a panacea for all the world's problems.[162] However, it might equally be seen as a new development, as an attempt to establish liberalism on a new global basis, significantly distinct from 19th century liberalism that was built on quite different levels of scientific and technological progress.[163]

Thanks to the phenomenon of globalization, the concept of the nation-state faces a severe crisis as a result of its exposure to competition from a growing number of increasingly powerful players. Today, giant multinational and transnational corporations are working to adapt economic systems and policies across the world to suit their needs and their own concept of how markets should work. These corporations control the technology of the information and communication revolution thanks to their possession of the biggest share of research and development (R&D) budgets. As a result they now – and perhaps since the 1990s – have forced the economies, countries and societies of the world to readjust to the realities of a new world molded by globalization.[164]

It is common knowledge that multinational corporations were the main players behind the establishment of the WTO in 1995, replacing GATT in order to forcefully achieve the liberalization of markets and international trade, flows of goods, liquid funds, bank bonds, media and advertising and publicity materials. At first glance, it seems that this liberalization has moved beyond the capacity of the nation-state, its power and authority. Many people have come to believe that globalization brings with it various consumer and entertainment products, as well as investments, and that there would be a positive outcome from the integration of Arab financial and stock markets into global markets. However, the reality is the entrenchment of technological, scientific, financial and cultural dependency that compounds political dependency and puts constraints on political maneuverability and thus increasingly undermines national political decision-making.[165]

There has been a significant decline in the role of the nation-state in the context of attempts to erase boundaries between political entities. This has been reinforced by the ICT revolution.[166] One of the consequences of this is that national governments are no longer able, as was previously the case, to control their economic development, which has become subject to the control of the market, and these governments now have to share their power and influence with other actors, such as NGOs, and international corporations and organizations.[167] Among the most important results in the context of globalization has been the boosting of production in light of growing technological innovation and competition among major powers as a result of economic globalization.[168]

The consequent impacts of globalization have forced the countries of the South, including the Arab World, to gradually loosen their grip on their own economic, social, political and cultural affairs,[169] by voluntarily ceding some of their symbols of sovereignty and handing over some of their roles to external forces represented in international financial institutions – which share the same orientations as multinational corporations – resulting in a number of Arab countries becoming akin to Myrdal's "soft states."[170]

In the same context, developing countries – including the Arab countries – suffer disproportionately in the global economy, and their situation has deteriorated under the influence of rapid globalization, their own accelerating economic liberalization, and integration into the global economy.[171] This sudden process of integration and early commitment to the 'rules' of globalization, liberalism and economic liberalization has had negative and often devastating impacts on the economies of developing countries, including in the Arab world.

It has created numerous obstacles to their development, rendered them incapable of protecting their national industries, led to higher costs for acquiring advanced knowledge and technologies, and exposed them to unbalanced competition from foreign imports and possible takeovers of national projects and key sectors by giant multinational corporations. The most serious consequence of all this is that it undermines the ability of developing countries to formulate and design policies, including those for development and trade, when decision-making has been transferred from the national level to the WTO.[172]

In addition, globalization has led to the emergence of a number of new global, regional and local forces, which have begun to compete politically with the nation-state. The most prominent of these new forces include: regional trade blocs; free trade areas and regional economic groupings such as ASEAN and NAFTA; and large financial, economic and trade institutions including the IMF, World Bank, WTO and multinational corporations.[173] These institutions have become so enormous and powerful that they are able to impose their will and policies on countries and shape the economic map of the world. This would mean that nation-states have lost their primary role of setting their own economic agendas—an important aspect of their sovereignty.[174]

Of course, the United States of America, which dominates the post-Cold War order, has worked to promote and deepen globalization in order to impose its own model on the world.[175]

Given the growing importance of the knowledge economy in a globalized world,[176] the nation-state is no longer able to protect itself against the invasion of the goods and services that penetrate its borders, and the related effects of incitement and rebellion against state authorities.[177] The growth in networking between different societies as a result of globalization has led to the creation of so-called electronic communities, and this in turn has created a type of loyalty that transcends nation-states' territorial boundaries, negatively affecting national loyalty.[178]

Debate regarding globalization has flourished since the dissolution of the Communist bloc and the lifting of the Iron Curtain. Societies and countries accustomed for decades to different lifestyles and political, economic, educational and cultural practices suddenly found themselves face to face with the realities and manifestations of globalization and the fears of associated hegemony—particularly since globalization has inspired the notion whereby the strongest – militarily, technologically and culturally – will necessarily dominate.

Strong economies dominate weaker ones, invade markets and prosper at the expense of these economies' opportunities for growth. What applies to the economy also applies to all other aspects of life – such as education, culture, politics and institutional and technological development – and the problematic question has become whether we should ask advanced countries to slow the pace of their progress so that the least developed may catch up, or ask underdeveloped countries to take sudden leaps forward to modernity in order to be reach a par with advanced countries?[179] The emergence of this problematic question has given rise to two outcomes: first, increasing fears of the effects of globalization and its consequences; second, growing controversy and debate about how to deal with this problem, particularly in light of the widening gap between the advanced and the least developed countries, as well as the search for ways to reduce the effects of hegemony, since globalization has transformed from being a process of participation and exchange of expertise and knowledge into a means for imposing hegemony and exploiting opportunities. This, some researchers argue, has fueled the rise of negative phenomena associated with globalization, such as violence and terrorism.[180]

The main impact of globalization on the structure of the new world order lies in the role it has played in reshaping many long-established practices. Globalization has redefined various concepts relating to the new world order that have had a profound effect on nation-states, sovereignty and borders, politics, and citizenship. These concepts have been shaken by globalization, even to the point of collapse.[181] Some researchers argue that the relationship between globalization and the national interests of states has specific indicators, including:[182]

1. Advancements in military technology in a number of countries, particularly the United States of America, enable them to reach and destroy any target in the world. As a

result, weaker countries are exposed to serious threats and the use of force by distant states in ways that were not possible in the past. This issue is also linked to the tremendous progress achieved in communications technology.

2. Advancements in WMDs, in addition to the proliferation of global travel, have enabled terrorists and their state sponsors to wreak havoc in powerful countries in a way unimaginable in the past. The relative accessibility of WMDs and of the ease movement of individuals have created new vulnerabilities and weaknesses that threaten national security in both strong and weak states alike.

3. The erosion of state sovereignty and the decline of conventional protection against intervention in the internal affairs of states have occurred for a variety of reasons, foremost among which are globalization and the communications revolution, and in particular the 24-hour news cycle, distributing instantaneous information regarding events and developments, commonly known as the "CNN Syndrome."[183] This has resulted in increased global awareness of distant events, which would previously pass unnoticed without arousing any reaction, especially in rich countries. As a result, the pressures of public opinion in any country not only affect its government, but also the governments or peoples of other countries. We have

already seen this in the political positions of major powers towards internal events in a number of Arab countries in recent years.[184]

4. Globalization of information allows people to remain informed regarding conflicts from the comfort of their living rooms, and to pass judgment on the performance of their troops on land or in the air, as well as in terms of human losses and civilian casualties. Those who prosecute war have tended to attach increasing importance to theaters of military operation. In recent years, we have seen how war, demonstrations and protests are be aired live from anywhere in the world. This world-wide broadcasting is no longer limited to global networks such as CNN, which was the first to air live TV coverage of military operations when it covered the liberation of Kuwait in 1991.

5. Global communication and trade networks have allowed elites to identify the best commodities, goods and technologies, contributing to a greater global awareness of consumer demand for particular goods. Given that the economic performance and technological bases of society constitute the infrastructure for military capability, any country that seeks to develop a sufficient military capability to ensure its security must keep up with advanced technology; this not only includes 'hard'

information, but also 'soft' information.[185] Thus, the development of the military capabilities of a country has become linked to the development of its information technology capabilities, its information network infrastructure, and free access to this network for various specialists to ensure the maximization of skills in all aspects of national security.[186]

6. The emergence of transnational cross-border issues, such as drug trafficking, terrorism, pandemics, smuggling, organized crime, global warming and human trafficking. These kinds of issues represent threats that could undermine the legitimacy of governments, jeopardize sea lanes, and endanger the safety of citizens at home and abroad because their impacts have become global. Although communication and transport technologies have brought forth a revolution in international trade, they have also minimized the barriers and costs to terrorists, as well as drug and people traffickers. This implies that the combination of globalization and information technology has provided individuals and groups with seemingly incredible power across the globe to pursue constructive, as well as subversive goals.[187]

7. The increasing role of multinational corporations has been the most notable result of the growing phenomenon of globalization, and these corporations are considered the

embodiment of pre-planned capitalism.[188] Such planning is carried out by a close-knit autonomous administrative elite who works to overcome situations of uncertainty and thereby controls the future of the company and maximize its potential advantages. This aspect of planning and organization represents one of the reasons for the clear danger posed by transnational corporations to the future of nation-states, not only because these corporations have more sophisticated planning and organizational apparatus than countries, but also because such effective planning and organization are coupled with these corporations' control of various resources and the expansion in their ranges of activities.[189] The heads of these corporations wield power and influence equivalent to – if not greater than – that of heads of state. They are usually quick to espouse the cultural values they adhere to, and even penalize those who disagree with them by unleashing the leviathan over which they preside—i.e., their 'giant' corporations. It is this fact that led Chester James Carville Jr., adviser to President William Jefferson "Bill" Clinton, to say: "I used to think if there was reincarnation, I wanted to come back as the president or the pope … But now I want to come back as the bond market. You can intimidate everybody."[190]

8. The emergence of new giant international economic players, the most influential of which is currently the BRICS, the advent of which are a victory for the

capitalist values that prevailed after the defeat of communism. New transformations in international relations took place as a result of the vacuum created by the fall of the Soviet Union and the end of the Cold War, which contributed to the successful domination of the global capitalist system over the destinies of peoples in the new global village.[191] These transformations reflect the inherent polarization that has become associated with the global expansion of capitalism over the past five centuries, and which will endure as long as the world remains wedded to capitalist principles.[192]

One of the most remarkable developments to influence the nature of the new world order was the catastrophic Cold War defeat of the Soviet Union. This was a result of the superiority of the democratic political system in the West over the rigid and totalitarian system of the East,[193] as well as the superiority of the Western market economy and its liberal financial and economic system. In addition, the extreme policies adopted by Ronald Wilson Reagan – who served as US president from January 20, 1981 to January 20, 1989 – played a significant role in accelerating the pace of the factors that would ultimately lead to the dissolution of the Soviet Union and communism. Other aggravating factors included the effects of the economic slump, the failure to catch up with the "third technological revolution" or the post-industrial era, as well as the rigidity of its economic management.[194] Hence, a transition to a market economy was an important element in the US vision for a new world order, stemming from the perception that capitalism was the best economic system for the world, just as democracy and the liberal political system prevailing in the West should represent the model for others to follow.[195]

9. Today, the new world order is characterized by a basic feature of the 21st century—namely the results of the information revolution. Such has been the flow of information in recent times that it has even been referred to as a 'knowledge explosion' in terms of the volume, means of collection, flow and retrieval of information.[196] The third technological revolution, mentioned previously, is the necessary prelude to all the changes that took place after World War II, before which the world settled on concepts and policies which many people treated as semi-immutable theories.[197] The ICT revolution refers to advances in communications that have taken place during the last quarter of the 20th century, and that are characterized by their speed, reach and widespread effects in the field of mass communications, from the form of the message itself to the means of their transmission within and between societies.[198] Indeed, the ICT revolution has reshaped our world in a way that necessitates a new mentality based on the qualitative change being witnessed in all aspects of

life—economy, politics, culture, education and social relations.[199] However, while part of the world is passing through an advanced stage of the technological revolution, another part is still lingering in the shadows and its technological achievement has yet to bridge this civilizational gap. There is no doubt that the ICT revolution has sometimes been exploited for aims other than those for which it was originally intended, and has sometimes been subject to censorship.

Modern media platforms have provided us with opportunities that were not available to previous generations.[200] The internet has dominated the world of information and communications and put an end to the dominance of traditional means of communication. Indeed, it is an amazing means of evolution and transition from one technology to another.[201] It allows much faster transmission of data and information to any place or person and does not require a passport or entry visa; it also opens new doors to the winds of social change as well as economic and political development—such is the process of evolution.[202]

Perhaps the most important outcome of the information and communications revolution is the apparently sudden achievement of human freedom with the single click of a mouse; the opportunity provided to us by the internet to publish whatever we want – be it humorous or serious, useful or harmful – has supported the greatest part of the free flow of information, something which humans have sought to achieve since the dawn of history. However, political, social, religious, economic and cultural constraints had previously prevented this freedom, which was seen as a departure from societal norms and customs.[203] Today, civilizational isolation in time or place no longer exists and it has become possible for any person anywhere to communicate with another in any part of the world through social media tools and other products of the ICT revolution.[204]

This revolution has helped humanity significantly in terms of rapid scientific advancement, and we should not forget that this revolution has benefited humanity[205] by facilitating the manufacture of high-quality consumer goods—many of which are produced by China at knock-down prices. This undoubtedly benefits all, especially those in the third world; however, it is also important to note that this revolution has led to the emergence of totally new kinds of social and economic interaction and the establishment of new societies.[206] Unlike its predecessors, this revolution has the ability to spread more rapidly and affect everyone's lives, providing people with access to information and knowledge anywhere in the world instantaneously.[207]

If the post-Westphalian international system has been based on the concept of the nation-state, then globalization has affected its structure by abolishing national boundaries and unifying economies, national cultures, technologies and governance. As a result, there are growing expectations that identities will expand beyond national boundaries, eventually contributing to the beginnings of a global society, and with increasing awareness of the benefits of cooperation across nations within the framework of regional and international institutions and organizations. Some believe that we are witnessing the end of the nation-state in modern times,[208] which represents a new historical era dominated by the growth of global market forces; it is the tide against which opposing governments and national economies have become helpless. Yet, there are some who question the veracity of these predictions, doubt the possibility of them becoming reality, and maintain that not only has the nation-state not been seriously weakened, there is no evidence for the emergence of a global identity that would replace the deep draw of nationalism. They argue that there are possibilities for structural developments in world governance and within individual economies without threatening the nation-state, which would still remain the major player instead of the emergence of a new world order that transcends nations.[209]

If it is difficult for some to support either of these viewpoints – for time alone could be sufficient to see one of them prevail – there are facts that are hard to ignore with regard to the effects of globalization on the new world order, including the fact that globalization undoubtedly brings with it calls for global coordination and collective action, and that expanding markets promote economic cooperation and trade among nations.[210] In addition, the effectiveness and reduced costs of communications, as a manifestation of globalization, strongly depends on the existence of global cooperation. Moreover, the solutions to various challenges – such as that posed by climate change – necessitate global cooperation. Such challenges do not differentiate between nations and populations, since security now transcends national borders and involves all countries.[211]

Based on the above, we can argue that the approach adopted by nation-states in defining the roles of global institutions in response to problems, plays a prominent role in deciding their own futures. Of course, the nation-state can choose not to do anything and leave all possibilities open until other coordination mechanisms have been developed by governmental and nongovernmental organizations. These states may seek to respond to global problems through local legislation or through coordination of local measures with those existing in other countries. They may resort to dealing with other countries directly in order to develop strategies to address global issues or to jointly establish global principles.[212] In all cases, the imperative for global collaborative effort has become more urgent when there is a need to exchange knowledge and establish consensus in taking decisions. However, it is usual for countries at first to choose the options that impose the least possible restrictions on their own sovereignty.

On the other hand, there are some who argue that the international institutions founded in the 1940s – such as the UN and its affiliated agencies – are creations born of the aftermath of a completely different war to confront threats no longer faced today,[213] and therefore such institutions have become obsolete and are not suitable for addressing contemporary challenges. They must be reformed or even be reinvented, and new institutions are required to deal with issues and challenges beyond the scope of existing international bodies—known in political literature as non-conventional threats.[214]

The idea of global government was raised in the 20th century in response to the two World Wars.[215] The argument for global governance is believed to have been based on the notion that establishing order among countries is no different from that which applies to individuals within a country; i.e. the existence of a higher authority in order to achieve a basic level of order, and to avoid war in particular. But critics of this idea say it impinges upon the freedoms of countries and nations, and hinders the freedoms of individuals who would be unable to attain political asylum from a despotic global government.[216]

Proponents of this view argue that the scenario of global government falls within the realm of the impossible, or even the undesirable. They believe that given the huge diversity of the world's various populations, envisaging a global version seems impossible, making any form of liberal democracy powerless to overcome existing obstacles in the current situation.[217] What backs this viewpoint is the fact that the world has never seen a global government, despite the long history of the concept itself. There has always been a current of opinion that advocates the need for global government, citing the universal state witnessed in the Roman period, or the principle of achieving a global state in the future that comes as a natural result of progress.[218]

In light of this heated intellectual debate about the impacts of globalization on the structure of the new world order, it is put forward here that this phenomenon may play the most prominent role in defining it in the future, at least in terms of the patterns of interaction between parties – but not necessarily the power relationship between them – and there is an abundance of debate and discussion on this in the West. We refer here to a vision put forward by Anne-Marie Slaughter[219] in her book *A New World Order*, in which she says the nation-state is not the only actor in the new world order, but it is still the most important; that the state is not disappearing, but disaggregating into its component institutions; and that these institutions still represent distinct national or state interests.[220] Slaughter argues that the new world order of government networks will not replace the existing infrastructure of international institutions, but will rather complement and strengthen it,[221] and as such she believes that states can be disaggregated for many purposes and in many contexts and still be completely unitary actors when necessary, such as in decisions to go to war.[222] Perhaps this could be the so-called paradox of globalization, where there seems to be a need for more governance at the global and regional levels, while there are parallel visions tending to reject centralization of power and decision-making.[223]

Given the cogent arguments opposing the idea of global government, it is difficult to talk about the emergence of any global administration at the expense of the role of the nation-state, irrespective of the decline of this role, or the emergence of a social contract between states, for the simple reason that states cannot agree among themselves to prevent wars or fend off dangers and confront common threats (be they security, environmental, cyber, cultural, economic or educational threats). It is difficult for states to agree upon a social contract based on delegating some of their jurisdiction and authority – such as maintaining internal security – to global government, in addition to myriad questions surrounding this idea, such as how this government could be set up and administered and how to determine its own jurisdiction and authorities.

Many international agencies do not function properly and do not produce their expected outcomes because of disparate international attitudes towards them. Above all, a wide spectrum of countries – especially those subjected to colonialism for long periods – will not easily succumb to the idea of obedience to a global entity managing their affairs, and they will inevitably see in it a return to thinly-veiled colonialism. How could these countries yield to a global administration if they are wary of the mere cultural, economic, commercial and educational manifestations of globalization? Frustrated people in the third world may see international organizations as nothing more than futile talking shops that provide no benefit to the poor and do not support the needy, but only serve the interests of the rich and powerful states dominating the new world order.[224] It is the view here that this largely explains the position taken by the Kingdom of Saudi Arabia in October 2013 when it rejected the revolving non-permanent seat on the United Nations Security Council in protest at the Council's position with regard to the crisis in Syria.

Such was the frustration with a strong Western elite over the removal of sovereignty from failed and troubled states across the world in order to prevent the spread of chaos. This Western elite believes that the threat of terrorism justifies the adoption of preventive and pre-emptive military action[225] and seeks to establish a new world order based on globalization, bypassing the principle of national sovereignty, and perhaps giving the West the right to seize control of unstable countries for security or humanitarian reasons.[226] Western intellectuals do not differ much on this; one can hardly find any difference between Fukuyama, Huntington or the neoliberals, since such ideas are shared by all shades of liberalism, even if justifications and arguments vary. The implication of this is that the defense of national sovereignty remains subject to the strength of the state and its possession of the necessary means to maintain this sovereignty and to confront any interference in its internal affairs. The world, in its pursuit of progress, becomes united in its perception of dangers and threats, and thus it is no longer in any country's interest to sponsor international terrorism, for example, and therefore find itself a common danger that unites the major powers against it. It is no longer internationally acceptable for any regime to violate human rights or to commit any transgressions that breach international law—if it does, it becomes a target for international humanitarian intervention on grounds of protecting civilians or other pretexts, particularly in cases where the motive of international humanitarian intervention might coincide with the interests of major powers, as in countries such as Iraq, Libya and Syria.

Based on the above, it could be argued that globalization is not only a manifestation of the new world order in a post-bipolar era, but also its primary driving force. There are those who believe that globalization is the true successor to the bipolar system of the Cold War, and that it will continue to be one of the most prominent factors governing the new world order in the foreseeable future. They argue that globalization is inevitable and that it is American, because the United States of America is the center and focal point of the world.[227]

There is no doubt that globalization imposed itself on the global agenda through the Millennium Summit of the United

Nations held at the UN General Assembly in New York on September 6–8, 2000 under the title "The Role of the United Nations in the Twenty-first Century."[228] The summit was attended by some 150 world leaders and acknowledged that globalization's "momentum cannot be resisted."[229] The report of the then UN Secretary-General, Kofi Atta Annan, contained a central message that globalization is a phenomenon with contradictory outcomes and dimensions.[230] It improves the standards of living in terms of income, education and health but concentrates these benefits among a small number of countries whilst further marginalizing others; globalization also opens the borders between countries, allowing an expansion of organized crime, terrorism, money laundering and the illicit trafficking of arms, drugs and people. In addition, globalization reflects scientific and technological advances, but in the absence of any controls, malicious individuals reap the benefits by inventing new types of illegal activities such as internet/cyber crime and computer viruses.[231]

The spread of information networks is one of the more profound aspects of the relationship between globalization and the new world order. This manifestation was described by the former US Secretary of State, Hillary Rodham Clinton, as the 'nervous system of the planet' in a speech delivered in January 2010 on internet freedom.[232]

What is noteworthy in this context, however, is that these networks have made governments and officials around the world more accountable, not only within their own countries but also among trans-border international organizations and agencies, such as the International Criminal Court (ICC), among others. This explains the remarks of former French Minister of Foreign Affairs, Bernard Kouchner, when he said the internet is "the most fantastic means of breaking down the walls that close us off from one another."[233] What all of this implies is that more freedom of information will lead to more democracy, liberalism and freedom of expression, and will exacerbate attempts by some countries to censor and control the content of information. This is especially so in light of the West's strong support for internet freedom, not only to benefit the economic interests of Western technology companies complaining about censorship and difficulties in protecting users' privacy, but also because internet freedom is a powerful tool for promoting so-called Western values.[234] This enhances existing efforts relating to the provision of support and assistance to local organizations in different countries of the world, since the West considers that to be in the interest of protecting basic human rights and enhancing the principle of accountability of ordinary individuals and officials anywhere on the planet.

In addition, the sweeping tide of globalization has also resulted in cross-border violations involving states and their authorities. The concept of the nation-state is now being questioned by both policymakers and transcontinental corporations, which are skeptical about its effectiveness and sustainability, to the extent that, "This will push multinational organizations and transnational regional agreements into ever-increasing important roles, because domestic national control is now clearly a pre-internet phenomenon."[235]

There are many doubts about the privacy of social media users and the possibility of being subject to monitoring and spying by major companies in order to amass consumer data, or by governments to control the content of information. In this context, reports show that automated processing at Google, for example, reviews users' emails on a daily basis, and special software scans the email messages looking for keywords. Google uses those keywords to target advertising at the sender and his or her contacts. This practice has given rise to the following questions: do employees at Google read those email messages, perhaps in the context of their own marketing research? How can we know whether they do? If we assume that we trust Google, does the American or the Chinese government, for example, read users' emails?[236]

Impact of the Attacks of September 11, 2001: A Black Swan Event

World politics underwent an abrupt and profound shift following the attacks of September 11, 2001. At the height of the information revolution during the 1990s,[237] the United States of America was in the midst of accelerated development, with the collapse of communism – the last rival of liberal democracy – the US economy was experiencing strong growth and democratic institutions started to steadily develop across the world. At that time, there was a prevailing conviction that technology deepens globalization and brings the global village closer together in a manner that renders the traditional nation-state irrelevant. However, a sudden and entirely different development occurred. The United States of America went on to wage a war against the Taliban and Al-Qaeda in Afghanistan after suffering an unprecedented attack on American soil. As a result, security considerations began to hamper the economy, which depends on open borders and the free movement of individuals and goods.[238]

Of course, it was not only the economy and trade that were affected. The September 11 attacks generated several outcomes in terms of global international relations, including a qualitative change in the shared interests among countries. Those attacks put the United States of America in need of assistance from other countries in its war on terror, and when a country asks another for assistance, it is usually in exchange for a favor.[239] Thus, it was not surprising that the United States of America paid more attention to requests from countries such as Turkey and Pakistan than it did before the attacks on the World Trade Center (WTC). Meanwhile, countries such as Sudan and Syria cooperated voluntarily with US counter-terror measures, mindful of the high cost of non-cooperation, and the fact that the United States of America had a new interest in assisting its allies in fighting terrorism and in punishing those countries defying it.[240]

This shift in the concept of interests was not limited to the United States of America. There was also a similar conceptual shift in several other countries, including China, which voted in favor of the UN resolution issued on September 28, 2001, that virtually granted the United States of America an open mandate to take any measures it deemed appropriate to attack areas used as havens by terrorists, even if those havens were provided by sovereign states. This is in total contrast to China's position when it opposed UN operations in Kosovo in 1999 on the grounds of concern about the violation of state sovereignty.[241] In addition, shared interests between China and India developed on the basis of their common concern over terrorist groups and Islamic extremism. An unexpected rapprochement took place between Beijing and New Delhi and was crowned by a visit by former Chinese Premier, Zhu Rongji, to India in January 2002—the first visit by a Chinese premier in a decade.[242]

Objectively speaking, the September 11, 2001 attacks were a bloody and untenable aggression that no-one could possibly defend, let alone justify or link to notions of freedom. Given the magnitude of the attacks, countries could no longer tolerate terrorism, and even tolerance with low-level terrorism has become more problematic. One of the most important consequences of the attacks was the public delegitimation of terrorism and the development of an international consensus.[243] Of course, that did not mean that all countries of the world suddenly renounced their support for terrorism, but what is meant here is the explicit support of terrorism, whether direct or indirect; even support under political cover has been more openly criticized. Major powers – the United States of America, EU, Russia and China – have become convinced that none of them could individually afford to fight terrorism without a concerted international effort, and this is what partly provides an introductory approach to understanding the formation of the broad international coalition against terrorism, where all major powers have realized that they have a shared interest in confronting this extremely dangerous phenomenon.[244]

In order to accurately understand the effects of the September 11, 2001 attacks, we should look at the description circulated in US literature at that time. Many American intellectuals considered the attacks as an exceptional event beyond historical or theoretical precedent,[245] while others argued that the United States of America found itself facing what could be called a new kind of 'virtuous war,' similar to the liberation of Kuwait, the Iraq War, or the Kosovo air campaign, where casualties were meant to be minimal as technical capability and ethical imperative could permit. Such wars draw on a combination of 'just war' and 'holy war.'

With regard to US strategic thinking, the severity of the September 11, 2001 attacks perhaps lies in the fact that the terrorism did not come from a rogue state, ballistic missiles or advanced biological, chemical or nuclear weapons, as US intelligence and national security experts had often warned, but instead from an evil terrorist network and hijackers belonging to Al-Qaeda. 19 members of Al-Qaeda carried out the worst attack on American soil by using hijacked civilian airliners.[246]

If the direct and indirect costs of the attacks were so vast as to become difficult to estimate, but every crisis represents an opportunity as well as a challenge, so the method with which the United States of America would respond to this challenge was important. The United States of America assumed the lead role in a loose global coalition of countries in its war on terror. Although the war was not clearly defined, the United States of America achieved quick strategic results,[247] including the destruction of one of the sources of global concern – the Taliban regime – and also gained access to new military bases in countries which were once part of the Soviet Union where the United States of America had little or no previous influence.[248]

The United States of America also managed to secure at least one important source of oil, and US global influence has grown since September 11, 2001. Thus, the war against the new global enemy known as terrorism has contributed to the expansion of American influence in the same way that the struggle against communism and the Soviet Union had done during the Cold War. In addition, the US response to those attacks has contributed to bringing about a substantial change in the application of international law, whereby the United States of America has succeeded in entrenching the principle of self-defense as an acceptable basis for action against potential terrorist attacks. Consequently, the United States of America has the right to resort to this *almost* established principle in perhaps less dangerous situations than the September 11, 2001 attacks,[249] although US claims to the right of pre-emptive strike were received with suspicion by the international community, since there was almost no existing support for the right of pre-emptive self-defense in international law.[250]

Analysis of the above reveals that since September 11, 2001 the United States of America has forged a path of unipolarity which it already had begun to create before the attacks. During its first eight months in power, the administration of George Walker Bush [Jr.] rejected or abandoned a number of international treaties,[251] including, for example: the Treaty on the Limitation of Anti-Ballistic Missile Systems, the Kyoto Protocol on Climate Change,[252] and the Rome Statute of the International Criminal Court, which was created in 2002.[253] Therefore, the pluralistic approach to dealing with international issues, as demonstrated by the global coalition against terrorism, did not mean that Bush was convinced of the importance of pluralism in the management of world affairs.[254] In fact, Washington refused to go to the UN

Security Council to obtain authorization for a military offensive in Afghanistan and other countries and regions, and chose instead to rely on a rather loose 'right to self-defense.'

However, what attracted attention was Bush's statement and assertion that the nations of the world "were either with the United States of America or against it."[255] That phrase ignored other countries' sovereign right of neutrality and placed the United States of America as the final arbitrator in deciding right and wrong. This constituted a vital turning point in the evolution of the new world order, especially after the US administration had been relatively successful in handling an early aspect of the war on terror when the President corrected the misunderstanding created by his use of the word 'crusade' which has hugely negative connotations for Muslims.[256] That word created a bad impression in the hearts of Muslims who felt that the American campaign against Afghanistan was nothing more than a manifestation of a US crusade waged against Muslims, followed by the Iraq War in March 2003, which consolidated that negative stereotype.

On more than one occasion, George Walker Bush [Jr.] publically declared his respect for Islam and differentiated between Islam and terrorism, and explained that his country was seeking to fight terrorism as much as it was seeking to find channels of understanding with Islam.[257] The aim of that step was to dispel rising fears not only in the Muslim world, but also in the West itself, that the invasion of Iraq was perceived by Muslims as a war against Islam—"a war of religion, for which Osama Bin Laden and George Bush were responsible."[258]

Global political interactions following the September 11, 2001 attacks resulted in the development of a unique form of power based on the outcome of those interactions on the one hand and the economic, political, technological and other realities of the contemporary world on the other. Hence, Joseph Samuel Nye argues that power today is distributed in a unipolar pattern resembling a complex three-dimensional chess game,[259] where the top dimension consists of military power. The middle dimension consists of economic power, which has already been multipolar in nature for more than a decade, involving the major players of the United States of America, Europe, Japan, and China (as well as India, Russia and Brazil) along with others which are gaining increasing importance. The lower dimension of the chessboard is the realm of transnational relations which include non-state actors such as banks, terrorist groups and electronic hackers, as well as untold global challenges such as pandemics and climate change.[260]

Attempts to Reform the United Nations

The post-Cold War era has seen prominent calls for reform of the UN to ensure its continuing role in effectively maintaining international peace and security. However, attempts improve its efficacy have been frustrated by a number of obstacles.

The UN, as the embodiment of international legitimacy and the global system, is based on two contradictory premises: the principle of sovereignty and equality among its member states, and the disproportionate weight of major countries which exert influence through their political, economic, military, and cultural strengths.[261] These states established and maintain the global system and its stability. With the end of the bipolar system, it has become clear that the relative strength of the UN and the Security Council during that period was exceptional. Under the new world order, however, the UN has become ineffective due to failures in implement its resolutions and open violation of the principles of its Charter.[262]

Indeed, the main obstacle facing the UN reform has been the desire of the United States of America to control it and prevent it from playing an active role in international relations that would undermine Washington's ability to dominate affairs in the international arena.[263]

The importance of the UN's role has been deliberately downplayed in official US circles, with talk of a direct American role in rewarding or punishing states – both economically and militarily – and curtailing the right of other countries to use the UN as an international platform to express their views, defend their causes or participate in the international decision-making.[264] The United States of America has adopted two approaches in dealing with the UN: financial pressure and non-payment of financial dues;

and manipulation of the UN Security Council to support US foreign policy.[265]

It is worth mentioning that UN reform is not a recent proposition. Committees in the 1960s, 1970s and 1980s presented studies on reforming the organization, which has 50,000–60,000 employees and spends around $10 billion annually.[266] Thus, the UN requires internal mechanisms to ensure non-duplication of programs and avoidance of contradiction between its specialized agencies. With regard to the poor political performance of the UN in international conflict resolution and peacekeeping, there are three political issues that member states – especially third-world countries that have suffered from UN actions – think should be taken into account; namely:[267]

1. Importance of expanding the UN Security Council's membership in light of the increase in UN membership.

2. Reducing and rationalizing the use of the right of veto.

3. Enhancing the UN Security Council's performance and achieving greater transparency in its working methods to dismiss the perception that it is some sort of private club engaging in clandestine operations.

Other researchers argue that activating the role of the UN should be done along two parallel tracks:[268]

1. Restoring the balance of the UN's affiliated bodies and agencies; ending the behavior of the United States of

America in pressuring small countries, and even some major countries; and expanding the permanent membership in the Security Council by including countries from influential international realms such as the Arab world, Africa, Southeast Asia and Latin America, in addition to Japan, Germany and India.

2. Improving the regulations, programs, and agencies of the UN to cope with growing human needs and the widening spread of conflicts, pandemics, poverty and malnutrition.

What should be stressed in this context is the extreme difficulty of the UN reforming process, if such a process is even entirely impossible, because the five permanent members have the right to veto any amendment or revision of the UN Charter.

The 2003 Invasion of Iraq and the New World Order

The military campaign led by the United States of America and its allies against Iraq on March 20, 2003 is viewed as one of the fundamental indications that the international system which was established after World War II had ended, and a new world order had emerged. The United States of America, Britain and their allies went to war against Iraq with complete disregard for the need to obtain international legitimacy. That war constituted the historic turning point that ushered in a new world order characterized by an unprecedented rise in American power and its exclusive superpower status.[265] The 2003 Iraq War also saw the application of a new security strategy, known as the 'Bush Doctrine,'[270] representing a considerable shift in US security policy and engagement with world affairs. The United States of America abandoned the deterrent and containment approaches espoused by the administration of William Jefferson "Bill" Clinton, and instead devised a pre-emptive strategy, striking against terrorist organizations and countries opposing US goals and interests— or even other countries seeking to acquire comprehensive power.

The US National Security Strategy presented to Congress by President George Walker Bush [Jr.] in September 2002, stated: "Our immediate focus will be those terrorist organizations of global reach and any terrorist or state sponsor of terrorism which attempts to gain or use weapons of mass destruction (WMD) or their precursors." It went on to state that the United States of America would defend itself, its people and interests by "[I]dentifying and destroying the threat before it reaches our borders. While the United States of America will constantly strive to enlist the support of the international community, we will not hesitate to act alone, if necessary, to exercise our right of self defense by acting preemptively against such terrorists, to prevent them from doing harm against our people and our country; and denying further sponsorship, support, and sanctuary to terrorists by convincing or compelling states to accept their sovereign responsibilities."[271] What happened to the regime of the former Iraqi president Saddam Hussein Al-Tikriti was a clear example of this American strategy.

Observers of US policy were not surprised by this document. George Walker Bush [Jr.] had already said in his speech on September 20, 2001 to the American public after the September 11 attacks that: "We must take the battle to the enemy, disrupt its plans and confront the worst threats before they emerge. In the world we have entered, the only path to safety is the path to action."[272] He also added that the United States of America "must uncover terror cells in 60 or more countries."[273] This implicitly means that Bush had planned to adopt the policy of "pre-emptive strikes"[274] against terrorism, terrorists and those countries sheltering them, at a time and place chosen by the United States of America, be there genuine or potential terrorist intent. This explains Bush's statement in his address to Congress on September 20, 2001, when he said: "If we wait for threats to fully materialize, we will have waited too long."[275] Bush reaffirmed his inclination towards a strategy of pre-emptive or preventive strikes in a speech to the Republican Party on June 15, 2002 in which he explained that the deterrence and containment of US foreign policy under the Truman Doctrine in 1947 was no longer sufficient.[276]

It is worth noting here that on March 12, 1947,[277] the 33rd American President, Harry S. Truman, declared a major new direction in US foreign policy, setting its guiding post-war principles. That direction was based on the intervention of the United States of America in world affairs in order to contain the spread of communism in the world, by force if necessary. The principle, later know as the Truman Doctrine,[278] represented an enormous commitment that the United States of America had never made before, and was an official declaration of the existence of the Cold War, which defined the balance of power in international relations for more than 40 years. The doctrine was based on dramatizing and exaggerating the Soviet threat and exploiting the fears of the American people.[279]

Two days after Bush's speech, former Secretary of State, Condoleezza Rice, explained the Bush Doctrine by saying: "It means forestalling certain destructive acts against you by an adversary ... There are times when you can't wait to be attacked to respond."[280]

Hence, we can see that the US National Security Strategy of the Bush administration outlined on September 17, 2002 had laid the theoretical groundwork for the war against Iraq.[281] By turning the strategy of preventive or pre-emptive war into practical reality, it reflected the dominance of the neoconservatives over US politics at that time.[282] A large body of political literature indicates that in the first year of the

George Walker Bush [Jr.] administration there was intensive work to finalize this strategic theory, which had been built on the parameters and developments of the post-Cold War world, whereas military theory in the previous era was based on the principle of 'mutual deterrence.' That theory became redundant and the Bush administration had to find a new effective strategy in the struggle against new threats; especially economic entities that have no boundaries, enemies which have no specific location, and organizations that hold an absolute belief in their faith. The United States of America was no longer facing one enemy, as was the case during the days of the Cold War. The nature of threat had changed and a set of dangers had emerged which made conventional deterrence options useless. The United States of America adopted this new strategy because its new enemies were far weaker than the Soviet Union, and so there was no hindrance to employing this strategy effectively against them.[283]

Following the emergence of this strategy, many experts and observers talked of a radical change in the US position towards the accepted principles of international relations. Some viewed this strategy as a flagrant breach of international law and an encroachment on the principle of sovereignty that had been recognized since the Peace of Westphalia[284] (which formed the basis for acknowledging the independence and equality of states in terms of rights and obligations). Thus, this strategy was considered a blatant American abandonment of the principles of respect for states' independence. Some researchers even felt that the Bush administration had ruined a long history of American contribution to the establishment of international rights organizations over nearly 200 years, and chose for the first time not to recognize the principles of international law and to embrace the principle of self-interest with regard to its goals and national security. Successive previous American administrations sought excuses to justify interference in other countries' affairs, whilst acknowledging and explicitly declaring their commitment to the principles of independence and non-interference in the internal affairs of other countries.[285]

With the Iraq War, many questions were raised in research circles around the world about global leadership after the US administration ignored the UN, particularly after the campaign by the conservative movement led by the former Vice-President Richard Bruce "Dick" Cheney[286] against it, and after the speech delivered by President George Walker Bush [Jr.] at the UN in which he warned the international organization that it would risk becoming irrelevant and could face the same fate as the League of Nations, explicitly indicating his country's willingness to ignore it and take unilateral military action against Iraq.[287] Some raised questions about the status of the United States of America in the new world order and the way it dealt with other countries, as well as the role of the UN and international law and their position within US policy. This was especially true after the emergence of new American attitudes towards certain major countries such as China, which was now defined as a 'strategic competitor' rather than a 'strategic partner' of the United States of America, as was the case during the Clinton presidency.

A kind of "cautious American confrontation"[288] with Chinese influence came into being, reflected in the collision between an American spy plane and a Chinese fighter above the Pacific Ocean and the subsequent emergency landing of the American aircraft at a Chinese airport without prior permission in April 2001.[289] China took a tough stance with regard to that incident and stated that the American aircraft had violated Chinese airspace. China said it had been observing US spying activities in the region and believed such activities would create unwarranted tensions in Sino–US relations, and expressly prohibited those aircraft to breach its airspace.[290] The Americans tried to convince the Chinese that the United States of America had strategic interests that required worldwide monitoring, via US satellites and spy planes. Bush's statement regarding that incident was the epitome of his strategic thinking when he said that the United States of America could not envision any power in the world that would prevent an American plane from flying in international airspace.[291]

This incident occurred some two years after of a wave of European anger caused by a statement made by former US Secretary of Defense Donald Henry Rumsfeld on January 22, 2003, describing France and Germany as 'Old Europe' in the context of their opposition to the US position on Iraq; and hence a specific American position was also formed in terms of how it dealt with its international partners.

What contributed to making the Iraq War so shocking to broad segments of civil society across the world, and so significant in terms of the strategic readjustment of America's role in the new world order, was the fact that the UN was there to prevent superpowers from resorting to the use of force at will in order to serve their own national interests. The Bush administration had acted as if the multilateral new world order was now an unreasonable constraint on its ability or desire to shape the world system.[292]

In light of the above, and regardless of the outcomes of the domestic situation of Iraq at later stages, the moment following the fall of Saddam Hussein Al-Tikriti's regime demonstrated an excessive sense of strength by the United States of America as an unmatched superpower in the world (whether in terms of its possession of the most advanced weaponry in the 21st century, its ability to launch such a huge military operation outside the United States of America in such short order, or its technological, information, or media and propaganda capabilities).[293]

Objectively, one can say that this overwhelming sense of American power was not a product of the historic moment following the invasion of Iraq, but instead had emerged years before. The extensive global reaction and sympathy extended to the United States of America after the September 11, 2001 attacks contributed to its view of itself as the sole superpower in the world. It sought to carve for itself a global role that would reflect its superiority. It was in this context that plans prepared by neoconservatives came to light within the framework of the Project for the New American Century (PNAC).[294] These plans helped pave the way for the aspirations of the Bush administration.[295]

This sense of overwhelming power may have contributed to frequent talk about the birth of a new empire. On March 19, 2003, when the first American smart bombs fell on Baghdad, Leon Sigmund Fuerth, the national security adviser to former US Vice-President Albert Arnold "Al" Gore and professor at George Washington University, published an article in the *Washington Post* in which he wrote of the birth of a new empire and presented an overview of the reality of America's place in the world.[296] This article expressed a specific situation that had become a reality on the ground—the United States of America wanted to prove globally that it had the upper hand, and the farthest reach, in influencing the rest of the world, particularly through its role in global oil markets after occupying Iraq and assuming full responsibility for making important decisions concerning the oil and gas industries.

Fuerth pointed out that irrespective of Americans' opinions and their approval – or lack thereof – for the establishment of an American empire, the reality indicated that the United States of America had indeed become an empire, and this consequently led to fissures in the ranks of its allies such as France and Germany. Particularly as the United States of America had hurt their pride by dispelling the illusion that they were able to reign in uncalculated American behavior.[297] Confirming the prevalence of such a sense of overwhelming power, Charles Krauthammer, a neoconservative,[298] wrote in 2004 that: "On December 26, 1991, the Soviet Union died and something new was born, something utterly new – a unipolar world dominated by a single superpower unchecked by any rival and with decisive reach in every corner of the globe. This is a staggering new development in history, not seen since the fall of Rome."[299]

After American failure over many foreign issues during the Bush administration, especially the Afghan and Iraq wars, some US researchers called for the use of soft power as opposed to hard power—a relatively new concept developed in the mid-1990s by Joseph Samuel Nye, Assistant Secretary of Defense in the Clinton administration. Nye explained this concept in his renowned book *Bound to Lead: the Changing Nature of America Power*,[300] where he defined the concept of soft power as the ability to attract and persuade. While hard power lies in the ability to force and coerce through a country's military power or economic might, soft power comes from the country's cultural, political, media or educational attraction as tools to achieve US interests, in addition to military power when necessary.

These debates emerged gradually in American political literature after the September 11, 2001 attacks; i.e. during the height of discussions about using military force to project American imperial power, and against the backdrop of the recognition by a number of researchers and officials of serious shortcomings in public diplomacy. Much criticism was leveled at US public relations diplomacy, pointing to the level of hatred for American policy which traditional diplomacy had failed to mitigate. The September 11, 2001 attacks also led to the widest and most comprehensive review of US foreign policy seen since World War II.[301] New debates surfaced at US political and intellectual levels regarding the traditional pillars of foreign policy. Those debates in turn branched out from the central question posed immediately after the collapse of the World Trade Center towers in New

York, which was: "why do they hate us?"[302] Calls increased for improving the image of the United States of America in the Arab and Muslim worlds, and many projects to win hearts and minds were devised.

In this context, a number of viewpoints emerged that saw the adoption of correct policy as insufficient, because the United States of America was hated and many hostile acts against it were a result of misunderstanding rather than actual bad policy; this fell under the area of public relations.[303] In the face of this, some officials – especially at the US State Department – quietly embarked on developing a conciliatory approach. Their efforts were focused on launching a public diplomacy campaign to influence Arab views and opinions about the United States of America and create a new system of assistance projects. These projects were topped by the Greater Middle East Project in February 2004, which was an initiative proposed by George Walker Bush [Jr.]. The initiative was controversial from the beginning and was received with objections and reservations from several Arab countries.[304] In its most ambitious version,[305] the initiative appeared bound to fail because many in the Middle East were skeptical about its stated objectives, especially as it was proposed at a time when the most visible signs of US policy in the region were the occupation of Iraq and growing US support for the policies of Israeli Prime Minister Ariel Sharon.[306]

When President Barack Hussein Obama took office,[307] talk was strongly revived about the need to discard the tough approach of US policy, and the term soft power[308] resurfaced. Joseph Samuel Nye pointed out that if the United States of America wanted to remain strong, Americans should also pay attention to their soft power, and argued that if it was possible to achieve one's objectives through the use of mere hard power, then for most of the great powers this would jeopardize their economic and political objectives.[309] Accordingly, Nye posited that not since Ancient Rome had one single nation acquired such economic, cultural and military power as the United States of America; but this power does not enable it resolve its problems or deal successfully with global challenges such as terrorism, environmental degradation, proliferation of WMDs, financial crises etc., as demonstrated in October 2013 when the US federal government faltered in meeting its financial obligations and was consequently forced into a partial shutdown. In light of this, however, Nye's argument for soft power, which he considers more effective in dealing with global challenges, could be re-understood.[310]

In all cases, the US strategic approach has changed substantially since the end of the administration of George Walker Bush [Jr.] and the election of President Barack Hussein Obama. In his announcement ending Operation Iraqi Freedom on August 31, 2010, Obama confirmed the responsibility of the

United States of America to sustain and strengthen its leadership in the world, but also stated that: "one of the lessons of our effort in Iraq is that American influence around the world is not a function of military force alone. We must use all elements of our power, including our diplomacy, our economic strength, and the power of America's example."[311] This approach is in sharp contrast to that of the previous administration and the Bush Doctrine, which will be linked forever with the Iraq War.[312] US policies during the second term of George Walker Bush [Jr.] revealed serious strategic mistakes committed in Iraq and an overestimation of the outcome expected from the use of US military force, leading to results opposite to those the American administration desired. Instead of boosting the status of the United States of America in the world, foreign policies adopted by the Bush administration seriously weakened it, and the position of the neoconservatives was indeed a disastrous misunderstanding of history.[313]

For example, US military intervention in Afghanistan and Iraq did not strengthen the status of the United States of America at the helm of the new world order as much as it aggravated the distress in the American economy. Current estimates show that the total cost to the United States of America of the Iraq and Afghanistan wars ranges between $4 and $6 trillion,[314] which is the highest in US history, in addition to damage inflicted on its moral standing and international reputation. In fact, the arrogant political rhetoric of the Bush administration severely damaged the constituents of American soft power across the world, notably the moral values and ideals which the United States of America has always sought to promote and reflect in its foreign policy.

Against this backdrop, it was self-evident that dramatic shifts in US strategic orientation would occur with the advent of the Obama administration, which has always stressed that the United States of America will continue to ensure global security through "our commitments to allies, partners, and institutions."[315] It appeared that the US National Security Strategy announced in May 2010 would clearly readjust American foreign policy. This strategy reaffirmed the US commitment to pursue its interests in a new world order where countries have certain rights and responsibilities. As a departure from the Bush administration's policies, the Obama administration's vision came up with a different direction based on the need for American engagement in international relations to uphold a just and sustainable international order.[316]

Several indications suggest that the conduct of the Obama administration and its approach to international relations are different from those of its predecessor, and are also consistent with the proposals of several US think-tanks at the time.[317] It is noteworthy that the approach of the United States of America towards Syria – for example – may have been entirely different had this crisis occurred during the administration of George Walker Bush [Jr.].

Secretary of State Hillary Rodham Clinton[318] laid out a different vision for US foreign policy after she assumed office, stressing the need to elevate diplomacy and development alongside defense—what she called a 'smart power' approach to solving global problems,[319] drawing on the intellectual approaches developed by Joseph Samuel Nye who used this term to mean the combination of hard and soft power in foreign policy in a way that brings American civilian power into better balance with American military power.[320]

Defense Secretary Robert Michael Gates[321] shared this strategic vision with Clinton. After taking office, Gates said that: "There has to be a change in attitude in the recognition of the critical role that agencies like the State Department and USAID play … for them to play the leading role that I think they need to play."[322] This new American strategic vision gained importance following the resignation of Donald Henry Rumsfeld, who was a prominent neoconservative and was known for his conviction that military power should be given priority in order to achieve desired goals—his name was associated with the Afghanistan and Iraq wars and many other controversial issues.

To implement the visions of both Clinton and Gates, Congress allocated funds to hire 1,108 new employees in the US State Department and Civil Service to enhance the Department's ability to achieve American interests and values. The US Agency for International Development also doubled its staff, hiring an additional 1,200 employees.[323] In addition, the Obama administration began building the US Agency for International Development into one of the world's leading development organizations, confirming its focus on civilian power in the Obama administration. Hillary Rodham Clinton considered this emphasis on civilian power to be in line with American history and tradition,[324] pointing to historical American roles in the Marshall Plan, the Peace Corps founded by former American President John Fitzgerald Kennedy[325] and the 'green revolution' for which the American scientist Norman Ernest Borlaug[326] was responsible.

In light of the above, it is clear that after the Afghanistan and Iraq wars, and the inauguration of President Obama in January 2009, American political discourse moved significantly away from unilateralism. There have emerged new forms of American leadership in the new world order, which have not yet fully materialized, with examples such as "leading from behind" during the international intervention in Libya, and the American management of the crisis in Syria.[327] The researcher Fareed Rafiq Zakaria stated that the intervention in Libya reflected a genuine international effort, with the United States of America initially playing the lead role but quickly moving to a support role.[328] However, that shift was not at all a full return to the pre-Iraq War approach, which was "the symbolic moment when America lapsed from being a hegemon with a responsibility for maintaining order into a revisionist imperial power bent on changing the rules of the game."[329]

Generally, there is near consensus among Western researchers that the Iraq War was a defining turning point in American foreign policy. To support this, one can refer, for example, to what Stephen Martin Walt, professor of international relations at Harvard University, wrote in his famous article, "The End of the American Era,"[330] published in the November/December 2011 issue of *The National Interest*, in which he discusses the effects of the Afghanistan and Iraq wars, pointing out that the debate is not about the collapse of American dominance, but rather about how long American influence in the world could possibly last. Walt argues that such influence was severely weakened by the wars in Iraq and Afghanistan and other fatal mistakes committed by the United States of America. As noted previously, the cost of those two wars ranges between $4 and $6 trillion,[331] while the end result would likely be an unstable quasi-democracy hostile to Israel and allied with Iran.[332]

In Afghanistan, what was achieved was much less than in Iraq, even if the American leaders tried to portray it as some kind of victory. The strenuous and costly US efforts to eliminate the Taliban and make Afghanistan a Western-style democratic state had failed. Walt argues that the United States of America had its own interests and should pursue them vigorously, but it should be more modest in its aims to rearrange the internal politics of other countries. He believes the most important lesson the United States of America has learned from the last decade was that it could not succeed in this, and it could in fact cause more problems for itself and its friends rather than have any chance of making things better. Moreover, he indicates that the United States of America needs to desist from telling other countries how to run their own affairs, and should only proffer advice without taking direct charge of governing countries such as Iraq and Afghanistan.[333]

Conclusion

This chapter sought to concentrate on several issues which have been absent in the ongoing research debates about both the new and old world orders. Among these issues, for example, is the link between the concept of the state, its creation and the emergence of sovereignty in its traditional form on the one hand, and the historical stages of the world order on the other. There is a clear need to deeply understand the world order and its working mechanisms from an historical perspective so that the world order does not appear to be simply academic, isolated from reality in the various stages of ancient and modern history. Of course, the objective of this chapter was not to establish the historical origin of American hegemony in this order, but rather to pinpoint some defining indicative milestones in its history, and to try to reveal its roots. The aim is to draw a comprehensive picture that could help in understanding both historical transformations and the nature of contemporary global realities.

In addition, the chapter carefully pondered some historic junctures which may be considered decisive in understanding the working philosophy of the new world order and the orientations of the sole superpower dominating it since the beginning of 1990s. In this context, the focus was on a thorough discussion of the phenomenon of globalization which, in the author's opinion, represents the most salient feature of the new world order—indeed it is accurately described by some researchers who consider globalization as the other "face" of this order, or at least the main driver of it at the levels of values, culture and economy. This chapter has also focused on historic events, because it would be difficult to understand the paths of the new world order without soundly understanding those events and analyzing their highly influential effects, such as the September 11, 2001 attacks and the American invasion of Iraq in March 2003.

This chapter provides the reader with an insightful cross-section of the global order in its various historical stages. This is a vital gateway to understand the developments occurring within the working mechanisms of the new world order. Such an understanding also reveals the level of American hegemony over this order, confirming that the world is still living at the height of the American age and that the recurrent debates about the limits of American power, or the emergence of shift in the structure of the new world order, may be prone to exaggeration—whether in estimating the elements of power that the United States of America possesses compared to its current or potential strategic rivals, or in understanding the deep value transformations taking place in the new world order, which are mostly in favor of continued American hegemony over this order in the near and medium terms.

The New World Order: Economy, Trade and Energy

Chapter IV

The New World Order:
Economy, Trade and Energy

Economic, financial and commercial strength, as well as energy resources, are undoubtedly among the most important foundations of the status and influence of individual states and blocs on the global stage, thereby representing major determinants of the hierarchy of power in the new world order. Historically, significant economic events have contributed to shaping major changes in the world system, a prime example being the Great Depression that struck following the collapse of stock prices in Wall Street on October 29, 1929, leading to devastating global consequences. Economic activities stalled, unemployment soared to unprecedented levels and countries moved toward commercial protectionism against imports.

Given the economic chaos that reigned in the aftermath of the Great Depression, it is no surprise to see the emergence of some attendant fanatic, nationalistic, and ethnocentric tendencies—such as the Nazi movement in Germany led by Adolf Hitler. Nazism gained currency in Germany because many Germans felt humiliated by the Treaty of Versailles, signed on June 28, 1919 following World War I.[1] The treaty imposed harsh economic, political and social sanctions on Germany,[2] as well as a raft of related, punitive economic and security requirements.[3]

It is also not surprising that the Great Depression continued in the United States of America for nearly a decade, which only began to recover after its entry into war against Nazi Germany in 1941 and the massive consequent war spending that created jobs and stimulated the economy.[4]

With the end of World War II on September 2, 1945, the economy also played a key role in shaping the new world system of the post-war period, particularly through two key initiatives. The first was the American Marshall Plan, announced on June 5, 1947, to rebuild Europe and stem the spread of Soviet influence. The plan continued for four years, from 1948 to 1952, and cost approximately US $12.7 billion.[5] It led to fundamental changes in the global role of the United States of America, as well as its economy and culture in peacetime. The Marshall Plan sowed the idea of European integration that led to the creation of the European Union, its growth and subsequent partial transformation into the monetary union of the euro zone.[6] The second initiative was the Bretton Woods Agreement signed in July 1944 to rebuild the post-war international economic system. The agreement established the IMF and the International Bank for Reconstruction and Development (IBRD) – known as the World Bank[7] – both of which have been leading global economic actors ever since. The agreement also included arrangements for exchange rates, obligating each country to peg its currency to the US dollar, which was convertible into gold on demand according to the Bretton Woods system. However, this collapsed between 1971 and 1973 when the United States of America unilaterally terminated convertibility of the dollar to gold, forcing a return to a flexible exchange rate system which made it easier for economies to adjust to oil shocks that first struck in 1973.[8]

Economics also played a key role in shaping the new world order when it directly brought about the collapse of the Eastern bloc and the Soviet Union. The restructuring policy (*Perestroika*) adopted by the then Soviet premier Mikhail Sergeyevich Gorbachev included an overhaul of the Soviet economic system, which had faced crisis and recession from the mid-1970s up to the early 1990s. The foundations of the communist system on which the Soviet Union was built collapsed, and the member states of the Union and its allies moved towards secession.[9]

Conversely, the early move toward economic reform in China not only saved it from collapse and disintegration, but also spurred its rise to influence on the world stage. China gradually introduced reforms from the end of 1978 at the hands of the reformist leader Deng Xiaoping, who led the country from 1978 to 1992 and introduced policies based on market economy. He began by reforming the agricultural sector, and then in the 1980s initiated a move towards privatization and a more significant role for the private sector, attracting foreign direct investment, reliance on exports and achieving integration into the world economy by joining the WTO in 2001.[10]

Economic transformations have also led to the emergence of other new influential powers on the world stage, such as the GCC countries—mainly as a result of their hydrocarbon production but also, more recently, for becoming significant international investors through their sovereign wealth funds, which are worth more than $2 trillion.[11] In addition, the power of many Southeast Asian countries – along with South Korea, Brazil, Chile and South Africa – has increased by virtue of economic reform and resilience in the face of financial crises, placing them in the category of 'emerging' market economies.[12]

To assess the structure of the new world order, it is necessary to explore the economic outlook for the main contenders for power, since their economic position and future – alongside their levels of education, scientific research, technology, military strength, economy, energy and logistics capabilities – represent important, if not paramount elements in determining the ranking of powers in the new world order. The focus here will be on the main powers of the order, ranked in the Introduction, which are: the United States of America China, the European Union and Russia; followed by Japan, India and Brazil; and then the rest of the world. Therefore, in order to assess their place in the global hierarchy, the past and projected future economic growth and performance of these countries must be evaluated, in addition to their government budgets and public debt, trade and transport infrastructure, and

348

conventional and unconventional hydrocarbon energy and renewable energy resources, as determinants of their future economic strength and position in the world order.

Economic Growth

The ranking of world powers presented above is validated by the economic growth enjoyed by the Unites States of America and others over the past 25 years. Table 4.1 illustrates the economic growth of these countries and groups in the form of average real GDP growth in five-year intervals, in addition to IMF forecasts for growth up to 2018.[13]

Table 4.1
Average Real GDP Growth, 1988–2018 (%)[14]

	1988–1992	1993–1997	1998–2002	2003–2007	2008–2012	2013–2018
World	3.22	3.35	3.23	4.79	2.91	4.20
United States of America	2.54	3.53	3.24	2.73	0.60	3.01
China	8.53	11.46	8.25	11.65	9.28	8.38
EU	2.45	2.14	2.71	2.72	-0.05	1.45
Eurozone	–	1.74	2.46	2.18	-0.23	1.17
Japan	4.45	1.44	0.14	1.85	-0.10	1.26
India	5.44	6.13	5.41	8.61	6.84	6.55
Brazil	-0.03	3.99	1.71	4.01	3.20	3.94
Russia	–	-5.55	4.18	7.50	1.93	3.61

During the past 25 years, the United States of America has faced a number of economic difficulties that testify to the resilience of its economic system and its ability to weather shocks, confirming it as the world's leading economy.[15] Over this period, the US has mainly relied on innovation – drawing on knowledge, technology and entrepreneurship – as a key economic driver.[16] An example of this is the rise of Silicon Valley in the southern region of the San Francisco Bay Area in Northern California, which has become renowned worldwide for its hosting of a large number of developers and manufacturers of integrated circuits and computer chips. The region now features all manner of high-tech businesses and is described as the global center of computing technology development, both in terms of hardware and software technologies.[17]

Another example is the rise and fall of companies working in the field of electronics (Sun Microsystems, Dell, Apple), the dominance of certain US companies over global software markets (Microsoft Corporation, Linux), and the rise of companies associated with the age of the Internet and smartphones, (Google, Yahoo, etc.).[18]

It seems clear that the United States of America dominates innovations in the high-tech sector, which is growing increasingly important as the world moves towards a new order.[19] However, the innovative capacity of the US economy is not confined to the field of information technology; it can also be seen across various sectors, ranging from the financial sector – where financial 'engineering' is employed, particularly in the field of financial derivatives[20] – to innovative techniques employed in the energy sector such as hydraulic fracturing, which has led to a boom in shale oil and gas production in the United States of America,[21] suggesting a noticeable change in the way conventional energy markets operate over the next 25 years—with significant global political, security and economic implications.

Figure 4.1
Average Real GDP Growth, 2008–2018 (%)[22]

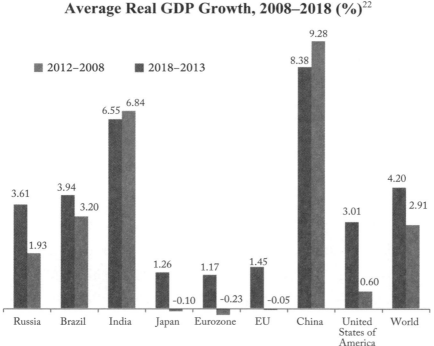

Figure 4.2

Share of Major Economies in World GDP (%)[23]

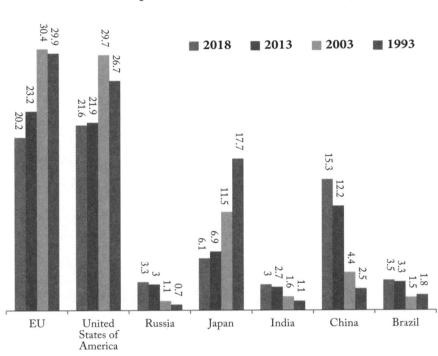

In addition to its reliance on innovation-based growth, the strength of the US economy is also evident in terms of its performance during the past 25 years, as well as its vast size, accounting for 21.9% of world GDP in 2013. This makes it more self-reliant than other economies, such as China, particularly with regard to investment and consumption.

Moreover, the American economy has withstood major crises such as 'Black Monday,'[24] and even the recent global financial crisis that began in 2007. Indeed, the US economy appears to be recovering faster than the European economy, for example. Its average real growth in GDP increased from 2.54% during the five years following the 1987 crisis (1988–1992) to 3.53% in the years 1993–1997. In addition, US economic growth is expected to reach 3.6% by 2015, against -0.3% and -3.1% during the two years following the 2007 crisis. Meanwhile, the European economy is expected to continue suffering more profoundly and for a longer period, and its rate of growth is not expected to exceed 1.7% by 2015 (compared to 0.5% and -4.2% during the two years following the 2007 crisis).[25]

As for China, despite the strong growth that has continued throughout the past 25 years under a reform process of gradual transformation towards a mixed system of centralized state planning and a market economy, the country suffers major weaknesses. Despite China's spectacular economic rise within a relatively short period (from 8th largest economy in 1988 to 2nd largest in 2013[26]), it still has a long way to go to catch up with advanced countries in terms of average per capita income. In this respect, China is still among the ranks of developing countries[27] and occupies a place comparable to Angola or Thailand, lower even than countries such as Peru and Turkmenistan, for example. Average per capita income in the United States of America, about $51,200 in 2013, is nearly eight times the average per capita income in China, which was estimated at around $6,629 in the same year.[28]

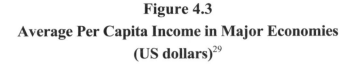

Figure 4.3
Average Per Capita Income in Major Economies
(US dollars)[29]

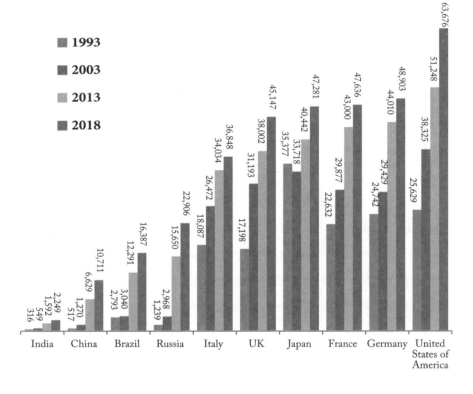

The Chinese economy still depends on traditional sectors such as heavy and light industry and agriculture, and is highly dependent on FDI and exports. This represents a major weakness, because the rise in living standards and income over time will undermine the competitiveness of China's economy against lower-cost competitors in the export market, such as Vietnam and the Philippines.[30] China is also disadvantaged by the current worldwide trend towards forming trade blocs against Chinese control over export markets, such as the move announced in 2013 to form the largest free-trade area in the world between the United States of America and the EU.[31] China also faces other problems, such as the need to open up its financial markets and make the value of its currency, the yuan (officially the renminbi), more reflective of market conditions.[32]

China could possibly face debt crises at the local government level, where total debt reached approximately $1.881 trillion in 2012 (22.9% of GDP), and is expected to reach $2.168 trillion by 2018 (16.5% of GDP).[33] China also faces the possibility of a real-estate price bubble burst, and problems among bank lenders.[34] Given that the Chinese economy has not really been tested by such crises in the past owing to the high level of government control over economic activity, any judgment on its resilience will have to be postponed until such time as it is seen to be truly tested.[35]

Moreover, China has a major weakness compared to the United States of America, which is its lack of adequate domestic energy resources required to sustain high economic growth,[36] and a lack of modern oil and gas production technology and infrastructure (when compared to their American counterparts).[37] China is attempting to overcome this problem by reaching overseas to create economic partnerships with oil-rich countries, mainly in Africa and certain parts of the Middle East,[38] in addition to attempts by certain Chinese companies to gain access to 'fracking' technology through cyber espionage targeting American firms.[39] It is worth noting that in July 2013 the United States of America accused foreign suspects of conspiring in a worldwide hacking and data breach that targeted American companies, including the NASDAQ, 7-Eleven, Visa, Discovery Financial Services, J.C. Penney and Dow Jones, causing hundreds of millions of dollars in losses, and making it the largest such incident in US history.[40]

China is also trying to minimize the risks arising from excessive dependence on exports as a driving force of the economy, and to counter criticism that it employs a policy of currency undervaluation to boost its exports, in what is often referred to as 'currency war.' Indeed, the new Chinese leadership has said it would follow more balanced economic policies through greater reliance on domestic demand and gradually reducing the country's dependence on exports.[41]

As for the European Union, despite upbeat expectations for greater economic integration and unity over the past 25 years – including the relative success in integrating Eastern European economies into Western Europe after the fall of the Berlin Wall in 1989, and in adopting a single common currency used by 17 of the 28 EU member states in 1999 – European economic performance following the 2007 global financial crisis has been questionable and invites pessimism about the future of EU economic cooperation in general and the euro zone in particular.[42]

The 2007 global financial crisis revealed serious weaknesses in the euro zone, one of which is that monetary union *per se* is not sufficient to achieve economic unity. Monetary union should have been supplemented by a fiscal and banking union.[43] Also, given the wide divergence in economic growth performance, job creation, government finances and public debt between Northern European countries (notably Germany and the Scandinavian countries) and Southern European countries (particularly Greece, Portugal, Cyprus and Spain) it is quite difficult to implement unified monetary and fiscal policies that suit the divergent economic structures of these countries.[44] There is no doubt that the weakness of states such as Greece and Portugal – and even France, Italy and Spain – places pressure on the euro exchange rate against other major currencies, but this pressure supports strong export-oriented economies such as Germany by enhancing the price competitiveness of their exports. However, since most European trade is conducted among the member countries of the Union, arguably Germany gains at the expense of Southern European countries, which suffer foreign trade deficits, negative economic growth rates and disturbingly high youth unemployment[45] (which in May 2013 reached 62.9% in Greece and 56.1% in Spain).[46]

Russia, meanwhile, has achieved relatively good levels of economic stability and growth over the past 15 years in particular. This is despite the severe economic crisis it suffered following the collapse of the Soviet Union on August 19, 1991, and the difficulties in transitioning from a centrally planned to a market economy, including corruption in the privatization of state-owned companies and the rise of illegal activities such as conventional organized crime and internet-related crimes. Russian average economic growth increased from -5.55% during 1993–1997 to 4.18% during 1998–2002, and to 7.50% during 2003–2007, stabilizing at 1.93% during 2008–2012.[47]

Russia has been successful owing to its endowment of raw materials, especially oil and natural gas. It has benefitted from the continued high price of natural gas, which represents an essential source of energy for the EU. In 2011, it provided the EU with about 51% of its oil supply and about 41% of its natural gas supply.[48] However, the Russian economy is still relatively small when compared to its American, Chinese and European counterparts. The size of the Russian economy is less than 14% of the US economy, about 25% of the Chinese economy, and less than 13% of the European economy.[49] Thus, if no tangible transformation of the Russian economic production structure takes place over the next 25 years – to make it more reliant on innovation and technology and better able to take advantage of its proximity to major Asian and European markets – Russia's relative weight in the new world order is unlikely to rise in terms of economic strength.

With respect to India and Brazil, both countries have managed to overcome economic crises over the past 25 years by implementing economic and social development programs under prudent leaderships. The two countries have become prominent pillars of the emerging economies, especially the BRICS group. However, they still have much to do in order to join the ranks of the advanced economies; for example, their levels of poverty and income inequality are still among the highest in the world. This situation was reflected by the recent protests in Brazil,[50] but both countries are witnessing significant development and growing regional power. Thanks to a focus on education, Indian students and professionals in the West excel in fields ranging from medicine to information technology and financial services. The development of human capital in India has also made it the largest provider of outsourcing services. With the expected 'reverse brain drain' that could result if improvements in living standards continue, India's economic power should carry on rising over the next 25 years.

As mentioned previously, Brazil has managed to overcome economic crises and has pursued policies leading to balanced development and social justice under the government of former president Luiz Inácio Lula da Silva. Brazil is known for its large size and diverse economy, with strengths in agriculture, manufacturing, tourism, and the production of raw materials.[51] It has borders with ten countries (Argentina, Bolivia, Colombia, French Guiana, Guyana, Paraguay, Peru, Suriname, Uruguay and Venezuela). With the improvement of social conditions and sustained pursuit of sound economic policies, Brazil is expected to rise in the new world order. Moreover, the nation holds 2% of global proven shale oil reserves off its coasts;[52] this could support the future development of Brazil, particularly in light of the expected increasing reliance of the United States of America on this source of energy in the future.[53]

The final potentially significant actor in the new world order is Japan. The country has experienced a prolonged period of anemic economic performance – in what is referred to as the 'lost decade,' and sometimes the 'lost two decades'[54] – where average economic growth has hardly exceeded two percent over the past 20 years. It has also begun to lose its relative technological advantage over its main Asian competitors (particularly South Korea and China) and faces continuing, intense energy crises, particularly following the 2011 disaster at Fukushima, which caused a sharp reduction in the production of many Japanese companies and a comprehensive review of national energy policy. However, it seems that under the leadership of Prime Minister Shinzo Abe Japan has started to take bolder steps towards restructuring its main economic policies—particularly its monetary and fiscal policies.[55] With the decline in the global position of the Japanese economy – from second largest in 1988 to third largest in 2010 – it could be argued that the economic factor behind the rise in Japanese soft power during the 1970s and 1980s is also the cause of its decline from the ranks of the second-tier states in the new world order to those of the third.

Energy

Conventional and Unconventional Hydrocarbon Energy

Over the past quarter-century the world has witnessed gradual, but significant, changes in the patterns of production and consumption of oil and gas—changes that are expected to bring about a realignment in the relative importance of major energy-producing regions to international political and economic powers that could have substantial implications for the composition of the new world order (see Appendices IV and V for the geographical distribution of world oil and gas reserves in 2012).

In this context, this part of the book will discuss the role of energy in the new world order by analyzing the situation of the most influential consumers and producers. Net consumers analyzed her include: the United States of America, the European Union, China, India and Japan; while major producing countries include the GCC states, the Americas, and the states of the former Soviet Union, particularly Russia. Special focus will be placed on critical issues for the future of energy and its role in the formation of the global order; with emphasis on unconventional sources of hydrocarbon energy, which new technology has rendered economically viable, namely: shale oil, shale gas, oil sands, and extra-heavy oil.[56] Finally, alternative and renewable energies are discussed, along with the role they could play in the balance of global energy supply and demand.

Table 4.2
Average Oil Imports, 1988–2012 (million barrels per day)[57]

	1988–1992	1993–1997	1998–2002	2003–2007	2008–2012
EU	10.95	10.78	11.23	12.16	11.77
United States of America	7.91	9.55	11.76	13.55	11.31
China	-0.37	0.44	1.44	3.35	5.10
Japan	5.19	5.71	5.53	5.29	4.59
India	0.52	0.86	1.45	1.86	2.50
Brazil	0.88	1.06	0.82	0.42	0.55
Russia	-5.04	-3.21	-4.17	-6.77	-7.36

Notes: imports calculated as daily consumption less daily domestic production.

Figure 4.4
Average Oil Imports, 2008–2012 (million barrels per day)[58]

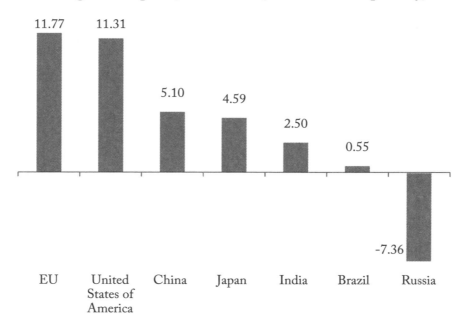

362

Table 4.2 shows that the past 10 years have seen a shift in oil import trends among major countries, with a decline in average imports by the United States of America and the EU (placing the USA second after the EU in terms of oil imports), compared to the preceding 15 years. Meanwhile, the imports of China and India have increased sharply, pushing China into third place, while Japan has dropped to fourth. As for Russia, it is a net exporter of oil and its export volumes have increased markedly during the past five years.

Table 4.3
Average Annual Imports of Natural Gas, 1988–2012
(billion cubic meters)[59]

	1988–1992	1993–1997	1998–2002	2003–2007	2008–2012
EU	137.21	157.75	209.07	275.40	301.86
Japan	47.62	58.79	70.94	81.86	99.59
United States of America	47.30	92.42	100.06	101.86	62.85
China	0.10	-1.04	-3.16	-1.32	16.36
Indian	0.00	0.00	0.00	5.33	12.58
Brazil	0.00	0.02	2.25	8.30	10.70
Russia	-163.60	-168.53	-171.62	-180.46	-171.38

Notes: imports calculated as annual consumption less annual domestic production.

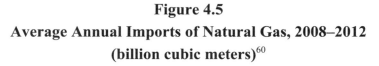

Figure 4.5

Average Annual Imports of Natural Gas, 2008–2012

(billion cubic meters)[60]

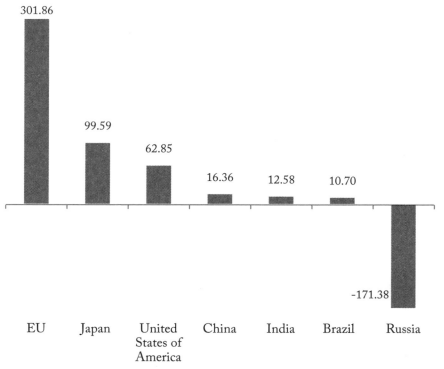

In terms of natural gas, the United States of America has witnessed a remarkable boom in its production. Its average annual imports declined by more than 40% over 2008–2012, compared to the previous five years (2003–2007).[61] Meanwhile, European and Japanese imports increased, and China became a net importer. Indian and Brazilian imports of natural gas increased, while Russia maintained its position as one of the major exporters of the world.

Figure 4.6
Oil and Natural Gas Prices, 1988–2012[62]

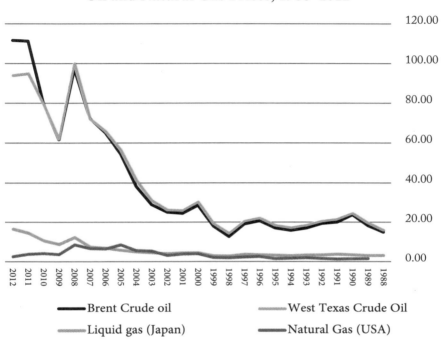

Notes: dollars per barrel for oil; dollars per million British thermal units for gas.

Considering the developments in the prices of oil and gas during the past 25 years, there is a clear trend towards increased consumption of gas in major countries (the United States of America, UK, Russia, China, Japan, India, Brazil, Germany, France and Italy) not only because it is a clean source of energy compared to oil, but also because of its relatively low price due to increased production, particularly in the United States of America, which is currently enjoying a shale gas boom.[63]

Figure 4.7
Value of Net Oil Imports, 1992–2018 (billion dollars)[64]

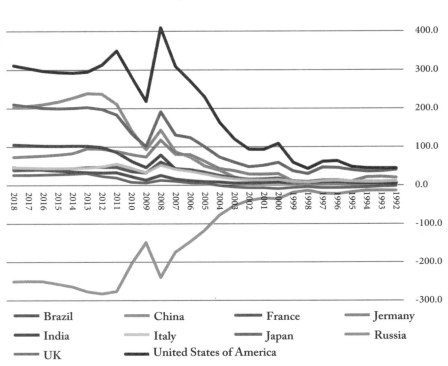

- —— Brazil
- —— China
- —— France
- —— Jermany
- —— India
- —— Italy
- —— Japan
- —— Russia
- —— UK
- —— United States of America

The New World Order and the Major Oil and Gas-Consuming Countries

United States of America

Since the beginning of the third millennium, the United States of America has witnessed a narrowing of the gap between consumption and production of both oil and gas, bringing the country ever-closer to self-dependence. Import dependence declined from about 61% in 2001 to 58% in 2011, and is expected to decline to less than 15% by 2035, according to the estimates of the International Energy Agency (IEA).[65] As for gas, US dependence on imported gas decreased from 11.8% in 2001 to 5.6% in 2011, leading to expectations that it will become a net exporter of gas by 2035.[66]

In this regard, it is worth noting that the narrowing of the gap between production and consumption of hydrocarbon energy in the United States of America is attributed to positive factors on both sides.[67] With respect to production, technological advances have made shale gas an important growing source of US energy. As for consumption, the use of oil in electricity generation has been almost completely abandoned in favor of natural gas,[68] and some modest progress has been achieved in the shift to energy-efficient means of transportation and those that use alternative energy, such as hybrid vehicles.

In addition to the decline in dependence on foreign oil and gas, the United States of America is witnessing a significant shift in sources of imported energy, relying mainly on the western hemisphere while reducing its dependence on Middle Eastern oil.[69] As a result of technological advances in the field of production from oil sands, and the economic feasibility brought about by current oil prices, the United States of America is increasingly shifting towards importing oil from Canada, which has the world's largest oil sands reserves. Canada and Venezuela together have more than half of all global oil sands reserves, and new offshore oil discoveries are being made in Central and South America; hence the United States of America is expected to continue to look to the rest of the western hemisphere as a source of energy imports. It is worth noting that since the dawn of the current millennium the dependence of the United States of America on the countries of the GCC as a source of oil has declined from 17% in 2001 to 13% in 2011, while its dependence on imports from other countries in the western hemisphere, especially Canada, Brazil and Colombia, increased from 50% to 55% during the same period.[70]

China

Unlike the United States of America, Chinese dependence on imported oil and gas, especially from the GCC countries, has increased in order to meet domestic demand. Strong economic growth since 2000 and rising per capita income have seen average energy consumption increase accordingly. China's dependence on imported oil increased from around 32% in 2001 to 58% in 2011, and is expected to reach 80% by 2035. As for gas, China has gone from being a country with a production surplus of 10.6% in 2001, to one with net imports of 21.6% in 2011. Furthermore, Chinese gas imports are expected to exceed 40% by 2035.[71] The increased Chinese dependence on oil and gas from the GCC countries necessarily means greater Chinese interest in the Gulf region and its security and stability, and provides the GCC states with a margin for political maneuver in their international affairs.

China is attempting to diversify its import sources; however, it is obviously moving towards increased reliance on oil from the GCC, while looking to neighboring countries for gas—especially Turkmenistan.[72] It may also be noted that almost one third of Chinese oil imports comes from Africa, and a further third comes from the GCC, while its oil imports from the former Soviet states and Iran together constitute about 22%.[73] With China's growing thirst for oil to fuel its economic growth, and with sanctions imposed on Iran, China is expected to rely increasingly on GCC oil, at least in the medium term. With respect to gas, China may rely increasingly on the development of supplies from Turkmenistan, in addition to negotiating more supply from Russia and working to secure supplies from Australia, Indonesia and Malaysia.[74]

European Union

The EU is increasingly dependent on imported oil and gas from Russia and other former states of the Soviet Union, North and sub-Saharan African countries, and the GCC states in order to meet domestic consumption—albeit growing at a slower rate than in China. EU oil import dependence increased from 78% in 2001 to 87.5% in 2011, and is expected to exceed 90% in 2035.[75] As for gas, the EU depended on imports to meet 48.5% of its demand in 2001, rising to 65.5% in 2011, and its gas dependence is expected to reach 90% by 2035.[76]

The EU's increased dependence on imported oil and gas has been accompanied by growing dependence on supplies from the states of the former Soviet Union and Africa. EU oil imports from the states of the former Soviet Union jumped from about 28% in 2001 to 51% in 2011,[77] while the GCC share declined from 18% in 2001 to 11% in 2011. With respect to gas, the share of natural gas supplies from the states of the former Soviet Union to the EU in 2011 reached 41%, while the GCC states provided only 16%.[78]

Major Hydrocarbon-Producing Blocs and the New World Order

The Cooperation Council for the Arab States of the Gulf (GCC)

The GCC is the only major group of countries whose share in world oil and gas production has increased (from 20.9% in 2001 to 23.9% in 2011) while its share of global proven reserves has declined (from 37.9% in 2001 to 29.9% in 2011).[79] With respect to gas, GCC reserves declined from 24.3% of global proven reserves in 2001 to 20.3% in 2011, while its share in world production grew from 6.4% in 2001 to 10.7% in 2011.[80]

With respect to the largest importers of Gulf oil, the list is topped by Japan, followed by China, South Korea, the United States of America, India and the EU. A shift in this order is expected by 2035, and will see China rise to the top of the list,

370

followed by India, Japan, South Korea and the EU, with the United States of America no longer featuring in the list of significant GCC energy export destinations.[81]

Western Hemisphere (North and South America)

The countries of the western hemisphere – the Americas – represent the only major group that has witnessed a significant favorable shift in its energy outlook. While their share of world oil production decreased from 27.6% in 2001 to 25.9% in 2011,[82] their share of proven oil reserves increased from 26% to 32.8% over the same period. Therefore, oil production is expected to continue for longer than was anticipated at the beginning of the millennium, hence explaining the US move toward increasing reliance on the western hemisphere for energy imports.[83]

States of the Former Soviet Union (FSU)

The states of the FSU comprise a major group that has witnessed a significant favorable shift in its gas outlook, with its share in world proven gas reserves increasing from 30.2% in 2001 to 35.8% in 2011. Over the same period its share in world production decreased from 26.5% to 23.7%, and therefore its production and exports are expected to continue for longer than previously projected.[84]

Developments in Unconventional Oil and Gas Production

Liquid fuels can be divided into two categories: first, conventional fuels, which include conventional crude oil in addition to associated gas and condensates. These types of fuel remain economical in production and consumption because their production costs are lower than unconventional sources; second, unconventional fuels, which include the following:

Shale Oil

Shale oil comes from organic residues contained in certain rocks. It is extracted by pyrolysis or hydrogenation of the rocks that contain oil. It is sometimes classified together with 'tight' oil which is trapped between formations of low-permeable rocks, often shale or non-porous sandstone.[85] Recent developments have occurred in the technology used to extract such resources, known as hydraulic fracturing or 'fracking' (fracturing source rock using pressurized liquid). The evolution of this method has made this source of energy more economically viable to exploit, but the technique faces criticism for its environmental impact, in some cases even being linked to earthquakes.[86] It is worth mentioning that the United States of America has around 76% of the world's proven shale oil resources, followed by China with around 7%, and Russia with 5%, as illustrated in Figure 4.8.

372

Figure 4.8

World Shale Oil Resources

(million barrels, and relative shares [%])[87]

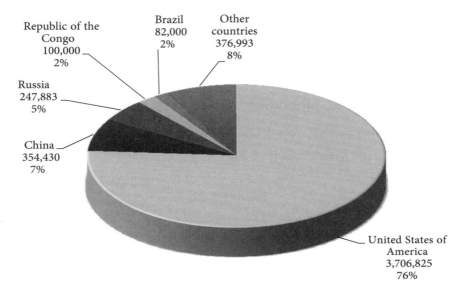

Extra-heavy Oil

This oil is usually found relatively close to the earth's surface, but its physical properties and the resultant difficulties faced in refining it mean that it has traditionally been considered economically unfeasible to exploit. However, current oil prices, as well as the emergence of new technologies – mainly patented by major Western oil companies such as ExxonMobil and Shell – have now made extra-heavy oil economically viable to produce. It is worth noting that Venezuela alone has more than 95% of the world's proven reserves of extra-heavy oil.[88]

Oil Sands: Natural Bitumen

Oil sands comprise a highly viscous mixture of sand, clay, water and petroleum.[89] Oil production from such sources was previously considered economically unfeasible, but new technologies and current oil prices have changed the situation. The bulk of world reserves are found in Canada (70%), and form an increasing proportion of exports to the United States of America. Meanwhile, Kazakhstan holds 17% of world reserves and Russia 12%, as shown in Figure 4.9.

Figure 4.9
World's Oil Sands Reserves
(million barrels, and relative shares [%])[90]

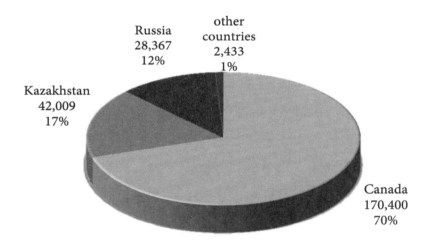

It is clear that the world's most important regions for reserves of unconventional liquids – whose production and consumption have recently become economical – are all in the western hemisphere. The United States of America holds most of the world's known shale oil resources (76%),[91] while Canada has the world's largest oil sands reserves (70%). Venezuela has the largest known extra-heavy oil reserves (more than 95%). It is noticeable that other countries in the Americas have reasonable reserves of these unconventional resources; Brazil, for example, holds 2% of the world's shale oil reserves.[92]

While world production is expected to remain dominated by conventional liquid fuels, their share in total production will decline from 95.4% in 2008 to 90.5% in 2025, and to 88.2% in 2035.[93]

Thus, for a major conventional oil-producing region like the Middle East, concern would not be linked to the decline of global demand for oil, but rather a shift in the relative importance of importers; for example, as the importance of exports to the United States of America decline, the importance of Asian countries as customers could increase. Also, in light of the concentration of 'new' resources in the Americas, and the stated US policy of reducing dependence on Middle Eastern oil since 1973, it is expected that the region's importance as a source of energy will decline, especially given US progress in terms of energy-efficient consumption, the emergence of new technologies, and a growing reliance on natural gas.[94]

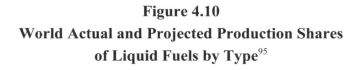

Figure 4.10
**World Actual and Projected Production Shares
of Liquid Fuels by Type**[95]

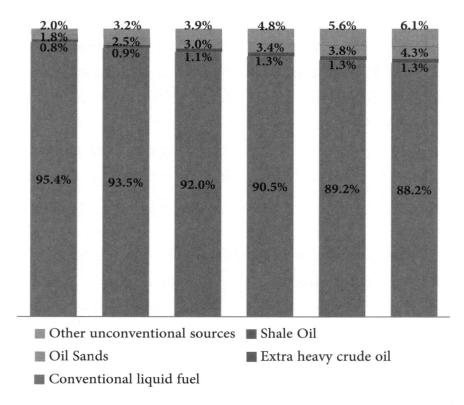

■ Other unconventional sources ■ Shale Oil
■ Oil Sands ■ Extra heavy crude oil
■ Conventional liquid fuel

Note: Shale oil is included in 2030–2035, but in such small proportions that it does not appear prominently in the figure.

Shale Gas and Tight Gas

Natural gas can be divided into two categories, similar to the categorization of liquid fuels. The first is conventional gas; the second is unconventional gas, which includes shale gas and tight gas. Shale and tight gas are trapped between reservoir rocks of very low permeability, but they have recently become economically feasible to exploit using fracking, as explained earlier.[96] This technology has been extremely influential in enabling the United States of America to increase its reliance on natural gas as a source of energy, particularly in electricity production. The US comes second to China in terms of proven reserves of shale gas – 19% and 13% respectively – as illustrated in Figure 4.11.

Figure 4.11

Technically Recoverable Shale Gas Resources from Major Geological Reservoirs (trillion cubic feet, and relative shares)[97]

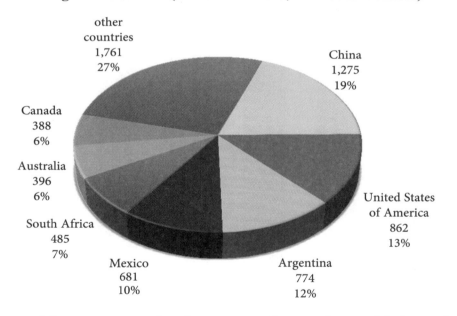

Most unconventional sources of natural gas (shale and tight gas) are found in the Americas. Four counties – the United States of America, Argentina, Mexico and Canada –

together account for about 41% of the total known reserves of shale gas.[98] As with liquid fuels, trends in natural gas production suggest an ongoing dominance of conventional gas over other types, but its share is projected to decrease from 88.2% in 2008 to 85.4% in 2015, 83.1% in 2025, and 81.1% in 2035, as shown in the Figure 4.12.[99]

Figure 4.12
World Actual and Projected Production of Natural Gas According to Production Technique[100] (relative share)

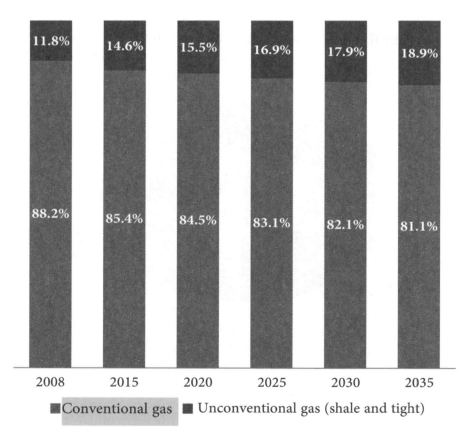

The Future of Energy in Light of Alternative and Renewable Energy Developments

Despite all the talk of a global trend towards reducing dependence on energy generated from fossil fuels – oil, gas and coal – because they are finite and contribute to environmental pollution and global warming, it is unlikely that the next 25 years will see any major change in the energy mix toward greater use of alternative or renewable sources.

Figure 4.13
Share of World Energy Production and Consumption
by Source, 2010/2030 (%)[101]

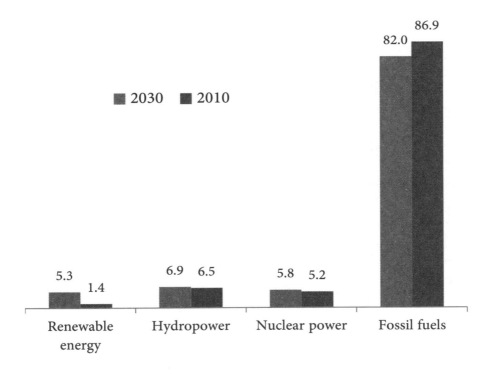

Table 4.4
Share of Energy Production and Consumption
by Region, 2010/2030[102]

	Share of consumption (%)		Share of production (%)	
	2010	2030	2010	2030
Fossil fuels (oil, gas, coal)				
North America	22.7	16.6	19.0	18.1
Central and South America	4.3	5.0	5.6	6.3
Europe and Eurasia	23.0	17.4	21.0	17.0
Middle East	6.8	8.8	15.3	16.9
Africa	3.4	3.9	7.7	7.6
Asia–Pacific	39.8	48.3	31.4	34.2
Nuclear energy				
North America	34.1	23.5	34.1	23.5
Central and South America	0.8	1.2	0.8	1.2
Europe and Eurasia	43.6	31.4	43.6	31.4
Middle East	0.0	0.5	0.0	0.5
Africa	0.5	0.6	0.5	0.6
Asia–Pacific	21.0	42.6	21.0	42.6
Hydropower				
North America	18.9	14.5	18.9	14.5
Central and South America	20.4	20.9	20.4	20.9
Europe and Eurasia	25.2	20.2	25.2	20.2
Middle East	0.5	0.9	0.5	0.9
Africa	2.9	3.9	2.9	3.9
Asia–Pacific	32.1	39.6	32.1	39.6
Renewable energy (wind, solar, etc)				
North America	26.8	21.8	26.8	21.8
Central and South America	6.7	4.2	6.7	4.2
Europe and Eurasia	42.8	29.9	42.8	29.9
Middle East	0.0	1.1	0.0	1.1
Africa	0.8	2.4	0.8	2.4
Asia–Pacific	22.9	40.7	22.9	40.7
Total energy				
North America	23.1	17.2	19.9	18.4
Central and South America	5.2	5.8	6.3	6.9
Europe and Eurasia	24.5	19.1	22.7	18.7
Middle East	6.0	7.4	13.3	14.0
Africa	3.2	3.6	6.9	6.7
Asia–Pacific	38.1	47.0	30.8	35.4

380

According to BP estimates (see Figure 4.13) fossil fuels will remain the primary energy source, with only a minimal decline in their relative global importance from 87% in 2010 to around 82% in 2030.[103] In contrast, dependence on alternative and renewable energy sources is expected to see a limited rise: renewable energy sources (solar energy, wind energy, water, etc.) will rise from 1.4% of total world energy sources in 2010 to about 5.3% in 2030, while nuclear energy will rise from 5.2% in 2010 to 5.8% in 2030, and hydropower will rise slightly from 6.5% in 2010 to 6.9% in 2030.[104] In light of the expected levels of production and consumption of these various sources in major regions of the world by 2030, a number of observations can be drawn, as illustrated in Table 4.4.

Figure 4.14
Expected Change in Energy Production Share
by Region, 2010–2030 (%)[105]

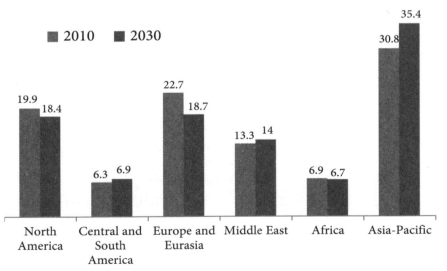

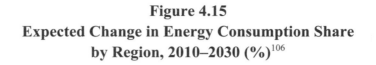

Figure 4.15
Expected Change in Energy Consumption Share
by Region, 2010–2030 (%)[106]

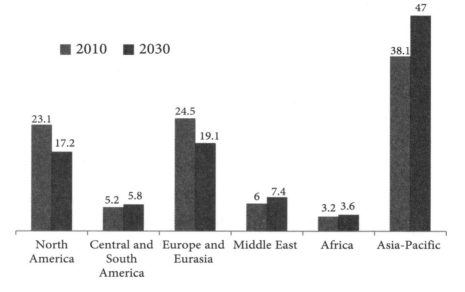

From Table 4.4 the following conclusions may be made:[107]

- North America's share in world energy production and consumption is expected to decrease across all sources between the years 2010 and 2030.[108] However, the decline in its share of world consumption (from 22.7% in 2010 to 16.6% in 2030) is expected to be much greater than in its share of production (from 19.0% in 2010 to 18.1% in 2030). Accordingly, North America is expected to become a net energy exporter by 2030 (this applies mainly to fossil fuels).

- The share of the Asia–Pacific in world consumption is expected to rise sharply. However, it will be severely constrained in its attempts to increase its share of world fossil fuel production, widening the gap between production and consumption and resulting in greater dependence on the rest of the world for energy supplies. Asia–Pacific consumption of fossil fuels is expected to rise from 39.8% of the global total in 2010 to 48.3% in 2030, while its share of world production is expected to witness a limited increase from 31.4% to 34.2% over the same period; this will likely be accompanied by an overall rise in its share of world consumption of all fuel types from 38.1% in 2010 to 47% in 2030, and a limited increase in its share in world production from 30.8% to 35.4% for the same period.[109]

- The contribution of Europe/Eurasia to total world production and consumption of energy from all sources is expected to fall, but the fall in consumption will be substantially more than in production, making it less dependent on the rest of the world for energy. The region's share in world energy consumption is expected to decrease from 24.5% in 2010 to 19.1% in 2030, while its share in world production will decline from 22.7% to 18.7% for the same period, and thus the gap is expected to narrow by 2030.[110]

- The Middle East's share in world energy consumption and production is expected to rise, but the region will remain a net energy producer. Its share of global energy consumption is expected to rise from 6% in 2010 to 7.4% in 2030, while production will increase from 13.3% to 14% for the same period.

- Central America and Africa are expected to become net energy exporters by 2030.

Figure 4.16

Expected Energy Production–Consumption Gap,
2010/2030 (million tons of oil equivalent)[111]

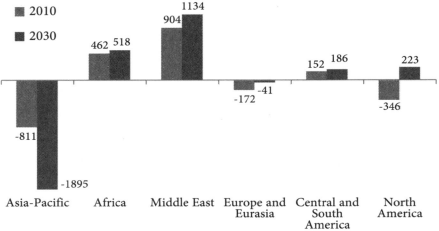

From Table 4.4 and Figure 4.16, a very important conclusion can be drawn with regard to the expected role of energy in the new world order, which is that while the global energy balance in 2010 shows an energy resource deficit in the Asia–Pacific, North America and Europe/Eurasia, and this deficit is adequately covered by sources from the Middle East, Africa and Central and South America, it is expected that by 2030 North America will achieve an energy surplus. The energy deficit in Europe/Eurasia is expected to narrow substantially, while in the Asia–Pacific region it is expected to increase. Therefore global energy markets in 2030 will be characterized by Asia–Pacific imports from the Middle East and Africa. This alignment of interests in the Middle East and Africa and the Asia–Pacific, and the end of American and European/Eurasian dependence on their traditional import sources will likely bring about a significant change in the priorities and nature of the strategic interests of major powers (the United States of America and China in particular) in geographic regions such as the Middle East. It is also likely that access to, and the securing of, energy sources will be a central issue in any indirect conflict that could arise between the United States of America and China (and perhaps India). This raises the possibility of strengthening the US role in the new world order, particularly given its current maritime dominance of the vital sea lanes through which Chinese trade must pass.[112]

Major Oil Companies and the Future of Energy in the New World Order

With the changing global demand for energy, and in light of both the enduring balance of power in terms of technological development among energy producers and other issues such as environmental concerns, there is much debate surrounding the role of major oil companies[113] in the new world order, and whether they will help in shaping that order or begin to decline in the face of energy conservation efforts and shifts toward alternative and renewable energies.

US oil giants such as ExxonMobil have continuously sought to preserve their place among the largest and most profitable companies in the world. In 2005, for example, ExxonMobil made a net profit of \$36.1 billion—the highest ever made.[114] Access to new oil reserves is the greatest strategic challenge facing such companies, forcing them to expand the scope of their interests to encompass development projects in politically unstable areas of Africa and Asia, particularly in those countries whose governments are unable to extract oil themselves.[115] These US companies and their European counterparts – such as Royal Dutch Shell and Total – continue to develop unconventional oil and gas extraction techniques – as noted above – whilst also diversifying in order to take the lead in developing renewable and alternative energies.[116] The technological superiority of Western oil companies compared with their counterparts in China and Russia suggests that these companies will likely retain their leading position for the foreseeable future. Indeed, it seems that there are many countries with unconventional oil and gas reserves that are unable to develop them, as in the case of Venezuela, for example.[117]

As mentioned above, US oil companies in particular are subject to regular bouts of electronic espionage to steal their industry secrets. The West's finger of blame in such cases usually points to Chinese companies seeking to bridge the technological gap and gain a key advantage in boosting their economic power in the new world order.[118] However, Chinese and Russian companies are unlikely to succeed in narrowing the gap with their US and European counterparts, and the West continues to lead the technological race in the development of hydrocarbon, renewable and alternative energies, which is expected to further entrench the dominance of the US position in the world order.

Government Budgets and Public Debt

Over the past 25 years, government budgets – and particularly their chronic deficits and the resulting accumulation of public debt – have played a significant role in shaping the global economic system. Debate on this subject has intensified in recent years in the aftermath of the global financial crisis of 2007 and the consequent financial burdens placed on governments in its wake—particularly those countries forced to expand government spending in order to rescue banks, invigorate their economies, and create jobs to address growing unemployment. This has led to chronic problems in combating the fiscal deficit, and brought to the fore the potential consequences of such high public debt, exemplified by the intractable disagreement between the administration of President Barak Obama and the US Congress that eventually led to a government shutdown in the period October 1–16, 2013.[119]

Ultimately, the countries identified as occupying the higher echelons of the new world order – the United States of America, China, Russia, the EU, Japan, India and Brazil – have all passed through debt crises – or are expected to face major crises in the near future – albeit each with a different set of causes, effects and circumstances.

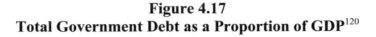

Figure 4.17
Total Government Debt as a Proportion of GDP[120]

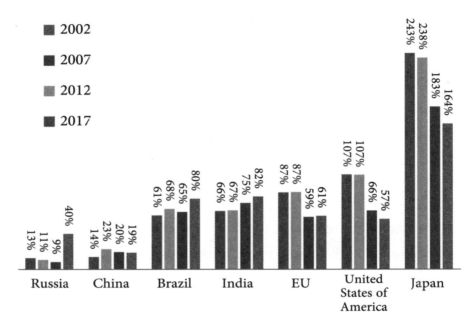

As for the United States of America (which has the largest government debt in the world in terms of value, exceeding $17 trillion for the first time in history on October 17, 2013) the net budget surplus achieved under the administration of William Jefferson "Bill" Clinton, which reached 1.5% of GDP in 2000, was turned into a deficit under the administration of George Walker Bush [Jr.], accompanied by huge military spending on the wars in Iraq and Afghanistan, the total cost of which was estimated to be between \$4 and \$6 trillion, as mentioned previously.[121] By the end of Bush's presidency in 2008, the fiscal deficit had reached 6.7% of GDP, leading to a rise in government debt from \$5.4 trillion in the year before he took office (2000) to \$10.8 trillion when he left.[122]

Following President Barack Hussein Obama's inauguration in 2009, the worsening of the global financial crisis that began in the US real-estate sector in 2007, and the subsequent follow-on effects on government bailout programs for the institutions and companies affected by the crisis and recession, US government debt climbed to \$17.6 trillion in 2013—equivalent to 108% of GDP.[123]

Despite the US debt and budget problems in 2012, including the so-called 'fiscal cliff' which has led to calls for automatic budget cuts to prevent the debt crisis from worsening, the controversy at times appears to comprise more partisan political bickering than actual substance as a crisis.[124] The US debt to GDP ratio is 108%—not as dangerously high as in the case of Japan, for example, which has the highest debt ratio in the world at 245%. Also, although one of the major credit rating agencies, Standard & Poor's,[125] downgraded US government debt on August 5, 2011 from AAA to AA+, two other major rating agencies, Moody's and Fitch, chose not to downgrade US debt. In fact, the cost of borrowing through American treasury bills and bonds has not gone up, but rather continued at levels considered among the lowest historically; hence, treasury bills and bonds have not lost their appeal as safe investment assets for investors, be they government, institutional or private.

Government finances and debt are therefore not expected to be one of the main weaknesses of the US economy over the next decade – provided bipartisan political squabbles can be avoided – especially when compared with the situation of its traditional potential competitors such as certain EU states and Japan. The main issue will remain the bipartisan conflict between the Republicans and Democrats over reducing the public deficit in order to curb the growth of public debt. The Republican Party believes that this could be achieved without imposing further tax burdens on American citizens and companies. As such, they propose the deficit could be reduced through significant cuts in government spending, even on social programs such as health. On the other hand, the Democratic Party sees the need to keep social programs intact, and to reduce the government deficit by increasing tax revenues.[126]

With respect to China, although the central government budget and debt seem quite moderate (China's fiscal deficit stands at 2.1% of GDP in 2013 and public debt representing 21.3% of GDP),[127] the Chinese government faces an altogether different problem relating to government debts at the local level, which have become a source of substantial criticism—for example, in the case of the extravagant spending of local officials on building and furnishing their offices. The latest government audit of 36 local departments in China, carried out in 2012, showed that they had increased their borrowing by 12.9% in just two years, bringing total local government borrowing to $624.6 billion.[128]

The local government debt problem is linked to the financing of this debt through borrowing from the banking system. This has resulted in major concerns about significant negative effects on the banking system resulting from its exposure to government debt, and has recently led to interbank liquidity problems. Since this represents a real threat to the Chinese economy in the near future, it is expected to also affect the orientation of the Chinese government towards financial openness to the outside world, jeopardizing potential foreign investment in financial instruments such as government bonds.

One of the noticeable effects of government finances and public debt on the balance of global power between the United States of America and China is that the latter is one of the largest foreign investors in US bonds.[129] Therefore, the trade/financial relationship between the two countries comprises a Chinese trade surplus and twin US deficits—fiscal and commercial.[130]

As a result of the huge trade surplus achieved by China in its commercial relations with the outside world, it has accumulated a huge financial surplus, of which it lends a substantial portion to the United States of America through the purchase of US government bonds. It seems that this relationship between the first and the second largest economic powers in the world will continue in the future. China has relied on exports as the main driver of its economy, and the United States of America has always depended on the advantage conferred by the dollar being the main global reserve currency, which gives it the unique advantage of being able to borrow without disrupting domestic price levels in the way that other countries might.

With regard to the EU, government finances and the debt crisis in the euro zone will be among the main factors negatively affecting economic strength, although the efforts led by Germany to recover the financial stability of governments and public debt give hope for reducing the risks of further such crises.[131] Historically, although European monetary union has led to the implementation of strict criteria in terms of budget deficits and debt-to-GDP ratios as preconditions for joining the EU, compliance has been lax and various rules have been violated. As a result, excessive government spending in some member countries like Greece and Portugal has led to the accumulation of huge debts.

The global financial crisis, which began in 2007, and the high cost of servicing debt, along with growing fears of default in light of the resultant economic slowdown, have all led to the inability of countries like Greece to service their debts. By the end of March 2013, Greek debt reached the highest level in the

EU at 160.5% of GDP.[132] The EU in general faces difficult choices on how to address this crisis. On one hand, the debt crisis has revealed the divergence between the financially conservative countries of the north – led by Germany – and the very clearly less financially conservative countries of the south. This has resulted in the following outcomes. First, the EU faced two choices: financial cooperation and collaboration in the absence of fiscal union between all member states and a lack of specific mechanisms to rescue states from government debt problems; or the expulsion of some countries from the Union, thereby risking its collapse. On the other hand, the most economically powerful and financially prudent country, Germany, has become the real leader of the Union in an economic sense, although this has raised criticism and objection – and even feelings of hatred – towards Germany in a number of the countries suffering financial problems.

Given the internal divisions within the EU over the need for fiscal union and collaboration, and the response of some countries – particularly those with strong financial positions – to the demands of their people that taxpayers should not foot the bill of excessive spending in other countries of the Union, the situation remains complicated and is expected to endure for some time. This will negatively affect the prospects for growth and will cast a shadow over the worsening unemployment – particularly among the young – in many member countries of the Union, which has reached record highs in countries such as

Greece (where youth unemployment hit 58.7% on July 31, 2013), and Spain (where it has reached 56.1%).[133]

In Japan too, government finances and public debt are fraught with complexity, as the country faces the highest ratio of government debt to GDP in the world (around 245% in 2013,[134] albeit about 95% of this debt is owned by local Japanese investors).[135] This extremely high ratio (by any international standard) has endured for a long time. In the midst of the continuing economic slowdown in Japan and the efforts of the new Japanese government to stimulate the economy through unconventional fiscal and monetary policies, debt reduction is expected to be one of the top priorities of the government in the near future. Although Japan still maintains investment-grade credit ratings from the three major rating agencies,[136] failure to find a sustainable solution to its economic problems could pose a significant risk to Japan's place in the new world order.

With respect to the three remaining countries – Russia, Brazil and India, which alongside China and South Africa form the BRICS group of the most significant emerging economies – some have witnessed historical financial problems. Russia faced a financial crisis in 1998 as a result of poor government finances, and the ensuing debt problems caused a significant decline in the value of the Russian currency, the ruble, which in turn resulted in excessive rates of inflation for a longer period.[137] Brazil also experienced a similar crisis during the 1990s as a result of irrational government spending causing a large fiscal deficit which was financed by local and external borrowing. This eventually led to a loss of confidence in the economy, a decline in the exchange rate of the national currency, and very high rates of inflation.[138] As a result of these problems and their severe economic and social impacts, these states can be expected to be keen to ensure the stability of government finances in the future and keep public debt within acceptable levels for fear of repeating past mistakes. Therefore, this experience is expected to set these countries on a path toward financial improvement in the future.

Trade and Transport

The role of external trade varies in importance among the major countries and groups which are expected to occupy the three top tiers in the structure of the new world order, in a manner that might reveal some potential strengths and weaknesses of the powers in the hierarchy presented in this book.

Considering imports of goods and services as a percentage of GDP in the aforementioned group of powers, the most dependent on the outside world as a driver of economic activity are the EU, China and Russia, while the United States of America is less dependent on the outside world—consequently, it is increasingly self-reliant, and therefore it is not surprising that financial and economic crises often originate from inside the United States of America and then, due to the relative size of the US economy, spread to other countries and regions that are more externally dependent, such as Europe. Similarly, the solution to such crises can also generally be found within the United States of America, through fiscal and monetary policies primarily designed to stimulate domestic demand for both consumption and investment—an uptick in US economic activity will generally have positive effects on many countries around the world.

Figure 4.18
Imports of Goods and Services
(% of GDP)[139]

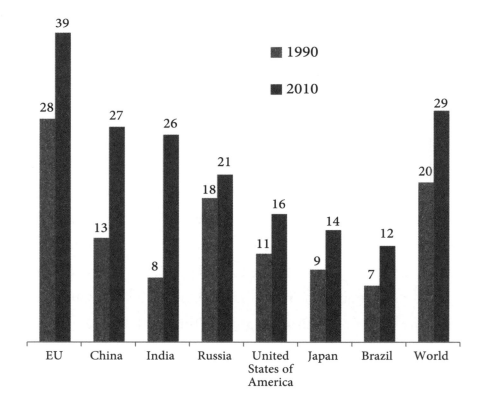

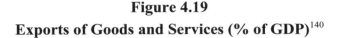

Figure 4.19
Exports of Goods and Services (% of GDP)[140]

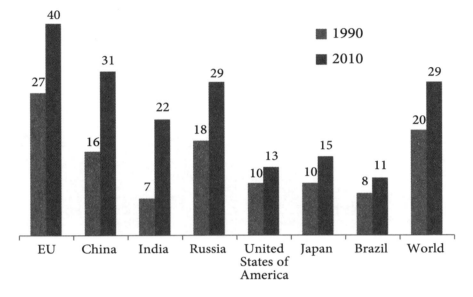

By examining the major trade partners of the top tier of the new world order, it appears that the prominent US partners are its two neighbors, Canada and Mexico, in addition to the EU, China and Japan. As for China, its largest trade partners are the United States of America and the EU in terms of imports. However, with the prospect of the largest ever free trade area being established between the US and EU at the beginning of 2014, China is expected to be strongly disadvantaged due to its dependence on exports to both. In addition, with current moves towards creating new economic blocs, and growing awareness among industrialized countries of the negative effects of China's excessive reliance on exports, the rapid growth of the Chinese economy is likely to be constrained in the new order.

Table 4.5
Major Trade Partners[141]

	Exports (%)		Imports (%)	
European Union	United States of America	17.0	China	17.3
	China	8.9	Russia	11.8
	Switzerland	8.0	United States of America	10.9
	Russia	7.1	Norway	5.5
	Turkey	4.7	Switzerland	5.5
Brazil	European Union	20.7	European Union	20.5
	China	17.3	United States of America	15.1
	United States of America	10.1	China	14.5
	Argentina	8.9	Argentina	7.5
	Japan	3.7	South Korea	4.5
China	European Union	18.8	European Union	12.1
	United States of America	17.1	Japan	11.2
	Hong Kong	14.1	South Korea	9.3
	Japan	7.8	Taiwan	7.2
	South Korea	4.4	United States of America	7.1
India	European Union	18.1	China	12.0
	United Arab Emirates	12.4	European Union	11.9
	United States of America	10.9	United Arab Emirates	7.7
	China	5.5	Switzerland	6.8
	Singapore	5.2	Saudi Arabia	6.1
Japan	China	19.7	China	21.5
	United States of America	15.5	European Union	9.4
	European Union	11.7	United States of America	8.9
	South Korea	8.0	Australia	6.6
	Taiwan	6.2	Saudi Arabia	5.9
Russia	European Union	44.4	European Union	40.3
	China	6.7	China	15.7
	Belarus	4.8	Ukraine	6.5
	Ukraine	3.5	Japan	4.9
	United States of America	3.0	Belarus	4.7
United States of America	Canada	19.0	China	18.4
	European Union	18.2	European Union	16.6
	Mexico	13.3	Canada	14.1
	China	7.0	Mexico	11.7
	Japan	4.5	Japan	5.9

398

Regarding the international trade balance between major countries and groups, the United States of America maintains a current account deficit, in contrast to the surpluses in China, Japan, Russia and the EU. Nonetheless, the overall EU surplus does not reflect the position of its individual members, since current accounts vary drastically from one country to another—Germany has a substantial surplus, while other countries, such as the United Kingdom, France and Italy, have deficits.

Figure 4.20

Current Account Balance (% of GDP)[142]

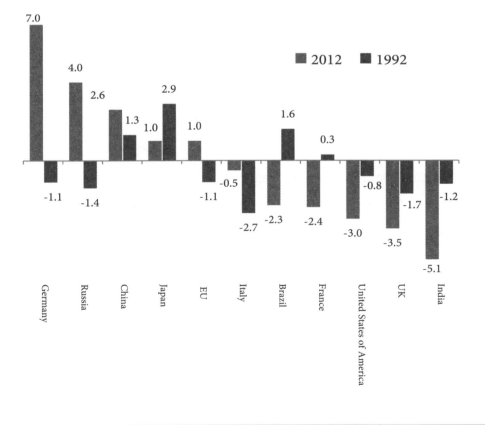

In terms of transport infrastructure and logistics, one of the most important developments that may affect the balance of power in the new world order would be the pursuit of new shipping routes for the main flows of international trade – including energy resources – away from international crisis zones. With the ongoing unrest in the Middle East, against the backdrop of the Iranian nuclear threat and escalating terrorist and extremist activities, and the inevitable resultant rises in the costs of insurance and shipping through major traditional waterways, it is not surprising that a Panama Canal expansion project was launched in 1999;[143] on completion, this will significantly affect the flow and cost of trade, and the links between West and East. The project seeks to double the capacity of the Canal by 2015, creating a new lane of traffic allowing larger ships to transit through this vital waterway, and in greater numbers. As a result, the cargo volume transiting the Canal is expected to grow by about 5% per annum to reach double the 2005 tonnage by 2025.[144] If this expansion succeeds in increasing the volume of traffic and the types of ships that can transit through the Canal, it will have a considerable impact in boosting US economic capabilities—and possibly military capabilities as well. The United States of America will have greater control over major navigation zones in the world, enabling it to reduce both the time and cost of the shipment of goods, and perhaps energy and military equipment, between the western and eastern hemispheres.

In China, where debate continues over whether the country is able to compete with the United States of America for the leading position in the hierarchy of the new world order, efforts are being made to find a solution to its weaknesses relative to the world's only superpower; namely, limited access to international sea and land transport lines. China is linking its railway network with that of Europe – and potentially the Middle East – in what has become known as the 'Iron Silk Road,' which will provide a means of transport at one third of the current cost of shipping.[145]

China is also working to find an outlet to the Indian Ocean in order to facilitate its access to oil resources in the Arabian Gulf by cooperating with Pakistan in the development and operation of Gwadar port, which some analysts argue could come to represent a Chinese naval base in the Indian Ocean.[146]

Also, China announced two major collaborative construction projects in Latin America in June 2013, both of which rival the Panama Canal expansion project. The first project, with an estimated cost of $20 billion, will see China construct a railway line in Honduras linking the Pacific and Atlantic coasts.[147] The second project is the construction of the Nicaragua Canal, which a Chinese developer will construct, together with an oil pipeline, two deep-water ports, a railway line and two airports. The estimated cost of the project is $40 billion; however, it has been proposed several times before without reaching the implementation stage.[148] Therefore, given the limited chances of success of these projects, as well as their limited global impact, it is unlikely that China will be able to catch up with the United States of America in terms of easy access and control over international maritime trade routes in the new world order, at least in the short or medium terms.

Conclusion

Throughout history, major economic events have understandably played a role in determining the rise and fall of major world powers and led to consequences that have changed the course of the formation of the world order. Some countries and international groups have risen to prominence and influence against the backdrop of key events such as the Great Depression, which began following the Wall Street stock market crash. The aftermath of the Great Depression contributed to the outbreak of World War II, which ended with the implementation of the Marshall Plan for the reconstruction of Europe, forming an important basis for an increasing global role of the United States of America in peacetime. The balance of global power has also been affected by economic events, such as the Bretton Woods Agreement governing the reconstruction of the post-war global financial order. The Agreement resulted in the establishment of international economic institutions through which a number of major countries exercised influence, particularly through the intervention of the International Monetary Fund (IMF) and the World Bank in developing countries' macroeconomic reform processes. In addition, particular events – such as the oil shocks of the 1970s, the economic crises experienced in the former Soviet Union and Eastern Europe, the creation of the European Union and the eurozone and its ensuing crises – have led to dramatic changes in international relations.

Taking into consideration the historical importance of economic factors in shaping the world order, an in-depth analysis of the key economic factors confirm the current hierarchy of powers in the new world order suggested in this study. With regard to economic growth, it may be noted that despite the spectacular expansion and rise of the Chinese economy during the past two decades, it is still only half the size of that of the United States of America, and remains in the league of developing countries in terms of its average per capita GDP. Furthermore, the US economy is flexible and highly reliant on internal forces and innovation for growth, as opposed to China's dependence on foreign investment and the exploitation of a low-cost labor advantage in export-oriented industries. These factors could make China more vulnerable to any future adverse economic shocks, especially if labor costs rise significantly. As for other major powers in the new world order, there are still doubts as to the possibility of the European Union and Japan achieving a growth performance that would warrant a rise in their relative influence at the expense of other powers. However, it is possible that the relative power of the Russian Federation, India and Brazil may rise – but in a limited fashion – if they are able to overcome the obstacles to achieving sustainable economic growth.

Developments in the energy sector in particular are expected to have a significant impact on the ranking of powers in the new world order. The rising independence of the United States of America in energy production – thanks to its exploitation of shale gas and oil resources, and its gradual shift to a reliance on unconventional energy sources from the western hemisphere (the Americas) – will give it a strong comparative advantage in the future. By the same token, energy is expected to be an area of relative weakness for powers such as China, India and Japan, in which energy consumption is rising significantly along with economic growth, rendering them more dependent on regions that may be relatively unstable, such the Middle East and Africa. As for the European Union and Russia, their energy interdependence will increase, with growing exports by the latter and rising imports by the former.

In addition, other economic factors such as governments' financial positions, trade and transport/logistics capabilities are expected to support a relative rise in US economic power, especially given the aim of the United States of America and the European Union to establish the world's largest free trade area. This could have tangible negative effects on emerging economies such as China and India. Moreover, the Panama Canal expansion is expected to boost US commercial maritime transport between East and West.

Jamal Sanad Al-Suwaidi

PUBLIC OPINION AND THE NEW WORLD ORDER: A SURVEY OF THE UAE POPULATION

Chapter V

Public Opinion and the New World Order: A Survey of the UAE Population

Public opinion polling seeks to identify prevailing opinions or beliefs among large segments of the public – whether citizens or expatriates – toward a certain social, cultural, economic or political issue of a local, national, regional or international nature.[1] Polls generally aim to achieve a number of targets, including the following:

- They provide the necessary information to formulate policies for adoption in various sectors. They also provide decision-makers with a picture of social, economic, political, cultural and educational conditions, before certain policies are applied. Polls also contribute to assessing the efficacy of such policies, and to what extent they accomplish their objectives following their implementation; hence, polls are considered a tool for community development.[2]

- Polls are also seen as a means to develop and enhance good governance, first by allowing political leaders and decision-makers to become better informed, providing them with a more detailed understanding of the needs and aspirations of the public, thereby increasing confidence between the public and both their leaders and institutions, and contributing to maintaining political stability in the community.[3] Second, polls provide decision-makers, researchers, or those interested in community issues (such as the media and others seeking objective information) with data on social topics and phenomena, such as unemployment, health care, education, etc., helping them to identify problems, set priorities, and ensure better management of the processes of economic and social development. They also give voice to every individual in the community to freely express their opinion on public affairs.

- Opinion polls produce a necessary body of data, upon which researchers may test their knowledge and theoretical models. Surveys and opinion polls are methodological tools adopted by all branches of the humanities and social sciences – political science, sociology, economics, demography, etc. – and are used to test hypotheses and interpret differences in attitudes, values, behavior, or understanding.

Until recently, opinion polls exploring these aspects of Arab countries were rare – especially in the GCC states – and limited either to individuals, or to researchers at a handful of universities.[4] Most foreign researchers[5] in the Arab region complain of the scarcity of surveys and opinion polls conducted since the 1970s. This lack of field research and polling data has given rise to simplistic and reductionist approaches to the reality of society and politics in the Arab and Muslim world, which are not based on objective scientific data but on stereotypical misconceptions of Arab society and culture. These stereotypes are frequently repeated in the Western media, and are mostly centered on the backwardness of the Arab reality and culture compared to the West, despite the presence of sophisticated cases of Arab development refuting and entirely undermining such notions—particularly in states such as the United Arab Emirates.[6]

These stereotypes paint individuals in Arab and Muslim societies as identical—a collective bloc holding uniform ideas and values governed by religion, customs, traditions, heritage and culture, and without any opinion other than that which their rulers or religious leaders provide them; hence, some posit that there is no utility in conducting polls in this region. This view served to delay research on Arab communities, and limited the intellectual product of researchers from the Arab region.[7] Beginning in the 1990s, change occurred in some Arab countries where it became possible for local think tanks and institutions to conduct field research that included questions about political culture, sometimes in coordination with global think tanks and institutions. For example, as part of its research activities, the Emirates Center for Strategic Studies and Research (ECSSR) in Abu Dhabi plays a vital role in identifying trends in local public opinion in the UAE regarding various local, regional and international issues.[8]

Since the terrorist attacks of September 11, 2001, interest in the Arab and Islamic world has increased significantly, as have the number and scope of opinion polls conducted by Arab governments, non-governmental organizations (NGOs), Western research centers and public opinion research units. These polls have aimed to correct the overwhelmingly narcissistic[9] emphasis of the first wave of post-September 11 surveys carried out by American organizations, which sought to gauge how Arabs feel about America, its policies and leaders; in short, how Arabs feel about the issues Americans care about. These polls produced results, but without any sense of the extent to which the issues mattered to the respondents. For instance, survey research has consistently found that economic and quality of life issues – rather than American policies or politics – are foremost among Arab concerns.[10]

This study attempts to uncover the views of the UAE public regarding the new world order, and to go beyond generalizations to interpret and explain various related opinions and attitudes. The focus will be on variables such as nationality, age – particularly the 18–40 and 40+ age groups – gender and education. These variables were selected to explain the potential variation in opinions and attitudes toward the attributes of the new world order. Moreover, the historical circumstances and events the region has witnessed – and continues to witness – will also have a bearing on the public's views and perceptions in the UAE.

One of the hypotheses of this study is that the political circumstances and events witnessed since the end of the Cold War, both in the region and worldwide, have contributed to the opinion of the population of the UAE – both citizens and non-citizens – and of other states toward the new world order, its principles, institutions and future. Significant events experienced in the region in recent times that have had major effects on the views of the population include the US occupation of Iraq in 2003, as well as the resulting regional power imbalance and ongoing sectarian conflict and tension. The other significant event was the US-led war in Afghanistan against al-Qaeda after the September 11 attacks. The US economy has been affected by these wars, which played significant roles in the 2007 financial crisis that spread beyond the United States of America to become a global financial downturn affecting numerous major economies. There is also no doubt that the so-called 'Arab Awakening,' which has been ongoing since 2011, has also influenced public opinion in the Arab world, for example, through the bloody conflict in Syria and the positions of the major powers in this regard. Also worthy of note is the rising economic role of emerging powers such as India and Brazil. These events and transformations have produced various strategic effects, creating a state of uncertainty about the new world order and the nature of the actors within it that resonates among the UAE public.

The cultural and economic openness and diversity that characterizes the UAE population – including citizens and non-citizens – make it an ideal model to study trends in world public opinion. Indeed, this mosaic of nationalities provides a rare opportunity to identify the impact of interaction between peoples in terms of their views and attitudes toward the prevailing value system in the new world order. Thus, significant conclusions can be reached regarding the long-standing hypotheses promoted by international relations theorists about the effects of globalization and freedom of travel and movement, as well as the social impacts of free-market economy, expatriate labor and its implications for existing cultures and values, and other concepts such as global citizenship. The UAE is an important model for identifying the economic potential for resolving the prevailing debate among researchers regarding the relationship between civilizations and cultures, particularly in light of its well-established model of humanitarianism and tolerance that dissuades civilizational or cultural antagonism and dissonance.

Methodology

The survey targeted citizens and non-citizens of the UAE aged 18 years and above, with multi-stage sample data being collected from a random sample of 1,500 residents of the UAE. The survey was designed in several stages by dividing the sample into different 'strata,' in accordance with the variables of the study. The population was identified according to place of residence (Emirate), nationality (UAE, Arab, Asian or Western), gender, age group (18–40 years old or above 40 years old), and finally according to education level (secondary or below, diploma or university, and postgraduate). The sample was designed to fully represent the population of the UAE through proportional representation of all segments of society according to the relative weight of each segment of the UAE population. A Z-test was applied to identify the differences between the response rates of the different groups in the sample. A Z-test is a statistical significance test for a group's differences in large samples that are normally distributed. The response rate was 98.7% and confidence in the results was 95%, with a 2.5% margin of error.

Field interviews were conducted with respondents from June 23 to July 3, 2013, in which the purpose of the study was explained using a specially prepared questionnaire (Appendix III). The questionnaire was distributed to respondents to complete, expressing their opinions without any influence or interference from those collecting or supervising the collection of data. It was designed to answer the questions and hypotheses raised by the study, and to achieve its goals. A pilot test of the survey was conducted in the field in which the questionnaire was distributed to a small sample of 150 respondents. Data from this small sample was not included in the results or analysis. The validity of both the content and construct of the questionnaire were tested, as was its reliability and consistency, using Cronbach's alpha. All the tests showed that the questionnaire was suitable for the purposes of the study.[11]

The quality of data collected in the field was verified after being validated and cleaned in SPSS (Statistical Package for the Social Sciences) statistics software to ensure accuracy, consistency, uniformity and integrity. The questionnaire aimed to gauge the attitudes and views of the UAE population on the new world order, its principles, institutions and prospects, and attempted to identify and explain any discrepancies.

Demographic Variables

The study sample comprised 1,500 individuals satisfying a number of demographic variables of interest to the study, as illustrated in Figure 5.1.

Nationality: nationality was selected as one of the most important variables in the study owing to its significance in forming the opinion of individuals on matters of international relations. If the state is the basic unit in the system of relations between countries, its position in the new world order will affect the opinion of individuals belonging to that state. With regard to this questionnaire, the nationality factor will add an international dimension to the study, enabling comparisons between nationalities. The proportion of UAE citizens in the sample is 35.9%, while Arabs account for 27.6%, Asians account for 28.5%, and Westerners 8.0%.

Figure 5.1
Demographic Variables of the Sample (%)
(Gender, Age Group, Nationality, Area of Residence, Educational Level)

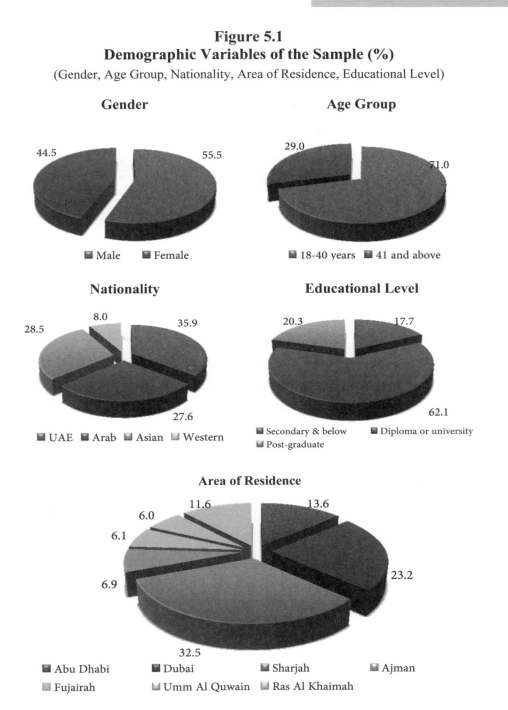

Gender

44.5   55.5

⬛ Male   ⬛ Female

Age Group

29.0   71.0

⬛ 18-40 years   ⬛ 41 and above

Nationality

8.0
28.5   35.9
27.6

⬛ UAE ⬛ Arab ⬛ Asian ⬛ Western

Educational Level

20.3   17.7
62.1

⬛ Secondary & below   ⬛ Diploma or university
⬛ Post-graduate

Area of Residence

11.6   13.6
6.0
6.1
6.9   23.2
32.5

⬛ Abu Dhabi   ⬛ Dubai   ⬛ Sharjah   ⬛ Ajman
⬛ Fujairah   ⬛ Umm Al Quwain ⬛ Ras Al Khaimah

Gender: the gender variable is important in social studies, especially those concerned with political aspects of social relations, as several studies have shown that male and female attitudes and interests differ in political affairs in general and in international politics in particular. The percentage of males in the sample is 55.5%, while the percentage of females is 44.5%.

Age: differences in opinion are expected to occur based on age. In this study, we used generation as the unit of analysis, given that each generation has its own experiences and circumstances which affect its way of thinking and attitude toward life. The 18–30 age group represented 34% of the sample; 31–40 year-olds represented 37%; those aged 41–50 represented 19.7%; and finally, those 51 years old and above accounted for 9.3%. At a later stage of the analysis the first and second age groups were merged, as were the third and fourth, producing two categories (18–40 at 71% of the sample; above 40 years at 29%).

Education level: there is no doubt that education plays a pivotal role in determining an individual's stance, expectations, interest in, and knowledge of international political affairs. Therefore, one may expect to see discrepancies in views on the issues raised in this survey based on the educational level of the respondents. The proportion of respondents who had completed secondary education (or below) was 17.7% of the sample, while those with diplomas or university degrees accounted for 62.1%, and respondents with postgraduate degrees accounted for 20.3%.

Place of residence: for the purposes of this study the place of residence was divided by Emirate, with Abu Dhabi accounting for 32.5% of the sample, Dubai for 13.6%, Sharjah 23.2%, Ajman, Fujairah and Umm Al-Quwain for 6.9%, 6.1%, and 6%, respectively, and finally Ras Al Khaimah accounted for 11.6%.

The questionnaire collected data on a number of themes: the extent to which respondents followed world affairs; their knowledge about the organizations and institutions of the new world order; the extent of their trust in those institutions; their viewpoint on the need for reform of such institutions and an expansion in their powers; opinions on the role of new world order institutions; the problems facing the world order that they considered to be most significant; attitudes toward globalization; the future of the new world order itself; and, finally, their opinions on the roles of young people and the internet in the new world order.

Results

Interest in World Affairs

A large proportion of respondents showed an interest in world news, with 80.5% of them stating that they followed world news, of which 38.4% always followed world news. A very small percentage (1.2%) claimed never to follow international news, whilst 18.3% occasionally followed world news.

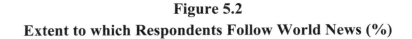

Figure 5.2
Extent to which Respondents Follow World News (%)

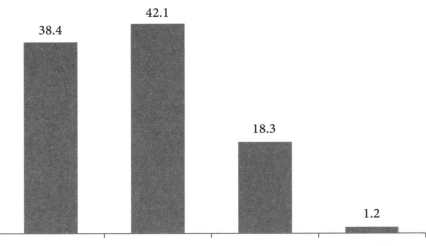

This high rate of interest in world news can be attributed to several factors, including the welcoming nature of the UAE – which is home to residents of around 200 different nationalities – and its cultural and ethnic diversity, which is not available in other countries.[12] The diversity of this sample reflects the variety and multicultural nature of respondents' interests, as residents of different nationalities follow news about their countries of origin as well as international news that directly or indirectly affects their status in the country hosting them. The other factor at play is how the era of globalization is characterized by an abundance of information and news flowing via several trans-border media channels.

Table 5.1
Demographic Breakdown of
World News Consumption (%)

Variable	Average	Gender		Nationality				Age Group		Educational Qualification		
		Male	Female	UAE	Arab	Asian	Western	18–40 years	Above 40 years	Secondary & below	Diploma or University	Post-graduate
Always follow	38.4	47.0	27.7	25.0	36.5	48.8	67.8	34.5	47.1	30.9	36.3	50.3
Often follow	42.1	37.6	47.6	45.9	43.8	39.8	28.0	42.9	40.5	40.1	44.2	36.3
Occasionally follow	18.3	14.5	23.0	26.3	19.2	11.2	4.2	21.1	11.7	29.0	18.4	12.7
Never follow	1.2	.9	1.7	2.8	.5	.2	0.0	1.5	0.7	0.0	1.1	0.7

Differences within the demographic variables showed significant variance according to gender, nationality, age and education. In terms of gender, males were more interested than females in following world news, as 84.7% of males said that they followed world news compared to 75.3% of females. This result confirms previous conclusions in international studies and polls on political culture,[13] in which it has been found that females are generally less interested in following politics in general, and particularly international politics.

In terms of nationality, Westerners were most interested in following world news (95.8% said they followed world news compared to 88.6% of Asians, 80.3% of Arabs, and 70.9% of UAE nationals).

Figure 5.3
Extent to which Respondents Follow World News
by Demographic Variable (%)

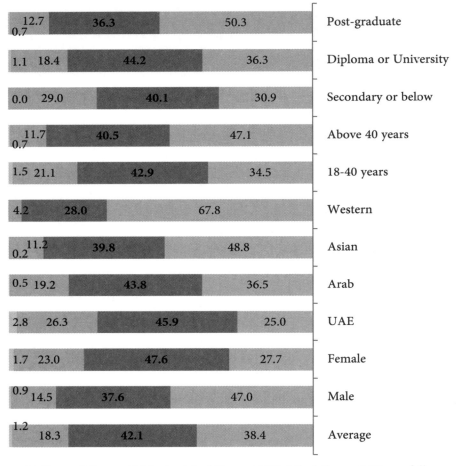

| | Always follow | Moderately follow | Slightly follow | Never follow |

In terms of age groups, the higher the age the more interest was reported in following world news—77.4% of 18–40 year olds said they followed world news, compared to 87.6% of those above 40.

In terms of respondents' levels of education, the survey found that those educated to postgraduate level were most interested in following world news, with 50.3% always following world news, compared to 36.3% of diploma or university degree holders, and 30.9% of those educated to secondary level or below.

Table 5.2
Choice of News Media
by Demographic Variable (%)

Variable	Average*	Gender		Nationality				Age Group		Educational Qualification		
		Male	Female	UAE	Arab	Asian	Westerner	18–40 years	Above 40 years	Secondary & below	Diploma or university	Higher Education
TV	72.6	74.8	71.5	76.5	76.6	67.5	66.4	66.1	73.5	78.3	71.5	74.5
Websites	43.3	45.1	41.8	39.6	47.9	43.9	46.2	41.3	45.1	38.3	42.1	54.4
Newspapers	41.1	45.5	36.6	36.3	35.3	48.9	59.7	34.3	41.6	35.7	40.3	50.3
Radio	28.0	31.4	24.2	23.9	23.7	34.2	42.0	25.5	28.8	24.3	28.5	30.2
Social Media	26.0	23.3	30.6	29.8	25.4	21.4	31.9	32.9	26.8	21.7	29.2	24.2

* Totals do not equal 100%, as respondents were free to choose more than one response.

Choice of Media

With regard to the media through which UAE residents chose to follow world news, television accounted for 72.6%, websites 43.3%, newspapers 41.1%, radio 28%, and social media 26.0%.

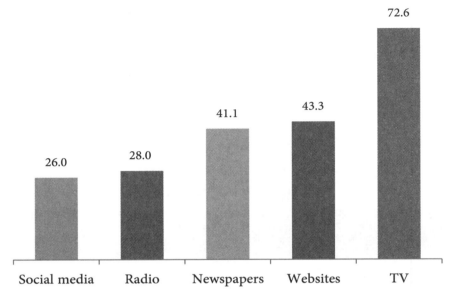

Figure 5.4
World News: Respondents' Choice of Media in General (%)

In determining media preferences by demographic, significant differences were found among all variables (gender, nationality, age and education).

The use of television as a means of receiving world news is higher among Arabs and the UAE citizens (76.6% and 76.5% respectively) than other nationalities. Also, males are more likely to receive news via television (74.8%) than females (71.5%), as are those above 40 years old (73.5%) compared to 18–40 year-olds (66.1%). Moreover, television usage is higher among those with secondary school or below qualifications (78.3%) than those with university degrees (71.5%) or postgraduate qualifications (74.5%).

Figure 5.5
Respondents' Choice of Media
by Demographic Variable (%)

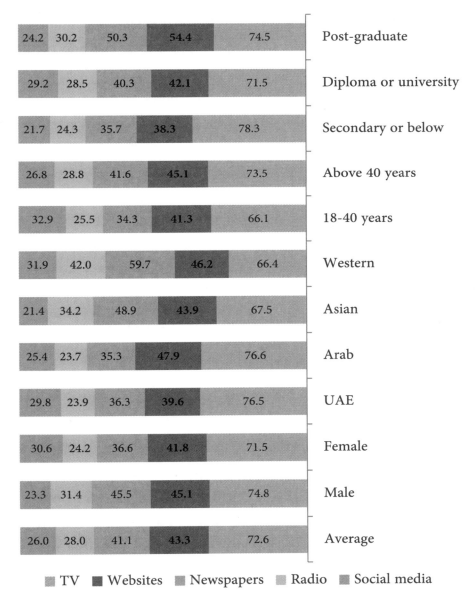

24.2	30.2	50.3	54.4	74.5	Post-graduate
29.2	28.5	40.3	42.1	71.5	Diploma or university
21.7	24.3	35.7	38.3	78.3	Secondary or below
26.8	28.8	41.6	45.1	73.5	Above 40 years
32.9	25.5	34.3	41.3	66.1	18-40 years
31.9	42.0	59.7	46.2	66.4	Western
21.4	34.2	48.9	43.9	67.5	Asian
25.4	23.7	35.3	47.9	76.6	Arab
29.8	23.9	36.3	39.6	76.5	UAE
30.6	24.2	36.6	41.8	71.5	Female
23.3	31.4	45.5	45.1	74.8	Male
26.0	28.0	41.1	43.3	72.6	Average

■ TV   ■ Websites   ■ Newspapers   ■ Radio   ■ Social media

The use of websites as a source of world news is higher among males (45.1%) than females (41.8%), among Arabs (47.9%) than UAE nationals (39.6%), among those in the higher education category (54.4%) than the secondary education or below category (38.3%), and among those over the age of 40 years (45.1%) compared to 18–40 year-olds (41.3%).

The use of social media to follow news is more common among females than males (30.6% vs. 23.3%), among Westerners (31.9%) over Asians (21.4%), as well as among those aged below 40 (32.9%) over those in the above 40 years category (26.8%), and among holders of university degrees (29.2%) over holders of secondary-level education or below (21.7%).

The remarkable aspect of these findings is that the percentage of those who follow news websites (43.3%) exceeded that of those who receive their news via newspapers (41.1%), and that the relative importance of radio has declined (28.0%).

Knowledge about New World Order Institutions

Knowledge about, and trust in the United Nations: when respondents were asked about the extent of their knowledge regarding the institutions of the new world order, 74.0% said they knew about the UN, with 30.6% of the sample claiming good knowledge, and 43.4% fair knowledge. 78.9% of males and 67.8% of females said they had good or fair knowledge of the UN. Westerners were the most knowledgeable about the UN (87.4%), while 64.1% of UAE nationals reported good or fair knowledge of the institution.

Figure 5.6
Knowledge about the UN
by Demographic Variable (%)

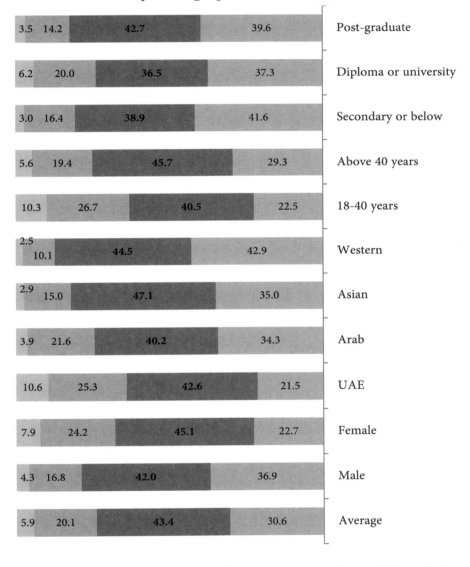

3.5	14.2	42.7	39.6	Post-graduate
6.2	20.0	36.5	37.3	Diploma or university
3.0	16.4	38.9	41.6	Secondary or below
5.6	19.4	45.7	29.3	Above 40 years
10.3	26.7	40.5	22.5	18-40 years
2.5 / 10.1	44.5	42.9		Western
2.9 / 15.0	47.1	35.0		Asian
3.9	21.6	40.2	34.3	Arab
10.6	25.3	42.6	21.5	UAE
7.9	24.2	45.1	22.7	Female
4.3	16.8	42.0	36.9	Male
5.9	20.1	43.4	30.6	Average

■ Good knowledge ■ Fair knowledge ■ Little knowledge ■ No knowledge

Knowledge about the UN among those aged above 40 years was 75%, compared to 63% among 18–40 year olds. Those with postgraduate qualifications were more knowledgeable regarding the UN (82.3%) than those with a university degree or diploma (73.8%).

The difference in the levels of knowledge regarding new world order institutions in general between gender and age group confirmed the findings of previous international studies.[14]

Indeed, a differences test revealed significant differences across all demographic variables (gender, nationality, age and educational qualification). When the respondents were asked to what extent they trusted the institutions of the new world order, their trust in the UN was 68.5% (15.7% highly trusted and 52.8% generally trusted).

71.4% of males and 64.8% of females expressed trust in the United Nations. Westerners were most likely to trust the UN (90.7%), while Arabs were least likely to trust the organization (57.4%).

Those in the 40+ age group showed greater trust in the UN (67.8%) than 18–40 year-olds (64%). Trust in the UN was also found to be higher among those educated to secondary level or below than holders of university degrees, at 74.6% and 67.3%, respectively.

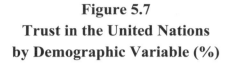

Figure 5.7
Trust in the United Nations
by Demographic Variable (%)

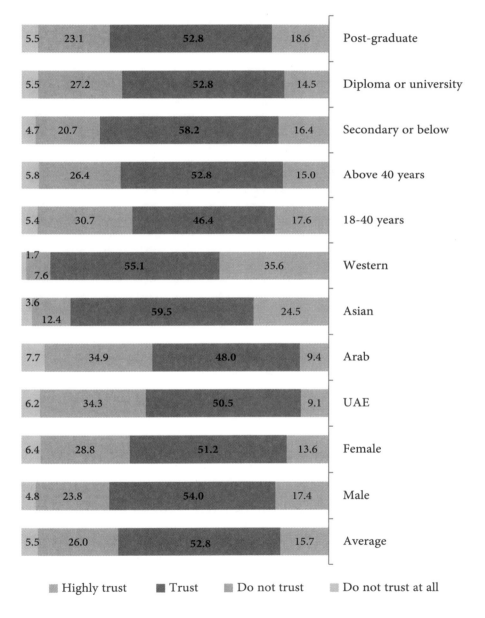

5.5 23.1 **52.8** 18.6		Post-graduate
5.5 27.2 **52.8** 14.5		Diploma or university
4.7 20.7 **58.2** 16.4		Secondary or below
5.8 26.4 **52.8** 15.0		Above 40 years
5.4 30.7 **46.4** 17.6		18-40 years
1.7 7.6 **55.1** 35.6		Western
3.6 12.4 **59.5** 24.5		Asian
7.7 34.9 **48.0** 9.4		Arab
6.2 34.3 **50.5** 9.1		UAE
6.4 28.8 **51.2** 13.6		Female
4.8 23.8 **54.0** 17.4		Male
5.5 26.0 **52.8** 15.7		Average

Highly trust ■ Trust ■ Do not trust ■ Do not trust at all

Figure 5.8
Knowledge about the UN Security Council
by Demographic Variable (%)

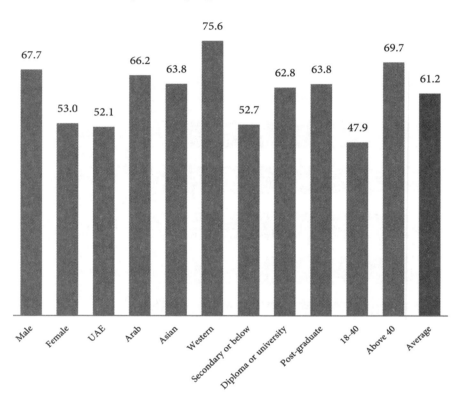

Knowledge about, and trust in the UN Security Council:
61.2% of respondents said they had knowledge of the UN
Security Council (UNSC), (24% good, and 37.2% fair). 67.7%
of males and 53.0% of females reported knowledge of the
Security Council. Westerners were the most knowledgeable
about the UNSC (75.6%) and UAE nationals the least (52.1%).
Knowledge about the UNSC among respondents above 40

years old was 69.7%, compared to 47.9% among 18–40 year olds. Those with postgraduate qualifications showed greater knowledge than those with secondary or lower qualifications, at 63.8% and 52.7%, respectively. Significant differences were found within all demographic variables (gender, nationality, age and educational qualification).

Figure 5.9
Trust in the UN Security Council
by Demographic Variable (%)

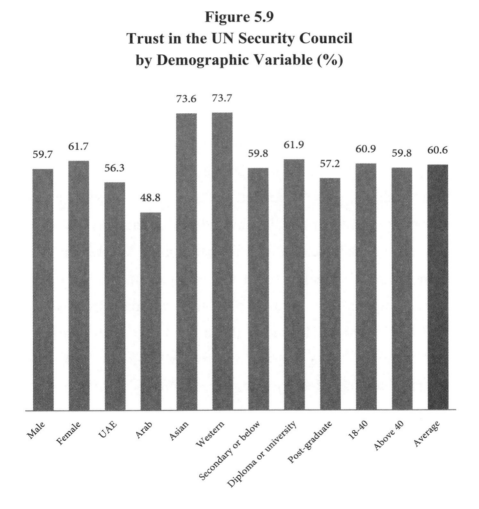

Trust in the UNSC in general was 60.6%. Again, significant differences were found within gender, nationality, and educational qualification; however, the difference was insignificant in terms of age.

61.7% of females vs. 59.7% of males expressed trust in the UNSC. In terms of nationality, Westerners ranked highest in their trust of the institution at 73.7%, versus 48.8% of Arabs. Trust in the UNSC was similar among the 18–40 and 40+ age groups, at 60.9% and 59.8% respectively. Trust in the UNSC among university graduates rose to 61.9%, versus 57.2% among postgraduates.

Knowledge about, and trust in the World Bank: knowledge about the World Bank was expressed by 58.1% of the sample (20% with a good knowledge, and 38.1% with a fair knowledge). 64.4% of males and 50.2% of females expressed knowledge of the World Bank. By nationality, Westerners were the most knowledgeable about the World Bank with a rate of 82.4%, compared to 46.6% of UAE nationals. Knowledge about the World Bank among those aged above 40 years was 64.8%, versus 46% among those aged 18–40. Likewise, postgraduates recorded a higher percentage (67.1%) than those with secondary or lower qualifications (47.3%).

Significant differences were found across all demographic variables (gender, nationality, age and educational qualification).

Figure 5.10
Knowledge about the World Bank
by Demographic Variable (%)

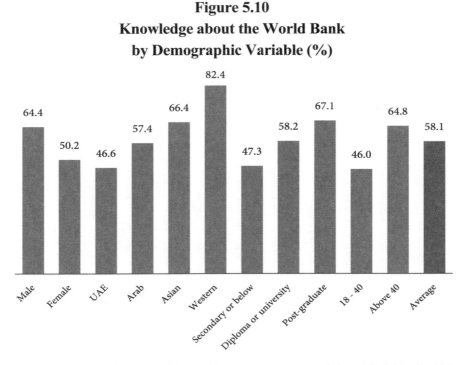

Trust in the World Bank was expressed by 59.2% (8.4% highly trust, and 50.8% trust). 60.9% of females vs. 57.8% of males showed trust in the World Bank. In terms of nationality, Asians ranked the highest in terms of their trust in the World Bank (74%) and Arabs the lowest (48.8%). Trust in the World Bank was similar among both age groups. Trust in the World Bank among postgraduates was 60.9%, compared to 57.5% among the category of those educated to secondary level or below.

Significant differences were found across the variables of gender, nationality, and educational qualification; however the difference was insignificant between age groups.

Figure 5.11
Trust in the World Bank
by Demographic Variable (%)

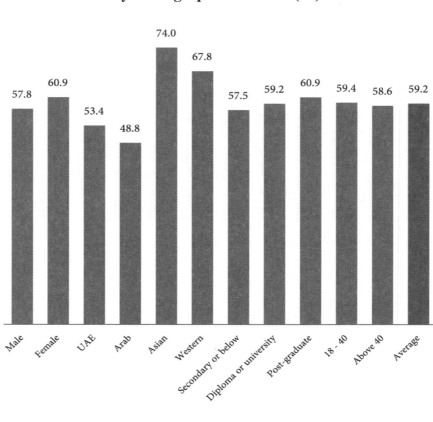

Knowledge about and trust in the International Monetary Fund (IMF): knowledge of the International Monetary Fund was expressed by 50.5% (17.7% reported a good knowledge, and 32.8% a fair knowledge). 57% of males and 42.4% of females said they had knowledge of the IMF. Westerners were the most knowledgeable about the Fund (73.9%), and UAE nationals the least (39.4%).

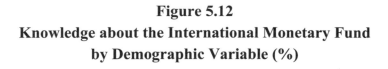

Figure 5.12
Knowledge about the International Monetary Fund
by Demographic Variable (%)

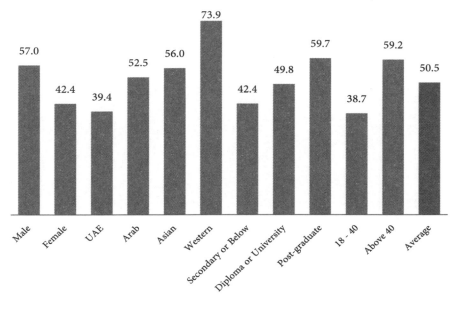

Knowledge about the IMF among those aged above 40 was 59.2%, compared to only 38.7% of 18–40 year-olds. Knowledge was proportional to education, with postgraduates recording 59.7% and university level respondents recording 49.8%, while those in the secondary or below category recorded only 42.4%. Significant differences were found in all demographic variables (gender, nationality, age and educational qualification).

When the respondents were asked to what extent they trusted the IMF, 55.7% of the sample expressed their trust in the institution (only 8.1% highly trust, and 47.6% trust).

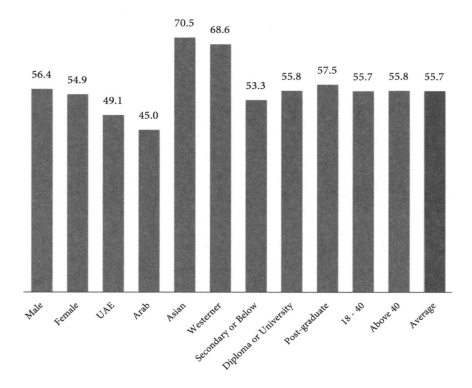

Figure 5.13
Trust in the International Monetary Fund by
Demographic Variable (%)

56.4% of males vs. 54.9% of females reported trust in the IMF. Asians ranked highest in terms of their trust in the IMF at 70.5%, compared to 45% of Arabs. Levels of trust were similar among the two age groups. Trust in the IMF among postgraduates was 57.5% versus 53.3% among those with secondary qualifications or less. Significant differences were found across all demographic variables (gender, nationality, age and educational qualification).

Knowledge about and trust in the International Court of Justice (ICJ): 49.9% of the respondents reported knowledge about the International Court of Justice (16.9% with good knowledge, 33% with fair knowledge). 55.2% of males and 43.3% of females said they had knowledge about the ICJ. Westerners were the most knowledgeable (68.1%) and UAE nationals the least knowledgeable (42.3%) about the ICJ.

Figure 5.14
Knowledge about the International Court of Justice by Demographic Variable (%)

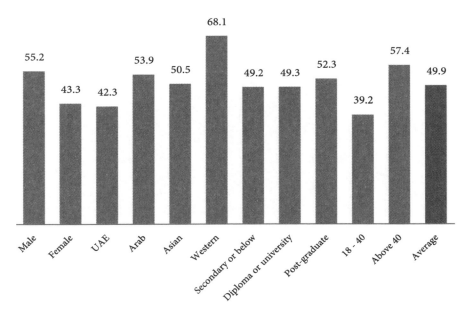

Knowledge about the ICJ – which as I mentioned in the chapter "The New World Order: Features and Concepts," is the principal judicial organ of the UN – among those above 40

years old was 57.4%, compared to only 39.2% among those aged 18–40. Knowledge about the ICJ increases among postgraduates (52.3%), but is almost equal to both the university and secondary or below categories (49.3 and 49.2%, respectively). Significant differences were found within all demographic variables. When respondents were asked to what extent they trusted the ICJ, 57.7% expressed trust in the institution (11.8% highly trust, and 45.9% trust).

Figure 5.15
Trust in the International Court of Justice
by Demographic Variable (%)

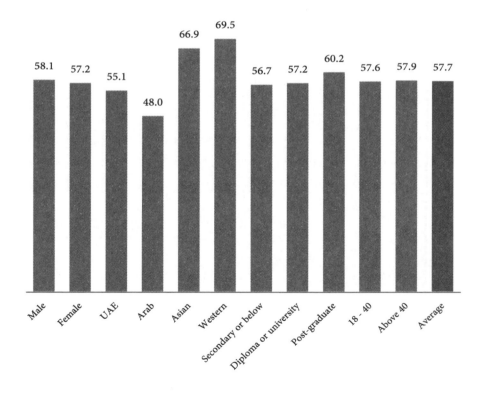

The data shows similar results for males and females, recording 58.1% and 57.2% respectively. Trust rates in the ICJ were also similar among the two age groups. Westerners ranked highest in terms of their trust in the ICJ (69.5%), and Arabs the lowest (48%). Trust in the ICJ among postgraduates was 60.2%, versus 56.7% for secondary or below. Significant differences were found only in the variables of nationality and educational qualification.

Knowledge about, and trust in the International Criminal Court (ICC): 47.4% of respondents recorded knowledge about the International Criminal Court (ICC) – as mentioned previously, the first tribunal with international jurisdiction and an unspecified time-frame to prosecute war criminals and perpetrators of atrocities against humanity – (14.2% professed a good knowledge, and 33.2% a fair knowledge). 53.7% of males and 39.5% of females said they had knowledge of the ICC. Westerners ranked the highest in terms of their knowledge about the ICC (66.4%), and UAE nationals the lowest (38.1%).

Knowledge of the ICC among those above 40 years old was 53.4%, falling to 37.6% among 18–40 year-olds. Knowledge was higher among postgraduates (50.3%) than the university and secondary or below categories (at 46.7% and 46.6%, respectively). Significant differences were found in all demographic variables. When asked to what extent they trusted the ICC, 56.3% of the respondents expressed their trust in this institution (only 9.2% highly trust, and 47.1% trust).

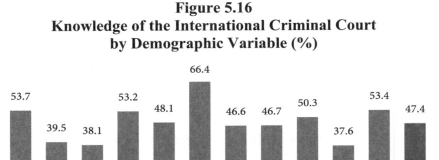

Figure 5.16
Knowledge of the International Criminal Court
by Demographic Variable (%)

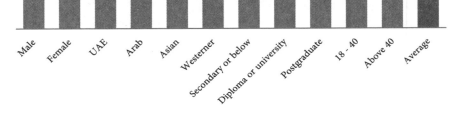

Figure 5.17
Trust in the International Criminal Court by Demographic (%)

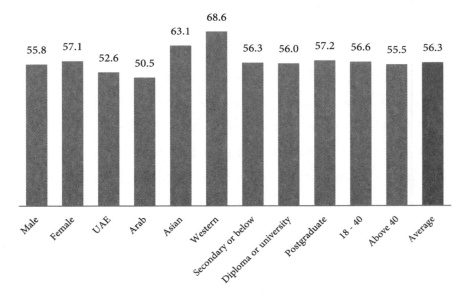

The results showed a similar rate of trust in the ICC among females and males (57.1% and 55.8%, respectively). Trust in the ICC was close among the two age groups, and also among those with different educational levels. Westerners were most likely to trust the ICC (68.6%), compared to 50% of Arabs. Significant differences were found only in the nationality variable.

Understanding Power Relations in the New World Order

The respondents were asked a question in order to discern their opinion on the nature of the new world order. The respondents' answers were divided into four categories; three of which returned similar results, reflecting the division of opinion about the world order.

According to 29.8% of the respondents, the new world order is dominated by a single power, meaning it is a unipolar system. A similar percentage of (29.6%) said that the new world order is "dominated by many powers," i.e. it is multipolar, while 28.8% of the respondents said it was not clearly defined. A small percentage (11.8%) said that it was "a system dominated by two powers," i.e., bipolar.

In terms of those who see the new world order as a multipolar system dominated by many powers, Asians ranked highest at 38.4%, followed by Westerners (34.5%), postgraduates (32.5%), those above 40 (31.6%), and males (30.6%).

Figure 5.18
Opinion on the Nature of the World Order in General (%)

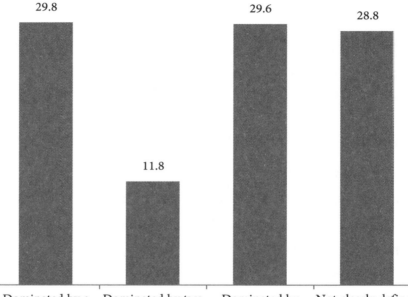

According to demographic variables, Westerners were most likely to view the new world order as unipolar (37%), followed by Arabs (35.6%). 36.3% of those with postgraduate qualifications, 34% of the over-40s, and 31.9% of males recorded the same view.

Westerners and Arabs were most likely to see the new world order as a bipolar system dominated by two powers, as these two categories recorded 17.6% and 13.1% respectively, and the rest of the groups were similar in their ranking at around 12%.

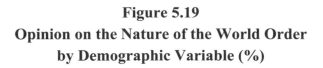

Figure 5.19
Opinion on the Nature of the World Order
by Demographic Variable (%)

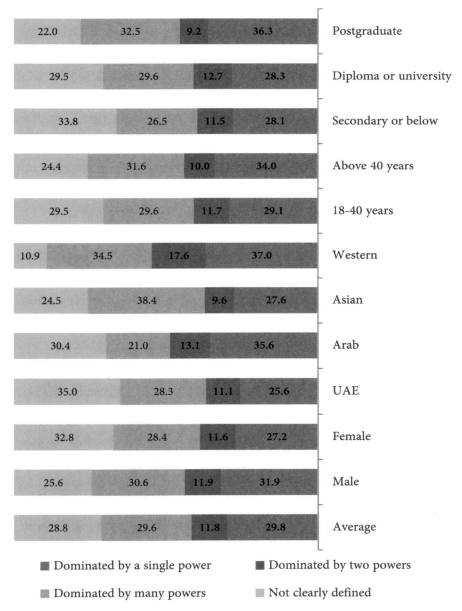

22.0	32.5	9.2	36.3	Postgraduate
29.5	29.6	12.7	28.3	Diploma or university
33.8	26.5	11.5	28.1	Secondary or below
24.4	31.6	10.0	34.0	Above 40 years
29.5	29.6	11.7	29.1	18-40 years
10.9	34.5	17.6	37.0	Western
24.5	38.4	9.6	27.6	Asian
30.4	21.0	13.1	35.6	Arab
35.0	28.3	11.1	25.6	UAE
32.8	28.4	11.6	27.2	Female
25.6	30.6	11.9	31.9	Male
28.8	29.6	11.8	29.8	Average

■ Dominated by a single power   ■ Dominated by two powers

■ Dominated by many powers   ■ Not clearly defined

UAE nationals and Arabs were most likely to be unsure of the nature of the new world order, at 35% and 30.4% respectively. Those educated to secondary level or below recorded 33.8%, and 18–40 year-olds recorded 29.5%.

The Most Significant Problems Facing the New World Order

Asked about the most significant problems facing the new world order, 68.1% of respondents reported that the economic and financial crisis topped the list of problems, followed by war, which accounted for 55.2%, terrorism and environmental issues, accounting for 42.5% and 39.6% respectively, and finally religious extremism at 37.6%.

Figure 5.20

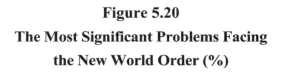

**The Most Significant Problems Facing
the New World Order (%)**

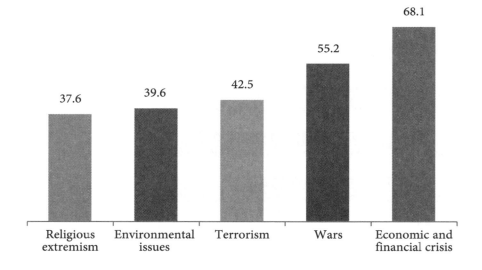

Evaluating the Role of New World Order Institutions

In general, 66.8% of the respondents agreed that the UN plays a positive role, and this percentage rises to 89% among Westerners and 85% among Asians, followed by UAE nationals and Arabs at 56.4% and 54.3%, respectively, as shown in Table 5.3.

Figure 5.21
Evaluating the Role of the
United Nations in the World (%)

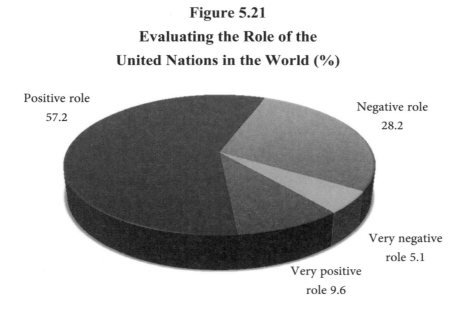

Positive role
57.2

Negative role
28.2

Very negative
role 5.1

Very positive
role 9.6

Dissatisfaction about the role of the UN among UAE nationals and Arabs in the sample may be due to the failure of the UN to find solutions to the many ongoing problems and conflicts in the region, mainly the Palestinian–Israeli conflict, upon which many decisions have been made but not enforced.

Table 5.3

Evaluation of the Role of the United Nations

in the World by Demographic Variable (%)

Variable	Average	Gender		Nationality				Age Group		Educational Qualification		
		Male	Female	UAE	Arab	Asian	Western	18–40 years	Above 40 years	Secondary & below	Diploma or University	Post-graduate
Very positive role	9.6	9.7	9.4	6.1	7.1	14.3	16.1	9.8	9.1	12.1	9.6	7.3
Positive role	57.2	59.7	54.0	50.3	47.2	70.7	72.9	55.8	60.4	52.2	56.8	62.6
Negative role	28.2	25.2	31.9	38.3	38.1	12.1	7.6	29.5	25.1	31.5	27.9	26.0
Very negative role	5.1	5.3	4.8	5.3	7.6	2.9	3.4	4.9	5.5	3.9	5.7	4.2

Further confirmation of the negative attitude of Arab and Muslim countries toward the UN is evident in the results of the June 2009 Pew Research Center's opinion poll "The United Nations: Between Strong Support and Harsh Criticism,"[15] which included 25 countries, and showed that 67% of the respondents in the Palestinian territories had an unfavorable view of the UN role, followed by 57% of Jordanians and Turks, and 56% of Egyptians. Despite this negative evaluation of its role, the Arab and Muslim public was not opposed to the existence of the UN in principle, but sought a strong international institution with adequate authority, but free from the influence of the major powers—particularly the United States of America.

This was expressed by one analyst who said: "While many people in Muslim countries express disappointment with the

UN, this actually masks their underlying desire for a UN that is robust and powerful."[16] The highest percentage of support for the role of the UN was recorded in South Korea (79%), followed by Kenya (76%) and France (74%).[17]

Expanding the Powers of the United Nations and Strengthening its Authority

A relatively small majority (56.8%) support the expansion of the UN's authority. 63.2% of males support such an expansion compared to 48.9% of females. Those aged above 40 exhibited the most support for the expansion of UN powers (60.7%) compared to 53.4% of 18–40 year-olds.

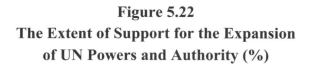

Figure 5.22
The Extent of Support for the Expansion
of UN Powers and Authority (%)

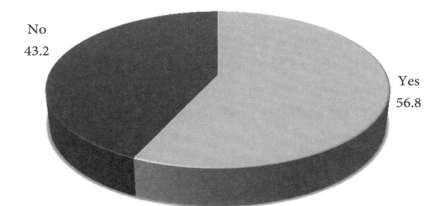

As for nationality, Asians ranked highest in terms of their support for the expansion of UN powers (69.9%), while UAE nationals showed the least support (49.4%). Regarding education level, those with postgraduate qualifications ranked highest in terms of their support (68.1%), compared to 53.6% of those educated to university/diploma level, as detailed in Table 5.4.

Table 5.4

Support for the Expansion of UN Powers and Authority by Demographic Variable (%)

Variable	Average	Gender		Nationality				Age Group		Educational Qualification		
		Male	Female	UAE	Arab	Asian	Western	18–40 years	Above 40 years	Secondary & below	Diploma or university	Postgraduate
Yes I support	56.8	63.2	48.9	49.4	53.0	69.9	57.8	53.4	60.7	55.8	53.6	68.1
No I don't support	43.2	36.8	51.1	50.6	47.0	30.1	42.2	46.6	39.3	44.2	46.4	31.9

Those respondents who favored broader UN power and authority were asked about their opinions as to which areas should benefit from such an expansion in powers. 59.3% of the respondents indicated that the UN should maintain its own standing peacekeeping force, while 31.5% said the organization should have the authority to enter countries in order to investigate suspected human rights violations. 9.2% of the respondents said that the UN should have the power to regulate the international arms trade.

448

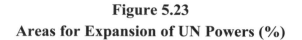

Figure 5.23
Areas for Expansion of UN Powers (%)

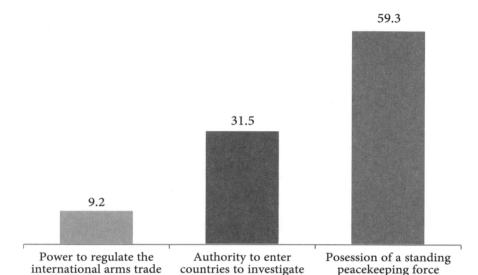

UAE nationals and Arabs were most supportive of a standing UN peacekeeping force (recording 66.1% and 66% in favor, respectively). This is likely due to the fact that peace in the Arab region has been elusive owing to the numerous crises and conflicts it has experienced. It should be noted that this result is similar to that of a question in a previous survey distributed in seven Muslim countries,[18] in which 64% showed support for such a force. According to a WorldPublicOpinion.org and Chicago Council on Global Affairs (WPO–CCGA) poll of 22 countries, the highest rate of support was recorded in Kenya (85%), followed by Nigeria (84%), Britain (79%), and the USA (72%).[19]

The respondents were asked a set of questions regarding the extent of their support or opposition to the use of powers currently granted to the UN in a variety of areas. Such questions included whether or not UN approval should be required in order to employ military force against the source of an international threat. Another question sought to determine views on to whether the UN should be given the authority to enter countries to investigate potential human rights violations. Respondents were also asked if the UN should be given the authority to use force to deliver humanitarian aid in the case of refusal by authorities of the country concerned. Answers to these questions were mostly favorable, as shown in Figure 5.24.

60.6% of respondents supported the need for UN approval to use military force against an international source of threat, and males were more in favor than females (67.7% vs. 51.9%). In terms of nationality, Asians were the most supportive (67.1%) regarding the need for UN approval for military force, followed by Arabs (64.7%), Westerners (56.4%), and finally UAE nationals (53.4%).

54.5% of the respondents said that they favor the option of the UN having the right to intervene in the internal affairs of countries to investigate human rights violations. Westerners exhibited the greatest support (71.8%), followed by Asians (67.6%), reflecting the general contemporary awareness of the issue of human rights and its importance in most countries of the world. According to the aforementioned questionnaire,

450

giving the UN authority to investigate human rights violations receives very high levels of support (65.0%)—the French recorded the highest rate (92%), followed by the British (86%), and Nigerians (83%). Egyptians recorded the highest rate of opposition to intervention (49%).[20]

Figure 5.24
Support for the Expansion
of Specific UN Powers (%)

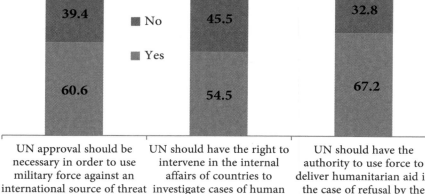

This was supported by the results of this study, with UAE nationals and Arabs recording low approval rates—43.5% and 50.4%, respectively. Perhaps this opinion reflects the sensitivity surrounding the idea of intervention by force in the internal affairs of countries for whatever reason, particularly as those in the Arab region recall events in Iraq following foreign intervention based on alleged possession of weapons of mass destruction and the pretext of protecting human rights. This sensitivity is also due to the fact that the issue of human rights is not a priority for the Arab public in light of current development-related problems.

The suggestion that the UN be given the authority to deliver humanitarian aid against the will of the authorities in a given country recorded the highest level of support (67.2%). Arabs and UAE nationals were the most supportive, at 70.1% and 67.6%, respectively.

The results of global opinion polls differ in terms of the international community's right, in accordance with Chapter VII of the UN Charter, to use military force. In a survey conducted in 18 countries by WPO–CCGA between 2006 and 2008[21] regarding the right of the UNSC to authorize military force, results indicated that 76% agreed to this right to defend a country that had been attacked. Also, a high proportion (76%) supported the use of force to prevent severe human rights violations and genocide—the highest rate was recorded in Kenya (90%), followed by Nigeria (88%) and France (85%).[22]

As for the need for UN approval to use force, the Pew Research Center poll revealed that opinions were divided. The idea was supported by 80% of respondents in Germany, 64% in Britain and 63% in France, but support was less prevalent in Jordan (47%) and Pakistan (38%).[23]

452

In the context of identifying public views and positions regarding the reform of international organizations, the respondents were asked to clarify to what extent they agreed that the number of countries with veto power in the UNSC should be increased. The results were unexpected, with less than half of the respondents (45.2%) supporting the idea, as illustrated in Figure 5.25.

Figure 5.25
Opinion on UNSC Expansion by Demographic Variable (%)

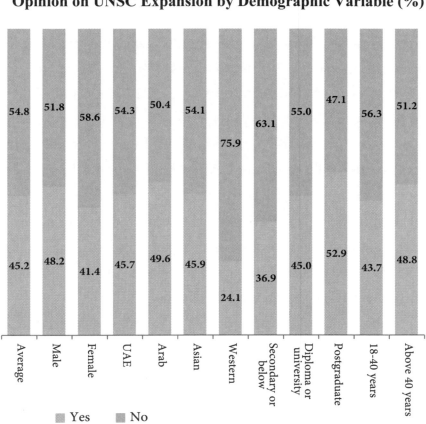

Western respondents were least supportive (24.1%), which is understandable given that the current composition of the UNSC benefits the interests of the West in general, with three out of the five countries having veto power being Western nations (the United States of America, the United Kingdom and France). Arabs and Asians were the most supportive at 49.6% and 45.9%, respectively. Support was higher among males than females (48.2% vs. 41.4%, respectively).

When those respondents who supported the expansion of the number of veto-holding members of the UNSC were asked which countries they thought should have the right to be permanent members, 90 respondents (39.1%) voted for the UAE, followed by India with 50 votes (21.7%), Saudi Arabia with 40 votes (17.4%), Egypt with 30 votes (13.0%) and finally Brazil with 20 votes (8.7%), as shown in Figure 5.26. The high response rate in favor of the UAE is likely due to the fact that the poll was conducted within the UAE, and the percentage of UAE respondents was 35.9% of the sample population, while the remaining 64.1% comprises expatriates residing in the UAE. However, both categories recognize the qualities that qualify the UAE to be granted this status.

In the context of respondents' evaluation of international organizations, they were asked about their opinion on the fairness of the ICC. The answers were divided roughly between people who believed it is fair and those who see it as unfair (51.3% vs. 48.7%).

454

Figure 5.26
Countries Nominated by Respondents
for Permanent UNSC Membership

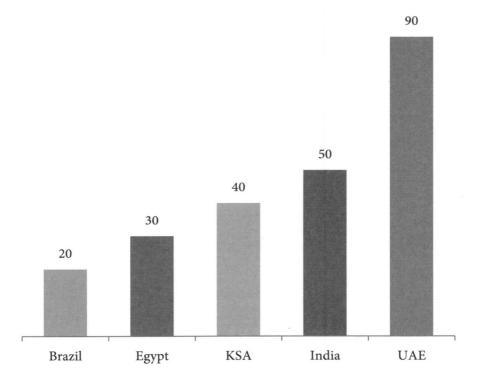

The percentage of females (53.8%) who considered the ICC's rulings fair was higher than that of males (49.4%). Asians were most likely to consider the ICC fair (57%), followed by Westerners (48.1%). There was no significant difference between the two age groups, as 51.9% of those aged above 40 years and 51.5% of 18–40 year-olds considered the ICC fair. There was also no significant difference between the views of those with different educational backgrounds.

Figure 5.27
Attitude toward ICC Rulings by Demographic Variable (%)

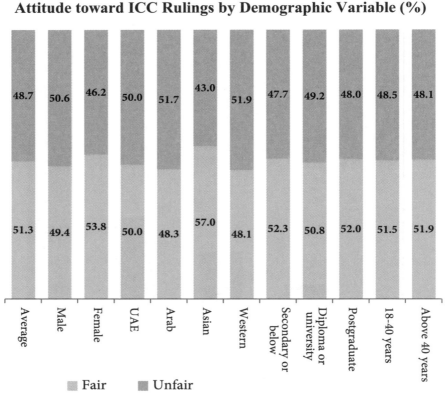

The high percentage of those who believe that the ICC's judgments are unfair raises questions about the credibility of this international institution and the extent of its neutrality and independence, namely the extent to which it is influenced by the dominant political forces in the new world order.

In terms of reform of international economic institutions, 81.4% of the respondents said there should be international bodies to regulate and control major financial institutions in order to achieve global financial stability. This might be due to the repercussions of the financial crisis that has affected most of the world's economies since 2007, particularly as one of its causes was the lack of controls and institutions to monitor financial transactions within and between countries.[24]

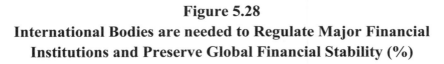

Figure 5.28
International Bodies are needed to Regulate Major Financial Institutions and Preserve Global Financial Stability (%)

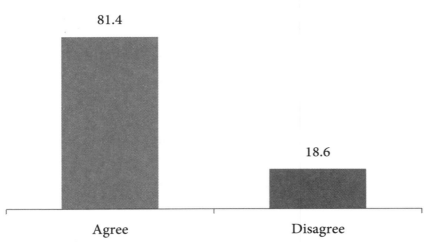

Respondents were also asked for their opinions on economic globalization and the resultant surge in the exchange of goods, services and investments between countries, and whether this has been beneficial or detrimental to their countries' economies. 54.8% of the respondents said that their countries had benefited from this increase in the exchange of goods, services and investments, while 25% said that economic globalization had been detrimental to their economies. The remaining 20.2% viewed the impact of economic globalization on their countries from a neutral point of view—neither beneficial nor detrimental.

A positive view of economic globalization was more prevalent among UAE nationals (60.3%)—this can be explained by the openness of the UAE economy and its high degree of global economic integration. This also applies to many Asian economies, with 57.5% of Asians reporting that their economies had benefited from globalization. However, only 46.1% of Arab respondents agreed, which is best explained by the stagnation and underdevelopment of most Arab economies.

Figure 5.29

Opinion on the Merits of Economic Globalization by Demographic Variable (%)

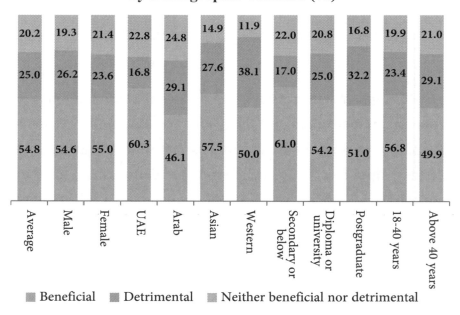

38.1% of Westerners considered globalization detrimental to the economies of their countries, which indicates the effects of the economic and financial crisis in the West—particularly in the euro zone economies.

Globalization has a cultural dimension, reflected in the speed and intensity of the movement of people, information, ideas, consumption patterns and lifestyle between countries, affecting indigenous cultures and identities. In order to identify the cultural impacts of globalization on the respondents, they were asked about the consequences of the increased movement of peoples on national identity, and the extent of the positive or negative effects of the phenomenon.

The results indicate that Westerners were most likely to view their national identity as being negatively affected by globalization (40.2%), which seems paradoxical at first glance, as the forces driving and dominating globalization are generally Western powers, which are seen by many outside the West as working to impose their economic and cultural model on the rest of the world, and thus threatening local cultures and identities. However, movement does not work in only one direction; in economic terms, for example, Western countries complain of competition from Asian products (especially from China) flooding Western markets. In terms of individual mobility, Western countries face the problem of a large influx of (legal and illegal) immigrants from different cultures. Hence, some sections of the populations of the West, and political elites representing right-wing and extreme right-wing parties, urgently and loudly voice their fears of the risks these immigrants pose to Western culture, lifestyle and national identity.

Figure 5.30
Impact of Globalization on National Identity
by Demographic Variable (%)

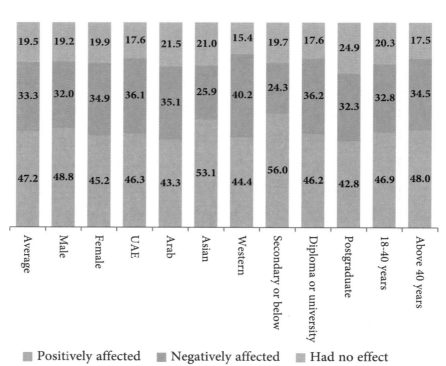

■ Positively affected   ■ Negatively affected   ■ Had no effect

Only one out of every three UAE nationals (36.1%) views globalization as a threat to their local culture and identity. This result represents another paradox; one might expect the figure to be much higher owing to the presence of large numbers of foreign migrants (by virtue of globalization and other historical

460

factors) in the UAE. This is perhaps evidence of the openness of UAE nationals to different cultures and their acceptance of 'the other,' as well as a sense that their culture is deep-rooted and impervious to the threats of globalization or co-existing cultures. Asians are the least likely to consider globalization a threat to their identity (25.9%).

Respondents above 40 years old were more likely to feel threatened by globalization (34.5%) than those aged 18–40 (32.8%); and females were more aware than males of the negative impacts of globalization on national identity (34.9% versus 32%).

Assessing the Dangers facing the New World Order

With respect to the proliferation of weapons of mass destruction, 73.3% of the respondents saw this as a major danger. UAE nationals and Arabs recorded the highest concern (83.6% and 77.1%, respectively), while Asians and Westerners recorded lower rates (63.6% and 59.8%, respectively). The high awareness among UAE nationals and Arabs of the danger posed by WMDs is due to regional instability, war and revolutions in which WMDs have been used, such as the Iran–Iraq War (1980–1988), the use of chemical weapons against the Kurds in Iraq, and their recent use in the Syrian civil war.[25] The region is witnessing an arms race and an attempt by certain countries to develop WMDs, including nuclear weapons. Along with Israel, which possesses a large arsenal of WMDs, Iran is working to acquire nuclear weapons, and there are unconfirmed reports of other countries in the Middle East seeking the same goal.[26]

57.5% of the respondents agreed that terrorism is a major danger facing the new world order, and females felt this threat more acutely than males (61.2% vs. 56.1%). However, in terms of nationality, UAE nationals ranked highest in considering terrorism as a major danger facing the new world order (62.4%), while Westerners were least likely to hold this view (52.9%). This result is somewhat surprising if we consider the fact that Western countries have suffered major acts of terrorism (New York on September 11, 2001, Madrid on March 11, 2004, and London on July 7, 2005).

Figure 5.31
Assessing the Dangers Facing the New World Order (%)

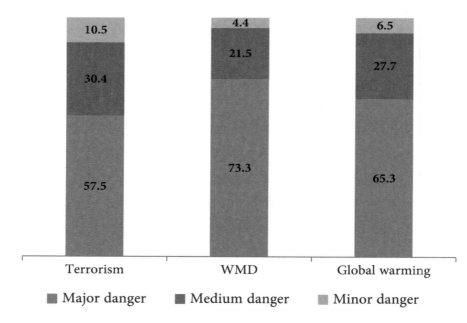

As for global warming, 65.3% of respondents said that the phenomenon represented a major danger to the new world order. 67.8% of women considered global warming a danger compared to 63.9% of men. Arabs are the most aware of the seriousness of global warming (70.3%), followed by UAE nationals (68.2%), and Asians at (64%). Ironically, Westerners were least aware of the seriousness of this phenomenon (44.5%), despite the common perception regarding their interest in the environment and risks that affect quality of life.

When asked whether they considered the US-led global war on terror to have been successful, 46.5% of respondents said it had (12% great success, and 34.5% medium success). This percentage rose among Westerners to 69.2% and among Asians to 56.1%, while it declined among UAE nationals and Arabs to 41.9% and 35.9%, respectively.

Figure 5.32
Assessing the Success of the US-led Global War on Terror

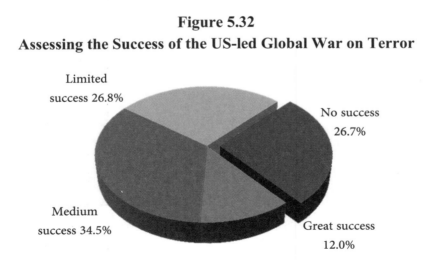

The Future of the New World Order

The respondents were asked about their vision regarding the future of the new world order, and their opinions as to which powers will likely dominate. More than half of the respondents (50.8%) believed that the world would be multipolar, 27.3% believed it would be bipolar, and only 21.9% said it would be unipolar. UAE nationals and Arabs make up the highest percentage of those who expect the world to be multipolar (57.6% and 54.2%, respectively), while this figure drops significantly among Asians (42.9%) and Westerners (37.4%). 43.5% of Westerners believed that the future order would be dominated by two powers, while 25.6 % of the Arabs foresaw a unipolar world.

This result is logical, as a multipolar world order will better serve the interests of the Arab region, especially considering how badly the region was affected in the bipolar Cold War era between 1947 and 1991. During this period the Arab world was politically and ideologically polarized and divided, leading to several disputes and conflicts among Arabs, such as the conflict in Yemen and other Arab–Arab conflicts which were – in some aspects – proxy conflicts between the two dominant poles in the world order at that time. After the collapse of the communist system and the dissolution of the Soviet Union on December 25, 1991, the international arena became a unipolar space under the United States of America in which conditions in the Arab world have not improved; the hallmark of this dominance was the Iraq War and the resulting sectarian and ethnic conflict that has further plagued inter-Arab relations.[27]

Figure 5.33
Opinion Regarding the New World Order
by Demographic Variable (%)

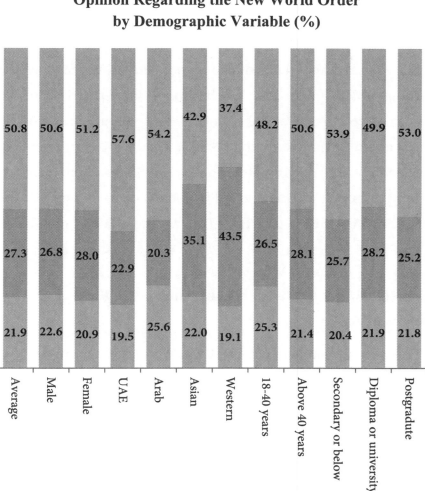

Dominated by a single power   Dominated by two powers
Dominated by many powers

Public opinion in the UAE regarding the nature of the new world order and its dominant forces is consistent with international public opinion, as the majority of the world's population rejects a unipolar or bipolar global system. This result was reached by two polls conducted in nine countries by the Bertelsmann Foundation,[28] in which respondents were asked about the global system most likely to achieve world peace. On average, 42% of the respondents favored a system without poles, under the leadership of the UN. The results according to citizens of the countries participating in the survey were as follows: Germany 68%, China 51%, Britain 47%, France 46% and Japan 33%. The second most popular system among respondents was one led by a balance of powers: United States of America 52%, Brazil 45%, India 37% and Russia 33%.[29]

The Role of the United States of America in the New World Order

When asked about the status of the United States of America and its role in the new world order, only one third of respondents (32.4%) said that the United States of America would continue to assume a leadership role, while almost half of respondents (49.6%) believed that the US role will be equal to that of other powers. The remainder (18%) believed that the United States of America would have no role at all in the new world order.

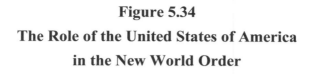

Figure 5.34

The Role of the United States of America

in the New World Order

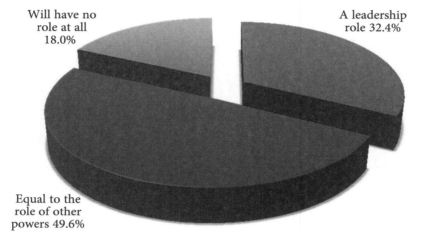

The results of the survey endorse the findings of global opinion polls. In 2006, WPO–CCGA[30] asked respondents in 15 countries to choose the ideal role for the United States of America in world affairs. Presented with various options, the least popular was that the United States of America should continue to be the sole superpower and preeminent world leader, with an average of only 11% choosing this option.[31]

Respondents were asked to what extent they agreed with the presence of a number of powers as poles in the new world order, and they were presented with the following options: the United States of America, Russia, China, or other powers.

Figure 5.35
Preferences Regarding the Influence
of Major Powers in the New World Order (%)

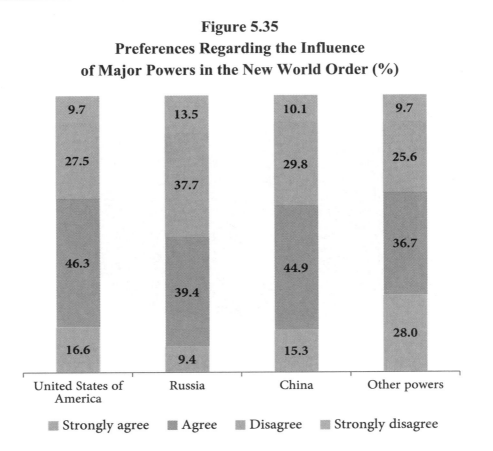

The results reveal a great desire to change the shape of the new world order and the powers controlling it, with 64.7% of the respondents reporting their support for powers other than the United States of America, China or Russia. 62.9% of the respondents were in favor of a role for the United States of America in the new world order, and 60.2% for China. However, less than half supported a pre-eminent Russian role in the new world order (48.8%).

468

UAE nationals and Arabs were least enthusiastic regarding Russia being a pole in the new world order (32.9% and 40.7% respectively), and in general did not show great enthusiasm for any of the aforementioned countries. Westerners ranked highest in supporting China as a pole in the new world order with (61.3%), while Arabs were the least supportive of the United States of America as a pole in the new world order (46.1%).

Most Significant Threats to the New World Order

The survey revealed that respondents believed the three most significant areas of concern in the new world order were human rights (63.6%), ethnic and sectarian conflicts (63.1%), and economy (63.1%).

Crime and disease/epidemics came in the middle of the list (35% and 31.9% respectively), while immigration came at the bottom of the list at 23.2%. 72.1% of UAE nationals believed that ethnic and sectarian conflicts were among the most significant issues threatening the new world order, while 75.6% of Asians cited human rights. 42.4% of Westerners considered immigration to be one of the most important issues facing the new world order, 67.2% of Arabs cited the economy, and 35% of UAE nationals cited crime as one of the most significant threats. Also, 34.8% of UAE nationals saw epidemics as one of the most important issues in the new world order.

Figure 5.36
Most Important Issues facing the New World Order (%)

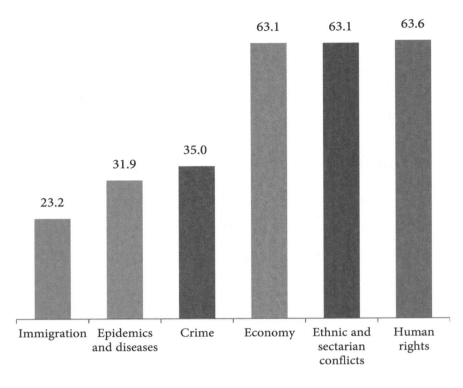

Young People, the Internet and the New World Order

The respondents were asked three questions about the internet and its impact on young people in the new world order. The vast majority (85%) believed that the internet made young people more aware of global issues, while 42.8% believed that it isolated young people from reality and its problems. Nearly half of the respondents (48.1%) believed that the internet made young people more extreme.

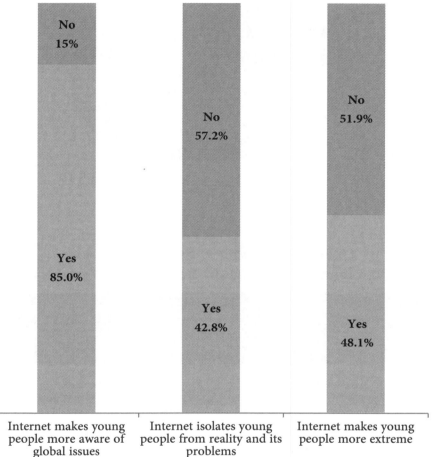

Figure 5.37
Young People, the Internet
and the New World Order

Internet makes young people more aware of global issues

Internet isolates young people from reality and its problems

Internet makes young people more extreme

The Role of Religion in Society and International Relations

70.3% of respondents believed that religion will have an important role to play in society and in international relations in general.

Figure 5.38

The Role of Religion in Society and International Relations

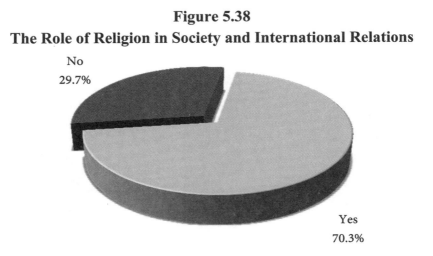

No
29.7%

Yes
70.3%

Table 5.5

**Opinion on the Role of Religion in Society
and International Relations by Demographic Variable (%)**

	Average	Gender		Nationality				Age Group		Educational Qualification		
		Male	Female	UAE	Arab	Asian	Western	18–40	Above 40	Secondary	Diploma or University	Post-graduate
Yes	70.3	69.8	75.2	82.0	72.1	68.1	46.1	74.8	65.8	79.1	72.9	63.2
No	29.7	30.2	24.8	18.0	27.9	31.9	53.9	25.2	34.2	20.9	27.1	36.8

Female respondents were more likely to believe that religion will play a greater role in the new world order than males, at 75.2%, and 69.8%, respectively. Likewise, respondents aged 18–40 were more likely to agree than their peers above 40, at 74.8% and 65.8%, respectively. In terms of nationality, UAE nationals ranked highest in this belief (82.0%) followed by Arabs (72.1%), while this percentage declined to 46.1% among Westerners. Respondents with a low

472

level of education (secondary or below) were more likely to believe religion would play greater role than those with postgraduate qualifications (79.1% and 63.2% respectively).

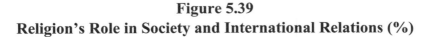

Figure 5.39
Religion's Role in Society and International Relations (%)

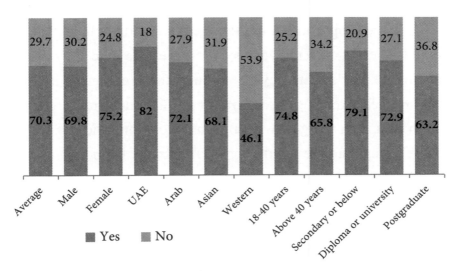

Conclusion

By examining the views and attitudes toward the new world order among the public in the United Arab Emirates, and taking into account variables that included: nationality, age, gender and educational level to explain the variation in the public's views and attitudes toward the new world order, the results showed that both the UAE citizens and expatriates are interested in following world news. This reflects the fact that the UAE is located in the center of events and also reflects its openness to the world and to different cultures. Results also showed high levels of knowledge regarding the various institutions of the global system, represented by the United Nations, the UN Security Council, the World Bank, the International Monetary Fund, the International Court of Justice and the International Criminal Court. Degrees of knowledge and confidence in these institutions varied among different nationalities in the UAE.

A large proportion of the sample population believe that the United Nations currently plays a positive role, and they are in favor of expanding its powers through the creation of its own standing peacekeeping force, granting it the authority to go into countries and investigate human rights violations and having the power to regulate the international arms trade. Respondents also believe that the UN's approval is needed in order to use military force against an international source of threat, that the UN should have the right to intervene in the internal affairs of countries to investigate cases of human rights violations and that the it should have the authority to use force to deliver humanitarian aid in the case of refusal from the concerned countries.

Nearly half of the public believe that these international organizations need to be reformed through expanding the UN Security Council and increasing the number of countries with Veto power. Respondents believe that the International Criminal Court rulings are fair, but the fact that nearly half of the public believes that the ICC is unfair raises questions about the credibility of this international institution and the extent of its neutrality and independence, namely the extent to which it is influenced by the dominant political forces in the world order.

As for understanding the relations between actors in the new world order, around one-third of the public believes that the new world order is unipolar, which is consistent with the hypothesis of this book that the US will assume the leadership of a global system shared by other superpowers of lower ranking. Around one-third of the public believes that the world order will be multipolar, and both results are consistent with our hypothesis. However, the fact that about one-third of the public does not recognize the nature of the new world order, raises questions about how uninformed the public is, and raises further questions about the extent of political knowledge among the public. These findings were confirmed again upon examining the public views regarding the nature of the new world order and its dominant powers, where about half of the sample believes that the world will be multipolar, and about one-third of the respondents believes that the United States of America will assume a leadership role within it. As for the position of the United States of America and its role in the new world order, about one-third of the public believes that the United States of America will take a leadership role, while half of the respondents believe it will have an equal role to that of other powers, a result not inconsistent with our hypothesis.

Statistical tests proved a significant discrepancy in opinion among the various groups represented in the sample. This was applicable to the vast majority of the hypotheses addressed by the survey, which confirms substantial differences in views on the basis of gender, nationality, education level and age—the variables adopted by the study to analyze variance among the views of respondents.

Jamal Sanad Al-Suwaidi

PROSPECTIVE STRUCTURAL CHANGES AND THEIR CONSEQUENCES FOR THE NEW WORLD ORDER

Chapter VI

Prospective Structural Changes and their Consequences for the New World Order

In essence, the new world order comprises a set of social, economic, political, geographic and cultural realities that govern relations within the international community and among its components—countries, peoples, individuals and civil society organizations. These realities, however, do not interact in a global vacuum; instead, they affect, and are affected by the prominent actors and components of this system, and particularly the single pole that dominates international politics and the aforementioned hierarchy of the new world order, as shown in Figure 1 (p. 55) of this book.

Recent circumstances have prompted the United States of America to rely on 'strategic partnerships,' forging international alliances to face regional and global threats—for example, the US-led international military alliance of 34 countries that repelled the Iraq occupation of Kuwait on August 2, 1990,[1] as well as the international coalition to fight global terrorism. However, the United States of America can be expected to rely increasingly on unilateralism in imposing its global policy in the coming decades, seeking to create the world it desires. This will apply particularly in cases where international consensus cannot be achieved, in order to maintain the US status as the only superpower but without abandoning its approach of forging joint alliances to face security challenges and risks which threaten international security, stability and its interests.

The US National Security Strategy, published on May 27, 2010, reflects the US vision of its global role,[2] one that seeks to strengthen its leadership in the new world order with a view to achieving its twenty-first century interests. To this end, the United States of America has adopted a dual-track approach: the first is to build US internal power; the second focuses on shaping a world order through which international challenges may be overcome via adaptable collaborative approaches and alliances,[3] while maintaining balance between hard and soft power resources—a combination known as 'Smart Power.'[4] At the same time, the United States of America will also follow an isolationist approach regarding issues that neither directly nor indirectly affect its strategic interests in its efforts to maintain its military, economic, technical and cultural superiority. It may also seek to draw its competitors toward involvement in marginal conflicts in order to drain their resources and divert them from US interests, thereby also avoiding the 'overstretch' that preceded the demise of previous empires—the Romans and Ottomans, among others.[5]

On the other hand, it appears, at least at first glance, that a clear division exists between two worlds, comprising a resurgent

South (including countries such as Malaysia and South Africa) in which there is evidence of progress in terms of growth, human development and poverty reduction, "… and a North in crisis—where austerity policies and the absence of economic growth are imposing hardship on millions of unemployed people and people deprived of benefits as social compacts come under intense pressure."[6]

However, this will not affect the ranking of powers in the new world order or its continuity for decades to come, as detailed in the Introduction to this volume. Even if China's economic growth were to reach 6.5% – versus 2.5% in the United States of America[7] – China would still be unable to compete with US influence, as it remains a developing country seeking to improve the living standards of millions of its citizens, while the United States of America is only working to address the slow pace of growth, public and private debt, and unemployment—"the United States of America remains the largest economy in the world in monetary terms and will remain so for the foreseeable future."[8]

Future Changes
and their Expected Consequences

The new world order will most likely continue to be governed in a unipolar fashion, perhaps beyond the next five decades, with the United States of America as the sole dominant superpower. Other global actors, such as China, the EU, Russia, Japan, India and Brazil may close the gap with the United States of America; but, there will remain a significant gulf in power and responsibility between the United States of America and other global players seeking to achieve, or merely maintain their interests.

The United States of America has proved its superiority in several areas, and shall be the undisputed leader of the new world order. This will have strategic implications for many countries and international organizations around the world, as a result of the profound structural changes in the new world order that can be expected as a result of the interaction between the orientations of the single pole and its other key elements and units. Such changes will lead to shifts in concepts, the deconstruction of positions and orientations, and variations in states' convergence, alliances and relations, as well as inter-state competition and conflict. The most important of these structural changes will be observed in the following spheres:

1. The Political Sphere

US relations with other countries are still affected by the strategic consequences of the September 11, 2001 attacks. Such relations are managed according to the principle laid down by former President George Walker Bush [Jr.] who famously said, "[I]f you are not with us you are against us."[9] Under this principle, the United States of America categorizes a group of

482

countries within the list of allies who enjoy its endorsement and support, while it categorizes others among current or potential enemies, which are thus are exposed to different degrees of sanctions and pressure according to the level of threat they pose to US interests, goals and strategies. The United States of America is expected to maintain this approach in the near and medium term, despite growing calls to adopt partnership formulas and to share international responsibilities and recognize the limits of its own power.

States, communities and individuals will be forced either to comply with the decisions and policies of the single pole, or face severe pressures and penalties. The leadership role of the United States of America will enable it to control movement within the new world order, and to oversee the interaction and relationships between its constituents,[10] relying on all four basic elements of power: a military force capable of deployment anywhere in the world; global economic strength; unprecedented cultural, educational, media and ideological influence; and the international political strength born of the previous three elements.[11]

The world is witnessing the ongoing spread of the values of democracy and political liberalism; individual empowerment; personal freedom; human and political rights; political pluralism and popular sovereignty; and respect for minorities; as well as increasing calls for the rights of peoples to choose their own political and social systems, and the growing role of cross-border civil society organizations to rival that of the state, allowing them to influence global public opinion. All of this will contribute to an increase in the number of democracies in the new world order, as countries respond to US political values, pressure from global civil society organizations, and the demands of young people, who represent high proportions of the population in such countries.[12]

The United States of America will also expand the US–Middle East Partnership Initiative for young leaders – which provides training and grants for young people to implement projects that benefit their communities – in order to build democracy, empower women and increase youth employment.[13] As previously mentioned in the chapter "The New World Order: Features and Concepts," it is estimated that around 1,275 young men and women from 22 different countries, most of them from the Middle East, have benefitted from the initiative during the past five years.[14]

However, all of the above suggests that a disconnect may arise between the accelerated pace of change and peoples' ability to adapt; thus, stability in the new world order will depend on the ability of societies to adjust,[15] as well as the extent of convergence between the orientations of individuals, communities and civil society organizations on the one hand, and the state and its government on the other.

Certainly, the role of the UN and its various international organizations, bodies and agencies will change as a result of attempts to balance American interests on one hand, and the interests of other international actors and emerging regional powers on the other.

2. The Economic Sphere

The world will witness a bolstering of economic blocs and a growing political role for sovereign wealth funds. The free trade zone that is expected to be established by the EU and the United States of America will increase the political influence of some developing powers in the new world order and will accelerate the transition toward a globalized economy.[16] This will occur against a backdrop of an increasing gap between opposing economic forces influencing the new world order, resulting in increasingly frequent global economic crises. The United States of America will capitalize on its expertise in managing such crises, remaining in control of a sizeable proportion of the global economy in the new world order. This will afford it a major role in promoting economic stability, while at the same time increasing its ability to impose economic sanctions.

The global economic system will become more influential in determining relationships and policies within the new world order in light of the growing economic prosperity of the BRICs and other emerging economies[17] and the declining role of traditional centers of global economic power. Europe cannot contain the intensifying debt crisis, and Japan's economy has been overtaken by that of China, which will have consequences for the mechanisms of doing business in the new world order.[18]

The following table shows the ranking of major countries' investments in sovereign wealth funds.

Table 6.1
World's Largest Sovereign Wealth Funds
by Assets under Management[19]

State	Total Assets in $ Billions
China	1,635.4
UAE	829.0
Norway	803.9
Saudi Arabia	681.2
Singapore	458.3
Kuwait	386.0
Kazakhstan	166.4
Qatar	115.0
United States of America	114.5
Australia	89.0

This raises a number of questions, such as: what will be the extent of the responsibility of these countries for maintaining the stability of the global economic system and meeting its challenges? To what extent will they participate in shouldering the burdens of economic leadership in the new world order alongside the United States of America? Will they employ their growing strength to achieve their own strategic interests or those of global, mutual concern? Will these countries adopt the principles of market economy, equal opportunities, and openness to free trade, or will they pursue a mixture of capitalism and socialism? And what role will these emerging economies play in the depletion of the world's natural resources?[20] As the UNDP points out, "global markets have played an important role in advancing progress. All newly industrializing countries have pursued a strategy of "importing what the rest of the world knows and exporting what it wants." But even more important are the terms of engagement with these markets. Without investment in people, returns from global markets tend to be limited."[21]

US influence in international financial institutions such as the IMF, World Bank and WTO will likely increase.[22] The United States of America controls the resolutions of these institutions—largely because it provides a sizeable proportion of their budgets, many of the decision-makers in these institutions are US citizens, and the US dollar is adopted as the global currency. The role of these institutions will increase in developing countries, where the central role of government in economic activities will be abolished in favor of liberal privatized economies, and all restrictions on free trade will be removed.[23] The new world order will also feature emergency mechanisms to maintain the flow of resources and ensure the continuity of development efforts in the face of global economic shocks and unexpected crises.

The Organization for Security and Cooperation in Europe (OSCE) Paris Summit – held on November 19–21, 1990 and involving 34 countries – adopted a declaration on the emergence of a new world order, entrenching the principles of democracy, personal and economic freedoms, and settling disputes through negotiation,[24] necessitating mutual economic cooperation between nations to strengthen relations, reject conflict, and achieve global democracy. However, the reality will be dictated by the preferred US vision of the international economic system; i.e., the United States of America will accept interdependence as long as it suits its economic interests and is based on the principles of liberal economy. This will give rise to regional and international economic blocs that submit to US dominance in the new world order, while elsewhere trade and economic conflicts will replace ideological and military ones.

On the other hand, the United States of America will also work over the next decade to reduce its dependence on oil from regions plagued by risk and instability, such as the Middle East. This may spell a decline in the importance of US foreign policy towards such regions, and subsequently in its influence over the events, developments and conflicts that may occur there, passing the burden of responsibility for these events and conflicts to the countries, peoples and community organizations of such regions.

3. The Military Sphere

The United States of America will maintain its military superiority in the new world order, as well as its pre-emptive strategy in facing major threats, with a tendency to pursue such objectives via alliances between various forces to support regional stability and security. At the same time, fourth generation warfare (4GW) will have a major impact in terms of defense postures, military strategies, and the structure of armed forces around the world.[25]

Global nuclear proliferation may continue, increasing related areas of instability. The United States of America will join China in its efforts to control conditions in Asia. Strategic balance at the global level will remain elusive; despite the growing economic and military power of Asia, Russia's desire to restore its position as a 'universal' player rather than just a global pole will continue unabated, while sub-state actors will pose a growing threat to international peace.

In its quest to maintain its military dominance and ensure the future of its human and military resources, the United States of America will adopt a strategy of 'fabricating the enemy,' in which it will implicate its rivals and adversaries in proxy wars. The role of the US military in this regard may be limited to containing such proxy conflicts, preventing them from spilling over or developing beyond US control. It will also seek to protect its friends and allies. Therefore, the world will likely become divided into zones of peace and war, the first including the United States of America, the EU, Canada and Japan, the second containing China, countries of the former Soviet Union and most countries in Asia, Africa and Latin America.

4. The Cultural and Media Sphere

As the United States of America clings to its strategy in all aspects of its role in the new world order, the ideological dimension is likely to be increasingly reflected in international relations, as well as in the cultural, educational and media spheres. The roles of religion and nationalism are expected to gain prominence with the increased overlap between communities, while some states will become more reluctant to fulfill their socio-economic obligations.

The 'Westernization of culture' – referring to the formulation of culture in accordance with that of the United States of America – may be a more accurate term than the 'globalization of culture' to describe the cultural evolution that will take place in the new world order. In the coming years, we will witness cultural Westernization based on the US interest in entrenching 'cultural dependency' as an important dimension of its relationships with other nations. American culture and lifestyle will dominate the world through movies, TV series, music, food and fashion, steering global culture in one direction at the expense of a rich global inter-cultural mix.[26] This approach, which represents a threat to national cultures, will inspire developing countries, and the Arab and Islamic countries in particular, to devise new and innovative mechanisms through which to maintain their cultural legacy, heritage, and national identity in the face of cultural globalization and the threat of cultural dependency on the United States of America.[27]

5. The Technological Sphere

The absorption rate of new technologies will become much more rapid. In the United States of America, for example, the introduction of electricity took 46 years, the telephone 35 years, radio 30 years, color TV 18 years, mobile communications 13 years, and the Internet just 7 years,[28] which indicates that, on a time line, the interval between the appearance of a new technology and its spread is shrinking, and the pace of technological change is accelerating. However, this will not be accompanied by a similar rate of acceleration in the adaptation to these innovations and their political, economic and social impacts. Therefore, countries will have to tap into technological advances for the benefit of their citizens and communities, or otherwise face a widening gap between states and peoples, and the effects of cross-border communication on internal stability.[29]

In the new world order, the United States of America can be expected to maintain its technological superiority – and achieve the greatest number of innovations – and its educational distinction (there are 4,140 universities in the United States of America, 83 of which were ranked among the top 400 universities in world in 2012).[30] US scientists and experts outnumber all others in every field, allowing the country to control the spread of advanced technologies and withhold them from countries opposing its interests and dominance in the new world order.[31]

6. The Social Sphere

The risks to global stability will increase as a result of a further deterioration in living conditions, particularly in the poorest countries of the world, due to population explosions and migration from rural to urban areas, swelling the ranks of the disadvantaged and rendering hundreds of millions of young people unemployed. Discontent will increase and be both aggravated and spread by modern means of communication, leading to rebellion against conventional authority. Meanwhile, resentment will grow as global inequalities become apparent, inspiring extremism, instability and insecurity.

Potential Modes of Strategic Influence on the New World Order

Robert Donald Kagan argues that the United States of America played a major role in forming the post-World War II system during the 1945–1990 period, a system characterized by an absence of war between international powers, the growth of the global economy, and a doubling in the number of democratic countries.[32] The United States of America assumed the helm of the new world order following the dissolution of the Soviet Union on December 25, 1991, and will continue to maintain order thanks to its possession of the requisite capabilities and its control of international mechanisms.[33]

By exploring these mechanisms, as well as the various forms of power adopted by the United States of America in the design and maintenance of the world order, one may foretell the most important aspects and mechanisms of US power in terms of its strategic impact on the countries of the world. Such mechanisms and patterns are used to ensure the continuation of American hegemony, whilst also encouraging any structural changes in the world order that the US may require. The most important of these mechanisms are:

1. Hard Power

Hard power involves a single power forcing others to change their positions by duress and threat, using a combination of material means to coerce a party to achieve certain objectives, either directly or indirectly, within a specific timeframe and context. In the case of a superpower, this is achieved through the threat or use of military force, or a mixture of diplomatic and economic sanctions, and regional or international isolation. Among the most prominent examples of US hard power are its actions against Afghanistan, Iraq and Kosovo, and in Pakistan and Libya.[34]

2. Soft Power

A superpower depends on soft power to influence others and encourage them to adopt a path that serves its interests by using financial and moral incentives as opposed to coercion and threat; it is the ability of a superpower to achieve its aims by persuasion rather than coercion, encouraging others to adopt policies and approaches that align with whatever objectives the superpower seeks to achieve.[35] The most important means of soft power include: humanitarian and development assistance; traditional and electronic media; cultural and ideological influence; tourism; assistance in resolving crises; and winning over domestic and international public opinion.

Strategic studies and research institutions play a leading role in soft power; in this context we may refer to US bodies such as the Carnegie Endowment for International Peace,[36] as well as other institutions in Qatar and Lebanon, and those concerned with democracy and human rights or bilateral/ multilateral public diplomacy.

There are three dimensions to public diplomacy: public communication, including via media messages based on specific policy objectives; strategic communication, through intensive political campaigns; and building an effective network of personal relationships with parties or individuals who enjoy direct or potential connections that may benefit the pursuit of a superpower's goals. This latter aim is achieved through scholarships, academic exchanges, training programs and conferences.[37] The US approach to achieving the disintegration of the Soviet Union is one of the most prominent examples of the use of soft power,[38] as is its role in the 'Arab Spring' countries – a contemporary example of how US soft power can change the political reality in other states – all in order to preserve US global dominance.

3. Smart Power

Smart power employs a combination of soft and hard power in order to achieve the desired outcome in cases in which neither would be effective or sufficient alone.[39] For example, where soft power alone cannot achieve a desired goal, the threat or use of a limited amount of hard power is employed.[40] Some experts believe that the United States of America should employ smart power to meet future challenges, such as reinvigorating its alliances and partnerships,[41] increasing the effectiveness of public diplomacy, supporting global development, promoting US free trade agreements, and facing the issues of energy security and climate change through technology investments.[42] Among the most prominent examples of the use of smart power by the United States of America is its approach to dealing with global terrorism, the impasse with Iran, and the indirect support for popular protests in Egypt and Tunisia.[43]

4. International Institutions and Bodies

International institutions and bodies play a vital role in entrenching the superpower's dominance over the new world order. The United States of America, for example, wields influence through the UNSC and international financial organizations. These institutions and bodies can impose pressure on states to comply with the norms of the new world order and yield to the will of the superpower dominating it. The decisions of the UNSC can legitimize the use of hard power by a superpower to achieve its interests, allow the formation of international military alliances to impose the will of the international community against any party, or issue resolutions to delegitimize failed or rogue states, subjecting them to international isolation and sanctions denying them access to strategic weapons or materials.

As for international financial organizations, they have the ability to provide or withhold loans, aid and support to economically distressed countries, which means that such countries must comply with accompanying restrictions and limitations. Such organizations have the capacity to intervene in the internal affairs of these countries and influence them according to the will of the superpower that indirectly controls these international institutions.[44]

5. Media

Media of all types – including visual, audio and print; conventional and modern; local and cross-border – have influential and active roles. The superpower dominating the new world order uses media effectively in order to influence domestic and international public opinion and hence uses it as a tool to pressure states and governments to change their positions. It also uses media to portray states and governments in a negative light abroad.[45] Such negative reportage encourages global civil society organizations to target such states and governments in order to force them to comply with their ideals. Media played a key role in the success of civil society organizations in mobilizing opponents across the world to stand up against globalization and the wars in Iraq and Afghanistan. Media has played a pivotal role in spotlighting undemocratic regimes' reactions toward peaceful protests, and has been instrumental in garnering sympathy among the international community with regard to individual events that led to the escalation of protests, such as the killing of the Egyptian Khaled Mohammed Saeed by Egyptian security forces, and the suicide of Tarek al-Tayeb Bouazizi in Tunisia after his humiliation at the hands of the Tunisian security forces.[46]

Pressure from international media was influential in encouraging the establishment of an international military alliance to intervene in Kosovo in 1999,[47] and has mobilized global sympathy for those affected by poverty, famine, desertification and drought in Africa. Cross-border media will therefore have a leading role to play in accelerating the processes of change and development in the new world order by mobilizing the attention of the masses on common issues.

Media, although a simple means, is also able to bypass the limits of space and time, as is evident in the shift from a reliance on reporters to a focus on audiovisual transmissions, capitalizing on new media technologies and modern means of social networking. Media can also highlight events via 'citizen journalists' whose circumstances place them at the site,[48] becoming an effective and influential asset in the fight against crime and in supporting preventive security across the world. For example, governments have been known to respond quickly to extradition demands as a result of pressure brought to bear by the mobilization of the global community.

6. The Internet

The significant role played by the internet in facilitating communication between the various elements of the new world order and its many components is well known. At the same time, however, the internet serves as a 'virtual global system,'[49] which comprises common values, provides the opportunity for greater understanding of citizenship rights, mobilizes efforts to achieve change and reform, and can support the formation of public solutions to global problems. The internet also represents the US domination of this virtual global system it has created, and which extends to every corner of the globe. The United States of America develops and controls the means of communication and cooperation between the elements in the system, and possesses the requisite educational, cultural, informational, cognitive, economic and security powers to manage the system according to its strategic interests. International relations – competition, cooperation, conflict and reconciliation – are played out within the internet, which can also be used to punish those who transgress its boundaries. It allows the transfer and circulation of print, visual and audio news, events, data, information and knowledge among billions of people via satellite, and ensures that the demands, opinions, attitudes and grievances of its users are presented to the largest possible number of people, creating global public opinion trends that can influence major powers in the new world order.[50]

The role of the internet as a virtual global system directly affects the vital interests and strategic objectives of states and governments in the new world order, particularly in light of the vulnerability of these countries and governments to the vagaries of domestic and international public opinion, and also because it serves as a means for the United States of America to achieve its interests and perpetuate its dominance.

7. Establishing New Blocs and Alliances

In light of the increasing interdependence and strategic partnership between powers in the new world order, one can expect the global system to witness a widening of the scope of alliances and blocs in various fields, particularly in terms of security/defense and economic cooperation.[51] Coalition is a foreign policy tool employed to achieve national security interests; as alliances are the product of contractual relationships, all members are bound to implement pre-arranged measures, representing an opportunity for achieving mutual goals, but also a restriction on the freedom of strategic movement of its members. The United States of America will seek to expand NATO to serve as one of a number of mechanisms for enforcing stability and security in the new world order.[52]

Speaking before a group of military, diplomatic and academic strategists participating at a Washington conference sponsored by the National Defense University on March 16–17, 2006,[53] the then Deputy US Secretary of Defense, Gordon Richard England (2004–2008), stressed that building and maintenance of international partnerships was a key aspect of US military strategy, and that the global war against terrorism, could be won by the United States of America, but only by "acting in partnership with coalition friends and allies."[54] Alliances shall be relied upon in the new world order to either support the position of the single superpower, or to stand up against it – particularly considering the great difficulty faced by any power or group of powers in acting as a strategic counterbalance to the United States of America – and impose their interests on the new world order.

8. Bilateral and Multilateral Agreements

The United States of America depends on bilateral and multilateral agreements to impose its military presence in a particular area or to achieve its economic interests over international parties.[55] This is clearly evident in the bilateral agreements the United States of America has established with more than 79 countries preventing them from applying the laws of the ICC on US citizens—whether civilian or military.[56] Other examples include multilateral economic agreements between the United States of America and Japan, Thailand and Hong Kong, securing economic benefits outside the scope of the WTO, in addition to agreements creating free zones between the United States of America and the GCC countries, and bilateral agreements on foreign investment.[57]

9. Parallel Diplomacy and Proxy War

In light of the continued complexity of the new world order environment, 'diplomacy by proxy' or 'parallel diplomacy'[58] has emerged as a means for the United States of America to maintain the coherence of this order. It comprises coordination with a major power to play a substitute diplomatic role for direct US diplomacy. The aim is to identify opportunities for, and obstacles to US strategic moves to achieve its interests and objectives, as well as to prepare the international environment for the success of its diplomacy or for the use of other tools to achieve its will. The most significant example of this is the US coordination with the EU to facilitate US diplomacy in dealing with the ongoing volatile situations in Egypt and Syria – which began with the protests and mass demonstrations that took place in January 2011 – whilst preserving US strategic interests and minimizing the visibility of its role. Another example is the role played by Turkey in convincing Iran to return to the negotiations on its nuclear program with the P5+1. The United States of America has also resorted to proxy war following the depletion of its military personnel and material capabilities by the conflict in Iraq and Afghanistan, with NATO carrying out the main operations in Libya. Proxy war is also being used in the ongoing war in Syria, which is weakening Syria militarily, economically and financially, destroying its infrastructure completely, and at the same time draining the capabilities of Iran, Lebanese Hezbollah, al-Qaeda and the Muslim Brotherhood without costing the United States of America any material or human losses or even affecting its image in the region.[59]

This pattern gives an indication of the approach that will be adopted by the United States of America in the coming period—a means of achieving its will without bearing any burden or being exposed to domestic or international public criticism.

10. Conference Diplomacy

Conference diplomacy has become an important mechanism of the new world order. The traditional role of diplomats has declined in favor of attending conferences to address crises and problems in the new world order. UN and civil society organizations have convened conferences to build international public opinion that can influence states' positions and governments' orientations, compelling them to yield to the will of the international community.[60] The future will see the United States of America rely increasingly on conference diplomacy to achieve its objectives and interests in the new world order. The focus of such global conferences will vary between security, defense, economics and politics in order to reach appropriate solutions that ensure US hegemony. This might be accompanied by the emergence of new international groupings within the global order with regional and global goals to challenge the US dominance or to influence its efforts and attitudes on issues of common global concern. The role of specialized UN organizations and agencies is expected to increase in promoting conference diplomacy to prepare the ground for new conventions and resolutions that will guide the new world order according to the US vision.[61] Thus, there will be less room for maneuver available to most states in the new world order as a result of the widening participation in these conferences, where the final say will be had by the powers that control the system. Hence, such states will need to be prepared to engage effectively in conference diplomacy in order to maximize gains and minimize losses, taking into account the important related role of local and global civil society organizations in this regard.

11. Direct and Indirect Military Intervention

Despite talk regarding the decline of the use of force in new world order relations, the United States of America will continue to resort to such means in dealing with threats to its strategic interests – at least for the next 25 years – without abiding by the fundamentals of international law or international conventions and norms. It will also establish international military alliances to achieve its immediate interests.

Global Repercussions and Strategic Effects

By identifying potential structural changes in the new world order and their implications for countries around the world, and by exploring the means and mechanisms that are likely to be used in the new world order to maintain its stability and continuity, a number of strategic effects on the elements and units of the new world order can be expected as a result of such structural changes and their implementation mechanisms. The most significant of such effects are explored below.[62]

1. The United Nations

The primary role of the United Nations and its international organizations and institutions in establishing a just peace in the world will witness significant decline in favor of the United States of America, which seeks to legitimize its behavior within the new world order and take advantage of UN mechanisms and organizations to achieve its own interests and entrench its dominance. The world's sole superpower will call for radical reform of the decision-making procedures of the UN and international organizations. This will increase its influence by supporting the efforts of its allies to assume important responsibilities within these organizations—especially the UNSC, in which the number of permanent members loyal to the United States of America will increase.[63]

2. The European Union

The financial crisis and the various related economic challenges facing many members of the EU – particularly Greece, Portugal, Italy and Spain – and the difficulties some of these countries are experiencing in finding effective solutions to these crises, raises questions about the prospects of their continuity within the EU. However the main forces controlling the EU – such as Germany, France and Britain – are moving in the orbit of the United States of America owing to their diplomatic and economic ties and the difficulty they face in defending their interests independently. The United States of America will seek to maintain the momentum of European unity,[64] as well as the expansion of NATO to become a US/EU military arm[65]—particularly considering the fact that the majority of EU countries have cut their defense budgets and reduced their military acquisitions. However, escalating nationalistic trends in Europe as a result of the increased level of unemployment in the most successful European countries have instigated hostility toward immigrants. This may drive French and German policies towards political extremism and national isolation, which may affect US efforts to maintain the unity of Europe in the new world order.[66]

Table 6.2
EU Members' Defense Budgets in 2011[67]

Country	EU Joining Date	Defense Budget (US $bn)
Austria	1995	2.08
Belgium	1952	2.82
Bulgaria	2007	1.01
Croatia	2013	0.935
Cyprus	2004	0.512
Czech Republic	2004	2.52
Denmark	1973	4.91
Estonia	2004	0.393
Finland	1995	3.43
France	1952	58.8
Germany	1952	44.2
Greece	1981	6.83
Hungary	2004	1.01
Ireland	1973	1.31
Italy	1952	21.0
Latvia	2004	0.292
Lithuania	2004	0.425
Luxemburg	1952	0.281
Malta	2004	0.60
Netherlands	1952	11.7
Poland	2004	9.43
Portugal	1986	2.83
Romania	2007	2.67
Slovakia	2004	1.07
Slovenia	2004	0.578
Spain	1986	15.3
Sweden	1995	6.21
United Kingdom	1973	63.7

3. South America

Most South American countries will be exposed to enormous pressure in the new world order to undertake development and political reform, and observe human rights and social justice, thereby raising the living standards of their populations and increasing per capita income, while at the same time augmenting efforts to combat organized crime and drugs and human trafficking, in addition to reducing immigration to the United States of America.[68]

4. Russia

Russia seeks to become a global player, but faces difficulty in returning to the status of a major pole in the new world order. It is therefore attempting to rebuild its military and economic capabilities, despite the many obstacles it faces in undertaking legal and legislative reform, and the modernization of its economy. Russia is also trying to become an active and influential political force in regional crises, but the United States of America is acting through the EU and NATO, as well as through its own indirect efforts, to curb the global influence of Russia. The United States of America is also pursuing the formation of a suitable geographic framework that may contain Russia in a larger collaborative context with Europe, so as to maintain sole US global dominance over the world order.

5. China

It is clear that China may be considered a global economic 'pole'; however it does not have the ability to engage at the same level in terms of its foreign policy. China cannot challenge US prominence in the new world order at any level—political, economic, cultural, technological or educational. This is because China lacks the military capability to keep pace with the United States of America, and also does not possess the soft power skills to influence the world culturally or politically in the way that the United States of America does, not least due to the difficulty of international communication in the Chinese language. The Chinese global identity is represented in terms of wealth—it seeks to build its wealth and maximize the gains and profits of that wealth in the belief that this will translate directly into power.[69]

The United States of America will attempt to come to some form of understanding with China in order to pave the way for a possible solution to the Taiwan issue, taking into account the fact that China could threaten the stability of the new world order in the context of the ongoing conflict with Japan over maritime boundaries and islands.[70] The United States of America is therefore seeking to involve China in a strategic dialogue with Japan in order to dispel any doubts surrounding its commitment to preserving Chinese unity, dealing with China from a perspective other than one based on economic and ideological competition, and integrating it into the global political community.[71]

If major strategic wars between the United States of America and Russia are relatively unlikely in light of the current situation, they may occur – perhaps even within two decades or more – between China and Russia, owing to regional conflicts and general rivalry, and between China and the United States of America against the backdrop of global Chinese strategic expansion and the US desire to curb China's role in order to preserve its dominant position in the world order.[72]

6. Japan

While Japan can become a military force as soon as circumstances allow – noting that its economic capacity has fallen against that of China – it remains a key ally of the United States of America and recognizes the US dominance over the new world order. Nonetheless, this will not prevent Japan from maintaining its global technological advancement compared to other major powers in the new world order. Through a close political relationship with Japan, the United States of America can work safely to accommodate China's regional aspirations, and at the same time defend against Chinese military action.[73]

7. India

The new world order considers India to be a relatively passive player regionally and globally, despite the capacities it enjoys in terms of manpower, democracy, and emerging economic and technological capabilities. The United States of America believes that the time has come to gradually involve India in discussing the future of stability in the region and the future of Central Asia as a whole, which involves the enhancement of US–Indian bilateral defense ties, and the adoption of a final, sustainable solution for the historic tensions and crises between India and Pakistan.[74] India must also reform its economy, despite the lack of solutions available to it and the political constraints it faces. The GCC countries have a significant role to play in supporting the strategic dialogue between the United States of America and India, particularly in light of their role in maintaining the stability of the Arabian Gulf region.[75]

8. Eurasia

It is time for the United States of America to "formulate and prosecute an integrated, comprehensive, and long-term geo-strategy for all of Eurasia. This need arises out of the interaction between two fundamental realities: America is now the only global superpower, and Eurasia is the globe's central arena."[76] In the short term the United States of America will seek to entrench democracy and perpetuate prevailing geopolitical pluralism in Eurasia. In the medium term the United States of America will focus on achieving a strategic balance that allows the establishment of a trans-Eurasian security system, characterized by further cooperation and coordination with the United States of America. Eventually, such a system may lead to the creation of real strategic partnerships in key areas in Eurasia, further entrenching US leadership of the new world order. The United States of America will then make certain that no state, or combination of states, will gain the capacity to expel the United States of America from Eurasia or even to diminish significantly its decisive, influential role in the region.[77] The United States of America may succeed in utilizing both alliances and conference diplomacy to gather the EU, China, Russia, Japan, India and Brazil to work alongside it in the context of the new world order, under the conviction that US national security has become linked to the broader security of the entire world order.[78]

9. The Middle East

The US approach toward the Middle East is based on four key dimensions: absolute security for Israel; political development; political Islam; and energy security.[79] Therefore, the United States of America will rely on certain regional powers to deal with these key dimensions, especially Israel, Turkey, Saudi Arabia, the UAE and Qatar—all of which are able to develop their economies and catch up with the tide of globalization.[80] However, Iran's capacity to destabilize the regional and international situation requires that the states of the new world order engage with Iran as part of the regional security system, and thwart its military nuclear ambitions and its quest to be recognized as a major regional power. There are also other questions that require answers, such as: can Saudi Arabia and the other GCC countries face the strategic challenges produced by ongoing regional changes and transformations, including the regime changes in some Arab countries and the accompanying rearrangement of foreign policies and patterns of regional alliances, besides the expected new regional security equations in light of an agreement between major powers and Tehran regarding its nuclear program?[81] What does the future hold for the Muslim Brotherhood and other Islamic–political currents in the region? Will continued US patronage of the Saudi role in supporting Sunnis in Lebanon, Iraq and Syria curb Iran's pursuit to expand its regional influence through the sectarian front?

10. Africa

Africa will rank highest in terms of population growth and the relative size of its youth demographic, as well as in terms of demand for water (40%), food (45%) and energy (53%), and the growing area affected by drought.[82] However, Africa remains a theater of competition between major powers, including the United States of America, which established the United States of America Africa Command (AFRICOM) to facilitate efficiency and flexibility in dealing with potential crises in the continent, as well as to monitor the activities of other world powers competing there[83]—particularly expansionist activity by China, but also that of France and Russia.

Conclusion

This chapter anticipates that US unipolarity will characterize the new world order for around the next five decades. Although the United States of America might be strategically challenged by certain major powers such as China, Russia, Japan, India and Brazil, this will not affect American hegemony over the new world order.

This unipolarity will affect the new world order in more than one respect. In the political sphere, the world will be divided into two parts: the first will comprise US allies, and hence will enjoy its support, while the second will represent adversaries of the United States of America, and will therefore be exposed to its sanctions. The United States of America will continue its support of values of democracy, freedom and human rights in the world, and this will undoubtedly affect the policies and role of the United Nations and its affiliated organizations. In the economic sphere, the world will witness a bolstering of economic blocs and a growing political role for sovereign wealth funds. Moreover, US influence in international financial institutions will likely increase. Washington will also work over the next decade to reduce its dependence on oil from regions plagued with risk and instability, such as the Middle East and the Arabian Gulf, which will spell a decline in the importance of US policy in such regions. In the military sphere, the United States of America will maintain its unrivalled military superiority and global nuclear proliferation may continue. Moreover, there may be an upsurge in proxy wars, fourth generation warfare and other mechanisms to achieve the universal US goals and interests in light of Washington's quest to maintain balance between its continued dominance over the new world order and the superiority of its military capabilities.

In the cultural and media sphere, the ideological dimension of international relations is likely to become more significant. The United States of America will pursue the Westernization of other cultures to perpetuate the concept of cultural dependency as one of the important dimensions of relations within the new world order. In the technological sphere, the absorption rate of new technologies will become much more rapid and the United States of America can be expected to maintain its technological superiority and achieve the greatest number of innovations to guarantee this. In the social sphere, the risks surrounding global stability will increase as a result of population growth, labor migration, unemployment, poverty and the spread of epidemics and other risks.

In the context of a world order characterized by its unipolarity, the United States of America will rely on several mechanisms to further its control and influence, the most important of which include smart power—combining hard and soft power capabilities. The United States of America will exploit the role of international institutions and bodies, especially the UN Security Council, as well as media and the Internet. It will also establish new alliances and blocs and resort to parallel diplomacy, proxy war, bilateral and multilateral agreements, conference diplomacy and direct and indirect military intervention.

As for the strategic implications of the structural changes expected for the new world order, they extend to different areas. The primary role of the United Nations will witness a significant decline in favor of the dominant superpower. The European Union will continue to move in the orbit of the United States of America. Most South American countries will be exposed to enormous pressure to undertake political reform. Russia will seek to become a global player but the United States of America will curb such pursuits. It is expected that within five decades China will become a global economic power, without the ability to effectively compete strategically with the United States of America in the leadership of the new world order. Japan will remain a key US ally. The United States of America will gradually involve India in discussing the future of stability in Asia. In the Middle East, Washington will

514

rely on a number of regional powers such as Israel, Turkey, Saudi Arabia, the United Arab Emirates and Qatar to deal with issues such as regional security, political Islam, political development and energy security. Finally, Africa will become a stage for international competition, especially between the United States of America and China.

THE NEW WORLD ORDER: FUTURE OUTLOOK

Chapter VII

The New World Order: Future Outlook

A number of recent theories refer to conspicuous changes in the fabric of the new world order in light of the rising roles of countries and blocs such as China and the EU. Such developments are expected to shape many of the new world order's features and lead to structural changes in the frameworks that govern both its leadership and the interaction of individuals, cross-border groups, states, and supranational groupings within it. These changes are likely to have substantial consequences for current means of maintaining alliances, managing conflicts, doing business, and overseeing production. Such changes are expected to affect mobility, social networking, and the identification of opinions and trends; moreover, they are likely to affect the considerations of individuals, civil society, the state, and international organizations in sovereign decision-making.

Three of these influential theories relate to the inability to control the course of local or international events—whether in the fields of politics, international relations, economics, business or even daily life. They are Moisés R. Naím's 'end of power'[1] thesis, the 'G-zero' theory of Ian Bremmer,[2] and the 'Black Swan' theory developed by Nassim Nicholas Taleb.[3]

The end of power theory, posited by Moisés R. Naím in his 2013 book of the same name, which was briefly reviewed in the Introduction to this volume, is based on the notion that power is shifting from West to East and North to South, from presidential palaces to public squares: "from large, stable armies to loose bands of insurgents, from formidable corporate behemoths to nimble agile start-ups," and – slowly but surely – from men to women.[4] But power, Naím says, is not merely shifting and dispersing. It is also decaying. Those in power today are more constrained in terms of how they may apply it, and more at risk of losing it than ever before.[5] They therefore retain power by erecting powerful barriers to keep challengers at bay. "Today, insurgent forces dismantle such barriers more quickly and easily than ever before, only to find that they themselves become vulnerable in the process"; power is shifting, "becoming harder to use and easier to lose." As a result, all leaders have less power than their predecessors, and the potential for upheaval is unprecedented.[6]

Naím attributes the reasons for the increasing ineffectiveness of power to three major changes that have affected traditional forms of authority through transformations in the basic elements of life: i.e., how, where, how long, and how well we live. He categorizes these changes through three consecutive 'revolutions.' First, the 'more' revolution, as the twenty-first century is literally – as mentioned previously – an age of profusion, with more people, more literacy, more goods and services in markets, and more political parties, etc.[7] Second, the 'mobility' revolution, as people around the globe move faster and more frequently than ever before, making them harder to manage. The third and final revolution is the 'mentality' revolution, which is represented in the profound changes in the mentality of the masses as a result of unprecedented access to resources and information which have allowed people to undergo a massive cognitive and emotional transformation.[8]

The G-zero theory was presented by Ian Bremmer in a number of articles and studies,[9] and was promoted by David F. Gordon, the former director of policy planning at the US State Department,[10] as well as professor of economics Nouriel Roubini, known for predicting the global financial crisis in 2007. This theory posits that we are now living in a so-called G-zero world,[11] one in which "no single country or bloc of countries has the political and economic leverage – or the will – to drive a truly international agenda."[12] The result, as the theory predicts, will be "intensified conflict on the international stage over vitally important issues, such as international macroeconomic coordination, financial regulatory reform, trade policy and climate change ..." to which we might add the Syrian and Iranian crises.[13] Such a vacuum will have far-reaching implications, as each government must work to build domestic security and prosperity to fit its own unique political, economic, geographic, cultural, and historical circumstances; "state capitalism is a system that must be unique to every country that practices it."[14] Ian Bremmer and David F. Gordon argue that in the G-zero world, the United States of America will remain for some time "first among equals but only that ... Rather than formulating and executing optimal solutions, the United States of America must resign itself to messier outcomes, in terms of the new world order's interactions and outcomes."[15] Ian Bremmer also believes that the result of living in a G-zero world is a lack of global leadership—a situation that has developed "just as growing numbers of transnational problems – Middle East turmoil, intensified territorial disputes, climate change, conflicts in cyberspace and poorly regulated cross-border financial flows – are gathering momentum."[16]

Nassim Nicholas Taleb's 'black swan' theory,[17] on the other hand, argues that highly influential events, such as the astonishing, rapid and unexpected success of Google, the attacks of September 11, 2001, World War I, the global economic and financial crisis, and the three most important contemporary technologies in the modern world – the computer, the internet, and the laser – can all be considered "black swans."[18]

A black swan is an 'outlier,' in that it "lies outside the realm of regular expectations, because nothing in the past can convincingly point to its occurrence. Second, it carries an extreme impact. Third, in spite of its outlier status, human nature makes us concoct explanations for its occurrence after the fact, giving an illusion that it is explainable and predictable."[19] Taleb suggests that rare events can contain structure: "… it is not easy to compute their probability, but it is easy to get a general idea about the possibility of their occurrence. We can turn these Black Swans into Gray Swans, so to speak, reducing their surprise effect."[20] Thus, Taleb argues that black swans are events which have extreme impacts affecting systems and developments, and are inherently of low predictability and hence difficult to manage.[21]

These theories may give the impression that the new world order will be based on the weakness of conventional powers, and the absence of a single power or powers capable of effectively managing the world order and controlling its resources, and furthermore that it is difficult to predict and prepare for those factors which play a major role in changing the course of history. However, there are some dynamics that may actually lend relative advantages in terms of power and influence to a limited number of countries, as well as other factors that could enable lower-tier states to catch up with pioneering powers, leading to a broader base of globally influential countries.

The most important factors suggesting the emergence of a limited number of powerful and influential states – or perhaps even one state – in the new world order, can be summarized as follows:

1. *The ever-accelerating pace of technological development in the realms of communication, defense, energy, economy, finance and trade:* such progress is led by a very limited

number of countries, including the United States of America, which suggests that the US will remain a single pole for some time, assuming the reins of leadership in the new world order. Undoubtedly, the new world order will be driven by development in the field of information technology—computing power is expected to increase eight thousand fold by 2026, according to [Gordon Earle] Moore's Law.[22] There is no doubt that whoever assumes global leadership in the development of information technology will be best equipped to apply both soft and hard power, augmenting its influence on the global arena. As a limited number of countries dominate the IT development field – with the United States of America occupying the top spot by a huge margin – it is expected that power in the new world order will be concentrated among a limited number of states, and perhaps even just one.[23]

2. *Returning to economic blocs and the concentration of wealth*: for a long period there was a global movement toward the liberalization of trade in goods and services, under rounds of negotiation organized by the WTO,[24] which is essentially controlled by the United States of America and the West. Such negotiations were accompanied by concrete efforts from the IMF to liberalize capital flows between countries and prevent exchange rates being used to achieve trade advantages. Such measures have been touted as the

best tools for developing countries to use in boosting their economic growth and raising living standards, thereby narrowing the gap separating them from developed countries. However, the global financial crisis, which began in 2007, reversed such efforts, and threatened the future of sustainable economic growth in many developing countries—especially export-oriented emerging markets. The move toward free trade was reversed, currency wars reemerged and a zero-sum mentality prevailed—where one party's gain must be at the direct expense of another's.[25]

Powerful new economic blocs are being established; the most prominent of which may materialize as a result of negotiations that began in mid-2013 between the United States of America and the EU to create the world's largest free trade zone (these are likely to be complete by end of 2014). It is expected that the resultant US–EU agreement will benefit both parties in terms of economic growth and job creation, providing more than one million jobs in the US and around 400,000 in the EU, while it will have significant adverse effects for China, which relies on exports to US and the EU markets.[26]

3. *Fragility in the foundations of economic, political and social systems in many emerging powers*: key emerging countries such as China, India and Brazil are still considered developing countries, as mentioned earlier –

with all the conventional problems that are common to other developing countries – and will require considerable time to raise the living standards of their citizens. This represents a dilemma, as high levels of income in these export-dependent countries may deprive them of their competitive advantages *vis-à-vis* other countries which still have low income levels. The systems of these emerging countries are yet to be tested by economic or financial shocks—a fact that raises legitimate questions over the degree of their resilience in the face of such crises.[27]

As for the factors that could lead a greater number of countries to join the ranks of the most powerful and influential states in the new world order, they can mainly be summarized as follows:[28]

1. *The increasing capability of certain economies in terms of counterfeiting and reverse engineering, and the difficulty of protecting intellectual property*: many questions have been raised in the West concerning Chinese firms in particular failing to respect intellectual property rights to technologies and innovations produced in developed countries, according to the EU and the United States of America. Chinese entities have also been accused of extensive cyber espionage, but most attacks do not appear to have been for military or political purposes; rather, the vast majority of

them have targeted Western companies – especially in the United States of America – in order to obtain innovative research.[29] Despite the legal and ethical issues associated with such activities, this helps countries such as China to narrow the technological gap between them and developed countries like the United States of America, Germany and Japan. Clear evidence of this fact is that most of the US companies targeted by Chinese hackers have been firms working in the field of energy—and especially those employing advanced fracking technology, such as ExxonMobil.[30] One company had all of its data on a ten-year, $1 billion research program copied by hackers in a single night. Estimates claim that global cyber-crime costs hacked companies around $110 billion a year.[31]

2. *Asymmetric conflict and fourth generation warfare (4GW)*: on the evolution of conflict, Moisés Naím cites a study conducted by Ivan Arreguin-Toft at Harvard University:[32] "… in the asymmetric wars that broke out between 1800 and 1849, the weaker side (in terms of soldiers and weapons) achieved its strategic goals in 12 percent of cases. But in the wars that erupted between 1950 and 1998, the weaker side prevailed more often: 55 percent of the time, and rising."[33] Hence, "the outcome of modern asymmetric conflicts is more likely to be determined by the interplay of

opposing political and military strategies than by blunt military force. Thus, a large, advanced army by itself no longer ensures that a country will achieve its strategic goals. One important factor behind this shift is the increasing ability of the weaker party to inflict casualties on its opponent at lower cost to itself."[34]

As a result of the changing balance of fortunes of major military powers in asymmetric conflicts – and especially against terrorist groups – the United States of America in particular began to develop a theory, 'fourth generation warfare (4GW),' in 1989. According to this theory the battlefield was unidentified geographically, "marked by greater dispersion, and likely to include the whole of the enemy's society."[35] It was also marked by the diminishing role of large military units which would "no longer be an overwhelming factor; in fact they … [were to] become a disadvantage."[36] Thus, reliance would be upon small, highly maneuverable, agile forces. 4GW aims to collapse the enemy internally, rather than physically destroy it, by targeting its culture and weakening it from the inside.[37] Of course, asymmetric conflict and 4GW make it difficult to evaluate the effectiveness of managing conflicts relying on the conventional military balance of power. Thus, this transformation may provide a tool to narrow the gap between major and minor military powers. At the same time, however, by virtue of the technical superiority of countries like the United States of America, this transformation may lend it even more advantage, allowing it to conduct conflicts with much less human and material cost than the traditional forms of warfare, rendering such conflicts less controversial both internally and externally.[38]

3. *A growing role and global impact of certain international organizations*: against the backdrop of the 2007 global financial crisis, the roles of certain international organizations (such as the IMF and the World Bank) have been placed in the spotlight after having been eclipsed, criticized, and pressured to re-examine their roles and global impact. With the revitalized roles of such organizations, a number of emerging countries, such as the BRICS and Saudi Arabia, began demanding a greater role in international decisions affecting the global economy. The IMF recently responded to the demands of such countries by reconsidering their roles.[39] With such organizations becoming more involved in decision-making that influences the international arena, it is expected that relatively small emerging countries, such as Brazil and Chile, are likely to have larger roles.

Likely Features of the New World Order

Anatoly Utkin argues that the new world order of the twenty-first century will see a convergence of the world's people, who will become ever more similar – like organizations – not only in terms of their clothing, language, culture, food, fashion, entertainment, and approaches to life, but also in their psychological DNA.[40] Utkin argues that people will converge and share common values, becoming one cosmic village, leading in the future to the elimination of boundaries between 'us' and 'them,' and drastically changing bio-molecular engineering science, cloning, the robotics industry, informatics and the world familiar to humans, whilst also guaranteeing our survival and success.[41]

Utkin also argues that easy access to media will weaken the role of the state and its organs, such as central banks and secret services. Just as the Protestants' need for the Church was practically made obsolete by the invention of the printing press, so will communications technology undermine the necessity of the state as an intermediary between the individual and the outside world.[42] As a result of the fear of terrorism – including nuclear terrorism – nations will concede sovereign rights to international organizations, which will stand up against authoritarian regimes, leading to the emergence of a post-nationalist civil society (under the pressure of a gradual decline in state sovereignty) where global governance will replace a number of individual governments' functions. On the domestic political front, the differences between the left and right of the political spectrum will vanish, and not only class division, but also class consciousness will disappear. What variances remain will mainly be between thinkers who are prepared for change and think in terms of global governance, and those who remain hampered by tradition, preconception, inertia, and opposition to change.[43]

Taking this view – with some reservation – a number of highly probable key features of the new world order can be identified as follows:[44]

A System Inclined toward Unipolarity

Unipolarity can be defined as the dominance of one superpower over the rest of the international community (which is organized in a hierarchical manner, as mentioned in the Introduction to this volume)—a state that exclusively controls international politics without contest from other major nations, and that monopolizes economic, technical, and military power, in some ways akin to the the United States of America today. Some observers believe that the world order may transform gradually over a long period from unipolarity to multipolarity, passing through two phases in the process. The first phase is genuine unipolarity where the United States of America governs the directions of international politics.[45] The second phase is 'soft' unipolarity, where relationships between major players in the international community evolve toward participation and cooperation in sharing international burdens and responsibilities.[46] A good example of soft unipolarity is the United States of America today under Barack Hussein Obama, whose approval rating stood at 41% in a CNN/ORC international survey, the results of which were announced on December 20, 2013.[47]

However, contrary to this view, it is highly likely that the new world order will not, in fact, evolve toward multipolarity, given the fact that this shift will require more than equal growth and development between the superpower dominating the new world order and the other major powers. Expansion in the three above-mentioned elements of power (economic, technical and military) should be faster among second-tier and possibly even third-tier states, than it is in the single superpower in order to allow for a balance of power and a greater role for emerging powers. Instead, unipolarity is expected to continue, but with an increasing role for sub-state entities such as issue-oriented non-governmental and civil society organizations—for example, in the fields of environment, personal freedoms and human rights. This expanding role for NGOs will be at the expense of official organizations and governments, so national and international decision-making will become increasingly influenced by sub-state groups utilizing contemporary mass media to promote their agendas and opinions.

In recent years China has been tipped as a future pole to balance the United States of America, marking the beginning of a shift to a multipolar international order; however, one may question whether China is able to catch up with the United States of America. Some observers believe that owing to the rapid and continuous growth of its economy China will be able to take the position of a second pole in the new world order during the next decade. Proponents of this view attribute their logic to the strong economic rise China has achieved during the past decade in particular, ranking as the world's second largest economy after the United States of America, up from the sixth position in 2000.[48] Economic expansion has resulted in convergence in terms of the relative size of the US and Chinese economies. In 2000 the US economy was more than eight times the size of China's, but this gap has since narrowed—to two and a half times by 2010, and to less than twice the size in 2013.[49] However, it is very difficult to imagine a convergence in economic, political and military elements of power between the United States of America and China; indeed, the gap between the two countries in terms of global power and influence may even become wider for the following reasons:[50]

1. Although the Chinese economy has grown much faster than the US economy over the past decade, and despite the fact that it has not been affected by the global financial and

economic crisis to the same degree as the United States of America or the EU, such substantial growth brings inherent vulnerabilities that could lead to sudden slowdowns in the performance of the Chinese economy, which in the future may hinder its ability to catch up with the United States of America.

The Chinese economy has relied upon two types of investment to achieve high growth rates over the past decade: state investment – particularly in infrastructure – and foreign direct investment (FDI), especially from the United States of America, Japan and a number of European countries. Conversely, the United States of America depends heavily on private – and largely domestic – investment. This puts China in a fragile situation in terms of its prospects for continued economic growth.

With regard to state investment, the general global trend is toward a reduction in the role of the state in the economy, as it is relatively inefficient compared to the private sector. Government involvement may also give rise to complex problems associated with competition with the private sector over financial resources. Moreover, inefficient management of government investment may lead to the accumulation of government debt and problems in public finances which could result in financial and economic crises and a loss of confidence in the economy reminiscent of the

European government debt crises in countries such as Greece. This represents an example of the negative impact an increase in government spending financed by debt can cause to a national economy, not to mention its potential to spark crises that might take decades to overcome.[51]

The second type of investment that China relies on as an engine for economic growth is FDI, the movements of which are prone to rapid shifts from one developing economy to another according to relative advantages in terms of labor cost, exchange rates, and tax/non-tax concessions. China could face a steep decline in FDI inflows, which may move away from China as changes occur which affect the factors that first made the economy attractive as a destination for investment.

In this context, two primary and controversial issues come to mind.[52] First is the cost of labor, since cheap labor and other highly concessional conditions in China were among the main reasons for foreign companies to invest there. However, China is witnessing increased growth, more openness to the outside world, a gradual rise in the living standards of the working class, and growing demands to improve employment conditions. These factors are expected to lead to increasing labor costs compared to neighboring competitors such as the Philippines and Vietnam. This in turn could lead to a significant shift in FDI away from China toward its regional competitors. The second issue is the exchange rate of the Chinese currency, the yuan – also known as the renminbi – (current exchange rate is 6.087 yuan to US dollar),[53] which has become increasingly controversial in light of the global inclination towards currency war.

2. It is expected that China will lose the current currency conflict, to the benefit of both the United States of America and the EU, which accuse China in particular of using the exchange rate policy to gain an unfair advantage for Chinese exports. Currency war, in this case launched by China through competitive currency devaluations, "is one of the most destructive and feared outcomes in international economics." In his book *Currency Wars: The Making of the Next Global Crisis,* James G. Rickards posits that currently there are three powers engaged in the new currency war which began in 2010: the United States of America, the eurozone and China. While no-one denies the importance of other major currencies, the dominance of the currencies of these three actors, accounting for about 60 percent of global GDP, creates a center of gravity to which all other economies and currencies become peripheral in some way. "In this currency war, there are three main battle lines: a dollar–yuan theater across the Pacific, a dollar–euro theater across the Atlantic, and a euro–yuan theater across the Eurasian landmass."[54]

The dollar–yuan front is perhaps the most important in terms of its potential effects on the relative strengths of the United States of America and China in the new world order. In this context, it should be noted that China has long undervalued the yuan. In 1983, the yuan was massively overvalued at 2.8 yuan to one dollar; however, this was at a time when exports made up a relatively small proportion of Chinese GDP.[55] During the following decade, China devalued the yuan several times and by 1993 the rate stood at 5.32 yuan to the dollar. On January 1, 1994, however, China massively devalued the yuan to 8.7 to the dollar, prompting the US Treasury to label China a 'currency manipulator.'[56]

Due to external pressures, the yuan was revalued a number of times, then pegged at 8.28 yuan to the dollar until 2004.[57] The Chinese Communist Party understood that the survival of the party and the continuation of political stability depended on job creation, and the surest way to rapid, massive job creation was through exports—the currency peg was a means to meet this objective. Sino-American relations had been cold for a long time, especially since the Tiananmen Square massacre,[58] when economic sanctions were imposed by the United States of America on China, leading to minimal FDI flows from US firms into China. However, the attacks on September 11, 2001 resulted in a thaw in

Sino-American economic relations. In 2002, bilateral trade and investment rose to $147.3 billion, compared to $75.4 billion in 1997.[59]

Table 7.1
Yuan Exchange Rate* against the US Dollar
during the Period 1970–2013[60]

Year	Year-end US Dollar–yuan Exchange Rate
1970	2.460
1975	1.970
1980	1.530
1985	3.200
1990	5.220
1995	8.318
2000	8.2772
2005	8.0702
2010	6.6000
2011	6.2939
2012	6.2301
2013	6.0867

* Exchange rate at the end of each year, except for 2013, which is calculated as of the end of October.

That year also marked the beginning of the ultra-low interest rate policy employed by the Chairman of the Federal Reserve, Alan Herbert Greenspan.[61] The policy sought to stimulate the US economy and respond to the challenges presented by the 2000 tech bubble collapse, the

2001 recession, the September 11, 2001 attacks and the Federal Reserve's fear of deflation. China, meanwhile, was exporting its deflation to the world through cheap labor, manipulating exchange rates so that the cost of Chinese goods – including labor costs – became relatively cheap compared to that of its competitors. For such purposes, China pegged its currency to the dollar and acquired massive quantities of US Treasury securities, as Chinese trade surpluses with the United States of America continued to grow. By 2011, total Chinese foreign reserves in all currencies amounted to $2.85 trillion, of which $950 billion were in US government obligations of one kind or another.[62]

Figure 7.1
Yuan–US Dollar Exchange Rate, 1970–2013

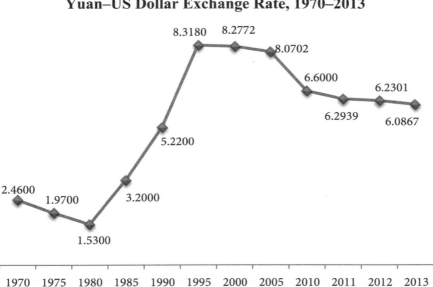

The United States of America recognized the negative impact of China's manipulation of exchange rates to make its exports to the US market and the rest of the world much larger than its imports and thereby accumulating surpluses in its current account. China used these surpluses to buy US government securities, effectively lending to the United States of America. Thus, the US urged China to increase the value of the yuan in order to reduce the growing US trade deficit with China and retard the massive accumulation of dollar-denominated assets by the People's Bank of China (PBOC). China complied and effected an increase in the yuan–dollar rate to 6.40 yuan in August 2011, compared to 8.28 yuan in 2004.[63] By mid-2013, the yuan had not moved strongly against the dollar, appreciating to about 6.12 yuan per dollar before August 2013, up by 4.4% over the past two years.[64]

In light of the current conflict over the use of the exchange rates to stimulate economies and pull them out of crises, the United States of America and the EU appear to be heading toward victory. On the one hand, it seems that the pressures brought on China to liberalize its exchange rate are gradually proving fruitful. As previously noted, China has already begun to allow an increase in the yuan rate, but more importantly, since 2011 China has started taking steps to partially internationalize its currency.[65] These developments have exposed the Chinese economy to two specific vulnerabilities: first, it is expected that the relative cost of goods produced in China for export will increase compared to that of its competitors due to the high price of the yuan. The second vulnerability is that the liberalization of trading in yuan could facilitate the transmission of the global financial crisis to the Chinese economy through the exchange rate.[66]

Moreover, it seems that the exchange rate battle has led to a shift in the global trend of multilateral liberalization of foreign trade – which was in the interest of China – towards exclusive-membership trading blocs. Perhaps the ultimate example of such a move is the announcement of negotiations between the United States of America and the European Union in mid-2013[67] to establish the world's largest free trade zone; negotiations for which are expected to be completed before the end of 2014.[68] Some studies have shown that such an agreement would be in the best interests of both parties, especially the US side, as it would result in almost 1.1 million more American jobs and boost US GDP per capita by 13.4%. As for the EU, the full implementation of an ambitious liberalization of transatlantic trade and investment could boost the EU economy by 119 billion euros ($159 billion) a year, leading to a 0.5% annual growth in EU GDP and about 400,000 new jobs. However, the agreement will inflict serious damage on non-members, including developing countries such as China, because imports from non-member states will drop significantly.[69]

3. The Chinese economic system continues to develop, and is yet to experience a major challenge, while the US economic system has reached a high stage of development and has not only managed to survive a number of financial and economic crises, but subsequently to maintain its primary position. Despite the criticism directed recently toward the capitalist system in general, and its application in the United States of America in particular, following the financial crisis and its repercussions in terms of job losses, the US economic system has demonstrated resilience in the face of numerous economic shocks, and maintained its key features as a free capitalist system based on private-sector initiative. The debate about the role of government in the US economic recovery may be misread as moving away from capitalism in search of new economic practices. However, it should be noted that this debate – especially in terms of government policies on taxation, expenditure and government debt – lies within the broad framework of the capitalist system, and is limited to the nature of indirect government intervention in economic activity through fiscal and monetary policy in time of crisis.[70]

Conversely, the Chinese economic system is believed by some observers to be moving gradually toward a mixture of state planning and capitalism,[71] as China begun to gradually decrease state control over the economy in favor of a more market-oriented economy and intensified its export activities since the beginning of the new millennium. Moreover, as stated earlier, the Chinese economy is untested in the face of serious economic and financial crises, so there is little evidence on which to base judgments regarding its flexibility and resilience to shocks. Such assessments are the natural consequence of the growing global pressure on China to open its financial sector to the outside world, and to increase the flexibility of make its currency.[72] Thus, the world may soon witness some economic and financial crises in China, such as real estate overvaluation (a 'property price bubble'), or a crisis either in local government debt or banking liquidity and loans. Unless and until the Chinese economic system proves resilient to such challenges, it will remain difficult to imagine it achieving a better position than that of the United States of America, which survived the Great Depression in 1929, Black Monday in 1987, the savings and loans crisis of 1989–1991, and the recent global financial crisis, which began in 2007. There is no doubt that one of the signs of the US economic system's relative superiority is that despite all these crises, the US dollar is still the world's reserve currency *par excellence*, and US Treasury securities remain one of the safest financial investments in global markets.[73]

4. The US economy is based on innovation, technology and services, which means it is a modern economy, while the Chinese economy is still based on traditional economic sectors such as agriculture and industry. Despite all that is said about China's global dominance over technology production – laptops, tablets, smart phones, etc.[74] – and the related concern that China might be in a position to use this mass production as a means to spy on the world, the vast majority of these products are American or European innovations, and the United States of America has an almost absolute monopoly over the operating systems that these devices depend on through the likes of Microsoft, Apple and Google.[75] Indeed, this provides an apt illustration of the different approaches toward growth and production between China and the United States of America—China produces the body, while the United States of America designs and manufactures the brain.

There is no doubt that the future of the global economy and the roles of its various components in the new world order will be increasingly dependent on technology and innovation. This will impart a relative advantage to the United States of America, and may increase the gap in terms of economic power between the United States of America and its adversaries, particularly China. The US economy is still the world leader in terms of spending on research and development (R&D),[76] not only in information technology but also in areas such as aircraft manufacturing, military industry and energy extraction (in particular through hydraulic fracturing).[77]

China is trying hard to catch up with the United States of America in the fields of technology and innovation, and its companies sometimes resort to controversial methods such as hacking to obtain technology secrets and as a means to undertake reverse engineering. However, such efforts have not been as successful as hoped.[78] It is therefore difficult to imagine a narrowing of the gap in light of the colossal US spending on research and development, and the inability of Chinese companies to keep pace with such spending, at least in the near or medium term, due to tighter restrictions on financial resources.

5. At the political level, it is unclear as to whether China is willing or able to play an effective leadership role in facing global crises. China's strategic allies differ in nature to those of the United States of America; the latter has proved quite capable of achieving balance between national and global interests, not to mention the crucial role it plays in international organizations, or its wide expertise in managing international politics.

Despite what is said about China's growing role in the global economy and the resultant growth in its significance regarding global issues, it is obvious that China does not seek to play a leadership role in the near future. It is clear from China's cautious movements with regard to international issues that it prefers to pursue a 'reactive' approach rather than seeking to lead. There is clear evidence of this in terms of current international issues such as the Syrian crisis, and through China's moves in Southeast Asia to counter potential US threats in the region. China has been at pains to paint itself as a still-developing state that retains its distance from international conflicts, but is ready to cooperate with other major powers in order to achieve world peace.[79]

China is also trying to forge new alliances and, unlike the United States of America, does not make loans or aid conditional on the practices of human rights and good governance. Instead it seeks out international groups in which the United States of America or the EU are not represented. China relies mainly on soft power in its alliances, promoting its peaceful Confucian culture to maintain its image in the world. At the same time, however, it is in some ways searching for a new identity in the face of an American cultural invasion.[80]

There is no doubt that China's reluctance to take on a leadership role stems largely from the costs associated with such a role, and its adverse effects on China's quest to promote itself as a peaceful country that does not wish to be involved in conflict. Besides, China is highly dependent on its exports as an engine to drive its economy and employment, which places restrictions on its involvement in foreign conflicts as such interventions might lead to China losing export markets.

However, it is noted that questions have been raised recently regarding China's growing presence in areas such Africa; Beijing's penetration of the continent has not been ideological but rather focused on commercial opportunism and the acquisition of natural resources. Sino-African bilateral trade has witnessed a huge boom, reaching $50 billion in 2006, compared to $1 billion in 2000,[81] making China the third largest trading partner of the African Continent after the United States of America and France. Perhaps the best example of the importance of Africa to the Chinese economy is the fact that in 2006 Angola overtook Saudi Arabia as China's premier supplier of oil.[82] Africa saw five significant visits by Chinese leaders between 2005 and 2007, and in the midst of China's entry into African markets its foreign policy operated with 'no political strings attached.' This approach, coupled with Beijing's willingness to provide assistance and concessional loans to African nations, has rendered it highly attractive to African leaders.

While African resources seem vital to the well-being of the Chinese economy, the continent also occupies an important place in China's global ambitions. The emergence of China as a major player in Africa and the impact of its presence there, effectively challenging Western superiority in the continent, constitute crucial components of this new relationship.[83] Barack Hussein Obama's visit to Africa in 2013 was of little economic significance compared to Chinese influence in Africa.[84]

6. In a military context, the United States of America retains absolute primacy in terms of its capability to mobilize forces beyond its borders, its overseas military bases, the power of its military alliances, and its technical superiority in military industry.

In his book, *The Next 100 Years: A Forecast for the 21st Century*, George Friedman predicts that the twenty-first century will be dominated by the United States of America, owing to its geographic position as well as its control over the world's oceans through its navy and military bases.[85] He states that North America has distinct advantages, in that it has coasts on both the Atlantic and Pacific oceans, and can meet the prohibitively high cost of maintaining navies that can patrol both of these oceans; ultimately, the fact that the United States of America is the dominant power in North America means it is also the dominant power in the international system, and will remain so for the next 100 years.[86] The United States of America seeks to preserve this domination of the world's oceans, partly by denying other powers the resources to invest in, and assemble a rival navy. The US achieves this by creating shifting alliances to tie down any potential regional hegemon.[87]

He notes that China is "an isolated country physically," with Siberia in the north and the Himalayas to the south, its access to external ports is mostly via the eastern part of the country, and thus it is difficult for China to expand further.[88] China has not been a major naval power for centuries, and it will not be able to achieve relative progress against the United States of America because building a navy is not only costly and time-consuming, but requires training to produce the military personnel capable of managing it.[89] These factors make it very difficult for China to even come close to developing naval forces that might compete with the United States of America in controlling the world's waterways, or in mobilizing significant military forces to areas of international conflict with strategic significance to China.[90]

Nothing is more indicative of the naval capacity gap than their respective carrier fleets. The United States of America has ten active aircraft carriers in service, it is building one more, and there are a further two in the planning stage.[91] In contrast, China has one aircraft carrier, and is currently building a second. However, the existing carrier is a retrofit of a Soviet ship, and owing to the age of the design it is very limited in terms of which aircraft can operate from it, as mentioned in the earlier chapter in this volume, "Factors Influencing the Structure of the New World Order."[92]

Furthermore, Chinese alliances are limited in terms of geography and influence compared to those of the United States of America, as mentioned previously. Most Chinese alliances are in Central Asia, away from those involving the United States of America and the EU.[93] As for the United States of America, it has multiple alliances based in all regions of the world, including NATO, which is the world's strongest.

Technological Advantages

The second feature of the new world order is the growing importance of technologically advanced and nonconventional systems of production and communication to replace decaying conventional systems, and an increasing reliance on genetic engineering, cloning and nanotechnology in finding solutions to key issues such as the provision of food, energy, medicine and the development of human capabilities.[94]

The past three decades have shown that technological developments can lead to drastic changes in the global balance of power, and that whoever takes the lead in this respect is able to substantially increase their negotiating power in the global arena. A clear example in this context is hydraulic fracturing,[95] which has allowed the United States of America to extract oil and shale gas, as already mentioned in Chapter IV. Since the infamous oil crisis, which began on October 15, 1973, the United States of America has always considered reducing its dependence on Middle Eastern oil to be an important strategic goal, and it has now begun to successfully achieve this through hydraulic fracturing. This may have a significant impact on the stability of various regions of the world.[96] As mentioned previously, US dependence on oil from the GCC has declined from 17% of supply in 2001 to 13% in 2011, while imports from other countries in the western hemisphere increased from 50% to 55% during the same period.[97] This dependence is expected to shrink gradually in the future with a higher degree of self-sufficiency, and movement toward bridging the gap using supply from neighboring countries. As detailed in Chapter IV, the western hemisphere contains the world's most important regions in terms of proven unconventional liquid fuel reserves. The United States of America has 76% of the world's proven reserves of shale oil, while Canada possesses 70% of oil sands reserves and Venezuela has the vast majority of the world's proven extra-heavy crude reserves, accounting for more than 95%.[98] Other countries in the Americas also possess unconventional resources—Brazil, for example, holds 2% of the world's shale oil reserves.[99]

As already mentioned, such unconventional gas sources include shale gas and tight gas, which are trapped between reservoir rocks of very low permeability, and have recently become economically feasible to exploit using "fracking." Also worthy of note is that such technology has been extremely influential in enabling the United States of America to increase its reliance on natural gas as a source of energy, particularly in electricity production. The US comes second to China in terms of proven reserves of shale gas—China with a share of 19%, and the United States of America with a share of 13%. Furthermore, most unconventional sources of natural gas are found in the Americas, with the United States of America, Argentina, Mexico and Canada together accounting for about 41% of the known reserves of shale gas.[100]

Elsewhere, high-tech breakthroughs in areas such as nanotechnology have overcome boundaries restricting human potential in terms of health and physical strength[101]—developments that could have implications for how future wars may be waged. Advances in cloning and genetic engineering, for example, have increased the potential for organ replacement, and may revolutionize the very concept. Other breakthroughs in terms of cybernetics offer the possibility of increasing physical strength, or providing instant real time information about one's environment. Google Glass is a good example of the latter technology that will soon be in mass production.[102] Such breakthroughs have raised philosophical questions about the transformation of human beings in the future to what science fiction describes as 'cyborgs.'[103] Moreover, innovations such as 3D printers may change the balance of power and concept of military supply, as demonstrated by the use of 3D printers to manufacture working firearms.[104]

In military terms, technology is also changing the balance of asymmetric conflicts. In April 2013 a missile was successfully destroyed by using a laser beam—a technology that is expected to be increasingly deployed in missile defense. This could result in drastic changes in the cost–benefit balance of conflicts—replacing a missile defense system that costs hundreds of thousands of dollars per shot with a laser that costs just a single dollar to fire.[105]

Increasing Pressure on the Capitalist System

There is no doubt that the 2007 global financial crisis, and the subsequent unemployment crisis – affecting young people in particular – has raised questions about the future of the capitalist system, which is based on the interaction of market forces and a reduced economic role of the state. However, unlike the communist system (which was based on centralized state planning and control of the factors of production, and which essentially collapsed along with the Berlin Wall and the Soviet Union, mainly due to the accompanying abandonment of personal motivation, innovation and development) the capitalist system has been tested repeatedly by major financial and economic crises, from the Great Depression in 1929 to the recent financial crisis which began in 2007, but has managed to survive and evolve, learning from the mistakes of the past.[106]

In this regard, however, the current financial and economic situations have brought to light a number of challenges that the capitalist system must meet in order to develop new mechanisms capable of dealing with the contemporary developments and breakthroughs the world has witnessed over the past two decades in terms of technology, telecommunications and logistics capabilities. The crisis also sheds light on a number of lessons learned from the experience of the past few years whose negative effects should be addressed.

Further technological development leads to increased difficulty in providing jobs for young people. In the capitalist system, the primary objective is profit maximization – the exact equivalent in conceptual terms to cost minimization[107] – which represents the one and only economic goal for production. This aim creates competition between the technological and human elements in the production process; i.e., with cost-saving technological developments, the need for the human element is reduced. The evolutions in robotics, control systems, and office management systems, and the availability of information through the internet, has rendered obsolete many of the functions performed by the human element. As technological development is expected to gain momentum, the human element will face ever more challenges to maintain its functions in a variety of areas, including medicine, engineering, office work and others. All these phenomena, in addition to huge population growth, especially in developing countries, will pose major challenges to the capitalist system, inevitably requiring it to develop in order to survive.[108]

Further developments in communications and social networking will lead to increased competition for jobs across international borders. In recent decades the world has witnessed greater attention directed at the detrimental effects of immigration from densely populated low-income countries to less heavily-populated high-income countries, particularly in terms of competition for jobs, often resulting in higher unemployment rates and lower living standards among nationals. This problem is clearly illustrated by the case of Mexican immigrants in the United States of America and African immigrants in EU countries. However, the new world order will also witness the emergence of problems stemming from a different kind of immigration between these two types of countries; for example, jobs being outsourced to countries where labor costs are lower.[109] As previously mentioned, the effects of developments in communication and transportation technologies in intensifying global competition for jobs is best described by the American journalist Thomas Loren Friedman in his book, *The World is Flat: A Brief History of the Twenty-First Century*:[110] "… clearly, it is now possible for more people than ever to collaborate and compete in real time with more other people on more different kinds of work from more different corners of the planet and on a more equal footing than at any previous time in the history of the world—using computers, e-mail, networks, social media, teleconferencing, and dynamic new software."[111]

Naturally, the new world order – which is increasingly globalized and eliminates many of the geographical barriers to labor mobility, not only physically but also through modern means of communication – represents a new challenge to the capitalist system. Economic policy-makers in industrialized countries will have to address the negative effects of this on youth employment as well as on the living standards of their citizens, which may require them to abandon the principles of free movement in the capitalist system.

Economic and financial openness resulting from globalization and technical progress have facilitated the transmission of crises from one country to another and weakened the control of institutions managing local economic policy based on macroeconomic conditions. There is no doubt that globalization and multilateral economic openness advocated by the capitalist system and formerly adopted by GATT – now the WTO – have contributed significantly to the transmission of financial and economic crises from one country to another and from one region to another across the world. Hence, it is not surprising that among the countries least affected by the recent global financial crisis were the least economically, financially and commercially open ones, such as North Korea, although such countries have structural problems caused by their economic isolation.[112]

This yields two important conclusions for the future of the capitalist system. First, economic openness to the outside world opens up new channels for the transmission of crises through activities such as the phenomenon of 'hot money' (the sudden movement of investments from one country to another), and the domino effect of the banking crisis, spreading from one state to another due to the interconnectedness and complexity of the global financial system. Second, economic openness weakens the capacity of local institutions to efficiently deal with financial and economic crises,[113] requiring greater regional and international cooperation and intervention. Therefore, international and regional economic institutions – the IMF, the World Bank, the Asian, African and American development banks, the UN Conference on Trade and Development (UNCTAD) and the WTO – are expected to assume a greater role in shaping domestic economic policies in the context of international coordination and the effects of individual nations' policies on the entire international community. However, this growing role will require international consensus to amend the objectives, powers and methods of these institutions in a manner consistent with the public interest, and – for many of them – avoid the mistakes of the past in order to restore the attractiveness of the global capitalist system.[114]

Furthermore, in order to achieve growth and prevent the outflow of jobs and investments under a free financial and trade system, it will be necessary to shift the focus from the ideal of global multilateral trade liberalization to the 'second best' policy of regional liberalization of trade, with a view to achieving the WTO's aspiration of global liberalization at a later stage.[115]

The Changing Nature of Conflict

The fourth feature is the decline in conventional military conflicts and the growing reliance on the rapid development of technology to facilitate unorthodox methods of conflict that are not only less costly in terms of men and materiel, but also less controversial. While continued US conventional military superiority will remain as a deterrent and a tool to strengthen negotiations relating to international conflicts (to be used only as a last resort), the United States of America is increasingly leading a process of change in military approach away from the conventional, in light of the experience it has gained from the wars of the past two decades, as mentioned previously. US 'wars' against terrorism have shown that conventional approaches and military strategies are often useless in asymmetric conflict with terrorist groups such as Al Qaeda.[116] The total cost of the US wars in Iraq and Afghanistan in particular were staggeringly high for the US economy—some observers estimate the total cost for these two wars at somewhere between $4 to $6 trillion, as mentioned previously.[117] Conventional military intervention also proved costly in terms of human losses, both for the United States of America and its allies, as well as for civilians in the countries of conflict, with a death toll of 6,668 US soldiers (4,474 in Iraq and 2,194 in Afghanistan),[118] and about 132,000 Iraqi and Afghan civilian victims during the first ten years of war.[119] In addition, these conflicts had moral repercussions in terms of the internal opposition to foreign military ventures in the United States of America and its allies, and the impression it created among people abroad as being a colonial war against Islam.[120]

Owing to the asymmetric conflict between the United States of America and cross-border extremist groups, the United States of America has assumed a leading role in changing the concepts and strategies of war, drawing on a combination of advanced technology, and conventional and nonconventional media, supported by an unprecedented level of global military dominance and based on the premise that the army should be 'smaller' and 'smarter.'[121] In light of US debt problems, it was initially agreed that military spending would be cut by nearly one trillion dollars over the next ten years.[122] From 1999 to 2011, annual US defense spending increased from $360 billion to $537 billion in constant dollars, in addition to other military expenses spent on operations in Afghanistan and Iraq. To achieve this without affecting the efficiency of the army in the face of threats, a plan is expected to be implemented to reduce the army and Marine Corps and redeploy naval forces so that they are easier to deliver through key sea lanes, accompanied by a greater reliance on remote operations, missile forces, drones and cost-saving technologies.[123]

As noted previously, there is a growing interest in 4GW theory, wherein targets are not merely military in nature, but also include an enemy's culture and society:[124] "fourth generation warfare seems likely to be widely dispersed and largely undefined; the distinction between war and peace will be blurred to the vanishing point. It will be nonlinear possibly to the point of having no definable battlefields or fronts. The distinction between 'civilian' and 'military' may disappear. Actions will occur concurrently throughout all participants' depth including their society as a cultural not just a physical entity."[125]

4GW will be technology-driven and "psychological operations may become the dominant operational and strategic weapon. Computer viruses may be used to disrupt civilian as well as military operations. A major target will be the enemy population's support of its government and the war. Television news may become a more powerful operational weapon than armored divisions."[126] As such, focus will shift from the enemy's front, which is the military, to its rear which is society. Moreover, some have suggested that the origins of 'idea-based' 4GW can be found in certain aspects of terrorism—techniques which could be employed in combination with high technology and social tools such as religion and ideology to undertake direct attacks on the culture of the enemy society from within.[127]

Other new realms of warfare are also developing. For example, 2008 witnessed a substantial turning point in terms of the evolution of contemporary threats, as the United States of America suffered its most serious cyber attack to date, in which the Department of Defense was compromised. The source of the attack was a flash drive connected to a military laptop at a US base in the Middle East.[128] The malicious computer code, delivered by an undisclosed foreign intelligence agency, uploaded itself onto a network run by US Central Command (CENTCOM). The spread of the code resulted in both classified and unclassified data being harvested from abroad. The Pentagon responded with an operation code-named Buckshot Yankee[129] to counter the attack, recognizing the fact that this was a 'game-changer' in terms of the threats faced by the military. The Department of Defense defined a new strategy, the basis of which was described by former Deputy Secretary of Defense William J. Lynn: "[T]he first of the pillars is that we need to – and have – recognized cyberspace for what it is: a new domain of warfare. Like land, sea, air, and space, we need to treat cyberspace as a domain we will operate in, that we will defend in, and that we will treat in a military doctrinal manner."[130]

Former US Secretary of Defense Leon Edward Panetta has warned that the United States of America faces major threats in terms of cyber warfare, and that it is only a matter of time before a 'cyber Pearl Harbor'[131] scenario, in which transportation systems and financial networks are attacked, alongside conventional hostile action. The United States of America may wage a pre-emptive strike to eliminate such a danger, and has undertaken an extensive revision of its rules of engagement to accommodate action in cyberspace.[132]

It is expected that the Middle East will be one of the main battlefields for this new form of conflict, particularly as the region has already experienced sophisticated cyber attacks during the past two years, including alleged US–Israeli attacks targeting Iran and Lebanon using highly complex generations of malware[133] – such as Stuxnet, Flame, and Gauss – to damage Iranian nuclear installations and spy on bank accounts in Lebanon. Furthermore, Aramco in Saudi Arabia and RasGas in Qatar were both struck by the Shamoon virus, which damaged around 30,000 computers in Aramco alone.[134]

There is no doubt that cyber warfare will be one of the most important fields of military operation in the new world order, especially considering its low cost, the difficulty of tracing belligerents, and the magnitude of the financial damage that may result from the use of cyberspace as a battlefield.

Hegemony of Values and Culture

The world is now living in a post-industrial, post-modern society that is increasingly dependent on digital technologies, as detailed in the author's previous work, *From Tribe to Facebook: The Transformational Role of Social Networks*. This has given rise to the birth of a 'digital citizen,' who asks himself 'what is next?' rather than the traditional 'what shall we do?'[135] Modern communications have permeated society to the extent that no-one can remain in isolation. Mankind today faces a torrent of information, ideas and opinions. Indeed, it could be said that an abundance of communication has come to characterize the age, and often constitutes a burden. This can drive users into isolation or indifference to the physical world, or even a heightened awareness of events that leads to a radical, obsessive behavior—the effects can be varied and sometimes conflicting. Some experts regard this glut in communication as enriching human intellect, while others consider it an assault on the mind, comprising psychological pressure and an aberration of fundamental beliefs.[136]

The world is living through a communications/social media revolution; by removing geographic and socio-economic barriers, this has eroded the strength of traditional social relations in favor of virtual relationships. Social networks have managed to create a live and interactive 'virtual community' that is similar in many ways to a physical community: "Remote continuous communication is possible without tangible obstacles. Therefore, an individual's life gradually becomes based on 'electronic communication' where living in a virtual world includes establishing a 'virtual family' within the 'virtual community.' These new cross-border relations lead to the emergence of new values and principles as a result of interaction between domestic traditions and norms and their foreign counterparts. This could lead to a form of 'globalization' of values and principles adopted by the majority of people, with the emergence of minorities resisting this orientation—sometimes moving towards radicalism in defiance."[137]

The effects on language are among the notable social impacts of cultural globalization through social networks and cross-border media (satellite TV channels etc.) that are expected to dominate the social character of the new world order. The global digital revolution has contributed to shaping the future of language; indeed, some researchers even talk of the possible emergence of a universal language due to a generational convergence of mentality and culture.[138]

For example, the Arabic language faces a threat from the proliferation of colloquial Arabic and slang, particularly via social networking, as well as the widespread use of English, and a question remains as to whether the Arabic language will be able to keep pace with technological and scientific development, or be consigned to a fate similar to that of Latin—remaining in written form only, unspoken, but with its vocabulary and grammar preserved.[139]

Some are convinced the Arabic language is incapable of keeping pace with science and technology, and consider the use of foreign languages (which they see as the universal medium of contemporary scientific thought) to be evidence of intellectual and civilizational superiority. Mastering these languages is essential in gaining knowledge from its original sources and combining this with Arab thought and knowledge. The problem is not the ability of the Arabic language to keep up with the times, but the absence of will to promote its use in scientific fields. Encouraging publishing and translation breeds respect for the Arabic language, protects it, and highlights the issues it faces. It also serves to liberate the language from the rigidity of readymade templates and reveals its true characteristics and ability to absorb modern sciences by digesting and reforming terminology.[140]

Social networks also have other impacts, including a widening of cultural, interactive and communication gaps within and between current and future generations—the higher the capacity, number of users, and potential of social networks, the wider the gap will be between each and subsequent generation, as noted in Chapter V of this volume, "Public Opinion and the New World Order: A Survey of the UAE Population." The world's population is forecast to reach more than 8 billion by 2026, of which three billion will be online. As each person has the ability to assume several online identities, there could potentially be billions of fictitious virtual identities; deconstructing these multiple identities could comprise a significant social problem.[141] We may also witness the increased isolation and social alienation of individuals, leading to diminishing loyalty toward family and society, the separation of individuals from their communities, and a trend toward narcissism and introversion; indeed, families will be the first structural aspect of society to suffer from this existential threat.

Furthermore, "new patterns of migration will also appear – including electronic migration – as a result of economic globalization and the growing dependence on outsourcing, allowing developed countries to take advantage of skilled labor anywhere in the world without having to relocate, and opening the door to 'virtual citizenship'."[142]

Thus, the social character of the new world order will likely be characterized by a convergence of cultures, customs and traditions in a mixture that may result in the obliteration of national and ethnic identities, and the development of a universal identity. Such an identity will not comprise a balance between the world's different cultures, as it will no doubt be disproportionately influenced by the culture from which innovation in social networks, media and entertainment has sprung; American culture will dominate, owing to the global influence of the US entertainment industry via American movies, TV programs and music. Moreover, the world's foremost social networks – Facebook and Twitter – are also

American, and US education and news channels such as CNN are highly influential.[143]

Some observers may view this imbalance in cultural globalization as being negative, but at the same time one must remember that American culture itself is derived from its own 'melting pot' of immigrant cultures.[144] Thus, a universal global culture with a heavy US influence in the new world order may be considered an expansion of an existing product of the interaction between cultures.

Conclusion

There are a number of features that are expected to be among the most important determinants of the new world order in the future, according to the hierarchal structure of powers illustrated in this book. This pyramidal structure suggests that the new world order will be occupied at the top by the United States of America followed in second place by China, the European Union and the Russian Federation, in third place by India, Japan and Brazil, and finally at the bottom of the pyramid, the rest of the world.

The first of these features is a new world order characterized by unipolarity, in which the United States of America takes the lead due to several factors that serve its interests, such as economic, political and geographic factors, as well as its supremacy in terms of energy, innovation and its military. It will be extremely difficult for competing countries, particularly China, to catch up with the United States of America to become a second 'pole' in the new world order.

The second feature of the new world order is the growing importance of technologically advanced and nonconventional systems of production and communication to replace decaying conventional systems, and an increasing reliance on genetic engineering, cloning and nanotechnology in finding solutions to key issues such as attaining food and water security, narrowing the gap in terms of energy resources, achieving breakthroughs in medicine and developing human capabilities.

The third feature of the new world order is that it will witness increasing pressure on the capitalist system to develop and enhance its sustainability and survival, particularly in light of the lessons learned from the recent global financial crisis, which began in 2007. It will also be a system in which there will be increasing pressure to resolve the problems arising from globalization and maximize its potential benefits and advantages.

The fourth feature of the new world order is a relative decline in the pursuit of conventional military conflict and a growing reliance on rapid technological development, means of communication and social media, to facilitate unorthodox methods of conflict that are not only less costly in terms of men and materiel, but also less controversial. However, this will occur under continued US conventional military superiority that will remain as a deterrent and a tool to strengthen the US negotiating position in international conflicts, to be used only as a last resort.

568

Moreover, humanity in the new world order will move toward a unified universal cultural and value system based on the US model, and the concept of international citizenship will prevail. Under this new world order those who oppose these stereotypical universal values will come together to form the extremist groups that may pose one of the greatest risks to the world order.

CONCLUSION

CONCLUSION

When I chose to title this work *Prospects for the American Age* I sought to not only provide my own analysis-based conclusions on this vital topic, but also to develop and convey a deep and insightful understanding of the new world order in a way that illustrates the major landmarks of this topic for an Arab audience—in an age when an appreciation of the interaction between international realities and the factors that govern and influence them is still lacking in certain Arab political circles. These actors still operate according to rules and considerations that are no longer effective given the rise of new, highly influential variables affecting world affairs.

Superpower rivalry is no longer an elitist topic, of interest only to a handful of countries, and the concerns of states are no longer separate from those of individuals. In the new world order, interests have overlapped and differences between nations and groups have faded away. At the same time, traditional geographical boundaries are becoming increasingly irrelevant, and concepts have evolved in accordance with the value system that governs this new order, contemporary international rivalries and conflicts, and the prevailing conditions in which these conflicts occur.

The data and statistics in this book testify to the huge gulf that separates the United States of America from the remaining major powers – such as the EU, China, Russia, Brazil, India and others – which aspire to compete in the coming decades and centuries. Furthermore, through its in-depth analysis this volume has sought to reveal the mechanisms at work behind the scenes in international relations, particularly in terms of the factors and variables that influence the behavior, policies and decisions of the United States of America and other major powers.

Although I have sought to tackle the subject of this book in an academic fashion throughout the preceding chapters, I will now present a number of significant concluding observations – based on my own point of view – whilst retaining the neutrality and objectivity of the former approach to the extent that human nature permits.

First, far from fading away or receding, globalization will continue to spread. The world is headed towards greater levels of interconnection and inter-communication in all fields; indeed, the flow and fluidity of the connections between different parts of the world have come to represent the hallmark of the increased movement of capital, investments, people, ideas, information, services and commodities. As a result, we may expect waves of fierce competition between economies over their share in this new realm of continuous interaction. Integration with the global economy is no longer an option one can avoid; instead, coping with globalization and all of its manifestations (particularly those of an economic and cultural nature) is increasingly becoming a pressing need. Following the dissolution of the voices of those who advocate alternative forms of globalization, and the failure of attempts to discourage its progress by focusing on its disadvantages or via protest movements and activities, globalization appears to have proved itself uncontainable, not to mention irresistible and inevitable.

With globalization having been so well-established, becoming an integral part of the interests of countries and emerging economies, globalization can no longer be described as being of a 'Western' or 'American' orientation. It may not be an exaggeration to say that China, not the United States of America, has benefitted most from the spread of globalization. Therefore, the debate is no longer about how to curb or rein in globalization, but about the best ways to address its negatives and maximize its returns in light of the neoliberalism of the age, which has seen a further decline in the role of states, accompanied by equal growth in the liberalization of markets, and which undermines the principles of social justice, further entrenching free market policies.

It is noteworthy that the globalization of international affairs and other issues have not been achieved only as a direct result of the interests of a particular group of states; rather, they have been inspired, in parallel, by the emergence of global challenges that mandate active international cooperation—pressing issues that can be addressed only through international frameworks based on understanding. Such issues include phenomena of a global nature such as climate change—the adverse effects of which neither West nor East, North nor South can escape.

Second, the difficulty in defining the new world order does not detract in any way from the realities of US hegemony over its various elements, or the major powers' explicit or implicit acceptance of the US and Western role. Hence, the essential question should not focus on the timeframe of the 'American age,' but on the methods of US and Western cultural and economic hegemony, and how the sole superpower confronts rivals' attempts to assume greater influence – or indeed leadership – in the new world order. The value of such an undertaking lies in the fact that the United States of America is experiencing economic difficulties that may not have much impact in bridging the gap with its significant competitors – China, in particular – but, to a certain extent, these difficulties do limit the ability of the United States of America to carry out the role of an apex power in a highly complex and competitive new world order. Perhaps, the reaction to the Syrian crisis proves the degree of complexity that has come to characterize the crises in this new world order.

In recent years, numerous political theses and treatises have sought to chart the end of the American age and the emergence of a post-US world without poles; however, the analysis of the consequences of the emergence of the new world reality described in Western literature is mainly linked to the economic rise of China and the recent economic crises faced by the West—particularly the financial and debt crises in the United States of America. These analyses are held hostage to predictions that the Chinese economy will overtake that of the United States of America, achieving global primacy in a matter of two to three decades (depending on the expert or specialist in question), with clear disregard to other determinants and measures of power, such as education, culture, military and technical superiority, economics, industry, energy and spending on research and development (R&D), all of which play strategic roles of equal significance in the 21st century.

All studies acknowledge the fact that the United States of America wields a level of power no other country in the world enjoys today, or has done in the past. The real question relates to the formula for governance of the new world order in the medium term, and whether this will merely be based on the survival of the United States of America as the single dominant power, or a new shared responsibility, with roles distributed among US partners or other world players. Will the new world order evolve to operate without singular governance, under the collective leadership of key actors and the United Nations? Or will another formula be reached that differs from that of the past? Will a balance of economic power take precedence over a military balance of power? It is difficult to offer answers to all these questions given the entanglement of interests and growing world problems, particularly those related to globalization and its cross-border impacts.

Third, this historical juncture in the evolution of the world order offers a glimpse of the features of the future, which will be discerned more accurately in the years and decades to come. It is indisputable that the increasing divergence in the positions of the major powers on the central issues of our times will leave its mark on key concepts such as international legitimacy, even altering the nature of these concepts in the future. Both Russia and China seek to commit the United States of America and its Western allies to working under the umbrella of international legitimacy represented by the UN; i.e., a return to the years before the US administration of President George Walker Bush [Jr.] invaded Iraq without a UN mandate in 2003.

The resultant polarization may either serve to push the new world order towards even greater US hegemony at the expense of international cooperation within the United Nations, or a decline in US influence by way of an implicit acknowledgment that it is unable to assume unilateral leadership of the world order, allowing other partners to participate and returning to the UN to developing and achieving international peace and security.

However, it is too early to say that the battle of wills between the United States of America and its allies – as well as with other major powers – will herald the advent of a multi-polar world order or the emergence of a formula for shared power and influence between the United States of America and other countries. Military solutions to world problems have contributed to the decline of US influence – especially after Iraq and Afghanistan – and are themselves the focus of controversy; hence, options other than the militarization of crises would be in the interest of the United States of America, which has shown a preference for smart power over hard power in achieving its strategic objectives.

The military and technical, logistics, scientific, cultural and educational superiority of the United States of America is not in doubt, nor its capacity for renewal and adaptation; however, we might question the possibility of the emergence of parallel powers in the leadership of the new world order during the next three decades.

The fourth observation relates to the growing speculation and expectations for the rise of China on the world stage. In the author's opinion, much analysis on this topic ignores the realities of power in the twenty-first century, and approaches the subject from an outdated perspective. Although the transition of power from one dominant state to another is familiar historically, according to the American thinker Joseph Samuel Nye, we should also take note of the changing elements upon which power is based in each era. The factors that enabled the empires of yesteryear to dominate are not the same as those that have enabled the United States of America to establish itself as the world's only superpower since the early 1990s. It is not sufficient to know how to climb to the top of the order; one must also know how to maintain one's dominant position. Domination today is more difficult than in the past, and the foundations of power are greater and more diverse; hence, today's superpower must dedicate substantial effort to maintain its position.

Predictions of imminent Chinese ascendance ignore key considerations, including how the state might exercise its new-found power. Many believe that a state's strategic position is a direct consequence of economic power, because the latter enables the acquisition of military and political power. This argument has merit, but it is very important also to consider how a state employs and manages its economic resources, as well as its ability to maintain its power by utilizing innovation to fuel growth and defend against economic crises. There is no evidence to suggest that China has the will or the inclination to assume leadership of the world order, at least for the foreseeable future. There are also doubts about China's ability to achieve the level of innovation-based growth witnessed by the US economy, as well as its ability to deal with economic crises.

As mentioned previously in Chapter II, "Factors Influencing the Structure of the New World Order," and Chapter IV, "The New World Order: Economy, Trade and Energy," the pillars of global dominance comprise industrial, military, technological, educational, cultural and economic progress, as well as energy and transport security. According to the statistics and data presented, no country other than the United States of America possesses the necessary combination of these elements—the world's other major powers possess some, but not all.

This does not mean that China will not seek to assume a prominent role in the new world order, as this remains a matter of political will and strategy in the future. In any eventuality, two vital variables can be identified: first is the economic rise of China and the projected imbalances in the global economic system that may result; second is how China approaches the issue of dominance and influence in the new world order. Although China's continued economic rise is likely, it will not necessarily allow it to replace the United States of America in terms of the running of world affairs. Of course, the outcome also depends on how the United States of America deals with challenges in the global arena, as well as China's stance on unilateral leadership in general.

The fifth observation relates to the need to discuss the future of the nation-state, particularly in light of the ongoing debate on the impacts of globalization on the power of the state in dealing both with non-state actors and the structure of the new world order. It is difficult to deny the decline of the traditional role of the nation-state, but far too early to consign the concept to the annals of history. It is true, however, that the state no longer wields the same control over its components and the elements of its sovereignty as in the past, but it is still a key player in terms of interactions within the new world order via international organizations and frameworks. This new pattern of coexistence between state and non-state actors has become a reality according to Harald Müller, who argues that the state should engage with more non-state actors since it is no longer possible to develop successful economic policies without the participation of banks, or secure energy supplies without involving oil companies, in the same way that issues such as verification of compliance with chemical weapons non-proliferation safeguards may be ineffective unless the chemical industry participates. Yet, we should be mindful that Müller suggests this interactive relationship applies only to democracies, arguing that totalitarian states will still exercise foreign policy without any regard for domestic public opinion.

Globalization has contributed to the weakening of a number of aspects of nation-state power. However, this does not necessarily affect the model as a whole. The effects of globalization on the nation-state are clear in the case of weak states – on the political, economic, cultural, educational and military levels – due to the fact that these countries do not have sufficient means to protect themselves from negative transcontinental influences and trends whilst positively engaging with and benefitting from globalization. When China is cited as a leading beneficiary of globalization (in light of its ability to leverage its role in the global economy) one must consider the fact that globalization is not necessarily a negative phenomenon; rather, the way in which a state deals with globalization will determine its character—surrender, retreat or self-defeat, or positive engagement and openness, accommodating the interests of the state and allowing it to achieve its objectives. The latter approach allows a state to avoid the potentially damaging aspects of globalization on its economy, culture and education sector.

An analysis of all available evidence will likely confirm that while the concept of the nation-state established by the treaties of Westphalia in 1648 has been significantly eroded, it still endures, albeit in a form shaped by the continuous interactions of international relations, technological revolutions and conceptual shifts witnessed since these treaties. In light of the immense human progress achieved in all fields, it is no longer acceptable to talk of a link between the new world order and a treaty that dates back more than four centuries. It is instead logical to study the nation-state in its modern form to determine the limits of its ability to cope with contemporary global realities and variables, as well as to understand the patterns of its interaction within the new world order. Indeed, a more apt approach is that of Saeed Al-Siddiki, who in his book *The State in a Changing World: The Nation-State and the Challenges of New Globalization* states that the concept of sovereignty – the cornerstone of the nation-state and of international law – shifts and transforms as a consequence of globalization, re-forming and rebuilding itself in each era in accordance with prevailing global realities. This development in our understanding of sovereignty, evolving alongside the structure of the new world order and the patterns of interaction between its major players, offers a more appropriate approach than the restrictive, traditional concept of the principle of state sovereignty.

The sixth observation relates to the extent to which the United States of America accepts the idea of power-sharing in the new world order as a result of its shrinking leadership and influence, and the emergence of new powers seeking leading roles, as has been discussed by numerous theorists and researchers. In this regard, the United States of America demonstrates a clear determination to maintain its position at the top of the world order and exerts tremendous efforts to that end—enhancing its capabilities, resources and sources of power so as to ensure uninterrupted control and hegemony, and expending significant effort in containing potential rivals, particularly China. The relationship between these two powers is too complicated and interdependent to understand in terms of theories of competition, both in light of the growing international challenges facing world security and stability, and the vast and growing overlap in interests. With such factors in mind, it would be naïve to jump to conclusions about the potential for military conflict between these two states in the next two decades. The magnitude of mutual interests is borne out by the statistics, and the complexity of international relations makes it difficult for the dominant pole in the new world order to engage in direct military conflict with another major power in that order without each side risking significant loss of prestige and influence. Most importantly, in the author's opinion, China is clearly convinced of the importance of the US role in the world order, shouldering as it does the responsibility and enormous economic burden of such a position, as well as difficult global problems such as crises in the realms of water, environment, food, poverty, terrorism, and ethnic and religious conflicts. This does not negate the possibility that China may seek to play a more central role in world affairs that more accurately reflects its growing economic power, but such an ambition – and its limits – will be determined by China's strategic vision and long-term objectives.

The seventh observation concerns the vulnerability of Arab states to various interactions within the new world order. The Arab region is a central arena and the focus of a variety of conflicts that are of direct relevance to US prospects in the global order. Prominent examples include the events in the Arab world in recent years that have toppled long-standing political regimes dating back to periods prior to the development of the new world order, such as Egypt, Libya, Yemen and Tunisia. Despite the fact that these regimes featured in US plans to control and dominate the world – to the extent that some of them played a vital role in enabling the United States of America to control parts of the world order and impose its control, as in the Gulf War to liberate Kuwait that ended on February 26, 1991 – the system of values that is considered an integral part of the structure of the new world order had a major role in the overthrow of these regimes. These values also influenced the US stance toward these regimes, leading to the crucial decision to abandon strategic allies such as former Egyptian President Muhammad Hosni Mubarak and Tunisia's Zine El-Abidine Ben Ali. Moreover, the United States of America has played a leading role in nurturing youth protest movements in these states in preparation for their removal—such regimes having become less relevant to US interests and strategy in the Middle East.

In light of the obstacles to development faced by many Arab states, it is difficult to say that the near future will herald

586

improvements in these countries' circumstances, particularly in light of the worsening internal crises developing in Egypt, Syria and Iraq, and the strategic expansion of regional non-Arab powers to fill the void left by the decline of the regional role of the traditional Arab powers, in addition to a strengthening in the standing of Turkey, Iran and Israel – which is now in the best strategic position since its creation – whose influence are increasing due to the absence of any significant resistance from Arab countries, which are preoccupied with internal crises or threats emanating from neighboring states. Meanwhile, growing US influence in the new world order is reflected positively on the standing, prestige and status of Israel. These tremendous strategic shifts occurring in the Arab world will no doubt contribute to drawing the boundaries of US power and the extent of its control over its traditional areas of influence.

What is more, the events that have led to the fall of several Arab regimes in recent years represent the end of the era of Arab nationalism and the rise of other influences and factors in determining the regional situation, such as ethnic, religious, doctrinal and sectarian identities. This has been reflected in the Palestinian–Israeli conflict, which no longer enjoys the same urgency it has for so many years. It may be too early to pass a categorical judgment on the status of the Palestinian issue in the collective Arab consciousness, but for Arab countries to retreat into themselves and concentrate on domestic affairs –

countries that have long played a leading role in defending Palestinian rights – creates controversy and raises questions about the real importance and future of this issue on the Arab agenda.

The eighth observation is extremely important, and concerns the role of the economy in the structure of the new world order in the short and medium terms. The statistics and economic data presented in detail in Chapter IV, "The New World Order: Economy, Trade and Energy," reveal the significant effect of the global economy on the balance of power. Economics will not simply be a factor in the calculation of states' roles and ranks in the new world order, but will become the central engine of change among small and mid-sized powers in the new world order. Indeed, we cannot but notice the growing economic and political influence of the BRICS group, or the broadening roles reserved for other emerging economies around the world.

In the midst of these developments, the economic downturn in the West has indirectly supported, to some degree, opportunities for countries to adopt alternative economic models in order to emerge, ascend and win influence in global decision-making. The most prominent example of this is China's mixed economic model, wherein capitalist values dominate over established communist traditions.

The financial crisis that began in the United States of America in 2007 has contributed to the restructuring of the global economy, highlighting the influence of economics in determining the structure of the new world order as a whole. It is perhaps no exaggeration to say that the real threat to US prestige and influence in the world comes not in the form of the growing military capability or political influence of rival powers, but rather the rapid economic ascent and influence of major powers such as China, the EU, Russia, India and Brazil. We should also take heed of the fact that the rise of the EU as a world power has to some extent been affected by the failure of attempts to supplant the US dollar with the euro as the major world currency. The financial crises faced by certain EU countries such as Greece, Portugal, Ireland, Spain and Italy have also played an influential role in curtailing European political ambitions.

It is necessary to note here that the globalization of the economy has made it difficult to pass absolute or definitive judgments on the rise and fall of individual economies; i.e., if economic globalization means greater interconnection and interdependence among the world's economies – especially major ones – then to say that the decline of an economy plays directly into the hands of its competitors is out of touch with reality.

Undoubtedly, one of the most important conclusions of this volume concerns US dominance of the global financial system, which has implications for the entire world – including states, regional blocs and international financial institutions –

particularly in terms of the repercussions arising from factors such as US government debt. The crisis caused by this debt, and the resultant, growing global threat (described earlier in this volume and leading to a shutdown of some US federal government activities and other profound economic implications) may again shake overall confidence in the global economy.

US debt – which exceeded its GDP to reach more than 17 trillion dollars in 2013 – and any further tremors of confidence in the US government's ability to service this debt, could lead to severe impacts on those states investing in US bonds, most notably China. A downgrade in the credit rating of the United States of America could raise interest rates, which would lead to a significant decline in the value of the holdings of countries such as China that may therefore lose a large proportion of their invested reserves.

To address its debt, the US administration must adopt bold measures to either increase taxes or reduce government spending; but such actions can slow the economic recovery and lead to a return to recession. With the increase in US debt, there are fears among investors (including banks, financial institutions and foreign governments) regarding related consequences, such as the US government resorting to selling bonds—its tool for borrowing. This process increases the holdings without any corresponding increase in production in the economy, which will lead to inflation.

It is worth noting here that inflation in the United States of America, particularly in wage terms, makes countries like China more attractive for investment owing to low labor costs. This encourages US companies to move their operations away from the United States of America to other countries, which in turn invest their surpluses in US government bonds. Similarly, the inflation that can result from the Federal Reserve's purchase of US Treasury bonds, combined with the loss of jobs resulting from off-shoring, render the United States of America vulnerable to both inflation and recession—so-called 'stagflation.' This situation leads to a dilemma for the US government, because attempting to cure the recession by pumping in more money will lead to higher inflation, while reducing expenditures or increasing taxes to reduce the recourse to borrowing from the Federal Reserve will lead to greater stagnation. Thus, the US government will be forced to postpone such therapeutic procedures by continuing to borrow, which could delay any solution to the debt problem to a later date, by which time the problem will have grown even bigger. This leads us to another important point; namely the nature of the next global economic crisis. Will it be linked to the problem of government debt, and particularly US debt? And how do we predict potential crisis scenarios?

These are the most important concerns in the new world order—the continuing issue of US Treasury bonds, the need to address the problem of US government debt, and the conflict between Republicans and Democrats over how best to solve these problems. The huge amount of US debt, and the fact that US bonds account for the most substantial investment of foreign reserves, mean that any future crisis will be one of global dimensions and could be unprecedented in its severity.

On the other hand, the next economic crisis may come from the East. As mentioned earlier in this volume, there are fears that financial crises could occur in China as result of local government debts or possibly the real-estate sector. Also, the Japanese government is considered the most indebted in the world in terms of debt-to-GDP ratio, and has undertaken expansionist policies that make it difficult to anticipate a decline in this debt. While potential crises in China or Japan may not have similar effects to one occurring in the United States of America, they will nonetheless have significant impacts on the global economy, owing to the considerable interconnection that now exists between the different components of the global financial system.

The ninth observation concerns the impact of developments in the field of energy on the balance of power in the new world order. Recently, the world has witnessed the emergence of a number of interesting developments in energy, both in terms of technological developments associated with the extraction of oil and gas (which have made some reserves economically viable), and in terms of the growing awareness of the effects of fossil fuel use on the environment and the need for rational consumption that have prompted numerous countries to adopt policies emphasizing reliance on cleaner forms of energy, including renewable and alternative energies, even by replacing oil and coal with natural gas. However, oil and natural gas remain the major energy sources of the world, and are expected to remain so for the foreseeable future. Therefore, developments in oil and natural gas continue to constitute major influences on the strengths and weaknesses of states and state groupings in terms of the availability of energy resources. There is no doubt that developments such as growing US energy self-sufficiency thanks to the use of hydraulic fracturing, and the fact that emerging countries such as China and India do not have access to such resources, will play a significant role in tipping the balance in favor of the United States of America, at least in energy terms. The expected US superiority in this field will also affect major oil and gas producing countries, particularly in the Middle East, and may have impacts on the relative importance of the region and its ability to maintain stability between the United States of America and its potential rivals from the East— particularly China.

It is also noteworthy that some energy-related developments in the Middle East could lead either to new forms of cooperation or disagreement between the states of the region and global powers. For example, a change in the global attitude towards Iran and the prospect of a normalization of relations with the international community could have important impacts on oil and gas markets. New discoveries in the region could also have significant implications, particularly in terms of natural gas reserves (for example, discoveries of Mediterranean gas fields in the territories of countries which have had tense relations in the past, such as Israel and Lebanon). Such developments could in the future affect the stability of the Middle East, which remains the global hub for hydrocarbon energy. Such developments will have both negative and positive impacts on key players in the new world order, according to the degree of their dependency on Middle East energy supplies.

Among the other developing aspects of the new world order is the potential role of the United States of America in the global energy market, by virtue of its increasing production of shale gas. With the remarkable developments in extraction techniques, and the potential for exporting supplies abroad, the United States of America is expected to become a net exporter in the future. Indeed, the United States of America has begun issuing licenses to export gas to countries with which it has no bilateral trade agreements. This may have future consequences as, contrary to oil, gas is sold on long-term contracts and prices vary from region to region. Currently, US natural gas prices are extremely low compared to those in China, Japan, South Korea and Qatar. Indeed, such is the disparity that the price of US gas is much less than half that of gas produced in these other states, which gives energy-dependent industries in the United States of America a substantial comparative advantage. However, some fear that an exaggerated trend towards exporting US gas would lead to a significant increase in gas supply prices to US industries, hence US companies would lose the advantage of access to cheap energy, which in turn could adversely affect the performance of the US economy as a whole. Therefore, shale developments in the United States of America, and the potential transfer of technology used in its extraction to other countries in the future, may have significant effects on the balance of global economic power in the new world order. However, such developments are still in their infancy, and may have significant impacts over the long term if the cost of gas production and volume of exports are reduced, while the focus here has been limited to the potential to meet local demand in order to maintain a competitive advantage for US industries.

In this context, there has been much debate as to the feasibility of replicating the US shale gas experience in other countries and regions of the world—particularly China, which would then be able to strengthen its energy situation and thereby overcome it biggest weakness compared to the United States of America. However, despite its extensive efforts, current realities suggest that it would be difficult for China to achieve any such success in the near future. Specifically, the extraction of shale gas in China requires relatively high-cost investments; while the costs of preparing a well for shale gas extraction in the United States of America is about $2–3 million, the cost of doing the same in China is about $16 million. This makes the extraction of shale gas in China cost effective only when energy prices are high. It is also worth mentioning that although China aims to complement domestic production by extracting shale gas to reach 5.6 billion cubic meters by 2015, such a scale might be practically impossible to achieve because it would require nearly $20 billion of investment. Even if China were to succeed in achieving this objective, its level of production would equate to less than three percent of current US production. Therefore, the United States of America is expected to continue to dramatically outperform China in terms of cost-effective production of shale gas.

This leads us to another question: will US superiority in shale gas production lead to tangible repercussions for the balance of the global natural gas market? In this regard, as mentioned earlier in this volume, there are two significant factors: first, the cost of natural gas in the United States of America is much less than in other key regions such as Europe and the Pacific (as a result of these two regions' use of liquefied natural gas, which is more expensive); second, the natural gas market has begun to show signs of a transition from dependence on long-term futures contracts to the spot market, which is expected to produce a more active and flexible market in the long term. Thus, it is possible that continued US superiority in shale gas production at relatively limited cost, together with an expansion in shale gas exports to the Pacific region, will have remarkable effects on the global flows of gas among different parts of the world, with less reliance among Pacific and European consumers on Middle Eastern or Russian supplies, and a greater dependency on US gas imports, with a trend towards falling global prices.

Finally, it should be noted that the hierarchy of the new world order (as outlined in Figure 1 of the Introduction), in which the United States of America remains dominant and unchallenged by China, will only be affected by three key factors in the foreseeable future: continued outstanding Chinese economic growth in the absence of major financial or economic crises; success in catching up with the United States of America in terms of the development of advanced technologies—turning from imitation to innovation; and any failure of the United States of America and the EU to strengthen their economic, trade and financial ties and exclude China from this international cooperative framework.

APPENDICES

APPENDICES

Appendix I: Abbreviations and Acronyms

AFRICOM	US Africa command
AIDS	acquired immunodeficiency disorder
APEC	Asia–Pacific Economic Cooperation
ASEAN	Association of South East Asian Nations
bcf	billion cubic feet
bcf/y	billion cubic feet per year
BRICS	Brazil, Russia, India, China, South Africa
CBN	chemical–biological–nuclear
CCGA	Chicago Council on Global Affairs
CENTCOM	US Central Command
CEO	Chief Executive Officer
CIA	Central Intelligence Agency
CNN	Cable News Network
DNA	Deoxyribonucleic acid
ECSSR	Emirates Center for Strategic Studies and Research
EU	European Union
FAO	UN Food and Agricultural Organization
FDI	Foreign Direct Investment
FSU	Former Soviet Union
GATT	General agreement on Tariffs and Trade
GCC	Cooperation Council of the Arab States of the Gulf
GDP	Gross Domestic Product
GNI	Gross National Income
GNP	Gross National Product

HDI	Human Development Index
IAEA	International Atomic Energy Agency
IBRD	International Bank for Reconstruction and Development
ICC	International Criminal Court
ICJ	International Court of Justice
ICT	information and communications technology
IEA	International Energy Agency
ILO	International Labor Organization
IMF	International Monetary Fund
IRI	International Republican Institute
IT	Information technology
kbpd	thousand barrels per day
KFC	Kentucky Fried Chicken
LLP	Limited Liability Partnership
mbpd	million barrels per day
MSF	Médecins Sans Frontières
NAFTA	North Atlantic Free Trade Agreement
NASDAQ	National Association of Securities Dealers Automated Quotations
NATO	North Atlantic Treaty Organization
NDI	National Democratic Institute
NGO	Non-governmental organization
NPA	Norwegian People's Aid
OPEC	Organization of the Petroleum Exporting Countries
OSCE	Organization for Security and Cooperation in Europe
PBOC	People's Bank of China
PNAC	Project for the New American Century

SPSS	Statistical Package for the Social Sciences
UAE	United Arab Emirates
UK	United Kingdom
UN	United Nations
UNCTAD	United Nations Conference on Trade and Development
UNDP	United Nations Development Program
UNESCO	United Nations Educational, Scientific and Cultural Organization
UNIDO	United Nations Industrial Development Organization
UNSC	United Nations Security Council
USA	United states of America
USAID	United States of America Agency for International Development
USS	United States of America' ship
USSR	Union of Soviet Socialist Republics
WHO	World Health Organization
WIPO	World Intellectual Property Organization
WMD	weapons of mass destruction
WTC	World Trade Center
WTO	World Trade Organization

Appendix II: Figures and Tables

1. Figures

604

2. Tables

Appendix III
Public Survey Regarding the New World Order

1. How often do you follow world news in general?

(1) Always   (2) Moderately   (3) Occasionally

(4) Never   (5) Other (please explain) ....

2. Through which media do you follow this news?

(1) TV   (2) Radio   (3) Newspapers

(4) Websites   (5) Social Media   (6) Other (please explain)................

3. How do you rate your knowledge about the following international organizations and entities?

Organization/Entity	Good Knowledge	Fair Knowledge	Little Knowledge	No Knowledge
United Nations				
Security Council				
World Bank				
International Monetary Fund				
International Court of Justice				
International Criminal Court				

4. Have you heard about the "New World Order"?

(1) Yes   (2) No   (3) Other (please explain) ....

610

5. How do you see the new world order?

(1) Dominated by a single power   (2) Dominated by two powers

(3) Dominated by many powers   (4) Not clearly defined

(5) Other (please explain) ....

6. From your viewpoint, what are the most significant problems facing the new world order? (Choose the top 3)

(1) Economic and financial crisis   (2) Environmental issues (pollution, water scarcity, global warming etc.)

(3) Wars   (4) Spread of epidemics and diseases

(5) Religious extremism   (6) Terrorism

(7) WMD proliferation   (8) Other (please explain) ....

7. Do you agree that the powers of the United Nations should be expanded?

(1) Yes   (2) No   (3) Other (please explain) ....

8. If the answer is "yes", in what areas should this expansion be?

a. Having a standing peacekeeping force.

b. Having the authority to go into countries to investigate human rights violations.

c. Having the power to regulate the international arms trade.

d. Other (please explain) ....

9. Do you agree that the approval of the United Nations is necessary in order to use military force against an international source of threat?

(1) Yes   (2) No   (3) Other (please explain) ....

10. **Do you agree that the United Nations should have the right to intervene in the internal affairs of countries to investigate cases of human rights violations?**

(1) Yes   (2) No   (3) Other (please explain) ....

11. **Do you agree that the United Nations should have the authority to use force to deliver humanitarian aid in the case of refusal from the concerned countries?**

(1) Yes   (2) No   (3) Other (please explain) ....

12. **The following list includes names of a number of international organizations and institutions; to what extent do you trust each of them?**

Organization/ Entity	Highly trust	Trust	Do not trust	Do not trust at all
United Nations				
Security Council				
World Bank				
International Monetary Fund				
International Court of Justice				
International Criminal Court				

13. How do you evaluate the role of the United Nations in the world?

(1) Very positive role   (2) Positive role   (3) Negative role

(4) Very negative role   (5) Other (please explain) ....

14. Do you agree that the number of countries having veto power in the Security Council should be increased?

(1) Yes   (2) No

15. If the answer is "yes", what country or countries would you prefer to see as permanent members in the Security Council?

....

16. How do you feel about the rulings of the International Criminal Court?

(1) Fair   (2) Unfair   (3) Other (please explain) ....

17. If we consider globalization as an upsurge in the exchange of goods, services and investments between countries, in your opinion has globalization been beneficial or detrimental to your country's economy?

(1) Beneficial   (2) Detrimental   (3) Neither beneficial nor detrimental

(4) Other (please explain) ....

18. If we also consider globalization as an upsurge in the movement of people, information and ideas between countries, how has it affected your national identity?

(1) Positively affected   (2) Negatively affected

(3) Had no effect   (4) Other (please explain) ....

19. From your viewpoint, how do you rate the issue of terrorism in the world order?

(1) A major issue   (2) An issue

(3) A small issue   (4) Other (please explain) ....

20. In your opinion, how successful was the US-led global war against terrorism?

(1) Great success   (2) Medium success   (3) Limited success

(4) No success   (5) Other (please explain) ....

21. How do you rate the danger of the proliferation of Weapons of Mass Destruction?

(1) Major danger   (2) Medium Danger   (3) Little Danger

(4) Other (please explain) ....

22. How do you rate the danger of the global warming phenomenon?

(1) Major danger   (2) Medium Danger   (3) Little Danger

(4) Other (please explain) ....

23. In order to achieve global economic and financial stability, there must be international bodies to regulate and control the major financial institutions.

(1) I agree   (2) I do not Agree   (3) Other (please explain) ....

24. How do you see the future world order?

(1) Unipolar   (2) Bipolar   (3) Multipolar

(4) Other (please explain) ....

25. How do you see the role of the United States in the world order in future?

(1) A leadership role   (2) Equal to the role of other powers

(3) Will have no role at all

26. To what extent do you agree that the following countries should be poles in the new world order

	Strongly agree	Agree	Disagree	Strongly disagree	Don't know
United States of America					
Russia					
China					
Other (explain)					

27. From your viewpoint, what are the most important issues that pose a threat to the world order in the future? (Choose the top 3)

(1) Ethnic and sectarian conflicts   (2) Human rights   (3) Immigration

(4) Economy   (5) Epidemics and disease   (6) Crime

Do you agree with the following statements?

28. The Internet makes young people more aware of global issues

(1) Yes   (2) No   (3) Other (please explain) ....

29. The Internet isolates young people from reality and its problems

(1) Yes   (2) No   (3) Other (please explain) ....

30. The Internet makes young people more extreme

(1) Yes   (2) No   (3) Other (please explain) ....

31. In your opinion, will religion have a greater role in society and in relations between countries?

(1) Yes   (2) No   (3) Other (please explain) ....

DEMOGRAPHIC DATA

32. Gender:

(1) Male   (2) Female

33. Nationality: (1) UAE   (2) Arab   (3) Asian   (4) Western   (5) Other: ....

34. Age: ....

35. Residence:

(1) Abu Dhabi   (2) Al Ain   (3) Western Region

(4) Dubai   (5) Sharjah   (6) Ajman

(7) Fujairah   (8) Umm Al Quwain   (9) Ras Al Khaimah

(10) Other (please explain) ....

36. Educational level:

(1) Below secondary   (2) Secondary

(3) Diploma or University   (4) Postgraduate

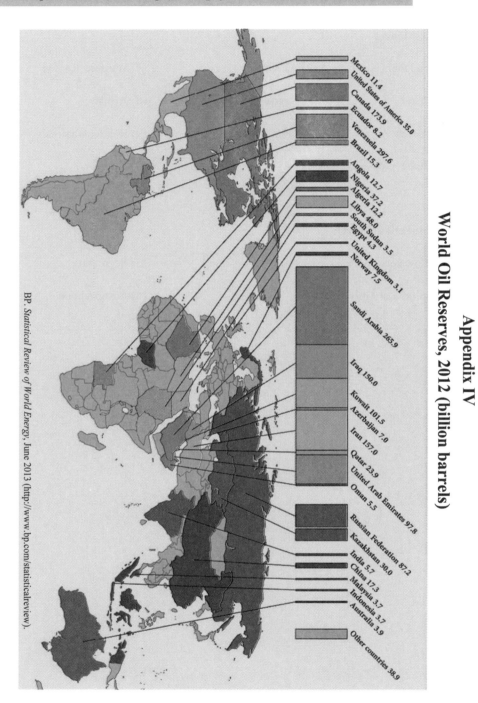

Appendix IV
World Oil Reserves, 2012 (billion barrels)

Mexico 11.4
United States of America 35.0
Canada 173.9
Ecuador 8.2
Venezuela 297.6
Brazil 15.3
Angola 12.7
Nigeria 37.2
Algeria 12.2
Libya 48.0
South Sudan 3.5
Egypt 4.3
United Kingdom 3.1
Norway 7.5
Saudi Arabia 265.9
Iraq 150.0
Kuwait 101.5
Azerbaijan 7.0
Iran 157.0
Qatar 23.9
United Arab Emirates 97.8
Oman 5.5
Russian Federation 87.2
Kazakhstan 30.0
India 5.7
China 17.3
Malaysia 3.7
Indonesia 3.7
Australia 3.9
Other countries 38.9

BP. *Statistical Review of World Energy*, June 2013 (http://www.bp.com/statisticalreview).

Appendix V

World Natural Gas Resources, 2010 (trillion cubic meters)

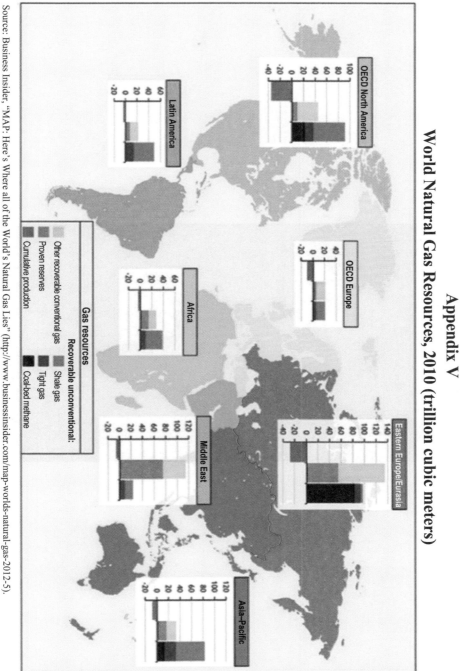

Source: Business Insider, "MAP: Here's Where all of the World's Natural Gas Lies" (http://www.businessinsider.com/map-worlds-natural-gas-2012-5).

NOTES

NOTES

Introduction

1. Fadeel Abunnasr, The *Global Citizen: Globalization, Globalism and the Just Global Order* [in Arabic]; (Beirut: Bissan for Publishing, Distribution and Information, 1st Edition, 2001), pp. 117–134.

2. For more on World War II, see R.A.C. Parker, *The Second World War: A Short History* (New York, NY: Oxford University Press, 1997), pp. 27–242.

3. K.R. Cox and T.J. Sinclair, *Approaches to World Order* (Cambridge: Cambridge University Press, 1996), pp. 191–196; F.M. Edoho (ed.), *Globalization and the New World Order* (New York, NY: Praeger Publishing, 1997), pp. 110–115.

4. David E. Long (ed.), *Gulf Security in the Twenty-First Century* (Abu Dhabi: The Emirates Center for Strategic Studies and Research, 1997); Joseph Moynihan, *Information Warfare: Concepts, Boundaries and Employment Strategies* (Abu Dhabi: The Emirates Center for Strategic Studies and Research, 1997); Mikhail Gorbachev, *The New World Order*, Emirates Lecture Series No. 15 (Abu Dhabi: The Emirates Center for Strategic Studies and Research, 1998); Richard Higgott, *Regionalization: New Trends in World Politics*, Emirates Lecture Series No. 13 (Abu Dhabi: The Emirates Center for Strategic Studies and Research, 1998); The Emirates Center for Strategic Studies and Research, *Global Strategic Developments: A Futuristic Vision* (Abu Dhabi: The Emirates Center for Strategic Studies and Research, 2012).

5. Mikhail Gorbachev, *Perestroika: New Thinking for Our Country and the World* [in Arabic]. Hamdi Abdelgawwad (trans.); (Cairo: Dar Al-Shorok, 1988), p. 162.

6. Ibid., p. 167.

7. Ibid., p. 169.

8. Ibid., pp. 170–71.

9. George H.W. Bush, "Operation Desert Storm Launched," address to the nation from the White House, January 16, 1991.

10. George H.W. Bush, Speech to Congress, The White House, March 6, 1991.

11. Joseph S. Nye, "What New World Order?" *Foreign Affairs* (Spring 1992), p. 90.

12. Ibid.

13. Ibid.

14. Lawrence Freedman, "Order and Disorder in the New World," *Foreign Affairs* vol. 71, no. 1, (special issue 1991), p. 121.

15. Ibid.

16. Ibid., pp. 121–122.

17. Samuel P. Huntington, *The Clash of Civilizations and The Remaking of World Order* (New York, NY: Simon & Schuster, 1996), p. 20.

18. Ibid., pp. 207–209.

19. Ibid., p. 321.

20. Ibid.

21. It is known that the Security Council is the organ that dominates the United Nations (UN) and most of its institutions, a fact that Fukuyama considers to be a mistake. The normal situation should be that the UN dominates, not just on the Security Council, which is one of its bodies, but also on the new world order as a whole.

22. Francis Fukuyama, *The End of History and The Last Man* (London: The Penguin Group, 1992), pp. 282–283.

23. Ibid., p. 283.

24. Zbigniew Brzezinski, *The Grand Chessboard: American Primacy and its Geostrategic Imperatives* (New York, NY: Basic Books, 1997), pp. 28–29.

25. Thomas L. Friedman, *The World is Flat: A Brief History of The Twenty-First Century* (New York, NY: Farrar, Straus and Giroux, 2005), pp. 48–172.

26. For more information on the extent of the impact of information technology systems on engagement between individuals, see: Jamal Sanad Al-Suwaidi, *From Tribe to Facebook: The Transformational Role of Social Networks* [in Arabic]; (Abu Dhabi: Emirates Center for Strategic Studies and Research, 2013), pp. 28–98.

27. Thomas L. Friedman, op. cit., pp. 48–160.

28. Ibid., pp. 316–317.

29. Ibid.

30. This role seems logical, considering the resources and capabilities of these states.

31. See the translation of Hassan A. El-Najjar's book *The Gulf War: Overreaction and Excessiveness* [in Arabic]; (Dalton, GA: Amazone Press, 2001), specifically Chapter Seven: "America Goes to War" (http://www.gulfwar1991.com).

32. Indeed, he repeated the term 'new world order' nearly 347 times on different occasions between August 1990 and March 1991. Ahmed Salem Al-Bursan, "The Greater Middle East Initiative: Political and Strategic dimensions" [in Arabic], *Al-Siyassa Al-Dawliya*, Issue 158 (October 2004), pp. 42–44.

33. Dumitru Chican, "Constructive Anarchy in the Context of the New Middle East," *Geostrategic Pulse* magazine, Issue 147, June 20, 2013, pp. 3–10.

34. Condoleezza Rice, Interview, *The Washington Post*, April 4, 2005, p. 13.

35. Abdelilah Belkeziz, "Creative Chaos: the Code Name of Fragmentation" [in Arabic], *Al-Kaleej*, May 11, 2012, p. 36.

36. United Nations Development Program (UNDP), *Millennium Development Goals: A Compact Among Nations to End Human Poverty, Human Development Report 2003* (New York, NY: United Nations Publications, 2003), p. 28.

37. It is noteworthy that a lot of the practices and features related to the new world order have already emerged. Civil society organizations possess an increasing power, enabling them to interfere in the affairs of countries. Moreover, global civil society has a real role to play in managing world affairs and building global positions towards issues and crises.

38. Fridah Aziz, *The New World Order and the 21st Century* [in Arabic]; (Damascus: Dar Al-Rasheed, 1994), p. 26.

39. Former US President George W. Bush was the first to use this expression in the aftermath of the attacks of September 11, 2001.

40. Mamdouh Mahmoud Mustafa, "The Concept of the 'International Order' Between Scientism and Normalcy" [in Arabic], *Strategic Studies* (Abu Dhabi: The Emirates Center for Strategic Studies and Research, 1998), pp. 10–12.

41. For more on US foreign policy during the post-bipolar stage, see: Amr Abdel-Ati, a review of the book *The World America Made* [in Arabic], Aljazeera.net website, May 13, 2013 (http://studies.aljazeera.net/bookrevision/2013/05/20135137202626736.htm).

42. Saad Haqqi Tawfiq, *New International Order: A Study of the Future of International Relations after the End of the Cold War*, [in Arabic]; (Amman: Alahliya for Publishing and Distribution, 1999), p. 42.

43. Boutros Boutros-Ghali, "The United Nations and the Containment of Ethnic Conflicts," [in Arabic] *Al-Siyassa Al-Dawliya*, Issue 115 (January 1994), p. 10.

44. See the biography of US President George H.W. Bush in: "American President: A Reference Resource," Miller Center, University of Virginia (http://millercenter.org/president/bush/essays/biography/5), accessed September 22, 2013.

45. Ibid., accessed November 4, 2013.

46. Anne-Marie Slaughter, *A New World Order* (Princeton, NJ: Princeton University Press, 2004), pp. 27–31.

47. Raslan Khasbulatov, *The Bloody Confrontation: A Testimony for History on the Collapse of the Soviet Union* [in Arabic], Abu-Bakr Youssef (trans.); (Cairo: Al-Ahram Center for Translation and Publishing, 1996), pp. 11–26.

48. George Friedman, "Beyond the Post-Cold War World," Sratfor, April 2, 2013 (http://www.stratfor.com/weekly/beyond-post-cold-war-world).

49. John Lamberton Harper, *The Cold War* (Oxford: Oxford University Press, 2011), pp. 21–64.

50. Ibid. pp. 81–89.

51. Laicie Heeley, "US Defense Spending vs. Global Defense Spending," The Center for Arms Control and Non-Proliferation, April 24, 2013 (http://arms controlcenter.org/issues/securityspending/articles/ 2012_topline_global_defense_spending). The defense spending of the European Union for 2011 amounted to 197.5 billion euros (around US$274.5 billion); Joachim Hofbauer, Priscilla Hermann and Sneha Raghavan, "European Defense Trends, 2012: Budgets, Regulatory Frameworks and the Industrial Base," CSIS Defense-Industrial Initiatives Group, Center for Strategic and International Studies (CSIS), December 2012, p. 4.

52. International Monetary Fund (IMF), "World Economic Outlook Database," April 2013 (http://www.imf.org/external/pubs/ft/weo/2013/01/weodata/index. aspx).

53. Bahgat Qarni, "From the International System to the World Order" [in Arabic], *Al-Siyassa Al-Dawliya*, Issue 161 (July 2005), pp. 40–45.

54. See the UN Regular Budget (http://www.un.org/ar).

55. See the biography of A. Gary Shilling, President of the US financial consultancy firm 'A. Gary Shilling & Co.,' see: "A. Gary Shilling," Bloomberg (http://www.bloomberg.com/view/bios/gary-shilling); and "A. Gary Shilling and Company, Inc." (http://www.agaryshilling.com).

56. "Six Reasons the US Will Dominate the World" [in Arabic], *Akhbar Al-Saah* bulletin, Issue 5187 (Abu Dhabi: The Emirates Center for Strategic Studies and Research, September 1, 2013), p. 4; see also the original: A. Gary Shilling, "Six Reasons the US Will Dominate," Bloomberg (http://www.bloomberg.com/news/2013-08-27/six-reasons-the-u-s-will-dominate.html), accessed August 31, 2013.

57. Ibid.

58. Ibid.

59. Congressional Budget Office, "Monthly Budget Review for August 2013," September 9, 2013 (http://www.cbo.gov/sites/default/files/cbo files/attachments/44552-%20MBR_2013_08.pdf), accessed November 18, 2013.

60. International Monetary Fund (IMF), "IMF Executive Board Concludes 2013 Article IV Consultation with the United States of America," Press Release no. 13/277, July 26, 2013 (http://www. imf.org/external/np/sec/pr/2013/pr13277.htm).

61. George Friedman, "Beyond the Post-Cold War World," Sratfor, April 2, 2013 (http://www.stratfor.com/weekly/beyond-post-cold-war-world).

62. Saleh Sulaiman Abdulazim, *China Goes Global: The Partial Power* [in Arabic], by David Shambaugh, Al-Jazeera Center for Studies, Doha, July 23, 2013, pp. 6–7 (http://studies.aljazeera.net/book revision/2013/07/201372371958283608.htm).

63. Amin Al-Mahdi, "The End of the Cold War Has Weakened National Sovereignty in Favor of Peoples" [in Arabic], *Al-Hayat*, July 27, 2003, p. 20.

64. Abdul Aziz Said, Charles O. Lerche Jr., and Charles O. Lerche III, *Concepts of International Politics in Global Perspective* [in Arabic], Naf'e Ayoub Lobbos (trans.); (Damascus: Publications of the Arab Writers Union, 1999), p. 174. See also: United Nations (UN), "Main Bodies," n.d. (http://www.un.org/ar/mainbodies).

65. See the text of the GCC Common Defense Agreement [in Arabic] at: (http://www.almeezan.qa/AgreementsPage.aspx?id=1527&language=ar).

66. For more information on global and regional economic groupings, see: Akef Soufan, *International and Regional Organizations* [in Arabic]; (Damascus: Qordoba Publishing, 2004), pp. 157–176; and Hussein Omar, *Directory of International Organizations* [in Arabic]; (Cairo: Dar el-Fikr el-Arabi, 1997), pp. 63–186.

67. United Nations (UN), *World Investment Report 2013* (New York, NY: UN Publications, 2013), pp. 199–201.

68. On the history of US intervention in Latin America see: William Blum, *Killing Hope: US Military and CIA Interventionism since World War II* (Monroe, ME: Common Courage Press, 1995).

69. The White House, "First Annual Report to the Congress on United States of America Foreign Policy for the 1970s," February 18, 1970, pp. 6–21.

70. David Shinn and Kerry Brown, *China and Africa: A Century of Engagement* (London: Chatham House, June 29, 2012), pp. 4–5.

71. Al-Sayyid Ameen Shalabi, "Henry Kissinger and the Diplomacy of Détente" [in Arabic], *Al-Siyassa Al-Dawliya*, Issue 46 (October 1976), pp. 52–54.

72. Ibid., 56–57.

73. Ahmed Yousef Al-Qurae, "Reviving the Hotline in a World at the Brink of the Abyss" [in Arabic], *Al-Ahram*, October 20, 2006 (http://yyy.ahram. org.eg/archive/2006/10/20/OPIN3.HTM), accessed September 23, 2013.

74. See: Bowker, "New Books, Titles and Editions" in *Book Publishing in the United Arab Emirates: A Survey and Analysis* (Sharjah: Emirates Publishers Association, 2011); *The Book Market in Greece* (Athens: National Book Centre of Greece, 2012).

75. For more information, see: Central Intelligence Agency (CIA), "Country Comparison: Education Expenditures," *The World Factbook* (Washington, DC: Central Intelligence Agency, 2013); (https://www. cia.gov/library/publications/the-world-factbook/rankorder/2206rank. html); and The World Bank, "Research and Development Expenditure (% of GDP)" (http://data.worldbank.org/indicator/GB.XPD.RSDV. GD.ZS) and (http://data.worldbank.org/products/wdi) accessed December 3, 2013. See also: Hermann Simon, "Why does Siemens apply for 6 times more patents than all of Spain? On the innovation gulf in Europe," Whiteboard (http://www.whiteboardmag.com/why-does-siemens-apply-for-6-times-more-patents-than-all-of-spain-on-the-innovation-gulf-in-europe/).

76. World Bank data years for each country listed: United States of America (2011), Russia (2011), China (2009), European Union (2010), India (2007), Brazil (2010), Japan (2010).

77. United Nations Development Program, Human Development Report 2013, op. cit., p. 198.

78. International Monetary Fund (IMF), "World Economic Outlook Database," op. cit.

79. United Nations Development Program, "Human Development Report 2013," op. cit., p. 2.

80. International Monetary Fund (IMF), "World Economic Outlook Database," op. cit.

81. United Nations Development Program, "Human Development Report 2013," op. cit., pp. 198–201.

82. International Institute for Strategic Studies (IISS), *The Military Balance 2013* (London: IISS, 2013); "Countries Ranked by Military Strength (2013)," GlobalFirePower.com (http://www.globalfirepower. com/countries-listing.asp); and Craig Hoyle, "World Air Forces 2013," Flightglobal.com December 13, 2012 (http://www.flightglobal.com/ blogs/the-dewline/2012/12/free-download-world-air-forces).

83. International Monetary Fund (IMF), "World Economic Outlook Database," op. cit.

84. Central Intelligence Agency (CIA), *The World Factbook* (Washington, DC: Central Intelligence Agency, 2013), p. 12; (https:// www.cia.gov/library/publications/the-world-factbook/geos/us.html).

85. US Central Intelligence Agency (CIA), "Country Comparison: Airports," *The World Factbook* (Washington, DC: Central Intelligence Agency, 2013); (https://www.cia.gov/library/publications/the-world-factbook/rankorder/2053rank.html); and National Highways Authority of India, "Indian Road Network" (http://www.nhai.org/roadnetwork. htm).

86. George Friedman, *The Next 100 Years: A Forecast for the 21st Century* (New York, NY: Anchor Books, 2010), p. 39.

87. For more details on the method of determining timings, see: (http://www.distancefromto.net).

88. George Friedman, op. cit., p. 40.

89. Ibid., pp. 40–41.

90. Ibid., p. 42.

91. See: "The British Burn Washington, DC, 1814," *Eyewitness to History* (http://www.eyewitnesstohistory.com/washingtonsack.htm), accessed September 22, 2013.

92. George Friedman, op. cit., pp. 42–44.

93. Ibid.

94. Ibid.

95. Ibid.

96. Ibid. p. 44.

97. Ibid., pp. 45–46.

98. On the concepts of balances of power and interests, see: Nizar Ismail Al-Hyali, *NATO's Role After the End of the Cold War* [in Arabic]; (Abu Dhabi: The Emirates Center for Strategic Studies and Research, 2003), pp. 20–24.

99. For more information on perfect peace and real peace, see: Richard Nixon, *1999 Victory Without War* (London: Sidgwicke & Jakson, 1988).

100. For instance, China faces many internal challenges as a result of its large population and the multiplicity of its ethnic and religious make-up. It also lacks the international diplomacy experience to address the world due to the limited international utility of the Chinese language. The same applies to the Russian Federation, whose economy still suffers from structural problems; see: Paul Salem and Matthew Ferchen, "The Chinese Economic Model: Policies and Best Practices," Carnegie Middle East Center, June 12, 2012, p. 2.

101. Saad Haqqi Tawfiq, op. cit., p. 58.

102. Philip Andrews-Speed, et al., "The Global Resource Nexus: The Struggles for Land, Energy, Food, Water and Minerals," Transatlantic Academy, May 2012), pp. 43–89.

103. Moisés Naím, *The End of Power: From Boardrooms to Battlefields and Churches to States, Why Being in Charge isn't What it Used to Be* (New York, NY: Basic Books, 2013), p. 1.

104. Ibid, p. 5.

105. Regarding oil production and consumption averages, see: BP, *BP Statistical Review of World Energy 2013*, June 2013, pp. 8–11.

106. Ibid.

107. For more information on global warming, see: Intergovernmental Panel on Climate Change (IPCC), "Working Group I Report –'The Physical Science Basis'," *Fourth Assessment Report: Climate Change 2007(AR4); (*Geneva: IPCC, 2010).

108. Naím, op. cit., p. 113.

109. Franklin B. Miles, "Asymmetric Warfare: An Historical Perspective" Strategy Research Project, US Army War College, Carlisle Barracks, 1999, pp. 2–16.

110. Naím, op. cit., p. 113.

111. Ibid., pp. 113–115.

112. Ibid.

113. Ibid., p. 54.

114. The World Bank, *Global Monitoring Report 2012: Food Prices, Nutrition and the Millennium Development Goals* (March 2013), p. 58.

115. Ibid., pp. 55–56.

116. Ibid.

117. Ibid., pp. 58–59.

118. Walter W. Powell and Kaisa Snellman, "The Knowledge Economy," *Annual Review of Sociology*, vol. 30, no. 1 (August 2004), p. 201.

119. "World Values Survey 2010–2012," revised master, October 2011 (WVS 2010-2012 Wave); (http://www.worldvaluessurvey.org/index_surveys), pp. 1–20.

120. Naím, op. cit., pp. 64–70.

121. For US political literature dealing with the concept of power change, see: Joseph S. Nye, "The Future of Power," *Public Affairs* (March/April 2011); Joseph S. Nye, "The Future of Power: Dominance and Decline in Perspective," *Foreign Affairs* (November/December 2010); Fareed Zakaria, "The Future of American Power," Council on Foreign Relations (May/June 2008); Christine Todd Whitman, "What is the Future of American Nuclear Power?" *Forbes*, December 10, 2012; Tyler Crowe, "What will Power America's Future? The Case for Oil," The Motley Fool, September 21, 2013; Aaron Friedberg, "The Future of American Power," *Political Science Quarterly*, vol. 109, no.1 (Spring 1994).

122. For more on 'smart power,' see: Richard L. Armitage and Joseph S. Nye, *CSIS Commission on Smart Power: A Smarter, More Secure America* (Washington, DC: CSIS, 2007), pp. 27–60.

123. On the principles and problems of humanitarian intervention, see: Joseph S. Nye, *Understanding International Conflicts: An Introduction to Theory and History* [in Arabic], Ahmad Al-Jamal and Magdi Kamel (trans.); (Cairo: The Egyptian Association for the Dissemination of Universal Culture and Knowledge, 1997); David Forsythe, *Human Rights and World Politics* [in Arabic], Mohammad Mustafa Ghoneim (trans.); (Cairo: The Egyptian Association for the

Dissemination of Universal Culture and Knowledge, 1993); Hassanein Tawfiq Ibrahim, "Globalization: Political Dimensions and Implications: An Initial Vision from the Perspective of Political Science" [in Arabic], *Alam el-Fikr* vol. 28, Issue 2 (October/December 1999); Gene M. Lyons and Michael Mastanduno, "International Intervention, State Sovereignty and Future of the International Community" [in Arabic], Mohammed Jalal Abbas (trans.), *International Social Science Journal* (UNESCO), no. 138 (November 1993); Omar Ismail Saadullah, *Human Rights and Peoples' Rights: The Relationship and Legal Developments* [in Arabic], (Algiers: Office of University Publications, 1991); and Ibrahim Ali Badawi Sheikh, "The United Nations and Human Rights Violations" [in Arabic], *Egyptian Journal of International Law*, vol. 36, Issue 36 (1980).

124. The right to humanitarian intervention is one of the most controversial principles of international relations in recent years, especially following the intervention of the international community to protect civilians in certain regions and countries, and not others. Thus, the codification and application of clear rules for this right has become an extremely urgent matter to ensure the rule of international law. See: Khaled Al-Moeini, 'Pretext of Humanitarian Intervention in International Relations' [in Arabic], Al-Jazeera.net website, April 9, 2012 (http://www.aljazeera.net/opinions/pages/ 032efaa9-0dad-4af0-9d00-ba9f6afc0adf).

125. "Assets under Management of the Largest Hedge Fund Firms in October 2011 (in billion US dollars)," Statista.com, n.d. (http://www.statista.com/statistics/273133/assets-under-management-of-the-largest-hedge-fund-firms).

126. During the period from 1945 to 2011, the number of sovereign states in the world increased from 41 to 194. See: US Central Intelligence Agency (CIA), "North America," *The World Factbook*, 1992–2013 (https://www.cia.gov/library/publications/the-world-factbook/geos/us.html), accessed August 21, 2013.

127. Hanaa Baidany, *The Concept of Despotism in Modern and Contemporary Islamic Political Thinking: A Comparative Study* [in Arabic]; (Cairo: Egyptian Lebanese Publishing House, 2012), pp. 45–77.

128. Jeffrey Haynes (ed.), *Religion and Democratizations* (London and New York, NY: Routledge, 2011), pp. 18–44.

129. Ibid.

130. "America Punishes Green Revolution Repressors: Iran is a Hypocrite," CNN Arabic website, July 9, 2011 (http://arabic.cnn.com/2011/world/6/9/iran.greenrev).

131. On the imposition of democracy in Haiti, see: "Operation Uphold Democracy-Haiti," Air University Library, Maxwell Airforce Base (http://www.au.af.mil/au/aul/bibs/haiti/haiti99.htm), accessed June 22, 2013.

132. Some researchers believe that the United States of America goes to the United Nations in certain cases when it has the support of the major powers, while ignoring it when it knows this support is not forthcoming. See: Ibrahim Abrash, "System Limits and the Legitimacy Crisis in the New World Order' [in Arabic], *Al-Mustaqbal Al-Arabi*, Issue 185 (1994); Mousa Al-Zoubi, *A New World Order or a New American Hegemony?* [in Arabic]; (Damascus: Dar al-Shadi, 1993), pp. 123–127; Abdul Khaliq Abdullah, "The New World Order: Facts and Illusions" [in Arabic], *Al-Siyassa Al-Dawliya*, Issue 124 (April 1996), pp. 46–49.

133. On governance and good governance, see: R.A.W. Rhodes, "The New Governance: Governing without Government," *Political Studies*, no. 44 (London: IISS, 1996).

134. See the text of United Nations Security Council Resolution 940 of 1994 (http://daccess-dds-ny.un.org/doc/UNDOC/GEN/N94/312/22/PDF/N9431222.pdf?OpenElement).

Chapter I

1. On the new world order and the circumstances of its emergence, see: Joseph R. Biden Jr., "How I Learned to Love the New World Order," *The Wall Street Journal*, April 23, 1992, p. A13.

2. Anne-Marie Slaughter, *A New World Order* (Princeton, NJ: Princeton University Press, 2004), p. A3.

3. Hussein Ali Zahir, *The Evolution of International Relations from Westphalia to Versailles* [in Arabic]; (Beirut: Dar Al-Mawasim for Printing, Publishing and Distribution, 1999), pp. 118–133.

4. Pierre Beaudry, "The Economic Policy that Made the Peace of Westphalia," *Executive Intelligence Review*, vol. 30, no. 21 (May 2003), pp. 64–78.

5. Ibid.

6. Ibid.

7. Paul Kennedy, *The Rise and Fall of the Great Powers* (London: Fontana Press, 1989), p. xxi.

8. Ibid.

9. Irving Werstein, *1914–1918: World War I* (New York, NY: Cooper Square Publishers, Inc., 1964).

10. Treaty of Versailles, Covenant of the League of Nations (http://ushistory.org).

11. United Nations (UN), "Charter of the United Nations," pp. 4–5 (http://www.un.org/en/documents/charter/index.shtml).

12. For more information, see: Christopher M. Meissner, "*A New World Order: Explaining the Emergence of the Classical Gold Standard*," Kings College (Cambridge: University of Cambridge, August 2001).

13. Zbigniew Brzezinski, *Out of Control: Global Turmoil on the Eve of the 21st Century* [in Arabic], Fadel al-Badri (trans.); (Amman: Al-Ahlia for Publishing and Distribution, 1998), pp. 86–90; Richard Haass, *The Opportunity: America's Moment to Alter History's Course* [in Arabic], Saad Kamel Elias (trans.); (Riyadh: Obeikan Publishing, 2007), pp. 42–45; and Samuel Huntington, *The Clash of Civilizations and the Remaking of World Order* [in Arabic], Abbas Hilal Kadhim (trans.); (Amman: Dar Al-Amal for Publishing and Distribution, 2006), pp. 21–22.

14. Marxist thought emerged after Karl Marx and Friedrich Engels released their book *The Communist Manifesto* in 1848, and also after Marx's famous book *Das Kapital* in 1867, vol. 3, which was edited and completed by Friedrich Engels in 1894. However, the spread of Marxism came when Vladimir Ilyich Ulyanov (Lenin) led the Bolshevik Revolution in Russia in 1917.

15. Francis Fukuyama, *The End of History and the Last Man* (London: The Penguin Group, 1992), pp. 25–29. See also: Bahgat Qarni, "From the International System to the World Order" [in Arabic], *Al-Siyassa Al-Dawliya*, Issue 161 (July 2005), p. 42.

16. Mohamed Hassanein Heikal, *The American Empire and the Raid on Iraq* [in Arabic]; (Cairo: Dar El Shorouk, 2009), pp. 128 et seq; and Henry Kissinger, *Diplomacy from the Cold War to the Present Day* [in Arabic], Omar Ayoubi (trans.); (Amman: Al Dar Al Ahlia for Distribution and Publication, 1995), pp. 521 et seq.

17. C.G. Jacobsen, *The New World Order's Defining Crises: The Clash of Promise and Essence* (London: Dartmouth Publishing Company, 1996), pp. 25–34.

18. George H.W. Bush, Speech at Maxwell Air Force Base, Montgomery, Alabama, The White House, April 13, 1992 (http://www.presidency.ucsb.edu/ws/?pid=19466#axzz2iEpfIVMS).

19. Paul W. Schroeder, "The New World Order: A Historical Perspective," *Washington Quarterly*, vol. 17, no. 2 (Spring 1994), pp. 25–27.

20. The World Trade Organization (WTO) was established in 1995 as the successor to the General Agreement on Tariffs and Trade (GATT), which was established after World War II. It is concerned with ensuring the movement of trade within the new world order with the greatest freedom. Therefore, it is responsible for the enactment of international laws relevant to the organization on trade between nations, and currently has 152 member states. See the official website of the World Trade Organization (http://www.wto.org).

21. Khosrow Fatemi (ed.), *The New World Order* (New York, NY: Pergamon, 2000), pp. 29–33.

22. Ali Eddin Hilal, "The New International Order: The Current Situation and Future Prospects" [in Arabic], *Alam el-Fikr* [The World of Thought], vol. 23, nos. III and IV (Kuwait: January/March and April/June 1995), pp. 9–24.

23. Ibid.

24. D. Held, *Democracy and the Global Order: From the Modern State to Cosmopolitan Governance* (Stanford, CA: Stanford University Press, 1996), pp. 11–13.

25. Ibid., p. 12.

26. Schroeder, op. cit., pp. 30–31.

27. Henry Kissinger, *Diplomacy from the Cold War to the Present Day* [in Arabic] Omar Ayoubi (trans.); (Amman: Al Dar Al Ahlia for Distribution and Publication, 1995); p. 527.

28. Henry Kissinger, *Does America Need a Foreign Policy?* (New York, NY: Simon & Schuster, 2001), p. 347.

29. Kauthar Abbas al-Rubaie and Marwan Salem Al-Ali, *The Future of the New International Order in Light of the Emergence of Rising*

Powers and its Impact on the Arab Region: The EU Model [in Arabic]; (Baghdad: Center for International Studies, 2009), p. 3.

30. Bart R. Kessler, *Bush's New World Order: The Meaning Behind the Words* (Montgomery, AL: US Air Command and Staff College, 1997), pp. 19–62.

31. Nazli Moawad Ahmed, "The Japanese Perception of the International System" [in Arabic], *Al-Siyassa Al-Dawliya*, Issue 101 (July 1990), pp. 57–61.

32. Qarni, op. cit., pp. 40–45. For other views regarding the definition of the global order, see: Rod Grubb, *Alternative Global Vision of a New World Order* (Northfield, MN: St. Olaf College, 1992), pp. 102–107.

33. Stephen M. Walt, "The End of the American Era," *The National Interest*, October 25, 2011 (http://nationalinterest.org/article/the-end-the-american-era-6037), accessed September 23, 2013. See also: Joseph Nye, "The Future of American Power" [in Arabic], in Joseph Nye, Hillary Clinton, Tim Dunne and Kledja Mulaj, "The Future of American Power," *International Studies*, issue no. 105 (Abu Dhabi: The Emirates Center for Strategic Studies and Research, 2012), pp. 7–24.

34. Ted Galen Carpenter, "The New World Disorder," *Foreign Policy* (Fall 1991), pp. 24–39. See also: Mounir Mahmoud Badawi Essayyed, "Modern Trends in the Study of the International System Since the End of the Cold War," research submitted to the Standing Committee for Political Science, Assiut University, Faculty of Commerce, 2004, p. 3.

35. Abdul Aziz Said, Charles O. Learche, Jr. and Charles O. Lerche, III, *Concepts of International Politics in Global Perspective* [in Arabic], Naf'e Ayoub Lobbos (trans.); (Damascus: Publications of the Arab Writers Union, 1999), pp. 221–222.

36. Ibid.

37. In this regard we point to the fact that in the international system, Russia or China could veto a resolution by the UN Security Council, as is the case for the United States of America, Britain and France. But in the new world order, we find that the United States of America has been able to pressure the UN Security Council to pass a resolution to use force in the cases of Somalia and Iraq following its occupation of Kuwait in 1990, but has in cooperation with its allies invaded Iraq in March 2003, without obtaining a mandate from the United Nations and ignoring objections from China and Russia.

38. For more details on the role of multinational companies, see: Mohamed Medhat Ghassan, *Multinational Companies and State Sovereignty* [in Arabic]; (Amman: Dar Al-Raya for Publishing and Distribution, 2013), pp. 9–10.

39. The mixed economy is an economic system based on a combination of more than one manifestation of the different economic systems. It usually involves companies owned by individuals or by the government. It also contains elements of the capitalist system and some of the features of the socialist system, such as social welfare, or a combination of elements of the planned economy and the market economy. The mixed system is defined as a degree of economic freedom combined with centralized economic planning. For more information, see: "The World is Looking for a New Economic System After the Failure of the Capitalist and Socialist Systems" [in Arabic], April 17, 2011 (http://alphabeta.argaam.com/article/detail/28833).

40. For more on liberalism and democracy in the new world order, see: Ash Jain, *Like-minded and Capable Democracies: A New Framework for Advancing a Liberal World Order*, IIGG Working Paper, US Council on Foreign Relations, January 2013 (http://i.cfr.org/content/publications/attachments/IIGG_WorkingPaper12_Jain.pdf).

41. We notice that the foreign policies of countries have started to take into account the strategic interests of the power dominating the new

world order to avoid contradicting it. Therefore they cannot rely on the policy of containment or waging internal wars away from the will of that dominant power.

42. United Nations, "The 1945 Statute of the International Court of Justice" [in Arabic]; (http://www.un.org/arabic/aboutun/statute.htm).

43. During the first ten years after the inception of the International Criminal Court (ICC), it investigated and convicted the perpetrators of crimes against humanity and war crimes in Uganda, the Democratic Republic of the Congo, Central African Republic, Kenya, Libya and Côte d'Ivoire, and genocide in Darfur, Sudan.

44. United Nations, "Rome Statute of the International Criminal Court," December 31, 2003 (http://www.un.org/Law/icc/index.html), accessed June 29, 2013.

45. "The African Union rejects the appearance of the Kenyan president before the Criminal Court of Justice," [in Arabic] Reuters, October 12, 2013 (http://ara.reuters.com/article/worldNews/idARACAE9B25 H220131012), accessed November 4, 2013.

46. Qarni, op. cit., p. 42.

47. Patrick Goodenough, "US Taxpayers Will Continue to Pay More Than One-Fifth of UN Budget," CNS News, December 28, 2012 (http://cnsnews.com/news/article/us-taxpayers-will-continue-pay-more-one-fifth-un-budget).

48. Noam Chomsky, *Rogue States: The Rule of Force in World Affairs* [in Arabic], Mahmoud Ali Issa (trans.); (Beirut: Dar Al Kitab Al Arabi, 2003), pp. 65–68.

49. Of particular importance is the role played by former US Secretary of State, Colin Powell, in presenting to the UN Security Council false information and pictures in order to get a UN resolution authorizing the United States of America to use force against Iraq. In addition, false satellite images of the military situation in Iraq during the

invasion of Kuwait were sent by US President George H.W. Bush to French President François Mitterrand to persuade him to participate in the international coalition against Iraq.

50. Fathi Hosni Atwa, "The return of Egyptian-Soviet relations" [in Arabic], *Al-Siyassa Al-Dawliya*, Issue 78 (October 1984), pp. 136–142.

51. Some researchers call this approach "the diffusion of American culture and development of the world."

52. Kissinger, 2001, op. cit., p. 411.

53. Robert Kagan, *The World America Made* (New York, NY: Knopf Doubleday Publishing Group, 2013), pp. 64–67.

54. On December 21, 2012 the US Senate approved by 81 votes to 14 votes the defense budget for the fiscal year starting in October 2012.

55. The military premises mentioned have been identified as a result of analysis of contemporary US military activity.

56. Michael J. Lostumbo et al., *Overseas Basing of US Military Forces: An Assessment of Relative Costs and Strategic Benefits* (Santa Monica, CA: RAND Corporation, 2013), pp. 22–32; US Department of Defense, *Base Structure Report, 2010*; Zachary Fillingham, "US Military Bases: A Global Footprint," *Geopolitical Monitor*, April 14, 2012, pp. 2–7.

57. "Aircraft Carrier Locations," *Gonavy.jp* (http://www.gonavy.jp/CVLocation.html), accessed October 7, 2013; and "USS Carl Vinson (CVN 70)," unofficial Navy Site (http://navysite.de/cvn/cvn70.html).

58. Jean-Loup Samaan, "A New Perspective on the Relationship between NATO and the Gulf States" [in Arabic], *NATO Review* (online); (http://www.nato.int/docu/review/2012/Arab-Spring/NATO-Gulf-Strategic-Dialogue/AR/index.htm).

59. It consists of a ground missile system deployed in several geographical points both inside and outside the United States of America, capable of shooting down any intercontinental ballistic missile targeting the territory of the United States of America or its allies. See: Hossam Eldin Mohamed Swailam, *US National Missile Defense System* [in Arabic]; (Abu Dhabi: The Emirates Center for Strategic Studies and Research, 2003), pp. 70–78.

60. International Monetary Fund (IMF), "World Economic Outlook Database," April 2013 (http://www.imf.org/external/pubs/ft/weo/2013/01/weodata/index.aspx).

61. US economic premises were prepared in accordance with their direct and indirect role in the management of the global economy in order to achieve US interests as the dominant power over the new world order.

62. The United States of America has defense agreements and military cooperation with most countries of the Cooperation Council for the Arab Gulf States (GCC), and bears significant material and military costs, although the region is not a major source of US energy and yet is a major energy source for China, India and the EU.

63. Kissinger, 2001, op. cit., pp. 350–351.

64. Ibid., p. 371.

65. For more information on US technological strength, see: National Center for Education Statistics, *Digest of Education Statistics Report*, 2012.

66. Richard LeBaron, a researcher on the Gulf states and former US ambassador to Kuwait, mentions in a detailed report on Saudi scholarships to the United States of America – published in *USA Today* March 2, 2013, p. A8 – that the popularity of the scholarship program with Saudi youth has increased significantly, with the total

number of male and female Saudi students on scholarships reaching 71,000 in 2012, up from just 6,000 in 2004.

67. Numbers are made on the basis of one year out of five for the period 1949/1950–1999/2000. Interval years have been estimated by assuming that the annual growth rate was constant for each five-year period. For the years 1999/2000–2011/2012, detailed annual data are available, see: Institute of International Education (IIE), "International Students: All Places of Origin" (http://www.iie.org/Research-and-Publications/Open-Doors/Data/International-Students/All-Places-of-Origin).

68. This is highlighted by rapid US intervention to manage the affairs of the new world order through engagement with global crises and conflicts as an actor and a hegemon, imposing solutions without waiting for the affected parties to reach solutions that may conflict with its interests.

69. Sam Carpenter, *Work the System: The Simple Mechanics of Making More and Working Less* (Austin, TX: Greenleaf Book Group, 2011), pp. 3–6. See also: Kamal El-Menoufi, *Theories of Political Systems* [in Arabic]; (Kuwait: Publications Agency, 1985), pp. 95–99.

70. Zbigniew Brzezinski, *The Choice: Global Domination or Global Leadership* (New York, NY: Basic Books, 2004), p. 4.

71. Ibid.

72. For more information on the working mechanisms within the global system, see: Gordana Yovanovich (ed.), *The New World Order: Corporate Agenda and Parallel Reality* (London: McGill-Queens University Press, 2003), pp. 23–122.

73. Fareed Zakaria, *The Post-American World* (New York, NY: W.W. Norton & Company, 2009), pp. 125–128.

74. Ibid.

75. Brzezinski, op. cit., pp. 88–89.

76. The current US President, Barack Hussein Obama, had criticized in Moscow on August 10, 2013 the return of what he called the rhetoric of confrontation, which dates back to the era of the Cold War between the United States of America and the Soviet Union. He also ruled out any return to that period against the backdrop of an escalation of hostile rhetoric between the two countries. Obama promised to launch a new era with respect to US intelligence agencies, and greater transparency. He denied any intention to spy on ordinary citizens inside or outside the country. Tension in the relationship between Washington and Moscow began after Edward Snowden – who fled the United States of America in May 2013 – took refuge in Moscow and was granted temporary political asylum in July of the same year after he revealed a huge US spying program that probably goes beyond US boundaries. The Snowden incident also raised tension between the United States of America and its European allies when they discovered that Washington was spying on their private communications, both as individuals and governments, and that this was taking place in a systematic manner for the benefit of commercial, political and security purposes. This prompted many European officials to publicly express their anger, such as Fleur Pellerin, the French minister responsible for SMEs and the Digital Economy, who said she was shocked by the "generalized surveillance of populations … that's an affair completely different from espionage; it's much more serious." For more, see: William Pfaff, "Europe is the Victim of US Espionage" [in Arabic], *Al-Ittihad*, July 14, 2013, p. 34. See also: "Obama Criticizes Russia and Promises A New Intelligence Era" [in Arabic], Al-Jazeera website (http://www.aljazeera.net/news/pages/970367d7-4449-41e8-b442-7c1ab5ceabe1), accessed August 10, 2013.

77. Emirates Center for Strategic Studies and Research (ECSSR), *Global Strategic Developments: A Futuristic Vision* (Abu Dhabi: ECSSR, 2012).

78. Brzezinski, op. cit., p. 141.

79. Ibid.

80. Samuel Huntington, *The Clash of Civilizations and the Remaking of World Order* [in Arabic], Abbas Hilal Kadhim (trans.); (Amman: Dar Al-Amal for Publishing and Distribution, 2006), p. 449.

81. Fukuyama, op. cit., pp. 204–206.

82. Ibid.

83. Noam Chomsky, *Power Systems: Conversations on Global Democratic Uprisings and the New Challenges to US Empire* (New York, NY: Metropolitan Books, 2013), pp. 164–166.

84. Brzezinski, op. cit., pp. 180–181.

85. The role of these centers emerged clearly in the setup and preparation for the recent Arab popular protests through the youth in Egypt and Tunisia in order to carry out the task of regime change, or at least to be a driver for the masses in both countries to overthrow the existing regimes. See: "The Democracy Lie: The National Democratic Institute," [in Arabic]; (http://ishtar-enana.blogspot.ae/2012/04/ndi.html).

86. Including young people from Egypt, Jordan, Lebanon, Libya, Pakistan, Syria, Turkey, the Occupied West Bank, Israel, Iraq, Afghanistan, Sudan, Tunisia, Indonesia, Kenya, Morocco, Nigeria, Somaliland, Serbia, Albania, Ukraine, and South Africa.

87. The Middle East Partnership Initiative (MEPI). It includes the US program "Tomorrow's Leaders" and the program of the US

Department of State's "Democracy Support Initiative and the Bureau of Democracy, Human Rights, and Labor in Washington."

88. On the concept of the analytical framework, see: Jim A. Kuypers, "Framing Analysis from a Rhetorical Perspective," in Paul D'Angelo and Jim A. Kuypers (eds), *Doing News Framing Analysis* (New York, NY: Routledge, 2010), pp. 286–311.

89. There is always a natural rivalry between human needs and the circumstances affecting them. The product of this is the emergence of a global system that evolves according to the relations of balance or imbalance in the strategic powers influencing this system.

90. Nye, op. cit., pp. 7–24.

91. Paul Kennedy, *The Rise and Fall of the Great Powers* (London: Fontana Press, 1989), pp. 693–695.

92. Ibid.

93. Fukuyama, op. cit., pp. 276–277.

94. Mustafa Kamel El-Sayed, "Civil society: The New Actor on the International Stage" [in Arabic], *Al-Siyassa Al-Dawliya*, vol. 41, Issue 161 (July 2005), pp. 67–68.

95. World Bank, "Risk and Vulnerability," Annual Bank Conference on Development Economics, Washington, DC, June 3–4, 2013, pp. 11–23.

96. On universal values and their dissemination, see the United Nations Development Program publications: *Human Development Report 1993*: "People's Participation"; *Human Development Report 1994*: "New Dimensions of Human Security"; *Human Development Report 1995*: "Gender and Human Development"; *Human Development Report 1999*: "Globalization with a Human Face"; *Human Development Report 2000*: "Human Rights and Human Development"; *Human Development Report*

2002: "Deepening Democracy in a Fragmented Word"; and *Human Development Report 2004*: "Cultural Liberty in Today's Diverse World."

97. Mustafa Kamel El-Sayed, op. cit., pp. 69–70.

98. United Nations Development Program (UNDP), *Human Development Report 2004*, op. cit., pp. 13–25, 139–249.

99. Stephen M. Walt, "The End of the American Era," *The National Interest*, October 25, 2011 (http://nationalinterest.org/article/the-end-the-american-era-6037).

100. Ibid.

101. United States of America Office of the Director of National Intelligence, "Reports and Publications" (http://www.dni.gov/index.php/newsroom/reports-and-publications).

102. On the effect of globalization on the role of the state, see: Burhan Ghalioun, "The Effect of Globalization on the Social Situation in the Arab Region" [in Arabic], a paper submitted to the Expert Meeting of the Economic and Social Commission for Western Asia, Beirut, December 19–21, 2005, pp. 3–5.

103. Mohamed Sa'ad Abu Amoud, "Globalization and the State" [in Arabic], *Al-Siyassa Al-Dawliya*, Issue no.161 (July 2005), p. 201.

104. Ibid.

105. Ibid., p. 202.

106. Ibid.

107. Talal Atrissi, "National Security and State Sovereignty in the Age of Globalization" [in Arabic], in *Globalization and its Influence on Society and State* (Abu Dhabi: The Emirates Center for Strategic Studies and Research, 2002), p. 47.

108. Ibid., pp. 61–63.

109. Hassan Abu Nimah, "Globalization and the International Order" [in Arabic], in *Globalization in the 21st Century: How Interconnected is the World?* 1st edition (Abu Dhabi: The Emirates Center for Strategic Studies and Research, 2009), p. 214.

110. Ibid., p. 215.

111. Ibid., p. 222.

112. Mohamed Sa'ad Abu Amoud, op. cit., p. 204

113. Talal Atrissi, op. cit., p. 63.

114. Hassan Abu Nimah, op. cit., p. 229.

115. Talal Atrissi, op. cit., p. 42.

116. Abdullah Bin Jabr Al-Otaibi, "Globalization and Interdependence in International Politics: A Realistic Viewpoint" [in Arabic], *El-Nahda*, Volume XI, Issue 3 (July 2010), p. 63.

117. Ibid., p. 64.

118. Ibid., pp. 87–88.

119. Abdul Nasser Gandali, *The Impact of the Cold War on the Major Trends and the International Order* [in Arabic]; (Cairo: Madbouli Bookshop, 2011), p. 566.

120. Ibid., p. 560.

121. Ibid., pp. 560–561.

122. Ibid., p. 564.

123. Ibid., p. 565.

124. Ibid., p. 568.

125. Mohammed Abel Kader Hatem, *Globalization: The Pros and Cons* [in Arabic]; (Cairo: General Egyptian Book Organization, 2005), p. 399.

126. Sayed Yaseen, *The Globalization Crisis and the Collapse of Capitalism* [in Arabic]; (Cairo: Nahdet Misr for Printing, Publishing and Distribution, March 2009), pp. 182–183.

127. Ibid., p. 195.

128. Ibid.

129. Nassif Youssef Hitti, "Shifts in the World Order, the New Intellectual Climate and its Reflection on the Arab Regional Order," *Al Mustaqbal Al-Arabi*, issue 165 (November 1992), p. 30.

130. Ibid.

131. Since the days of Marxism, the term 'ideology' has became identified as: "a pattern of beliefs, ideas and values relating to political, social, economic, cultural and moral aspects, which dominates a society in a certain era, and forms the attitudes of individuals and the perceptions of society." See: Ahmad Mahmoud Subhi and Safaa Abdel-Salam Jafar, *Philosophy of Civilization (Greek, Islamic, Western)* [in Arabic]; (Beirut: Dar al-Nahda al-Arabiya for Printing and Publishing, 1999), p. 195.

132. Fukuyama, op. cit., pp. 3–11.

133. Al Sayed Weld Abah, *The World after September 11, 2001: The Intellectual and Strategic Problematic* [in Arabic]; (Beirut: Arab Scientific Publishers, 2004), p. 15.

134. Mohammed Abdul Shafie Issa, "Development and Five Illusions" [in Arabic], *Al Siyassa Al Dawliya* no. 133 (July 1998), p. 90.

135. Humaid Hamad al-Sadoun, *Chaos of the New World Order and its Effects on the Arab Regional Order* [in Arabic]; (Beirut; Amman: Dar Al-Tali'a Al-Arabia for Publishing, 2001), p. 4.

136. Alyson J.K. Bailes, "The Future of International Order: A European Perspective," seminar hosted by the Center for Democratic Control of Armed Forces, Geneva, November 20, 2003, pp. 7–9.

137. Hassan Nafaa, "The United Nations in Half a Century" [in Arabic], *Alam Al-Maarifa* series, issue. 202 (Kuwait: National Council for Culture, Arts and Letters, 1995), p. 304; see also: Mohamed Hassanein Heikal, *The American Empire and the Raid on Iraq* [in Arabic]; (Cairo: Dar Al Shorok, 2003), p. 128.

138. Nafaa, op. cit. p. 304.

139. Yassin Al Sayed, "Civilizations between Dialogue, Conflict and the Alliance" [in Arabic], *Al-Ahram*, May 13, 2010 (http://digital.ahram.org.eg/articles.aspx?Serial=133748&eid=448), accessed October 30, 2013.

140. "Samuel Huntington's Clash of Civilizations," in Center for Strategic Studies, Research and Documentation, *The Clash of Civilizations* [in Arabic]; (Beirut: CSSRD, 1995), p. 21.

141. Ibid., p. 21.

142. Ibid., p. 22.

143. Ibid.

144. Ibid.

145. Hassan Aourid, *Islam, the West and Globalization* [in Arabic]; (Casablanca: Al Zaman Newspaper Publications, 1999), p. 33.

146. Al Sayed Ahmed Faraj, *Dialogue of Civilizations under American Hegemony: is it Possible?* [in Arabic]; (Cairo: Dar Al Wafaa, 2004), p. 22.

147. Ibid.; see also Fukuyama, op. cit.

148. Fukuyama, op. cit., p. 9.

149. Ibid.

150. Redwan Al Sayyed, "Dialogue in the Face of Calls of a Clash of Civilization and the End of History" [in Arabic], *Asharq Al Awsat*, July 18, 2008, p. 11.

151. Abdulaziz bin Othman Altwaijri, "Dialogue for Coexistence" [in Arabic]; (Cairo: Dar Al Shorok, 1998), p. 24.

152. Ibid.

153. Mohammad Madhi, "'Why Don't You Understand Us?' Versus the Question 'Why Do They Hate Us?'" [in Arabic], *Swissinfo.ch* (http://www.swissinfo.ch/ara/detail/content.html?cid=1094502).

154. Ismail Sabri Moukalled, *International Strategy and Policy* [in Arabic], 2nd ed. (Beirut: Arab Research Foundation, 1985), p. 117.

155. Ibid.

156. Anwar Mohammed Gargash, "Let's Reject the Logic of the Clash of Civilizations" [in Arabic], *Al Ittihad*, February 20, 2006 (http://www.alittihad.ae/wajhatdetails.php?id=18295), accessed October 30, 2013.

157. Mohamed Sayed Ahmed, "The Escalation of Terrorism and the Clash of Civilizations" [in Arabic], *Al Arabi* no. 518 (January 2002), p. 153.

158. Quoted in Zarfawi Omar, "The Clash of Civilizations: A Theory or an Ideology" [in Arabic], *Kalema* no. 39 (Spring 2003); (http://kalema.net/v1/?rpt=96&art).

159. Mustafa Mohammed Al Tahhan, "Is it the End of History" [in Arabic], *Al-Mujtama'a Al Thaqafi* ["Culture Community"] no. 1313 (1998), p. 45.

160. Ibid.

161. "Clash of Civilizations Author Samuel Huntington Dies at Age 81" [in Arabic], *Reuters*, December 27, 2008 (http://ara.reuters.com/article/entertainmentNews/idARACAE4BQ0TE20081227).

162. Muhannad Ali Saqqor, "Fukuyama from the End of History to its Beginning ... A Turning Shift," *Al Wehda*, March 10, 2011 (http://wehda.alwehda.gov.sy/_archive.asp?FileName=446896330201 10312144413).

163. Ibid.

164. Anthony Giddens, *The Third Way: The Renewal of Social Democracy* [in Arabic], Ahmed Zayed (trans.), et al. (Cairo: Supreme Council of Culture, 1999), pp. 42–44.

165. Yassin Al-Sayed, "The Third Way: New Political Ideology" [in Arabic], *Al-Siyassa Al-Dawliya* no. 195 (January 1999), p. 61.

166. Maxime Rodinson, *Europe and the Mystique of Islam* [in Arabic], Rouger Veinus (trans.); (London: I.B. Tauris, 1987), p. 3

167. Hasan Al-Shami, "Essence of the Clash of Civilizations between Islam and the West" [in Arabic], Modern Discussion website, issue 3713, April 30, 2012 (http://www.ahewar.org/debat/show.art.asp?aid =305633).

168. Ibid.

169. Ali Al-Quraishi, "The Dialogue of Civilizations and the Need to Rein in Arrogant Identities" [in Arabic], *Al Arabi* no. 525 (August 2002), p. 164.

170. Mohamed Khaled Al-Shayyab, *Arab Society between the Authority of State and the Tyranny of Religion* [in Arabic]; (Amman: Ward Books for Publishing and Distribution, 2004), p. 70.

171. Ibid.

172. For more details, see: Wajih Kawtharani, "The Future of the Islamic Political Project: Fundamentalism or Islamic Partisan" [in Arabic], *Ma'alomat* no. 3, (May 1993), pp. 2–4.

173. Suleiman Haritani, *Employing the Taboo* [in Arabic]; (Damascus: Dar Al Hasad Publishing and Distribution, 2000), p. 355.

174. Bernard Lewis, *The Political Language of Islam* [in Arabic], Abdulkarim Mahfouz (trans.); (Damascus: Dar Jaafar for Studies and Publishing, 2001), p. 119.

175. Abdelilah Belkeziz, "After the Collapse of the Soviet Union, What to Do?" [in Arabic], *Al Mustaqbal Al Arabi* no. 154 (December 1991), pp. 14–16.

176. Kamal Issa, "Why the West Fights Islam?" *Al Watan Voice*, February 19, 2006 (http://pulpit.alwatanvoice.com/articles/2006/02/19/37734.html).

177. For more information, see: Abdullah Al Daim, "The New Barbarians: Would the Third World People Become the neo-Barbarians in the New International Order?" [in Arabic], *Al Mustaqbal Al Arabi* no. 106 (June 1992); (http://www.abdeldaim.com/moreinfo.php?b=4&sub_id=332), accessed October 28, 2013.

178. Abdel Wahab El-Messiri, "Islam and the West," *Al Jazeera.net*, September 26, 2004 (http://www.aljazeera.net/opinions/pages/12d34a40-f90b-4192-9a35-a9315b4e9132), accessed October 30, 2013.

179. Rasoul Mohammad Rasoul, "The West and Islam: A Look into the Contemporary German Orientalism" [in Arabic], *Kalema* no. 30 (Winter 2001), p. 99.

180. Ibid.

181. Thomas Friedman, "From Beirut to Jerusalem to New York: It is World War III" [in Arabic], *ASharq Al Awsat* no. 8327, September 15, 2001, p. 9.

182. Ibid., p. 8.

183. Ibid.

184. Ibid.

185. Abdulaziz Hamid Al-Jaboury, "Problems and Prospects of Co-existence between Nations," in Emirates Center for Strategic Studies and Research (ECSSR), *Islam and the West: a Civilized Dialogue* [in Arabic]; (Abu Dhabi: The Emirates Center for Strategic Studies and Research, 2012), p 226.

186. Abdel Wahab Badrakhan, "About the Relationship of the West with Islam" [in Arabic], Emirates Center for Strategic Studies and Research (ECSSR) website (http://www.ecssr.com).

187. Ibid.

188. Ahmed Subhy Mansour, "Does Congressman Tancredo Really Want to Bomb Mecca?" [in Arabic], Modern Discussion Website, issue 1271, July 30, 2005 (http://www.ahewar.org/debat/show.art.asp?aid= 42099).

189. Badrakhan, op. cit.

190. Ibid.

191. Ibid.

192. Omar Masqawi, "Between the Muslim Women's Veil in France and Europe and the Veil of Conscience in Palestine" [in Arabic], *Al Mustaqbal*, January 7, 2004, p. 4.

193. Hassan Hanafi, "Islam and the West: Theoretical Confusion," in ECSSR, *Islam and the West: A Cvilized Dialogue*, op. cit., pp. 71–73.

194. Ibid., pp. 78–80.

195. Fattouh Haikal, "Fitna Film ... Attempt to Distort the Tolerant Image of Islam" ECSSR website, April 17, 2008 (http://www.ecssr.com).

196. Ghassan Salamé, *State and Society in the Arab Levant* [in Arabic]; (Beirut: Center for Arab Unity Studies, 1987), p. 130.

197. Wahdan Wahdan, "Ethnic Conflicts and National Security" [in Arabic], Dr. Saleh Al Khathlan Forums, April 28, 2010 (http://www. sas445.com/vb/showthread.php?t=2163).

198. Ibid.

199. Abdulsalam Ibrahim Baghdadi, *National Unity and the Problem of Minorities in Africa* [in Arabic]; (Beirut: Center for Arab Unity Studies, First Edition, 1987), p. 180.

200. Ahmad Wahban, "Ethnic Conflicts and the Stability of the Modern world: A Study of Minorities and Ethnic Groups and Movements" [in Arabic]; (Alexandria: El Dar El Gamaya, 2003/2004), p. 75.

201. Jalal Hassan Moustafa and Nawshirwan Hussein Saeed, "Ethnic Conflict: Reasons and Solution, Kirkuk as a Case Study" [in Arabic], *Kirkuknow.com* (http://kirkuknow.com/arabic/?p=11225), accessed on October 28, 2013.

202. Ibid.

203. Kadhim Shabib, "The Sectarian Issue: Multiple Identities in One State" [in Arabic]; (Beirut: Dar Al Tanweer Printing, Publication and Distribution) 2011, p. 86.

204. Ibid.

205. Mahmoud Saleh Al Karwi, "The Status of Religion in the Moroccan Monarchy System" [in Arabic], *Arab Journal of Political Science* no. 19 (Summer 2008), p. 16.

206. Mohammed Saadi, *The Future of International Relations: From the Clash of Civilizations to the Humanization of Civilization and Peace Culture* [in Arabic]; (Beirut: Center for Arab Unity Studies, 1st ed., 2006) p. 92.

207. Abdul Hussein Shaaban, "Islam in International Politics: Dialogue of Civilizations and International Terrorism" [in Arabic], *Arab Journal of Political Science* no. 15 (Summer 2007), p. 160.

208. Moustafa and Saeed, op. cit.

209. Ibid.

210. Shabib, op. cit., pp. 87–88.

211. Ibid.

212. Moustafa and Saeed, op. cit.

213. Shabib, op. cit., p. 91.

214. Hamdy Abdel Rahman Hassan, "Ethnic and Political Conflicts in Africa: Reasons, Patterns and Future Prospects" [in Arabic], *African Qira'at [Readings]* no. 1 (October 2004); (http://www.siironline.org/alabwab/derasat(01)/607.htm), accessed December 5, 2013.

215. Shabib, op. cit., pp. 143–145.

216. Riyadh Aziz Hadi, "From One Party to Multipartism [in Arabic]; (Baghdad: The General House of Cultural Affairs, 1995), p. 64.

217. Shabib, op. cit., pp. 175–178.

218. Hassan, op. cit.

219. Basheer Zainulabdeen, "The Sectarian Challenge in Syria," working paper presented during the conference "The Challenges of the post-Arab Spring" (http://albayan.co.uk/Files/adadimages/malfat%20pdf/libya/002abidine.pdf).

220. Hassan, op. cit.

221. Shabib, op. cit., pp. 271–274.

222. Mohamed Mahfood, "Education and Progress" [in Arabic], *Al-Riyadh*, November 10, 2010 (http://www.alriyadh.com/2010/11/10/article575924.html).

223. For more information see: Gill Graeme, *The Dynamics of Democratization* (London, Macmillan Press, 2000), pp. 4–7.

224. For more information see: Mark Robinson, "Economic Reform and The Transition to Democracy," in Robin Luckham and Gordon White (eds.), *Democratization in The South: The Jagged Wave* (Manchester: Manchester University Press, 1996), pp. 70–72.

225. Manar El-Shorbagy, "The United States of America and the Iraqi Question: the GCC Dilemma" [in Arabic], in Ahmed Ibrahim Mahmoud (ed.), *The Gulf and the Iraqi Question: From the Invasion*

of Kuwait to the Occupation of Iraq 1990–2003 [in Arabic]; (Cairo: Al-Ahram Center for Political & Strategic Studies, 2003), p. 51.

226. Elias Hanna, "Institutionalization of the Bush Doctrine" [in Arabic], *AlJazeera.net*, October 3, 2004 (http://www.aljazeera.net/opinions/pages/165e161b-e5c9-41b1-bcf4-b2850fd2287a), accessed on October 28, 2013.

227. Mohamed El-Sayed Saeed, *The Stalled Democratic Transition in Egypt* (Cairo: Merritt Publishing House, 2006), pp. 88–89, and "How Arabs Say No," *Al-Ahram*, December 9, 2002.

228. George H. Nash, *The Conservative Intellectual Movement In America* (Wilmington, DE: Intercollegiate Studies Institute, 1998), p. 250.

229. Ibid.

230. "Arab Strategic Report, 2002/2003" [in Arabic]; (Cairo: Al-Ahram Center for Political & Strategic Studies, 2003), p. 140.

231. Ibid.

232. Yusuf El-Hassan, "The Religious Dimension of the American Policy Regarding the Arab–Zionist Conflict" [in Arabic]; (Beirut, Center for Arab Unity Studies 1990), pp. 81–88

233. For more information see the Fox News website (http://www.foxnews.com/index.html). The most prominent programs on this network include: *The O'Reilly Factor*, presented by Bill O'Reilly; the *Sean Hannity Show*; and *The Kelly File* hosted by Megyn Kelly.

234. "Arab Strategic Report, 2002/2003," op. cit. p. 135.

235. Ibrahim Khaled, "The Main Characters in the Neoconservatives" [in Arabic], *Al Wasat*, March 6, 2007 (http://www.alwasatnews.com/1642/news/read/219544/1.html), accessed on October 28, 2013.

236. El Sayed Amin Shalaby, "From the Cold War to the Search for a New International System" [in Arabic]; (Cairo: General Egyptian Book Organization, The Family Library, 2005), pp. 135–150.

237. Ibid., p. 10.

238. Altwaijri, op. cit., p. 24.

239. Ammar Ali Hasan, "Flaws of Dialogue among Civilizations" [in Arabic], *Al Ittihad*, wajhat, May 24, 2013, p. 32.

240. Ibid.

Chapter II

1. Samuel P. Huntington, *The Clash of Civilizations and the Remaking of World Order* [in Arabic], Abbas Hilal Kadhim (trans.); (Jordan: Dar Al-Amal for Publishing and Distribution, 2006), p. 28.

2. Ibid.

3. Huntington indicates that there is disagreement between scholars as to the exact number of human civilizations, both past and present, but he is generally in favor of the classification that identifies at least 12 major civilizations, seven of which no longer exist (the Mesopotamian, Egyptian, Cretan, Greco-Roman, Byzantine, Middle American, and Andean). Five civilizations remain: the Chinese, Japanese, Indian, Islamic and Western. He believes that it is feasible in the modern world to add to these five civilizations both the Catholic Latin American and the African civilizations; Huntington, 2006, op. cit. pp. 51–59.

4. For a biography of Francis Fukuyama, see "Francis Fukuyama: Biography," Stanford University (http://fukuyama.stanford.edu), accessed July 12, 2013.

5. Francis Fukuyama, "History and September 11," in Ken Booth and Tim Dunne (eds.), *Worlds in Collision: Terror and the Future of Global Order* [in Arabic]; (Abu Dhabi: The Emirates Center for Strategic Studies and Research, 2005), p 41.

6. Ibid., p. 42.

7. Ibid.

8. Abdul Wahab El-Messiri, "Americanization, Cocacola-ization and Secularization" [in Arabic], *Al Jazeera.net*, May 29, 2007 (http://www.aljazeera.net/opinions/pages/52ef6867-ef25-4fce-8de4-4c34a30e4b79), accessed July 12, 2013. See also: Jafer Hassan Atrisi, *Americanization of Nations and the Clash of Civilizations: The New*

International System and Individual Leadership [in Arabic]; (Beirut: Dar Al-Hadi, 2002), pp. 75–93

9. "Dialogues with the Intellectual and Researcher Slavoj Žižek," in Mohamed Milad (trans.), *Will the World Slide into the Abyss?* [in Arabic]; (Damascus: Dar Al-Hewar for Publishing and Distribution, 2009), pp. 171–180.

10. On November 30, 1999, tens of thousands of demonstrators gathered in the city of Seattle in the United States of America to protest against the World Trade Organization (WTO) Ministerial Conference. Demonstrations continued for nearly five days, and turned into a symbol of the growing opposition to capitalist globalization. For more, see: Nir Nader, "The Committed Documentary on the Anti-globalization Seattle Events" [in Arabic], *Al-Hewar Al-Motamadden* (Modern Discussion) website, December 9, 2001 (http://www.ahewar.org/debat/show.art.asp?aid=341), accessed July 27, 2013. On anti-globalization movements around the world, see Samir Amin and Francois Houtard, *Countering Globalization: Popular Organizations, Movements in the World* [in Arabic]; (Cairo: Madbouly Bookshop, 2004), pp. 14–182. See also Parag Khanna, *The Second World: Empires and Influence in the New Global Order* [in Arabic], Dar Al-Tarjamah (trans.); (Beirut: Arab Scientific Publishers; Dubai: Mohamed bin Rashid Al Maktoum Foundation, 2009), pp. 27–30

11. Bahman Baktiari, "Globalization and Religion," in Emirates Center for Strategic Studies and Research (ECSSR), *Globalization in the 21st Century: How Interconnected is the World?* [in Arabic]; (Abu Dhabi: ECSSR, 2009), p. 176.

12. Ibid., p. 177.

13. Samuel P. Huntington, "The Clash of Civilizations?" *Foreign Affairs*, vol. 72, no. 3 (Summer 1993); (http://www.foreignaffairs.com/articles/48950/samuel-p-huntington/the-clash-of-civilizations).

14. Mohammed Abed Al-Jabri, *Issues in Contemporary Arab Thought* [in Arabic]; (Beirut: Center for Arab Unity Studies, 1997), pp. 93–103.

15. A famous principle founded by the Italian thinker and philosopher Machiavelli (1469–1527). Among his most famous books is *The Prince*, a work in which he aimed to write instructions and guidance for rulers. In the book, published posthumously, he endorsed the idea that all that is useful is necessary. The book has become an important reference in the study of political science and humanities, and its principles later gave rise to utilitarianism and political realism. See Niccolò Machiavelli, *The Prince* [in Arabic], Mohamed Lutfi Jom'a (trans.); (Limassol: Cordoba for Publishing, Documentation and Research, 1998), pp. 51–174.

16. Confucius (551–479 BC) was a Chinese philosopher, a pioneering thinker and teacher; Abdelmjid Amrani, *The Future of the Dialogue of Civilizations and Globalization* [in Arabic]; (Dubai: The Cultural and Scientific Foundation, 2004), pp. 33–38. See also: Sinolingua, *Confucius: A Sage from China: His Life and Wisdoms* [in Arabic]; Chinese Sages Series (Beirut: Arab Scientific Publishers, 2009), pp. 170–210.

17. Al-Jabri, op. cit., p. 97.

18. Harald Müller, *Das Zusammenleben der Kulturen: ein Gegenentwurf zu Huntington* [in Arabic], Abu Hashhash (trans.); (Beirut: Dar Al-Kitab Al-Jadeed Al-Mottahedah, 2005), pp. 23–49.

19. Al-Jabri, op. cit., p. 91.

20. Emil Amin, "Coexistence of Cultures: Müller in the Face of Huntington" [in Arabic], *Asharq Al-Awsat*, Issue 12362, October 2, 2012 (http://www.aawsat.com/details.asp?section=17&article=6978 64&issueno= 12362), accessed August 19, 2013.

21. Ibid.

22. Redwan al-Sayyed, "Civilizations: From Dialogue to Coalition, and the New Turkish Policies" [in Arabic], *Asharq Al-Awsat* no., Issue 11091, April 10, 2009 (http://www.aawsat.com/leader.asp?section=3&article=514609&issueno=11091), accessed August 18, 2013.

23. Ibid.

24 Edward W. Said, "The Clash of Ignorance" [in Arabic], in Mohamed Milad (trans.), Will the World Slide into the Abyss? (Damascus: Dar Al-Hewar for Publishing and Distribution, 2009), pp. 43–52.

25. Ibid.

26. Huntington, op. cit., 2006, p. 33.

27. Mohamed Sa'adi Al-Hassan, "The Role of Culture in Building Dialogue Among Nations" [in Arabic], *Emirates Lecture Series* no. 154 (Abu Dhabi: The Emirates Center for Strategic Studies and Research, 2013), p. 16.

28. Walid Salim Abdel Hay, *Future Status of China in the International Order 1978–2010* [in Arabic]; (Abu Dhabi: The Emirates Center for Strategic Studies and Research, 2000), p. 27.

29. The term 'dialogue of civilizations' is more widely used in the context of countries and among intergovernmental institutions. However, the term 'civilization' is broader and more comprehensive than 'culture.' It encompasses the various aspects of human progress in its material, moral, intellectual, cultural and religious dimensions. See: Ali Bin Ibrahim Al-Namlah, *The East and the West: Premises and Determinants of Relations* [in Arabic]; (Beirut: Bissan for Publishing, Distribution and Information, 2010), pp. 265–294.

30. Ammar Ali Hassan, "Defects of the Dialogue of Civilizations" [in Arabic], *Al-Ittihad*, Viewpoints, May 24, 2013 (http://www.alittihad.ae/wajhatdetails.php?id=72641).

31. The first to field this idea was the intellectual Roger Garaudy in his pioneering project to bring together different cultures on the basis of a

common understanding among the peoples of the earth in his book *For A Dialogue of Civilizations*, published in French in 1977; Roger Garaudy, *Pour un dialogue des civilizations* [in Arabic], 5th ed., Adel Al-Awwa (trans.); (Beirut: Editions Oueidat, 2003), pp. 215–228.

32. In his book *The World is Flat*, Thomas Friedman deals with the accelerating technical and social transformations witnessed by the world on the basis that they have 'flattened' the world as a result of various events that have brought about global convergence, including: the fall of the Berlin Wall, the rise of the Netscape Navigator browser and the subsequent dot.com boom, the emergence of common software platforms, and the rise of outsourcing. Together, these events contributed to the rise of economies such as China and India in the global economy. See: Thomas Friedman, *The World is Flat: A Brief History of the Twenty-First Century* [in Arabic]; (Beirut: Dar Al-Kitab Al-Arabi, 2006), pp. 9–56.

33. Bahman Baktiari, "Globalization and Religion," op. cit, p. 177, cites Thomas L. Friedman, "Anyone, Anything, Anywhere," *The New York Times*, The Opinion Pages, September 22, 2006.

34. Al-Hassan, op. cit., p. 4.

35. Nassim Al-Khoury, *Arab Media and the Collapse of Linguistic Authorities* [in Arabic]; (Beirut: Centre for Arab Unity Studies, 2005), p. 429.

36. Jamal Sanad Al-Suwaidi, *From Tribe to Facebook: The Transformational Role of Social Networks* [in Arabic]; (Abu Dhabi: Emirates Center for Strategic Studies and Research, 2013), p. 60.

37. Al-Hassan, op. cit., p. 16.

38. There are approximately four million German Muslims, representing about five percent of the population and around a quarter of all immigrant origin in Germany (http://www.almania.diplo.de/Vertretung/almania/ar/02/04IslamD/InegrationFeb-10Seite.html). On the subject of Muslims in Germany see: Jørgen S. Nielsen, *Muslims in*

Western Europe [in Arabic]; (Beirut: Dar Al-Saqi in collaboration with Al-Babtain Translation Center, 2005), pp. 53–76. See also: Mustafa Abel Aziz Morsi, *Arab Immigrants' Issues in Europe* [in Arabic]; (Abu Dhabi: The Emirates Center for Strategic Studies and Research, 2010), pp. 137–144.

39. For more on the Cooperation Council for the Arab States of the Gulf (GCC), see: Jamal Sanad Al-Suwaidi (ed.), *The Gulf Cooperation Council: Prospects for the Twenty-first Century* [in Arabic]; (Abu Dhabi: The Emirates Center for Strategic Studies and Research, 1999).

40. "200 Nationalities Co-exist Peacefully in the UAE" [in Arabic], *Albayan*, December 14, 2011 (http://www.albayan.ae/across-the-uae/accidents/2011-12-14-1.1554891), accessed October 30, 2013.

41. Fukuyama, op. cit., 2005., pp. 47–48.

42. Ibid., p. 48.

43. Ibid.

44. Ibid.

45. For more on the Shiite sect, see: Mohamed Abu Zahra, *History of Islamic Denominations in Politics and Doctrines and the History of Jurisprudential Denominations* [in Arabic], (London: Dar Al-Hadith, 1987); Salah Abu Saud, *Shiites: Political Emergence and Religious Doctrine* [in Arabic], (Al-Giza: Al-Nafezah Bookshop, 2004), pp. 33–59, 273–277; and Mohamed Emara, *Trends of Islamic Thinking* [in Arabic], 3rd ed. (Cairo: Dar el-Shorouk, 2008), pp. 201–244.

46. This argument would ultimately lead to the division of the world according to what George W. Bush's characterization of being "either with us or against us," exacerbating tensions between religions and civilizations.

47. Martin Asser, "Blasphemous Cartoons: What is their Content?' [in Arabic], BBC website, February 18, 2006 (http://news.bbc.co.uk/hi/arabic/news/newsid_4728000/4728052.stm), accessed October 30, 2013.

48. "Norwegian *Magazinet* Apologizes for Publishing Blasphemous Cartoons of the Prophet" [in Arabic], Al-Jazeera.net, February 11, 2006 (http://www.aljazeera.net/news/pages/2a92ade9-3f1b-4862-bd07-f2e3d848e63c).

49. For more on the UAE's position toward terrorism, see: "The UAE Renews its International Commitments to Combat Terrorism at UN" [in Arabic], news report, Emirates News Agency (WAM), October 9, 2013 (http://www.wam.ae/servlet/Satellite?c=WamLocAnews&cid=1290006801383&pagename=WAM%2FWAM_A_PrintVersion), accessed October 30, 2013. See also the official statements issued by the UAE Ministry of Foreign Affairs: (http://www.mofa.gov.ae/Mofa/portal/31a66f92-3f6c-4ff0-86f7-90e656ef73fd.aspx), accessed on October 30, 2013.

50. Abdul Sattar Ibrahim Al-Hiti, "The Dialogue: The Self and the Other" [in Arabic], *Al-Ummah Book* series no. 99, undated, posted on the Umm Al-Qura University website (http://uqu.edu.sa/page/ar/59175), accessed July 23, 2013.

51. Among efforts that deserve encouragement is the United Nations Alliance of Civilizations (UNAOC), an international movement that encourages intercultural and interreligious dialogue and aims to provide a model of coexistence between human beings. See the official website of the Alliance of Civilizations (http://www.unaoc.org).

52. Joseph S. Nye, "The Future of American Power" [in Arabic], in: Joseph S. Nye, Hillary Clinton, Tim Dunne and Kledja Mulaj, "The Future of American Power" (trans.), *International Studies* no. 105

(Abu Dhabi: The Emirates Center for Strategic Studies and Research, 2012), p. 7.

53. Abdul Aziz Said, Charles O. Lerche, Jr. and Charles O. Lerche III, *Concepts of International Politics in Global Perspective* [in Arabic], Naf'e Ayoub Lobbos (trans.); (Damascus: Publications of the Arab Writers Union, 1999), p. 143–144.

54. On the Peace of Westphalia and its consequences, see: Mohammed Ali Al-Qoozi, *International Relations in Modern and Contemporary History* [in Arabic]; (Beirut: Dar Al-Nahda Al-Arabiya, 2002), pp. 63–90. See also: Hussain Ali Daher, *The Development of International Relations from Westphalia to Versailles* [in Arabic]; (Beirut: Dar al-Mawasim for Printing, Publishing and Distribution, 1999), pp. 118–121.

55. Condoleezza Rice, "Balance of Power: Concept and Practice" [in Arabic], *Al-Ittihad*, Viewpoints, March 23, 2003 (http://www.alittihad.ae/wajhatdetails.php?id=18972).

56. Ibid.

57. Nizar Ismail Al-Hyali, *NATO's Role After the End of the Cold War* [in Arabic]; (Abu Dhabi: The Emirates Center for Strategic Studies and Research, 2003), p. 20.

58. The idea of creating a balance between international powers became a reality after the Treaty of Utrecht, which recognized Philip V as the King of Spain; but Philip was removed from the line of succession to the French throne so that Spain and France would not be united under one ruler. Austria won most of the fiefdoms in Spain, Italy and the Netherlands and French hegemony over Europe effectively ended. As a result of this treaty, Britain inherited the Spanish colonies in Gibraltar and Menorca (one of the Balearic Islands), and a contract to supply all the Spanish colonies in America with African slaves. France also ceded to British claims to Hudson Bay, Newfoundland

and Nova Scotia in the Acadians. For more, see: "The Treaties of Utrecht (1713)," *Heraldica.org* (http://www.heraldica.org/topics/france/utrecht.htm).

59. Al-Hyali, op. cit., p. 21.

60. Ismail Sabri Maklad, *Strategy and International Politics: The Basic Concepts and Facts* [in Arabic]; (Beirut: Arab Research Foundation, 1979), p. 108.

61. Michael Byers, "Terror and the Future of International Law" [in Arabic], in Booth and Dunne, op. cit., p. 160.

62. Ibid., p. 161.

63. Noam Chomsky, "Washington Above International Law—America: The Rogue State." [in Arabic], in Mohamed Milad (trans.) *Will the World Slide into the Abyss?* (Damascus: Dar Al-Hewar for Publishing and Distribution, 2009), pp. 11–12.

64. United Nations (UN), "Chapter VII: Action with Respect to Threats to the Peace, Breaches of the Peace, and Acts of Aggression," Chapter VII of the Charter of the United Nations (http://www.un.org/ar/documents/charter/chapter7.shtml).

65. Ibid.

66. Article 51 of the United Nations Charter reads: "Nothing in the present Charter shall impair the inherent right of individual or collective self-defense if an armed attack occurs against a Member of the United Nations, until the Security Council has taken the measures necessary to maintain international peace and security. Measures taken by Members in the exercise of this right of self-defense shall be immediately reported to the Security Council and shall not in any way affect the authority and responsibility of the Security Council under the present Charter to take at any time such action as it deems

necessary in order to maintain or restore international peace and security," ibid.

67. Byers, op. cit., p. 161.

68. Mahmood Saleh Al-Adli, *International Legitimacy Under the New World Order* [in Arabic]; (Alexandria: Dar Al-Fikr Al-Gamei, 2003), p. 21.

69. Madeleine Albright was the first woman to assume the post of Secretary of State in the United States of America after being nominated by President Clinton on December 5, 1996 during his second term. She took office on January 23, 1997 to the become the 64th US Secretary of State. She remained in office until January 20, 2001. Previously, she had served as the US Permanent Representative to the United Nations, from January 27, 1993 to January 21, 1997. For more information, see: US Department of State, "Biography: Madeleine Korbel Albright," State Department archive (http://secretary.state.gov/www/albright/albright.html).

70. Chomsky, op. cit., p. 13.

71. The White House, "William J. Clinton" (http://www.whitehouse. gov/about/presidents/williamjclinton).

72. Chomsky, op. cit.

73. Former UN Secretary-General Kofi Annan travelled to Baghdad in February 20–23, 2003, in an effort to defuse the deepening political crisis with the Government of Iraq over the issue of UN weapons inspections. Most UN staff returned to Baghdad after being temporarily transferred to Amman and Erbil due to security conditions.

74. Al-Hyali, op. cit., p. 24.

75. Abdul Hussein Shaaban, "The Big Paradoxes between Savage Capitalism and the Capitalism with a Human Face" [in Arabic], *Al-*

Eqtisadiah no. 6185, September 17, 2010 (http://www.aleqt.com/2010/09/17/article_443170.html), accessed July 12, 2013.

76. "David Cameron," The History Channel (http://www.history.co.uk/biographies/david-cameron).

77. "Cameron: Britain must 'Sort Out' its Economy if it wants to 'Carry Weight in the World' [in Arabic], BBC website, November 16, 2010 (http://www.bbc.co.uk/arabic/worldnews/2010/11/101115_cameron_economy_tc2.shtml), accessed July 14, 2013. On the relationship between the economy and the world, see: Martin Jacques, *When China Rules the World: The End of the Western World and the Birth of a New Global Order* [in Arabic], Fatma Nasr Mohamed (trans.); (Cairo: Sotour Publishing House, 2010), p. 16.

78. US National Intelligence Council (NIC), "Global Trends 2025: A Transformed World," Office of the Director of National Intelligence, November 2008 (http://www.dni.gov/files/documents/Newsroom/ReportsandPubs/2025_Global_Trends_Final_Report.pdf), accessed July 13, 2013.

79. Ibid.

80. V.E. Korolev, *Emperor of All the Earth* [in Arabic], Muntajab Younes (trans.); (Damascus: Dar Aladdin Publishing, 2006), p. 214.

81. Tim Dunne and Kledja Mulaj, "America After Iraq" [in Arabic], in: Nye, et al., op. cit., p. 47.

82. Korolev, op. cit., p. 30.

83. Ibid., p. 240.

84. European Union (EU), "Energy Markets in the European Union in 2011," European Commission, Directorate-General for Energy (Luxembourg: Publications Office of the European Union, 2012); (http://ec.europa.eu/energy/gas_electricity/doc/20121217_energy_market_2011_lr_en.pdf), p. 15.

85. Korolev, op. cit., p. 240.

86. "Assafir Publishes a Comprehensive Report on the Meeting between Bandar and Putin: Take the Investments and the Oil Price and give us Syria" [in Arabic], *Assafir* Issue 12558, August 21, 2013 (http://www.assafir.com/Article.aspx?EditionId=2543&articleId=1693 &ChannelId=61387&Page=2#Comments), accessed October 30, 2013.

87. BRICS, a grouping established in 2011 that includes Brazil, Russia, India, China and South Africa, previously referred to as BRIC before the inclusion of South Africa in 2010; see "BRICS and its Aims," *AlJazeera.net*, March 30, 2012 [in Arabic]; (http://www.aljazeera.net/ news/pages/5522ec81-6341-4fe6-a9ad-bab8ae41d46c).

88. Peter Day, "The Global Change in Economic Power [in Arabic]," BBC News online, September 20, 2005 (http://news.bbc.co.uk/hi/ arabic/business/newsid_4264000/4264154.stm).

89. Ibid.

90. On the circumstances of the outbreak of World War I, see: Issa Al-Hassan, *World War I: Proceedings of the War that Ended the Lives of Millions* [in Arabic]; (Amman: Al-Ahlia for Publishing and Distribution, 2009), pp. 7–30.

91. Paul Kennedy, *The Rise and Fall of the Great Powers* (London: Fontana Press, 1989).

92. The 1979 oil crisis took place in the wake of the Islamic Revolution in Iran. Oil exports stopped temporarily and then were restarted at a more limited volume, prompting prices to increase. In 1980, in the wake of the Iraq–Iran war, oil production in Iran almost came to a halt. Iraqi oil production was also severely reduced. For more, see: Safaa Gamaleddin, "The Energy Crisis and the Policies of Western

Industrialized Countries" [in Arabic], *Al-Siyassa Al-Dawliya*, Issue 68, (April 1982), pp. 147–150. See also: The Middle East Institute, *The 1979 "Oil Shock:" Legacy, Lessons, and Lasting Reverberations*, (Washington, DC: Middle East Institute, 2009), pp. 38–40, 57–59.

93. Deng Xiaoping led the People's Republic of China between 1978 and 1992 towards the adoption of market economics. He is the advocate of the "right–opportunist" approach, and was considered among those leading Chinese politicians who supported relations with the United States of America. He believed that maintaining smooth relations with Washington was a central dimension in Chinese foreign policy, and that Chinese economic development required a stable international environment. He pursued a pragmatic policy epitomized by his famous observation that it doesn't matter whether a cat is white or black, as long as it catches mice. For more, see: Abdel Hay, op. cit., pp. 145–186.

94. "China becomes the World's Second-largest Economy" [in Arabic], *Aljazeera.net*, December 26, 2009 (http://www.aljazeera.net/ebusiness/pages/991facb5-0e94-43b6-96d1-e6e180577519), accessed October 29, 2013.

95. Jacques, op. cit., p. 238.

96. Gérard Chaliand, Michel Jan, "Vers un Nouvel Ordre du Monde" [in Arabic], Mohamed Saadi (trans.), *Strategic Visions*, Issue 4 (Abu Dhabi: The Emirates Center for Strategic Studies and Research, September 2013), p. 166.

97. John Naisbitt, "From Nation States to Networks" [in Arabic], in Rowan Gibson (ed.), *Rethinking the Future* [in Arabic], Translated Studies no. 21 (Abu Dhabi: The Emirates Center for Strategic Studies and Research, 2004), p 259.

98. Al-Suwaidi, op. cit., 2013, p. 78.

99. Naisbitt, op. cit., p. 261.

100. Bilal Al-Hassan, "Bush Seeks to Impose a New World Order" [in Arabic], *Asharq Al-Awsat*, Issue 8713, October 6, 2002 (http://www.aawsat.com/leader.asp?section=3&article=128462&issue no=8713).

101. Eurozone Portal; (http://www.eurozone.europa.eu).

102. European Union (EU), "Treaty of Maastricht on European Union" (http://europa.eu/legislation_summaries/institutional_affairs/treaties/treaties_maastricht_en.htm).

103. Michael Mandelbaum, *The Ideas That Conquered the World: Peace, Democracy and Free Markets in the Twenty-first Century* [in Arabic], Ola Ahmed Eslah (trans.); (Cairo: International House for Cultural Investments, 2009), p. 350.

104. Howard Schneider, "How Globalization Mixed the Calculations of the Founders of the Single European Currency" [in Arabic], *Asharq Al-Awsat*, Issue 12332, September 2, 2012 (http://aawsat.com/details.asp?section=6&article=693397&issueno=12332#.UrmTlv2IoSs).

105. Increased talk of the rise of China at the expense of the United States of America is associated with the effects of the financial crisis that began in the United States of America in 2007 and had profound effects from which the US economy still suffers. For more, see: Tareq Lissaoui, 'The Story of the Rise and Growth of China runs in Parallel to the Story of the Decline of the Dream of the American Empire" [in Arabic], *Al-Quds Al-Arabi,* October 25, 2013 (http://www.alquds.co.uk/?p=96781); Fadeel Al-Ameen, "Does China's Rise Mean America's Decline? [in Arabic], *Asharq Al-Awsat*, Issue 11447, April 1, 2010 (http://www.aawsat.com/leader.asp?section=3&articlee=563434&issueno=11447#.Um-48vmnpmg), accessed October 29, 2013.

106. Amr Abdel Ati, "Transformations of the International System and the Future of American Hegemony" [in Arabic], *Al-Siyassa Al-Dawliya*, Issue 183 (January 2011), pp. 203–206.

107. "Delivery of the First Aircraft Carrier to the Chinese Army" [in Arabic], *Al-Jazeera.net*, September 23, 2012 (http://www.aljazeera. net/news/pages/ffefb2ff-3df3-4999-ad20-e77462e588b8).

108. "Xinhua: China builds a Second Larger Aircraft Carrier" [in Arabic], Reuters, April 24, 2013 (http://ara.reuters.com/article/worldNews/ idARACAE9B28Z V20130424).

109. Sayed Yaseen, "Historical Transformations of the International System" [in Arabic], *Al-Arabiya* website, October 25, 2009: (http://www.alarabiya.net/views/2009/10/25/89147.html), accessed July 7, 2013.

110. For more on the views of British researcher Martin Jacques, see: (http://www.martinjacques.com/), accessed October 30, 2013.

111. Martin Jacques, *When China Rules the World: The End of the Western World and the Birth of a New Global Order* [in Arabic], Fatma Nasr Mohamed (trans.); (Cairo: Sotour Publishing House, 2010), pp. 404–446.

112. Nye, op. cit., p. 10.

113. Yaseen, op. cit.

114. Bates Gill, "China as an Emergent Center of Global Power" [in Arabic], in Graeme P. Herd (ed.), *Great Powers and Strategic Stability in the 21st Century: Competing Visions of World Order* (trans.); (Abu Dhabi: The Emirates Center for Strategic Studies and Research, 2013), pp. 261–264.

115. Ibid., p. 264.

116. The most famous borough of New York City, and site of the attacks on the World Trade Center on September 11, 2001 (http://www1. nyc.gov), accessed July 14, 2013.

117. "Wall Street," *Investopedia* (http://www.investopedia.com/terms/w/wallstreet.asp), accessed July 14, 2013.

118. Mandelbaum, op. cit., p. 16.

119. Ibid., p. 18.

120. International Monetary Fund (IMF), "Currency Composition of Official Foreign Exchange Reserves (COFER), (In US$ millions)" updated June 28, 2013 (http://www.imf.org/External/np/sta/cofer/eng/cofer.pdf). See also Philip Coggan, "Expect China to Shape the Next Bretton Woods Pact" [in Arabic], *Asharq Al-Awsat*, Issue 12124, February 7, 2012: (http://www.aawsat.com/leader.asp?section=3&article=662509&issueno=12124), accessed August 28, 2013.

121. Ibid.

122. Martin Jacques, "What Kind of Superpower Could China Be?' [in Arabic], BBC website, October 26, 2012 (http://www.bbc.co.uk/arabic/worldnews/2012/10/121028_china_superpower.shtml). Some media sources quoted the then Chinese Premier Zhou Enlai as saying that he was referring by his comment to the student riots which took place in Paris in 1968, i.e. a few years prior to his statement; Richard McGregor, "Zhou's Cryptic Caution Lost in Translation," *Financial Times*, June 10, 2011 (http://www.ft.com/cms/s/0/74916db6-938d-11e0-922e-00144feab49a.html#axzz2oOZtuTbS).

123. Jacques, op. cit., 2010, p. 465.

124. "What does Xi Jinping's China Dream Mean?" [in Arabic], BBC website, June 6, 2013 (http://www.bbc.co.uk/arabic/worldnews/2013/06/130606_china_xi_dream.shtml).

125. Byers, op. cit., p. 157.

126. Mark Mardell, "Will the Rise of the Rest Mean the Decline of the US?" [in Arabic], BBC website, April 30, 2013 (http://www.bbc.co.uk/arabic/worldnews/2013/04/130429_us_decline.shtml), accessed July 12, 2013 .

127. Kate Randall, "US Congress Passes $633 Billion Military Spending Bill," December 21, 2013, World Socialist Website (https://www.wsws.org/en/articles/2013/12/21/ndaa-d21.html).

128. "Hagel: US Army Budget will continue to Account for 40% of Defense Spending," *El-Watan* June 1, 2013 (http://www.elwatan news.com/news/details/192536), accessed July 23, 2013.

129. For more on global military spending, see: the Stockholm International Peace Research Institute (http://www.sipri.org); and Global Firepower (GFP); (http://www.globalfirepower.com).

130. Federation of American Scientists (FAS), "Country Rankings: 1997" (http://www.fas.org/man/docs/wmeat98/rank98.pdf).

131. Kenneth N. Waltz, "The Continuity of International Politics" [in Arabic], in Booth and Dunne, op. cit., p. 454.

132. Mohammed Yacoub Abdel Rahman, *Humanitarian Intervention in International Relations* [in Arabic]; (Abu Dhabi: The Emirates Center for Strategic Studies and Research, 2004), p. 134.

133. The White House, "President Barack Hussein Obama" (http://www.whitehouse.Gov/administration/president-obama).

134. Richard A. Clarke and Robert K. Knake, *Cyber War: The Next Threat to National Security and What to Do About It* [in Arabic], Translated Studies (Abu Dhabi: The Emirates Center for Strategic Studies and Research, 2012), p. 319.

135. David E. Sanger and Thom Shanker, "Broad Powers Seen for Obama in Cyberstrikes," *New York Times*, February 3, 2013 (http://www.nytimes.com/2013/02/04/us/broad-powers-seen-for-obama-in-cyber strikes.html?_r=0), accessed October 30, 2013.

136. Ibid.

134. The Chief Executive Officer of Kaspersky Lab, which specializes in computer security.

138. The remarks were made during a speech delivered before the Third Annual International Cyber Security Conference of the Yuval Ne'eman Workshop for Science, Technology and Security in Israel in June 2012.

139. Rabie Mohamed Hamed, "Israel and Steps to Dominate the Arena of Cyberspace in the Middle East: A Study on the Preparations and Work Themes of the Jewish State in the Internet Age (2002–2013)" [in Arabic], *Strategic Visions*, Issue 3 (Abu Dhabi: The Emirates Center for Strategic Studies and Research, June 2013), p. 81.

140. US Department of Commerce, "Gross Domestic Product by Industry Data Show Information Technology Drove Economic Growth in the Late 1990s: New Estimates Based on the North American Industry Classification System, "Bureau of Economic Analysis, BEA 04-51, November 15, 2004 (http://www.bea.gov/newsreleases/industry/gdp industry/2004/naics.htm).

140. Robert J. Shapiro and Aparna Mathur, *The Contributions of Information and Communication Technologies to American Growth, Productivity, Jobs and Prosperity* (September 2011), pp. 11–12 (http://www.tiaonline.org/gov_affairs/fcc_filings/documents/Report_ on_ICT_and_Innovation_Shapiro_Mathur_September_8_2011.pdf).

141. Thomas E. Copeland, 'The Information Revolution and National Security' [in Arabic], *International Studies* no. 46 (Abu Dhabi: The Emirates Center for Strategic Studies and Research, 2003), p. 9.

142. Jamal Sanad Al-Suwaidi, "Introduction: Human Resource Development in a Knowledge-Based Economy" [in Arabic], in *Human Resource Development in a Knowledge-Based Economy* (Abu Dhabi: The Emirates Center for Strategic Studies and Research, 2004), p. 11.

143. "Panetta Warns of a Cyber Pearl Harbor" [in Arabic], *Aljazeera.net*, October 12, 2012 (http://www.aljazeera.net/news/pages/e6948a4c-d6dd-4712-9681-2e71714c186e).

144. Al-Suwaidi, op. cit., 2013, p. 91.

145. "Richard Clarke," Belfer Center for Science and International Affairs, Harvard University (http://belfercenter.ksg.harvard.edu/experts/1621/Richard_clarke.html).

146. Clarke and Knake, op. cit, p. 49.

147. Ibid.

148. Hamed, op. cit., p. 71.

149. Riad Saouma, *Opportunities for Change After the Failure of Radical Liberalism and the Fall of Unipolarity* [in Arabic]; (Beirut: Dar al-Farabi, 2009), p. 27.

150. Ibid., p. 28.

151. Al-Suwaidi, op. cit., 2013, p. 29.

152. Sayed Abu Daif Ahmad, *A Crumbling Empire: The Future of American Hegemony and the International System* [in Arabic]; (Cairo: Dar Al Talae for Publishing and Distribution, 2009), p. 327.

153. Anne-Marie Slaughter, *A New World Order* [in Arabic], Ahmed Mahmoud (trans.); (Cairo: National Center for Translation, 2011), pp. 5–50.

154. Zbigniew Brzezinski, *Grand Chessboard: American Primacy and its Geostrategic Imperatives* (New York, NY: Basic Books, 1997).

155. "A Billion Searches in Google Monthly" [in Arabic], Sky News Arabia website, February 3, 2013 (http://www.skynewsarabia.com/web/article/75208).

156. Fawzi Hassan, "Non-governmental Organizations and the Globalization of the International System" [in Arabic], *Albayan*, May 23, 2013 (http://www.albayan.ae/opinions/articles/2013-05-23-1.188 8730), accessed July 7, 2013.

157. Jeremy Rifkin, *The Age of Access: The New Culture of Hypercapitalism, Where All of Life is a Paid-for Experience* [in Arabic], Translated Studies (Abu Dhabi: The Emirates Center for Strategic Studies and Research, 2003), pp. 294–300.

158. On the concept of power diffusion, see: Joseph S. Nye, *Bound to Lead: The Changing Nature of American Power* [in Arabic], Abdulqader Othman (trans.); (Amman: Jordan Book Centre, 1991) pp. 163–167.

159. Joseph S. Nye, "The Reality of Virtual Power" [in Arabic], *Aleqtisadiah*, February 5, 2011 (http://www.aleqt. com/2011/02/05/article_500244.print), accessed July 23, 2013.

160. Ibid.

161. Joseph S. Nye and John D. Donahue, *Governance in a Globalizing World* [in Arabic], Mohammed Sharif Tarah (trans.); (Riyadh: Obeikan Bookshop, 2002), p. 126.

162. Mohamed Ibrahim el-Sakka, "The Asian Crisis" [in Arabic], *Al-Eqtisadiah* (http://www.aleqt.com/2010/08/13/article_429207.html), accessed October 29, 2013.

163. Nizam Barakat, "Implications of the September Incidents for the International System" [in Arabic], *Aljazeera.net*, October 3, 2004 (http://www.aljazeera.net/home/print/787157c4-0c60-402b-b997-178 4ea612f0c/452a9426-53ea-4f74-a70b-897bb6eef613).

164. Fukuyama, op. cit., 2005, pp. 47–49.

165. Sebestyen L.V. Gorka, "Religious Fundamentalism and Terrorism" [in Arabic], in Emirates Center for Strategic Studies and Research (ed.), *Globalization in the 21st Century: How Interconnected is the World?* (Abu Dhabi: ECSSR, 2009), pp. 238–239.

166. Ibid.

167. Thomas J. Biersteker, "Targeting Terrorist Finances: The New Challenges of Financial Market Globalization" [in Arabic], in Booth and Dunne (eds.), op. cit, p. 101.

168. Tony Saich, "Globalization, Governance, and the Authoritarian State: China" [in Arabic], in Nye and Donahue, op. cit., pp. 289–290.

169. After 15 years of intensive effort, the 142 member countries of the World Trade Organization (WTO) approved the Protocol of Accession of the People's Republic of China to the WTO at the Fourth Ministerial Conference held in Doha on November 10, 2001. On December 11, China officially became the 143rd member of the WTO. Its membership constitutes a symbol of a new stage in China's 'open-door' policy.

170. China signed the International Covenant on Economic, Social and Cultural Rights on October 27, 1997. It also signed the International Covenant on Civil and Political Rights on October 5, 1998. Both Covenants are part of the legally binding international and regional human rights compacts.

171. Nye and Donahue, op. cit., p 289.

172. Ibid., p. 375.

173. Ranjit Dwivedi, "Environmental Movements in the Global South: Issues of Livelihood and Beyond" [in Arabic], Shohrat El-Alem (trans.), *Al-Thaqafa Al-Alamiya* [World Culture] no. 111, 2002, p. 220.

174. Shukrani Al-Hussein, "Climate Justice: Towards a New Social Justice" [in Arabic], *Strategic Visions* no. 1 (Abu Dhabi: The Emirates Center for Strategic Studies and Research, 2012), p. 110.

175. Ibid., p. 109.

176. Iman Ahmad, "Patterns and Roles of Non-state Actors in the Arab Region" [in Arabic], *Al-Siyassa Al-Dawliya*, Issue no.185 (July 2011), pp. 88–91.

177. William C. Wohlforth, "The Stability of a Unipolar World" [in Arabic], International Studies no. 36 (Abu Dhabi: The Emirates Center for Strategic Studies and Research, 2001), p. 7.

178. Ibid.

179. Ibid., p. 8.

180. Ibid., p. 9.

181. Majed Ahmed Zamili, "The Balance of International Power" [in Arabic], Al-Hewar Al-Motamadden [Modern Discussion] website on June 4, 2011 (http://www.ahewar.org/debat/show.art.asp?aid=261 834), accessed July 3, 2013.

182. William A. Rugh, "Bush and the Task of Radical Change in Foreign Policy Approach" [in Arabic], *Al-Ittihad*, Viewpoints December 5, 2003 (http://www.alittihad.ae/wajhatdetails.php?id=1632), accessed August 22, 2013.

183. Byers, op. cit., p. 159.

184. Noam Chomsky, *Hegemony or Survival: America's Quest for Global Dominance* [in Arabic], Sami Kaaki (trans.); (Beirut: Dar Al Kitab Al Arabi, 2004), p. 19.

185. Ibid., p. 20.

186. Ibid., p. 21.

187. Ibid.

188. Ibid., p. 23.

189. Ibid., p. 24–25.

190. Ibid.

191. Ibid., p. 25.

192. Ibid., p. 26.

193. Majed Ayef, "The New World Order" [in Arabic], Al-Hewar Al-Motamadden [Modern Discussion] website, September 26, 2012 (http://www.ahewar.org/debat/show.art.asp?aid=325822), accessed July 7, 2013.

194. Anatoly Utkin, *The World in the 21st Century* [in Arabic]; Younes Kamel Deeb and Hashem Hammadi (trans.); (Damascus: Dar Al Markaz Al Thaqafi for Printing and Publishing, 2007), pp. 293–295.

195. Driss Lagrini, "China's Transformations and the Future of the International System" [in Arabic], in *Aafaq Al-Mustaqbal*, no. 17 (Abu Dhabi: The Emirates Center for Strategic Studies and Research, January 2013), p. 17.

196. Masaoud Daher, "Expected Shifts in the New World Order" [in Arabic], in *Al-Bayan*, December 7, 2011 (http://www.albayan.ae/opinions/articles/2011-12-07-1.1550208), accessed July 7, 2013.

197. Ibid.

198. Al-Hassan, op. cit., 2002.

199. Ibid.

200. "These are the reasons for the return of American unipolarity" [in Arabic], *Akhbar Al-Saah* bulletin, Issue 5152 (Abu Dhabi: The Emirates Center for Strategic Studies and Research, July 20, 2013), p. 4; and Jan Techau, "What if Unipolarity Came Back?" Judy Dempsey's Strategic Europe, Carnegie Europe, July 16, 2013 (http://carnegieeurope.eu/strategiceurope/?fa=52411), accessed August 29, 2013.

201. Ibid.

Chapter III

1. Muhammad Aziz Shukri, [in Arabic] *Global International System Between Theory and Reality* (Beirut: Dar Al-Fikr, 1973), p. 49.

2. Ramesses II led several military campaigns northward to attack the Levant. In the second Battle of Kadesh during the fourth year of his reign (1274 BC), the Egyptian troops under his command engaged with the troops of the Hittite king, Muwatallis, but over the years that followed neither party was able to defeat the other. Therefore, in the 21st year of his reign (1258 BC), Ramesses II concluded a treaty with Hattusili III, which was the oldest peace treaty in history. For more about Ramesses II, see: Wael Fikri, "Summary," *Encyclopedia of Ancient Egypt* (Cairo: Madbooli Bookshop, 2009), pp. 379–430; see also the Egyptian State Information Service [in Arabic] at: (http://www.sis.gov.eg/Ar/Templates/Articles/tmpArticles.aspx?CatI D=585).

3. For more information, see: Nabeel Abdul-Ameen Al-Rubaie [in Arabic] "The Umma Kingdom: Ancient Civilization of Mesopotamia," *Al-Hiwar Al-Mutamaddin* July 12, 2013 (http://m.ahewar.org/s.asp?aid=368300&r=0&cid=0&u=&i=0&qK), accessed August 23, 2013.

4. Isam Al-Atiyya, *Public International Law* [in Arabic]; (Baghdad: Baghdad University Press, 1983), p. 153.

5. Confucius, or "Master Kong," was born in 551 BC and was the first Chinese philosopher who established a philosophical doctrine encompassing all the Chinese traditions of social and moral behavior. His philosophy emphasized personal morality and the existence of a government that serves the people according a higher moral ideal. For more information, see Alban G. Widgery, *Interpretations of History: Confucius to Toynbee*, Zawqan Qarqoot (trans.); (Beirut: Dar Al-Qalam, 1979), pp. 9–46.

6. History shows that the Ancient Greek cities were familiar with the codes of neutrality, the ransom of prisoners of war, and arbitration to solve differences arising between them. The Ancient Greeks also followed certain rules of war such as the treatment of prisoners of war and prohibition on attacking places of worship. It also signed a number of famous peace treaties, such as the Thirty Years' Peace Treaty between Sparta and Athens in 446 BC, and the Fifty Years' Peace Treaty in 431 BC. For more information, see: Gustave Glotz, *The Greek City & Its Institutions*, 1st edition, Muhamamd Mandoor (trans.); (Cairo: National Center For Translation, 2011), pp. 317–324.

7. According to the founding myth, Rome came in existence in 753 BC. During its height of power in the 2nd century AD, it controlled most of the Italian peninsula, half of Europe, most of the Middle East and North African coast. It became one of the largest empires in the ancient world and contributed to the development of international law. It was the first 'state' to set guidelines that governed its relations with other states. In addition, there was a Roman law for peace and war, and it was the first to introduce the concept of a 'just war.' Roman envoys, who were Rome's ambassadors at the same time, assumed the task of adjudicating on infringements by any other state towards Rome, and deciding on Rome's right to wage a just war. The law was purely Roman and Rome remained committed to it when dealing with other states. For more details, see: [in Arabic]; (http://aljsad.com/forum52/thread114870). For more on the concept of 'just war,' see: Mansoor Abdul Hakeem, *The Latest World War is the Last War on Earth* (Damascus & Cairo: Dar Al-Kitab Al-Arabi, 2008), pp. 371–387.

8. Fathiyya Al-Nabrawi and Muhammad Nasr Muhanna, [in Arabic] *Principles of International Political Relations* (Alexandria: Munsh'at AL-Ma'arif, n.d.), pp. 263–270.

9. Mohammed Ali Al-Qoozi, *International Relations in Modern and Contemporary History*, (Beirut: Dal Al-Nahda Al-Arabiyya, 2002), pp. 63–90; Muhammad Al Ismail, "Harbingers of the European

Renaissance," [in Arabic] *Aafaqcenter.com*, March 19, 2012 (http://aafaqcenter.com/index.php/post/1081), accessed October 30, 2013; A.J.P. Taylor, *The Struggle for Mastery in Europe 1848–1918*, [in Arabic] Fadil Jatkar (trans.); (Abu Dhabi: Abu Dhabi Authority for Culture and Heritage, Kalima Project for Translation and Arab Cultural Center, 2009), pp. 19–42.

10. 19th century Europe was characterized by various important events such as the establishment of the French Empire under Napoleon and its fall; the industrial revolution; libertarian revolutions; the establishment of the modern nation-state in Italy and Germany; in addition to the development of the concept of freedom and its role in colonial competition among European countries and their struggle over the Ottoman Empire. See: Mufeed Al-Zaidi, *Encyclopedia of Modern and Contemporary History of Europe: From the French Revolution to the First World War, Part III, 1789–1914* [in Arabic]; (Amman: Dar Usama for Publishing and Distribution, 2004), pp. 659–722.

11. For more about the Ancient Greek cities, see: Gustave Glotz, *The Greek City*, Muhammad Mandoor (trans.); (Cairo: National Center for Translation, 2011), pp. 29–92; Laila Halawa, "Sovereignty: the Dialectics of State and Globalization," [in Arabic] *onislam.net*, May 8, 2005 (http://www.onislam.net/arabic/madarik/concepts/99415-2005-05-08%2022-00-47.html), accessed August 12, 2013.

12. Laila Halawa, "Sovereignty: the Dialectics of State and Globalization," [in Arabic] *onislam.net*, May 8, 2005 (http://www.onislam.net/arabic/madarik/concepts/99415-2005-05-08%2022-00-47.html), accessed August 12, 2013.

13. "Zenith and Prosperity, Part I: Political Development," [In Arabic] *Reference History Book of the Islamic State Volume III* (Tunis: Arab Organization for Education, Culture and Science, 2006), p. 10.

14. It is common knowledge that systems of government, like other aspects of civilization, cannot be examined in a piecemeal fashion. Thus, one cannot study the Abbasid administration in isolation from the administration during the Umayyad era, since each are interconnected and complement each other. They must be studied holistically if we want to understand and interpret them, taking into account the dynamics of history, which highlights the impact of preceding events on the subsequent ones. For example, the shift towards the Sasanian system of government – which was an absolute monarchy and characterized in Persia by considerable centralization, ambitious urban planning, agricultural development, and technological improvements; however, below the king a powerful bureaucracy carried out much of the affairs of government – started during the reign of the Umayyad Caliph, Hisham ibn Abd Al-Malik, and became more apparent in the early Abbasid era. The formation of a regular professional army began during the era of the Umayyad Caliph, Marwan ibn Muhammad, and the early Abbasids expanded on the notion. For more about this topic, see: Farooq Umar Fawzi, *The History of Islamic Systems: A Study of the Development of the State Central Institutions in Early Islamic Centuries* [in Arabic]; (Amman: Dar Al-Shurooq for Publishing and Distribution, 2010), pp. 1–50.

15. Farooq Umar Fawzi, *Studies in Islamic History: Research on Systems and Politics during the Early Islamic Centuries* [in Arabic], (Amman: Dar Majdalawi, 2006), p. 167.

16. Ibid., p. 188.

17. Ibid., p. 202.

18. Ibid., 193.

19. For more about the concept of Cosmopolitanism, see: Paul Hopper, *Understanding Cultural Globalization*, Tal'at Al-Sha'ib (trans.); (Cairo: National Center for Translation, 2011), pp. 207–235; Tom G. Palmer, "Globalization, Cosmopolitanism, and Personal Identity,"

Etica & Politica/Ethics & Politics vol. 2 (2003); (http://www.open starts.units.it/dspace/bitstream/10077/5455/1/Palmer_E%26P_V_200 3_2.pdf), accessed October 29, 2013.

20. Muhammad Saeed Talib, *A Study on the Emergence of the Arab Nation: History and Ideology* [in Arabic]; (Damascus: Al-Dar Al-Wataniyya Al-Jadeeda, 2009), p. 348.

21. Ibid., p. 349.

22. The *Mawali* in the Umayyad period were non-Arab Muslims, or those who converted to Islam in the lands conquered by the Arabs. For more details, see: Muhammad Umar Shaheen, *History of the Mawali and their Role in Social and Economic Life in Early Islam and the Umayyad State* (Beirut: Dar Al-Kutub Al-Ilmiyya, 2011), pp. 24–42.

23. Muhammad Saeed Talib, op. cit., p. 193.

24. Farooq Umar Fawzi, *The History of Islamic Systems: A Study of the Development of Central Institutions in the State in Early Islamic Centuries* [in Arabic]; (Amman: Dar Al-Shurooq for Publishing and Distribution, 2010), pp. 45–48.

25. Ibid., p. 46.

26. Ibid., p. 47.

27. Andrew Wheatcroft, *The Ottomans* (London: Penguin Group, 1993), p. 23.

28. Donald Quataert, *The Ottoman Empire 1700–1922*, Ayman Al-Arminazi (trans.); (Riyadh: Obeikan Publishing, 2004), p. 8.

29. Halil İnalcık, *History of the Ottoman Empire Classical Age*, Muhammad M. Al-Arnaoot (trans.); (Tripoli: Dar Al-Madar Al-Islami, 2002), pp. 30–31.

30. Muhammad Shakir, "Part VIII: The Ottoman Era," [in Arabic] *Islamic History* (Beirut: Al-Maktab Al-Islami, 2000), p. 5.

31. Ibid.

32. Ibid., p. 31.

33. İnalcık, op.cit., p. 11.

34. Ibid. p. 17.

35. Yilmaz Oztuna, *Encyclopedia of Political, Military and Civilizational History of the Ottoman Empire 629–1231 (Hijri) 1431–1922* vol. 1 [in Arabic], Adnan Mahmoud Salman (trans.), revised by Mahmoud Al-Ansari (Beirut: Arab Encyclopedia House, 2010), p. 7.

36. Zain Al-Abideen Shams Al-Deen Najm, *History of the Ottoman State* [in Arabic]; (Amman: Dar Al-Massira, 2010), p. 11.

37. Oztuna, op. cit., pp. 8–9.

38. Fathiyya Al-Nabrawi and Muhammad Nasr Muhanna, op. cit., p. 263.

39. The Spanish Empire spanned about five centuries, starting with the first voyages to the Americas in 1492 until the loss of its last African colonies in 1975. It was one of the most prominent global empires in history.

40. For more about the Spanish Empire, see: "The Spanish Empire," *latinlibrary.com* (http://www.thelatinlibrary.com/imperialism/notes/Spanishempire.html). See also: "History of the Spanish Empire," *History World* (http://historyworld.net/wrldhis/PlainTextHistories.asp?historyid=ab49), accessed October 30, 2013.

41. For more about the fall of Granada, see Shakib Arslan, *The End of Arab History in Andalusia* (Giza: Al-Nafiza Bookshop, 2011), pp. 147–245; Khalid Al-Soofi, *History of the Arabs in Spain, the End of the Umayyad Caliphate in Andalusia* (Beirut: Al-Jamal publications, 2011), pp. 63–94; Abdul-Mun'im Al-Hashimi, *The Andalusian Caliphate* [in Arabic]; (Beirut: Dar Ibn Hazm for Printing, Publishing and Distribution, 2007), pp. 581–589.

42. "Charles V: Holy Roman Emperor (1500–1558)," *Heritage History* (http://www.heritage-history.com/www/heritage.php?Dir=characters& FileName=charles5s.php).

43. Christopher Columbus, *biography.com* (http://www.biography.com/ people/christopher-columbus-9254209).

44. Protestantism emerged as a new reformist movement against Catholic orthodoxy, which began in Germany by Martin Luther and then spread to Europe. The religious reform movement was generally against the papal authority and influence of clergymen in Rome. For more information, see: Sami Al-Shaikh Muhammad, "The Protestant Reform Movement (Luther, Zwingli and Calvin)," [in Arabic] *Alwatanvoice*, January 8, 2006 (http://pulpit.alwatanvoice.com/ articles/2006/01/08/35520.html), accessed October 30, 2013; and Dahham Hassan, "Religious Reform Movement in Europe," [in Arabic] *Minbar Al-Hurriyya*, November 1, 2010 (http://minbaral hurriyya.org/index.php/archives/2679), accessed October 30, 2013.

45. The Thirty Years' War was considered a conflict within the Holy Roman Empire, the second largest empire in Europe after the Russian territories, which some considered then as part of the European continent. The number of casualties of the Thirty Years' War in Europe was estimated at 1.8 million soldiers and at least 3.2 million civilians. The Germanic states lost more than a fifth of their population. This number of victims was equivalent, as a proportion of population, to more than the total number of victims in Europe during two World Wars. For more information, see: Dr. Hussein Ali Zahir, *The Evolution of International Relations from Westphalia to Versailles* [in Arabic], (Beirut: Dar Al-Mawasim for Printing, Publishing and Distribution, 1999), pp. 118–121.

46. The Treaty of Westphalia represented a new course in international relations. It came after a series of wars between Catholic and Protestant countries which lasted for almost 30 years, starting in 1635.

The war took the form of an international European conflict that eclipsed any religious dimension. The Treaty established a pattern of relationships based on cooperation instead of the use of force, and hence was seen as the first framing of the rules of international law. The Treaty established several international principles, the most important of which was the recognition of the principle of sovereignty as an international term, implying the legal capacity of the state. It also endorsed the principle of non-interference in the internal affairs of states, established a system of permanent embassies, developed a system of consular affairs, and set up the rules for the sanctity of international borders and frontiers. In addition, it recognized the newly emerging countries in the aftermath of the collapse of the Holy Roman Empire and its disintegration into many states. See: "The Peace of Westphalia," *History Learning Site* (http://www.history learningsite.co.uk/peace_of_westphalia.htm).

47. "Portugal: Historical Setting Library of Congress Country Study," *About.com* (http://lcweb2.loc.gov/frd/cs/pttoc.html); and Mufeed Al-Zaidi, "Part I, History of Europe in the Middle Ages (1789–1914)," [in Arabic] *Encyclopedia of Modern and Contemporary History of Europe* (Amman: Dar Usama for Publishing and Distribution, 2004), pp. 405–416.

48. Muhammad Al-Sayyid Saeed, *The Future of the Arab System after the Gulf Crisis*, [in Arabic] A'lam Al-Ma'rifa Series, No. 158 (Kuwait: the National Council for Culture, Arts and Letters, February 1992), pp. 10–11.

49. Ismail Sabri Maqlad, *International Political Relations, Theory and Reality* 4th edition [in Arabic]; (Assiut: Assiut University, 2007), p. 34.

50. Hedley Bull, *The Anarchical Society: A Study of Order in World Politics* (New York, NY: Columbia University Press, 1977), p. 59.

51. Abdul Aziz Said, Charles O. Lerche Jr., and Charles O. Lerche III, *Concepts of International Politics in Global Perspective*, Nafi'Ayyoob Labbas (trans.); (Damascus: Publications of the Arab Writers Union, 1999), pp. 163–164.

52. The Conference of Westphalia, in which delegates from France, the Holy Roman Empire and Sweden participated, marked the beginning of organized relations between European countries. Although political and economic relations between European countries existed before then, they were volatile and non-institutionalized. The importance of the Conference lay in the fact that it saw the launch of conference diplomacy, which has become an effective tool for the implementation of countries' foreign policy, conflict resolution and solidification of international cooperation. The Conference also recognized the principle of equality among countries regardless of their political systems or religious doctrines. It also endorsed the principle of permanent diplomatic missions, and thus endorsing some of the most important rules of diplomacy such as immunity and privilege. It also established the principle of balance of power between countries of Europe by deterring states from seeking to expand at the expense of others. For more about the Treaty of Westphalia, see: Mohammed Ali Al-Qoozi, *International Relations in Modern and Contemporary History*, [in Arabic]; (Beirut: Dal Al-Nahda Al-Arabiyya, 2002), pp. 63–90; and Hussein Ali Zahir, *The Evolution of International Relations from Westphalia to Versailles* [in Arabic]; (Beirut: Dar Al-Mawasim, 1999), pp. 118–121.

53. Abdul Aziz Said, Charles O. Lerche Jr., and Charles O. Lerche III, op. cit., p. 165.

54. Richard Clarke and Robert Knake, *Cyber War: The Next Threat to National Security and What To Do About It* [in Arabic]; (Abu Dhabi: Emirates Center for Strategic Studies and Research, 2012), pp. 215–256.

55. Al-Hayali, op. cit., p. 11.

56. Riyad Al-Samad, [in Arabic] *International Relations in the 20th Century* (Beirut: Arab Institution for Research, Publishing and Distribution, 1983), pp. 220–240.

57. Ibid., p. 220. Also see: Michael J. Hogan, *The End of the Cold War: Its Meaning and Implications*, Muhammad Usama Al-Qawtali (trans.); (Damascus: Ministry of Culture, 1998), pp. 21–41; and Sameeh Abdul Fattah, *The Collapse of the Soviet Empire: A New Unipolar World System* [in Arabic]; (Amman: Dar Al- Shurooq for Publishing and Distribution, 1996), pp. 47–65.

58. William C. Wohlforth, *The Stability of a Unipolar World* [in Arabic] International Studies Series, No. 36 (Abu Dhabi: The Emirates Center for Strategic Studies and Research, 2001), p. 7.

59. Joseph S. Nye, "The Future of American Power: Dominance and Decline in Perspective," *Foreign Affairs*, vol. 89, issue 6 (November/ December 2010), p. 12.

60. The Allies of World War II consisted of several countries, including: Britain, France, China and Poland. After the Japanese attack on Pearl Harbor, the United States of America joined the Allies in the war against the Axis powers, followed by the former Soviet Union. For more about the causes of World War II and its outcomes, see: Issa Al-Hassan, *The Second World War: Causes, Facts and Results* [in Arabic]; (Amman: Al-Ahliyya for Publication and Distribution, 2009), pp. 9–39.

61. Abdul Jaleel Zaid Marhoon, "Europe and the Future of German Centrism," [in Arabic] *Al-Riyadh*, May 10, 2002 (http://www. alriyadh.com/2002/05/10/article27856.html), accessed March 29, 2013.

62. For more about the Yalta Conference, see: Ali Subh, *International Struggle in Half a Century: 1945–1995* (Beirut: Dar Manhal for Printing and Publishing, 2006), pp. 15–17; and Encyclopaedia Britannica, "Yalta Conference" (http://global.britannica.com/EB checked/topic/651424/Yalta-Conference), accessed October 30, 2013.

63. Sameeh Abdul Fattah, *The Collapse of the Soviet Empire: A New Unipolar World System*[in Arabic]; (Amman: Dar Al-Shurooq for Publishing and Distribution, 1996), p. 23.

64. In February 1945, former American President Franklin Roosevelt, Soviet President Joseph Stalin and British Prime Minister Winston Churchill signed the Yalta Agreement, which is considered the founding basis of the right of veto enjoyed by the five permanent member countries of the United Nations Security Council, which had not then taken its present shape. For more details, see: Ali Subh, *International Struggle in Half a Century*, op. cit., pp. 26–32.

65. Al-Sayyid Ameen Shalabi, "From the Cold War to the Search for a New World Order," [in Arabic] *Al-Siyassa Al-Dawliyya,* No. 179, (January 2010), pp. 32–36.

66. Waheed Abdul Majeed, "Thirty Years after Bandung Conference: the Third World between the United States of America and the Soviet Union," [in Arabic] *Al-Siyassa Al-Dawliyya*, no. 80, (April 1985), pp. 155–175.

67. North Atlantic Treaty Organization (NATO) is one of the largest military alliances in history. It was founded in 1949 under the North Atlantic Treaty, which was signed by 12 countries in Washington on April 4, 1949. See: Kazim Hashim Ni'ma, *NATO: Expansion to the East and Dialogue with the South and Arab National Security* (Tripoli: Academy of Graduate Studies, 2003), pp. 15–79.

68. In mid-May 1955 in Warsaw, a conference was convened by the Eastern Bloc countries (Soviet Union, Poland, Czechoslovakia, East

Germany, Romania, Bulgaria, Albania and Hungary) after which an agreement was issued for mutual cooperation and assistance, and unification of military leadership. Thus, the Warsaw Pact was formed to confront the North Atlantic Treaty Organization (NATO) and to finalize a number of bilateral agreements linking all member countries (except Albania which had not signed any bilateral agreement with any of the mentioned countries, and Romania which had not signed a bilateral agreement with East Germany). The official name of the Warsaw Pact was the "Treaty of Friendship, Cooperation, and Mutual Assistance." At first, the Pact was to remain for 20 years, and extended for a further ten years if member countries agreed. The Pact stipulated the formation of a unified military command for member countries, and the stationing of Soviet military units in their territories. For more details, see: Ali Subh, op. cit., pp. 119–125.

69. Dwight Eisenhower was the 34th American President, serving from January 20, 1953 to January 20, 1961.

70. The Eisenhower Doctrine refers to a speech by President Dwight Eisenhower on January 5, 1957, as part of a "Special Message to Congress on the Situation in the Middle East." Under the Eisenhower Doctrine, a country could request American economic assistance or aid from the American military forces if it found itself threatened by armed aggression from another country. Eisenhower singled out the Soviet threat in his doctrine by declaring the commitment of US forces "to secure and protect the territorial integrity and political independence of such nations, requesting such aid, against overt armed aggression from any nation controlled by international communism." For more about this Doctrine, see: "Eisenhower Doctrine, 1957" Office of the Historian, US Department of State (http://history.state.gov/milestones/1953-1960/eisenhower-doctrine), accessed October 30, 2013.

71. The deployment of Soviet nuclear missiles in Cuba 50 years ago represented the worst crisis in the Cold War and perhaps the most dangerous moment in human history, where the world was on the

verge of a nuclear war. The American Secretary of Defense at the time, Robert McNamara, stated during a conference in Havana in 2002: "For many years, I considered the Cuban missile crisis to be the best managed foreign policy crisis of the last half-century, but I now conclude that, however astutely the crisis may have been managed, by the end of those extraordinary 13 days, luck also played a significant role in the avoidance of a nuclear war." The former director of the KGB's Cuban office, Nikolai Leonov, considered the peaceful ending to be a miracle, as he said: "It is almost as if some divine intervention occurred to help us save ourselves." For more details, see: "In 1952 and after 50 Years: the Cuban Missile Crisis Almost Drew the World into a Nuclear War," [in Arabic] *Al-Wasat,* October 10, 2012; (http://www.alwasatnews.com/3686/news/read/707685/1.html). Also see: Al-Sayyid Ameen Shalabi, "From the Cold War to the Search for a New World Order," [in Arabic] *Al-Siyassa Al-Dawliyya,* no. 179 (January 2010), pp. 32–36; and Ali Subh, *International Struggle in Half a Century,* op. cit, pp. 160–163.

72. Bahjat Qurani, "From International System to World System," *Al-Siyassa Al-Dawliyya,* no. 161 (July 2005), p. 41.

73. Ahmad Yousuf Al-Qarie, "Revival of the Hotline in a World on the Brink," [in Arabic] *Al-Ahram,* October 20, 2006 (http://yyy.ahram.org.eg/archive/ 2006/ 10/20/OPIN3.HTM).

74. Qurani, op. cit., p. 41.

75. Joseph S. Nye, "The Cuban Missile Crisis at 50," [in Arabic] *Saudi Al-Iqtisadiyya,* October 15, 2012 (http://www.aleqt.com/2012/10/15/article_701626.html), accessed July 27, 2013.

76. Lester Thurow, *Head to Head: The Coming Economic Battle Among Japan, Europe, and America,* Muhammad Fareed (trans.); (Abu Dhabi: The Emirates Center for Strategic Studies and Research, 1996), p. 237.

77. Boris Yeltsin was the first President of the Russian Federation after the disintegration of the Soviet Union, serving from July 10, 1991 to December 31, 1999.

78. Salama Keela, "We Are in a New World Taking Shape" [in Arabic], Al- Jazeera Net, April 15, 2013 (http://www.aljazeera.net/opinions/pages/2bb55e44-4dee-4661-83db-f71c6350cef6), accessed July 27, 2013; also see: Muhammad Al-Sayyid Saeed and Ahmad Ibrahim Mahmood "Chaos and Stability in the International System: Trends in the Evolution of International System in Post-Cold War Era," [in Arabic] *Arab Strategic Report 1995* (Cairo: Al-Ahram Center for Political and Strategic Studies, 1996), p. 17.

79. Mechanisms of domination and influence emerged when President H.W. Bush [Sr.] announced during the Gulf crisis on September 11, 1990, the establishment of a new world order. Security, military, economic, political and cultural arrangements implicitly reflecting the rules of this new order were formulated. See: Salama Keela, op. cit. (http://www.aljazeera.net/opinions/pages/2bb55e44-4dee-4661-83db-f71c6350cef6), accessed July 27, 2013; and Robert A. Pastor, *A Century's Journey: How The Great Powers Shape the World*, Hashim Ahmad Muhammad (trans.); (Cairo: National Center for Translation, 2010), p. 292.

80. Such use of the United Nations in essence was not contradictory to the US desire for unilateralism and its tendency to work in isolation from the United Nations, meaning that Washington resorted to the United Nations when it needed it, and to work in isolation when it chose to do so.

81. Muhammad Al-Sayyid Saeed and Ahmad Ibrahim Mahmood, "Chaos and Stability in the International System," op. cit., pp. 17–18.

82. Francis Fukuyama, *The End of History and the Last Man*, Hussein Ahmad Ameen (trans.); (Cairo: Al-Ahram Center for Translation and Publishing, 1993), p. 9.

83. "The Bolshevik Revolution 1917," *thenagain.com* (http://www. thenagain.info/webchron/easteurope/octrev.html), accessed October 30, 2013.

84. Qurani, op. cit., p. 42.

85. Keela, op. cit.

86. Noam Chomsky, "Washington Above International Law—America: The Rogue State" [in Arabic], in Mohamed Milad (trans.) *Will the World Slide into the Abyss?* [in Arabic]; (Damascus: Dar Al-Hewar for Publishing and Distribution, 2009), p. 20.

87. "US Military Spending Over the Years," *davemanual.com* (http://www.davemanuel.com/2010/06/14/us-military-spending-over-the-years).

88. Chomsky, 2009, op. cit., p. 20.

89. Jalal Khasheeb, "Major Directions of American Strategy after the Cold War," [in Arabic] Al-Hiwar Al-Mutamaddin, no. 3818, August 13, 2012 (http://www.ahewar.org/debat/show.art.asp?aid=319828), accessed September 3, 2013.

90. Julius Nyerere (1922–1999) was one of most respected political figures in Africa. For more information, see: "Biography: Julius Kambarage Nyerere," Marxists.org (http://www.marxists.org/subject/africa/nyerere/biography.htm).

91. Sir Winston Churchill was British Prime Minister from May 1940 to July 1945. For more details, see: "Winston Churchill," *Biography.com* (http://www.biography.com/people/winston-churchill-9248164).

92. Noam Chomsky, *World Orders, Old and New* Safwan Akkash (trans.); (Damascus: Dar Fussilat for Studies, Translation and Publishing, 2000), p. 20.

93. Woodrow Wilson was the 28th American President, serving from March 4, 1913 to March 4, 1921.

94. Nizar Ismail Al-Hyali, *NATO's Role After the End of the Cold War* [in Arabic]; (Abu Dhabi: The Emirates Center for Strategic Studies and Research, 2003), p. 12.

95. In an address on the occasion of sending American troops to the Arabian Gulf after the Iraqi invasion of Kuwait on August 2, 1990, former American President George H.W. Bush [Sr.] hinted at the intention of the United States of America to create a new world order. In this context, he talked about a "new era" and an "era of freedom" and a "time of peace for all peoples"; these are the basic features of the new world order from the American perspective. On September 11, 1990, he referred to the establishment of a "new world order."

96. James Baker was the 61st American Secretary of State in the administration of President George H.W. Bush [Sr.], serving from January 20, 1989 to August 23, 1992.

97. Chomsky, 2000, op. cit., p. 23.

98. Ibid., p. 23.

99. Al-Hayali, op. cit., p. 13.

100. Faris Ishti, "The New International System between Order and Hegemony," [in Arabic] *Al-Manar*, no. 56 (1998), p. 27.

101. Abdul Mun'im Saeed, *Arabs and the New World Order: Proposed Options*, [in Arabic] Strategic Papers Series, no. 3, (Cairo: Al-Ahram Center for Strategic Studies, 1991), p. 26.

102. Muhammad Yaaqoob Abdul Rahman, "Humanitarian Intervention in International Relations," op. cit., pp. 125–140.

103. Abdul Azeem Jabr Hafiz, [in Arabic] "The New International System and the United States of America," (http://www.alitthad.com/paper.php?name=News&file=article&sid=18636).

104. George H.W. Bush, "Address Before the 45th Session of the United Nations General Assembly in New York, New York October 1, 1990," the American Presidency Project, University of California, Santa Barbara (http://www.presidency.ucsb.edu/ws/index.php?pid=18883).

105. Majid A'if, "The New World Order," [in Arabic] *Al-Hiwar Al-Mutamaddin*, no. 3862, September 26, 2012 (http://www.ahewar.org/debate/show.art.asp?aid=325822K), accessed August 27, 2013.

106. Muhammad Al-Sayyid Saeed, "The Idea of the New World Order between Tyranny and Participation," [in Arabic] *Al-Arabi*, no. 403 (June 1992); (http://www.alarabimag.com/Article.asp?ART=532&ID=272), accessed July 27, 2013.

107. Chomsky, 2003, op. cit., pp. 63–66.

108. Najah Al-Ashry, *Globalization and Hegemony* [in Arabic]; (Tripoli: Nasser International University, 1999), pp. 22–24.

109. Kawthar Abbas Al-Rubaie, *The Evolution of the Concept of American National Security, Strategic Studies* [in Arabic] series, No. 35 (Baghdad: Center for International Studies, 2002), p. 10.

110. Muhammad Al-Sayyid Saeed and Ahmad Ibrahim Mahmood, "Chaos and Stability in the International System," op. cit., p. 39.

111. Mohammed Yacoub Abdel Rahman, *Humanitarian Intervention in International Relations* [in Arabic]; (Abu Dhabi: The Emirates Center for Strategic Studies and Research, 2004), p. 128.

112. Ministry of Defense, French Republic, "Armée de Terre" (http://www.defense.gouv.fr/terre).

113. The common European currency (the euro) is an example in this context, in which some researchers see it as a symbol of the erosion of state sovereignty since it was launched on January 1, 1999.

114. The euro, for example, restricts the freedom of member countries of the Eurozone to adopt monetary and fiscal policies independent of other members. In fact, monetary policies are made by all members for reasons and considerations related to institutional cohesion of monetary union.

115. Shukrani Al-Hussein, "Climate Justice: Towards a New Perspective for Social Justice," [in Arabic] *Strategic Visions* vol. 1, Issue 1 (December 2012), p. 109.

116. Ibid.

117. Saeed Marzooq Al-Siddiqi, "Tightening Border Controls and Building Fences to Fight Immigration: A Comparison between American and Spanish policies," [in Arabic] *Strategic Visions* vol. 1, Issue 3 (June 2013), p. 92.

118. Ibid.

119. Qurani, op. cit., pp. 40–45.

120. Cited in: Muhammad Saadi Al-Hassan, "A Book Review: War in the Name of Humanity: Kill or Let Die," [in Arabic]; (*La guerre au nom de l'humanité. Tuer ou laisser mourir*) *Strategic Visions* vol. 1, Issue 1 (December 2012), pp. 126–129.

121. Some researchers argue that humanitarian intervention is an old phenomenon in the history of international relations. They cite the first written treaty in the history of mankind, which dates back to 1258 BC, between Ramesses II and the king of the Hittites, which

stipulated that: "If a man or two men, or three men flee from the country of Egypt, and if they come to the country of the Hittites, then the king of the country of the Hittites has to take hold of them and to order them to be taken to Ramesses II. As for their crime, it should not be imputed; their tongue and their eyes are not to be pulled out; their ears and their feet are not to cut off; their houses with their wives and their children are not to be destroyed. This equally applies to those who flee from the country of the Hittites to the country of Egypt." Some researchers see this treaty as a confirmation of the historical dimension of humanitarian invention in international relations, which aims to sanctify and protect human life in times of peace and war. For more about humanitarian intervention in international relations, see: Ghassan Abdul Hadi Ibrahim, *Al-Hiwar Al-Mutamaddin*, no. 319, September 16, 2005 (http://www.ahewar. org/debat/show.art.asp?aid=45630); and Muhammad Yaaqoob Abdul Rahman, op. cit., pp. 27–28.

122. Al-Hassan, op. cit., p. 129.

123. "Jihawaiyya" – the Arabic equivalent of Regionalism – is used in Morocco, Algeria and Tunisia, mainly in an administrative political context. "Jihawaiyya" is used as a translation of the French words *régional, régionalisme* and *région*, depending on the context.

124. Nassif Yusuf Hitti, "Shifts in International System, and the New Intellectual Climate and its Implications for the Arab Regional System," [in Arabic] *Al-Mustaqbal Al-Arabi*, no. 165 (November 1992), p. 31.

125. Some theorists believe that democratic values and systems – which are based on dialogue, conflict management, discussion and exchange of opinions to reach acceptable solutions and agreement between parties – allow the resort to arbitration whenever necessary to reach compromises involving all parties. These are protective safeguards that prevent democracies from slipping into the zone of military conflict. For more about the definition of democracy, see: Jawad Al-Hindawi,

Constitutional Law and Political Systems [in Arabic]; (Beirut: Dar Al-Aarif Publications, 2010), pp. 61–85. Also see: Muhsin Bagir Al-Musawi, *Shura and Democracy* [in Arabic]; (Beirut: Dar Al-Hadi Printing, Publishing and Distribution, 2003), pp. 263–285.

126. For more information on the World Conference on Human Rights, June 14–25, 1993 in Vienna, visit the website of the Office of the United Nations High Commissioner for Human Rights (http://www.ohchr.org/AR/AboutUs/Pages/ViennaWC.aspx).

127. The final document of the Conference agreed in Vienna, which was endorsed by the 48th Session of the General Assembly of the United Nations (Resolution 48/121 of 1993), reaffirmed the principles that had been developed during the past 45 years and further strengthened the foundation for additional progress in the area of human rights, and the recognition of interdependence between democracy and human rights. For example, it prepared the way for future cooperation by international organizations and national agencies in the promotion of all human rights, including the right to development. Similarly, the Conference took historic new steps to promote and protect the rights of women, children and indigenous peoples by supporting the creation of a new system; nominating a special rapporteur on violence against women; calling for the universal ratification of the Convention on the Rights of the Child by the year 1995; and recommending the proclamation by the General Assembly of an international decade of the world's indigenous peoples; a recommendation which the General Assembly has implemented.

128. The General Assembly of the United Nations created the post of High Commissioner for Human Rights on December 20, 1993 pursuant to resolution 48/141. The Secretary-General of the United Nations nominated Mr. José Ayala Lasso as the first High Commissioner. He assumed office on April 5, 1994.

129. In his speech before the General Assembly of the United Nations on 23rd of September 23, 2010, President Barack Hussein Obama stated:

"... freedom, justice and peace for the world must begin with freedom, justice, and peace in the lives of individual human beings. And for the United States of America, this is a matter of moral and pragmatic necessity. As Robert Kennedy said, "the individual man, the child of God, is the touchstone of value, and all society, groups, the State, exist for his benefit." So we stand up for universal values because it's the right thing to do. But we also know from experience that those who defend these values for their people have been our closest friends and allies, while those who have denied those rights – whether terrorist groups or tyrannical governments – have chosen to be our adversaries." Remarks by the President to the United Nations General Assembly, September 23, 2010, Office of the Press Secretary, The White House (http://www.whitehouse.gov/the-press-office/2010/09/23/remarks-president-united-nations-general-assembly). For more details, see "President Obama's Address to U.N. General Assembly," [in Arabic] the White House, Office of the Press Secretary, September 23, 2010 (http://iipdigital.usembassy.gov/st/arabic/texttrans/2010/09/20100923163440x0.2680584.html#axzz2aht cXXY).

130. Hassan Nafaa, "The Changing International Priorities and the Arab World," [in Arabic] in Ahmed Yusuf Ahmed, et al., *The Arab World and Global Developments*, (Cairo: Center for Arab Research and Studies, 1991), pp. 93–134.

131. Muhammad Al-Sayyid Saeed, "Introduction" in Ahmed Yusuf Ahmed, et al., *The Arab World and Global Developments* (Cairo: Center for Arab Research and Studies, 1991), p. 19.

132. Ibid.

133. Majid Kayyali, "Shift in American Political Strategy from the Occupation of Iraq to Calls for Change in the Region," [in Arabic] *Shu'un Arabiyya* no. 114 (Summer 2003), pp. 25–27.

134. The Group of 8 includes: the United States of America, Japan, Germany, Russia, Italy, the United Kingdom, France and Canada.

135. For more on the Greater Middle East Initiative, see: Ahmad Saleem Al-Barsan, "The Greater Middle East Initiative: Political and Strategic Dimensions," [in Arabic] *Al-Siyasa Al-Dawliyya* no. 158 (October 2004), pp. 42–44.

136. Muhammad Abdul Aati, "The Greater Middle East Initiative," [in Arabic] Al-Jazeera Net, May 21, 2004 (http://aljazeera.net/news/pages/13e60cb3-caed-44d5-a289-14e3a6facb79); and Al-Sayyid Ameen Shalabi, "Promotion of Democracy from Bush to Obama," [in Arabic] *Al-Masri Al-Yawm*, November 8, 2010 (http://www.almasryalyoum.com/node/230413).

137. Muhammad Abdul Aati, "The Greater Middle East Initiative and the Arab Summit," Al-Jazeera Net, October 3, 2004 (http://www.aljazeera.net/home/print/466530fd-e741-4721-acd2-a85c1ce6092a/315 1aab2-5b13-4eed-92eb-04db51f 5550c).

138. Noam Chomsky, "America Fears Democracy in Arab Spring Countries," [in Arabic], *Al-Jazeera Net*, October 27, 2012 (http://www.aljazeera.net/news/pages/c4ec8953-89d6-4803-aa43-6a93 7c0414a8). Also see: Muhammad Madi, "American Swinging between Support for Democracy and Reliance on Dictatorships," [in Arabic] *Swissinfo*, June 28, 2013 (http://www.swissinfo.ch/ara/detail/content.html?cid=36187292).

139. Kenneth Waltz, "The Continuity of International Politics" in Ken Booth and Tim Dunne (eds) *Worlds in Collision* (New York, NY: Palgrave Macmillan, 2002), pp. 451–457.

140. Ibid., p. 454.

141. Ibid., p. 455.

142. US Department of State, "Anti-Ballistic Missile Treaty," (http://www.state.gov/www/global/arms/treaties/abm/abm2.html).

143. Waltz, op. cit., p. 458.

144. Abdul Qadir Muhammad Fahmi, *The International Political System: A Study on Theoretical Origins and Contemporary Characteristics* [in Arabic]; (Baghdad: the General House of Cultural Affairs, 1995), pp. 88–89.

145. Al- Hayali, op. cit., p. 22.

146. William C. Wohlforth, *The Stability of a Unipolar World*, [in Arabic] International Studies Series, No. 36 (Abu Dhabi: The Emirates Center for Strategic Studies and Research, 2001), p. 8.

147. Ibid.

148. Francis Fukuyama, *State-Building: Governance and World Order in the 21st century*, Mujab Al-Imam (trans.); (Riyadh: Obeikan Publishing, 2007), p. 166.

149. Ibid.

150. Ibid.

151. The White House, "President Bush Delivers Graduation Speech at West Point," June 1, 2002 (http://georgewbush-whitehouse.archives.gov/news/releases/2002/06/20020601-3.html).

152. William Schneider, "Bush's Role for America: The World's Top Cop," [in Arabic] *Al-Sharq Al-Awsat*, no. 8602, June 17, 2002 (http://www.aawsat.com/details.asp?issueno=8435&article=108683), accessed August 23, 2013.

153. William Cohen, "Globalization Today: How Interconnected is the World?" in *Globalization In The 21st Century: How Interconnected Is The World?* (Abu Dhabi: Emirates Center for Strategic Studies and Research, 2009), p. 22.

154. Hassan Hanafi and Sadiq Jalal Al-Azm, [in Arabic] *What is Globalization?* (Beirut; Damascus: Dar Al-Fikr Al-Mu'asir, 1999), p. 125.

155. Ibid.

156. Ramzi Zaki, "The Road to Seattle – Impacts of Globalization and the Illusions of Chasing the Mirage," [in Arabic] *Al-Nahj*, no. 21 (Winter 2000), p. 7.

157. Ibid.

158. Al-Sayyid Yaseen et al., *Arabs and Globalization* (Beirut: Center for Arab Unity Studies, 1998), p. 319.

159. Remon Haddad, *International Relations: International Relations Theory, International Relations Characters; Chaos or Order Under Globalization* [in Arabic]; (Beirut: Dar Al-Haqeeqa, 2000), pp. 275–286.

160. Ibid., p. 287.

161. Ibid., 279.

162. Samir Amin, *Empire of Chaos* Sana Abu Shaqra (trans.); (Beirut: Dar Al-Farabi, 1991), pp. 12, 79.

163. Ibid., p. 79.

164. Ahmad Thabit, *Globalization: Interactions and contradictions of International Transformations,* [in Arabic] Political Research Series no. 119 (Cairo: Center for Political Research and Studies, Cairo University, April 1992), p. 2.

165. Ibid.

166. Thomas Friedman, *The Lexus and the Olive Tree: Understanding Globalization,* Laila Zaidan (trans.); (Cairo: Al-Dar Al-Wataniyya Publishing and Distribution, 1999), p. 3.

167. Jessica T. Mathews, "Power Shift," *Foreign Affairs* (January/February 1997), p. 56.

168. Ibrahim Al-Isawai, "Economic Globalization between Inevitable Continuation and Potential Decline," [in Arabic] *Al-Nahda,* no. 1 (1999), pp. 125–126.

169. Jalal Amin, "Globalization and the State," [in Arabic] *Al-Mustaqbal Al-Arabi*, no. 228 (February 1998), p. 30.

170. Soft state was a notion floated by the Swedish Nobel laureate economist, Karl Gunnar Myrdal, in his two books: *Asian Drama: An Inquiry into the Poverty of Nations* (1968), and *The Challenge of World Poverty* (1970). Myrdal believes that this term or theory is an accurate diagnostic description of poor conditions in many third world countries that suffer from what he calls symptoms of soft state, and it is the source of affliction and a primary cause of poverty and underdevelopment. By soft state he means the state that issues laws and does not implement them, not only because of the loopholes in these laws but also because no-one in these countries respect laws, whether from the upper or lower class, due to misuse of power, corruption and nepotism. He even believes that restrictions in these countries are only imposed in order to be taken by some as a means for getting rich by breaking them. These countries have poor tax collection, and positions become a means for getting rich, and corruption and bribes are widespread. Corruption is rampant in different parts of the executive, legislative, political and judiciary authorities and universities, in such a way that corruption becomes "a way of life." According to Myrdal, the soft state appears under conditions where certain classes of society acquire power and influence so that they can impose their will on the rest of society. It is also remarkable that the soft state is characterized by the existence of

laws and regulations that ostensibly look democratic and fair, but these laws are only enforced upon the poor and lower classes. The soft state is also a country where not everyone owes allegiance to the homeland, but rather to one's class and family. For more about the concept of the soft state, see: Jalal Amin, *The Soft State in Egypt* [in Arabic]; (Cairo: Sina Publishing, 1993), pp. 5–10. See also: Arup Maharatna, "In Resurrection of Gunnar Myrdal's Asian Drama," *Mainstream Weekly*, vol. XLVIII, no. 18, April 24, 2010 (http://www.mainstreamweekly.net/article2035.html).

171. Ramzi Zaki, "Impacts of Globalization and the Delusions of Chasing the Mirage," [in Arabic] *Al-Nahj* no. 57 (2000), p. 18.

172. Ibid.

173. Abdul Khaliq Abdullah, "Globalization: its Roots and Branches and How to Deal with it," *Alam Al Fikr* no. 28 (October 1999), p. 67.

174. Ibid.

175. Noam Chomsky, "Market Democracy in a Neoliberal Order: Doctrines and Reality," Iman Shams (trans.), *Shu'un Al-Awsat*, No. 71 (April 1998).

176. Knowledge-based economy is one mainly based on production, dissemination and the use of knowledge and information, i.e. knowledge is the prime engine of a country's economic growth. See: Abdul Rahman Al-Hashimi and Faiza Muhammad Al-Izzawi, [in Arabic] *Curriculum and Knowledge Economy* (Amman: Dar Al-Masseera for Publication, Distribution and Printing, 2007), pp. 21–58; Ribhi Mustafa Alian, *Knowledge Economy* [in Arabic]; (Amman: Dar al-Safaa for Publication and Distribution, 2011), pp. 96–122.

177. Jacques Attali, *Lignes d'horizon*, Muhammad Zakariyya (trans.); (Beirut: Dar Al-Ilm Lil-Malayeen, 1992), p. 61.

178. Marie Guéhenno, *End of Democracy*, Haleem Tosson (trans.); (Cairo: Al-Shurooq Bookshop, 1995), pp. 10–15.

179. Hassan Abu Nimah, "Globalization and the International System" in *Globalization In The 21st Century: How Interconnected Is The World?* op. cit., pp. 216–217.

180. Ibid., p. 219.

181. Ibid., p. 220.

182. Graham Allison, "The Impact of Globalization on National and International Security," in *Governance in a Globalizing World*, Joseph Nye and John Donahue (eds), Muhammad Sharif Al-Tarh (trans.); (Riyadh: Obeikan Publishing, 2002), pp. 116–132.

183. In 1991, CNN was the only cable news channel that broadcast the events of the Second Gulf war live. On September 11, 2001, it was the first cable news channel to break the news of attacks on World Trade Center.

184. Allison, op. cit., pp. 125–127.

185. For more about the concept of Hard and Soft information, see: Mitchell A. Petersen, "Information: Hard and Soft," Kellogg School of Management, Northwestern University, July 2004 (http://www.kellogg.northwestern.edu/faculty/petersen/htm/papers/softhard.pdf).

186. Allison, op. cit., p. 128.

187. Ibid., p. 132.

188. Muhammad Al-Sayyid Saeed, "Transnational Corporations and the Future of the Phenomenon of Nationalism," [in Arabic] *A'lam Al-Ma'rifa* series, no. 107 (Kuwait: National Council for Culture, Arts and Letters, November 1986), pp. 56–60.

189. Ibid.

190. Hans-Peter Martin and Harald Schumann, "The Global Trap: Globalization and the Assault on Democracy and Prosperity," Adnan

Abbas Ali (trans.), *A'lam Al-Ma'rifa* series, no. 238 (Kuwait: National Council for Culture, Arts and Letters, October 1998), p. 136.

191. Samir Amin, *An Intellectual Autobiography* [in Arabic]; (Beirut: Dar Al-Aadab, 1993), p. 79.

192. Ibid.

193. Francis Fukuyama, "The End of History," *The National Interest* (Summer 1989), pp. 3–18.

194. Ibid.

195. Ghassan Al-Izzi, *Power Politics: The Future of the International System and the Great Powers* [in Arabic]; (Beirut: Center for Arab Unity Studies, 2000), pp. 161–163.

196. Salma Al-Saeedi, *Smart School is the School of the 21st Century* [in Arabic]; (Cairo: Dar Farha for Printing, Publishing and Distribution, 2002), p. 55.

197. Ibrahim Ismat Mutawie, *Human Development Through Education and Learning* [in Arabic]; (Cairo: Dar Al-Fikr Al-Arabi, 2002) p. 24.

198. Samia Muhammad Jabir and Ni'mat Ahmad Uthman, *Communication and Media (Information Technology),* [in Arabic]; (Alexandria: Dar Al-Maarifa Al-Jami'iyya, 2000), p. 108.

199. Mustafa Kazim, "Information and Communication Revolution Reshaped Our World," [in Arabic] BBC website, December 31, 2007: (http://news.bbc.co.uk/hi/arabic/news/newsid_7166000/7166241.stm), accessed September 2, 2013.

200. Ibid.

201. Ibid.

202. Ibid.

203. Shakir Al-Nabulsi, "A Critique of the Ideology of Information and Communication Revolution," [in Arabic] *Al-Hiwar Al-Mutamaddin* October 24, 2010 (http://www.ahewar.org/debat/show.art.asp?aid= 232949), accessed September 2, 2013.

204. Jamal Sanad Al-Suwaidi, *From Tribe to Facebook: the Transformational Role of Social Networks* [in Arabic]; (Abu Dhabi: Emirates Center for Strategic Studies and Research, 2013), p. 115.

205. Ibid., p. 116.

206. International Telecommunication Union, World Summit on the Information Society: Geneva 2003 and Tunis 2005 (http://www.itu. int/wsis/indexar.html).

207. Ibid.

208. Pippa Norris, "Global Governance and Cosmopolitan Citizens," in *Governance in a Globalizing World*, op. cit., p. 222.

209. Ibid., p. 223.

210. Cary Coglianese, "Globalization and Design of International Institutions," in *Governance in a Globalizing World*, op. cit., p. 405.

211. Al-Hussein, op. cit., p. 99.

212. Coglianese, op. cit., p. 412.

213. Anne-Marie Slaughter, *A New World Order*, Ahmad Mahmood [in Arabic]; (Cairo: National Center for Translation, 2011), p. 21.

214. Unconventional security threats are those issues threatening the survival of populations and nations and their well being. They often arise from non-military factors such as climate change, resource scarcity, infectious diseases and pandemics, natural disasters, irregular migration, hunger, people smuggling, drug trafficking and cross-border crime. See: Vijay Sakhuja, *The Strategic Dynamics of the Indian Ocean* [in Arabic], Emirates Lectures Series, no. 156 (Abu

Dhabi: The Emirates Center for Strategic Studies and Research, 2013), p. 26.

215. Bull, op. cit., p. 346.

216. Ibid., p. 347.

217. Slaughter, op. cit., p. 21.

218. Bull, op. cit., p. 346.

219. Anne-Marie Slaughter is well known in the field of political science and international relations. She is a professor at Princeton University and served as Director of Policy Planning for the US State Department at the beginning of Obama administration. She has made recognized contributions to the study of the world order and US foreign policy.

220. Slaughter, op. cit., pp. 33–34.

221. These networks are groups or organizations interconnected at various levels. Senior officials such as heads of states and governments network with each other and achieve good results and find common positions through collective negotiation and discussion, such as the G7. They do not have any formal status as an international organization but are based on institutional relationships among a number of leaders. These networks are not alliances or treaty partners. There are also other networks of finance ministers, defense ministers, bank chairmen, capital markets directors, insurance companies etc. These networks are trans-governmental but they are not organizations formed among countries; they are not formed under a treaty or executive agreements, and they take no specific place in international law.

222. Slaughter, op. cit., p. 50.

223. Ibid., p. 21.

224. Thomas Volgy, Zlatko Sabic, Petra Roter and Andrea Gerlak, *Mapping the World Order,* Atif Mu'tamad and Izzat Zayyan (trans.); (Cairo: National Center for Translation, 2011), p. 12.

225. "Pre-emptive or Preventive" wars are those initiated to prevent a possible attack from another party, particularly in case when the other party's offensive intentions are discovered. Thus, both wars assume the presence of a premeditated intention for an attack from an adversary. However, at the implementation level, preventive war means initiation of a military attack regardless of how far the adversary is effectively prepared to launch the intended offensive. Pre-emptive war is launched against forces effectively deployed by the adversary in preparation for war. Thus, pre-emptive war is launched when there is an imminent aggression, while preventive war is initiated to thwart a potential threat, and often based on opaque evidence. This means that pre-emptive war could be classified within legitimate self-defense acts under international law, while it is difficult to say so about preventive war. See: James J. Wirtz and James A. Russell, "US Policy on Preventive War and Preemption," (http://cns.miis.edu/npr/pdfs/101wirtz.pdf).

226. Some researchers, including Francis Fukuyama, argue that the erosion of the principle of sovereignty has not come as a result of security interventions in the aftermath of the September 11, 2001 attacks. It has basically resulted from humanitarian interventions in Kosovo, Bosnia, Rwanda, Somalia, East Timor and Congo, and other parts of the world which had witnessed bloody massacres and serious violations of human rights, pushing the international community to intervene to protect the citizens of weak and failing states from the cruelty of their rulers. Thus, if the West had the right to intervene to protect others for humanitarian reasons, then it would be its right and duty to intervene to defend itself and protect its citizens for security reasons.

227. Nevine Mussaad, "International Relations and the Future of the World Order in the Stage of Globalization," [in Arabic] in *Globalization and its Influence on Society and State* (Abu Dhabi: The Emirates Center for Strategic Studies and Research, 2002), p. 156.

228. United Nations, Millennium Report of the UN Secretary-General (Kofi Annan) entitled "We the People: the Role of United Nations in the Twenty-first Century," [in Arabic]; (http://www.un.org/arabic/millennium/sg/report/report0.htm).

229. In his report, Kofi Annan literally said of globalization: "Its integrative logic seems inexorable, its momentum irresistible" (http://www.un.org/arabic/millennium/sg/report/report0.htm).

230. Mussaad, op. cit., p. 171.

231. For more details, see the section titled "Globalization and Governance" in the Millennium Report of the former Secretary-General of the United Nations, op. cit.

232. Daniel Calingaert, "Challenges for International Policy," in *Liberation Technology: Social Media and the Struggle for Democracy*, [in Arabic] Larry Diamond and Marc Plattner (eds); (Abu Dhabi: The Emirates Center for Strategic Studies and Research, 2013), p. 267.

233. Ibid.

234. Some scholars argue that Western civilization has developed six features that have made Europe and subsequently the United States of America rise to global dominance and civilizational superiority for decades. These features are: 1) competition; 2) science; 3) property rights; 4) modern medicine; 5) the consumer society—meaning a model of civilization centering around the consumer market, its expansion, increase of production and free interplay of supply and demand; and 6) the work ethic— work as primary way to achieve

self-actualization, material wealth, social status and political influence at the same time. For more on this part, see: "Six Values the West Added to Civilizations," [in Arabic] *Al-Bayan,* United Arab Emirates, November 20, 2011 (http://www.albayan.ae/one-world/new-books/2011-12-20-1.1558037), accessed July 30, 2013.

235. Thomas L. McPhail, *Global Communication,* Abdul Hakeem Ahmad Al-Khuzami (trans.); (Cairo: Dar Al-Fajr for Publishing and Distribution, 2012), p. 478.

236. "Social Networking Sites on the Internet – A Source of Great Threat to Individual Privacies: Companies, Governments and Thieves Use them to Extract Information," [in Arabic] *Al-Sharq Al-Awsat* March 16, 2010 (http://www.aawsat.com/details.asp?issueno=11700&article=561211), accessed September 4, 2013.

237. Francis Fukuyama, "History and September 11," in Ken Booth and Tim Dunne (eds.), *Worlds in Collision: Terror and the Future of Global Order* [in Arabic]; (Abu Dhabi: The Emirates Center for Strategic Studies and Research, 2005), p. 39.

238. Ibid.

239. Robert Keohane, op. cit., pp. 189.

240. Ibid., 190.

241. Ibid., 192.

242. "History of Relations between China and India," CNTV Arabic website, May 21, 2013 (http://arabic.cntv.cn/2013/05/21/ARTI1369104581220531.shtml), accessed October 30, 2013.

243. Robert Keohane, op. cit., p. 187.

244. The wide international coalition lineup against terrorism can be understood in light of common interests among major powers in fighting this dangerous phenomenon. China, for example, fights what it considers Islamic extremism in Xinjiang region, and Russia

confronts extremist fundamentalist groups in Chechnya, in addition to its animosity towards the Afghan Taliban.

245. James Der Derian, "In Terror: Before and After 9/11," in *Worlds in Collision: Terror and the Future of Global Order*, op. cit., p. 139.

246. Some Western experts and scholars see the attacks of September 11, 2001 as the worst attacks on American homeland, and consider it worse than the Pearl Harbor attack.

247. Michael Cox, "Meanings of Victory: American Power after the Towers," in *Worlds in Collision: Terror and the Future of Global Order*, op. cit., p. 205.

248. Ibid.

249. Michael Byers, "Terror and the Future of International Law," in *Worlds in Collision: Terror and the Future of Global Order*, op. cit., p. 165.

250. Customary International Law, like International Treaty Law, is the main source of Public International Law. While international treaties are written conventions in which states establish certain rules, Customary International Law is derived from unwritten "general practices accepted as law." To set a certain rule as customary, two elements are required: an objective element reflected in state practice, and a subjective element reflected in the international community's belief that such practice is required as a matter of law. The objective element is often referred to as the 'state practice,' and the subjective element as 'legal opinion.' For more details, see International Committee of the Red Cross, "Customary international humanitarian law," October 29, 2010 (http://www.icrc.org/ara/war-and-law/treaties-customary-law/customary-law/overview-customary-law.htm).

251. The United States of America refused to sign some of these treaties, such as the Kyoto Protocol, based on its own concept of the shared responsibility principle, which states that all nations, regardless of the

level of their industrial and economic progress, are responsible for environmental degradation and global warming. Accordingly, what eventually matters are the consequential outcomes, not the reasons or actors. This in turn requires integrated collective solutions through concerted efforts from both affected states and actors. Thus, the United States of America believes that the Protocol does not differentiate between the responsibilities of states, and this is unacceptable from its viewpoint. For more on this topic see: Shukrani Al-Hussein, op. cit., pp. 98–111.

252. For more on the Kyoto Protocol, see: United Nations (UN), Framework Convention on Climate Change (http://unfccc.int/kyoto_ protocol/items/2830.php).

253. United Nations, "Rome Statute of the International Criminal Court" (http://legal.un.org/icc/statute/romefra.htm).

254. Byers, op. cit., pp. 158–159.

255. Alan Woods, "George Bush and the Crusades," [in Arabic] *Al-Hiwar Al-Mutamaddin* no. 495, May 22, 2003 (http://www.ahewar.org/ debat/show.art.asp?aid=7556), accessed July 29, 2013.

256. Ibid.

257. Saeed Ukasha, "How the Americans Perceived the Events of September 11," [in Arabic] *Al-Dimuqratiyya* January 1, 2002 (http://digital.ahram.org.eg/articles.aspx?Serial=794078&eid=410), accessed July 29, 2013.

258. Pascal Boniface, "Why Victory in the War on Terror Remains Elusive?" Opinion Articles, the Emirates Center for Strategic Studies and Research website, July 30, 2005 (http://www.ecssr.com), accessed July 30, 2013.

259. Nye, 2010, op. cit., p. 8.

260. In mid-2009, for example, an intellectual controversy emerged about the responsibility of globalization for the spread of the virus that caused 'swine flu,' and its effectiveness in combating it. Some laid the blame on globalization and argued that it had failed in confronting and controlling the disease, despite its extensive reach into various parts of the world. However, others took a contrary view.

261. Ahmad Abu Al-Wafa, "The United Nations and the New World Order," [in Arabic] *Al-Siyassa Al-Dawliyya*, no. 122 (October 1996), pp. 78–79.

262. Ibid., p. 81.

263. Laila Sharaf, [in Arabic] commentary remarks in "Recent Developments in the United States of America and their Arab implications," *The Arabs and the World After September 11* (Beirut: Center for Arab Unity Studies, 2004), p. 29.

264. Ibid.

265. Ibid., p. 30.

266. Muhammad Waleed Iskaf, "Reforming the United Nations or International Legitimacy," *Al-Hiwar Al-Mutamaddin*, September 4, 2005 (http://www.ahewar.org/debat/show.art.asp?aid=44693), accessed August 30, 2013.

267. Ibid.

268. Ibid.

269. Abdul Ghaffar Al-Duwaik, "Failure of Bush's Pre-emptive Doctrine: War Is Not Won by Military Strategy Alone," [in Arabic] *Al-Ahram* January 11, 2004 (http://www.ahram.org.eg/archive/2004/1/11/FILE 10.HTM), accessed August 16, 2013.

270. For more about the Bush Doctrine, see: Elias Hanna, "Institutionalization of the Bush Doctrine," [in Arabic] *Al-Jazeera Net*, October 3, 2004 (http://www.aljazeera.net/home/print/7dcab3c3-3422-4c8b-b091-049383f5dada/165e161b-e5c9-41b1-bcf4-b2850fd2287a).

271. The White House, "The National Security Strategy of the United States of America," Washington, DC, September 2002, p. 6; see also: V.I. Korolev, *Emperor of All the Earth* [in Arabic], Muntajab Younes (trans.); (Damascus: Dar Aladdin Publishing, 2006), p. 191.

272. Yassir Qutaishat, "Pre-emptive Strike as a New Strategy in International Relations: War on Iraq as an Example," [in Arabic] *Minbar Al-Hurriyya*, December 4, 2009 (http://minbaralhurriyya.org/index.php/archives/2204), accessed August 16, 2013.

273. Ibid.

274. Ibid.

275. Ibid.

276. Adil Al-Safti, "Getting Rid of the Bush doctrine – A Task Awaiting the Congress," [in Arabic] *Al-Ittihad,* Opinion Page, June 8, 2007, p. 33.

277. Adil Al-Safti, "Power Politics – from Truman to the Bush Doctrine," *Al-Ittihad*, [in Arabic] Opinion Page, (Abu Dhabi: August 3, 2007); (http://www.alittihad.ae/wajhatdetails.php?id=30075).

278. "The Truman Doctrine," *History Learning Site* (http://www.history learningsite.co.uk/truman_doctrine.htm); "The Truman Doctrine," *Johndclare.net* (http://www.johndclare.net/cold_war8_TrumanDoctrine.htm).

279. Adil Al-Safti, "Getting Rid of the Bush doctrine – A Task Awaiting the Congress," op. cit., p. 33.

280. Qutaishat, op. cit.

281. Muhammad Madi, "The Dominance of the Neoconservatives," [in Arabic] *swissinfo.ch* July 12, 2003 (http://www.swissinfo.ch/ara/detail/content.html?cid=3307084), accessed August 16, 2013.

282. The Neoconservative current in the United States of America consists of many political figures and intellectuals who theorize on ways and strategies that ensure American global dominance in the 21st century. The role of the Neoconservatives in the US policy-making process became well-established in the aftermath of the September 11, 2001 attacks. For more information, see: Ahmad Mahir, "The Neoconservatives in America – What is their Philosophy and How Do They Plan?" [in Arabic] *Al-Sharq Al-Awsat,* no. 9642, April 22, 2005 (http://aawsat.com/leader.asp?section=3&article=294962&issueno=9642), accessed October 30, 2013. Also see: Ibrahim Khalid, "Main Figures in the Neoconservatives Current," *Al-Sharq Al-Wasat,* no. 1642, March 6, 2007 (http://www.alwasatnews.com/1642/news/read/219544/1.html), accessed October 30, 2013.

283. Korolev, op. cit., p. 188.

284. Ibid., p. 190.

285. Ibid., p. 192.

286. "Cheney, Richard Bruce," Biographical Directory of the United States of America Congress (http://bioguide.congress.gov/scripts/biodisplay.pl?index=C000344).

287. For more on the speech of former American President George W. Bush (Jr.) at the General Assembly of the United Nations in September 2002, see: (http://archives.cnn.com/2002/US/09/12/bush.transcript).

288. Muhammad Al-Sayyid Saleem, "The Reality and Future of Alliances in Asia," *Al-Siyassa Al-Dawliyya* no. 183 (January 2011); (http://

digital.ahram.org.eg/articles.aspx?Serial=409097&eid=306), accessed August 16, 2013.

289. In April 2001, a mid-air collision occurred between a US Navy Lockheed EP-3 surveillance plane and two Chinese fighter aircraft which were intercepting it. As a result, one of the Chinese aircraft crashed into the sea and its pilot was lost. The US Navy aircraft made an emergency landing at an airport on Hainan Island and its crew were safe. The incident, known as the "Hainan Island incident," led to a diplomatic row between the United States of America and China. For more information, see: (http://defense-arab.com/vb/threads/59636/), accessed October 30, 2013.

290. For more about the Hainan incident, see: "China Resentfully Rejects an Offer from Washington to Compensate it for the Hainan Incident," *Al-Sharq Al-Awsat* August 13, 2001 (http://www.aawsat.com/details.asp?issueno=8070&article=52257).

291. Muhammad Saad Abu Aamood, "Towards a Multipolar International System: China-US Relations," *Al-Siyassa Al-Dawliyya*, no. 145, vol. 37 (July 2001), p. 101.

292. Joseph Nye, Hillary Clinton, Tim Dunne and Kledja Mulaj, "The Future of American Power," *International Studies*, issue no. 105 (Abu Dhabi: The Emirates Center for Strategic Studies and Research, 2012), p. 46.

293. Korolev, op. cit., p. 266.

294. For more about the new American century, see Information Clearing House (http://www.informationclearinghouse.info/article1665.htm).

295. Jacques, 2010, op. cit, p. 13.

296. Korolev, op. cit., p. 270.

297. Ibid., p. 272.

298. For more information on the American conservative theorist Charles Krauthammer, see: "Charles Krauthammer: Prize Writer," *Mitchellbard.com* (http://www.mitchellbard.com/articles/kraut.html); "Charles Krauthammer," *Washington Post* Opinions, February 24, 2011 (http://www.washingtonpost.com/charles-krauthammer/2011/02/24/ADJkW7B_page.html).

299. Jacques, 2010, op. cit, p. 14.

300. Joseph S. Nye, *Bound to Lead: The Changing Nature of American Power* (New York, NY: Basic Books, 1991), pp. 173–201; and Joseph S. Nye, *Soft Power: The Means to Success in World Politics*, Muhammad Tawfeeq Al-Bujairmi (trans.); (Riyadh: Obeikan Publishing, 2004).

301. Mu'taz Salama, *Political Reform: American Policy and the Arab Responses*, Strategic Papers Series, No. 153, (Cairo: Al-Ahram Center for Strategic Studies, 2005); (http://acpss.ahram.org.eg/ahram/2001/1/1/SBOK48.HTM), accessed August 19, 2013.

302. This was a famous question circulating in American intellectual and research circles immediately after the September 11, 2001 attacks. It was first posed by President George W. Bush (Jr.), when asked in one of his speeches, and he answered: "I can't understand why they hate us; because I know how good people we are." For more about the September 11 attacks and their effect on the American policy, see: Al-Shaikh Jaafar Hassan Atreesi, *Americanization of Nations and Clash of Civilizations: The New World Order and Solo Leadership* [in Arabic]; (Beirut: Dar Al-Hadi, 2002), pp. 192–291.

303. Majid Ahmad Al-Zamili, [in Arabic] "Diplomacy and its Impact on International Relations," *Al-Hiwar Al-Mutamaddin* no. 4223, September 22, 2013 (http://www.ahewar.org/debat/show.art.asp?aid =379192), accessed October 30, 2013; and "Djerejian Chairs a Committee to Review Public Relations Diplomacy to Improve

America's Image in the Muslim World," *Al-Sharq Al-Awsat* no. 8957, June 7, 2003 (http://www.aawsat.com/details.asp?issueno=8800& article=175177#.UnJS0Plgd8E), accessed October 30, 2013.

304. Tamara Cofman Wittes, "The New US Proposal for a Greater Middle East Initiative: An Evaluation," *Middle East Memo*, no. 2, May 10, 2004 (http://www.brookings.edu/research/papers/2004/05/10middle east-wittes).

305. For the text of the Greater Middle East Project, see CNN [in Arabic]; (http://arabic.cnn.com/2004/arab.2004/3/1/grandmiddleeast.document).

306. William Quandt, "Greater Middle East Initiative – Illusion of Slogans and Difficulty of Trade-offs," [in Arabic] *Al-Ittihad*, Opinion Pages, (Abu Dhabi: March 7, 2006); (http://www.alittihad.ae/wajhatdetails. php?id=18627).

307. See the biography of President Barack Hussein Obama at: The White House, "President Barack Hussein Obama" (http://www.whitehouse. gov/administration/president-obama).

308. Jawdat Hoshiar, "Joseph Nye and the Theory of Soft Power," *Al-Hiwar Al-Mutamaddin* July 18, 2013 (http://www.m.ahewar.org/s. asp?aid=369043&r=0&cid=0&u=&i=0&q=).

309. Nye, *Soft Power: The Means to Success in World Politics*, op. cit., pp. 19–63.

310. Yahya Al-Yahyawi, "Obama and the Concept of Smart Power," *Hespress* March 10, 2009 (http://hespress.com/opinions/11560.html), accessed March 18, 2013.

311. Tim Dunne and Klejda Mulaj, "America after Iraq," *International Affairs* (November 2010), op. cit., p. 45.

312. Ibid.

313. Ibid.

314. This cost includes about $2 trillion in direct expenses related to *Operation Enduring Freedom* (OEF) which started in Afghanistan in 2001, *Operation Iraqi Freedom* (OIF) which started in Iraq in 2003 and *Operation New Dawn* (OND) which started in Afghanistan in 2010. These direct expenses cover direct combat operations, reconstruction efforts, and other direct war spending by the Department of Defense, State Department, Department of Veterans Affairs and US Social Security Administration. In addition to that, total cost include costs of long-term health care; cost of disability allowance for active-duty service members, veterans and their families; costs of military replenishment, in addition to social and economic burden on the US economy. See: Linda J. Bilmes, "The Financial Legacy of Iraq and Afghanistan: How Wartime Spending Decisions Will Constrain Future National Security Dudgets," Harvard Kennedy School, *Faculty Research Working Paper Series*, RWP13-003, March 2013, pp 1–2 (https://research.hks.harvard.edu/publications/workingpapers/citation.aspx?PubId=8956).

315. Dunne and Mulaj, 2010, op. cit., p. 59.

316. Ibid.

317. In 2008 the Brookings Institution argued that US foreign policy should undergo a change at the global level in the post-Bush era. The change should involve ending the militarization of US foreign policy and transforming the United States of America into a reliable international partner, through various mechanisms entirely within the bounds of soft power, notably concentrating on international peace-keeping efforts.

318. Hillary Clinton was the United States of America Secretary of State from January 20, 2009 to February 1, 2013.

319. Hillary Clinton, "Leading Through Civilian Power: Redefining American Diplomacy and Development," *The Future of American Power*, op. cit., p. 25.

320. For more about Joseph Nye's concept of smart power, see: Joseph Nye, "Smart Power," *The Huffington Post* (http://www.huffington post.com/joseph-nye/smart-power_b_74725.html).

321. Robert Gates was the United States of America Secretary of Defense from December 18, 2006 to 2011. For more details, see: "Robert Gates," *Biography.com* (http://www.biography.com/people/robert-gates-40993). His book, *Duty: Memoirs of a Secretary at War*, was published by Knopf in 2014.

322. Hillary Clinton, "Leading Through Civilian Power: Redefining American Diplomacy and Development," op. cit., p. 25.

323. For more about the United States of America Agency for International Development (USAID), see: (http://www.usaid.gov).

324. Hillary Clinton, "Leading Through Civilian Power: Redefining American Diplomacy and Development," op. cit., p. 43.

325. John F. Kennedy was the 35th US President serving from January 20, 1961 to November 22, 1963.

326. Norman Borlaug was an American professor and considered the father of the 'Green Revolution.' He studied at the University of Minnesota and worked at the Rockefeller Foundation where he carried out several research projects for the International Maize and Wheat Improvement Center. He was awarded the Nobel Peace Prize in 1970. The Green Revolution helped in doubling agricultural produce between 1960 and 1990, and benefited Asia, Africa and Latin America. The Nobel Foundation credited him with saving the lives of hundreds of millions from starvation worldwide. The Green Revolution prevented the occurrence of a global famine in the 20th

century. For more about Norman Borlaug, see: "Norman Borlaug – Biographical," The Nobel Prize (http://www.nobelprize.org/nobel_ prizes/peace/laureates/1970/borlaug-bio.html).

327. Although the United States of America sought to partly hand over leadership of the military operation in Libya to NATO, it seemed that the Allies were reluctant to take full responsibility, and left the US military to shoulder the bulk of responsibility for operations, particularly in regard to leadership, command and control, and information gathering.

328. Fareed Zakaria, "Does the US Really Want to Own Libya?" [in Arabic] *Al-Sharq Al-Awsat* April 1, 2011, no. 11812 (http://www. aawsat.com/leader.asp?section=3&issueno=11812&article=615259), accessed August 16, 2013.

329. Dunne and Mulaj, 2010, op. cit., p. 51.

330. Stephen M. Walt, "The End of the American Era," *The National Interest*, October 25, 2011 (http://nationalinterest.org/article/the-end-theamerican-era-6037).

331. Linda J. Bilmes, "The Financial Legacy of Iraq and Afghanistan: How Wartime Spending Decisions Will Constrain Future National Security Budgets," Harvard Kennedy School, *Faculty Research Working Paper Series*, RWP13-003, March 2013, pp 1–2 (https://research.hks. harvard.edu/publications/workingpapers/citation.aspx?PubId=8956).

332. An interview with Stephen Walt by Jacqueline Shoen, "Stephen Walt Calls for Balance of Power in Politics: Iran and the Bomb"; *Al-Majalla*, December 30, 2010 (http://www.majalla.com/arb/2010/12/ article55226239), accessed March 18, 2013.

333. Ibid.

Chapter IV

1.   Conan Fischer and Alan Sharp (eds.), *After the Versailles Treaty: Enforcement, Compliance, Contested Identities* (New York, NY: Routledge, 2009), p. 5.

2.   Ibid., pp. 11–17

3.   The Treaty of Versailles required Germany to accept responsibility for the war and its effects, and to pay financial compensation for all damage suffered by the civilian population and governments of the Allied Powers and their property during the period of the war with Germany and its allies. The treaty also forced Germany to make substantial territorial concessions by handing over a number of provinces to France, Belgium, Poland and Czechoslovakia, and not to seek any union with Austria. It imposed controls and restrictions on the German military, forcing it to disarm, dismantle military fortifications, and disband its airforce, heavy artillery and submarine forces. It required that Germany dismantle its ammunition factories and submit its naval fleet to the Allied powers. Germany was also compelled to cede control of its colonies to the Allied powers, to build warships for the Allied powers to replace the ones it sank, and provide France with huge amounts of coal to compensate for the mines it destroyed. A committee from the Allied forces was formed to oversee these military restrictions and to strip the German armed forces of their military character. Ibid., pp. 103–107.

4.   Louis Hyman, "How Did World War II End the Great Depression?" Bloomberg, December 16, 2001 (http://www.bloomberg.com/news/2011-12-16/how-did-world-war-ii-end-the-great-depression-echoes.html).

5.   For more details about the plan, see: Martin A. Schain, *The Marshall Plan Fifty Years Later* (New York, NY: Palgrave MacMillan, 2001), p. 149.

6.   Ibid., pp 29–34.

7. See: International Monetary Fund (IMF), "The End of the Bretton Woods System (1972–81)" (http://www.imf.org/external/about/histend.htm).

8. Ibid.

9. For more details, see: David M. Koltz and Fred Weir, *Revolution from Above: The Demise of the Soviet System* (New York, NY: Routledge, 1997), pp. 71–91.

10. For more details see: Barry Naughton, et al., "A Political Economy of China's Economic Transition," in Loren Brandt and Thomas G. Rawski (eds.), *China's Great Economic Transformation* (Cambridge: Cambridge University Press, 2008), pp. 91–135.

11. Sovereign Wealth Fund Institute, "Sovereign Fund Rankings," September 3, 2013 (http://www.swfinstitute.org/fund-rankings).

12. "Ins and outs: Acronyms BRIC Out All Over," *The Economist*, September 18, 2008 (http://www. economist.com/node/12080703).

13. International Monetary Fund (IMF), "World Economic Outlook Database," April 2013 (http://www.imf.org/external/pubs/ft/weo/2013/01/weodata/index.aspx).

14. Ibid.

15. Robert Kagan, *The World America Made* (New York, NY: Knopf Doubleday Publishing Group, 2012), pp. 130–133.

16. For more information about the role of innovation as a driver of economy see: Bronwyn H. Hall and Jacques Mairesse, "Empirical Studies of Innovation in the Knowledge Driven Economy: An Introduction," NBER Working Paper Series, Working Paper no. 12320, National Bureau of Economic Research, June 2006 (http://www.nber.org/papers/w12320).

17. For more information, see: John Markoff, "Searching for Silicon Valley," *New York Times*, April 17, 2009 (http://travel.nytimes.com/2009/04/17/travel/escapes/17Amer.html?pagewanted=1&_r=0), D9.

18. For more on the 20 biggest tech firms in the Fortune 500 see: Rick Whiting, "The 25 Biggest Tech Companies on the Fortune 500," CRN, May 14, 2013 (http://www.crn.com/slide-shows/channel-programs/240154736/the-25-biggest-tech-companies-on-the-fortune-500.htm).

19. SelectUSA, "The Software and Information Technology Services Industry in the United States of America" (http://selectusa.commerce. gov/industry-snapshots/software-and-information-technology-services-industry-united-states).

20. International Association of Financial Engineers (IAFE), "What is a Financial Engineer?" IAFE Guide to Financial Engineering Programs (http://www.iafeguide.org/financial-engineer.php).

21. For more on hydraulic fracturing see: Carl T. Montgomery and Michael B. Smith, "Hydraulic Fracturing: History of an Enduring Technology," December 2010 (http://www.spe.org/jpt/print/archives/2010/12/10Hydraulic.pdf), pp. 26–41.

22. International Monetary Fund (IMF), World Economic Outlook Database, April 2013 (http://www.imf.org/external/pubs/ft/weo/2013/01/weodata/index.aspx).

23. IMF, op. cit.

24. In finance, Black Monday refers to Monday, October 19, 1987. The stock market crash began in Hong Kong and spread around the world as markets opened causing a 22.61% drop in the Dow Jones Industrial Average index, which was considered the biggest drop ever in history.

25. IMF, op. cit.

26. According to the IMF's World Economic Outlook Database updated in April 2013, China was in eighth place globally in terms of GDP denominated in US dollars, behind the United States of America, Japan, Germany, France, Italy, the UK and Canada; but it climbed to second place in 2010, replacing Japan; IMF, op. cit.

27. Ibid.

28. Ibid.

29. Ibid.

30. "Surging Wages Threaten Economy's Competitiveness," *China Daily*, April 10, 2012 (http://www.chinadaily.com.cn/business/2013-04/10/content_16390012.htm).

31. "Europe and the United States of America Launch Negotiations on the Largest Free Trade Zone in the World" [in Arabic], *Al-Khaleej* (UAE), June 18, 2013 (http://www.alkhaleej. ae/portal/e38575a3-ba54-4004-ade2-79061a2a9718.aspx).

32. "China Starts First Steps in Internationalization of the Yuan and Allows its Circulation in the United States of America" [in Arabic], *Al-Sharq Al-Awsat*, January 13, 2011 (http://www.aawsat.com/details.asp?section=6&issueno=11734&article=603581#.UfYfDdLTyE4).

33. IMF, op. cit.

34. Institute of New Economic Thinking, "Why is China Auditing Local Government Debt Again?" July 29, 2013 (http://ineteconomics.org/china-economics-seminar-0/why-china-audit-local-government-debt-again).

35. Fareed Zakaria, "Can China Change its Economic Course?" *The Washington Post*, WP Opinions, July 17, 2013 (http://articles.washingtonpost.com/2013-07-17/opinions/40632962_1_china-s-growth-gdp).

36. Yanqing Wu, "Resource and Energy Problems in China," Energy and Environmental Studies of Shanghai Jiao Tong University (http://ncrs.cm.kyushu-u.ac.jp/assets/files/Newsletter/volume_3/jp/NCRS_NLJ Vol3_19SJTU.pdf), p. 4.

37. Richard Lester and Edward Steinfeld, "China's Real Energy Crisis," *Harvard Asia Pacific Review*, vol. 9, no. 1 (Winter 2007); (http://www.hcs.harvard.edu/~hapr/winter07_gov/lester.pdf), p. 35.

38. Ian Taylor, *China's Oil Diplomacy in Africa* [in Arabic], International Studies no. 63 (Abu Dhabi: The Emirates Center for Strategic Studies and Research [ECSSR], 2007), p. 16.

39. "Difference Engine: Hackers' Paradise," *The Economist*, March 11, 2013 (http://www.economist.com/blogs/babbage/2013/03/crimeware ?fsrc=scn/tw/te/bl/differenceenginehackersparadise).

40. Jennifer Booton, "Major Corporations attacked in Historic Hacking Case," Fox Business, July 25, 2013 (http://www.foxbusiness.com/ technology/2013/07/25/major-companies-victims-in-biggest-hacking-case).

41. "Developing by Relying on its Own Strength, Reform and Innovation," China Internet Information Center (http://www.china. org.cn/english/features/book/152764.htm).

42. Barry Eichengreen, "Can the Euro Area Hit the Rewind Button?" University of California at Berkley, July 23, 2011 (http://emlab. berkeley.edu/~eichengr/can_euro_area_7-23-11.pdf), p. 2.

43. Larry Elliott, "Eurozone Crisis Demands One Banking Policy, One Fiscal Policy – and One Voice," *The Guardian*, Economics Blog, April 1, 2013 (http://www.theguardian.com/business/economics-blog/ 2013/apr/01/eurozone-crisis-banking-fiscal-union).

44. David Wessel, "Euro Zone Confronts Limits of 'One-Size-Fits-All' Policies," *The Wall Street Journal*, March 17, 2011 (http://online.wsj. com/article/SB10001424052748704396504576204531942846492.html).

45. "Eurozone Crisis: Beggar Thyself and Thy Neighbor," Research on Money and Finance (http://researchonmoneyandfinance.org/media/ reports/eurocrisis/e_summary_eng.pdf), p. 2.

46. European Union (EU), "Euro Area Unemployment Rate at 12.1%," Eurostat News Release No. 126/2013, August 30, 2013. (http://epp. eurostat.ec.europa.eu/cache/ITY_PUBLIC/3-30082013-AP/EN/3-300 82013-AP-EN.PDF), p. 4.

47. IMF, op. cit.

48. See: European Union (EU), "Monthly and Accumulated Crude Oil Imports (volumes and prices) by EU and non EU Country," Market Observatory for Energy, European Commission, Directorate-General for Energy (http://ec.europa.eu/energy/observatory/oil/import_export _en.htm).

49. IMF, op. cit.

50. Simon Romero and William Neuman, "Sweeping Protests in Brazil Pull in an Array of Grievances," *The New York Times*, June 20, 2013 (http://www.nytimes.com/2013/06/21/world/americas/brazil-protests. html?pagewanted=all&_r=0).

51. Juan de Onis, "Brazil's Big Moment," *Foreign Affairs*, vol. 87, no. 6 (November/December 2008); (http://www.foreignaffairs.com/articles/ 64610/juan-de-onis/brazils-big-moment).

52. World Energy Council (WEC), "Survey of Energy Resources 2010," November 2010 (http://www.worldenergy.org/publications/3040.asp).

53. Amy Myers Jaffe, "The Americas, Not the Middle East, will be the World Capital of Energy," *Foreign Policy*, vol. 90, no. 5, September/ October 2011 (http://www.foreignpolicy.com/articles/2011/08/15/the_ americas_not_the_middle_east_will_be_the_world_capital_of_energy).

54. The term "Lost Decade" was initially used to refer to the period following the burst of the asset price bubble in Japan between 1991 and 2000, but that period was then expanded with the continuation of weak economic performance to include the period 2001–2010, becoming known as the "Lost Two Decades."

55 . "Not so Super: The "Third Arrow" of Reform has Fallen well short of its Target; Time for Shinzo Abe to Rethink," *The Economist,* Abenomics, June 15, 2013 (http://www.economist.com/news/ leaders/21579464-third-arrow-reform-has-fallen-well-short-its-target-time-shinzo-abe-rethink-not).

56. For the categorization of innovative sources of hydrocarbon energy, see: WEC, op. cit., pp. 93, 123, 151.

57. BP, *BP Statistical Review of World Energy*, June 2013 "Historical Data Workbook" (http://www. bp.com/statisticalreview).

58. Ibid.

59. Ibid.

60. Ibid.

61. Ibid.

62. Ibid.

63. For more about shale gas boom in the United States of America and its impact on the economy, see: PricewaterhouseCoopers (PwC), "Shale Gas: A Renaissance in US Manufacturing?" December 2011 (http://www.pwc.com/en_US/us/industrial-products/assets/pwc-shale-gas-us-manufacturing-renaissance.pdf), pp. 2–6.

64. IMF, op. cit.

65. WEC, op. cit

66. Ibid.

67. US Department of Energy (DoE) / Energy Information Administration (EIA), "Electricity in the United States of America" (http://www.eia.gov/energyexplained/index.cfm?page=electricity_in the_united_states).

68. Ibid.

69. Jaffe, op. cit.

70. US Department of Energy (DoE) / Energy Information Administration (EIA), "US Imports by Country of Origin" (http://www.eia.gov/dnav/pet/pet_move_impcus_a2_nus_ep 00_im0_mbbl_m.htm).

71. US Department of Energy (DoE) / Energy Information Administration (EIA), "China: Analysis" (http://www.eia.gov/countries/cab.efm?fips =CH).

72. "China Secures Larger Turkmen Gas Supplies," Reuters, September 3, 2013 (http://uk.reuters.com/article/2013/09/03/gas-turkmenistan-china-idUKL6N0GZ31W20130903).

73. US DoE/EIA, "China: Analysis" op. cit.

74. Ibid.

75. EU, Market Observatory for Energy, op. cit. For expected changes in patters of consumption and imports by 2035, see: US Department of Energy (DoE) / Energy Information Administration (EIA), *Annual Energy Outlook 2012* (http://www.eia.gov/forecasts/aeo/pdf10383 (2012).pdf), pp. 74–75.

76. EU, Market Observatory for Energy, op. cit.

77. Ibid.

78. Ibid.

79. BP, op.cit.

80. Ibid.

81. US DoE/EIA, *AEO 2012*, op. cit., pp. 74–75.

82. BP, op. cit.

83. Ibid.

84. Ibid.

85. US Department of the Interior, "About Oil Shale," Oil Shale and Tar Sands Programmatic EIS (http://ostseis.anl.gov/guide/oilshale/index.cfm).

86. PwC, op. cit., pp. 2–6.

87. WEC, op. cit.

88. Ibid., p. 141.

89. Ibid., p. 123.

90. Ibid., p. 139.

91. Ibid., p. 110

92. Ibid.

93. US DoE/EIA, *AEO 2012*, op. cit., p. 210.

94. Jaffe, op. cit.

95. US Department of Energy (DoE) / Energy Information Administration (EIA), *International Energy Outlook, 2011*, p. 26 (http://www.eia. gov/forecasts/archive/ieo11/pdf/0484(2011).pdf).

96. For categorization of innovative sources of hydrocarbon Energy, see: PwC, op. cit., pp. 93,123, 151.

97. US Department of Energy (DoE) / Energy Information Administration (EIA), "World Shale Gas Resources: An Initial Assessment of 14 Regions outside the United States of America," April 2011 (http://www.eia.gov/analysis/studies/worldshalegas/archive/2011/pdf/ fullreport.pdf), p. 4.

98. Ibid.

99. US EIA, *IEO*, 2011, op. cit., p. 50.

100. Ibid.

101. BP, op. cit.

102. Ibid.

103. Ibid.

104. Ibid.

105. Ibid.

106. Ibid.

107. Ibid.

108. Ibid.

109. Ibid.

110. Ibid.

111. Ibid.

112. Kagan, op. cit., p. 76.

113. Such companies include: BP; Shell; Gulf Oil; Texaco; ExxonMobil; Chevron and Total.

114. Steve Coll, *Private Empire: ExxonMobil and American Power* (New York, NY: Penguin, 2012), p. 318.

115. Ibid.

116. Shell has spent $2.2 billion developing alternative energies, carbon capture and storage (CCS) technologies, and carbon dioxide-related R&D over the past five years. For more details, see: Shell, "About Shell" (http://www. shell.com/global/aboutshell/at-a-glance.html).

117. Tom Gjelten, "Venezuela's Next Leader Faces Tough Choice on Oil Program," NPR, April 11, 2013 (http://www.npr.org/2013/04/11/17 6843567/venezuela-s-next-leader-faces-tough-choice-on-oil-program).

118. As mentioned above, electronic espionage has caused millions of dollars in losses, and international efforts are underway to counter it. Such efforts may take the form of lawsuits, as in the US in June 2013, when the government filed suits against individuals involved in worldwide hacking dating back to 2007 that targeted international companies, including major US companies. For more details, see: Booton, op. cit.

119. Richard McGregor, "US Budget Politics: America Goes Dark," *Financial Times* October 4, 2013 (http://www.ft.com/cms/s/0/83610 290-2cd6-11e3-a0ac-00144feab7de.html#axzz2h73gcJkT).

120. IMF, op. cit.

121. Linda J. Bilmes, "The Financial Legacy of Iraq and Afghanistan: How Wartime Spending Decisions Will Constrain Future National Security Budgets," Harvard Kennedy School, Faculty Research Working Paper

Series, RWP13-003, March 2013, pp 1–2 (https://research.hks. harvard.edu/publications/ workingpapers/citation.aspx?PubId=8956).

122. IMF, op. cit.

123. Ibid.

124. For more about the "fiscal cliff" and related issues, see: John Wasik, "Fiscal Cliff Follies: Four Myths," *Forbes*, November 29, 2013 (http://www.forbes.com/sites/johnwasik/2012/11/29/fiscal-cliff-follies-four-myths).

125. For further details on government debt ratings, see the websites of the three major rating agencies: Standard and Poor's (http://www.standardandpoors.com/ratings/en/us); Moody's (https://www.moodys.com/researchandratings); and Fitch (http://www.fitchratings.com).

126. For details about the disagreement between the Republicans and the Democrats over fiscal policy, see: Connie Cass, "Fiscal Cliff: Why Can't Democrats and Republicans Agree?" Associated Press (AP), *USA Today*, December 31, 2012 (http://www.usatoday.com/story/news/politics/2012/12/29/fiscal-cliff-guide/1798027).

127. IMF, op. cit.

128. "Audit Office Shines Light on Local Government Debt," *The Wall Street Journal*, June 11, 2013 (http://blogs.wsj.com/chinarealtime/2013/06/11/audit-office-shines-light-on-local-government-debt/).

129. Zhang Yuwei, "China's US T-bill holdings hit record in May," *China Daily*, July 17, 2013 (http://usa.chinadaily.com.cn/epaper/2013-07/17/content_16787441.htm); and ibid.

130. For more details about the US twin deficits, see: Nouriel Roubini, "The Unsustainability of the US Twin Deficits," CATO Institute (http://www.cato.org/sites/cato.org/files/serials/files/cato-journal/2006/5/cj26n2-13.pdf), pp. 343–356.

131. Michael Stothar, Angela Merkel's Victory Prompts Mixed Response in Europe, *The Financial Times*, September 23, 2013 (http://www.ft.com/intl/cms/s/0/490142a6-2441-11e3-a8f7-00144feab7de.html#axzz2h73gcJkT).

132. European Union (EU), "First Quarter of 2013 Compared with Fourth Quarter of 2012," Eurostat News Release no. 114, July 22, 2013 (http://epp.eurostat.ec.europa.eu/cache/ITY_PUBLIC/2-22072013-AP/EN/2-22072013-AP-EN.PDF), p. 4.

133. European Union (EU), "Euro Area Unemployment Rate at 12.1%," Eurostat News Release, no. 118/2013, July 31, 2013 (http://epp.eurostat.ec.europa.eu/cache/ITY_PUBLIC/3-31072013-BP/EN/3-31072013-BP-EN.PDF).

134. IMF, op. cit.

135. Hiroko Tabuchi, "In Japan, a Tenuous Vow to Cut," *The New York Times*, September 1, 2011 (http://www.nytimes.com/2011/09/02/business/global/japan-seeks-answers-to-debt-load-without-angering-voters.html?pagewanted=all&_r=0).

136. In mid-2013, Standard & Poor's rated Japanese government debt at "AA-," Fitch at "A+" and Moody's at "Aa3."

137. Public Broadcasting Service (PBS), "Russia's Crisis: Will Russia Survive its Economic and Political Crisis?" (http://www.pbs.org/newshour/forum/september98/russia.html).

138. Third World Network, "The Brazilian Economic Crisis" (http://www.twnside.org.sg/title/brazil-cn.htm).

139. IMF, op. cit.

140. Ibid.

141. World Trade Organization (WTO), "Trade Profiles 2013," April 2013 (www.wto.org/english/res_e/booksp_e/anrep_e/trade_profiles13_e.pdf).

142. IMF, op. cit.

143. For more details, see: David Kashi, "Panama Canal Expansion Can Increase US Maritime Industry by Shipyards Building Smaller Vessels to Unload Cargo in a Feeder System or Short Sea Shipping System to East Coast Ports," *International Business Times* August 27, 2013 (http://www.ibtimes.com/panama-canal-expansion-can-increase-us-maritime-industry-shipyards-building-smaller-vessels-unload).

144. For details of the Panama Canal expansion plan, see: Canal De Panmamá, "Proposal for the Expansion of the Panama Canal: 3rd Set of Locks Project," April 24, 2006 (http://www.acp.gob.pa/eng/plan/documentos/propuesta/acp-expansion-proposal.pdf), pp. 3–6.

145. Dexter Roberts, Henry Meyer, and Dorothee Tschampa, "The Silk Railroad of China–Europe Trade," *Businessweek*, December 20, 2012 (http://www.businessweek.com/articles/2012-12-20/the-silk-railroad-of-china-europe-trade).

146. Ghulam Ali, "China's Strategic Interests in Pakistan's Port at Gwadar," East Asia Forum, March 24, 2013 (http://www.eastasia forum.org/2013/03/24/chinas-strategic-interests-in-pakistans-port-at-gwadar).

147. Rebecca Conan, "Chinese Firms to Develop US$20bn Panama Canal Alternative in Hondorus," *Business News Americas*, June 21, 2013 (http://www.bnamericas.com/news/infrastructure/chinese-firm-to-develop-us20bn-panama-canal-alternative-in-honduras1).

148. Adam Williams, "Nicaragua's Canal: Chinese Tycoon Wang Jing Wants to Build It," *Bloomberg Businessweek*, June 27, 2013 (http://www.businessweek.com/articles/2013-06-27/nicaraguas-canal-chinese-tycoon-wang-jing-wants-to-build-it).

Chapter V

1. Nizar Mihoub, *"Public Opinion ... Voice of the People,"* [in Arabic] the International Association of Public Relations, 2012 (http://www. ipra-ar.org/alpha/topic/view.php?id=21), accessed November 26, 2013.

2. Mark Tessler. *Public Opinion in the Middle East*: *Survey Research and Political Orientations of Ordinary Citizens* (Bloomington, IN: Indiana University Press, 2011), p. xii.

3. Ibid.

4. Ibid., p. xi.

5. William Zartman, "Political Science," in Leonard Binder (ed.), *The Study of the Middle East: Research and Scholarship in the Humanities and Social Sciences* (New York, NY: Boulder, 1987); Michael Hudson, "The Political Culture Approach to Arab Democratization," in Rex Brynen, Bahgat Korany, and Paul Noble (eds.), *Political Liberalization and Democratization in the Arab World* (Boulder, CO: Lynne Rienner Publishing, 1995), p. 69.

6. The development and evolution witnessed in the UAE provides an apt example of this; Osman Siraj Eldeen Fateh Al Rahman, "Social Welfare between the International Conventions and Treaties and the Domestic laws: United Arab Emirates as a Model" [in Arabic], *Strategic Visions*, vol. 1, issue 4, Emirates Center for Strategic Studies and Research, September 2013, pp. 52–69; and Yousef Al-Bastanji, "UNDP Issues its Global Development Report from Abu Dhabi: UAE Ranked First in the Arab Region, 30th Globally in terms of Human Development" [in Arabic], *Al-Ittihad*, January 9, 2012); (http://www. alittihad.ae/details.php?id=2633&y=2012).

7. Shibley Telhami, *The World Through Arab Eyes: Arab Public Opinion and the Reshaping of the Middle East* (New York, NY: Basic Books, June 2013), p. 5.

8. For more details about ECSSR's activities, see: (http://www.ecssr. ac.ae/).

9. Mark Lynch, "Why Arab Public Opinion Matters," *Foreign Policy Review*, August 3, 2013, p. 1.

10. Ibid., p. 2.

11. E.G. Carmines and R.A. Zeller, *Reliability and Validity Assessment* (Newbury Park, CA: Sage Publications, 1991); (http://www.uky.edu/~clthyn2/PS671/carmines_zeller_671.pdf).

12. From the speech of H.H Lt. General Sheikh Saif bin Zayed Al Nahyan, Deputy Prime Minister and Minister of the Interior, at the closing session of the first Government Summit, February 12, 2013 in Dubai, United Arab Emirates. "Saif bin Zayed: 'Our Wise Leadership Turned Visions into Strategic Decisions'," [in Arabic], *Al-Ittihad*, February 13, 2013); (http://www.alittihad.ae/details.php?id=15512&y=2013), accessed October 30, 2013.

13. Sidney Verba, Nancy Burns and Kay Lehman Schlozman, "Knowing and Caring about Politics: Gender and Political Engagement," *Journal of Politics*, vol. 59, issue 4 (November 1997), pp. 1051–1072 (http://dx.doi.org/10.2307/2998592).

14. "Women Worldwide know less about Politics than Men," Economic and Social Research Council, UK, July 3, 2013 (http://www.esrc.ac.uk/news-and-events/press-releases/26789/women_worldwide_know_less_about_politics_ than_men.aspx); Richard R. Lau and David P. Redlawsk, "Older but Wiser? Effects of Age on Political Cognition," *The Journal of Politics*, vol. 70, Issue 1 (January 2008), pp. 168–185.

15. Pew Research Center, "25-Nation Pew Global Attitudes Survey," Pew Global Attitude Project, July 23, 2009 (http://www.pewglobal.org/files/2009/07/Pew-Global-Attitudes-Spring-2009-Report-1-July-23-11am.pdf).

16. Steven Kull, quoted in: "People in Muslim Nations Conflicted About UN," WorldPublicOpinion.org, December 2, 2008 (http://www.worldpublicopinion.org/pipa/articles/btunitednationsra/575.php).

17. Ibid.

18. Ibid.

19. Ibid.

20. Ibid.

21. Ibid.

22. Ibid.

23. Pew Research Center, "25-Nation Pew Global Attitudes Survey," Pew Global Attitude Project, July 23, 2009, op. cit. (http://www.pew global.org/files/2009/07/Pew-Global-Attitudes-Spring-2009-Report-1-July-23-11am.pdf).

24. James Crotty, "Structural Causes of the Global Financial Crisis: A Critical Assessment of the New Financial Architecture," *Cambridge Journal of Economics* no. 33, 2009, pp. 563–580.

25. Seth Carus, "Chemical Weapons in the Middle East," *Policy Focus* no. 9, Washington Institute for Near East Policy, December 1988, (http://www.washingtoninstitute.org/policy-analysis/view/chemical-weapons-in-the-middle-east).

26. "The Nuclear Question in the Middle East," Working Group Summary Report no. 4, Center for International and Regional Studies, Georgetown University School of Foreign Service, Qatar, 2012 (http://www12.georgetown.edu/sfs/qatar/cirs/NuclearQuestionSummary Report.pdf).

27. The focus on the struggle among international powers and their impact on the Arab region does not exclude the fact that there are other internal reasons fueling differences within the Arab system.

28. Bertelsmann Stiftung, "Topics: Encouraging Social Change," January 2008 (http://www.bertelsmann-stiftung.de/cps/rde/xbcr/SID-746191A F-2CA45334/bst/xcms_bst_dms_23678_23679_2.pdf)

29. Ibid.

30. Ibid.

31. Ibid.

Chapter VI

1. Mona Hamdan, "Will Syria Join the List of US Military Interventions" [in Arabic] *Al Hayat*, July 28, 2013 (http://alhayat.com/Details/545929), accessed September 22, 2013.

2. The White House, *National Security Strategy*, May 2010 (http://www.whitehouse.gov/sites/default/files/rss_viewer/national_security_strategy.pdf).

3. Ibid., pp. 41–49.

4. Joseph S. Nye, "The Future of American Power: Dominance and Decline in Perspective," *Foreign Affairs*, vol. 89, issue 6 (November/December 2010), pp. 2–11.

5. Paul Kennedy, *The Rise and Fall of the Great Powers* (London: Fontana Press, 1989), pp. 1–17. Also see: Amr Abdel-Ati, "American Unilateralism between Continuity and Demise" [in Arabic], *Al-Siyassa Al-Dawliya*, Issue 173, (Cairo: July 2008), p. 223.

6. United Nations Development Program, *Human Development Report 2013: The Rise of the South; Human Progress in a Diverse World* (New York, NY: UN publications, 2013), p. 1.

7. Arvind Subramanian, *Eclipse: Living in the Shadow of China's Economic Dominance* (Washington, DC: Peterson Institute for International Economics, 2013), pp. 89–108.

8. UNDP, op. cit., p. 2.

9. Elias Hanna, "Institutionalization of the Bush Doctrine" [in Arabic], AlJazeera.net, October 3, 2004 (http://www.aljazeera.net/opinions/pages/165e161b-e5c9-41b1-bcf4-b2850fd2287a), accessed October 28, 2013.

10. Mounir Mahmoud Badawi Elsayed, "Modern Trends in the Study of the International System since the End of the Cold War" [in Arabic], paper presented to the Standing Committee on Political Science, Faculty of Commerce, Assiut University, 2004, p. 7.

11. Ismail Sabri Moukalled, *International Political Relations: Theory and Reality* [in Arabic]; (Assiut: Assiut University, 2007), pp. 56–57.

12. In this context, we may refer to the US position towards the popular protests that have occurred in some Arab countries in recent years, as a result of which the administration of President Barack Hussein Obama was forced to abandon historic allies such as former Egyptian President Hosni Mubarak, and to respond to the demands of the Egyptian street at the time, out of its concern over its image as a sponsor of freedom and democratic values.

13. The Middle East Partnership Initiative (MEPI), "Leaders for Democracy Fellowship Program" (http://mepi.state.gov/opportunities/mepi-exchange-programs/leaders-for-democracy-fellowship.html).

14. Ibid.

15. Al Jazeera Centre for Studies, book revision: "Global Trends 2030: Alternative Worlds," [in Arabic] reviewed by Walid Abdulhay, March 25, 2013, p. 4.

16. The sixth special session of the United Nations General Assembly was held on April 1974; on May 1, 1974, two documents were released: the first included a declaration on the establishment of a new international economic system, and the second was an agenda for the establishment of such a system, but the intention was to achieve economic integration at the regional level and promote active attempts to establish economic groupings for specific goals. The international economy remained under exclusive US dominance until, after more than two decades, China began to take a greater share of this dominance.

17. For more details on the rise of emerging economies and their impact on the global economic system, see: "The Emerging Economies are Demanding a Greater Role in Financial Policies" [in Arabic], BBC Arabic, September 4, 2009 (http://www.bbc.co.uk/arabic/business/

2009/09/090904_ah_emerging_economies_tc2.shtml), accessed September 22, 2013.

18. Despite the cohesion of the Eurozone, which has avoided disintegration and collapse, European monetary union still faces many challenges. Meanwhile the Japanese economy continues to suffer the effects of its own problems.

19. Sovereign Wealth Fund Institute, "Fund Rankings" (http://www. swfinstitute.org/fund-rankings/), accessed December 3, 2013.

20. For more information on developments and interactions in the new world order, see: Mohammad Medhat Ghassan, "Multinational Companies and State Sovereignty," op. cit., pp. 58-60; also see Benn Steil and Manuel Hinds, "Money, Markets, and Sovereignty" [trans. in Arabic]; (Abu Dhabi: The Emirates Center for strategic Studies and Research, 2013).

21. UNDP, op. cit., p. 5.

22. This influence is mainly associated with the fact that these international financial institutions are one of the tools of US hegemony over the 'financial nervous system' of the new world order.

23. It has been noted that the corridors of the World Trade Organization (WTO) in recent years have echoed with complaints and criticisms directed against the restrictions imposed by some countries on the freedom of trade and movement of investment and financial flows— frustrating the aim of achieving greater flow and liquidity in globalized economic activity. For more information see: "The Constant and the Changing in the Global Economic System," [in Arabic], *Lebanese National Defense Magazine*, October 2000, pp. 2–8.

24. The Cold War ended with the Malta Summit between Mikhail Gorbachev and George H.W. Bush on December 4, 1989. Germany was reunited on October 3, 1990. The Eastern and Western blocs participated in the Paris Conference on November 19–20, 1990,

where they announced the end of the Cold War. The Warsaw Pact was dissolved on November 3, 1990, and the Comecon was dissolved on June 28, 1991. The Soviet Union was disbanded in December 1991.

25. For more information about the shape and effects of fourth generation warfare, see: William S. Lind, "Understanding Fourth Generation War," *Military Review*, September–October 2004, pp. 12–16

26. Mounir Mahmoud Badawi Elsayed, "Modern Trends in the Study of the International System since the End of the Cold War" [in Arabic], paper presented to the Standing Committee on Political Science, Faculty of Commerce, Assiut University, 2004, p. 16.

27. For more information on cultural invasion and dependency, see: Shaker Al Nabulsi, "The Manifestations and Mechanisms of Cultural Invasion in Contemporary Arab Thought" [in Arabic], Modern Discussion website, September 29, 2008 (http://www.ahewar.org/debat/show.art.asp?aid=148626).

28. Figures are based on the number of years before use of the said technologies had been adopted by 25% of the US population. US National Intelligence Council (NIC), "Global Trends 2030: Alternative Worlds," Office of the Director of National Intelligence, December 2012 (http://www.dni.gov/files/documents/GlobalTrends_ 2030.pdf).

29. The acceleration of technological advance in the new world order suggests that its pursuit seems inevitable if states seek to communicate with the rest of the world and provide a decent life for their citizens; otherwise, technological (and thus cultural and economic) isolation will be the alternative.

30. National Center for Education Statistics, *Digest of Education Statistics Report*, 2012 (http://nces.ed.gov/programs/digest/2012menu_tables.asp).

31. Ibid.

32. Robert Kagan, *The World America Made* (New York, NY: Knopf Doubleday Publishing Group, 2012), op. cit., pp. 52–55.

33. Ibid.

34. The United States of America has used all forms of military force in Afghanistan, Iraq, Kosovo and Pakistan; it has also provided military support to the opposition forces in Syria and Libya.

35. A clear example is the events of the "Arab Spring" in Egypt and Tunisia, as some US research centers and social networking and media companies played a key role in mobilizing young people toward change.

36. Jan Techau "Germany must stop Moralising and Embrace Espionage," *Financial Times*, October 13 2013 (http://carnegieendowment.org/# /slide_508_ germany-must-embrace-espionage).

37. Joseph S. Nye, "Soft Power: The Means to Success in World Politics" [in Arabic], Mohamed Tawfiq Al-Bujairami (trans.); (Riyadh: Obeikan Library, 2007), pp. 180–181.

38. For more details about soft power, see: Ibid., pp. 207–215.

39. Richard L. Armitage and Joseph S. Nye, *CSIS Commission on Smart Power: A Smarter, More Secure America* (Washington, DC: CSIS, 2007), pp. 27–60.

40. Ibid., pp. 64–66.

41. One of the characteristics of smart power is that it allows the United States of America – with its massive capabilities – to vary the use of its sources of strength between soft power and hard power on a case-by case basis, depending on US interests and the anticipated result of using one source or another.

42. Richard L. Armitage and Joseph S. Nye, "A Smarter, More Secure America," op. cit., pp. 27–60.

43. The United States of America relied on US media and research centers, and on training young cadres how best to employ peaceful demonstrations, etc.

44. There is much evidence of the use of international institutions and bodies to entrench US hegemony over the new world order; for example, the International Monetary Fund in recent years has adopted rules and standards based on noncooperation with governments that do not enjoy domestic popularity, not to mention military regimes or governments who, according to specialized US reports, violate human rights.

45. US media plays an influential role in foreign policy, whether in terms of building attitudes and shaping domestic public opinion in the United States of America, or in terms of directing international public opinion and shaping attitudes regarding crises and issues affecting US strategic interests.

46. Middle East News Agency, (http://portal.mena.org.eg/#ad-image-0K), accessed September 22, 2013.

47. Anne-Cécile Robert, "A Disturbing Shift in International Relations," *Al-Ahram*, October 5, 2013 (http://digital.ahram.org.eg/Policy.aspx?Serial=1425387), accessed September 22, 2013.

48. Jamal Sanad Al Suwaidi, op. cit., pp. 121–133.

49. For more information about the Internet's effects in various fields: see: Ibid., pp. 53–93.

50. For more information about the future of the virtual space and its role in global decision-making, see: Ibid., pp. 121–133.

51. For more about the role of alliances and their influence in the global order, see: Mamdouh Mahmoud Mustafa Mansour, "International Coalition Policies: A Study in the Origins of the International Coalition Theory" [in Arabic]; (Alexandria: Alexandria University,

1995), pp. 160–163; Muhammad Aziz Shukri, "Alliances and Blocs in International Politics" [in Arabic], Alam Al-Maarifa series (Kuwait: National Council for Culture, Arts and Letters, 2008); and Al Sayed Mustafa Ahmad Abu Al Khair, "The General Theory of Military Alliances and Blocs in Accordance with the Rules of General International Law" [in Arabic]; (Beirut: Center for Arab Unity Studies, 2010).

52. In light of US defense budget cuts and the reduced role of the military in some areas in the world, and the administration's obvious attempt to focus its efforts towards Asia, the alternative is NATO, which is controlled by the United States of America.

53. Jacquelyn S. Porth, "Defense Official Says International Alliances Key to US Strategy," Bureau of International Information Programs (IIP), US State Department, March 21, 2006 (http://iipdigital.us embassy.gov/st/english/article/2006/03/20060320132430sjhtrop0.93 39716.html#axzz2jwLrsaKd).

54. Ibid.

55. A good example is the ongoing process of negotiations between the United States of America and the European Union to establish a free trade zone, for more details, see: "Negotiations between the United States of America and the European Union to Establish a Free Trade Zone," BBC, February 13, 2013 (http://www.bbc.co.uk/arabic/business/2013/02/130213_eu_us_trade.shtml).

56. For more on the position of the United States of America towards the International Criminal Court, see: Kenneth Roth, "The United States of America versus the International Criminal Court: No Global System is based on Exception," Modern Discussion website, issue 190, July 15, 2012 (http://www.ahewar.org/debat/show.art.asp?aid =2140).

57. It is noted that recent years have witnessed increasing negotiations on the establishment of free trade zones between the United States of

America and many countries and economic blocs outside the scope of the World Trade Organization.

58. Proxy diplomacy will become a popular form of international relations in the new world order, where the United States of America commissions major powers to manage negotiations or dialogue with a third party, whereby the superpower can identify the strengths and weaknesses in the third party's diplomacy. Then the superpower can intervene at the right time to maintain its hegemony in the new world order, and sustain its cohesion, thereby protecting the success of its direct diplomacy. Parallel diplomacy is also a method that will spread in the new world order to indirectly achieve the interests of the superpower, whereby the tools of soft power, public diplomacy and civil society play an influential diplomatic role parallel to that of direct diplomacy.

59. Patterns of American leadership have changed in recent years: during the military intervention in Libya, it settled for leading from behind and left the European Union to play the major role in this operation, while it went on to call for 'surgical' strikes if it decided to punish the regime of Syrian President Bashar al-Assad for the use of chemical weapons against unarmed civilians.

60. Recent years have witnessed an increase in the participation of civil society organizations in international conferences convened to discuss global issues or crises, reflecting the growing influence of these organizations in shaping public attitudes towards such issues.

61. This role of the United Nations and its specialized agencies is mainly associated with the vision of the dominant power in the new world order, in the sense that the UN role will grow or shrink according to the vision of the United States of America.

62. These global repercussions are the product of analytical studies and projections regarding expected structural changes in the new world order and their positive or negative implications, whether direct or indirect, on various regions and on the United Nations.

63. Countries that join the UN Security Council will not have veto powers, which will remain in the hands of the conventional five major members, including the United States of America.

64. The US approach in this regard is mainly due to a desire to reduce its responsibilities towards maintaining or ensuring European security in light of the American pivot-to-east-Asia strategy, and in light of the intensified US military presence there to face emerging Chinese power and preserve growing American interests in the region.

65. In *The Choice*, Brzezinski argues that the two sides of the Atlantic should work together to chart a global course that ensures significant improvement of global affairs, and that the European Union should be aware that it is more secure when linked to the global security system dominated by the United States of America; Zbigniew Brzezinski, *The Choice: Global Domination or Global Leadership* (New York, NY: Basic Books, 2004), pp. 220–221.

66. This speculation comes as a result of current and future conditions affecting the European countries in the medium- and long-term.

67. The International Institute for Strategic Studies (IISS), *The Military Balance 2012* (London: IISS, 2012), pp. 90–168.

68. Owing to the close vicinity of South American countries to the United States of America, the US side is showing considerable interest in these countries, particularly regarding negative phenomena and practices there, such as organized crime, drug trafficking and illegal immigration, which affects the United States of America directly.

69. David Shambaugh, *China Goes Global: The Partial Power* (New York, NY: Oxford University Press, 2013), pp. 189–201.

70. Ahmed Taher, "The Future of Sino-American Relations" [in Arabic], *Al Siyassa Al Dawliya* no. 193, (July 2013), pp. 134–138.

71. Henry A. Kissinger, "The Future of US-Chinese Relations: Conflict is a Choice, not a Necessity," *Foreign Affairs*, March/April 2012

(http://www.foreignaffairs.com/articles/137245/henry-a-kissinger/the-future-of-us-chinese-relations).

72. Brzezinski, *The Choice,* op. cit., p. 12.

73. Brzezinski, *The Grand Chessboard: American Primacy and Its Geostrategic Imperatives* [in Arabic]; (Cairo: Merit Publishing House, 2003), p. 203.

74. In his book, *The Choice*, op. cit., pp. 12–13, Brzezinski argues that a major regional war is likely to break out between India and Pakistan.

75. Henry Kissinger, Does America Need a Foreign Policy? (New York, NY: Simon & Schuster, 2001), op. cit., pp. 302–303.

76. Brzezinski, *The Grand Chessboard,* op. cit., p. 188.

77. Ibid., pp. 192–193.

78. Brzezinski, *The Choice*, op. cit., p. 25.

79. National Intelligence Council, Global Trends 2030: Alternative Worlds, op. cit., pp. 74–75.

80. Ibid., pp. 75–78.

81. Ibid.

82. Ibid., pp. 31–38.

83. Colonel Robert Killebrew (ret.), "AFRICOM Stands Up," *Small Wars Journal*, op. ed., October 9, 2008 (http://www.africom.mil/NEWS ROOM/Article/6331/us-africa-command-stands-up).

Chapter VII

1. As a reference to the theory, See: Moisés Naím, *The End of Power: From Boardrooms to Battlefields and Churches to States, Why Being in Charge isn't What it Used to Be* (New York, NY: Basic Books, 2013).

2. Ian Bremmer and Nouriel Roubini, "A G-Zero World: The New Economic Club Will Produce Conflict, Not Cooperation," *Foreign Affairs*, vol. 90, no. 2, March/April 2011 (http://www.foreignaffairs.com/articles/67339/ian-bremmer-and-nouriel-roubini/a-g-zero-world).

3. Nassim Taleb, *The Black Swan* [in Arabic]; (Beirut, Arabic Scientific Publishers, Inc., 2009).

4. Naím, op. cit., p. 1.

5. Ibid., p. 2.

6. Ibid., p. 10.

7. Ibid., p. 11.

8. Ibid.

9. "G-zero" is an expression based on the various global "groups" of major economies that meet and cooperate on a periodic basis: the G-7 (which includes the United States of America, the United Kingdom, Germany, France, Italy, Canada and Japan), the G-8 (which also includes the Russian Federation), and the G-20, which features the world's twenty largest economies (Argentina, Australia, Brazil, Canada, China, France, Germany, India, Indonesia, Italy, Japan, Mexico, Russia, Saudi Arabia, South Africa, Turkey, South Korea, the United Kingdom, the United States of America and the European Union).

10. Bremmer and Roubini, op. cit.

11. Ibid.

12. Ibid.

13. For examples of issues relating to the G-zero world, see Diane Francis, "Welcome to the G-zero World," *Financial Post*, September 6, 2013 (http://opinion.financialpost.com/2013/09/06/welcome-to-the-g-zero-world/).

14. Bremmer and Roubini, op. cit.

15. Ian Bremmer and David Gordon, "The G-Zero Order," *The New York Times*, The Opinion Pages, October 26, 2011 (http://www.nytimes.com/2011/10/27/opinion/27iht-edbremmer27.html), accessed July 27, 2013.

16. Ian Bremmer, "From G8 to G20 to G-Zero: Why No One Wants to Take Charge in the New Global Order," *New Statesman*, June 11, 2013 (http://www.newstatesman.com/politics/politics/2013/06/g8-g20-g-zero-why-no-one-wants-take-charge-new-global-order), accessed July 27, 2013.

17. According to Nassim Taleb, the term Black Swan was used in Ancient Greece to symbolize something that does not exist—it stemmed from a common conviction that all swans were white. After the discovery of Australia, an explorer sighted a black swan, undermining the belief among Europeans that swans were only white. Hence the book's title, "The Black Swan" refers to that which is thought to be improbable or unlikely to occur.

18. Taleb, op. cit., p. 268.

19. Ibid., p. 10.

20. Ibid., p. 330.

21. Ibid. pp. 14–15.

22. Based on Gordon Moore's 1965 prediction that processing power would double every 18 months. Fadil Delio, *New Information and Communication Technology (NTIC/NICT): Concept, Uses, Prospects* [in Arabic]; (Amman: Dar Al Thaqafa, 2010), p. 173.

23. Richard Florida, "The World's Leading Nations for Innovation and Technology," *The Atlantic Cities*, October 3, 2011 (http://www.the atlanticcities.com/technology/2011/10/worlds-leading-nations-innovation-and-technology/224/).

24. Multiple attempts were made to reach an agreement on global multilateral trade liberalization under the General Agreement on Tariffs and Trade (GATT), which since 1995 has been known as the World Trade Organization. Seven rounds of negotiations occurred under the GATT, and two under the WTO—one in Uruguay and the other in Doha. The last round was the most disappointing; for more details visit: (http://www.wto.org/).

25. Manuel F. Ayau, *Not a Zero-Sum Game: The Paradox of Exchange* (Guatemala: Universidad Francisco Marroquin, 2007), pp. 18–19.

26. "US, EU Start Free-trade Talks Today" [in Arabic], *Al Ittihad*, July 8, 2013 (http://www.alittihad.ae/details.php?id=65041&y=2013).

27. Fareed Zakaria, "Can China Change its Economic Course?" *The Washington Post*, WP Opinions, July 17, 2013 (http://articles. washingtonpost.com/2013-07-17/opinions/40632962_1_china-s-growth-gdp).

28. The following section reflects a classification based on technical, military and economic aspects of power.

29. "Difference Engine: Hackers' Paradise," *The Economist*, March 11, 2013 (http://www.economist.com/blogs/babbage/2013/03/crimeware ?fsrc=scn/tw/te/bl/differenceenginehackersparadise).

30. INTEK, Inc., "Secure Fuels from Domestic Resources, Profiles of Companies Engaged in Domestic Oil Shale and Tar Sands Resource and Technology Development," 5th ed., prepared for the US Department of Energy (DoE), Naval Petroleum and Oil Shale Reserves, Office of Petroleum Reserves, September 2011 (http://energy.gov/sites/prod/files/2013/04/f0/SecureFuelsReport2011.pdf), p. 2.

31. "Difference Engine: Hackers' Paradise," *The Economist*, March 11, 2013 (http://www.economist.com/blogs/babbage/2013/03/crimeware ?fsrc=scn/tw/te/bl/differenceenginehackersparadise).

32. Moisés Naím, op. cit., p. 5.

33. Ibid.

34. Ibid.

35. William S. Lind, Keith Nightengale, John F. Schmitt, Joseph W. Stutton, and Gary I. Wilson, "The Changing Face of War: Into the Fourth Generation," *Marine Corps Gazette*, vol. 73, no. 10, October 1989 (http://www.mca-marines.org/files/The%20Changing%20Face%20of%20War%20-%20Into%20the%20Fourth%20Generation.pdf), pp. 22–26

36. Ibid., p. 26.

37. Ibid.

38. Ibid.

39. International Monetary Fund (IMF), "IMF Governance Structure, Directors Back Reforms to Overhaul IMF Quotas and Voice," IMF Survey online, March 28, 2008 (http://www.imf.org/external/pubs/ft/survey/so/2008/NEW032808A.htm).

40. Anatoly Utkin, *The World in the 21st Century* [in Arabic]; (Damascus: Dar Al Markaz Al Thaqafi for Printing and Publishing, 2007), p. 8.

41. Ibid.

42. Ibid.

43. Ibid.

44. The following section is based on the military, economic and technical elements of power detailed previously.

45. Saad Haqqi Tawfiq, *New World Order* (Amman: Al Ahlia for Publishing and Distribution, 1999), p. 130.

46. Ibid., pp. 130–148.

47. Paul Steinhauser, "President Ends Year At All-Time CNN Polling Low," CNN, December 20, 2013 (http://politicalticker.blogs.cnn.com/2013/12/20/president-ends-year-at-all-time-cnn-polling-low/).

48. International Monetary Fund (IMF), "World Economic Outlook Database," April 2013 (http://www.imf.org/external/pubs/ft/weo/2013/01/weodata/index.aspx).

49. Ibid.

50. For more views regarding Chinese strengths and weaknesses vis-à-vis the United States of America, see "A Point of View: What Kind of Superpower Could China Be?" *BBC News*, October 19, 2012 (http://www.bbc.co.uk/news/magazine-19995218).

51. For more details about the crisis in Greece, see: Georgia Kaplanoglou and Vassilis T. Rapanos, "The Greek Fiscal Crisis and the Role of Fiscal Governance," GreeSE Paper No. 48, Hellenic Observatory Papers on Greece and Southeast Europe, London School of Economics and Political Science, and Hellenic Observatory, European Institute, June 2011(http://www.lse.ac.uk/europeanInstitute/research/hellenicObservatory/pdf/GreeSE/GreeSE48.pdf), pp. 5–8.

52. For more details see: Yuqing Xing, "Why is China so Attractive for FDI? The Role of Exchange Rates," May, 2004, International Development Program, International University of Japan, pp. 21–22 (http://faculty.washington.edu/karyiu/confer/beijing03/papers/xing.pdf).

53. The exchange rate of the yuan against major currencies, see: "Bank of China, Exchange Rate," Bank of China (http://www.boc.cn/sourcedb/whpj/enindex.html), accessed November 4, 2013.

54. James Rickards, *Currency Wars: The Making of the Next Global Crisis* (New York, NY: Portfolio Penguin, 2011), pp. 98–99.

55. Ibid., p. 101.

56. Ibid.

57. Ibid., p. 102.

58. For more information about the events in Tiananmen Square see Nicholas D. Kristof, "A Reassessment of How Many Died in the Military Crackdown in Beijing," *New York Times*, June 21, 1989 (http://www.nytimes.com/1989/06/21/world/a-reassessment-of-how-many-died-in-the-military-crackdown-in-beijing.html).

59. Rickards, op. cit., p. 101.

60. Data sources for 1970, see (http://www.chinability.com/Rmb.htm# exchange_rates); for 1975–1995, see (http://intl.econ.cuhk.edu.hk/ exchange_rate_regime/index.php?cid=8); for 2000–2013, see (http:// www.federalreserve.gov/releases/h10/hist/dat00_ch.htm).

61. Ibid.

62. Ibid., p. 104.

63. Rickards, op. cit., p. 106.

64. "Markets, Currencies," *Financial Times*, July 29, 2013 (http:// markets.ft.com/RESEARCH/markets/DataArchiveFetchReport?Cate gory=CU&Type=3SPT&Date=07/29/2013).

65. "China Takes First Step in the Internationalization of the Yuan and allows its use in America" [in Arabic], *Asharq Al Awsat*, January 13, 2011, see (http://www.aawsat.com/details.asp?section=6&issueno= 11734&article=603581#.UfYfDdLTyE4).

66. World Economic Forum (WEF), "Euro, Dollar, Yuan Uncertainties: Scenarios on the Future of the International Monetary System," World Scenario Series, June, 2012, p. 12.

67. "EU and US Negotiators begin Talks aimed at Creating the World's Largest Free Trade Zone" [in Arabic], *Al Khaleej* June 18, 2013 (http://www.alkhaleej.ae/portal/e38575a3-ba54-4004-ade2-79061a2a 9718.aspx).

68. "The European Union and the United States of America: Towards the Largest Free Trade Zone" [in Arabic], *Russia Today* website, July 10, 2013 (http://arabic.rt.com/news/620782).

69. "EU and US Launch Talks to Create the Biggest Free Zone in the World" [in Arabic], *Alroeya*, June 18, 2013 (http://www.alroeya. com/node/34792).

70. For more details on the role of fiscal and monetary policy in time of economic crisis, see Federal Reserve Bank of St. Louis, "Monetary and Fiscal Policy in Times of Crisis," *Economic Information Newsletter*, March 2011 (http://research.stlouisfed.org/pageone-economics/uploads/newsletter/2011/201103_ClassroomEdition.pdf).

71. For more information on the nature of the Chinese economy, see Yuchun Yuan, "The Mixed Economy in China: Through Rhetorical Perspective," Master's degree thesis, Texas A&M University (http://repository.tamu.edu/bitstream/handle/1969.1/1207/etd-tamu-20 03B-2003070714-Yuan-1.pdf?sequence=1).

72. For more details about the liberalization of China's financial sector, see Haihong Gao and Ulrich Volz, "Is China Ready to Open its Capital Account?" East Asia Forum, March 29, 2012 (http://www.eastasia forum.org/2012/03/29/is-china-ready-to-open-its-capital-account/).

73. Thomas Kenny, "How Safe are US Treasuries?" About.com (http://bonds.about.com/od/governmentandagencybonds/a/How-Safe-Are-U-S-Treasuries.htm).

74. Statistics show that China made more than a billion mobile phones in the first 11 months of 2012, along with 314.5 million PCs, 116.1 million monitors, and 114 million TV sets; Jack Schofield, "China's 2012 Electronics Production includes more than a Billion Mobile Phones," ZDNet blog (http://www.zdnet.com/chinas-2012-electronics-production-includes-more-than-a-billion-mobile-phones-7000009294/).

75. According to NetMarketShare.com, statistics published in July 2013 show that Microsoft and Apple together accounted for 95.5% of computer operating systems, while Apple, Google and Microsoft account for 84.7 of smart phone operating systems. For more details, see (http://www.netmarket share.com/)

76. According to the statistics of the Organization for Economic Cooperation and Development (OECD) issued in 2012, the United States of America spent $366 million in 2009 (in 2005 PPP prices) on research and development (R&D), while China's spending was limited to 140.6 million. For more details, see Organization for Economic Cooperation and Development (OECD), "OECD Factbook 2013" (http://www.oecd-ilibrary.org/economics/oecd-factbook_1814 7 364).

77. For more information about US technological superiority, see "Maintaining US 'Overwhelming Technological Advantage' over Adversaries," March 27, 2013, Homeland Security News Wire, (http://www.homelandsecuritynewswire.com/dr20130327-maintaining-u-s-overwhelming-technological-advantage-over-adversaries).

78. See the link: "Difference Engine: Hackers' Paradise," *The Economist*, March 11, 2013 (http://www.economist.com/blogs/babbage/2013/03/crimeware?fsrc=scn/tw/te/bl/differenceenginehackersparadise).

79. Zhaoxing Li, "Setting the Record Straight on China's Global Ambitions," *Europe's World* (Autumn 2011); (http://europesworld. org/2011/10/01/setting-the-record-straight-on-chinas-global-ambitions/#.UrmDAf2IpaQ).

80. Eric Follah and Wieland Wagner, "China Seeks Role as Second Superpower," Spiegel Online International, February 11, 2012, p. 19 (http://www.spiegel.de/international/world/global-ambitions-china-seeks-role-in-world-as-second-superpower-a-864358.html).

81. Chris Alden, *China in Africa: A Partner or a Competitor?* [in Arabic], translated by Othman Al Jabali Al Mathlouthi (Beirut: Arab Scientific Publishers, Inc. 2009), p. 19.

82. Winnie Zhu, "Angola Overtakes Saudi Arabia as Biggest Oil Supplier to China," Bloomberg, April 21, 2008 (http://www.bloomberg.com/apps/news?pid=newsarchive&sid=aqJ3Wjxs.OWs).

83. Chris Alden, *China in Africa: A Partner or a Competitor?*, op. cit., p. 20.

84. T. Chase Meacham, "Obama Africa Trip 2013: Why Obama's $100 Million African Trip Isn't a Big Deal," June 15, 2013, Policymic.com (http://www.policymic.com/articles/49001/obama-africa-trip-2013-why-obama-s-100-million-african-trip-isn-t-a-big-deal).

85. George Friedman, *The Next 100 Years: A Forecast for the 21st Century* (New York, NY: Anchor Books, 2009), pp. 5–9.

86. Ibid., p. 5.

87. Ibid.

88. Ibid., p. 6.

89. Ibid.

90. Ibid., p. 7.

91. US NAVSEA Shipbuilding Support Office (NAVSHIPSO), "Naval Vessel Register" (http://www.nvr.navy.mil/).

92. John Reed, "Is this China's Second Aircraft Carrier?" *Foreign Policy*, National Security, August 3, 2013 (http://killerapps.foreignpolicy. com/posts/2013/08/02/spotted_china_is_building_a_second_aircraft _carrier).

93. Eric Follah and Wieland Wagner, "China Seeks Role as Second Superpower," Spiegel Online International, February 11, 2012, p. 19 (http://www.spiegel.de/international/world/global-ambitions-china-seeks-role-in-world-as-second-superpower-a-864358.html).

94. For more discussions about the effect of technology on the future of the human race, see Reena Jana, "What Three Tech Trends will Affect Our Lives in 2020, Future Hunting with Intel's Brian David Johnson," *Designmind: Radical Openness* (issue 17); (http://designmind.frog design.com/articles/radical-openness/what-three-tech-trends-will-affect-our-lives-in-2020.html).

95. United States of America Environmental Protection Agency (EPA), "Natural Gas Extraction: Hydraulic Fracturing" (http://www2.epa. gov/hydraulicfracturing#improving).

96. Ibid.

97. US Department of Energy (DoE) / Energy Information Administration (EIA), "Petroleum and Other Liquids: US Imports by Country of Origin" (http://www.eia.gov/dnav/pet/pet_move_impcus_a2_nus_ep 00_im0_mbbl_m.ht).

98. World Energy Council (WEC), *2010 Survey of Energy Resources* (http://www.worldenergy.org/publications/3040.asp)

99. US Department of Energy (DoE) / Energy Information Administration (EIA), *"International Energy Outlook 2011"*. (http://www.eia.gov/ forecasts/archive/ieo11/pdf10484 (2011).pdf)

100. Department of Energy (DoE) / Energy Information Administration (EIA), "World Shale Gas Resources: An Initial Assessment of 14 Regions Outside the United States of America," April 2011.

101. "Are We Becoming Cyborgs?" *The New York Times*, November 30, 2012 (http://www.nytimes.com/2012/11/30/opinion/global/maria-po pova-evgeny-morozov-susan-greenfield-are-we-becoming-cyborgs. html?pagewanted=all&_r=0).

102. For more information about Google Glass, see (http://www.google. com/glass/start/).

103. "Are We Becoming Cyborgs?" *The New York Times*, November 30, 2012 (http://www.nytimes.com/2012/11/30/opinion/global/maria-popova -evgeny-morozov-susan-greenfield-are-we-becoming-cyborgs.html?page wanted= all&_r=0).

104. Alex Hern, "A Gun Made on a 3D Printer has been Fired: Let's Look at this in Perspective," *The Guardian*, May 6, 2013 (http://www. theguardian.com/commentisfree/2013/may/06/3d-printer-gun-has-been -fired).

105. "Navy's New Cost-Saving Weapon: A Laser That Can Shoot Drones from the Sky," The Blaze, April 9, 2013 (http://www.theblaze.com/

stories/2013/04/09/navys-new-cost-saving-weapon-a-laser-that-can-shoot-drones-from-the-sky/).

106. Larry Elliott, "Global Financial Crisis: Five Key Stages 2007–2011," *The Guardian*, August 7, 2011 (http://www.theguardian.com/business /2011/aug/07/global-financial-crisis-key-stages).

107. Beck A. Taylor, "On the Equivalency of Profit Maximization and Cost Minimization: A Note on Factor Demands" (http://capone.mtsu. edu/jee/pdf/taylor.PDF), pp. 3–4.

108. Richard M. Cyert and David C. Mowery (eds.), "Technology and Employment: Innovation and Growth in the US Economy," The National Academies Press, 1987 (http://www.nap.edu/catalog.php? record_id=1004), pp. 86–88.

109. Thomas L. Friedman, *The World is Flat: A Brief History of the Twenty-First Century* (New York, NY: Farrar, Straus and Giroux, 2005), p. 8.

110. Ibid.

111. Ibid.

112. "10 Countries Least Affected by the US Economic Crisis," Businesspundit.com, October 8, 2008 (http://www.businesspundit. com/10-countries-least-affected-by-the-us-financial-crisis/).

113. Danny M. Leipziger, "Institutional Reforms and the Shifting Global Economic Order," The North–South Institute, June 2011, pp. 2–6 (http://www.nsi-ins.ca/content/download/Leipziger2011.pdf).

114. Ibid., pp. 6–13.

115. Linda Low, "The Political Economy of Trade Liberalization," *Asia–Pacific Development Journal*, vol. 11, no. 1 (June 2004); (www.unescap.org/pdd/publications/apdj_11_1/low.pdf), pp. 3–13.

116. Joseph E. Stiglitz and Linda J. Bilmes, *The Three Trillion Dollar War: The True Cost of the Iraq Conflict* (New York, NY: W.W. Norton & Company, 2008), p. x.

117. Linda J. Bilmes, "The Financial Legacy of Iraq and Afghanistan: How Wartime Spending Decisions Will Constrain Future National Security Budgets," Harvard Kennedy School, *Faculty Research Working Paper Series*, RWP13-003, March 2013, pp 1–2 (https://research.hks. harvard.edu/publications/workingpapers/citation.aspx?PubId=8956).

118. "Faces of the Fallen," *The Washington Post* (http://apps.washington post.com/national/fallen/), accessed August 1, 2013.

119. Spencer Ackerman, "Afghanistan, Iraq Wars Killed 132,000 Civilians, Report Says," *Wired*, June 29, 2011 (http://www.wired.com/danger room/2011/06/afghanistan-iraq-wars-killed-132000-civilians-report-says/).

120. "Accused Fort Hood Massacre Suspect says US at War against Islam," July 28, 2013 (http://www.upi.com/Top_News/US/2013/07/28/Accused-Fort-Hood-massacre-suspect-says-US-at-war-against-Islam/UPI-61641374989300/).

121. Michael E. O'Hanlon, *Healing the Wounded Giant: Maintaining Military Preeminence while Cutting the Defense Budget* (Salem, VA: R.R. Donelly, 2013), pp. 3–12.

122. Andrew F. Krepinevich Jr., "Strategy in a Time of Austerity," *Foreign Affairs*, vol. 91, no. 6, November/December 2012 (http://www.foreignaffairs.com/articles/138362/andrew-f-krepinevich-jr/strategy-in-a-time-of-austerity).

123. Ibid.

124. First generation warfare reflects the tactics of the era of the smoothbore musket and troops being arranged in line and column, depending on maximum firepower and manpower; second generation

warfare was based on operational planning and fire and maneuver, with mass firepower replacing mass manpower; Third generation warfare increased the focus on maneuver and firepower over attrition (e.g. *blitzkrieg*); see: William S. Lind, Keith Nightengale, John F. Schmitt, Joseph W. Stutton, and Gary I. Wilson, "The Changing Face of War: Into the Fourth Generation," op. cit., p. 23.

125. Ibid., pp. 25–26.

126. Ibid., p. 26.

127. Ibid.

128. William J. Lynn III and Nicholas Thompson, "Foreign Affairs LIVE: The Pentagon's New Cyberstrategy," *Foreign Affairs*, October 1, 2010 (http://www.foreignaffairs.com/discussions/news-and-events/foreign-affairs-live-the-pentagons-new-cyberstrategy).

129. Ibid.

130. Ibid.

131. US Department of Defense (DoD), "Remarks by Secretary Panetta on Cybersecurity to the Business Executives for National Security, New York City," October 11, 2012 (http://www.defense.gov/transcripts/transcript.Aspx?transcriptid=5136).

132. Ibid.

133. "Cyber attack hits Qatar's RasGas" [in Arabic], BBC Arabic Website, 31 August, 2012 (http://www.bbc.co.uk/arabic/scienceandtech/2012/08/120831_computer-virus.shtml).

134. Ibid.

135. Nassim Al-Khoury, *Arab Media and the Collapse of Linguistic Authorities* [in Arabic]; (Beirut: Centre for Arab Unity Studies, 2005), p. 429.

136. Hadi Noman Al-Haiti, "Incoming International Satellite TV Communication and Potential Political Effects on the Arab World" [in

Arabic], *Al-Mustaqbal Al-Arabi* no. 34 (Beirut: Centre for Arab Unity Studies, 2003).

137. Jamal Sanad Al-Suwaidi, *From Tribe to Facebook: the Transformational Role of Social Networks* [in Arabic]; (Abu Dhabi: Emirates Center for Strategic Studies and Research [ECSSR], 2013), p. 62.

138. Al-Khoury, op. cit. p. 429.

139. Al-Suwaidi, op. cit., p. 65.

140. Maha Nasser Kheir Bek, "The Arabic language and Sciences of the Era," *Al-Arabi* magazine (Kuwait), no. 554/1, 2005 (http://www.alarabimag.com/Article.asp?ART=9122&ID=115).

141. Delio, op. cit, p. 177.

142. Al-Suwaidi, op. cit., pp. 113–115.

143. Lance Whitney, "America: A Nation Obsessed With Tech," CNET, September 2, 2009 (http://news.cnet.com/8301-10797_3-10332910-235.html).

144. "Melting Pot' America," BBC News online, May 12, 2006 (http://news.bbc.co.uk/2/hi/americas/4931534.stm).

BIBLIOGRAPHY

BIBLIOGRAPHY

"10 Countries Least Affected by the US Economic Crisis." *Businesspundit. com*, October 8, 2008 (http://www.businesspundit.com/10-countries-least-affected-by-the-us-financial-crisis).

"200 Nationalities Co-exist Peacefully in the UAE" [in Arabic]. *Albayan*, December 14, 2011 (http://www.albayan.ae/across-the-uae/accidents/2011-12-14-1.1554891).

"A Billion Searches in Google Monthly" [in Arabic]. Sky News Arabia website, February 3, 2013 (http://www.skynewsarabia.com/web/article/75208).

"A Point of View: What Kind of Superpower Could China Be?" *BBC News*, October 19, 2012 (http://www.bbc.co.uk/news/magazine-19995 218).

"A. Gary Shilling and Company, Inc" (http://www.agaryshilling.com).

"A. Gary Shilling." Bloomberg (http://www.bloomberg.com/view/bios/gary-shilling).

"Accused Fort Hood Massacre Suspect says US at War Against Islam." *UPI.com*, July 28, 2013 (http://www.upi.com/Top_News/US/2013/07/28/Accused-Fort-Hood-massacre-suspect-says-US-at-war-against-Islam/UPI-61641374989300/).

"Aircraft Carrier Locations." Gonavy.jp (http://www.gonavy.jp/CV Location.html), accessed October 7, 2013.

"America Punishes Green Revolution Repressors: Iran is a Hypocrite." CNN Arabic website, July 9, 2011 (http://arabic.cnn.com/2011/world/6/9/iran.greenrev).

"American President: A Reference Resource." Miller Center, University of Virginia (http://millercenter.org/president/bush/essays/biography/5), accessed September 22, 2013.

"Arab Strategic Report, 2002/2003" [in Arabic]; (Cairo: Al-Ahram Center for Political & Strategic Studies, 2003).

"Are We Becoming Cyborgs?" *The New York Times*, November 30, 2012 (http://www.nytimes.com/2012/11/30/opinion/global/maria-popova-evgeny-morozov-susan-greenfield-are-we-becoming-cyborgs.html?pagewanted=all&_r=0).

"Assafir Publishes a Comprehensive Report on the Meeting between Bandar and Putin: Take the Investments and the Oil Price and give us Syria" [in Arabic]. *Assafir* Issue 12558, August 21, 2013 (http://www.assafir.com/Article.aspx?EditionId=2543&articleId=1693&ChannelId=61387&Page=2#Comments).

"Assets under Management of the Largest Hedge Fund Firms in October 2011 (in billion US dollars)." Statista.com, n.d. (http://www.statista.com/statistics/273133/assets-under-management-of-the-largest-hedge-fund-firms/).

"Audit Office Shines Light on Local Government Debt." *The Wall Street Journal*, June 11, 2013 (http://blogs.wsj.com/chinarealtime/2013/06/11/audit-office-shines-light-on-local-government-debt/).

"Bank of China, Exchange Rate." Bank of China (http://www.boc.cn/sourcedb/whpj/enindex.html).

"Biography: Julius Kambarage Nyerere." *Marxists.org* (http://www.marxists.org/subject/africa/nyerere/biography.htm).

"BRICS and its Aims." AlJazeera.net, March 30, 2012 [in Arabic]; (http://www.aljazeera.net/news/pages/5522ec81-6341-4fe6-a9ad-bab8ae41d46c).

"Cameron: Britain must 'Sort Out' its Economy if it wants to 'Carry Weight in the World'" [in Arabic]. BBC website, November 16, 2010 (http://www.bbc.co.uk/arabic/worldnews/2010/11/101115_cameron_economy_tc2.shtml), accessed July 14, 2013.

"Charles Krauthammer." *Washington Post* Opinions, February 24, 2011 (http://www.washingtonpost.com/charles-krauthammer/2011/02/24/ADJkW7B_page.html).

"Charles Krauthammer: Prize Writer." *Mitchellbard.com* (http://www.mitchellbard.com/articles/kraut.html).

"Charles V: Holy Roman Emperor (1500–1558)." *Heritage History* (http://www.heritage-history.com/www/heritage.php?Dir=characters&FileName=charles5s.php).

"Cheney, Richard Bruce." Biographical Directory of the United States Congress (http://bioguide.congress.gov/scripts/biodisplay.pl?index=C000344).

"China becomes the World's Second-largest Economy" [in Arabic]. Aljazeera.net, December 26, 2009 (http://www.aljazeera.net/ebusiness/pages/991facb5-0e94-43b6-96d1-e6e180577519), accessed October 29, 2013.

"China Resentfully Rejects an Offer from Washington to Compensate it for the Hainan Incident." *Al-Sharq Al-Awsat* August 13, 2001 (http://www.aawsat.com/details.asp?issueno=8070& article=52257).

"China Secures Larger Turkmen Gas Supplies." *Reuters*, September 3, 2013 (http://uk.reuters.com/article/2013/09/03/gas-turkmenistan-china-idUKL6N0GZ31W20130903).

"China Starts First Steps in Internationalization of the Yuan and Allows its Circulation in the United States of America" [in Arabic]. *Al-Sharq Al-Awsat*, January 13, 2011 (http://www.aawsat.com/details.asp?section=6&issueno=11734&article=603581#.UfYfDdLTyE4).

"China Takes First Step in the Internationalization of the Yuan and allows its Use in America" [in Arabic]. *Asharq Al Awsat*, January 13, 2011 (http://www.aawsat.com/details.asp?section=6&issueno=11734&article=603581#.UfYfDdLTyE4).

"Christopher Columbus." *biography.com* (http://www.biography.com/people/christopher-columbus-9254209).

"Clash of Civilizations Author Samuel Huntington Dies at Age 81" [in Arabic]. Reuters, December 27, 2008 (http://ara.reuters.com/article/entertainmentNews/idARACAE4BQ0TE20081227).

"Countries Ranked by Military Strength (2013)." GlobalFirePower.com (http://www.globalfirepower.com/countries-listing.asp);

"Cyber attack hits Qatar's RasGas" [in Arabic]. BBC Arabic Website, August 31, 2012 (http://www.bbc.co.uk/arabic/scienceandtech/2012/08/120831_computer-virus.shtml).

"David Cameron." The History Channel (http://www.history.co.uk/biographies/david-cameron).

"Delivery of the First Aircraft Carrier to the Chinese Army" [in Arabic]. Al-Jazeera.net, September 23, 2012 (http://www.aljazeera.net/news/pages/ffefb2ff-3df3-4999-ad20-e77462e588b8).

"Developing by Relying on its Own Strength, Reform and Innovation." China Internet Information Center (http://www.china.org.cn/english/features/book/152764.htm).

"Difference Engine: Hackers' Paradise." *The Economist*, March 11, 2013 (http://www.economist.com/blogs/babbage/2013/03/crimeware?fsrc=scn/tw/te/bl/differenceenginehackersparadise).

"Djerejian Chairs A Committee to Review Public Relations Diplomacy to Improve America's Image in the Muslim World." *Al-Sharq Al-Awsat* no. 8957, June 7, 2003 (http://www.aawsat.com/details.asp?issueno=8800&article=175177#.UnJS0Plgd8E).

"Egyptian State Information Service" [in Arabic]; (http://www.sis.gov.eg/Ar/Templates/Articles/tmpArticles.aspx?CatID=585).

"Eisenhower Doctrine, 1957." Office of the Historian, US Department of State (http://history.state.gov/milestones/1953-1960/eisenhower-doctrine).

"EU and US Launch Talks to Create the Biggest Free Zone in the World" [in Arabic]. *Alroeya*, June 18, 2013 (http://www.alroeya.com/node/34792).

"EU and US Negotiators begin Talks aimed at Creating the World's Largest Free Trade Zone" [in Arabic]. *Al Khaleej* June 18, 2013 (http://www.alkhaleej.ae/portal/e38575a3-ba54-4004-ade2-79061a2 a9718.aspx).

"Euro area Unemployment Rate at 12.1%." Eurostat News Release No. 126/2013, August 30, 2013. (http://epp.eurostat.ec.europa.eu/cache/ITY_PUBLIC/3-30082013-AP/EN/3-30082013-AP-EN.PDF), p. 4.

"Europe and the United States of America Launch Negotiations on the Largest Free Trade Zone in the World" [in Arabic]. *Al-Khaleej*, June 18, 2013 (http://www.alkhaleej.ae/portal/e38575a3-ba54-4004-ade2-79061a2a9718.aspx).

"Eurozone Crisis: Beggar Thyself and Thy Neighbor." Research on Money and Finance (http://researchonmoneyandfinance.org/media/reports/eurocrisis/e_summary_eng.pdf).

"Faces of the Fallen." *The Washington Post* (http://apps.washingtonpost.com/national/fallen).

"First Quarter of 2013 Compared with Fourth Quarter of 2012." Eurostat News Release no. 114, July 22, 2013 (http://epp.eurostat.ec.europa.eu/cache/ITY_PUBLIC/2-22072013-AP/EN/2-22072013-AP-EN.PDF), p. 4.

"Francis Fukuyama: Biography." Stanford University (http://fukuyama.stanford.edu), accessed July 12, 2013.

"Hagel: US Army Budget will continue to Account for 40% of Defense Spending" [in Arabic]. *El-Watan* June 1, 2013 (http://www.elwatan news.com/news/details/192536).

"History of Relations between China and India." CNTV, May 21, 2013 (http://arabic.cntv.cn/2013/05/21/ARTI1369104581220531.shtml).

"History of the Spanish Empire." *History World* (http://historyworld.net/ wrldhis/PlainTextHistories.asp?historyid=ab49).

"In 1952 and after 50 Years: the Cuban Missile Crisis Almost Drew the World into a Nuclear War." *Al-Wasat,* October 10, 2012 (http://www. alwasatnews.com/3686/news/read/707685/1.html).

"Ins and outs: Acronyms BRIC Out All Over." *The Economist*, September 18, 2008 (http://www.economist.com/node/12080703).

"Maintaining US 'Overwhelming Technological Advantage' over Adversaries." March 27, 2013, Homeland Security News Wire (http:// www.homelandsecuritynewswire.com/dr20130327-maintaining-u-s-overwhelming-technological-advantage-over-adversaries).

"Management Team; Eugene Kaspersky." Kaspersky Lab (http://www. kaspersky.com/about/management_team).

"Markets, Currencies." *Financial Times*, July 29, 2013 (http://markets.ft. com/RESEARCH/markets/DataArchiveFetchReport?Category=CU& Type=3SPT&Date=07/29/2013).

"Melting Pot' America." BBC News online, May 12, 2006 (http://news. bbc.co.uk/2/hi/americas/4931534.stm).

"Monthly and Accumulated Crude Oil Imports (volumes and prices) by EU and non EU Country." Market Observatory for Energy, European Commission, Directorate-General for Energy (http://ec.europa.eu/ energy/observatory/oil/import_export_en.htm).

"Navy's New Cost-Saving Weapon: A Laser That Can Shoot Drones from the Sky." *The Blaze*, April 9, 2013 (http://www.theblaze.com/stories/

2013/04/09/navys-new-cost-saving-weapon-a-laser-that-can-shoot-drones-from-the-sky).

"Negotiations between the United States and the European Union to Establish a Free Trade Zone." *BBC.co.uk*, February 13, 2013 (http://www.bbc.co.uk/arabic/business/2013/02/130213_eu_us_trade.s html).

"Norman Borlaug – Biographical." The Nobel Prize (http://www. nobelprize.org/nobel_prizes/peace/laureates/1970/borlaug-bio.html).

"Norwegian *Magazinet* Apologizes for Publishing Blasphemous Cartoons of the Prophet" [in Arabic]. Al-Jazeera.net, February 11, 2006 (http://www.aljazeera.net/news/pages/2a92ade9-3f1b-4862-bd07-f2e3d848e63c).

"Not so Super: The 'Third Arrow' of Reform has Fallen well short of its Target; Time for Shinzo Abe to Rethink." *The Economist,* June 15, 2013 (http://www.economist.com/news/leaders/21579464-third-arrow-reform-has-fallen-well-short-its-target-time-shinzo-abe-rethink-not).

"Obama Criticizes Russia and Promises A New Intelligence Era" [in Arabic]. Al-Jazeera website (http://www.aljazeera.net/news/pages/970367d7-4449-41e8-b442-7c1ab5ceabe1), accessed August 10, 2013.

"Operation Uphold Democracy-Haiti." Air University Library, Maxwell Airforce Base (http://www.au.af.mil/au/aul/bibs/haiti/haiti99.htm), accessed June 22, 2013.

"Panetta Warns of a Cyber Pearl Harbor" [in Arabic]. Aljazeera.net, October 12, 2012 (http://www.aljazeera.net/news/pages/e6948a4c-d6dd-4712-9681-2e71714c186e).

"People in Muslim Nations Conflicted About UN." WorldPublicOpinion. org, December 2, 2008 (http://www.worldpublicopinion.org/pipa/articles/btunitednationsra/575.php).

"Portugal: Historical Setting Library of Congress Country Study." *About.com* (http://lcweb2.loc.gov/frd/cs/pttoc.html).

"President Bush Delivers Graduation Speech at West Point." The White House, June 1, 2002 (http://georgewbush-whitehouse.archives.gov/news/releases/2002/06/20020601-3.html).

"President Obama's Address to U.N. General Assembly." The White House, Office of the Press Secretary, September 23, 2010 (http://iipdigital.usembassy.gov/st/arabic/texttrans/2010/09/20100923 16 3440x0.2680584.html#axzz2ahtcXXYb).

"Proposal for the Expansion of the Panama Canal: 3rd Set of Locks Project." Canal De Panmamá, April 24, 2006 (http://www.acp.gob.pa/eng/plan/documentos/propuesta/acp-expansion-proposal.pdf).

"Richard Clarke." Belfer Center for Science and International Affairs, Harvard University (http://belfercenter.ksg.harvard.edu/experts/1621/richard_clarke.html).

"Robert Gates." *Biography.com* (http://www.biography.com/people/robert-gates-40993).

"Saif bin Zayed: 'Our Wise Leadership Turned Visions into Strategic Decisions'" [in Arabic]. *Al-Ittihad*, February 13, 2013 (http://www.alittihad.ae/details.php?id=15512&y=2013).

"Six Reasons the US Will Dominate the World" [in Arabic]. *Akhbar Al-Saah* bulletin, Issue 5187 (Abu Dhabi: ECSSR, September 1, 2013).

"Six Values the West Added to Civilizations" [in Arabic]. *Al-Bayan,* November 20, 2011 (http://www.albayan.ae/one-world/new-books/2011-12-20-1.1558037).

"Social Networking Sites on the Internet – A Source of Great Threat to Individual Privacies: Companies, Governments and Thieves Use them to

Extract Information" [in Arabic]. *Al-Sharq Al-Awsat* March 16, 2010 (http://www.aawsat.com/details.asp?issueno=11700&article=561211).

"Surging Wages Threaten Economy's Competitiveness." *China Daily*, April 10, 2012 (http://www.chinadaily.com.cn/business/2013-04/10/content_16390012.htm).

"The African Union rejects the appearance of the Kenyan president before the Criminal Court of Justice" [in Arabic]. Reuters agency, October 12, 2013 (http://ara.reuters.com/article/worldNews/idARACAE9B2 5H220131012), accessed November 4, 2013.

"The Bolshevik Revolution 1917." *thenagain.info* (http://www.thenagain. info/webchron/easteurope/octrev.html).

"The British Burn Washington, DC, 1814." *Eyewitness to History* (http://www.eyewitnesstohistory.com/washingtonsack.htm), accessed September 22, 2013.

"The Constant and the Changing in the Global Economic System" [in Arabic], *Lebanese National Defense Magazine* (October 2000).

"The Democracy Lie: The National Democratic Institute" [in Arabic]; (http://ishtar-enana.blogspot.ae/2012/04/ndi.html).

"The Emerging Economies are Demanding a Greater Role in Financial Policies" [in Arabic]. BBC Arabic, September 4, 2009 (http://www. bbc.co.uk/arabic/business/2009/09/090904_ah_emerging_economies_ tc2.shtml).

"The European Union and the United States: Towards the Largest Free Trade Zone" [in Arabic]. *Russia Today*, July 10, 2013 (http://arabic. rt.com/news/620782).

"The Manifestations and Mechanisms of Cultural Invasion in Contemporary Arab Thought" [in Arabic]. Modern Discussion website, September 29, 2008 (http://www.ahewar.org/debat/show.art.asp?aid=148626).

"The Nuclear Question in the Middle East." Working Group Summary Report no. 4, Center for International and Regional Studies, Georgetown University School of Foreign Service, Qatar, 2012 (http://www12.georgetown.edu/sfs/qatar/cirs/NuclearQuestion SummaryReport.pdf).

"The Peace of Westphalia." *History Learning Site* (http://www.history learningsite.co.uk/peace_of_westphalia.htm).

"The Spanish Empire." *latinlibrary.com* (http://www.thelatinlibrary.com/ imperialism/notes/spanishempire.html).

"The Treaties of Utrecht (1713)." Heraldica.org (http://www.heraldica. org/topics/france/utrecht.htm).

"The Truman Doctrine." *History Learning Site* (http://www.history learningsite.co.uk/truman_doctrine.htm);

"The Truman Doctrine." *Johndclare.net* (http://www.johndclare.net/cold_ war8_TrumanDoctrine.htm).

"The UAE Renews its International Commitments to Combat Terrorism at UN" [in Arabic]. Emirates News Agency (WAM), October 9, 2013 (http://www.wam.ae/servlet/Satellite?c=WamLocAnews&cid=12900 06801383&pagename=WAM%2FWAM_A_PrintVersion), accessed October 30, 2013.

"The World is Looking for a New Economic System After the Failure of the Capitalist and Socialist Systems" [in Arabic]. April 17, 2011 (http://alphabeta.argaam.com/article/detail/28833).

"These are the reasons for the return of American unipolarity" [in Arabic]. *Akhbar Al-Saah* bulletin, Issue 5152 (Abu Dhabi: The Emirates Center for Strategic Studies and Research, July 20, 2013).

"Topics: Encouraging Social Change." Bertelsmann Stiftung, January 2008 (http://www.bertelsmann-stiftung.de/cps/rde/xbcr/SID-746191 AF-2CA45334/bst/xcms_bst_dms_23678_23679_2.pdf)

"Treaty of Versailles." Covenant of the League of Nations (http://us history.org).

"US Military Spending Over the Years." *davemanual.com* (http://www.davemanuel.com/2010/06/14/us-military-spending-over-the-years).

"US, EU Start Free-trade Talks Today" [in Arabic]. *Al Ittihad*, July 8, 2013 (http://www.alittihad.ae/details.php?id=65041&y=2013).

"USS Carl Vinson (CVN 70)." Unofficial Navy Site (http://navysite.de/cvn/cvn70.html).

"Wall Street." Investopedia (http://www.investopedia.com/terms/w/wall street.asp), accessed July 14, 2013.

"What does Xi Jinping's China Dream Mean?" [in Arabic]. BBC website, June 6, 2013 (http://www.bbc.co.uk/arabic/worldnews/2013/06/130606_china_xi_dream.shtml).

"Winston Churchill." *biography.com* (http://www.biography.com/people/winston-churchill-9248164).

"Women Worldwide know less about Politics than Men." Economic and Social Research Council, UK, July 3, 2013 (http://www.esrc.ac.uk/news-and-events/press-releases/26789/women_worldwide_know_less_about_politics_than_men.aspx).

"World Values Survey 2010–2012." revised master, October 2011 (WVS 2010-2012 Wave); (http://www.worldvaluessurvey.org/index_surveys).

"Xinhua: China builds a Second Larger Aircraft Carrier" [in Arabic]. Reuters, April 24, 2013 (http://ara.reuters.com/article/worldNews/id ARACAE9B28ZV20130424).

"Yalta Conference." Encyclopaedia Britannica (http://global.britannica.com/EBchecked/topic/651424/Yalta-Conference).

A'if, Majid. "The New World Order" [in Arabic]. *Al-Hiwar Al-Mutamaddin*, no. 3862, September 26, 2012 (http://www.ahewar.org/debate/show.art.asp?aid=325822K).

Aati, Muhammad Abdul. "The Greater Middle East Initiative and the Arab Summit." Al-Jazeera Net, October 3, 2004 (http://www.aljazeera.net/home/print/466530fd-e741-4721-acd2-a85c1ce6092a/3151aab2-5b13-4eed-92eb-04db51f 5550c).

Aati, Muhammad Abdul. "The Greater Middle East Initiative" [in Arabic]. *Al-Jazeera Net*, May 21, 2004 (http://aljazeera.net/news/pages/13 e60cb3-caed-44d5-a289-14e3a6facb79).

Abah, Al Sayed Weld. *The World after September 11, 2001: The Intellectual and Strategic Problematic* [in Arabic]; (Beirut: Arab Scientific Publishers, 2004).

Abdel Hay, Walid Salim. *Future Status of China in the International Order 1978–2010* [in Arabic]; (Abu Dhabi: The Emirates Center for Strategic Studies and Research, 2000).

Abdel Rahman, Mohammed Yacoub. *Humanitarian Intervention in International Relations* [in Arabic]; (Abu Dhabi: The Emirates Center for Strategic Studies and Research, 2004).

Abdel-Ati, Amr. "American Unilateralism between Continuity and Demise" [in Arabic]. *Al-Siyassa Al-Dawliya*, Issue 173 (July 2008).

Abdel-Ati, Amr. "Review of *The World America Made*" [in Arabic]. Aljazeera.net website, May 13, 2013 (http://studies.aljazeera.net/bookrevision/2013/05/20135137202626736.htm).

Abdul Hakeem, Mansoor. *The Latest World War is the Last War on Earth* (Damascus & Cairo: Dar Al-Kitab Al-Arabi, 2008).

Abdullah, Abdul Khaliq. "Globalization: its Roots and Branches and How to Deal with it." *Alam Al Fikr* no. 28 (October 1999).

Abdullah, Abdul Khaliq. "The New World Order: Facts and Illusions" [in Arabic]. *Al-Siyassa Al-Dawliya*, Issue 124 (April 1996).

Abrash, Ibrahim. "System Limits and the Legitimacy Crisis in the New World Order' [in Arabic]. *Al-Mustaqbal Al-Arabi*, Issue 185 (Beirut: 1994).

Abu Amoud, Mohamed Sa'ad. "Globalization and the State" [in Arabic]. *Al-Siyassa Al-Dawliya*, Issue no.161 (Cairo: July 2005).

Abu Saud, Salah. *Shiites: Political Emergence and Religious Doctrine* [in Arabic]; (Al-Giza: Al-Nafezah Bookshop, 2004).

Abu Zahra, Mohamed. *History of Islamic Denominations in Politics and Doctrines and the History of Jurisprudential Denominations* [in Arabic]; (London, Cyprus: Dar Al-Hadith, 1987).

Abunnasr, Fadeel. The *Global Citizen: Globalization, Globalism and the Just Global Order* [in Arabic]; (Beirut: Bissan for Publishing, Distribution and Information, 1st Edition, 2001).

Ackerman, Spencer. "Afghanistan, Iraq Wars Killed 132,000 Civilians, Report Says." *Wired*, June 29, 2011 (http://www.wired.com/danger room/2011/06/afghanistan-iraq-wars-killed-132000-civilians-report-says).

Ahmad, Iman. "Patterns and Roles of Non-state Actors in the Arab Region" [in Arabic]. *Al-Siyassa Al-Dawliya*, Issue no.185, July 2011.

Ahmad, Sayed Abu Daif. *A Crumbling Empire: The Future of American Hegemony and the International System* [in Arabic]; (Cairo: Dar Al Talae for Publishing and Distribution, 2009).

Ahmed, Ahmed Yusuf, et al. *The Arab World and Global Developments* (Cairo: Center for Arab Research and Studies, 1991).

Ahmed, Mohamed Sayed. "The Escalation of Terrorism and the Clash of Civilizations" [in Arabic]. *Al Arabi* no. 518 (Kuwait: January 2002).

Ahmed, Nazli Moawad. "The Japanese Perception of the International System" [in Arabic]. *Al-Siyassa Al-Dawliya*, Issue 101 (July 1990).

Al-Abideen, Zain and Najm Shams Al-Deen. *History of the Ottoman State* [in Arabic]; (Amman: Dar Al-Massira, 2010).

Al-Adli, Mahmood Saleh. *International Legitimacy Under the New World Order* [in Arabic]; (Alexandria: Dar Al-Fikr Al-Gamei, 2003).

Al-Ameen, Fadeel. "Does China's Rise Mean America's Decline? [in Arabic]. *Asharq Al-Awsat*, Issue 11447, April 1, 2010 (http://www. aawsat.com/leader.asp?section=3&article=563434&issueno=11447#. Um-48vmnpmg).

Al-Ashry, Najah. *Globalization and Hegemony* [in Arabic]; (Tripoli: Nasser International University, 1999).

Al-Atiyya, Isam. *Public International Law* [in Arabic]; (Baghdad: Baghdad University Press, 1983).

Al-Barsan, Ahmad Saleem. "The Greater Middle East Initiative: Political and Strategic Dimensions" [in Arabic]. *Al-Siyasa Al-Dawliyya* no. 158 (October 2004).

Al-Bastanji, Yousef. "UNDP Issues its Global Development Report from Abu Dhabi: UAE Ranked First in the Arab Region, 30th Globally in terms of Human Development" [in Arabic]. *Al-Ittihad*, January 9, 2012 (http://www.alittihad.ae/details.php?id=2633&y=2012).

Al-Bursan, Ahmed Salem. 'The Greater Middle East Initiative: Political and Strategic dimensions' [in Arabic]. *Al-Siyassa Al-Dawliya*, Issue 158 (Cairo: October 2004).

Al-Daim, Abdullah. "The New Barbarians: Would the Third World People Become the neo-Barbarians in the New International Order?" [in Arabic]. *Al Mustaqbal Al Arabi* no. 106, June 1992 (http://www. abdeldaim.com/moreinfo.php?b=4&sub_id=332).

Alden, Chris. *China in Africa: A Partner or a Competitor?* [in Arabic], Othman Al Jabali Al-Mathlouthi (trans.); (Beirut: Arab Scientific Publishers, Inc. 2009).

784

Al-Duwaik, Abdul Ghaffar. "Failure of Bush's Pre-emptive Doctrine: War Is Not Won by Military Strategy Alone" [in Arabic]. *Al-Ahram* January 11, 2004 (http://www.ahram.org.eg/archive/2004/1/11/FILE 10.HTM).

Al-Haiti, Hadi Noman. "Incoming International Satellite TV Communication and Potential Political Effects on the Arab World" [in Arabic]. *Al-Mustaqbal Al-Arabi* no. 34 (Beirut: Centre for Arab Unity Studies, 2003).

Al-Hashimi, Abdul Rahman and Faiza Muhammad Al-Izzawi. *Curriculum and Knowledge Economy* [in Arabic]; (Amman: Dar Al-Masseera for Publication, Distribution and Printing, 2007).

Al-Hashimi, Abdul-Mun'im. *The Andalusian Caliphate* [in Arabic]; (Beirut: Dar Ibn Hazm for Printing, Publishing and Distribution, 2007).

Al-Hassan, Bilal. "Bush Seeks to Impose a New World Order" [in Arabic]. *Asharq Al-Awsat*, Issue 8713, October 6, 2002 (http://www.aawsat.com/leader.asp?section=3&article=128462&issueno=8713).

Al-Hassan, Issa. *The Second World War: Causes, Facts and Results* [in Arabic]; (Amman: Al-Ahliyya for Publication and Distribution, 2009).

Al-Hassan, Issa. *World War I: Proceedings of the War that Ended the Lives of Millions* [in Arabic]; (Amman: Al-Ahlia for Publishing and Distribution, 2009).

Al-Hassan, Mohamed Sa'adi. "A Book Review: War in the Name of Humanity: Kill or Let Die" (*La guerre au nom de l'humanité. Tuer ou laisser mourir*); [in Arabic]. *Strategic Visions* vol. 1, Issue 1 (Abu Dhabi: The Emirates Center for Strategic Studies and Research, December 2012).

Al-Hassan, Mohamed Sa'adi. "The Role of Culture in Building Dialogue Among Nations" [in Arabic]. *Emirates Lecture Series* no. 154 (Abu Dhabi: The Emirates Center for Strategic Studies and Research, 2013).

Al-Hindawi, Jawad. *Constitutional Law and Political Systems* [in Arabic]; (Beirut: Dar Al-Aarif Publications, 2010).

Al-Hiti, Abdul Sattar Ibrahim. "The Dialogue: The Self and the Other" [in Arabic]. *Al-Ummah Book* series no. 99, undated, posted on the Umm Al-Qura University website (http://uqu.edu.sa/page/ar/59175), accessed July 23, 2013.

Al-Hussein, Shukrani. "Climate Justice: Towards a New Perspective for Social Justice" [in Arabic]. *Strategic Visions* vol. 1, Issue 1 (Abu Dhabi: The Emirates Center for Strategic Studies and Research, December 2012).

Al-Hyali, Nizar Ismail. *NATO's Role After the End of the Cold War* [in Arabic]; (Abu Dhabi: The Emirates Center for Strategic Studies and Research, 2003).

Ali, Ghulam. "China's Strategic Interests in Pakistan's Port at Gwadar." East Asia Forum, March 24, 2013 (http://www.eastasiaforum.org/2013/03/24/chinas-strategic-interests-in-pakistans-port-at-gwadar).

Alian, Ribhi Mustafa. *Knowledge Economy* [in Arabic]; (Amman: Dar al-Safaa for Publication and Distribution, 2011).

Al-Isawai, Ibrahim. "Economic Globalization between Inevitable Continuation and Potential Decline" [in Arabic]. *Al-Nahda,* no. 1 (1999).

Al-Ismail, Muhammad. "Harbingers of the European Renaissance" [in Arabic]. Aafaqcenter.com, March 19, 2012 (http://aafaqcenter.com/index.php/post/1081), accessed October 30, 2013.

Al-Izzi, Ghassan. *Power Politics: The Future of the International System and the Great Powers* [in Arabic]; (Beirut: Center for Arab Unity Studies, 2000).

Al-Jabri, Mohammed Abed. *Issues in Contemporary Arab Thought* [in Arabic]; (Beirut: Center for Arab Unity Studies, 1997).

Al-Karwi, Mahmoud Saleh. "The Status of Religion in the Moroccan Monarchy System" [in Arabic], *Arab Journal of Political Science* no. 19 (Summer 2008).

Al-Khoury, Nassim. *Arab Media and the Collapse of Linguistic Authorities* [in Arabic]; (Beirut: Centre for Arab Unity Studies, 2005).

Al-Mahdi, Amin. "The End of the Cold War Has Weakened National Sovereignty in Favor of Peoples" [in Arabic]. *Al-Hayat*, July 27, 2003.

Al-Moeini, Khaled. "Pretext of Humanitarian Intervention in International Relations" [in Arabic]. Al-Jazeera.net website, April 9, 2012 (http://www.aljazeera.net/opinions/pages/032efaa9-0dad-4af0-9d00-ba9f6afc0adf).

Al-Musawi, Muhsin Bagir. *Shura and Democracy* [in Arabic]; (Beirut: Dar Al-Hadi Printing, Publishing and Distribution, 2003).

Al-Nabrawi, Fathiyya, and Muhammad Nasr Muhanna. *Principles of International Political Relations* [in Arabic]; (Alexandria: Munsh'at AL-Ma'arif, n.d.).

Al-Nabulsi, Shakir. "A Critique of the Ideology of Information and Communication Revolution" [in Arabic]. *Al-Hiwar Al-Mutamaddin* October 24, 2010 (http://www.ahewar.org/debat/show.art.asp?aid=232949).

Al-Namlah, Ali Bin Ibrahim. *The East and the West: Premises and Determinants of Relations* [in Arabic]; (Beirut: Bissan for Publishing, Distribution and Information, 2010).

Al-Otaibi, Abdullah Bin Jabr. "Globalization and Interdependence in International Politics: A Realistic Viewpoint" [in Arabic]. *El-Nahda*, Volume XI, Issue 3 (July 2010).

Al-Qarie, Ahmad Yousuf. "Revival of the Hotline in a World on the Brink." *Al-Ahram*, October 20, 2006; [in Arabic]; (http://yyy.ahram.org.eg/archive/2006/10/20/OPIN3.HTM).

Al-Qoozi, Mohammed Ali. *International Relations in Modern and Contemporary History* [in Arabic]; (Beirut: Dar Al-Nahda Al-Arabiya, 2002).

Al-Qurae, Ahmed Yousef. "Reviving the Hotline in a World at the Brink of the Abyss" [in Arabic]. *Al-Ahram*, October 20, 2006 (http://yyy.ahram.org.eg/archive/2006/10/20/OPIN3.HTM).

Al-Quraishi, Ali. "The Dialogue of Civilizations and the Need to Rein Arrogant Identities" [in Arabic]. *Al Arabi* no. 525 (August 2002).

Al-Rahman, Osman Siraj Eldeen Fateh. "Social Welfare between the International Conventions and Treaties and the Domestic laws: United Arab Emirates as a Model" [in Arabic]. *Strategic Visions*, vol. 1, issue 4 (September 2013).

Al-Rubaie, Kauthar Abbas, and Marwan Salem Al-Ali. *The Future of the New International Order in Light of the Emergence of Rising Powers and its Impact on the Arab Region: The EU Model* [in Arabic]; (Baghdad: Center for International Studies, 2009).

Al-Rubaie, Kawthar Abbas. *The Evolution of the Concept of American National Security,* [in Arabic] *Strategic Studies Series*, No. 35 (Baghdad: Center for International Studies, 2002).

Al-Rubaie, Nabeel Abdul-Ameen. "The Umma Kingdom: Ancient Civilization of Mesopotamia" [in Arabic]. *Al-Hiwar Al-Mutamaddin* July 12, 2013 (http://m.ahewar.org/s.asp?aid=368300&r=0&cid=0&u=&i=0&qK).

Al-Sadoun, Humaid Hamad. *Chaos of the New World Order and its Effects on the Arab Regional Order* [in Arabic]; (Amman: Dar Al-Tali'a Al-Arabia for Publishing, 2001).

Al-Saeedi, Salma. *Smart School is the School of the 21st Century* [in Arabic]; (Cairo: Dar Farha for Printing, Publishing and Distribution, 2002).

Al-Safti, Adil. "Getting Rid of the Bush doctrine – A Task Awaiting the Congress" [in Arabic]. *Al-Ittihad,* Opinion Page, June 8, 2007.

Al-Safti, Adil. "Power Politics – from Truman to the Bush Doctrine" [in Arabic]. *Al-Ittihad*, Opinion Page, August 3, 2007 (http://www.alittihad.ae/wajhatdetails.php?id=30075).

Al-Samad, Riyad. *International Relations in the 20th Century* [in Arabic]; (Beirut: Arab Institution for Research, Publishing and Distribution, 1983).

Al-Sayed, Mustafa and Ahmad Abu Al-Khair. "The General Theory of Military Alliances and Blocs in Accordance with the Rules of General International Law" [in Arabic]; (Beirut: Center for Arab Unity Studies, 2010).

Al-Sayed, Yassin. "Civilizations between Dialogue, Conflict and the Alliance" [in Arabic]. *Al-Ahram* newspaper, May 13, 2010 (http://digital.ahram.org.eg/articles.aspx?Serial=133748&eid=448).

Al-Sayyed, Redwan. "Civilizations: From Dialogue to Coalition, and the New Turkish Policies" [in Arabic]. *Asharq Al-Awsat* no., Issue 11091, April 10, 2009 (http://www.aawsat.com/leader.asp?section=3&article=514609&issueno=11091).

Al-Sayyed, Redwan. "Dialogue in the Face of Calls of a Clash of Civilizations and the End of History" [in Arabic]. *Asharq Al Awsat*, July 18, 2008.

Al-Sayyid, Muhammad Saeed and Ahmad Ibrahim Mahmood. "Chaos and Stability in the International System: Trends in the Evolution of International System in Post-Cold War Era" [in Arabic]. *Arab Strategic Report 1995* (Cairo: Al-Ahram Center for Political and Strategic Studies, 1996).

Al-Sayyid, Muhammad Saeed. "The Idea of the New World Order between Tyranny and Participation" [in Arabic]. *Al-Arabi*, no. 403

(June 1992); (http://www.alarabimag.com/Article.asp?ART=532& ID=272).

Al-Sayyid, Muhammad Saeed. "Transnational Corporations and the Future of the Phenomenon of Nationalism" [in Arabic]. *A'lam Al-Ma'rifa* series, no. 107 (Kuwait: National Council for Culture, Arts and Letters, November 1986).

Al-Sayyid, Muhammad Saeed. *The Future of the Arab System after the Gulf Crisis*, [in Arabic]. A'lam Al-Ma'rifa Series, No. 158 (Kuwait: the National Council for Culture, Arts and Letters, February 1992).

Al-Sayyid, Muhammad Saleem. "The Reality and Future of Alliances in Asia." *Al-Siyassa Al-Dawliyya* no. 183 (January 2011); (http://digital. ahram.org.eg/articles.aspx?Serial=409097&eid=306).

Al-Sayyid, Yaseen, et al. *Arabs and Globalization* (Beirut: Center for Arab Unity Studies, 1998).

Al-Shaikh, Jaafar Hassan Atreesi. *Americanization of Nations and Clash of Civilizations: The New World Order and Solo Leadership* [in Arabic]; (Beirut: Dar Al-Hadi, 2002).

Al-Shaikh, Sami Muhammad. "The Protestant Reform Movement (Luther, Zwingli and Calvin)" [in Arabic]. *Alwatanvoice*, January 8, 2006 (http://pulpit.alwatanvoice.com/articles/2006/01/08/35520.html).

Al-Shami, Hasan. "Essence of the Clash of Civilizations between Islam and the West" [in Arabic]. Modern Discussion website, Issue 3713, April 30, 2012 (http://www.ahewar.org/debat/show.art.asp?aid= 305633).

Al-Shayyab, Mohamed Khaled. "Arab Society between the Authority of State and the Tyranny of Religion" [in Arabic]; (Amman: Ward Books for Publishing and Distribution, 2004).

Al-Siddiqi, Saeed Marzooq. "Tightening Border Controls and Building Fences to Fight Immigration: A Comparison between American and Spanish policies" [in Arabic]. *Strategic Visions* vol. 1, Issue 3 (Abu Dhabi: The Emirates Center for Strategic Studies and Research, June 2013).

Al-Soofi, Khalid. *History of the Arabs in Spain, the End of the Umayyad Caliphate in Andalusia* (Beirut: Al-Jamal publications, 2011).

Al-Suwaidi, Jamal Sanad (ed.). *The Gulf Co-operation Council: Prospects for the Twenty-first Century* [in Arabic]; (Abu Dhabi: The Emirates Center for Strategic Studies and Research, 1999).

Al-Suwaidi, Jamal Sanad. *From Tribe to Facebook: the Transformational Role of Social Networks* [in Arabic]; (Abu Dhabi: Emirates Center for Strategic Studies and Research [ECSSR], 2013).

Al-Tahhan, Mustafa Mohammed. "Is it the End of History" [in Arabic]. *Al-Mujtama'a Al Thaqafi* ["Culture Community"] no. 1313 (1998).

Altwaijri, Abdulaziz bin Othman. "Dialogue for Coexistence" [in Arabic]; (Cairo: Dar Al Shorok, 1998).

Al-Wafa, Ahmad Abu. "The United Nations and the New World Order" [in Arabic]. *Al-Siyassa Al-Dawliyya*, no. 122 (October 1996).

Al-Yahyawi, Yahya. "Obama and the Concept of Smart Power." *Hespress* March 10, 2009 (http://hespress.com/opinions/11560.html).

Al-Zaidi, Mufeed. "Part I, History of Europe in the Middle Ages (1789–1914)" [in Arabic]. *Encyclopedia of Modern and Contemporary History of Europe* (Amman: Dar Usama for Publishing and Distribution, 2004).

Al-Zaidi, Mufeed. *Encyclopedia of Modern and Contemporary History of Europe: From the French Revolution to the First World War, Part III, 1789–1914* [in Arabic]; (Amman: Dar Usama for Publishing and Distribution, 2004).

Al-Zamili, Majid Ahmad. "Diplomacy and its Impact on International Relations" [in Arabic]. *Al-Hiwar Al-Mutamaddin* no. 4223, September 22, 2013; (http://www.ahewar.org/debat/show.art.asp?aid =379192).

Al-Zoubi, Mousa. *A New World Order or a New American Hegemony?* [in Arabic]; (Damascus: Dar al-Shadi, 1993).

Amin, Emil. "Coexistence of Cultures: Müller in the Face of Huntington" [in Arabic]. *Asharq Al-Awsat*, Issue 12362, October 2, 2012; (http://www.aawsat.com/details.asp?section=17&article=697864&iss ueno=12362).

Amin, Jalal. "Globalization and the State" [in Arabic]. *Al-Mustaqbal Al-Arabi*, no. 228 (February 1998).

Amin, Jalal. *The Soft State in Egypt* [in Arabic]; (Cairo: Sina Publishing, 1993).

Amin, Samir, and Francois Houtard. *Countering Globalization: Popular Organizations, Movements in the World* [in Arabic]; (Cairo: Madbouly Bookshop, 2004).

Amin, Samir. *An Intellectual Autobiography* [in Arabic]; (Beirut: Dar Al-Aadab, 1993).

Amin, Samir. *Empire of Chaos* [in Arabic]. Sana Abu Shaqra (trans.); (Beirut: Dar Al-Farabi, 1991).

Amrani, Abdelmjid. *The Future of the Dialogue of Civilizations and Globalization* [in Arabic]; (Dubai: The Cultural and Scientific Foundation, 2004).

Andrews-Speed, Philip, et al. "The Global Resource Nexus: The Struggles for Land, Energy, Food, Water and Minerals." Transatlantic Academy, May 2012.

Aourid, Hassan. *Islam, the West and Globalization* [in Arabic]; (Casablanca: Al Zaman Newspaper Publications, 1999).

Arab League Educational, Cultural and Scientific Organization (ALECSO). *Reference History Book of the Islamic State*, Vol. 3 [In Arabic]; (Tunis: ALECSO, 2006).

Armitage, Richard L., and Joseph S. Nye. *CSIS Commission on Smart Power: A Smarter, More Secure America* (Washington, DC: Center for Strategic and International Studies [CSIS], 2007).

Arslan, Shakib. *The End of Arab History in Andalusia* (Giza: Al-Nafiza Bookshop, 2011).

Asser, Martin. "Blasphemous Cartoons: What is their Content?' [in Arabic]. BBC website, February 18, 2006; (http://news.bbc.co.uk/hi/arabic/news/newsid_4728000/4728052.stm), accessed October 30, 2013.

Ati, Amr Abdel. "Transformations of the International System and the Future of American Hegemony" [in Arabic]. *Al-Siyassa Al-Dawliya*, Issue 183 (January 2011).

Atrisi, Jafer Hassan. Americanization of Nations and the Clash of Civilizations: The New International System and Individual Leadership [in Arabic]; (Beirut: Dar Al-Hadi, 2002).

Attali, Jacques. *Lignes d'horizon*, Muhammad Zakariyya (trans.); (Beirut: Dar Al-Ilm Lil-Malayeen, 1992).

Atwa, Fathi Hosni. "The Return of Egyptian-Soviet Relations" [in Arabic]. *Al-Siyassa Al-Dawliya*, Issue 78 (October 1984).

Ayau, Manuel. F. *Not a Zero-Sum Game: The Paradox of Exchange* (Guatemala: Universidad Francisco Marroquin, 2007).

Ayef, Majed. "The New World Order" [in Arabic]. Al-Hewar Al-Motamadden [Modern Discussion] website, September 26, 2012; (http://www.ahewar.org/debat/show.art.asp?aid=325822).

Aziz, Fridah. *The New World Order and the 21st Century* [in Arabic]; (Damascus: Dar Al-Rasheed, 1994).

Badrakhan, Abdel Wahab. "About the Relationship of the West with Islam" [in Arabic]; (http://www.ecssr.com).

Baghdadi, Abdulsalam Ibrahim. *National Unity and the Problem of Minorities in Africa* [in Arabic]; (Beirut: Center for Arab Unity Studies, First Edition, 1987).

Baidany, Hanaa. The Concept of Despotism in Modern and Contemporary Islamic Political Thinking: A Comparative Study [in Arabic]; (Cairo: Egyptian Lebanese Publishing House, 2012).

Bailes, Alyson J.K. "The Future of International Order: A European Perspective." seminar hosted by the Center for Democratic Control of Armed Forces, Geneva, November 20, 2003.

Barakat, Nizam. "Implications of the September Incidents for the International System" [in Arabic]. Aljazeera.net, October 3, 2004; (http://www.aljazeera.net/home/print/787157c4-0c60-402b-b997-1784ea612f0c/452a9426-53ea-4f74-a70b-897bb6eef613).

Beaudry, Pierre. "The Economic Policy that Made the Peace of Westphalia." *Executive Intelligence Review*, vol. 30, no. 21 (May 2003).

Bek, Maha Nasser Kheir. "The Arabic language and Sciences of the Era." *Al-Arabi* magazine (Kuwait), no. 554/1, 2005; (http://www.alarabi mag.com/Article.asp?ART=9122&ID=115).

Belkeziz, Abdelilah. "After the Collapse of the Soviet Union: What to Do?" [in Arabic]. *Al Mustaqbal Al Arabi* no. 154 (December 1991).

Belkeziz, Abdelilah. "Creative Chaos: the Code Name of Fragmentation" [in Arabic]. *Al-Kaleej*, May 11, 2012.

794

Biden, Joseph R. Jr. "How I Learned to Love the New World Order." *The Wall Street Journal*, April 23, 1992.

Bilmes, Linda J. "The Financial Legacy of Iraq and Afghanistan: How Wartime Spending Decisions Will Constrain Future National Security Dudgets." Harvard Kennedy School, *Faculty Research Working Paper Series*, RWP13-003, March 2013 (https://research.hks.harvard.edu/publications/workingpapers/citation.aspx?PubId=8956).

Blum, William. *Killing Hope: US Military and CIA Interventionism since World War II* (Monroe, ME: Common Courage Press, 1995).

Boniface, Pascal. "Why Victory in the War on Terror Remains Elusive?" Opinion Articles, the Emirates Center for Strategic Studies and Research website, July 30, 2005 (http://www.ecssr.com).

Booth, Ken, and Tim Dunne (eds.). *Worlds in Collision: Terror and the Future of Global Order* [in Arabic]; (Abu Dhabi: The Emirates Center for Strategic Studies and Research, 2005).

Booton, Jennifer. "Major Corporations attacked in Historic Hacking Case." *Fox Business*, July 25, 2013; (http://www.foxbusiness.com/technology/2013/07/25/major-companies-victims-in-biggest-hacking-case).

Boutros-Ghali, Boutros. "The United Nations and the Containment of Ethnic Conflicts" [in Arabic]. *Al-Siyassa Al-Dawliya*, Issue 115 (January 1994).

BP. "BP Statistical Review of World Energy." June 2013; (http://www.bp.com/statisticalreview).

Bremmer, Ian and David Gordon. "The G-Zero Order." *The New York Times*, Opinion Pages, October 26, 2011; (http://www.nytimes.com/2011/10/27/opinion/27iht-edbremmer27.html).

Bremmer, Ian and Nouriel Roubini. "A G-Zero World: The New Economic Club Will Produce Conflict, Not Cooperation." *Foreign Affairs*, vol. 90, no. 2 (March/April 2011); (http://www.foreignaffairs. com/articles/67339/ian-bremmer-and-nouriel-roubini/a-g-zero-world).

Bremmer, Ian. "From G8 to G20 to G-Zero: Why No One Wants to Take Charge in the New Global Order." *New Statesman*, June 11, 2013 (http://www.newstatesman.com/politics/politics/2013/06/g8-g20-g-zero-why-no-one-wants-take-charge-new-global-order).

Brynen, Rex, Bahgat Korany, and Paul Noble (eds.). *Political Liberalization and Democratization in the Arab World* (Boulder, CO: Lynne Rienner Publishing, 1995).

Brzezinski, Zbigniew. *Out of Control: Global Turmoil on the Eve of the 21st Century* [in Arabic]. Fadel al-Badri (trans.); (Amman: Al-Ahlia for Publishing and Distribution, 1998).

Brzezinski, Zbigniew. *The Choice: Global Domination or Global Leadership* (New York, NY: Basic Books, 2004).

Brzezinski, Zbigniew. *The Grand Chessboard: American Primacy and its Geostrategic Imperatives* (New York, NY: Basic Books, 1997).

Brzezinski, Zbigniew. *The Grand Chessboard: American Primacy and Its Geostrategic Imperatives* [in Arabic]; (Cairo: Merit Publishing House, 2003).

Bull, Hedley. *The Anarchical Society: A Study of Order in World Politics* (New York, NY: Columbia University Press, 1977).

Bush, George H.W. "Address before the 45th Session of the United Nations General Assembly in New York, New York October 1, 1990." The American Presidency Project, University of California, Santa Barbara (http://www.presidency.ucsb.edu/ws/index.php?pid=18883).

Bush, George H.W. "Operation Desert Storm Launched." Address to the nation from the White House, January 16, 1991.

Bush, George H.W. Speech at Maxwell Air Force Base, Montgomery, Alabama, The White House, April 13, 1992 (http://www.presidency. ucsb.edu/ws/?pid=19466#axzz2iEpfIVMS).

Bush, George H.W. Speech to Congress, The White House, March 6, 1991.

Carmines, E.G. and R.A. Zeller. *Reliability and Validity Assessment* (Newbury Park, CA: Sage Publications, 1991); (http://www.uky.edu/~ clthyn2/PS671/carmines_zeller_671.pdf).

Carpenter, Sam. Work the System: The Simple Mechanics of Making More and Working Less (Austin, TX: Greenleaf Book Group, 2011).

Carpenter, Ted Galen. "The New World Disorder." *Foreign Policy* (Fall 1991).

Carus, Seth. "Chemical Weapons in the Middle East." *Policy Focus* no. 9, Washington Institute for Near East Policy, December 1988; (http://www.washingtoninstitute.org/policy-analysis/view/chemical-weapons-in-the-middle-east).

Cass, Connie. "Fiscal Cliff: Why Can't Democrats and Republicans Agree?" Associated Press (AP), *USA Today*, December 31, 2012; (http://www.usatoday.com/story/news/politics/2012/12/29/fiscal-cliff-guide/1798027).

Center for Strategic Studies, Research and Documentation. *The Clash of Civilizations* [in Arabic]; (Beirut: CSSRD, 1995).

Chaliand, Gérard, and Michel Jan. "Vers un Nouvel Ordre du Monde" [in Arabic]. Mohamed Saadi (trans.), *Strategic Visions*, Issue 4 (Abu Dhabi: The Emirates Center for Strategic Studies and Research, September 2013).

Chican, Dumitru. "Constructive Anarchy in the Context of the New Middle East." *Geostrategic Pulse* magazine, Issue 147, June 20, 2013.

Chomsky, Noam. "America Fears Democracy in Arab Spring Countries" [in Arabic]. *Al-Jazeera Net*, October 27, 2012; (http://www.aljazeera.net/news/pages/c4ec8953-89d6-4803-aa43-6a937c0414a8).

Chomsky, Noam. "Market Democracy in a Neoliberal Order: Doctrines and Reality." Iman Shams (trans.), *Shu'un Al-Awsat*, No. 71 (April 1998).

Chomsky, Noam. *Hegemony or Survival: America's Quest for Global Dominance* [in Arabic]. Sami Kaaki (trans.); (Beirut: Dar Al Kitab Al Arabi, 2004).

Chomsky, Noam. *Power Systems: Conversations on Global Democratic Uprisings and the New Challenges to US Empire* (New York, NY: Metropolitan Books, 2013).

Chomsky, Noam. *Rogue States: The Rule of Force in World Affairs* [in Arabic]. Mahmoud Ali Issa (trans.); (Beirut: Dar Al Kitab Al Arabi, 2003).

Chomsky, Noam. *World Orders, Old and New* Safwan Akkash (trans.); (Damascus: Dar Fussilat for Studies, Translation and Publishing, 2000).

Clarke, Richard A., and Robert K. Knake. *Cyber War: The Next Threat to National Security and What to Do About It* [in Arabic]. Translated Studies (Abu Dhabi: The Emirates Center for Strategic Studies and Research, 2012).

Cofman Wittes, Tamara. "The New US Proposal for a Greater Middle East Initiative: An Evaluation." *Middle East Memo*, no. 2, May 10, 2004; (http://www.brookings.edu/research/papers/2004/05/10middleeast-wittes).

Coggan, Philip. "Expect China to Shape the Next Bretton Woods Pact" [in Arabic], *Asharq Al-Awsat*, Issue 12124, February 7, 2012 (http://www.aawsat.com/leader.asp?section=3&article=662509&issue no=12124).

Coll, Steve. *Private Empire: ExxonMobil and American Power* (New York, NY: Penguin, 2012).

Committee of the Red Cross. "Customary international humanitarian law." October 29, 2010; (http://www.icrc.org/ara/war-and-law/treaties-customary-law/customary-law/overview-customary-law.htm).

Conan, Rebecca. "Chinese Firms to Develop US$20bn Panama Canal Alternative in Hondorus." *Business News Americas*, June 21, 2013; (http://www.bnamericas.com/news/infrastructure/chinese-firm-to-develop-us20bn-panama-canal-alternative-in-honduras1).

Cooperation Council of the Arab States of the Gulf (GCC). "GCC Common Defense Agreement" [in Arabic]; (http://www.almeezan.qa/AgreementsPage.aspx?id=1527&language=ar).

Copeland, Thomas E. "The Information Revolution and National Security" [in Arabic]. *International Studies* no. 46 (Abu Dhabi: The Emirates Center for Strategic Studies and Research, 2003).

Cox, K.R. and T.J. Sinclair. *Approaches to World Order* (Cambridge: Cambridge University Press, 1996).

Crotty, James. "Structural Causes of the Global Financial Crisis: A Critical Assessment of the New Financial Architecture." *Cambridge Journal of Economics* no. 33 (2009).

Crowe, Tyler. "What will Power America's Future? The Case for Oil." *The Motley Fool,* September 21, 2013.

Cyert, Richard M. and David C. Mowery (eds.). "Technology and Employment: Innovation and Growth in the US Economy"

(Washington, DC: The National Academies Press, 1987); (http://www.nap.edu/catalog.php?record_id=1004).

D'Angelo, Paul, and Jim A. Kuypers (eds.). *Doing News Framing Analysis* (New York, NY: Routledge, 2010).

Daher, Hussain Ali. *The Development of International Relations from Westphalia to Versailles* [in Arabic]; (Beirut: Dar al-Mawasim for Printing, Publishing and Distribution, 1999).

Daher, Masaoud. "Expected Shifts in the New World Order" [in Arabic]. *Al-Bayan*, December 7, 2011; (http://www.albayan.ae/opinions/articles/2011-12-07-1.1550208).

Day, Peter. "The Global Change in Economic Power [in Arabic]." BBC News online, September 20, 2005; (http://news.bbc.co.uk/hi/arabic/business/newsid_4264000/4264154.stm).

de Onis, Juan. "Brazil's Big Moment." *Foreign Affairs*, vol. 87, no. 6 (November/December 2008); (http://www.foreignaffairs.com/articles/64610/juan-de-onis/brazils-big-moment).

Delio, Fadil. *New Information and Communication Technology (NTIC/NICT): Concept, Uses, Prospects* [in Arabic]; (Amman: Dar Al Thaqafa, 2010).

Diamond, Larry, and Marc Plattner (eds.). *Liberation Technology: Social Media and the Struggle for Democracy* [in Arabic]; (Abu Dhabi: The Emirates Center for Strategic Studies and Research, 2013).

Dwivedi, Ranjit. "Environmental Movements in the Global South: Issues of Livelihood and Beyond" [in Arabic]. Shohrat El-Alem (trans.), *Al-Thaqafa Al-Alamiya* [World Culture] no. 111, 2002.

Edoho, F.M. (ed.). *Globalization and the New World Order* (New York, NY: Praeger Publishing, 1997).

Eichengreen, Barry. "Can the Euro Area Hit the Rewind Button?" University of California at Berkley, July 23, 2011 (http://emlab. berkeley.edu/~eichengr/can_euro_area_7-23-11.pdf).

El-Hassan, Yusuf. "The Religious Dimension of the American Policy Regarding the Arab-Zionist Conflict" [in Arabic]; (Beirut, Center for Arab Unity Studies 1990).

Elliott, Larry. "Eurozone Crisis Demands One Banking Policy, One Fiscal Policy – and One Voice." *The Guardian*, Economics Blog, April 1, 2013; (http://www.theguardian.com/business/economics-blog/2013/ apr/01/eurozone-crisis-banking-fiscal-union).

Elliott, Larry. "Global Financial Crisis: Five Key Stages 2007–2011." *The Guardian*, August 7, 2011; (http://www.theguardian.com/business/ 2011/aug/07/global-financial-crisis-key-stages).

El-Menoufi, Kamal. *Theories of Political Systems* [in Arabic]; (Kuwait: Publications Agency, 1985).

El-Messiri, Abdel Wahab. "Islam and the West." Al Jazeera.net, September 26, 2004; (http://www.aljazeera.net/opinions/pages/12d 34a40-f90b-4192-9a35-a9315b4e9132).

El-Messiri, Abdul Wahab. "Americanization, Cocacola-ization and Secularization" [in Arabic]. Al Jazeera.net, May 29, 2007; (http://www.aljazeera.net/opinions/pages/52ef6867-ef25-4fce-8de4- 4c34a30e4b79).

El-Najjar, Hassan A. *The Gulf War: Overreaction and Excessiveness in Killing and Destruction* [in Arabic]; (Dalton, GA: Amazone Press, 2001).

El-Sakka, Mohamed Ibrahim. "The Asian Crisis" [in Arabic]. *Al-Eqtisadiah* (http://www.aleqt.com/2010/08/13/article_429207.html).

Elsayed, Mounir Mahmoud Badawi. "Modern Trends in the Study of the International System since the End of the Cold War" [in Arabic].

Paper presented to the Standing Committee on Political Science, Faculty of Commerce, Assiut University, 2004.

El-Sayed, Mustafa Kamel. "Civil Society: The New Actor on the International Stage" [in Arabic]. *Al-Siyassa Al-Dawliya*, vol. 41, Issue 161 (July 2005).

Emara, Mohamed. *Trends of Islamic Thinking* [in Arabic], 3rd ed. (Cairo: Dar el-Shorouk, 2008).

Emirates Center for Strategic Studies and Research (ECSSR). *Global Strategic Developments: A Futuristic Vision* (Abu Dhabi: ECSSR, 2012).

Emirates Center for Strategic Studies and Research (ECSSR). *Globalization and its Influence on Society and State* [in Arabic]; (Abu Dhabi: ECSSR, 2002).

Emirates Center for Strategic Studies and Research (ECSSR). *Globalization in the 21st Century: How Interconnected is the World?* [in Arabic]; (Abu Dhabi: ECSSR, 2009).

Emirates Center for Strategic Studies and Research (ECSSR). *Human Resource Development in a Knowledge-Based Economy* [in Arabic]; (Abu Dhabi: ECSSR, 2004).

Emirates Center for Strategic Studies and Research (ECSSR). *Islam and the West: a Civilized Dialogue* [in Arabic]; (Abu Dhabi: ECSSR, 2012).

Emirates Publishers Association (EPA). *Book Publishing in the United Arab Emirates: A Survey and Analysis* (Sharjah: EPA, 2011);

Essayyed, Mounir Mahmoud Badawi. "Modern Trends in the Study of the International System Since the End of the Cold War." Research submitted to the Standing Committee for Political Science, Assiut University, Faculty of Commerce, 2004.

European Union (EU). "Energy Markets in the European Union in 2011." European Commission, Directorate-General for Energy (Luxembourg: Publications Office of the European Union, 2012); (http://ec.europa. eu/energy/gas_electricity/doc/20121217_energy_market_2011_lr_en. pdf).

European Union (EU). "Treaty of Maastricht on European Union" (http://europa.eu/legislation_summaries/institutional_affairs/treaties/tr eaties_maastricht_en.htm).

Fahmi, Abdul Qadir Muhammad. *The International Political System: A Study on Theoretical Origins and Contemporary Characteristics* [in Arabic]; (Baghdad: the General House of Cultural Affairs, 1995).

Faraj, Al Sayed Ahmed. *Dialogue of Civilizations under American Hegemony: is it Possible?* [in Arabic]; (Cairo: Dar Al Wafaa, 2004).

Fatemi, Khosrow (ed.). *The New World Order* (New York, NY: Pergamon, 2000).

Fattah, Sameeh Abdul. *The Collapse of the Soviet Empire: A New Unipolar World System* ([in Arabic]; (Amman: Dar Al-Shurooq for Publishing and Distribution, 1996).

Fawzi, Farooq Umar. *Studies in Islamic History: Research on Systems and Politics during the Early Islamic Centuries* [in Arabic]; (Amman: Dar Majdalawi, 2006).

Fawzi, Farooq Umar. *The History of Islamic Systems: A Study of the Development of Central Institutions in the State in Early Islamic Centuries* [in Arabic]; (Amman: Dar Al-Shurooq for Publishing and Distribution, 2010).

Federal Reserve Bank of St. Louis. "Monetary and Fiscal Policy in Times of Crisis." *Economic Information Newsletter*, March 2011; (http:// research.stlouisfed.org/pageone-economics/uploads/newsletter/2011/ 201103_ClassroomEdition.pdf).

Federation of American Scientists (FAS). "Country Rankings: 1997"; (http://www.fas.org/man/docs/wmeat98/rank98.pdf).

Fikri, Wael. *Encyclopedia of Ancient Egypt* (Cairo: Madbooli Bookshop, 2009).

Fillingham, Zachary. "US Military Bases: A Global Footprint." *Geopolitical Monitor*, April 14, 2012.

Fischer, Conan and Alan Sharp (eds.). *After the Versailles Treaty: Enforcement, Compliance, Contested Identities* (New York, NY: Routledge, 2009).

Florida, Richard. "The World's Leading Nations for Innovation and Technology." *The Atlantic Cities*, October 3, 2011 (http://www.the atlanticcities.com/technology/2011/10/worlds-leading-nations-innovation-and-technology/224).

Follah, Eric and Wieland Wagner. "China Seeks Role as Second Superpower." *Spiegel Online International*, February 11, 2012 (http://www.spiegel.de/international/world/global-ambitions-china-seeks-role-in-world-as-second-superpower-a-864358.html).

Forsythe, David. *Human Rights and World Politics* [in Arabic]. Mohammad Mustafa Ghoneim (trans.); (Cairo: The Egyptian Association for the Dissemination of Universal Culture and Knowledge, 1993).

Francis, Diane. "Welcome to the G-zero World." *Financial Post*, September 6, 2013 (http://opinion.financialpost.com/2013/09/06/welcome-to-the-g-zero-world).

Freedman, Lawrence. "Order and Disorder in the New World." *Foreign Affairs* vol. 71, no. 1 (special issue 1991).

Friedberg, Aaron. "The Future of American Power." *Political Science Quarterly*, vol. 109, no.1 (Spring 1994).

Friedman, George. "Beyond the Post-Cold War World." Sratfor, April 2, 2013; (http://www.stratfor.com/weekly/beyond-post-cold-war-world).

Friedman, George. *The Next 100 Years: A Forecast for the 21st Century* (New York, NY: Anchor Books, 2009).

Friedman, Thomas L. "From Beirut to Jerusalem to New York: It is World War III" [in Arabic]. *ASharq Al Awsat* no. 8327, September 15, 2001.

Friedman, Thomas L. *The World is Flat: A Brief History of The Twenty-First Century* (New York, NY: Farrar, Straus and Giroux, 2005).

Friedman, Thomas L. *The World is Flat: A Brief History of the Twenty-First Century* [trans. in Arabic]; (Beirut: Dar Al-Kitab Al-Arabi, 2006).

Friedman, Thomas. *The Lexus and the Olive Tree: Understanding Globalization,* Laila Zaidan (trans.); (Cairo: Al-Dar Al-Wataniyya Publishing and Distribution, 1999).

Fukuyama, Francis. "The End of History." *The National Interest* (Summer 1989).

Fukuyama, Francis. *State-Building: Governance and World Order in the 21st Century*, Mujab Al-Imam (trans.); (Riyadh: Obeikan Publishing, 2007).

Fukuyama, Francis. *The End of History and The Last Man* (London: The Penguin Group, 1992).

Fukuyama, Francis. *The End of History and the Last Man* [in Arabic]. Hussein Ahmed Amin (trans.); (Cairo: Al-Ahram Center for Translation and Publishing, 1993).

Gamaleddin, Safaa. "The Energy Crisis and the Policies of Western Industrialized Countries" [in Arabic]. *Al-Siyassa Al-Dawliya*, Issue 68 (Cairo: April 1982).

Gandali, Abdul Nasser. *The Impact of the Cold War on the Major Trends and the International Order* [in Arabic]; (Cairo: Madbouli Bookshop, 2011).

Gao, Haihong and Ulrich Volz. "Is China Ready to Open its Capital Account?" East Asia Forum, March 29, 2012; (http://www.eastasia forum.org/2012/03/29/is-china-ready-to-open-its-capital-account).

Garaudy, Roger. *Pour un dialogue des civilizations* [in Arabic], 5th ed. Adel Al-Awwa (trans.); (Beirut: Editions Oueidat, 2003).

Gargash, Anwar Mohammed. "Let's Reject the Logic of the Clash of Civilizations" [in Arabic]. *Al Ittihad*, February 20, 2006; (http://www. alittihad.ae/wajhatdetails.php?id=18295).

Ghalioun, Burhan. "The Effect of Globalization on the Social Situation in the Arab Region" [in Arabic]. Paper submitted to the Expert Meeting of the Economic and Social Commission for Western Asia, Beirut, December 19–21, 2005.

Ghassan, Mohamed Medhat. *Multinational Companies and State Sovereignty* [in Arabic]; (Amman: Dar Al-Raya for Publishing and Distribution, 2013).

Gibson, Rowan (ed.). *Rethinking the Future* [in Arabic]. Translated Studies No. 21 (Abu Dhabi: The Emirates Center for Strategic Studies and Research, 2004).

Giddens, Anthony. *The Third Way: The Renewal of Social Democracy* [in Arabic]. Ahmed Zayed, et al. (trans.); (Cairo: Supreme Council of Culture, 1999).

Gjelten, Tom. "Venezuela's Next Leader Faces Tough Choice on Oil Program." NPR, April 11, 2013; (http://www.npr.org/2013/04/11/1768 43567/venezuela-s-next-leader-faces-tough-choice-on-oil-program).

Glotz, Gustave. *The Greek City & Its Institutions*, 1st ed. Muhamamd Mandoor (trans.); (Cairo: National Center for Translation, 2011).

Goodenough, Patrick. "US Taxpayers Will Continue to Pay More Than One-Fifth of UN Budget." CNS News, December 28, 2012; (http://cnsnews.com/news/article/us-taxpayers-will-continue-pay-more-one-fifth-un-budget).

Gorbachev, Mikhail. *Perestroika: New Thinking for Our Country and the World* [in Arabic]. Hamdi Abdelgawwad (trans.); (Cairo: Dar Al-Shorok, 1988).

Gorbachev, Mikhail. *The New World Order*. Emirates Lecture Series No. 15 (Abu Dhabi: The Emirates Center for Strategic Studies and Research, 1998).

Graeme, Gill. *The Dynamics of Democratization* (London, Macmillan Press, 2000).

Grubb, Rod. *Alternative Global Vision of a New World Order* (Northfield, MN: St. Olaf College, 1992).

Guéhenno, Marie. *End of Democracy*, Haleem Tosson (trans.); (Cairo: Al-Shurooq Bookshop, 1995).

Haass, Richard. *The Opportunity: America's Moment to Alter History's Course* [in Arabic]. Saad Kamel Elias (trans.); (Riyadh: Obeikan Publishing, 2007).

Haddad, Remon. *International Relations: International Relations Theory, International Relations Characters; Chaos or Order Under Globalization* [in Arabic]; (Beirut: Dar Al-Haqeeqa, 2000).

Hadi, Riyadh Aziz. "From One Party to Multipartism [in Arabic]; (Baghdad: The General House of Cultural Affairs, 1995).

Hafiz, Abdul Azeem Jabr. "The New International System and the United States of America" [in Arabic]; (http://www.alitthad.com/paper.php?name=News&file=article&sid=18636).

Haikal, Fattouh. "Fitna Film ... Attempt to Distort the Tolerant Image of Islam." ECSSR website, April 17, 2008 (www.ecssr.com).

Halawa, Laila. "Sovereignty: the Dialectics of State and Globalization" [in Arabic]. Onislam.net, May 8, 2005 (http://www.onislam.net/arabic/madarik/concepts/99415-2005-05-08%2022-00-47.html).

Hall, Bronwyn H. and Jacques Mairesse. "Empirical Studies of Innovation in the Knowledge Driven Economy: An Introduction." NBER Working Paper Series, Working Paper no. 12320, National Bureau of Economic Research, June 2006; (http://www.nber.org/papers/w12320).

Hamdan, Mona. "Will Syria Join the List of US Military Interventions" [in Arabic]. *Al Hayat*, July 28, 2013; (http://alhayat.com/Details/545929).

Hamed, Rabie Mohamed. "Israel and Steps to Dominate the Arena of Cyberspace in the Middle East: A Study on the Preparations and Work Themes of the Jewish State in the Internet Age (2002–2013)" [in Arabic]. *Strategic Visions*, Issue 3 (Abu Dhabi: The Emirates Center for Strategic Studies and Research, June 2013).

Hanafi, Hassan and Sadiq Jalal Al-Azm. *What is Globalization?* [in Arabic]; (Beirut; Damascus: Dar Al-Fikr Al-Mu'asir, 1999).

Hanna, Elias. "Institutionalization of the Bush Doctrine" [in Arabic]. *AlJazeera.net*, October 3, 2004; (http://www.aljazeera.net/opinions/pages/165e161b-e5c9-41b1-bcf4-b2850fd2287a).

Haritani, Suleiman. *Employing the Taboo* [in Arabic]; (Damascus: Dar Al Hasad Publishing and Distribution, 2000).

Harper, John Lamberton. *The Cold War* (Oxford: Oxford University Press, 2011).

Hassan, Ammar Ali. "Defects of the Dialogue of Civilizations" [in Arabic]. *Al-Ittihad*, Viewpoints, May 24, 2013; (http://www.alittihad.ae/wajhatdetails.php?id=72641).

Hassan, Dahham. "Religious Reform Movement in Europe" [in Arabic]. *Minbar Al-Hurriyya*, November 1, 2010 (http://minbaralhurriyya.org/index.php/archives/2679).

Hassan, Fawzi. "Non-governmental Organizations and the Globalization of the International System" [in Arabic]. *Albayan*, May 23, 2013 (http://www.albayan.ae/opinions/articles/2013-05-23-1.1888730).

Hassan, Hamdy Abdel Rahman. "Ethnic and Political Conflicts in Africa: Reasons, Patterns and Future Prospects" [in Arabic]. *African Qira'at [Readings]* no. 1, October 2004 (http://www.siironline.org/alabwab/derasat(01)/607.htm).

Hatem, Mohammed Abel Kader. *Globalization: The Pros and Cons* [in Arabic]; (Cairo: General Egyptian Book Organization, 2005).

Haynes, Jeffrey (ed.). *Religion and Democratizations* (London and New York, NY: Routledge, 2011).

Heeley, Laicie. "US Defense Spending vs. Global Defense Spending." The Center for Arms Control and Non-Proliferation, April 24, 2013; (http://armscontrolcenter.org/issues/securityspending/articles/2012_topline_global_defense_spending).

Heikal, Mohamed Hassanein. *The American Empire and the Raid on Iraq* [in Arabic]; (Cairo: Dar El Shorouk, 2009).

Held, D. *Democracy and the Global Order: From the Modern State to Cosmopolitan Governance* (Stanford, CA: Stanford University Press, 1996).

Herd, Graeme P. (ed.). *Great Powers and Strategic Stability in the 21st Century: Competing Visions of World Order* (trans.); (Abu Dhabi: The Emirates Center for Strategic Studies and Research, 2013).

Hern, Alex. "A Gun made on a 3D Printer has been Fired: Let's Look at this in Perspective." *The Guardian*, May 6, 2013; (http://www.theguardian.com/commentisfree/2013/may/06/3d-printer-gun-has-been-fired).

Higgott, Richard. *Regionalization: New Trends in World Politics*, Emirates Lecture Series No. 13 (Abu Dhabi: The Emirates Center for Strategic Studies and Research, 1998).

Hilal, Ali Eddin. "The New International Order: The Current Situation and Future Prospects" [in Arabic]. *Alam el-Fikr* [The World of Thought], vol. 23, nos. III and IV (January/March and April/June 1995).

Hitti, Nassif Youssef. "Shifts in the World Order, the New Intellectual Climate and its Reflection on the Arab Regional Order" [in Arabic]. *Al Mustaqbal Al-Arabi*, Issue 165 (November 1992).

Hofbauer, Joachim, Priscilla Hermann and Sneha Raghavan. "European Defense Trends, 2012: Budgets, Regulatory Frameworks and the Industrial Base." CSIS Defense-Industrial Initiatives Group, Center for Strategic and International Studies (CSIS), December 2012.

Hogan, Michael J. *The End of the Cold War: Its Meaning and Implications*, Muhammad Usama Al-Qawtali (trans.); (Damascus: Ministry of Culture, 1998).

Hopper, Paul. *Understanding Cultural Globalization*. Tal'at Al-Sha'ib (trans.); (Cairo: National Center for Translation, 2011).

Hoshiar, Jawdat. "Joseph Nye and the Theory of Soft Power." *Al-Hiwar Al-Mutamaddin* July 18, 2013; (http://www.m.ahewar.org/s.asp? aid=369043 &r=0&cid=0&u=&i=0&q=).

Hoyle, Craig. "World Air Forces 2013." Flightglobal.com December 13, 2012; (http://www.flightglobal.com/blogs/the-dewline/2012/12/free-download-world-air-forces).

Huntington, Samuel P. "The Clash of Civilizations?" *Foreign Affairs*, vol. 72, no. 3 (Summer 1993); (http://www.foreignaffairs.com/articles/489 50/samuel-p-huntington/the-clash-of-civilizations).

Huntington, Samuel P. *The Clash of Civilizations and The Remaking of World Order* (New York, NY: Simon & Schuster, 1996).

Huntington, Samuel. *The Clash of Civilizations and the Remaking of World Order* [in Arabic]. Abbas Hilal Kadhim (trans.); (Amman: Dar Al-Amal for Publishing and Distribution, 2006).

Hyman, Louis. "How Did World War II End the Great Depression?" *Bloomberg.com*, December 16, 2001 (http://www.bloomberg.com/news/2011-12-16/how-did-world-war-ii-end-the-great-depression-echoes.html).

Ibrahim, Hassanein Tawfiq. "Globalization: Political Dimensions and Implications: An Initial Vision from the Perspective of Political Science" [in Arabic]. *Alam el-Fikr* vol. 28, Issue 2 (October/December 1999).

İnalcık, Halil. *History of the Ottoman Empire Classical Age*, Muhammad M. Al-Arnaoot (trans.); (Tripoli: Dar Al-Madar Al-Islami, 2002).

Institute of International Education (IIE). "International Students: All Places of Origin"; (http://www.iie.org/Research-and-Publications/Open-Doors/Data/International-Students/All-Places-of-Origin).

Institute of New Economic Thinking. "Why is China Auditing Local Government Debt Again?" July 29, 2013; (http://ineteconomics.org/china-economics-seminar-0/why-china-audit-local-government-debt-again).

INTEK, Inc. "Secure Fuels from Domestic Resources, Profiles of Companies Engaged in Domestic Oil Shale and Tar Sands Resource and Technology Development." 5th ed., September 2011; (http://energy.gov/sites/prod/files/2013/04/f0/SecureFuelsReport2011.pdf).

Intergovernmental Panel on Climate Change (IPCC). "Working Group I Report –'The Physical Science Basis'." *Fourth Assessment Report: Climate Change 2007(AR4)*; (Geneva: IPCC, 2010).

International Association of Financial Engineers (IAFE). "What is a Financial Engineer?" *IAFE Guide to Financial Engineering Programs* (http://www.iafeguide.org/financial-engineer.php).

International Institute for Strategic Studies (IISS). *The Military Balance 2013* (London: IISS, 2013).

International Institute for Strategic Studies (IISS). *The Military Balance 2012* (London: IISS, 2012).

International Monetary Fund (IMF). "Currency Composition of Official Foreign Exchange Reserves (COFER); (In millions of US dollars)." June 28, 2013; (http://www.imf.org/External/np/sta/cofer/eng/cofer.pdf).

International Monetary Fund (IMF). "IMF Executive Board Concludes 2013 Article IV Consultation with the United States." Press Release no. 13/277, July 26, 2013; (http://www.imf.org/external/np/sec/pr/2013/pr13277.htm).

International Monetary Fund (IMF). "IMF Governance Structure, Directors Back Reforms to Overhaul IMF Quotas and Voice." IMF Survey online, March 28, 2008; (http://www.imf.org/external/pubs/ft/survey/so/2008/NEW032808A.htm).

International Monetary Fund (IMF). "The End of the Bretton Woods System (1972–81)"; (http://www.imf.org/external/about/histend.htm).

International Monetary Fund (IMF). "World Economic Outlook Database," April 2013; (http://www.imf.org/external/pubs/ft/weo/2013/01/weodata/index.aspx).

Ishti, Faris. "The New International System between Order and Hegemony" [in Arabic]. *Al-Manar*, no. 56 (1998).

Iskaf, Muhammad Waleed. "Reforming the United Nations or International Legitimacy." *Al-Hiwar Al-Mutamaddin*, September 4, 2005; (http://www.ahewar.org/debat/show.art.asp?aid=44693).

Issa, Kamal. "Why the West Fights Islam?" *Al Watan Voice*, February 19, 2006; (http://pulpit.alwatanvoice.com/articles/2006/02/19/37734.html).

Issa, Mohammed Abdul Shafie. "Development and Five Illusions" [in Arabic]. *Al Siyassa Al Dawliya* no. 133, July 1998, p. 90.

Jabir, Samia Muhammad and Ni'mat Ahmad Uthman. *Communication and Media (Information Technology)* [in Arabic]; (Alexandria: Dar Al-Maarifa Al-Jami'iyya, 2000).

Jacobsen, C.G. *The New World Order's Defining Crises: The Clash of Promise and Essence* (London: Dartmouth Publishing Company, 1996).

Jacques, Martin. "What Kind of Superpower Could China Be?' [in Arabic]. BBC website, October 26, 2012; (http://www.bbc.co.uk/ arabic/worldnews/2012/10/121028_china_superpower.shtml).

Jacques, Martin. *When China Rules the World: The End of the Western World and the Birth of a New Global Order* [in Arabic]. Fatma Nasr Mohamed (trans.); (Cairo: Sotour Publishing House, 2010).

Jaffe, Amy Myers. "The Americas, Not the Middle East, will be the World Capital of Energy." *Foreign Policy*, vol. 90, no. 5 (September/ October 2011); (http://www.foreignpolicy.com/articles/2011/08/15/ the_americas_not_the_middle_east_will_be_the_world_capital_of_ energy).

Jain, Ash. *Like-minded and Capable Democracies: A New Framework for Advancing a Liberal World Order*. IIGG Working Paper, US Council on Foreign Relations, January 2013; (http://i.cfr.org/content/ publications/attachments/IIGG_WorkingPaper12_Jain.pdf).

Jana, Reena. "What Three Tech Trends will Affect Our Lives in 2020, Future Hunting with Intel's Brian David Johnson." *Designmind: Radical Openness* (issue 17); (http://designmind.frogdesign.com/ articles/radical-openness/what-three-tech-trends-will-affect-our-lives-in-2020.html).

Joseph Nye and John Donahue (eds.). *Governance in a Globalizing World.* Muhammad Sharif Al-Tarh (trans.); (Riyadh: Obeikan Publishing, 2002).

Kagan, Robert. *The World America Made* (New York, NY: Knopf Doubleday Publishing Group, 2012).

Kaplanoglou, Georgia and Vassilis T. Rapanos. "The Greek Fiscal Crisis and the Role of Fiscal Governance." GreeSE Paper No. 48, Hellenic Observatory Papers on Greece and Southeast Europe, London School of Economics and Political Science and Hellenic Observatory, European Institute, June 2011; (http://www.lse.ac.uk/european Institute/research/hellenicObservatory/pdf/GreeSE/GreeSE48.pdf).

Kashi, David. "Panama Canal Expansion Can Increase US Maritime Industry by Shipyards Building Smaller Vessels to Unload Cargo in a Feeder System or Short Sea Shipping System to East Coast Ports." *International Business Times* August 27, 2013; (http://www.ibtimes.com/panama-canal-expansion-can-increase-us-maritime-industry-shipyards-building-smaller-vessels-unload).

Kawtharani, Wajih. "The Future of the Islamic Political Project: Fundamentalism or Islamic Partisan" [in Arabic]. *Ma'alomat* no. 3, May 1993.

Kayyali, Majid. "Shift in American Political Strategy from the Occupation of Iraq to Calls for Change in the Region" [in Arabic]. *Shu'un Arabiyya* no. 114 (Summer 2003).

Kazim, Mustafa. "Information and Communication Revolution Reshaped Our World" [in Arabic]. *BBC.co.uk* December 31, 2007; (http://news.bbc.co.uk/hi/arabic/news/newsid_7166000/7166241.stm).

Keela, Salama. "We Are in a New World Taking Shape" [in Arabic]. Al-Jazeera Net, April 15, 2013; (http://www.aljazeera.net/opinions/pages/2bb55e44-4dee-4661-83db-f71c6350cef6).

Ken Booth and Tim Dunne (eds) *Worlds in Collision* (New York, NY: Palgrave Macmillan, 2002).

Kennedy, Paul. *The Rise and Fall of the Great Powers* (London: Fontana Press, 1989).

Kenny, Thomas. "How Safe are US Treasuries?" *About.com* (http://bonds. about.com/od/governmentandagencybonds/a/How-Safe-Are-U-S-Treasuries.htm).

Kessler, Bart R. *Bush's New World Order: The Meaning Behind the Words* (Montgomery, AL: US Air Command and Staff College, 1997).

Khalid, Ibrahim. "Main Figures in the Neoconservatives Current." *Al-Sharq Al-Wasat,* no. 1642, March 6, 2007; (http://www.alwasatnews. com/1642/news/read/219544/1.html).

Khanna, Parag. *The Second World: Empires and Influence in the New Global Order* [in Arabic]. Dar Al-Tarjamah (trans.); (Beirut: Arab Scientific Publishers; Dubai: Mohamed bin Rashid Al Maktoum Foundation, 2009).

Khasbulatov, Raslan. *The Bloody Confrontation: A Testimony for History on the Collapse of the Soviet Union* [in Arabic]. Abu-Bakr Youssef (trans.); (Cairo: Al-Ahram Center for Translation and Publishing, 1996).

Khasheeb, Jalal. "Major Directions of American Strategy after the Cold War" [in Arabic]. *Al-Hiwar Al-Mutamaddin*, no. 3818, August 13, 2012; (http://www.ahewar.org/debat/show.art.asp?aid=319828).

Killebrew, Colonel Robert (ret.) "AFRICOM Stands Up." *Small Wars Journal*, op. ed., October 9, 2008; (http://www.africom.mil/NEWS ROOM/Article/6331/us-africa-command-stands-up).

Kissinger, Henry A. "The Future of US-Chinese Relations: Conflict is a Choice, not a Necessity." *Foreign Affairs* (March/April 2012); (http://www.foreignaffairs.com/articles/137245/henry-a-kissinger/the-future-of-us-chinese-relations).

Kissinger, Henry A. *Diplomacy from the Cold War to the Present Day* [in Arabic]. Omar Ayoubi (trans.); (Amman: Al Dar Al Ahlia for Distribution and Publication, 1995).

Kissinger, Henry A. *Does America Need a Foreign Policy?* (New York, NY: Simon & Schuster, 2001).

Koltz, David M. and Fred Weir. *Revolution from Above: The Demise of the Soviet System* (New York, NY: Routledge, 1997).

Korolev, V.I. *Emperor of All the Earth* [in Arabic] Muntajab Younes (trans.); (Damascus: Dar Aladdin Publishing, 2006).

Krepinevich Jr., Andrew F. "Strategy in a Time of Austerity." *Foreign Affairs*, vol. 91, no. 6 (November/December 2012); (http://www.foreignaffairs.com/articles/138362/andrew-f-krepinevich-jr/strategy-in-a-time-of-austerity).

Kristof, Nicholas D. "A Reassessment of How Many Died in the Military Crackdown in Beijing." *New York Times*, June 21, 1989; (http://www.nytimes.com/1989/06/21/world/a-reassessment-of-how-many-died-in-the-military-crackdown-in-beijing.html).

Lagrini, Driss. "China's Transformations and the Future of the International System" [in Arabic]. *Aafaq Al-Mustaqbal*, no. 17 (Abu Dhabi: The Emirates Center for Strategic Studies and Research, January 2013).

Lau, Richard R. and David P. Redlawsk. "Older but Wiser? Effects of Age on Political Cognition." *The Journal of Politics*, vol. 70, Issue 1 (January 2008).

LeBaron, Richard, and Stefanie Hausheer. "Americans Must Do More to Welcome Saudi Scholarship Students." US News, March 1, 2013; (http://www.usnews.com/opinion/blogs/world-report/2013/03/01/americans-must-do-more-to-welcome-saudi-scholarship-students).

Leipziger, Danny M. "Institutional Reforms and the Shifting Global Economic Order." The North–South Institute, June 2011; (http://www.nsi-ins.ca/content/download/Leipziger2011.pdf).

Lester, Richard and Edward Steinfeld. "China's Real Energy Crisis." *Harvard Asia Pacific Review*, vol. 9, no. 1 (Winter 2007); (http://www.hcs.harvard.edu/~hapr/winter07_gov/lester.pdf).

Lewis, Bernard. *The Political Language of Islam* [in Arabic]. Abdulkarim Mahfouz (trans.); (Damascus: Dar Jaafar for Studies and Publishing, 2001).

Li, Zhaoxing. "Setting the Record Straight on China's Global Ambitions." *Europe's World* (Autumn 2011); (http://europesworld.org/2011/ 10/01/setting-the-record-straight-on-chinas-global-ambitions/#.Urm DAf2IpaQ).

Lind, William S. "Understanding Fourth Generation War." *Military Review* (September/October 2004).

Lind, William S., Keith Nightengale, John F. Schmitt, Joseph W. Stutton and Gary I. Wilson. "The Changing Face of War: Into the Fourth Generation." *Marine Corps Gazette*, vol. 73, no. 10 (October 1989); (http://www.mca-marines.org/files/The%20Changing%20Face%20of %20War%20-%20Into%20the%20Fourth%20Generation.pdf).

Lissaoui, Tareq. 'The Story of the Rise and Growth of China runs in Parallel to the Story of the Decline of the Dream of the American Empire" [in Arabic]. *Al-Quds Al-Arabi,* October 25, 2013; (http://www.alquds.co.uk/?p=96781).

Long, David E. (ed.). *Gulf Security in the Twenty-First Century* (Abu Dhabi: The Emirates Center for Strategic Studies and Research, 1997).

Lostumbo, Michael J., et al. Overseas Basing of US Military Forces: An Assessment of Relative Costs and Strategic Benefits (Santa Monica, CA: RAND Corporation, 2013).

Low, Linda. "The Political Economy of Trade Liberalization." *Asia–Pacific Development Journal*, vol. 11, no. 1 (June 2004); (http://www.unescap.org/pdd/publications/apdj_11_1/low.pdf).

Luckham, Robin, and Gordon White (eds.). *Democratization in The South: The Jagged Wave* (Manchester: Manchester University Press, 1996).

Lynch, Mark. "Why Arab Public Opinion Matters." *Foreign Policy Review*, August 3, 2013.

Lynn, William J. III and Nicholas Thompson. "Foreign Affairs LIVE: The Pentagon's New Cyberstrategy." *Foreign Affairs*, October 1, 2010; (http://www.foreignaffairs.com/discussions/news-and-events/foreign-affairs-live-the-pentagons-new-cyberstrategy).

Lyons, Gene M., and Michael Mastanduno. "International Intervention, State Sovereignty and Future of the International Community" [in Arabic]. Mohammed Jalal Abbas (trans.), *International Social Science Journal* (UNESCO), no. 138 (November 1993).

Machiavelli, Niccolò. *The Prince* [in Arabic]. Mohamed Lutfi Jom'a (trans.); (Limassol: Cordoba for Publishing, Documentation and Research, 1998).

Madhi, Muhammad. "'Why Don't You Understand Us?' Versus the Question 'Why Do They Hate Us?'" [in Arabic]. Swissinfo.ch (http://www.swissinfo.ch/ara/detail/content.html?cid=1094502).

Madi, Muhammad. "American Swinging between Support for Democracy and Reliance on Dictatorships" [in Arabic]. Swissinfo.ch, June 28, 2013; (http://www.swissinfo.ch/ara/detail/content.html?cid=36187292).

Madi, Muhammad. "The Dominance of the Neoconservatives" [in Arabic]. *swissinfo.ch* July 12, 2003; (http://www.swissinfo.ch/ara/detail/content.html?cid=3307084).

Maharatna, Arup. "In Resurrection of Gunnar Myrdal's Asian Drama." *Mainstream Weekly*, vol. XLVIII, no. 18, April 24, 2010; (http://www.mainstreamweekly.net/article2035.html).

Mahfood, Mohamed. "Education and Progress" [in Arabic]. *Al-Riyadh*, November 10, 2010; (http://www.alriyadh.com/2010/11/10/article 575924.html).

Mahir, Ahmad. "The Neoconservatives in America – What is their Philosophy and How Do They Plan?" [in Arabic] *Al-Sharq Al-Awsat,* no. 9642, April 22, 2005; (http://aawsat.com/leader.asp?section=3& article=294962&issueno=9642).

Mahmoud, Ahmed Ibrahim (ed.). *The Gulf and the Iraqi Question: From the Invasion of Kuwait to the Occupation of Iraq 1990–2003* [in Arabic]; (Cairo: Al-Ahram Center for Political & Strategic Studies, 2003).

Majeed, Waheed Abdul. "Thirty Years after Bandung Conference: the Third World between the United States and the Soviet Union" [in Arabic]. *Al-Siyassa Al-Dawliyya*, no. 80 (April 1985).

Maklad, Ismail Sabri. *Strategy and International Politics: The Basic Concepts and Facts* [in Arabic]; (Beirut: Arab Research Foundation, 1979).

Mandelbaum, Michael. *The Ideas That Conquered the World: Peace, Democracy and Free Markets in the Twenty-first Century* [in Arabic]. Ola Ahmed Eslah (trans.); (Cairo: International House for Cultural Investments, 2009).

Mansour, Ahmed Subhy. "Does Congressman Tancredo Really Want to Bomb Mecca?" [in Arabic]. Modern Discussion Website, Issue 1271, July 30, 2005 (http://www.ahewar.org/debat/show.art.asp?aid=420 99).

Mansour, Mamdouh Mahmoud Mustafa. "International Coalition Policies: A Study in the Origins of the International Coalition Theory" [in Arabic]; (Alexandria: Alexandria University, 1995).

Maqlad, Ismail Sabri. *International Political Relations, Theory and Reality* 4th edition [in Arabic]; (Assiut: Assiut University, 2007).

Mardell, Mark. 'Will the Rise of the Rest Mean the Decline of the US?' [in Arabic]. BBC website, April 30, 2013; (http://www.bbc.co.uk/arabic/worldnews/2013/04/130429_us_decline.shtml).

Marhoon, Abdul Jaleel Zaid. "Europe and the Future of German Centrism." *Al-Riyadh*, May 10, 2002; [in Arabic]; (http://www.alriyadh.com/2002/05/10/article27856.html).

Markoff, John. "Searching for Silicon Valley." *New York Times*, April 17, 2009; (http://travel.nytimes.com/2009/04/17/travel/escapes/17Amer.html?pagewanted=1&_r=0).

Martin, Hans-Peter and Harald Schumann. "The Global Trap: Globalization and the Assault on Democracy and Prosperity." Adnan Abbas Ali (trans.), *A'lam Al-Ma'rifa* series, no. 238 (Kuwait: National Council for Culture, Arts and Letters, October 1998).

Masqawi, Omar. "Between the Muslim Women's Veil in France and Europe and the Veil of Conscience in Palestine" [in Arabic]. *Al Mustaqbal*, Beirut, January 7, 2004.

Mathews, Jessica T. "Power Shift." *Foreign Affairs* (January/February 1997).

McGregor, Richard. "US Budget Politics: America Goes Dark." *Financial Times* October 4, 2013; (http://www.ft.com/cms/s/0/83610290-2cd6-11e3-a0ac-00144feab7de.html#axzz2h73gcJkT).

McGregor, Richard. "Zhou's Cryptic Caution Lost in Translation." *Financial Times*, June 10, 2011; (http://www.ft.com/cms/s/0/74916db6-938d-11e0-922e-00144feab49a.html#axzz2oOZtuTbS).

McPhail, Thomas L. *Global Communication,* Abdul Hakeem Ahmad Al-Khuzami (trans.); (Cairo: Dar Al-Fajr for Publishing and Distribution, 2012).

Meacham, T. Chase. "Obama Africa Trip 2013: Why Obama's $100 Million African Trip Isn't a Big Deal." June 15, 2013, *Policymic.com*; (http://www.policymic.com/articles/49001/obama-africa-trip-2013-why-obama-s-100-million-african-trip-isn-t-a-big-deal).

Meissner, Christopher M. *A New World Order: Explaining the Emergence of the Classical Gold Standard* (Cambridge: King's College, University of Cambridge, August 2001.).

Middle East Institute (MEI). *The 1979 "Oil Shock:" Legacy, Lessons, and Lasting Reverberations*. Viewpoints Special Edition, September 1, 2009.

Middle East Partnership Initiative (MEPI). "Leaders for Democracy Fellowship Program" (http://mepi.state.gov/opportunities/mepi-exchange-programs/leaders-for-democracy-fellowship.html).

Mihoub, Nizar. "Public Opinion ... Voice of the People" [in Arabic]. The International Association of Public Relations, 2012; (http://www.ipra-ar.org/alpha/topic/view.php?id=21).

Milad, Mohamed (trans.). *Will the World Slide into the Abyss?* [in Arabic]; (Damascus: Dar Al-Hewar for Publishing and Distribution, 2009).

Miles, Franklin B. "Asymmetric Warfare: An Historical Perspective." Strategy Research Project, US Army War College, Carlisle Barracks, 1999.

Ministry of Defense, French Republic. "Armée de Terre"; (http://www.defense.gouv.fr/terre).

Montgomery, Carl T. and Michael B. Smith. "Hydraulic Fracturing: History of an Enduring Technology." December 2010; (http://www.spe.org/jpt/print/archives/2010/12/10Hydraulic.pdf).

Morsi, Mustafa Abel Aziz. *Arab Immigrants' Issues in Europe* [in Arabic]; (Abu Dhabi: The Emirates Center for Strategic Studies and Research, 2010).

Moukalled, Ismail Sabri. *International Political Relations: Theory and Reality* [in Arabic]; (Assiut: Assiut University, 2007).

Moukalled, Ismail Sabri. *International Strategy and Policy* [in Arabic], 2nd ed. (Beirut: Arab Research Foundation, 1985).

Moustafa, Jalal Hassan, and Nawshirwan Hussein Saeed. "Ethnic Conflict: Reasons and Solution, Kirkuk as a Case Study" [in Arabic]. Kirkuknow.com (http://kirkuknow.com/arabic/?p=11225).

Moynihan, Joseph. *Information Warfare: Concepts, Boundaries and Employment Strategies* (Abu Dhabi: The Emirates Center for Strategic Studies and Research, 1997).

Mu'taz, Salama. *Political Reform: American Policy and the Arab Responses*, Strategic Papers Series, No. 153 (Cairo: Al-Ahram Center for Strategic Studies, 2005); (http://acpss.ahram.org.eg/ahram/2001/1/1/SBOK48.HTM).

Müller, Harald. *Das Zusammenleben der Kulturen: ein Gegenentwurf zu Huntington* [in Arabic]. Abu Hashhash (trans.); (Beirut: Dar Al-Kitab Al-Jadeed Al-Mottahedah, 2005).

Mussaad, Nevine. "International Relations and the Future of the World Order in the Stage of Globalization" [in Arabic] in *Globalization and its Influence on Society and State* (Abu Dhabi: The Emirates Center for Strategic Studies and Research, 2002).

Mustafa, Mamdouh Mahmoud. "The Concept of the 'International Order' Between Scientism and Normalcy" [in Arabic]. *Strategic Studies* (Abu Dhabi: The Emirates Center for Strategic Studies and Research, 1998).

Mutawie, Ibrahim Ismat. *Human Development Through Education and Learning* [in Arabic]; (Cairo: Dar Al-Fikr Al-Arabi, 2002).

Nader, Nir. "The Committed Documentary on the Anti-globalization Seattle Events" [in Arabic]. *Al-Hewar Al-Motamadden* (Modern Discussion) website, December 9, 2001; (http://www.ahewar.org/debat/show.art.asp?aid=341), accessed July 27, 2013.

Nafaa, Hassan. "The Changing International Priorities and the Arab World" [in Arabic] in Ahmed Yusuf Ahmed, et al., *The Arab World and Global Developments* (Cairo: Center for Arab Research and Studies, 1991).

Nafaa, Hassan. "The United Nations in Half a Century" [in Arabic]. *Alam Al-Maarifa* series, Issue. 202 (Kuwait: National Council for Culture, Arts and Letters, 1995).

Naím, Moisés. *The End of Power: From Boardrooms to Battlefields and Churches to States, Why Being in Charge isn't What it Used to Be* (New York, NY: Basic Books, 2013).

Nash, George H. *The Conservative Intellectual Movement In America* (Wilmington, DE: Intercollegiate Studies Institute, 1998).

National Book Centre of Greece. *The Book Market in Greece* (Athens: NBCG, 2012).

National Center for Education Statistics. *Digest of Education Statistics Report*, 2012; (http://nces.ed.gov/programs/digest/2012menu_tables.asp).

National Highways Authority of India. "Indian Road Network"; (http://www.nhai.org/roadnetwork.htm).

Naughton, Barry, et al. "A Political Economy of China's Economic Transition" in Loren Brandt and Thomas G. Rawski (eds.), *China's Great Economic Transformation* (Cambridge: Cambridge University Press, 2008).

Ni'ma, Kazim Hashim. *NATO: Expansion to the East and Dialogue with the South and Arab National Security* (Tripoli: Academy of Graduate Studies, 2003).

Nielsen, Jørgen S. *Muslims in Western Europe* [in Arabic]; (Beirut: Dar Al-Saqi in collaboration with Al-Babtain Translation Center, 2005).

Nixon, Richard. *1999 Victory Without War* (London: Sidgwicke & Jakson, 1988).

Nye, Joseph S. "Bound to Lead: The Changing Nature of American Power." Library of Congress Cataloging-in-Publication Data, 1990.

Nye, Joseph S. "The Cuban Missile Crisis at 50" [in Arabic]. *Saudi Al-Iqtisadiyya*, October 15, 2012; (http://www.aleqt.com/2012/10/15/article_701626.html).

Nye, Joseph S. "The Future of American Power: Dominance and Decline in Perspective." *Foreign Affairs*, vol. 89, issue 6 (November/December 2010).

Nye, Joseph S. "The Future of Power." *Public Affairs* (March/April 2011).

Nye, Joseph S. "The Reality of Virtual Power" [in Arabic]. *Aleqtisadiah* February 5, 2011; (http://www.aleqt.com/2011/02/05/article_500244.print).

Nye, Joseph S. "What New World Order?" *Foreign Affairs* (Spring 1992).

Nye, Joseph S. *Bound to Lead: The Changing Nature of American Power* (New York, NY: Basic Books, 1991).

Nye, Joseph S. *Bound to Lead: The Changing Nature of American Power* [in Arabic]. Abdulqader Othman (trans.); (Amman: Jordan Book Centre, 1991).

Nye, Joseph S. *Soft Power: The Means to Success in World Politics* [in Arabic]. Muhammad Tawfeeq Al-Bujairmi (trans.); (Riyadh: Obeikan Publishing, 2004).

Nye, Joseph S. *Understanding International Conflicts: An Introduction to Theory and History* [in Arabic]. Ahmad Al-Jamal and Magdi Kamel (trans.); (Cairo: The Egyptian Association for the Dissemination of Universal Culture and Knowledge, 1997).

Nye, Joseph S., and John D. Donahue. *Governance in a Globalizing World* [in Arabic]. Mohammed Sharif Tarah (trans.); (Riyadh: Obeikan Bookshop, 2002).

Nye, Joseph, Hillary Clinton, Tim Dunne and Kledja Mulaj. "The Future of American Power." *International Studies*, Issue no. 105 (Abu Dhabi: ECSSR, 2012).

Nye, Joseph. "Smart Power." *The Huffington Post*; (http://www.huffing tonpost.com/joseph-nye/smart-power_b_74725.html).

O'Hanlon, Michael E. *Healing the Wounded Giant: Maintaining Military Preeminence while Cutting the Defense Budget* (Salem, VA: R.R. Donelly, 2013).

Omar, Hussein. *Directory of International Organizations* [in Arabic]; (Cairo: Dar el-Fikr el-Arabi, 1997).

Omar, Zarfawi. "The Clash of Civilizations: a Theory or an Ideology" [in Arabic]. *Kalema* no. 39, Spring 2003; (http://kalema.net/v1/?rpt=96 &art).

Organization for Economic Cooperation and Development (OECD). "OECD Factbook 2013"; (http://www.oecd-ilibrary.org/economics/ oecd-factbook_18147364).

Oztuna, Yilmaz. *Encyclopedia of Political, Military and Civilizational History of the Ottoman Empire 629–1231 (Hijri) 1431–1922,* vol. 1 [in Arabic]. Adnan Mahmoud Salman (trans.), revised by Mahmoud Al-Ansari (Beirut: Arab Encyclopedia House, 2010).

Palmer, Tom G. "Globalization, Cosmopolitanism, and Personal Identity." *Etica & Politica* (Ethics & Politics) vol. 2, 2003; (http://www. openstarts.units.it/dspace/bitstream/10077/5455/1/Palmer_E%26P_ V_2003_2.pdf).

Parker, R.A.C. *The Second World War: A Short History* (New York, NY: Oxford University Press, 1997).

Pastor, Robert A. *A Century's Journey: How The Great Powers Shape the World*, Hashim Ahmad Muhammad (trans.); (Cairo: National Center for Translation, 2010).

Petersen, Mitchell A. "Information: Hard and Soft." Kellogg School of Management, Northwestern University, July 2004; (http://www. kellogg.northwestern.edu/faculty/petersen/htm/papers/softhard.pdf).

Pew Research Center. "25-Nation Pew Global Attitudes Survey." Pew Global Attitude Project, July 23, 2009; (http://www.pewglobal.org/ files/2009/07/Pew-Global-Attitudes-Spring-2009-Report-1-July-23- 11am.pdf).

Pfaff, William. "Europe is the Victim of US Espionage" [in Arabic]. *Al-Ittihad*, July 14, 2013.

Porth, Jacquelyn S. "Defense Official Says International Alliances Key to US Strategy." Bureau of International Information Programs (IIP), US State Department, March 21, 2006; (http://iipdigital.usembassy.gov/ st/english/article/2006/03/20060320132430sjhtrop0.9339716.html#ax zz2jwLrsaKd).

Powell, Walter W., and Kaisa Snellman. "The Knowledge Economy." *Annual Review of Sociology*, vol. 30, no. 1 (August 2004).

PricewaterhouseCoopers (PwC). "Shale Gas: A Renaissance in US Manufacturing?" December 2011; (http://www.pwc.com/en_US/us/ industrial-products/assets/pwc-shale-gas-us-manufacturing- renaissance.pdf).

Public Broadcasting Service (PBS). "Russia's Crisis: Will Russia Survive its Economic and Political Crisis?"; (http://www.pbs.org/newshour/ forum/september98/russia.html).

Qarni, Bahgat. "From the International System to the World Order" [in Arabic], *Al-Siyassa Al-Dawliya*, Issue 161 (July 2005).

Quandt, William. ["Greater Middle East Initiative – Illusion of Slogans and Difficulty of Trade-offs." in Arabic] *Al-Ittihad*, Opinion Pages, March 7, 2006; (http://www.alittihad.ae/wajhatdetails.php?id=18627).

Quataert, Donald. *The Ottoman Empire 1700–1922*. Ayman Al-Arminazi (trans.); (Riyadh: Obeikan Publishing, 2004).

Qurani, Bahjat. "From International System to World System." *Al-Siyassa Al-Dawliyya*, no. 161 (July 2005).

Qutaishat, Yassir. "Pre-emptive Strike as a New Strategy in International Relations: War on Iraq as an Example" [in Arabic]. *Minbar Al-Hurriyya*, December 4, 2009; (http://minbaralhurriyya.org/index.php/archives/2204).

Randall, Kate. "US Congress Passes $633 Billion Military Spending Bill." World Socialist Website, December 21, 2013; (https://www.wsws.org/en/articles/2013/12/21/ndaa-d21.html).

Rasoul, Rasoul Mohammad. "The West and Islam: A Look into the Contemporary German Orientalism" [in Arabic]. *Kalema* no. 30, Winter 2001.

Reed, John. "Is this China's Second Aircraft Carrier?" *Foreign Policy*, National Security, August 3, 2013; (http://killerapps.foreignpolicy.com/posts/2013/08/02/ spotted_china_is_building_a_second_aircraft_carrier).

Rhodes, R.A.W. "The New Governance: Governing without Government." *Political Studies*, no. 44 (London: IISS, 1996).

Rice, Condoleezza. "Balance of Power: Concept and Practice" [in Arabic]. *Al-Ittihad*, Viewpoints, March 23, 2003); (http://www.alittihad.ae/wajhatdetails.php?id=18972).

Rice, Condoleezza. Interview, *The Washington Post*, April 4, 2005.

Rickards, James. *Currency Wars: The Making of the Next Global Crisis* (New York, NY: Portfolio Penguin, 2011).

Rifkin, Jeremy. *The Age of Access: The New Culture of Hypercapitalism, Where All of Life is a Paid-for Experience* [in Arabic]. Translated Studies (Abu Dhabi: The Emirates Center for Strategic Studies and Research, 2003).

Robert, Anne-Cécile. "A Disturbing Shift in International Relations." *Al-Ahram*, October 5, 2013 (http://digital.ahram.org.eg/Policy.aspx?Serial=1425387).

Roberts, Dexter, Henry Meyer, and Dorothee Tschampa. "The Silk Railroad of China–Europe Trade." *Businessweek*, December 20, 2012; (http://www.businessweek.com/articles/2012-12-20/the-silk-railroad-of-china-europe-trade).

Rodinson, Maxime. *Europe and the Mystique of Islam* [in Arabic]. Rouger Veinus (trans.); (London: I.B. Tauris, 1987).

Romero, Simon and William Neuman. "Sweeping Protests in Brazil Pull in an Array of Grievances." *The New York Times*, June 20, 2013; (http://www.nytimes.com/2013/06/21/world/americas/brazil-protests.html?pagewanted=all&_r=0).

Roth, Kenneth. "The United States versus the International Criminal Court: No Global System is based on Exception." Modern Discussion website, issue 190, July 15, 2012; (http://www.ahewar.org/debat/show.art.asp?aid=2140).

Roubini, Nouriel. "The Unsustainability of the US Twin Deficits." CATO Institute; (http://www.cato.org/sites/cato.org/files/serials/files/cato-journal/2006/5/cj26n2-13.pdf).

Rugh, William A. "Bush and the Task of Radical Change in Foreign Policy Approach" [in Arabic]. *Al-Ittihad*, Viewpoints December 5, 2003; (http://www.alittihad.ae/wajhatdetails.php?id=1632).

Saad Abu Aamood, Muhammad. "Towards a Multipolar International System: China-US Relations." *Al-Siyassa Al-Dawliyya*, no. 145, vol. 37 (July 2001).

Saadi, Mohammed. The Future of International Relations: From the Clash of Civilizations to the Humanization of Civilization and Peace Culture [in Arabic]; (Beirut: Center for Arab Unity Studies, 1st ed., 2006).

Saadullah, Omar Ismail. *Human Rights and Peoples' Rights: The Relationship and Legal Developments* [in Arabic]; (Algiers: Office of University Publications, 1991).

Saeed, Abdul Mun'im. *Arabs and the New World Order: Proposed Options*, [in Arabic] Strategic Papers Series, no. 3 (Cairo: Al-Ahram Center for Strategic Studies, 1991).

Saeed, Mohamed El-Sayed. "How Arabs Say No." *Al-Ahram*, December 9, 2002.

Saeed, Mohamed El-Sayed. *The Stalled Democratic Transition in Egypt* (Cairo: Merritt Publishing House, 2006).

Said, Abdul Aziz, Charles O. Lerche, Jr. and Charles O. Lerche, III. *Concepts of International Politics in Global Perspective* [in Arabic]. Naf'e Ayoub Lobbos (trans.); (Damascus: Publications of the Arab Writers Union, 1999).

Sakhuja, Vijay. *The Strategic Dynamics of the Indian Ocean* [in Arabic] Emirates Lectures Series, no. 156 (Abu Dhabi: The Emirates Center for Strategic Studies and Research, 2013).

Salamé, Ghassan. *State and Society in the Arab Levant* [in Arabic]; (Beirut: Center for Arab Unity Studies, 1987).

Salem, Paul, and Matthew Ferchen. "The Chinese Economic Model: Policies and Best Practices." Carnegie Middle East Center, June 12, 2012.

Samaan, Jean-Loup. "A New Perspective on the Relationship between NATO and the Gulf States" [in Arabic]. *NATO Review* online; (http://www.nato.int/docu/review/2012/Arab-Spring/NATO-Gulf-Strategic-Dialogue/AR/index.htm).

Sanger, David E., and Thom Shanker. "Broad Powers Seen for Obama in Cyberstrikes." *New York Times*, February 3, 2013; (http://www.ny times.com/2013/02/04/us/broad-powers-seen-for-obama-in-cyber strikes.html?_r=0).

Saouma, Riad. Opportunities for Change After the Failure of Radical Liberalism and the Fall of Unipolarity [in Arabic]; (Beirut: Dar al-Farabi, 2009).

Saqqor, Muhannad Ali. "Fukuyama from the End of History to its Beginning ... A Turning Shift." Al Wehda, Syrian newspaper unit March 10, 2011; (http://wehda.alwehda.gov.sy/_archive.asp?FileName=44689633020110312144413).

Schain, Martin A. *The Marshall Plan Fifty Years Later* (New York, NY: Palgrave MacMillan, 2001).

Schneider, Howard. "How Globalization Mixed the Calculations of the Founders of the Single European Currency" [in Arabic]. *Asharq Al-Awsat*, Issue 12332, September 2, 2012; (http://aawsat.com/details.asp?section=6&article=693397&issueno=12332#.UrmTlv2IoSs).

Schneider, William. "Bush's Role for America: The World's Top Cop" [in Arabic]. *Al-Sharq Al-Awsat*, no. 8602, June 17, 2002; (http://www.aawsat.com/details.asp?issueno=8435&article=108683).

Schofield, Jack. "China's 2012 Electronics Production includes more than a Billion Mobile Phones." ZDNet blog; (http://www.zdnet.com/chinas-2012-electronics-production-includes-more-than-a-billion-mobile-phones-7000009294).

Schroeder, Paul W. "The New World Order: A Historical Perspective." *Washington Quarterly*, vol. 17, no. 2 (Spring 1994).

SelectUSA. "The Software and Information Technology Services Industry in the United States"; (http://selectusa.commerce.gov/industry-snapshots/software-and-information-technology-services-industry-united-states).

Shaaban, Abdul Hussein. "Islam in International Politics: Dialogue of Civilizations and International Terrorism" [in Arabic]. *Arab Journal of Political Science* no. 15 (Summer 2007).

Shaaban, Abdul Hussein. "The Big Paradoxes between Savage Capitalism and the Capitalism with a Human Face" [in Arabic]. *Al-Eqtisadiah* no. 6185, September 17, 2010; (http://www.aleqt.com/2010/09/17/article_443170.html).

Shabib, Kadhim. "The Sectarian Issue: Multiple Identities in One State" [in Arabic]; (Beirut: Dar Al Tanweer Printing, Publication and Distribution, 2011).

Shaheen, Muhammad Umar. *History of the Mawali and their Role in Social and Economic Life in Early Islam and the Umayyad State* (Beirut: Dar Al-Kutub Al-Ilmiyya, 2011).

Shakir, Muhammad. "Part VIII: The Ottoman Era" [in Arabic]. *Islamic History* (Beirut: Al-Maktab Al-Islami, 2000).

Shalabi, Al-Sayyid Ameen. "From the Cold War to the Search for a New World Order" [in Arabic]. *Al-Siyassa Al-Dawliyya,* No. 179 (January 2010).

Shalabi, Al-Sayyid Ameen. "From the Cold War to the Search for a New International System" [in Arabic]; (Cairo: General Egyptian Book Organization, The Family Library, 2005).

Shalabi, Al-Sayyid Ameen. "Henry Kissinger and the Diplomacy of Détente" [in Arabic]. *Al-Siyassa Al-Dawliya*, Issue 46 (October 1976).

Shalabi, Al-Sayyid Ameen. "Promotion of Democracy from Bush to Obama" [in Arabic]. *Al-Masri Al-Yawm*, November 8, 2010; (http://www.almasryalyoum.com/node/230413).

Shambaugh, David. *China Goes Global: The Partial Power* (New York, NY: Oxford University Press, 2013).

Shambaugh, David. *China Goes Global: The Partial Power* [in Arabic]. Saleh Sulaiman Abdulazim (trans.); (Doha: Al-Jazeera Center for Studies, July 23, 2013).

Shapiro, Robert J., and Aparna Mathur. *The Contributions of Information and Communication Technologies to American Growth, Productivity, Jobs and Prosperity* (Sonecon, September 2011); (http://www.

tiaonline.org/gov_affairs/fcc_filings/documents/Report_on_ICT_and_Innovation_Shapiro_Mathur_September_8_2011.pdf).

Sharaf, Laila. Commentary remarks in "Recent Developments in the United States and their Arab implications" [in Arabic]. *The Arabs and the World After September 11* (Beirut: Center for Arab Unity Studies, 2004).

Sheikh, Ibrahim Ali Badawi. "The United Nations and Human Rights Violations" [in Arabic]. *Egyptian Journal of International Law*, vol. 36, Issue 36 (1980).

Shell. "About Shell"; (http://www.shell.com/global/aboutshell/at-a-glance. html).

Shilling, A. Gary. "Six Reasons the US Will Dominate." Bloomberg; (http://www.bloomberg.com/news/2013-08-27/six-reasons-the-u-s-will-dominate.html).

Shinn, David, and Kerry Brown. *China and Africa: A Century of Engagement* (London: Chatham House, June 29, 2012).

Shoen, Jacqueline. "Stephen Walt Calls for Balance of Power in Politics: Iran and the Bomb." *Al-Majalla*, December 30, 2010; (http://www. majalla.com/arb/2010/12/article55226239).

Shukri, Muhammad Aziz. "Alliances and Blocs in International Politics" [in Arabic]. Alam Al-Maarifa series (Kuwait: National Council for Culture, Arts and Letters, 2008).

Shukri, Muhammad Aziz. *Global International System Between Theory and Reality* [in Arabic]; (Beirut: Dar Al-Fikr, 1973).

Simon, Hermann. "Why does Siemens apply for 6 times more patents than all of Spain? On the innovation gulf in Europe," Whiteboard (http://www.whiteboardmag.com/why-does-siemens-apply-for-6-times-more-patents-than-all-of-spain-on-the-innovation-gulf-in-europe/).

Sinolingua. *Confucius: A Sage from China: His Life and Wisdoms* [in Arabic]; Chinese Sages Series (Beirut: Arab Scientific Publishers, 2009).

Slaughter, Anne-Marie. *A New World Order* (Princeton, NJ: Princeton University Press, 2004).

Slaughter, Anne-Marie. *A New World Order* [in Arabic] Ahmad Mahmood (trans.); (Cairo: National Center for Translation, 2011).

Soufan, Akef. *International and Regional Organizations* [in Arabic]; (Damascus: Qordoba Publishing, 2004).

Sovereign Wealth Fund Institute. "Sovereign Fund Rankings." September 3, 2013; (http://www.swfinstitute.org/fund-rankings).

Steil, Benn and Manuel Hinds. *Money, Markets, and Sovereignty* [in Arabic]; (Abu Dhabi: The Emirates Center for strategic Studies and Research, 2013).

Steinhauser, Paul. "President Ends Year At All-Time CNN Polling Low." CNN, December 20, 2013; (http://politicalticker.blogs.cnn.com/2013/12/20/president-ends-year-at-all-time-cnn-polling-low/).

Stiglitz, Joseph E. and Linda J. Bilmes. *The Three Trillion Dollar War: The True Cost of the Iraq Conflict* (New York, NY: W.W. Norton & Company, 2008).

Stothar, Michael. "Angela Merkel's Victory Prompts Mixed Response in Europe." *The Financial Times*, September 23, 2013; (http://www.ft.com/intl/cms/s/0/490142a6-2441-11e3-a8f7-00144feab7de.html#axzz2h73gcJkT).

Subh, Ali. *International Struggle in Half a Century: 1945–1995* (Beirut: Dar Manhal for Printing and Publishing, 2006).

Subhi, Ahmad Mahmoud, and Safaa Abdel-Salam Jafar. *Philosophy of Civilization (Greek, Islamic, Western)* [in Arabic]; (Beirut: Dar al-Nahda al-Arabiya for Printing and Publishing, 1999).

Subramanian, Arvind. *Eclipse: Living in the Shadow of China's Economic Dominance* (Washington, DC: Peterson Institute for International Economics, 2013).

Swailam, Hossam Eldin Mohamed. *US National Missile Defense System* [in Arabic]; (Abu Dhabi: The Emirates Center for Strategic Studies and Research, 2003).

Tabuchi, Hiroko. "In Japan, a Tenuous Vow to Cut." *The New York Times*, September 1, 2011; (http://www.nytimes.com/2011/09/02/business/global/japan-seeks-answers-to-debt-load-without-angering-voters.html?pagewanted=all&_r=0).

Taher, Ahmed. "The Future of Sino-American Relations" [in Arabic]. *Al Siyassa Al Dawliya* no. 193 (July 2013).

Taleb, Nassim. *The Black Swan* [in Arabic]; (Beirut, Arabic Scientific Publishers, Inc., 2009).

Talib, Muhammad Saeed. *A Study on the Emergence of the Arab Nation: History and Ideology* [in Arabic]; (Damascus: Al-Dar Al-Wataniyya Al-Jadeeda, 2009).

Tawfiq, Saad Haqqi. *New International Order: A Study of the Future of International Relations after the End of the Cold War*, [in Arabic]; (Amman: Alahliya for Publishing and Distribution, 1999).

Taylor, A.J.P. *The Struggle for Mastery in Europe 1848–1918* [in Arabic]. Fadil Jatkar (trans.); (Abu Dhabi: Abu Dhabi Authority for Culture and Heritage, Kalima Project for Translation and Arab Cultural Center, 2009).

Taylor, Beck A. "On the Equivalency of Profit Maximization and Cost Minimization: A Note on Factor Demands"; (http://capone.mtsu.edu/jee/pdf/taylor.PDF).

Taylor, Ian. *China's Oil Diplomacy in Africa* [in Arabic], International Studies no. 63 (Abu Dhabi: The Emirates Center for Strategic Studies and Research [ECSSR], 2007).

Techau, Jan. 'What if Unipolarity Came Back?' Judy Dempsey's Strategic Europe, Carnegie Europe, July 16, 2013; (http://carnegieeurope.eu/strategiceurope/?fa=52411).

Techau, Jan. "Germany must stop Moralising and Embrace Espionage." *Financial Times*, October 13 2013; (http://carnegieendowment.org/#/slide_508_germany-must-embrace-espionage).

Telhami, Shibley. *The World Through Arab Eyes: Arab Public Opinion and the Reshaping of the Middle East* (New York, NY: Basic Books, June 2013).

Tessler, Mark. *Public Opinion in the Middle East*: *Survey Research and Political Orientations of Ordinary Citizens* (Bloomington, IN: Indiana University Press, 2011).

Thabit, Ahmad. *Globalization: Interactions and contradictions of International Transformations* [in Arabic] Political Research Series no. 119 (Cairo: Center for Political Research and Studies, Cairo University, April 1992).

The White House, "President Barack Obama"; (http://www.whitehouse. Gov/administration/president-obama).

The White House. "First Annual Report to the Congress on United States Foreign Policy for the 1970s." February 18, 1970.

The White House. "President Barack Obama"; (http://www.whitehouse. gov/administration/president-obama).

The White House. "The National Security Strategy of the United States of America." Washington, DC, September 2002.

The White House. "William J. Clinton"; (http://www.whitehouse.gov/about/presidents/williamjclinton).

The White House. *National Security Strategy*, May 2010; (http://www. whitehouse.gov/sites/default/files/rss_viewer/national_security_strate gy.pdf).

The World Bank. "Research and Development Expenditure (% of GDP)"; (http://data.worldbank.org/indicator/GB.XPD.RSDV.GD.ZS).

The World Bank. *Global Monitoring Report 2012: Food Prices, Nutrition and the Millennium Development Goals* (March 2013).

Third World Network. "The Brazilian Economic Crisis" (http://www.twnside.org.sg/title/brazil-cn.htm).

Thurow, Lester. *Head to Head: The Coming Economic Battle among Japan, Europe, and America,* Muhammad Fareed (trans.); (Abu Dhabi: The Emirates Center for Strategic Studies and Research, 1996).

Ukasha, Saeed. "How the Americans Perceived the Events of September 11" [in Arabic]. *Al-Dimuqratiyya* January 1, 2002; (http://digital.ahram.org.eg/articles.aspx?Serial=794078&eid=410).

United Nations (UN). "Chapter VII: Action with Respect to Threats to the Peace, Breaches of the Peace, and Acts of Aggression." Chapter VII of the Charter of the United Nations; (http://www.un.org/ar/documents/charter/chapter7.shtml).

United Nations (UN). "Charter of the United Nations"; (http://www.un.org/en/documents/charter/index.shtml).

United Nations (UN). "Framework Convention on Climate Change" (http://unfccc.int/kyoto_protocol/items/2830.php).

United Nations (UN). "Main Bodies," n.d.; (http://www.un.org/ar/main bodies).

United Nations (UN). "Rome Statute of the International Criminal Court." December 31, 2003; (http://www.un.org/Law/icc/index.html).

United Nations (UN). "The 1945 Statute of the International Court of Justice" [in Arabic]; (http://www.un.org/arabic/aboutun/statute.htm).

United Nations (UN). "We the People: the Role of United Nations in the Twenty-first Century" [in Arabic]. Millennium Report of the UN Secretary-General; (http://www.un.org/arabic/millennium/sg/report/report0.htm).

United Nations (UN). *World Investment Report 2013* (New York, NY: UN Publications, 2013).

United Nations Development Program (UNDP). "Cultural Liberty in Today's Diverse World." *Human Development Report 2004.*

United Nations Development Program (UNDP). *Human Development Report 2013: The Rise of the South; Human Progress in a Diverse World* (New York, NY: UN publications, 2013),

United Nations Development Program (UNDP). *Millennium Development Goals: A Compact Among Nations to End Human Poverty, Human Development Report 2003* (New York, NY: United Nations Publications, 2003).

United Nations Security Council (UNSC). "UNSC Resolution 940 of 1994"; (http://daccess-dds-ny.un.org/doc/UNDOC/GEN/N94/312/22/PDF/N9431222.pdf?OpenElement).

US Central Intelligence Agency (CIA). *The World Factbook* (Washington, DC: Central Intelligence Agency, 2013); (https://www.cia.gov/library/publications/the-world-factbook/).

US Congressional Budget Office. "Monthly Budget Review for August 2013," September 9, 2013; (http://www.cbo.gov/sites/default/files/cbo files/attachments/44552-%20MBR_2013_08.pdf).

US Department of Commerce. "Gross Domestic Product by Industry Data Show Information Technology Drove Economic Growth in the Late 1990's: New Estimates Based on the North American Industry Classification System." Bureau of Economic Analysis, BEA 04-51,

November 15, 2004 (http://www.bea.gov/newsreleases/industry/gdp industry/2004/naics.htm).

US Department of Defense (DoD). "Remarks by Secretary Panetta on Cybersecurity to the Business Executives for National Security, New York City." October 11, 2012; (http://www.defense.gov/transcripts/ transcript.aspx?transcriptid=5136).

US Department of Defense (DoD). *Base Structure Report, Fiscal Year 2010 Baseline.* Office of the Deputy Undersecretary of Defense (Installations & Environment), 2010.

US Department of Education Institute of Education Sciences. *Digest of Education Statistics Report.* National Center for Education Statistics, 2012.

US Department of Energy (DoE) / Energy Information Administration (EIA). *Annual Energy Outlook 2012*; (http://www.eia.gov/forecasts/ aeo/pdf10383(2012).pdf).

US Department of Energy (DoE) / Energy Information Administration (EIA). "China: Analysis"; (http://www.eia.gov/countries/cab.efm? fips=CH).

US Department of Energy (DoE) / Energy Information Administration (EIA). "Electricity in the United States"; (http://www.eia.gov /energyexplained/index.cfm?page=electricity_inthe_united_states).

US Department of Energy (DoE) / Energy Information Administration (EIA). "Petroleum and Other Liquids: US Imports by Country of Origin"; (http://www.eia.gov/dnav/pet/pet_move_impcus_a2_nus _ep00_im0_mbbl_m.ht).

US Department of Energy (DoE) / Energy Information Administration (EIA). "US Imports by Country of Origin"; (http://www.eia.gov/ dnav/pet/pet_move_impcus_a2_nus_ep00_im0_mbbl_m.htm).

US Department of Energy (DoE) / Energy Information Administration (EIA). "World Shale Gas Resources: An Initial Assessment of 14 Regions outside the United States." April 2011; (http://www.eia.gov/ analysis/studies/worldshalegas/archive/2011/pdf/fullreport.pdf).

US Department of Energy (DoE) / Energy Information Administration (EIA). *International Energy Outlook 2011*; (http://www.eia.gov /forecasts/archive/ieo11/pdf10484(2011).pdf).

US Department of Energy (DoE) / Energy Information Administration (EIA). *World Shale Gas Resources: An Initial Assessment of 14 Regions Outside the United States* (April 2011).

US Department of State. "Anti-Ballistic Missile Treaty"; (http://www. state.gov/www/global/arms/treaties/abm/abm2.html).

US Department of State. "Biography: Madeleine Korbel Albright." State Department archive; (http://secretary.state.gov/www/albright/albright. html).

US Department of the Interior. "About Oil Shale." Oil Shale and Tar Sands Programmatic EIS; (http://ostseis.anl.gov/guide/oilshale/index. cfm).

US Environmental Protection Agency (EPA). "Natural Gas Extraction: Hydraulic Fracturing"; (http://www2.epa.gov/hydraulicfracturing# improving).

US National Intelligence Council (NIC). "Global Trends 2025: A Transformed World." Office of the Director of National Intelligence, November 2008; (http://www.dni.gov/files/documents/Newsroom/ Reports%20and%20Pubs/2025_Global_Trends_Final_Report.pdf).

US National Intelligence Council (NIC). "Global Trends 2030: Alternative Worlds." Office of the Director of National Intelligence, December 2012; (http://www.dni.gov/files/documents/GlobalTrends_2030.pdf).

US National Intelligence Council (NIC). "Global Trends 2030: Alternative Worlds" [in Arabic]. Al Jazeera Centre for Studies, book revision, reviewed by Walid Abdulhay, March 25, 2013.

US NAVSEA Shipbuilding Support Office (NAVSHIPSO). "Naval Vessel Register"; (http://www.nvr.navy.mil/).

US Office of the Director of National Intelligence. "Reports and Publications"; (http://www.dni.gov/index.php/newsroom/reports-and-publications).

Utkin, Anatoly. *The World in the 21st Century* [in Arabic]. Younes Kamel Deeb and Hashem Hammadi (trans.); (Damascus: Dar Al Markaz Al Thaqafi for Printing and Publishing, 2007).

Verba, Sidney, Nancy Burns and Kay Lehman Schlozman. "Knowing and Caring about Politics: Gender and Political Engagement." *Journal of Politics*, vol. 59, issue 4 (November 1997); (http://dx.doi.org/10.2307/2998592).

Volgy, Thomas, Zlatko Sabic, Petra Roter and Andrea Gerlak. *Mapping the World Order,* Atif Mu'tamad and Izzat Zayyan (trans.); (Cairo: National Center for Translation, 2011).

Wahban, Ahmad. "Ethnic Conflicts and the Stability of the Modern World: A Study of Minorities and Ethnic Groups and Movements" [in Arabic]; (Alexandria: El Dar El Gamaya 2003–2004).

Wahdan, Wahdan. "Ethnic Conflicts and National Security" [in Arabic]. Dr. Saleh Al Khathlan Forums, April 28, 2010; (http://www.sas445.com/vb/showthread.php?t=2163).

Walt, Stephen M. "The End of the American Era." *The National Interest*, October 25, 2011; (http://nationalinterest.org/article/the-end-the-american-era-6037).

Wasik, John. "Fiscal Cliff Follies: Four Myths." *Forbes*, November 29, 2013; (http://www.forbes.com/sites/johnwasik/2012/11/29/fiscal-cliff-follies-four-myths).

Werstein, Irving. *1914–1918: World War I* (New York, NY: Cooper Square Publishers, Inc., 1964).

Wessel, David. "Euro Zone Confronts Limits of 'One-Size-Fits-All' Policies." *The Wall Street Journal*, March 17, 2011; (http://online.wsj.com/article/SB10001424052748704396504576204531942846492.html).

Wheatcroft, Andrew. *The Ottomans* (London: Penguin Group, 1993).

Whiting, Rick. "The 25 Biggest Tech Companies on the Fortune 500." CRN, May 14, 2013; (http://www.crn.com/slide-shows/channel-programs/240154736/the-25-biggest-tech-companies-on-the-fortune-500.htm).

Whitman, Christine Todd. "What is the Future of American Nuclear Power?" *Forbes*, December 10, 2012.

Whitney, Lance. "America: A Nation Obsessed With Tech" CNET, September 2, 2009; (http://news.cnet.com/8301-10797_3-10332910-235.html).

Widgery, Alban G. *Interpretations of History: Confucius to Toynbee.* Zawqan Qarqoot (trans.); (Beirut: Dar Al-Qalam, 1979).

Williams, Adam. "Nicaragua's Canal: Chinese Tycoon Wang Jing Wants to Build It." *Bloomberg Businessweek*, June 27, 2013; (http://www.businessweek.com/articles/2013-06-27/nicaraguas-canal-chinese-tycoon-wang-jing-wants-to-build-it).

Wirtz, James. J. and James A. Russell. "US Policy on Preventive War and Preemption." James Martin Center for Non-Proliferation Studies (http://cns.miis.edu/npr/pdfs/101wirtz.pdf).

Wohlforth, William C. *The Stability of a Unipolar World* [in Arabic]. International Studies Series, No. 36 (Abu Dhabi: The Emirates Center for Strategic Studies and Research, 2001).

Woods, Alan. "George Bush and the Crusades" [in Arabic]. *Al-Hiwar Al-Mutamaddin* no. 495, May 22, 2003; (http://www.ahewar.org/debat/show.art.asp?aid=7556).

World Bank. "Risk and Vulnerability." Annual Bank Conference on Development Economics, Washington, DC, June 3–4, 2013.

World Economic Forum (WEF). "Euro, Dollar, Yuan Uncertainties: Scenarios on the Future of the International Monetary System." World Scenario Series (June 2012).

World Energy Council (WEC). *2010 Survey of Energy Resources*; (http://www.worldenergy.org/publications/3040.asp).

World Trade Organization (WTO). "Trade Profiles 2013." April 2013; (www.wto.org/english/res_e/booksp_e/anrep_e/trade_profiles13_e.pdf).

Wu, Yanqing. "Resource and Energy Problems in China." Energy and Environmental Studies of Shanghai Jiao Tong University; (http://ncrs.cm.kyushu-u.ac.jp/assets/files/Newsletter/volume_3/jp/NCRS_NLJ Vol3_19SJTU.pdf).

Xing, Yuqing. "Why is China so Attractive for FDI? The Role of Exchange Rates." May, 2004, International Development Program, International University of Japan; (http://faculty.washington.edu/karyiu/confer/beijing03/papers/xing.pdf).

Yassin, Al Sayed. "Historical Transformations of the International System" [in Arabic]. *Al-Arabiya* website, October 25, 2009; (http://www.alarabiya.net/views/2009/10/25/89147.html).

Yassin, Al Sayed. "The Third Way: New Political Ideology" [in Arabic]. *Al-Siyassa Al-Dawliya* no. 195 (Cairo: January 1999).

Yassin, Al Sayed. *The Globalization Crisis and the Collapse of Capitalism* [in Arabic]; (Cairo: Nahdet Misr for Printing, Publishing and Distribution, March 2009).

Yovanovich, Gordana (ed.). *The New World Order: Corporate Agenda and Parallel Reality* (London: McGill-Queens University Press, 2003).

Yuan, Yuchun. "The Mixed Economy in China: Through Rhetorical Perspective." Master's degree thesis, Texas A&M University; (http://repository.tamu.edu/bitstream/handle/1969.1/1207/etd-tamu-2003B-2003070714-Yuan-1.pdf?sequence=1).

Yuwei, Zhang. "China's US T-bill holdings hit record in May." *China Daily*, July 17, 2013; (http://usa.chinadaily.com.cn/epaper/2013-07/17/content_16787441.htm).

Zahir, Hussein Ali. *The Evolution of International Relations from Westphalia to Versailles* [in Arabic]; (Beirut: Dar Al-Mawasim for Printing, Publishing and Distribution, 1999).

Zainulabdeen, Basheer. "The Sectarian Challenge in Syria." Working paper presented during the conference "The Challenges of the post-Arab Spring"; (http://albayan.co.uk/Files/adadimages/malfat%20pdf/libya/002abidine.pdf).

Zakaria, Fareed. "Can China Change its Economic Course?" *The Washington Post*, WP Opinions, July 17, 2013; (http://articles.washingtonpost.com/2013-07-17/opinions/40632962_1_china-s-growth-gdp).

Zakaria, Fareed. "Does the US Really Want to Own Libya?" [in Arabic] *Al-Sharq Al-Awsat* April 1, 2011, no. 11812; (http://www.aawsat.com/ leader.asp?section=3&issueno=11812&article =615259).

Zakaria, Fareed. "The Future of American Power." Council on Foreign Relations (May/June 2008).

Zakaria, Fareed. *The Post-American World* (New York, NY: W.W. Norton & Company, 2009).

Zaki, Ramzi. "Impacts of Globalization and the Delusions of Chasing the Mirage" [in Arabic]. *Al-Nahj* no. 57 (2000).

Zaki, Ramzi. "The Road to Seattle – Impacts of Globalization and the Illusions of Chasing the Mirage" [in Arabic]. *Al-Nahj*, no. 21 (Winter 2000).

Zartman, William. "Political Science" in Leonard Binder (ed.), *The Study of the Middle East: Research and Scholarship in the Humanities and Social Sciences* (New York, NY: Boulder, 1987).

Zhu, Winnie. "Angola Overtakes Saudi Arabia as Biggest Oil Supplier to China." *Bloomberg*, April 21, 2008; (http://www.bloomberg.com/apps/news?pid=newsarchive&sid=aqJ3Wjxs.OWs).

INDEX

INDEX

858

global number 55
United States
    Arab students (1949–
        2012) 123
    current number 55
Utrecht, Treaty of 197

V

Venezuela 367–8, 373, 375, 551
Versailles, Treaty of 345–6

W

war on terror
    and Bush Doctrine 172
    as aid to US expansion 315
    UAE public opinion on 463
    US need for assistance 312
warfare
    asymmetric conflicts 527–9,
        553, 558–9
    changing nature of 217–18,
        558–62
    declining international role
        258–9
    fourth generation (4GW)
        527–8, 560
    and global broadcasting 295
    pre-emptive action 307
    and technology 553, 558
    see also cyber warfare
Warsaw Pact 100, 119, 152,
    262, 264
Washington Treaty 262
water resources 22
welfare state 151
West
    intervention in failed states
        307–8
    falling population 162
    and Islam
        historical legacies 163–4

solution to problem
    between 162–3, 165
    tensions with Islam 160–2
    view of Islam 159–60
    Muslim communities in 162,
        164, 192
western hemisphere
    oil production share (2001–11)
        371
    oil reserves share (2001–11)
        371
Westphalia, treaties of 26, 96–7,
    134, 141, 176, 196–7, 256, 258
Wilson, Woodrow 267
WMDs (weapons of mass
    destruction) 22, 153
    false US Iraqi evidence 114
    as justification for
        intervention 77
    as political tool 106
    UAE citizens' concerns 461–2
    see also nuclear weapons
women
    empowerment of 74–5, 280,
        484
    rights of 80–1, 115
World Bank 38, 41, 49
    and globalization 141
    political power of 231, 265,
        403
    UAE public knowledge
        about/trust in 432–4
    US influence over 120, 487
world order
    concept of 257
    interconnectedness of 259–60
    major 20th century conflicts
        151–3
    origins of
        overview 256–60
        Cold War era 261–84